P9-CJN-495

DATE DUE

DE 23 '94			
MR 10 '95			
MR 25 '97			
AP 11 '97			
JE 9 '97			
NO 7 00			
DE 15 '04			

DEMCO 38-296

Tenth Edition

LABOR ECONOMICS

AND

LABOR RELATIONS

Lloyd G. Reynolds
Yale University

Stanley H. Masters
*State University of New York
at Binghamton*

Colletta H. Moser
Michigan State University

Prentice Hall
Englewood Cliffs, New Jersey 07632

Library of Congress Cataloging in-Publication Data

Reynolds, Lloyd G.
    Labor economics and labor relations / Lloyd G. Reynolds, Stanley H. Masters, Colletta H. Moser.—10th ed.
      p.   cm.
    Includes bibliographical references and index.
    ISBN 0-13-517376-0
    1. Labor economics. 2. Industrial relations. I. Masters, Stanley, H. II. Moser, Colletta H. III. Title.
HD4901.R47 1991
331'.0973—dc20
                                           90-40155
                                               CIP

Editorial/production supervision and
   interior design: *Carol Burgett*
Cover design: *Patricia Kelly*
Cover photo: *K. Hayden/Stock Imagery*
Prepress buyer: *Trudy Pisciotti*
Manufacturing buyer: *Bob Anderson*

©1991, 1986, 1982, 1978, 1974, 1970, 1964, 1959, 1956, 1954, 1949 by Prentice-Hall, Inc.
A Paramount Communications Company
Englewood Cliffs, New Jersey 07632

Printed in the United States of America

10 9 8 7 6 5 4 3

ISBN 0-13-517376-0

PRENTICE-HALL INTERNATIONAL (UK) LIMITED, *London*
PRENTICE-HALL OF AUSTRALIA PTY. LIMITED, *Sydney*
PRENTICE-HALL CANADA INC., *Toronto*
PRENTICE-HALL HISPANOAMERICANA, S.A., *Mexico*
PRENTICE-HALL OF INDIA PRIVATE LIMITED. *New Delhi*
PRENTICE-HALL OF JAPAN, INC., *Tokyo*
SIMON & SCHUSTER ASIA PTE. LTD., *Singapore*
EDITORA PRENTICE-HALL DO BRASIL, LTDA. *Rio de Janeiro*

To Beth

CONTENTS

4   HUMAN CAPITAL: EDUCATION AND JOB TRAINING   77

5   DEMAND   112

6   INVESTMENTS BY FIRMS IN WORKERS   142

7   WAGE DETERMINATION   171

13   UNIONS, POLITICS, AND THE LAW   353

14   THE DECLINE OF PRIVATE-SECTOR UNIONS   380

15   COLLECTIVE BARGAINING: UNION AND MANAGEMENT GOALS   412

16   BARGAINING   431

17   COLLECTIVE BARGAINING: ISSUES AND OUTCOMES   457

PREFACE

Branches of applied economics go through cycles of growth and decline. In the 1930s and 1940s, labor economics was a major area of study. Unions were organizing many new areas. This development was analyzed primarily from a historical, institutional perspective, rather far away from the more theoretical mainstream of economics. As the union movement stabilized in the 1950s, labor became a backwater area of the discipline.

By the 1960s, labor economics had made a dramatic revival. New theories brought the field closer to the microeconomic center of the discipline. Since the late 1960s, the growing supply of microeconomic data sets, together with good theory, has made possible much more penetrating analysis of worker, household, and firm behavior. Economic models and quantitative techniques have also been applied with increasing success to collective bargaining and its economic impact. Questions that used to be discussed in qualitative terms are now subjected to statistical estimation. While the numerous studies in these areas have greatly increased our knowledge of labor markets and the behavior of workers, unions, and employers, the field has sometimes put a premium on mathematical sophistication at the expense of first-hand observation and common sense.

In this edition, we seek to combine the strengths of both the early and the more recent traditions of labor economics. We make use of much recent literature, both theoretical and empirical. At the same time, we try to ensure that all topics are covered from a practical as well as a theoretical perspective. Thus, while the text is aimed primarily at students taking labor economics courses in economics departments, it should also be useful in many courses on industrial relations taught in business and management schools.

Theory becomes most interesting, as well as most useful, when we consider how it can contribute to informed discussion of policy issues. Especially in the labor economics section of the book, the reader will find a heavy emphasis on policy issues. A new chapter on American workers in a world economy, focusing on the policy responses to widespread illegal immigration and increased foreign competition in product markets, has been added. Substantial revisions have been made in the chapters on discrimination, the slow growth of productivity and real wage rates, and the determination of wage rates and benefits, all issues that have received and are likely to continue to receive much attention in the policy arena.

The section of the book that has been most heavily revised is the discussion of unions, an area of labor where there have been major changes in the economy over the past decade or so. Two chapters in this section are completely new for this edition, one on the decline of private-sector unions and the other featuring case studies in collective bargaining. The latter chapter discusses how collective bargaining has changed in four industries: automobiles, agricultural machinery, steel, and trucking. Other chapters that have been extensively revised for this edition include those on the evolution of American unions; unions, politics, and the law; issues in collective bargaining; bargaining in the public sector; and union wage effects. In making these revisions, we emphasize how unions and collective bargaining have changed in recent years. We also stress the contribution that economics and economic theory can make in analyzing these issues.

We provide several pedagogical aids in each chapter: a chapter summary, highlighting important issues and conclusions; a list of key concepts, which are defined in a glossary at the end of the book; a set of review questions, which should also be useful for class discussion; and selected readings, for those who wish to pursue a particular subject in greater depth.

This edition has been improved as a result of the suggestions of many readers. We welcome critical comments that will help to improve the quality of future editions.

LABOR ECONOMICS
AND
LABOR RELATIONS

LABOR ECONOMICS: INSTITUTIONS AND THE MARKET

You have already taken a course in introductory economics. There you learned that there are demand curves and supply curves for labor, which determine an equilibrium wage rate for each job in the economy. What more is there to say? What can a course in labor economics add to what you already know?

General economics views people mainly as consumers and asks, What economic arrangements will yield greatest consumer satisfaction? But most adults are also producers, who spend one-third or more of their waking hours at work. Labor economics focuses on the world of work, on people's behavior in choosing and changing jobs, on the nonmonetary as well as the monetary rewards for work. It asserts that producer satisfaction is as important as consumer satisfaction. Moreover, the two objectives conflict. An economy that provided the easiest and most pleasant jobs for everyone would not provide the largest consumable output. Balancing producer and consumer satisfactions is a central economic issue.

In addition, labor markets have peculiarities not found in markets for goods. The geometry of supply-demand diagrams makes the two kinds of market appear similar, but this is misleading. We shall review the simple labor market model found in every elementary text. That, however, is only a starting point, and we shall devote several chapters to exploring the complications the simple model leaves out.

Wages and other terms of employment are not determined solely through market dealings between workers and employers. Market results are supplemented, and at times overridden, by institutional rules imposed by business organizations, trade unions, and governments. The trade union is a way of pooling employees' strength for joint negotiation with the employer, usually called collective bargaining. This bargaining has complex economic effects, which require more thorough analysis than is possible in an elementary text.

SOME PECULIARITIES OF LABOR MARKETS

The structure of labor markets will occupy us for many chapters to come. But as a beginning, let us note some ways in which labor markets differ from markets for wheat or steel sheets or men's shoes.

1. Multiplicity of Markets. We often speak of *the* labor market. But in reality there are thousands of markets for different kinds of work. These differ widely in skill level—from restaurant dishwashers to top surgeons. They differ also in geographic scope—from local markets for most blue-collar and white-collar occupations, to national markets for college teachers and business executives, to international markets for doctors, scientists, and engineers.

These thousands of markets, however, are interrelated. Just as product markets are linked by consumers' choices among goods, so labor markets are linked by workers' choices among jobs. People, and especially young people, will move from one occupation to another if they can gain by so doing, and they will move geographically for the same reason.

But while the walls around labor markets are porous, the walls still exist. Movement is not easy or costless. We can, on paper, construct a system of competitive labor markets in which barriers to movement would be at a minimum. At the other extreme, we can construct a system in which movement among markets is impossible, as in J. E. Cairnes's model of "noncompeting groups." The real world falls somewhere between these extremes. What are the main barriers to mobility in practice? If we assume that free choice of jobs is desirable, how might existing barriers be reduced? These are central issues in labor market analysis.

2. No Central Clearinghouse. For many goods there is a single point of sale. That is true of wheat, corn, sugar, and other basic materials sold on commodity exchanges. Even where there are many points of sale, as with retail sale of consumer goods, communication among these points is close enough to hold price differences within narrow bounds.

In labor markets the communication network is usually less well developed. So if we speak of "the market for machinists in Cincinnati," we are speaking figuratively rather than literally. Each plant that hires machinists is to some extent a separate market, and information flows are not fast or accurate, especially on the workers' side of the market. This situation increases workers' costs of job search and makes people less willing to change jobs except under pressure of necessity. It also means the wages and other conditions of employment can differ considerably among employers, with no tendency for these differences to vanish over the course of time.

There are, to be sure, institutions that perform a clearinghouse function: (1) local offices of the state employment service, at which all workers receiving unemployment compensation are required to register for work, but at which employers are *not* required to register vacant jobs, though many may do so voluntarily; (b) private employment agencies, which are particularly active in the area of white-collar employment; (c) the local union office, which refers workers to vacant jobs in some industries, notably building construction, merchant shipping, and long-shoring. Most of the labor market traffic, however, bypasses these institutions. When workers are asked how they found their present job, the two most common answers are "heard it from a friend" or "just walked in and applied."

3. Workers not Standardized. Here, again, there is a marked contrast with product markets. Many goods, especially raw materials and semifinished goods, are completely standardized. Even where there are several brands of a good, they are usually quite similar in physical characteristics.

But when a company has to select among applicants for a job, it is dealing with people whose productive capacity differs and is largely unknown. Workers differ in age, sex, and racial origin. Under federal law, discrimination among applicants on the basis of race or sex is unlawful; but that does not mean it has been entirely eliminated. Workers differ also in intelligence, manual dexterity, physical strength and energy, work motivation, and other characteristics that affect productivity on the job. Employers appraise these characteristics as best they can, sometimes by tests administered in the personnel office, sometimes by taking years of education as an indicator of intelligence and motivation (a practice whose reliability and legality has recently been challenged). Mistakes are bound to be made, however, and so final selection is usually made after a probationary period of work on the job.

Workers differ also in amount and type of formal education, years of work experience, and amount of specific job training. Each worker is a combination of native abilities and "raw labor power" plus specific skills acquired through education and training. This second component is commonly called human capital. It resembles physical capital in that it costs something to acquire but yields a return through higher earnings in later years. Young people and their parents have to decide how much to invest in acquiring human capital. Employers also have to decide how much it pays to invest in training workers on the job, balancing training costs against expected returns. In selecting workers to hire, employers need to consider not only the present skills of the worker but also how quickly the worker can learn new skills and, if the employer invests in such training, whether the worker is likely to stay with the firm long enough for the employer to earn a good return on the investment.

4. Continuity of Employment Relation. In buying and selling goods, each day is a new experience. What a consumer or a business buys today need have no relation to what was bought yesterday or may be bought tomorrow. But in the purchase of labor, continuity does matter. A company that decided each morning whether to keep its present work force or to hire a completely new crew would not be acting economically. Indeed, it probably could not get anyone to work for it.

A worker is normally hired with an expectation of permanence, subject to good behavior. This arrangement has advantages for both employer and worker. The worker will often have gone through a training period and in any event will have become more productive through experience on the job. The company thus "has an investment in the worker," and this investment would be lost by replacing the worker, even with someone of comparable native ability. In addition, turnover of workers disrupts work teams whose members have become friends and learned to work harmoniously.

The worker, too, typically prefers continuity to change. Familiarity with work routines, work conditions, and work associates makes life more secure and pleasant. Additional years of service usually bring important benefits: longer vacations, larger pension rights, and greater security against layoffs. So losing a job one had expected to keep is a real hardship. Most workers have substantial job tenure, and length of tenure normally increases with age.

5. *Workers Deliver Themselves Along with Their Labor.*   Buyers and sellers of a good stand apart from the objects in which they deal. These have no direct effect on their personal life. But the seller of labor must be physically present. This means that the conditions under which work is carried on are an important part of the bargain. These conditions are partly physical—heat or cold, noise, dust, risks of injury from machinery. But they are also social—pace of work, closeness of supervision, fairness of treatment by supervisors.

The "employment package" thus has many components in addition to the wage. There are tradeoffs among these components in each worker's mind. One cannot say that a worker will seek the higest wage available in the market. Rather, he or she will seek the job that offers the greatest *net advantage,* considering all wage and nonwage terms of employment. By the same token, the employer has numerous options in competing for labor. Raising the wage will attract more new applicants and help to retain present employees. But an improvement in any other condition of employment will also help to attract labor. The fact that one company offers a higher wage level than another does not prove that its total employment package is superior. It may be offering more money to compensate for other unattractive features of the job.

The complexity of the employment package complicates the problem of job search. Some important conditions of employment, especially those involving human relations, can be learned only after one is actually on the job. So a worker, on the basis of limited information, takes a job that *looks* satisfactory. But after a few weeks of work, which reveal the full range of nonwage conditions, the worker may decide that the choice was mistaken and so quits and tries again. The employer, of course, is also experimenting on the basis of limited information. A company takes on a worker who *looks* trainable and productive. But during the probationary period this turns out not to be so, and the worker is let go. Labor turnover in the economy is not just purposeless waste. Much of it is an inevitable accompaniment of imperfect information on both sides of the market, which means that job shopping often involves "shopping by working."

These considerations explain some additional facts of life in the labor market. Turnover is much higher among young workers than among older workers, because for young people uncertainty on both sides of the market—will they like the work? can they do the work?—is unusually great. Turnover is higher among short-service workers than among long-service workers. If a worker is going to quit, or if the worker is dismissed for unsatisfactory performance, it usually happens after a short period of service. Long tenure is an indication of job satisfaction and good performance. It also may indicate that the employer has invested in training the worker and has provided the worker with strong incentives to remain with the firm so that the employer can earn a good return on the investment.

6. Worker's Inferiority in "Bargaining Power." It is usually said that labor markets differ from other markets in that the scales are tilted in favor of the buyer. For reasons we shall discuss in later chapters, at the going wage there are usually more workers seeking jobs than there are vacancies available. The worker, with limited resources, needs a job badly and quickly. The employer can afford to wait and can pick and choose among a surplus of applicants. Thus the employer has a dominant voice in setting conditions of employment.

Under nonunion conditions, there usually is no "bargaining" in the ordinary sense. The employer defines a package of wage and nonwage conditions of employment. The worker can take it or leave it. The worker's "bargaining power," then, really means his or her ability to refuse or quit a job; and this decision depends on the alternatives open to the worker.

A worker's ability to quit depends, first, on the state of demand for labor. Demand for a particular kind of labor may fall because of lagging sales in a particular company or industry. Demand for most kinds of labor fluctuates with the swings of the business cycle. So workers quit their jobs most readily at cycle peaks, and the quit rate drops sharply during recession.

Ability to quit or to bargain for better terms without quitting depends also on individual skill and ability. A worker of average ability in a low-skilled occupation is readily replaceable and has little leverage. But a person in a high-skilled occupation or a person of outstanding ability in any occupation can make demands on the employer, and the employer may comply rather than lose such a valuable employee. The most visible examples are star athletes and artistic performers; but business executives, professional people, and skilled craft workers often have considerable bargaining power.

Thus assertions that workers are inferior in bargaining power must be viewed with some caution. The statement is probably true for most workers most of the time. But many workers do have individual bargaining power, and their number increases when general demand for labor is high.

THE ROLE OF ORGANIZATIONAL RULES

What Markets Can and Cannot Do

With all the peculiarities described above, labor markets do operate. Indeed, they perform economic functions that one can scarcely imagine being performed without them.

The labor market is a reasonably effective instrument both for determining relative wage rates and for raising the general wage level as national output rises. The great increase in real wages in the United States over the past century is not due in any large measure to union activity or government decree. It has occurred mainly because employers were able and impelled to keep raising their wage offers in the market year after year: able because development of new machinery and production methods was steadily increasing output per worker-hour; impelled because the labor market forces each company to bid against others to hold its share of the labor supply. The labor market is the main mechanism by which increases in productivity have been translated into higher wages and living standards.

The market also does reasonably well in determining relative wage levels for different plants, industries, occupations, and regions. One can always find many queer or inequitable wage rates; but viewed broadly and over the long run, the national wage structure is not unreasonable.

Finally, the labor market is the only device we have for sorting out many millions of workers with varying skills and interests among the multitude of different jobs in the economy. Any attempt to do so by administrative methods, in addition to encroaching on personal liberty, would be hopelessly cumbersome and inefficient. Even Communist countries rely mainly on wage inducements in the markets to secure a desirable allocation of the labor force.

Recognition that the labor market does some things well, however, should not blind us to the things it does poorly or cannot do at all. It is not highly effective, for example, in regulating working conditions—physical conditions, safety and sanitation, work speeds, treatment by supervisors, and other personnel policies. The market still sets limits in the sense that if plant conditions become too bad, workers have the option of leaving. But these limits may be quite wide. Working conditions are hard for the market to evaluate and control because they are intangible, qualitative, hard for the worker to discover before he or she is on the job, and hard to bargain about on an individual basis. Workers conclude that the effective remedy is not individual bargaining or quitting (the market solution) but group pressure through a union.

The market cannot ensure that there will be sufficient aggregate demand for labor, so that most workers can obtain jobs for which they have the appropriate skills. Neither can the market provide any income protection for those who cannot find jobs because of disability, lack of skill, or inadequate demand. To deal with these issues, the federal government has assumed responsibility for managing aggregate demand and, with the states, for providing some assistance to those who suffer from serious difficulties in the labor market.

An important fact of life is that most workers regard resort to the market—that is, a change of employers—as a disaster rather than an opportunity. They typically want to continue with their present employer. They regard as academic advice the suggestion that they can improve the company's behavior by leaving it. They prefer to change the company's behavior without leaving.

Albert Hirschman has labeled these alternatives *exit* and *voice*. Exit involves punishing the company by quitting but at the same time punishing yourself. The alternative preferred by most workers is to achieve a greater voice in determining employment conditions while remaining on the job. The traditional method of achieving voice is through union organization.

Contenders for Rule-Making Authority

The need for administrative rules arises partly from the size of employing units. "The employer" is usually a company rather than a person, and may have many thousands of employees. The same is true of a government department. A large enterprise is bound together by an elaborate hierarchy of authority, which specifies the powers and responsibilities of everyone from company president to laborer. It is bound together also by a network of rules governing output and cost targets; products, equipment, and production methods; division of labor and design of jobs; types and amount of compensation; hiring, promotion, and discharge; and many other things.

A large enterprise will have hundreds or even thousands of specialized jobs, some of which may exist only in this enterprise. New workers are typically recruited for the bottom jobs and work their way up to higher jobs as they gain experience. Vacancies in higher jobs are filled mainly through internal promotion, often called the internal labor market. How are wages for these jobs to be determined, given the fact that there is no outside market for them? Wages paid by other companies for similar work may provide some guidance. But the decision is essentially an administrative decision.

The contenders for rule-making authority are the business firm, the trade union, and government. There are situations in which one or another of these plays an almost exclusive role. In nineteenth-century Britain and America, business managers had a dominant voice, with little interference from unions or government. In contemporary Yugoslavia or Israel, labor organizations have a powerful voice. In the Soviet Union and other Communist countries, government decisions predominate.

More commonly, however, authority is divided. The three contestants share rule-making power in a pluralistic system, as in Western Europe, North America, and Australia. The exact division of authority varies from country to country, and changes over the course of time. In the United States, unions and government agencies have more voice today than they had in 1930.

But while all three groups have a finger in the pie, each has certain areas of decision within which it has a comparative advantage and therefore a preponderant voice. Even in strongly unionized economies management retains a large measure of administrative authority. It typically has exclusive control over, or at least the right to take initial action concerning, production organization, production methods, production volume and labor requirements, recruitment and hiring of labor, assignment of workers to specific jobs, appointment of supervisors, determination of work speeds, establishment of shop rules and application of penalties for violating them, layoffs, and other personnel matters. Management acts; the union protests or appeals. The union may eventually secure a reversal of the decision, but the power to act retains much of its pristine potency.

The specific function of unionism is to police in-plant decisions and actions of management. This means negotiating a general framework of rules within which management action is confined (the union contract) and ensuring equitable application of these rules to individual cases (the grievance procedure). Rules concerning the conditions under which a worker may be penalized, demoted, or discharged are of prime importance, as are rules concerning layoffs, rehiring, promotion, and other matters of job tenure. Though unions also influence wages and working conditions, their distinctive function is to establish a system of industrial jurisprudence through which the individual can seek redress from harmful decisions by management.

Government has the ability to establish minimum standards that voters consider sufficiently important to be enforced on everyone. This may mean either bringing laggards up to the market level or establishing standards in areas where the market is not very effective. Government is an efficient mechanism for devising protection against loss of income through unemployment, old age, total or partial disability, and other causes. It is now generally agreed that government has responsibility for maintaining adequate total demand for labor. Finally, only government can prescribe rules to govern union and employer conduct in collective bargaining.

Institutions Versus the Market

Do market pressures or administrative judgments predominate in determining terms and conditions of employment? Great battles have been fought over this issue. "Neoclassical economists" asserted the dominance of market forces while "institutional economists" asserted the importance of managerial judgment and union-management negotiation. These debates have now subsided and, looking back, it appears that much ink was spilled to little purpose.

Especially in the long run, institutional decisions are more likely to supplement the labor market than to compete with it. They do so, first, by giving a precise answer to questions on which the market gives only general guidance. The problem of setting a wage rate for a specialized, semiskilled job found only in one company is a good example. Comparisons with similar work elsewhere might suggest a wage in the range of $8.00 to $9.00 an hour. But this is not good enough. Somebody—management or management and union negotiators—has to decide that the wage should be exactly $8.75. Judgment and bargaining are especially important in determining nonwage terms of employment, where market guidelines are more vague.

Second, market and institutional pressures often work in the same direction. Management decisions or union contract terms set a seal of approval on changes that were in the cards on economic grounds. For example, as hourly wage rates rise most people will choose to work fewer hours, for reasons explained in Chapter 3. So over the past century in the United States one would have expected a substantial drop in working hours, and this drop has in fact occurred. But unions have given this natural economic development the appearance of a social movement by campaigning first for a ten-hour day and then for an eight-hour day. Such campaigning, however, does not demonstrate that hours have fallen faster with unions than without them.

Another example is the shrinkage of the wage differential between skilled and unskilled blue-collar workers. An important reason is that as a growing percentage of young people finish high school, fewer of them are willing to accept unskilled jobs. This drop in supply should have produced a rise in the wage of unskilled laborers relative to skilled craftspersons. But unions in steel, automobiles, and other manufacturing industries have also favored a reduction of the skilledunskilled differential as a matter of policy. Here, again, contract terms have largely ratified a normal market result.

We should not deny that institutional pressures can make a difference. But the difference is usually less than it seems, and to estimate its size requires careful analysis.

EXPLANATION, PREDICTION, AND POLICY

In this book we are concerned mainly with the *positive economics* of the labor market. Positive economics tries to explain economic events, in this case the pattern of employment and the relative rates of pay for different jobs. We do this by building simplified models of reality. The need for simplification arises because reality is very complex, and it is impossible to deal with all the complications at once. Model building is a way of focusing on a few key characteristics and then adding complications one at a time.

Having constructed a market for a particular kind of labor, as we shall do in Chapter 2, we next ask how it would operate. What would be the market rate of wages? How would this rate change if there were a shift in the demand for, or supply of, this kind of labor? Suppose that a union or a government agency imposed a wage rate or altered the supply of labor. What then? This is *economic theorizing,* rather like piano finger exercises, requiring close attention but easily learned by practice.

But does theory work? The test is to check its predictions against statistical data. *Example:* the number of young people entering the labor force increased sharply during the 1970s and then declined in the 1980s as the baby-boom cohort, born from 1946 to 1960, became teenagers and then adults. The standard market model, developed in Chapter 2, predicts that this situation will *lower* the wages of teenagers relative to adults in the seventies and then *increase* them in the eighties. So we look at wage statistics. Sure enough, the relative earnings of people sixteen to twenty-four years old did fall during the 1970s. There is no evidence of a corresponding increase in the 1980s, however, perhaps because of nonmarket factors, such as the decline in the importance of the legal minimum wage, an issue we discuss in Chapter 5.

A model that gives a reasonable explanation of the past is also useful in predicting the future. As the preceding example indicates, however, judgment must also be used in determining whether any important factors not included in the model may be changing now or may change in the future.

Positive economics focuses on the questions of *what happened, why it happened,* and *what is likely to happen next.* It does not address the question of *what should be done about it.* Private markets often produce results that some people do not like, and government is urged to take corrective action. Is a proposed government action beneficial or harmful?

At this point we enter the area of *normative economics,* also called *welfare economics.* Modern welfare economics teaches that a government action can be given unqualified approval only if (1) it brings gains to some people without losses to anyone else or (2) it brings gains to some and losses to others; but the gainers are required to compensate the losers and, after doing so, are still better off than before.

An illustration of type 1 is action to improve the labor market. The state employment services now have a computer network by which information on job vacancies in one part of the country can be sent instantly to any other part of the country. This benefits both employers and job seekers, with no harm to anyone else. Or suppose that the U.S. Bureau of Labor Statistics (BLS) forecasts the demand for various types of skills ten years from now. To the extent that the forecasts are accurate, they can help young people to train for promising careers and to avoid dead ends.

Type 2 cases are less common, because compensation of losers is usually not feasible. But suppose a company wants to install new machinery that is more productive but also more dangerous, hence involving a loss to workers operating the machinery. Government requires the company to add safety devices to the machines, so that the danger to workers is no greater than before. If after the safety devices have been added, installation of the machines still lowers production costs, the installation is beneficial.

Most frequently, however, gainers and losers are not identical and compensation is not feasible. A community subsidizes a new employer who will provide jobs for many residents. This subsidy benefits the firm, its employers, and many local merchants. On the other hand, it increases traffic congestion and pollution. The dollar costs are borne by all taxpayers, including those who mainly value a quiet, pretty town as well as those who profit economically from the new industry. Is such a policy desirable? Since some gain and others lose, there is no clear answer to this question unless we can compare the magnitude of the gains and losses, a comparison that may be possible in dollar terms but not in terms of total satisfaction or *utility.* We can make judgments based on our own values, but these are personal rather than professional judgments. As a practical matter, prospective gainers and losers fight it out through the political process.

PLAN OF THE BOOK

We begin with a simple introductory model of the labor market, based on the traditional assumptions of competitive economic theory. Then we devote two chapters each to the supply and demand for labor. Next we consider the determination of wage rates in a world that is more complex but also more realistic than that of the simple introductory model. We move on to examine several important policy issues: discrimination in employment, changes in average wage rates, unemployment, and foreign competition.

In the second half of the book we focus on the unionized sector of the economy, which includes almost 40 percent of government employment but only a little over 10 percent of private employment. We look first at the growth and decline of trade unions in the United States, including changes in the legal environment in which unions and employers must operate. Next we devote five chapters to collective bargaining, including issues of goals, strategy, and the role of strikes. In this section we also compare developments in collective bargaining in the public and private sectors. In the concluding two chapters we face the question of how much difference unions make to the operation of the economy. What are the effects on job security, labor mobility and turnover, relative rates of pay, working conditions, productivity, profits, and the balance of political power? To what extent can each of these effects be judged beneficial or harmful? The object is not to conclude that unionism is desirable or undesirable but rather to help students in constructing their own balance sheet.

SUMMARY

1. Labor economics takes off from the concept of a labor market, which is treated in summary fashion in the elementary course. A course in labor economics goes beyond this by examining the following: the complicated nature of labor supply and demand; the special features of labor markets and the complexity of actual wage and employment decisions; the extent to which organizational rules developed by employers or through employer-union negotiation serve to override or supplement market forces; and a range of policy issues, including employment discrimination, unemployment, and poverty.

2. Labor markets differ in important respects from commodity markets: (a) there is no single market for a particular kind of labor; (b) worker information about jobs and employer information about workers is quite imperfect; (c) workers differ widely in ability and preferences, and jobs differ widely in skill requirements and working conditions; (d) the employment relation is usually expected to continue for an extended period, and change of employment involves substantial cost to both sides; and (e) the employment contract is multidimensional, involving a wage rate, benefits, working conditions, and a likelihood of permanence.

3. The labor market sets broad limits to what an employer can do and still retain the number of workers it needs. But the market cannot determine terms of employment in detail. Under nonunion conditions this determination is made by company management. Where a union exists, most terms of employment are decided by union-management negotiation. For the most part, these organizational rules serve to supplement the market rather than to override it.

4. Economists can contribute to a discussion of labor market policies by developing models, tested on the basis of past data, that can be used to help predict the consequences of a proposed course of action. A decision about whether the action is desirable, however, usually involves an ethical or political judgment, most commonly a judgment about equitable distribution of income; and this judgment goes beyond the bounds of economics.

KEY CONCEPTS

LABOR
LABOR ECONOMICS
LABOR MARKET
ORGANIZATIONAL RULE

EXIT
VOICE
POSITIVE ECONOMICS
NORMATIVE ECONOMICS

REVIEW QUESTIONS

1. What do you think labor economics is about or should be about? What are the main issues that should be discussed in the course?

2. Would it be useful and feasible to set up a central clearinghouse for labor in each locality? How would you go about it?

3. What problems confront the worker in searching for a job and the employer in recruiting and selecting workers? Why does the process necessarily involve labor turnover and unemployment?

4. There are industries in which "casual labor" is hired on a day-to-day basis. How will the policies of an employer in such an industry differ from those of an employer hiring labor on a permanent basis?

5. Evaluate the argument that the "bargaining power" of the individual worker is necessarily less than that of the employer.

6. What is the "market solution" for inferior working conditions in a particular company? Why might the company's employees prefer some other solution?

7. Why is the labor market usually supplemented by institutional rules in determining wages and other terms of employment?

8. What does *positive economics* try to do, and by what methods?

9. What is *normative economics?* Give several examples of (a) government actions that can be judged economically beneficial and (b) government actions on which economics cannot provide a judgment.

READINGS

BROWN, E. H. PHELPS, *The Economics of Labor.* New Haven, Conn.: Yale University Press, 1962.

HIRSCHMAN, ALBERT, *Exit, Voice, and Loyalty.* Cambridge, Mass.: Harvard University Press, 1973.

MCNULTY, PAUL, *The Origin and Development of Labor Economics.* Cambridge, Mass.: MIT Press, 1980.

A FIRST LOOK
AT LABOR MARKETS

In this chapter we begin by outlining a few of the main changes in the composition of employment over the past several decades. Then we develop a simplified model of a competitive labor market and show how this model can be used to help explain the employment trends that have been occurring.

After developing the competitive model, we go on to look at situations in which competition is restricted in one way or another. Suppose that only so many people can enter an occupation because of a state licensing system. Or suppose that there is only one employer of labor in an area. Or suppose a trade union demands and obtains a wage rate above the competitive level. We will find that demand-supply analysis is still useful, though the results differ from those of a competitive market. The simple model developed in this chapter is only a starting point, but it is a necessary one. In later chapters we shall remove the simplifications one by one and thus approach the complexity of actual labor markets in a systematic way.

CHANGES IN EMPLOYMENT BY INDUSTRY AND OCCUPATION

Over the past several decades there have been many significant trends in the labor market. There has been an increase in the employment of women, discussed in Chapters 3 and 8, and an increase in the education and skill of the average worker, discussed in Chapter 4. In the empirical part of this chapter, we consider two other important changes: (1) a decline in the percentage of workers employed in goods-

TABLE 2-1   Employment (%) by Sector and Major Industry Group, 1929–89

	1929	1947	1982	1989
Agriculture	19.9	12.1	3.4	2.7
Industry	39.7	42.1	33.8	32.5
Services	40.4	45.8	62.7	64.8
Industry				
Mining	2.2	1.7	1.0	0.6
Construction	5.0	5.2	5.8	6.5
Manufacturing	22.8	26.7	20.4	18.5
Transportation, communications, and public utilities	13.8	7.4	6.6	6.9
Services				
Wholesale trade	3.8	4.5	4.1	3.9
Retail trade	12.9	13.9	16.7	16.7
Finance, insurance, and real estate	3.4	3.2	6.3	6.8
Government	6.9	11.8	15.4	14.9
Other services	14.3	13.5	20.1	22.4

Source: Data for 1929 are from *Historical Statistics of the United States;* for 1947, *Employment and Training Report of the President;* and for 1982 and 1989, from Bureau of Labor Statistics, *Employment and Earnings,* January 1983 and January 1990, respectively (Washington, D.C.: Government Printing Office).

producing industries and an increase in the percentage employed in service industries and (2) a corresponding shift in employment by type of occupation, with white-collar work predominating increasingly over blue-collar jobs.

1. Employment by Industry.   Changes in this respect since 1929 are shown in Table 2-1. Most striking is the long-run decline of agriculture, which now employs only about 3 percent of the labor force. The industrial sector grew in relative importance until the end of World War II, when it employed 42 percent of the labor force, but its share has now dropped by ten percentage points. The most striking development since 1947 is the rise of what Fuchs has labeled "the service economy."[1] The proportion of the labor force employed in service industries, which was still less than half in 1947, has now risen to nearly two-thirds.

2. Employment by Occupation.   A different classification of the labor force is in terms of the kind of work done—clerical, professional, laborer, and so on. Changes in this respect since 1930 are shown in Table 2-2. The most striking feature of Table 2-2 is the growing predominance of the service-type occupations (which are largely, though not entirely, synonymous with white-collar employment) over goods-type occupations. As a percentage of total employment, the former group pulled ahead of the latter around 1955 and has continued to widen its lead. Note the especially sharp increase in demand for professional people, technicians, clerical workers, and other service workers.

---

[1]Victor R. Fuchs, *The Service Economy* (New York: National Bureau of Economic Research, 1984).

TABLE 2-2   Occupational Distribution (%) of the U.S. Labor Force, Selected Years, 1930–1989

	1930	1960	1982A	1982B	1989
Service-type occupations	36.5	55.5	67.4	67.8	70.0
Professional, technical, and kindred workers	7.1	11.4	17.0	15.6	16.3
Managers, officials, and proprietors (excluding farm)	7.7	10.7	11.5	10.7	12.7
Clerical and kindred workers	9.3	14.8	18.5	16.6	15.7
Sales workers	6.5	6.4	6.6	11.3	12.0
Service workers	5.9	12.2	13.8	13.6	13.3
Goods-type occupations	63.3	44.2	32.4	32.2	30.0
Precision production, craft and repair workers	13.4	13.0	12.3	11.8	11.8
Operatives and kindred workers	16.4	18.2	12.9	12.1	11.2
Laborers (excluding farm and mine)	11.4	5.4	4.5	4.5	4.1
Farmers and farm laborers	22.1	7.8	2.7	3.8	2.9

Note: The sources are the same as for Table 2-1. In 1983 the occupational definitions were changed. Column 1982A presents the figures for the old definitions, and column 1982B presents them for the new definitions. As can be seen, the main change is to increase the number of sales workers. We use the old names for the occupations except for the precision production, craft, and repair category.

To analyze why these changes have been occurring, we need to develop a theory of the labor market. First, we should discuss what we mean by a labor market.

The Scope of Labor Markets

A labor market is not necessarily, or even usually, a single place. True, there are places that are directly involved in labor recruitment and placement—union offices in the building or printing trades, the central hiring hall for longshoremen or seamen, the local office of the state employment service in each community. But these places are not synonymous with *the* labor market, since their use is usually not obligatory, and much of the flow of labor bypasses them.

The standard definition of *market* is an area within which buyers and sellers are in sufficiently close communication that price tends to be the same throughout the area. Such an area may vary in size from a neighborhood to the whole world. In the case of labor, the size of the market area varies with the skill level involved. Top administrators and professional people enjoy a national (even to some extent an international) market. The number of qualified people being small, employers find it feasible and desirable to recruit from all parts of the country. Accurate information about openings, salaries, and so on, is usually available through personal contacts and professional associations. The cost of moving from one part of the country to another is small relative to potential gains in income and professional advancement.

For most manual, clerical, and subprofessional jobs, the locality is the relevant market area. A worker who is settled in one community is unlikely to know much about, or to be very interested in, jobs in distant cities. Homeowners, in particular, are usually unwilling to move except in response to prolonged unemployment. Their market horizon is limited to the area within which they can readily commute to work. As auto transport has increasingly superseded public transport, however, commuting areas have become larger and more flexible. Towns that at one time were quite distinct are now merged into a common market. Moreover, nearby localities are linked by the *possibility* that people might move, in response to a substantial divergence in wage levels or employment opportunities.

A locality is not a *single* market but contains many specialized markets. In Seattle there are markets for typists, for aircraft welders, for schoolteachers, for janitors, and for hundreds of other occupations. Again, markets for "neighboring" occupations are linked by the possibility of labor transfer from one to the other. Occupationally as well as geographically, markets are linked in an intricate network, within which one can distinguish certain ridgelines at the boundaries of commuting areas and clearly defined skill groups.

In a certain sense, each employing unit can be regarded as a separate market. The specialized production jobs in a large manufacturing plant, for example, are typically filled by internal promotion rather than outside recruitment. The employer looks to the present employees as his source of supply, and workers look to this "internal market" for their prospects of advancement.

Features of the Simplified Market

What do we mean by a fully competitive labor market? The definition resembles that of pure competition in a product market. Its main features are the following:

1. There are many workers in the market and also many employers, so that no one has an appreciable influence on the market wage.
2. Workers and employers are free to enter or leave the market at will, and workers can move freely from one employer to another.
3. There is no organization on either side of the market. Employers do not combine to beat down the wage, nor do workers organize to raise it. Further, there is no wage fixing by government.
4. Workers and employers are well informed. Workers know about vacant jobs, the wage rates they pay, and other terms of employment. Employers know about workers available for employment, and they know what wage it will take to attract them.
5. Economic motivation is dominant. Other things equal, a worker will prefer a higher wage to a lower one. Other things equal, an employer will prefer more profit to less.

Two other simplifications will hold good for all the markets discussed in this chapter, whether competitive or noncompetitive.

1. The attractiveness of a job is measured solely by its hourly wage rate. Other job conditions are taken as given and constant.

2. All job vacancies are filled through the market. We ignore the fact that in practice many vacancies are filled through internal promotion.
3. Workers are interchangeable in the eyes of the employer and are of equal efficiency. We overlook the fact that in practice, employers have hiring preferences based on age, experience, and other factors; that workers differ considerably in efficiency; and that to achieve full efficiency on a particular job the worker usually requires a training period.

One other point should be emphasized before we proceed. In analyzing the wage rate for a particular kind of labor, we assume that *everything else in the economy remains constant.* More specifically, all product prices, interest rates, and wage rates offered by other employers remain constant. This technique was developed by Alfred Marshall of Cambridge, who called it "the method of *ceteris paribus*"—other things equal. By using it, we separate out the market in which we are interested from all the other markets to which it is related. Another term for this technique is *partial equilibrium analysis,* as distinct from *general equilibrium analysis,* which views the market network as a whole.

When we draw a supply-demand diagram for a particular company or industry, we show the wage rate on the vertical axis and the quantity of labor employed on the horizontal axis. The assumption that *all other wages are constant* gives this vertical axis a special significance. As we move up the vertical axis, this means that the wage rate is rising *relative to all other wages in the economy;* and conversely for a reduction in wages.

Unless this point is borne clearly in mind, one can readily fall into misstatements and confusion. For example, it is *not* correct to say: "If company *A*'s wage rate rises, more people will prefer to work there." But it would be correct to say (under our assumptions): "If company *A*'s wage rate rises *relative to other wage rates,* more people will prefer to work there." Again it is *not* correct to say: "If company *A*'s wage level rises, it will hire fewer workers." But it is generally true (under our assumptions) that "if company *A*'s wage level rises, *all prices and other wage rates remaining unchanged,* it will hire fewer workers."

DEMAND, SUPPLY, AND WAGES

Market Demand

Total demand for secretaries, machinists, or any other job is the sum of the demands of all employers in the market. We add the demand curves of all the employers to obtain the total, or *market demand curve,* for the occupation. We must begin, then, by asking what these employer demand curves look like.

The vertical axis of our diagram measures the wage rate for the occupation, while the horizontal axis shows the number of workers employed. We assert as a general principle that demand curves for labor slope downward to the right, that is, the number employed is related *inversely* to the wage rate. Following is a short explanation of why that is true. A more detailed explanation will be given in Chapter 5.

Why is it reasonable to suppose that if a company is obliged to pay a higher wage rate, it will hire fewer workers? First, the wage increase will raise the cost of production, and in time this will be reflected in higher prices for the company's products. But since product demand curves slope downward to the right, the higher price (other things equal) will reduce the company's sales. It will have to reduce its production schedules and hence will need fewer workers.

The force of this point may be more apparent if we suppose that the wage increase hits many employers at the same time. Suppose all bituminous coal companies are obliged to raise miners' wages by 10 percent. This will certainly raise mining costs and coal prices. Since coal competes with other fuels, more buyers will now choose gas, oil, or some other fuel. Coal sales will be reduced and mining employment will fall.

The second consideration is that labor is combined with other factors in production, notably with capital equipment; and labor and capital are to some extent interchangeable. If the cost of labor rises while the cost of capital remains unchanged, the company can reduce production costs by using more capital and less labor, that is, by greater mechanization of production. Again, the number of workers employed will fall. The growing mechanization of U.S. factories and offices owes much to the ingenuity of scientists and engineers. But it also owes much to the pressure of steadily rising wages. It is mainly higher labor costs that have stimulated management to set engineers to work inventing more mechanized production methods.

We repeat, then, that an individual employer's demand curve for labor will slope downward to the right. But what is true of the parts must be true of the whole. When we add up the demands of all employers, the market demand curve for the kind of labor in question will also slope downward to the right. It will look like *D* in Figure 2-1. Given this demand, the number employed will depend on the wage rate.

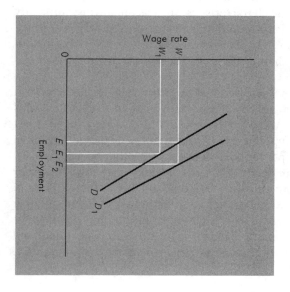

FIGURE 2-1   The Labor Demand Schedule

At a wage of W, E workers will be employed. At the lower wage, W_1, employment would be E_1.

We must observe the usual cautions in speaking of "demand" or "a change in demand." Demand is not a single *quantity*. It is a *schedule,* such as D, showing alternative quantities of employment at alternative rates of wages. If the wage rate falls from W to W_1 and, in response, employment increases from E to E_1, some might say demand for labor has risen. *That is incorrect.* Demand, in the proper sense of schedule D, has remained unchanged. An increase in demand means that the whole schedule has shifted to a higher level, such as D_1. If this happens, even if the wage rate, W, remains unchanged, employment will increase from E to E_2. An increase in demand means that for every possible wage rate, employment will now be higher than before. The opposite is true for a decrease in demand.

Market Supply

Turning to the other side of the market, let us look at a worker trying to choose among alternative occupations. The wage rate is not the only criterion of occupational choice. Occupations differ in many other respects—in public esteem, in working hours and degree of effort, in regularity of employment, in the pleasantness of the work, in the scope they offer for originality and initiative. Each person will evaluate these characteristics differently. But each person will tend to select the occupation that on balance seems to offer greatest *net* advantage.

Suppose now that we wish to chart a labor supply curve for a particular occupation. Since the wage rate is far from the only consideration in job choices, it may seem arbitrary to single it out for special consideration. But there are reasonable grounds for doing so. First, wages are measurable, while many other dimensions of an occupation are not. Second, income is for most people an important consideration in job choices. Third, the wage rate is one of the more flexible characteristics of an occupation. Some characteristics, such as the intrinsic difficulty and pleasantness of the work, are deep-rooted and change only slowly. The wage can vary from month to month. So it is plausible to take it as a variable in our analysis and to assume that other characteristics of the job are constant over the period in question.

Remember also that the characteristics of all other jobs in the economy, including their wage rates, are given and constant. A movement up the vertical axis in Figure 2-2 is an increase in the wage for this occupation *relative* to all other occupations. The upward sloping supply curve S says that the higher the relative wage for this occupation, the more people will choose it over other occupations. A higher wage for an occupation will increase its net advantage relative to other occupations. So some people who previously did not think it quite attractive enough will now switch over and choose it in preference to something else. If the relative wage rises still higher, some more people will switch over, and so on.

A rising supply curve is still more plausible if we bring in educational and training costs. There are few occupations that do not involve some training cost,

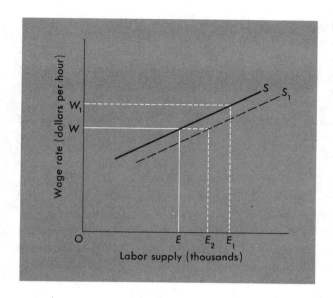

FIGURE 2-2   The Labor Supply
Schedule

and for the higher occupations the cost is very substantial. The returns may also be substantial, but they are uncertain, so they will be evaluated differently by different individuals. People will differ in their estimate of the most likely rate of return, in their attitude toward risk and uncertainty, in their actual ability for the occupation in question, and in their confidence in their own ability. Therefore, if the true (but unknown) return to investment in training for an occupation is 10 percent, some people will choose it and some will not. But we can be reasonably sure that if the rate of return rises to 12 percent, returns to all other occupations remaining unchanged, *more* people will choose it than previously. Supply is positively related to prospective earnings.

We must observe the usual cautions in interpreting the supply schedule. Suppose the wage in Figure 2-2 rises from W to W_1, everything else remaining unchanged. By looking at the supply curve, we see that the number who prefer this occupation will rise from E to E_1. *This is not an increase in labor supply.* It is simply a movement to another point on the same supply schedule.

An increase in supply means that the whole schedule has shifted rightward to a new location, such as S_1, so that at every possible wage more people now prefer this occupation. At a wage of W, for example, the number wishing to enter the occupation is now E_2 rather than E.

While labor supply curves normally slope upward, their shape differs from one situation to the next. An important consideration is that supply adjustments take time. This is especially characteristic of professional and technical occupations with a long training period. At any moment the number of trained chemical engineers is fixed, and a higher wage will have no immediate effect on numbers. In the short run, the supply curve is vertical. However, an increase in the relative wage for chemical engineers will lead more college freshmen to enroll in this specialty, which will increase supply four years later.

Both the supply and demand curves, indeed, have a *time dimension.* It takes time for more people to enter an occupation that requires a substantial amount of training. So supply is more responsive over several years than over a few months. On the demand side, it takes time for a wage increase to produce price increases, a consumer response through lower sales, and a producer response through changed production methods. So the employment response to a wage change will be greater over several years than over a short period.

Market Equilibrium

Labor demand and supply schedules intersect to determine how many will be employed in each occupation and how much they will be paid. Let us see how it would work out if all labor markets were purely competitive. This analysis will provide a benchmark against which we can later measure the effect of departures from competition.

Figure 2-3 shows the market demand and supply schedules for a particular occupation. Then, by the usual reasoning, we can predict that the market will move toward point *A,* corresponding to a wage rate *W.* If for some reason the wage starts out above *W,* there will be more people seeking work than employers are willing to hire. Some of these workers will offer to work for less, and there will be downward pressure on the wage rate until it reaches the level *W.* Conversely, if the wages start out below *W,* the number of workers employers want to hire will be greater than the available supply. Some employers will offer a little more money to attract the

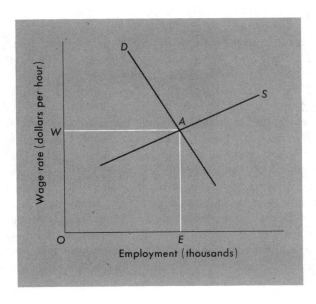

FIGURE 2-3   Equilibrium in a Competitive Labor Market

workers they need. There will be upward pressure on the wage rate, continuing until it reaches *W*.

With a wage of *W* and an employment of *E*, the market is in *equilibrium*. This is a state of balance, in which the number employers wish to hire just equals the number willing to work. It will continue until there is a change in the *D* or *S* schedule. The wage *W* is often called the *competitive wage,* or the market-clearing wage.

A word should be added about the supply of labor to the individual company. A competitive market, by definition, is one in which there are many buyers and sellers of labor, each being small relative to the size of the market. Each company, then, can increase or decrease its employment without affecting the market wage. It must pay as much as others are paying, otherwise it will get no labor at all. But at the market wage it can hire as many workers as it needs. Thus the supply schedule of labor to a single company is a *horizontal straight line at the level W.*

Figure 2-3 relates to only one kind of work in the economy, occupation *A*. But we can draw similar demand-supply diagrams for occupations *B, C, D,* and so on, through every type of work performed in the economy. There will be an equilibrium wage and employment for each occupation. Thus the structure of relative wage rates is completely determined, and so is the occupational distribution of the labor force.

This may seem no great feat until one thinks about how labor would be allocated in the absence of a competitive market. Suppose some federal official had to decide for the American economy as of 2000 how many people should be schoolteachers, how many should be bricklayers, how many should be accountants, and so on. That would be a staggering problem. Yet a competitive market system solves the problem rapidly and inconspicuously.

We can show also that the competitive market solution is optimal, both in terms of national output and in terms of people's satisfaction from work. In output terms, correct allocation requires that the value of extra output produced by an extra hour of a particular kind of labor be the same in every employing unit. In other words, the value of the worker's marginal product (VMP) must be the same for each employer. The need for this condition is obvious. If the value of a bricklayer's marginal product is higher in company *A* than in company *B*, then national output can be increased by shifting labor from *B* to *A*. As this process goes on, marginal productivity will fall in company *A* and rise in Company *B*. When it becomes equal in the two companies, nothing can be gained by further shifting.

The proof that this condition is satisfied under pure competition is straightforward. The market price of any type of labor will be the same to all producers. But each producer, to maximize profit, will employ labor only up to the point at which $VMP = W$. Since *W* is the same for all producers, *VMP* must also be the same.

Output is not everything. It is also desirable that the tasks performed by members of the community should be so allocated among them as to involve a minimum of sacrifice, because everybody is doing the work in which his or her net advantage is highest. If this condition is met, we can be sure that no switching of two people between jobs could benefit one person without either harming the other or causing a drop in output. And this condition will be met if people are able to make a free and informed choice among jobs.

Consider Ms. *A*, whose income is below Ms. *B*'s. Then *A* must have chosen her job, in preference to *B*'s, either because, lacking aptitude for *B*'s occupation, she could not have earned *B*'s income in it, or because she sees other disadvantages in *B*'s job that more than offset the higher wage. In neither case would there be a gain from moving *A* to *B*'s job. In the first case output would fall, and in the second case *A* would feel worse off than before.

USING THE MODEL: SHIFTS IN DEMAND AND SUPPLY

Labor Surpluses and Shortages

You will often read that there is a *surplus* or a *shortage* of a particular kind of labor. These terms are used loosely in popular discussion and lead to much confusion. First, they have no meaning except in a labor market context. The five-year development plan of a Third World country may project, usually on the basis of international comparisons, that the country in 1995 will "need" so many doctors, engineers, teachers, and so on. If the number estimated to be available in 1995 is below these targets, there is said to be a shortage. But the targets themselves are pulled out of the air. *Need* has no meaning apart from a market demand schedule. The question is, Who is willing to pay how much for the kind of labor in question?

Second, surplus and shortage can be defined only *at a price,* that is, at a particular wage rate. There is always some wage rate at which the quantity demanded would equal the quantity supplied. This is the equilibrium wage discussed earlier—the wage that just clears the market. But there may be restrictions that prevent the actual wage from reaching the equilibrium level.

Look at the market shown in Figure 2-4. The equilibrium wage for this kind of labor is W. But suppose for some reason the actual wage is W_1. The number of workers wanting jobs at this rate is considerably larger than the number demanded, so there is a surplus, shown by the distance between the S and D curves.

But how can the wage remain at W_1? Why don't the unemployed workers, by offering to work for less, eventually force the wage down to W? The commonest reasons are trade unionism and legal regulation of wages. If the union contract specifies a wage of W_1, the employer is not free to attract additional workers by lowering wages. The same is true of a minimum wage set by government.

At wage W_2, on the other hand, the number willing to work at that wage falls short of the number demanded, and there is a labor shortage. Again, the question is how such a situation can continue. Why don't employers offer to pay more and bid up the wage until it reaches W and the shortage disappears? Cases of a wage held deliberately below equilibrium are relatively rare. One example is the long-term shortage of nurses in many areas. Another is military service. For most of

FIGURE 2-4   Effect of Enforcing a Nonequilibrium Wage

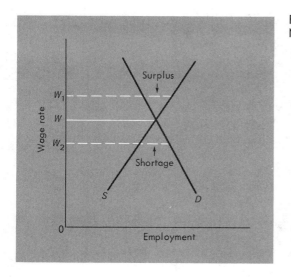

our history the government paid enlisted men in the services considerably less than they could have earned in civilian life. Since the number willing to enlist fell short of requirements, the draft system was used to make up the difference. In the early 1970s, however, the draft fell into disfavor, and government adopted an all-volunteer system. To attract the required number of volunteers, it was necessary to raise military pay close to the civilian level.

Shortage is also sometimes used to describe a situation in which the demand schedule is shifting to the right but the supply schedule is shifting less rapidly, and so the wage rate for the occupation is rising relative to wages in general. The necessity for above-average wage increases may lead employers to complain of a shortage, even though the market is actually in equilibrium at each point in time. A case in point was the much-proclaimed "doctor shortage" of the 1950s and 1960s, during which doctors' earnings rose well above those of other professions. We have shown that competitive labor markets yield an optimal allocation of the labor force *at a specific moment.* We can show also that the competitive market is an effective mechanism for *reallocating the labor force over time* in response to changes in demand and supply conditions.

Suppose, for example, that the supply curve in Figure 2-5 shifts from S to S_1. At any given wage, more people than before are now available for this kind of work. This could happen for several reasons. The supply curve could be for a white-collar occupation requiring high school graduation, and the proportion of each age group who finish high school could be rising. Or the job could have become easier, or other nonwage conditions could have improved. Or certain groups (women, black workers, and so on) formerly excluded from this kind of work may now be admitted, increasing the available supply.

Remember that everything else in the economy is being held constant. Moving to the right along the employment axis means an increase in employment in this occupation relative to all other occupations. Moving upward on the wage axis

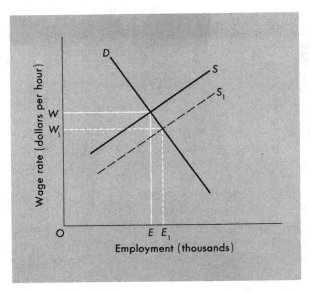

FIGURE 2-5 Supply Shifts, Wages, and Employment

means a higher wage for this occupation relative to all others. If supply shifts from S to S_1, employment will rise to E_1 and the relative wage level will fall to W_1. This result may seem odd, because we rarely see a wage rate falling in actuality. We live in an inflationary economy, in which most wages are rising continually. But a particular wage can fall relatively by *rising less rapidly* than wages in general.

We conclude that *increased labor supply to an occupation—other things remaining unchanged—will raise employment and lower the relative wage in that occupation. A decrease in labor supply will reduce employment and raise relative wages.*

Now consider the effects of a shift in demand. Demand for the occupation shown in Figure 2-6 rises from D to D_1, the supply curve remaining unchanged. What will happen? We can predict that employment and relative wages will both rise. But employment may not rise at once if it takes time to train workers for the occupation. In the short run, with the number of trained workers fixed at E, the equilibrium wage level will shoot up to W_2. As new trainees enter the occupation, however, employment will expand, and relative wages will subside toward the equilibrium level W_1.

The effect of a decline in demand could be seen by sketching in a demand curve to the left of D. Employment and relative wages will both decline.

We conclude that *increased demand for a particular occupation, other things being equal, will raise both employment and the relative wage in that occupation. A decline in demand will reduce employment and relative wages.*

Shifts in demand for a particular kind of labor are dominated by shifts in demand for the product that labor is making. As demand for U.S.-made textiles has declined in the face of import competition, the demand schedule for textile workers has shifted to the left. As demand for fast-food meals has risen, the demand sched-

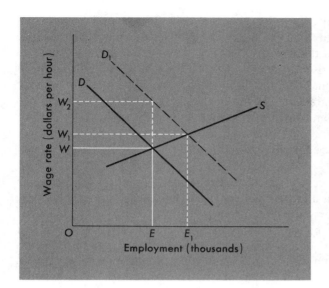

FIGURE 2-6 Demand Shifts, Wages, and Employment

ule for restaurant workers has shifted to the right. These shifts produce both a reallocation of employment and a change in relative wage rates.

Another possibility, common in practice, is when the demand and supply schedules are both shifting. For example, during the 1950s and 1960s demand for college graduates was rising because of the growing demand for technical, administrative, and professional services. Supply was also rising, as the percentage of high school graduates deciding to go on to college continued to increase. For a generation, however, the demand schedule moved faster, and the supply schedule lagged behind.

This sort of situation is illustrated in Figure 2-7. The *D* and *S* schedules

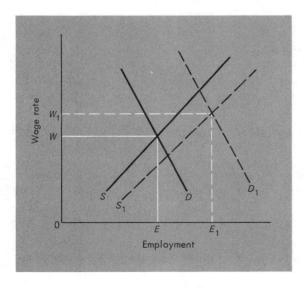

FIGURE 2-7 Demand and Supply Shifting Together

show demand and supply for college graduates in 1945. The D_1 and S_1 schedules show the market situation in 1965. In the new equilibrium, many more college graduates are employed, and their relative earnings (compared, say, with those of high school graduates) have risen from W to W_1. We'll see in Chapter 4 that this is not the end of the story. Around 1970 the supply schedule finally caught up, and the relative earnings of college graduates began to drop. By the 1980s the cycle had started over again, with demand again increasing relative to supply.

The Changing Pattern of Employment

We saw earlier that a rise in demand for a particular kind of labor will produce an increase in both employment and the relative wage. But which will change more? Will the main impact be on employment or on wage rates?

The answer depends on the elasticity of labor supply curves. Suppose, for example, that labor demand curves were completely elastic (horizontal). Then a rightward or leftward shift of a particular demand curve would be fully reflected in employment, and there would be no change in relative wage rates. This assumptions is implicit in many employment forecasting models, which project future employment levels entirely on the basis of demand shifts, with no attention to wage rates.

Suppose, on the other hand, that labor supply curves sloped upward rather steeply. Then a demand increase for a particular occupation would leave little effect on employment but would produce a marked increase in its relative wage.

The research evidence suggests that labor supply curves are in fact quite elastic. Thus the main impact of demand shifts is on the pattern of employment rather than on the wage structure. A study by Richard Freeman of three-digit occupations over the decade 1960–70 found that the variation of changes in employment was considerably larger than the variation of changes in wage rates.[2] This view is also supported by studies of labor mobility, which show a large amount of job shifting within the labor force.

At the beginning of this chapter we discussed how employment has been changing by industry and employment. Recall that the percentage of workers in agriculture and industry has declined while the number in service industries and occupations have increased. Now we want to see how we might explain these changes.

As we indicated above, changes in labor demand are more important than in supply. Changes in labor demand, in turn, depend mainly on changes in product demand.

There are two main reasons for changes in product demand: (1) differing income elasticities of demand (as per capita income rises, demand for medical care rises faster than demand for potatoes); (2) differing productivity trends. If productivity is rising unusually fast in industry A, its unit cost of production will be falling

---

[2]Richard Freeman, "An Empirical Analysis of the Fixed-Coefficient Manpower Requirements Model, 1960–1970," *Journal of Human Resources* (Spring 1980), pp. 176–99.

unusually rapidly. This will be reflected in prices, and the products of industry *A* will become cheaper relative to other products. Cheaper prices will encourage consumers to buy more of *A*'s products than before and less of other things.

The clearest tendency is a long-run decline in the relative importance of agriculture. The proportion of the labor force engaged in agriculture falls from 70 percent or more in the least developed countries to 10 percent or less in the most advanced. This does not, of course, mean any decrease in agricultural output. It means, rather, such a great rise in agricultural productivity that the population can be fed by a much smaller segment of the labor force. One farm family, instead of feeding few more than itself, can now feed ten other families as well.

Industries engaged in commodity production—manufacturing, mining, construction—increase sharply in importance as economic growth proceeds, but this increase does not continue indefinitely. After a certain point, the proportion of the labor force engaged in these industries levels off and moves along on a plateau. In most advanced industrial countries this plateau level is between 30 and 40 percent of the labor force, though in a few countries (Britain, Sweden, West Germany) it approaches 50 percent.

With agriculture continuing to decline in relative importance as development proceeds, and with commodity production leveling off, what takes up the slack in the labor force? The answer is found in industries producing services of every sort—wholesale and retail trade, banking and finance, recreation and entertainment, professional and other personal services, and government. Except for domestic service, which declines in the long run, the proportion of the labor force employed in service activities rises steadily as national income rises. Almost two-thirds of the United States labor force is now employed in the service industries.

What are the reasons for this growing preponderance of service employment? It is often asserted that the income elasticity of demand for services *as a group* is higher than that for goods *as a group*. After reviewing the evidence for the United States, Fuchs finds little support for this view. Indeed, commodity output in real terms has risen just about as fast as output of services since 1929. The decisive factor, then, is the differing movement of output per worker in the two sectors. Put differently, the amount of labor needed for a given volume of output has been shrinking much faster in industry and agriculture than in the service industries. This trend has led to a steadily shrinking proportion of the labor force in the agricultural and industrial sectors.

William Baumol has put this point in a dramatic parable.[3] Consider an economy with two sectors. In one sector (which we may call *S* for services, though Baumol does not), productivity never rises. In the other sector (which we call *G* for goods), productivity rises at a constant rate. Wages in *both sectors* rise at the same rate, geared to the rate of productivity increase in the *G* sector.

What will happen? (1) If the ratio of real output in the two sectors remains constant, the proportion of the labor force employed in the *G* sector will approach

---

[3]William J. Baumol, "Macroeconomics of Unbalanced Growth: The Anatomy of Urban Crisis," *American Economic Review* (June 1967), pp. 415–26.

zero, while the proportion in the *S* sector will approach 100 percent. As this happens, the rate of productivity increase in the economy will also approach zero. (2) Cost (and hence price) per unit of output in the *S* sector will rise without limit. Output of goods with a demand that is price-elastic will decline and perhaps ultimately vanish. As examples Baumol cites fine handmade goods, fine restaurants, live theatrical and concert performances, and "stately homes" requiring domestic servants. (3) Activities for which demand is income-elastic and price-inelastic, such as education and marketing services, will absorb a steadily increasing proportion of the labor force and of GNP. Since many of these are public-sector activities, pressure on state and local government budgets will be intense.

The rise of the service economy has other implications. (1) Economic evolution is often portrayed as a movement toward ever larger and more impersonal production units. This view is based almost entirely on the (now declining) goods sector. Most service activities have a relatively small scale of plant, and self-employment is common. (2) In the same vein, it is often said that the impersonal, routinized, and mechanized conditions of modern industry have squeezed the intrinsic interest out of labor, and that workers must increasingly find satisfactions off the job. But in the growing service sector, many activities require a high level of skill and training, involve personal contact with the consumer, and permit a wide variety of satisfying work activity. (3) Service industries employ a high proportion of white-collar workers, a high proportion (almost 50 percent) of women workers, and a high proportion (more than one-fourth) of part-time workers. This is reshaping the composition of the labor force and the character of labor markets.

RESTRICTIONS ON COMPETITION

We have discussed a simple competitive model of the labor market and have seen how, with some additional assumptions, this model can be used to help explain some of the major trends in employment.

Although the competitive model is useful in analyzing many issues, it has often been criticized on the ground that its assumptions are far from reality. We shall consider these criticisms in later chapters. At this point we can show that the demand-supply apparatus remains useful even when one or more of the requirements for competition is violated. We will consider three examples: (1) restrictions on entrance to an occupation, (2) the market power exercised by a single buyer of labor, and (3) wage fixing by collective bargaining. Another interesting case—the government minimum wage—will be analyzed in Chapter 5.

Restrictions on Labor Supply

The competitive model assumes that anyone wishing to enter an occupation can do so, but that is not always true. There are state licensing systems for many occupations, usually managed by those already in the field, which can be used to hold down the number admitted. For example, there are usually local restrictions on the

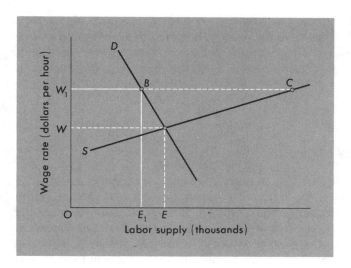

FIGURE 2-8   A Restriction on Labor Supply

number of taxicab drivers in a city that lead to reduced numbers and higher prices of cab fares. A taxi medallion in New York City has been known to sell for as much as a seat on the New York Stock Exchange.

In Figure 2-8 D is the demand schedule for a certain occupation, while S shows the number who would *prefer* to enter it at various wage levels. If entrance were free, E people would be employed in this occupation at a wage level W. Because of some supply restriction, however, only E_1 people can actually get into this field. Running up to the demand schedule, we see that this number can be employed at a wage of W_1, well above the competitive level.

Note that where supply is fixed, *the wage level is determined solely by demand.* An upward shift of the demand schedule would raise the wage rate, while a downward shift would reduce it, but in neither case would there be any effect on employment. The control of supply blocks the normal allocative function of the market.

Those who would prefer to work in this occupation but cannot gain admission, shown by the distance E_1E, will not remain unemployed. They will have to seek employment in other occupations, and the increase in labor supply to these occupations will lower their equilibrium wage. Thus the wage structure is distorted on two counts: (1) an artificially high wage for the occupation in which the supply restriction occurs and (2) an artificially low wage in other occupations in which entrance is unrestricted. Moreover, the forcing of people into occupations in which their marginal productivity is lower reduces national output.

Employers' Monopsony Power

Under pure competition, each employer is too small a buyer of labor to influence the wage. He or she can buy as much or as little labor as required at the market rate. Then the labor supply curve is horizontal.

Suppose, however, that the company's employment is a large part of total employment in its area. At the extreme, suppose it is the dominant employer in a "company town." In this case, it can no longer assume that unlimited labor is available at a standard wage. It will normally have to raise wages to attract additional workers from other companies and areas. It is faced with an *upward sloping labor supply curve* such as S_L in Figure 2-9. An employer with such a supply curve is called a monopsonist.

What does the curve S_L show? For any level of employment, it shows the wage rate—the *average cost of labor*—needed to attract that number of workers. But if the average cost of labor is rising, the *marginal cost* must be rising even faster. Look at it this way: To attract an extra hundred workers, the employer must offer a higher wage to those workers. But since it is impractical to have two wage levels in the same plant, the employer must also pay the higher wage to everyone he or she was previously employing. So the cost of additional labor is higher than appears at first glance. The marginal cost of labor rises along the line MC_L.

As we shall discuss in Chapter 5 the employer's labor demand schedule is identical with labor's marginal revenue productivity schedule where the worker's marginal revenue product, MRP, is the extra revenue the employer gets by employing an additional worker. It is shown in Figure 2-9 by $D_L = MRP_L$. What will it pay the employer to do in these circumstances? To maximize profit, he or she should hire only up to the point at which the cost of hiring an additional worker equals that worker's revenue product. In Figure 2-9 this is point B, where $MRP_L = MC_L$, and corresponds to an employment of E_1. If the employer goes beyond this, so that $MRP_L < MC_L$, he or she is losing money on each additional person employed.

Looking now at the labor supply curve, we see that E_1 workers can be hired at a wage rate W_1, so this will be the company's wage level. There is now a gap,

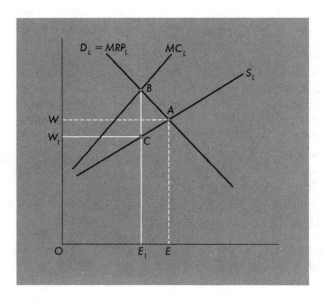

FIGURE 2-9   A Monopsonistic Buyer of Labor

shown by the distance BC, between labor's marginal revenue product (BE_1) and its wage (CE_1). The size of this gap depends on the shape of the labor supply curve. It is easy to see that if the supply curve in Figure 2-9 were steeper, the MC curve would also rise more rapidly, B would be higher up on the demand curve, both wages and employment would be lower, and the gap BC would be larger. The common sense of this is that the more firmly workers are tied to a particular occupation or area, the greater is the employer's power over the wage level, its monopsony power.

The one-company town is perhaps not as common today as in former times. In small communities, however, there are often a few substantial employers who cooperate closely on personnel matters. In such cases a monopsony wage might result from open or tacit agreement among employers to hold down the wage level. Adam Smith thought that employers were "always and everywhere" engaged in this sort of conspiracy. While *always* is too strong, *commonly* might be accurate.

Trade Unions

In the markets considered thus far, workers are unorganized. This does not mean, however, that the worker has no influence on the wage rate. True, the employer takes the initiative in making a wage offer. The worker takes it or leaves it. The worker's "bargaining power" consists of an ability to quit a job or refuse a job offer that does not meet his or her minimum standards. Bargaining power is greater for high-skilled workers than for low-skilled workers, greater during boom periods than during recession, and greater in a large competitive market than in a company town. But the employer's power over wages is always limited by workers' supply decisions.

But there is another way in which workers can seek to influence the wage rate: by forming a union and driving a single bargain with the employer. A union is a complex organization, but among other things, it is a wage-raising organization. Unless union members believe they are getting higher wages with the union than without it, they are apt to lose interest and drop out.

Unions might raise wages in two ways, only one of which is important in practice. They might try to control the supply of labor. The skilled crafts require considerable training and experience and are often learned in advance of employment, either through vocational school courses or apprentice training programs. Control of the number admitted to such programs could conceivably be used to restrict the supply of labor. Such restriction would produce an above-equilibrium wage rate, as explained in the previous section. This has not happened in practice, partly because there are so many ways in which one can learn a skilled trade.

For the most part, unions operate not by controlling the *supply of labor* but by controlling the *employer*. They demand and secure a wage above the competitive level by threatening the employer with strike sanctions. Later in the book we will see that unions differ considerably in their wage-raising ability. On the average, however, it appears that union members in the private sector currently earn about 20 percent more than nonunion workers with the same training, skill, and other personal characteristics.

The economic consequences can be read off from our earlier labor-surplus diagram, Figure 2-4. Suppose the union raises wages from W to W_1. We see from the demand curve that employers will hire fewer workers than before. Also, the number who would like to work at a wage of W_1 is considerably larger than the number employed—there is a labor surplus. These surplus workers will have to seek jobs elsewhere, driving down the relative wage in other occupations. Unions thus create a *wage gap*, both by raising wages on union jobs and by depressing wages on nonunion jobs.

The labor surplus, however, may present the union with a problem. These workers would still prefer to work in this occupation if they could get the wage W_1. Many of them, indeed, would be willing to work for less than W_1. This creates a possibility that nonunion employers will spring up to employ them at less than the union scale. Thus the union must be able to keep the industry organized, which is sometimes difficult. Where employers are numerous, small, and migratory, as in the clothing industry or house building, the organizing task is difficult and the union's wage-raising power is small.

There is one exception to the principle that union wage raising will reduce employment. This exception is the case of employer monopsony power, discussed in a previous section. Look again at Figure 2-9. Suppose the workers organize a union and persuade the employer to agree to a higher wage—for example, the wage W. The employer's freedom of decision is now restricted. Any portion of S_L lying below the bargained wage is irrelevant. S_L and therefore MC_L become horizontal along the line WA. The employer will now move to the point at which this line intersects the demand curve, which will mean an employment of E.

Thus we reach an apparently paradoxical result: Starting from a monopsony situation, it is possible to raise the wage rate up to W with no reduction in employment, in fact with an increase in employment. While such "company-town" cases exist, they are probably not very common. They do not overthrow the presumption that union wage raising is typically accompanied by a drop in employment.

SUMMARY

1. The percentage of workers in agriculture and industry has declined in recent decades, while the percentage in service industries has increased. Similarly there has been an increase in employment in service-oriented and a decline in goods-producing occupations.

2. A competitive labor market requires many buyers and sellers, freedom to enter or leave the market, no organization on either side of the market, no wage fixing by government, full information about market conditions, and economic motivation. Additional assumptions used in this chapter are that the wage rate is the sole measure of job attractiveness, all job vacancies are filled through the market, and all workers are interchangeable to employers and of equal efficiency.

3. The market demand schedule for a particular kind of labor slopes downward from left to right; an increase in the relative wage rate will decrease the number employed.

4. The market supply schedule for a particular kind of labor slopes upward from left to right; an increase in the relative wage rate will lead more workers to choose that occupation.

5. The intersection of the demand and supply schedules determines an equilibrium wage rate and employment level for each occupation. The totality of labor markets thus determines the structure of relative wage rates and the occupational distribution of the labor force.

6. This distribution of the labor force is optimal, in the sense that it maximizes both national output and people's satisfaction from work.

7. An increase in labor supply to an occupation will tend to increase employment in that occupation and to reduce its relative wage.

8. An increase in labor demand for an occupation will tend to increase employment in that occupation and to raise its relative wage. The main impact of demand shifts is on employment, and such shifts largely explain the marked changes in employment by industry and occupation over the past fifty years.

9. If entrance to an occupation is restricted, its wage may remain permanently above the competitive level.

10. A company that is the only employer of labor in an area is called a *monopsonist*. A monopsonist will pay less than the competitive wage rate and employ fewer workers. The same thing is true of a small number of employers who coordinate their wage policies.

11. A trade union may be able to compel an employer to pay more than the competitive wage rate. The usual result is to reduce employment and create a labor surplus in the occupation; but there is an exception when the union serves as an offset to monopsony power.

KEY CONCEPTS

LABOR MARKET, COMPETITIVE
EQUILIBRIUM ANALYSIS, PARTIAL
EQUILIBRIUM ANALYSIS, GENERAL
DEMAND FOR LABOR, FIRM
DEMAND FOR LABOR, MARKET

DEMAND FOR LABOR, CHANGE IN
SUPPLY OF LABOR, FIRM
SUPPLY OF LABOR, MARKET
SUPPLY OF LABOR, CHANGE IN
EQUILIBRIUM, LABOR MARKET

EQUILIBRIUM WAGE
LABOR SURPLUS
LABOR SHORTAGE

MONOPSONY
TRADE UNION

REVIEW QUESTIONS

1. Discuss the geographic size of the labor market for a bituminous coal miner, a computer programmer, a high school mathematics teacher, an aeronautical engineer.
2. What are the main assumptions used in constructing the simplified market models of this chapter?
3. Explain why a union may move the wage rate either closer to, or farther away from, the rate that would prevail under pure competition.
4. What is meant by employers' monopsony power? Under what conditions might one expect such power to be substantial?
5. What are the main factors to be considered in making a rational choice among occupations?
6. Is it plausible to assume that the supply curve of labor to an occupation always slopes upward? Explain.
7. Explain why, under pure competition, the allocation of labor among occupations and the relative wage rates for these occupations are simultaneously determined.
8. In what sense can the allocation of labor that would be achieved under pure competition be regarded as optimal?
9. Explain the meaning and the main effects of (a) an increase in demand for a particular kind of labor. (b) an increase in supply of a particular kind of labor.

READINGS

SCITOVSKY, TIBOR, *Welfare and Competition,* rev. ed. Homewood, Ill.: Richard D. Irwin, 1971.

STIGLER, GEORGE J., *The Theory of Price,* 4th edition. New York: Macmillan Publishing Co., 1987.

LABOR SUPPLY DECISIONS

In this chapter we discuss decisions about working. The quantity of labor available in the economy depends on personal decisions about *whether* to work and *how much* to work. We emphasize that these decisions are made in a lifetime perspective and are usually made within a household framework. There is now a well-developed body of theory in which households are viewed as deciding simultaneously on allocation of time of family members between market work and home production, investment in education and job training, consumption and saving, number and timing of children. Labor supply decisions must be understood as part of this larger decision set.

After developing the principles of labor supply, we use them to interpret the rapid increase in the percentage of working women in recent decades, the decline in labor force participation among men, the long downtrend of working hours in the United States, and the effect of tax and income maintenance policies on how much people work.

MEASURING LABOR SUPPLY

Labor, like capital, can be defined either as a *stock* of productive instruments at a point in time or as a *flow* of services yielded by these instruments over time. In the stock sense, *labor* is the totality of people counted as in the labor force, with whatever skills and productive capacity they possess at the moment. This is the human capital of the nation, a concept going back to Adam Smith. The individuals included in this stock are heterogeneous and hard to add up in a meaningful way; but that is equally true of machines, buildings, and other capital goods.

In a flow sense, *labor* is the number of worker-hours available for production over a period of time. Some members of the labor force work twenty hours a week, others work sixty, and others, everything in between. Moreover, customs about hours of work change over time. Over the past century there has been a large drop in hours worked per person per year. So the supply of available worker-hours has risen more slowly than the number of persons in the labor force.

There is also an important *quality* dimension to labor supply. The flow of labor services is very heterogeneous. It includes worker-hours of corporation presidents' time, research chemists' time, bricklayers' time, farm laborers' time. In recent decades the percentage of managerial, professional, and technical workers has risen substantially, while the proportion of low-skilled workers has declined. This has been accompanied by a large increase in the proportion of young people completing high school, college, and postgraduate programs. The average *quality* of the worker-hour flow has increased.

Because of these complications, our discussion will proceed by stages. We begin by looking briefly at the numbers, the stock aspect of labor supply. Who are in the labor force and what are they doing? Then we examine the flow dimension, workers' decisions about how much or how little work to do.

THE POPULATION BASE

A country's population sets outside limits to the size of its labor force. The population of the United States has increased throughout its history but at widely varying rates. Population grows partly through natural increase, through the excess of births over deaths within the country. And birth rates behave in a somewhat unpredictable way, a fact that has frustrated efforts to predict population growth very far in the future.

Fluctuations in birth rates are reflected in fluctuations in labor force growth; but there is a long lag, because it takes close to twenty years for young people to finish school and enter the labor force. Thus the 1946–60 baby boom shows up in a higher rate of labor force growth, beginning in about 1962 and continuing through the 1970s (see Figure 3-1). The labor force, previously growing at about 1 percent a year, began to grow at better than 2 percent a year. The high unemployment rates among young people during the 1970s arose partly from the fact that the labor market was suddenly faced with absorbing much larger inflows of young people than it had been geared to in the past.

Reduced birth rates after 1960 have now slowed the growth of the labor force. This will have important labor market effects, possibly including a rise in relative wage rates for young people as they become scarcer, as well as a drop in their unemployment rate.

The U.S. population has also grown through immigration, which like natu-

FIGURE 3-1 Annual Rates of Increase in Population and Labor Force, 1947–88
Source: *Statistical Abstract of the United States* (Washingon, D.C.: Government Printing Office, 1980); and *Economic Report of the President* (Washington, D.C.: Government Printing Office, 1989).

ral increase, has fluctuated over the years. It reached a flood tide from 1890 to 1914, was cut sharply by World War I and the immigration laws of the early 1920s, remained at a low level through 1945, and then rose substantially in the post-1945 period. The impact of immigration on the labor force is more direct and immediate than that of natural increase, as most immigrants are adults who go directly into the labor force.

An unusual feature of the past two decades has been the large number of illegal aliens entering and living in the United States, an issue discussed in Chapter 11. A side effect of illegal immigration is that our statistics on population and the labor force are no longer precise, since in the nature of the case, illegal aliens prefer to remain invisible. In general, they occupy the lowest rungs on the occupational ladder.

PARTICIPATING IN THE LABOR FORCE

Definition and Measurement

The percentage of a country's population or of a subgroup in the population that is in the labor force at a particular time is termed its *labor force participation rate,* usually shortened to *participation rate.* In the United States a complete enumeration is made every ten years in connection with the decennial census. Between censuses the Bureau of the Census conducts a monthly survey of a small sample of households carefully selected to represent different sections of the country. On the basis of information obtained from these households, estimates are made of the total labor force, employment, and unemployment in the country as a whole. This

Monthly Report on the Labor Force is the standard source for current labor force information.

An individual is counted as being in the labor force if he or she is able to work and either is working, is temporarily on layoff from a job, or is "actively seeking" work. This apparently simple definition leaves considerable room for doubt in many cases. What about a man who says he is able to work but whom employers judge to be so incapable that they are unwilling to hire him? What about a woman who is not "actively" seeking work because she believes there are no jobs available in her area but who would accept a job if offered? What about a coal miner in a depressed mining area who is willing to take a mining job but no other kind of work? Added to these logical problems is the fact that the census interviewer may see only one family member and has to take that person's word about the status of other people in the household. This leaves room for a good deal of

TABLE 3-1   Labor Force Participation Rates by Age and Sex, United States, 1890, 1947, and 1989

SEX AND AGE GROUP	1890	1947	1989
Males			
Total	89.3	86.8	76.4
16–17	61.5*	52.2	46.3
18–19		80.5	69.2
20–24	90.8	84.9	85.3
25–34	99.0	95.8	94.4
35–44		98.0	94.5
45–54	98.2	95.5	91.1
55–64		89.6	67.2
65+	74.1	47.8	16.6
Females			
Total	21.0	31.8	57.4
16–17	26.9*	29.5	44.5
18–19		52.3	62.5
20–24	32.1	44.9	72.4
25–34	18.0	32.0	73.5
35–44		36.3	76.0
45–54	15.7	32.7	70.5
55–64		24.3	45.0
65+	10.7	8.1	8.4
Total, both sexes	56.1	58.9	66.5

*These rates cover all persons aged 14–19, while subsequent rates cover those 16–19 only. If we had a comparable 16–19 rate for 1890, it would presumably be considerably higher than that shown.

Source: Data for 1890 are from Clarence D. Long, *Labor Force, Income and Employment* (New York: National Bureau of Economic Research, 1950), Appendix A. Data for 1947 are from Howard N. Fullerton Jr., "The 1985 Labor Force: BLS' Latest Projection," *Monthly Labor Review* (November 1985), p. 22. Data for 1989 are from *Employment and Earnings,* January 1990, p. 162.

misunderstanding and faulty reporting. Another problem is that millions of workers n the United States go into and out of the labor force quite frequently.

As a result of these and other difficulties, there is a considerable range of error in published reports on the size of the labor force. While we shall follow the convention of using a single labor force figure, it would be better to think in terms of a zone around the reported figure, which in a country as large as the United States may number several million people.

Participation Rates in the United States

What is the evidence on actual labor force participation in the United States? Table 3-1 shows participation rates for subgroups in the population in 1890, 1947, and 1989.

Reading across the table, we see the marked changes that have occurred over the years. Among men, labor force participation in the youngest age groups has declined considerably because young people on the average now complete more years of education. The sharp decline in participation rates among older men suggests that retirements are now occurring at a considerably earlier age. The most striking feature of the table is the sharp increase in the proportion of women who are in the labor force. In 1890 only one-fifth of women aged sixteen and over were at work. Today the proportion is more than one-half, and in the age groups twenty-five to forty-four it is about three-quarters.

THE COMPOSITION OF THE LABOR FORCE

The developments discussed in the last two sections have substantially changed the makeup of the U.S. labor force. Because of the large size of the baby-boom cohort, there was an unusually high proportion of young people in the labor force in the 1960s and 1970s. Now, as this cohort has grown older, there is an unusually high proportion who are middle aged. The sharp increase in women's labor force participation rates and the drop in men's rates have raised the proportion of women workers relative to men.

The size of these shifts is indicated by Table 3-2. Traditionally, men aged twenty-five to sixty-four were regarded as the core of the labor force, and in 1951 they still formed 55 percent of it. Today they form only 43 percent, and the percentage is still falling. Women, who in 1951 made up only about 30 percent of the labor force now form more than 45 percent of it.

This shift in the makeup of the labor force has had consequences that we will discuss at several points in later chapters. For example, the increasing percentage of women in the labor force has led to increasing concern about their employment opportunities and about the extent of labor market discrimination against women.

Now that we have seen how the labor force has been changing, let us look next at the economic theory of labor supply. After developing this theory, we shall show how it can help explain the changes in labor supply.

TABLE 3-2   Shifts in Labor Force Composition, 1951–89

SEX AND AGE GROUP	PERCENT OF LABOR FORCE IN EACH GROUP	
	1951	1989
Male		
16–19	3.8	3.3
20–24	6.4	6.1
25–64	55.2	43.7
65+	3.9	1.6
Female		
16–19	2.8	3.1
20–24	4.4	5.4
25–64	22.6	35.6
65+	0.9	1.1
Total male	69.2	54.8
Total female	30.8	45.2

Source: *Employment and Training Report of the President* (Washington, D.C.: Government Printing Office, 1982) and *Employment and Earnings* (January 1990).

The traditional analysis of labor supply views the worker as faced with a market wage and with choosing the workweek that will yield maximum satisfaction at that wage. The decision is an *individual* decision, and the result is a two-way division of time between working hours and leisure hours. Let us begin by asking what this simple model can tell us. Later on we will take account of the fact that most workers are members of families, whose decisions about work and consumption are interdependent.

THE SIMPLEST MODEL OF LABOR SUPPLY

A person works in order to earn income. Income can be used to purchase many items, from automobiles to textbooks to beer. Another such item is leisure, that is, time not spent working for money. To simplify the analysis, we shall assume that all time is spent either as leisure or working for pay. (Other possibilities, including time spent at school or looking after young children, will be considered later.) This assumption allows us to analyze labor supply decisions as decisions about the demand for leisure. Any factor that affects the demand for leisure must also affect labor supply. If the demand for leisure increases, labor supply must decrease, and vice versa. We first discuss this decision and then give a more precise graphical analysis.

A person's demand for leisure will depend on three things: income, the price of leisure, and personal preferences. There are considerable differences among people in work-leisure preferences. There are workaholics, and there are others who prefer to go fishing. Other things equal, the former will work more hours per year than the latter. But in short-run reasoning we usually take preferences as given and stable, and focus on the effect of income and price changes.

An increase in income normally raises the demand for goods. There are a few goods ("inferior goods") for which demand falls as income rises, but these are exceptional. There is no reason to think that leisure is an inferior good. So, as income rises, a person will "buy" more leisure as well as more clothes and entertainment. One buys more leisure by offering fewer hours of work in the market. Thus an increase in income, by itself, means a decrease in labor supply. This is called the *income effect.*

What is the price of leisure? Getting an extra hour of leisure means working an hour less, and giving up the income that might have been earned in that hour. So the price of leisure can be taken as equal to the market wage for the worker's particular skill.

The next question, then, is how a change in the market wage will affect labor supply. Suppose the worker's wage rate rises from $8 an hour to $10 an hour. Will she work more hours, or fewer?

The wage increase has two effects that pull in opposite directions. It means, first, that the price of leisure has risen. To take an hour off from work now costs the worker $10 rather than $8. Following the principle that one usually buys less of a good when its price has risen relative to other goods, we might expect the worker to "buy" less leisure, that is, to work longer hours. This is called the *substitution effect.*

On the other hand, the wage increase makes the worker better off than before. She can now afford to buy more of everything, *including* leisure. This income effect, as we have seen, will incline her to work fewer hours than before.

If the substitution effect predominates, the worker will work more hours than before. But if the income effect predominates, she will work fewer hours. We cannot say on logical grounds which effect will outweigh the other.

We do expect that for some individuals the substitution effect will predominate and for others the income effect. If a person is not working initially, an increase in the wage rate that she can earn will have no income effect. The increase in the wage rate will have a substitution effect, however, since a higher wage increases the price (opportunity cost) of leisure. Thus a higher wage rate will cause more people to seek employment.

For the average person who is already employed, the income effect may be stronger than the substitution effect. The fact that in the past average hours worked per week have fallen as real wage rates have risen is often cited as evidence that the income effect predominates for those in the labor force.

A Graphical Analysis

To make the analysis of labor supply decisions more precise, we develop a graphical analysis. First we need to show the worker's preferences for income versus leisure. This can be done by constructing a preference map. An indifference curve on this map, such as I_1 in Figure 3-2, shows different combinations of income and leisure

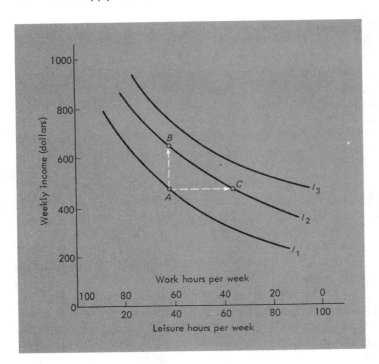

FIGURE 3-2 Preference for Income versus Leisure

that would be equally acceptable to the worker. Put differently, it shows how much leisure the person is prepared to sacrifice for additional income of *x* dollars per week. This is the only precise sense in which one can speak of "desire for income." Naturally, everyone "desires" income if it can be had for nothing. The strength of this desire can be tested only by asking how much leisure the worker is prepared to give up in return. The answer will differ at different *points* on the indifference curve. If the person is already working fifty hours a week, it will doubtless take more income to induce him to put in an extra hour than would be the case if he were working thirty hours a week. We show this by drawing the indifference curve concave upward.

Higher indifference curves, as usual, represent successively higher levels of satisfaction. I_2 in Figure 3-2 is preferable to I_1. Why? Because a worker moving up from, say, point A toward I_2 can have as much income as before and more leisure (point C), or as much leisure as before and more income (point B), or some intermediate combination yielding more of both income and leisure. By the same reasoning, I_3 is preferable to I_2 and so on.

Knowing a worker's preference map does not tell us how many hours he will actually work. To discover this we must also know the hourly wage rate for the job. Suppose it is $10 an hour. Then if he worked the physically feasible maximum—say, 100 hours per week—he could earn $1,000 (point A in Figure 3-3). If he does not work at all, he will earn nothing (point B in Figure 3-3); and he can do anything in between. The line *AB* indicates his *budget constraint*. The market permits him to choose any point on AB—or, for that matter, any point *below AB*. But he will not choose a point below AB, because this would mean working for less than the market wage. Nor can he choose any point *above AB*, because the market wage for his job is not high enough.

Now what point will the worker actually choose? He wants to achieve maximum satisfaction, that is, to reach the highest indifference curve his budget constraint permits. In Figure 3-3 this is I_2. The point C, at which AB just touches I_2, is the point of maximum satisfaction.

The fact that this is the best the worker can do can be demonstrated in either of two ways. First, note that at the point of tangency, C, the *slopes* of AB and I_2 are equal. These slopes have a special significance. The slope of I_2 at any point indicates how much income the worker is willing to sacrifice in order to get a little more leisure. It measures the worker's (subjective) *marginal rate of substitution* between income and leisure. The slope of AB, on the other hand, is an objective fact given by the market. It indicates the rate at which he can actually substitute income for leisure. When the two slopes are equal, the subjective marginal rate of substitution exactly equals the objective, or feasible, rate. This defines a position of maximum satisfaction.

Second, consider what will happen if the worker tries to move away from point C. Any other point on I_2, such as point D, would yield the same level of satisfaction. But point D is unattainable because it lies above his budget constraint. Indeed, all points on I_2 other than C are unattainable. The worker is free to move

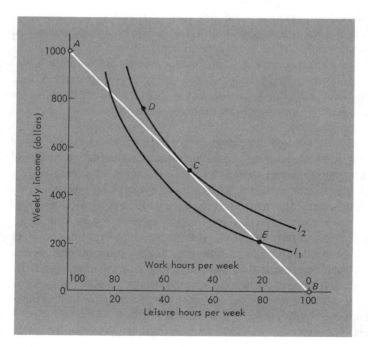

FIGURE 3-3 The Choice of a Workweek

up or down *AB,* say to a point such as *E.* But *E* lies on a lower indifference curve, indicating less satisfaction, so the worker will prefer to stay at part *C.* Since any feasible move away from *C* will reduce his satisfaction, this point indicates his optimum workweek.

There is one case where the optimal hours of work need not involve a tangency between an indifference curve and the budget line. If a person puts a very high value on extra hours of leisure, it may be optimal for the person not to work at all. In terms of the graphical analysis, if the slope of a person's indifference curve is always steeper than the slope of the budget line, the point of maximum satisfaction will not be at a point of tangency but instead will be at the extreme end of the budget line. This case is usually referred to as a *corner solution.* In this way hours of leisure are at their maximum, and there is no labor supply. Such a person will not be in the labor force.

Now that we have defined the worker's optimum position, let us see how this position will be affected by changes in the budget line. In this analysis we shall assume that the person does work (that is, that the optimal position is at a point of tangency rather than at a corner solution). A similar but slightly more complex analysis applies to the decision of whether to participate in the labor force.

Suppose first that the worker is not dependent solely on earnings but has income from other sources. A rich relative has left some property that yields interest or dividends; or the worker is eligible for Social Security payments from government (which are assumed to be independent of the person's hours of work). How will decisions to work be affected.

The effect is illustrated in Figure 3-4. The hourly wage this worker can earn in the market is shown by the slope of the line *AB.* If she were dependent solely on earnings, the highest indifference curve she could reach would be I_1, and she would choose to work the number of hours shown by the point *E.*

But in fact the worker has income of *BC* dollars from some other source. She will have this much income even if she does nothing; but of course she will have more if she chooses to work. Her budget constraint is shifted upward from *AB* to *CD.* These two lines are parallel, because their slope depends on the wage rate, and the wage rate has not changed.

Being better off, the worker can now reach the higher indifference curve I_2 and will choose point *F,* at which the budget line is tangent to this curve. Note that she is now working fewer hours than before. This tells us that leisure is a "normal good," which yields satisfaction, and thus has a positive income elasticity of demand. With more income, the worker "buys" more leisure as well as more goods.

We could repeat this experiment by giving the worker larger and larger amounts of "other income," enabling her to reach still higher indifference curves. In this way we could trace out a locus of intersection points, which would run upward to the northeast, work hours declining with increasing affluence. This result is the income effect. Increased income reduces the hours a person offers in the labor market, given the assumption that leisure is a normal good.

Consider next the effect of a change in the market wage. Suppose the

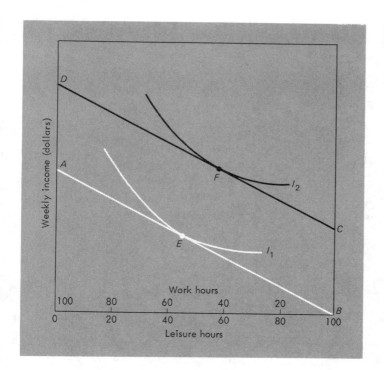

FIGURE 3-4   The Effect of
Nonwage Income on Hours

worker's wage rises from \$10 to \$12 per hour. The response to such a wage change is illustrated in Figure 3-5 by drawing a new budget constraint, A_1B. By working the maximum possible hours, the worker can now earn \$1,200 per week instead of \$1,000. The new budget line lies above the old one, except at the point where hours worked per week is zero. As long as the person was originally working, the new budget line enables the worker to reach a higher indifference curve, I_3. The point of maximum satisfaction is now C_1, where A_1B *is tangent to* I_3.

   As a result of the wage increase, the budget line has shifted from AB to A_1B. This shift can be broken down into an income increase represented by the dashed line, A_2B_2, which is parallel to the original budget line, *AB,* and tangent to the new indifference curve, I_3, at point C_2. The difference in hours worked between C and C_2 represents the income effect of the wage increase. The shift from the budget line A_2B_2 to A_1B represents a change in the wage rate *holding satisfaction constant,* since for each of these budget lines the equilibrium (tangency) point is on the same indifference curve, I_3. Therefore, the difference in hours worked between C_1 and C_2 represents the substitution effect of the original wage increase. This substitution effect must lead to greater hours of work, as long as the indifference curve is concave upward.

   At C_1 the person is working fewer hours than he or she was originally at point C. In this case the income effect of the wage increase is larger than the substitution effect. But as noted earlier, this is not a logical necessity. It depends on the slope of I_3. A little pencil experimentation will convince you that it is possible to

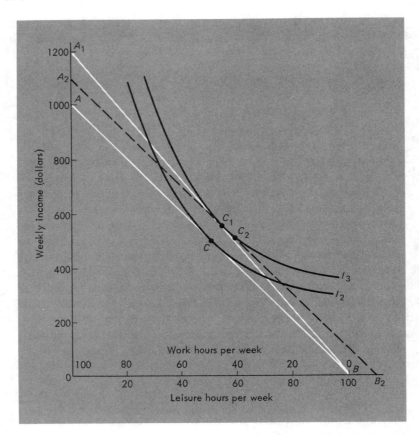

FIGURE 3-5 The Effect of a Wage Change on Hours

draw I_3 so that it would be tangent to A_1B somewhere to the left of C, with the worker putting in more hours than before.

This illustration used a wage increase, but we could construct a case of the opposite sort. Suppose the government levies a proportional tax of 10 percent on the worker's earnings. This tax amounts to a 10 percent cut in hourly take-home pay. The fact that leisure now costs less will incline the worker to "buy" more leisure. So the *substitution effect* will make for a reduction in hours of work. On the other hand, the worker is now poorer and can afford less of everything, including leisure. So the *income effect* will make for an increase in hours of work. Once more we cannot predict on logical grounds which effect will predominate.

What Scope for Choice?

Some may think that we have overestimated the role of individual choice in determining hours of work. Certainly, people can decide whether they want to work at all, the labor force participation decision. But given the fixity of employers' operating schedules, union contracts, and wage-hour legislation, does the individual worker have much scope to adjust hours?

There are two broad answers to this question. Even at a particular time, there is more scope for variation of hours than might appear at first glance. And over the course of time, employer and union policies are responsive to worker preferences.

Elements of flexibility include, first, the fact that the labor force includes self-employed business and professional people with considerable freedom to adjust hours and income. Many doctors and lawyers as well as farmers, grocers, and other small business proprietors work well beyond the standard forty hours a week.

Second, while the forty-hour workweek is commonest for wage-salary workers, some industries operate on a shorter schedule and others on a longer one. In a typical year, 25 to 30 percent of wage-salary workers are on schedules calling for forty-one hours a week or more. Long weeks are especially prevalent in agriculture and trade. On the other hand, workweeks below forty hours are found in some branches of manufacturing, in building construction, and in government service. Employment for less than a full year is also common in some occupations, including teaching and outdoor construction crafts as well as in certain industries, such as seasonal resorts. Thus people have some freedom to choose the amount they want to work by choosing among industries and occupations.

Third, there is the possibility of overtime work. When business activity is high, many employers find it cheaper to pay overtime rates to some of their present employees than to bear the cost of recruiting and training new workers. Sometimes overtime is compulsory, but often it is voluntary.

Fourth, there has been a rapid growth of opportunities for part-time work. The number of workers on voluntary part-time schedules has been rising three times as fast as the labor force. There has been a rapid growth in the number of teenage workers and women workers, who often prefer part-time work, and also a rapid expansion of employment in clerical, sales, and service occupations, which can use part-time workers. The growing supply of people willing to work part time at low hourly rates has probably encouraged employers to restructure their jobs in this way.

At present about one-fourth of all wage-salary jobs are part time. These are primarily sales, clerical, and service jobs. About half of all sales and service workers are on part-time schedules. About two-thirds of the part-time workers are women, while the remainder are young men plus a few older men. Part-time work seems to be especially attractive to married women with small children, since it can be more readily combined with child care. Of married women in the labor force with children under eighteen, about one-third are on part-time schedules, while for other adult women the proportion is only about one-quarter.[1]

---

[1]William V. Deuterman, Jr., and Scott Campbell Brown, "Voluntary Part-time Workers: A Growing Part of the Labor Force," *Monthly Labor Review* (June 1978), pp. 3–10; Carol Leon and Robert W. Bednarrik, "A Profile of Women on Part-time Schedules," *Monthly Labor Review* (October 1978), pp. 3–12; and Ralph E. Smith, ed., *The Subtle Revolution: Women at Work*, Chap. 3.

Fifth, it is possible to hold two jobs, a practice commonly known as moonlighting. There are presently about five million moonlighters, making up 5 percent of the labor force. About half of these people hold two wage-salary jobs. About a million combine a wage-salary job with work in agriculture, while another million combine a paid job with some other form of self-employment. Moonlighting is especially prevalent among teachers, police officers, fire fighters, farmers, and service workers.

Sixth, it is clear that some people reduce their annual hours of work by taking time off during the year. They follow the advice of an old airline commercial to "sneak a week" now and then. Taking leave without pay is possible on some jobs. For those who are changing jobs, the time spent between positions depends, in part, on the worker's preferences. The choice of a job may be influenced by the length of vacation and the number of holidays as well as by the wage rate.

Over the course of time, changes in workers' views about the desirable work-week and workyear influence union and management policies. In the case of the union, this influence is exerted through political channels. Union officials are elected leaders who need the support of their members to remain in office. When the bulk of the membership becomes convinced, say, that a thirty-five-hour week is preferable to a forty-hour week, this will soon become official union policy.

Workers' preferences also affect their choice of employers, thereby influencing employer policies. An employer competing for labor offers a "package" of wages, hours, and conditions that is attractive enough to recruit the number and quality of workers wanted. The hours component of the package will conform to prevailing practice—say, a forty-hour week, six paid holidays, and two weeks' paid vacation for those with five years of service. Suppose now that workers' preferences shift, so that many want a thirty-five-hour week or four weeks' vacation. Some employers incorporate these new specifications in their package, but some do not. Those who do not will find—wage rates and other components remaining equal— that they are attracting fewer workers and have a higher quit rate. There will be pressure on them to come into line, particularly during periods of high employment when labor is scarce. The older concept of a "normal" work schedule will be eroded gradually by the force of competition for labor.

A LIFETIME PERSPECTIVE

In the simple model presented above we have assumed a short-run perspective. Labor supply decisions are made on the basis of current wage rates and current income. What is decided today has no bearing on what is decided tomorrow. In fact, however, many labor supply decisions do take account of expected future events.

First consider income and substitution effects. The income effect on labor supply depends not only on current income but also on expected future income and on wealth accumulated from the past. Retirement decisions, for example, depend on both the current income available to the retiree *and* on how such pension income is expected to change in the future. Thus the income effect depends on expected long-term income more than on current income. This is an example of the *permanent-income hypothesis,* the hypothesis that economic decisions are based on long-run as well as short-run income.

The wage effect also depends not only on the current wage rate but also on expected future wage changes. Assume that a worker suddenly can earn a higher wage rate, but that this higher rate will be only for a short period. For example, the worker may be temporarily reassigned to a higher-paying position to fill in while a coworker is hospitalized. The reassigned worker has an economic incentive to work more while the wage is high, thereby substituting work now for leisure later. The worker might postpone a vacation until after the higher wage is no longer available. Such substitution of work hours across time periods is called the *intertemporal substitution effect.*

For a temporary change in the wage rate, the income effect will be small because of the permanent-income hypothesis, and the substitution effect will be larger than usual because of the intertemporal substitution effect. Thus a wage increase is more likely to increase labor supply in the short run if the wage change is expected to be temporary rather than permanent.

Pensions and Retirement

A typical pension from an employer provides an annual retirement income that depends on the employee's years of service with the firm and on his or her highest earnings.[2] If the employee works an extra year, he will receive a larger pension in the future since he will have an additional year of service and because his earnings are likely to be highest in his final year of employment. At first glance, this increase in retirement income appears to provide an incentive for the employee to postpone his retirement.

From an economic point of view, however, we might expect the worker to be more concerned with the net worth or asset value of the pension than with the annual income that it will provide. Despite the increase in the annual payments, often working an extra year will reduce the net worth of a worker's pension. The worker will not receive any pension income until he retires. If his age of retirement has no effect on how long he lives, then an employee who works an extra year will receive his pension for one less year. For those whose life expectancy is relatively short (e.g., perhaps twenty years), the loss of a year of pension income may have an effect on the pension's asset value that is greater than that of the higher annual retirement income.

In deciding whether to retire now or to work an extra year, the rational worker should consider her monetary compensation for that year to be her salary plus any change in the asset value of her pension. By the age of sixty, most employer pension plans decline in asset value if the employee continues working. Thus

---

[2]For further discussion of issues involving pensions, see Edward P. Lazear, "Retirement from the Labor Force," in *Handbook of Labor Economics,* vol. 1, ed. Orley Ashenfelter and Richard Layard, (Amsterdam: North Holland, 1986), pp. 305–57.

most pensions provide an incentive for a relatively early retirement. As a result, recent legislation abolishing compulsory retirement by employers may not lead to any appreciable change in the average retirement age. In fact, some firms may redesign their pension plans to provide a greater incentive for early retirement if many employees continue working past what had been the age of compulsory retirement.

Social Security

The largest retirement program in this country is Social Security. Until a few years ago, after age sixty-five a worker gained very little in annual benefits if she worked an extra year. By postponing her benefits, she would take a financial loss. The 1983 amendments to the Social Security Act increase the reward for retiring after age sixty-five, which should encourage many workers to retire later. This incentive effect is important because of the way Social Security is financed.

Like many private pensions, Social Security benefits are paid out of current revenue (in this case, Social Security taxes) rather than from funds put aside for this worker, based on the past Social Security payments of the worker and his employer. In other words, we have what is called a *pay-as-you-go* approach. At the present time members of the large baby-boom generation are in their prime earning years, contributing substantial Social Security taxes, more than enough to pay the retirement benefits for the smaller generation who are of retirement age. But in about twenty years the baby-boomers will start to retire. At that time there will be fewer workers to pay the taxes to finance that retirement. To reduce this problem, the 1983 amendments are phasing in incentives to retire later, incentives whose overall effect should be to reduce the Social Security benefits paid out to retired workers.

LABOR SUPPLY AND HOUSEHOLD PRODUCTION

The theory of labor supply developed thus far is a theory of individual behavior. It ignores the fact that most adults marry and form family units. For such people both labor supply and consumption decisions are made, at least partly, on a family basis. This interdependence of individual decisions occurs whenever individuals share housing arrangements and thus share in responsibility for such activities as preparing meals and keeping the home clean. Individuals who share housing are referred to as a *household*. Since the 1960s economists, such as Gary S. Becker and Kelvin J. Lancaster, have devoted considerable attention to the analysis of household decision making and household production.[3]

Economics traditionally distinguished production from consumption. Production was something that went on in business, while consumption was something

---

[3]Becker, *The Economic Approach to Human Behavior* (Chicago: University of Chicago Press, 1976), which among other things includes Becker's 1965 paper, "A Theory of the Allocation of Time"; Lancaster, "A New Approach to Consumer Theory," *Journal of Political Economy* (1966), pp. 132–57; and *Consumer Demand* (New York: Columbia University Press, 1971).

that went on in households. But what exactly is "consumption"? How do we consume a movie? We have to buy a *good,* the movie ticket, for cash. But we also have to spend a certain amount of *time.* And if you think about any other type of consumption, you will find that time is involved. It takes time to shop for food, cook it, and get it to the table. It takes time to mow the lawn and to do repairs around the house. It takes time to watch TV or go to a football game.

So what are people in a household really doing? They are buying goods in the market. Then, by adding time to these goods, they produce what Becker and Lancaster call *commodities*—the movie, or the meal on the table—which are the ultimate objects of satisfaction or *utility.* The household, in short, is a little factory. Like a business, it has a stock of capital goods—the house, furniture, kitchen equipment, automobile, and so on. It has a certain amount of labor power, the time of the various family members. By combining this time and capital with market goods, which can be considered raw materials, it manufactures commodities that yield utility.

The object is to maximize utility, to produce the bundle of commodities that yields greatest satisfaction to family members. The size of this bundle is limited by the family's *income,* which determines how many goods the family can buy. But it is limited also by the amount of *time* available to be combined with these goods. These two constraints reduce to one, because *time can be converted into income* through work in the market. The total resource constraint, which Becker calls *full income,* is the amount that could be earned if family members devoted the maximum feasible time to market work. In fact, they will not do this. They will sacrifice some income to achieve additional utility, since consumption requires time as well as income. But such forgone earnings must be regarded as an opportunity cost.

The implications of this approach are far-reaching. To mention only a few:

1. Instead of a simple choice between work and leisure, there is a more complex time-allocation problem. The possibilities include sale of labor time in the market, use of time in household production, and use of time for education and training that will raise earning power in the future. There is, in fact, no place for "free time" in this system.

   Analysis of household decisions, then, requires examining time used for all purposes. Some of the results are interesting. One study found that married women without jobs average 57 hours a week on housework. Full-time employed married women, on the other hand, average 34 hours a week on housework and 37 hours a week on the job, for a total of 71 hours. Married women workers do work harder. Interestingly, husbands do *not* spend any more time on housework if the wife is working—they spend about 11 hours a week in either case. If the wife is working, less housework gets done.[4]

2. All household decisions are interdependent. The family decides simultaneously on how much time each family member will sell in the market, on savings and purchase of capital assets, on how many children to have and how much to invest in them, on purchase of market goods *versus* do-it-yourself activity, on the assortment of mar-

---

[4]Clair Vickery, "Women's Economic Contribution to the Family," in Smith, *Subtle Revolution,* pp. 159–200. Also see Francine D. Blaù and Marianne Ferber, "Women in the Labor Market: The Last Twenty Years," *Women and Work* (1985), pp. 19–49.

ket goods bought, and on how to combine these goods with time in producing commodities. The unifying thread is that they all involve uses of time and are limited by the family's full income.

3. The labor supply decisions of one family member depend partly on the opportunities open to other members. When a wife's earnings opportunities exceed those of her husband, it is efficient to allocate more of the husband's time to consumption activities. An increase in the relative market efficiency of any family member will produce a reallocation of time by all other members.

A special kind of interdependence exists where husband and wife are employed in professional or executive occupations with a national market. The geographic area that offers the best opportunities for the wife is unlikely to be the best for the husband. A compromise is necessary. If the aim is to maximize family income, and if the wife's salary is lower than the husband's, it will be the wife's preferences that give way. The result could be to restrict the range of work opportunities available to women, and to depress their relative earnings.[5]

THE SUPPLY OF HOURS RECONSIDERED

Let's look again at decisions about hours of work and see what the household approach can add to our understanding of those decisions. The fuzzy concept of "leisure" now disappears from the picture. Time not spent at work is spent in the household where, in conjunction with market goods, it produces commodities that yield satisfaction.

There are two important facts about these commodities. First, they differ in the mix of time and goods required to produce them. Television watching involves much time relative to the goods used up. It is *time intensive*. On the other hand, wearing a mink coat takes a lot of goods and not much time. This commodity is *goods intensive*.

Second, time and goods are usually substitutable in the production of each commodity. A meal eaten in a fast-food restaurant may contain exactly the same items as a meal cooked and eaten at home; but the mix of time spent and money spent is different. The commodity of visiting a relative a thousand miles away can be produced by driving there or by taking a plane. The car is cheaper, but it takes more time.

Now let's consider how a person's division of time between market work and household production will be affected by the kinds of change we examined earlier.

Other Income

Suppose that the household's full income is increased by additional income not derived from wages. Such nonwage income includes interest payments, dividends, and transfer payments such as Social Security. An increase in nonwage income will lead to greater consumption of most commodities (the only exceptions being "inferior goods" with negative income elasticity of demand). But consumption of more

---

[5]See Robert H. Frank, "Why Women Earn Less: The Theory and Estimation of Differential Overqualification," *American Economic Review* (June 1978), pp. 360–73.

commodities requires more time as well as more cash outlay. And some of the commodities with a high income elasticity of demand ("luxuries") are quite time intensive: playing golf, time on the beach, vacations, travel. So time spent in consumption will increase, and hours worked must fall. This reinforces our earlier conclusion that higher income has a negative effect on labor supply.

Increase in the Wage Rate

A wage increase means a higher hourly value of time, and this higher value applies to time spent in the household as well as on the job. There will be two effects on the household's production and consumption of commodities: (1) Time-intensive commodities will become more expensive relative to goods-intensive commodities. This will cause a shift away from time-intensive commodities in the household's consumption pattern. (2) In the production of each commodity, goods will be substituted for time, since time has become relatively more expensive. People will make greater use of the fast-food chain, electric dishwashers, and other ways of saving time as time becomes more valuable.

For both reasons, time devoted to consumption will fall and hours worked will increase. This is the substitution effect of the higher wage. But the higher wage also increases household income, and this income effect will tend to reduce hours worked. Just as in the earlier section, we cannot predict on logical grounds which effect will outweigh the other.

You may find these results not very startling, and not very different from those yielded by the simple model. But they are somehow more satisfying, because they rest on a more inclusive view of human activity. People off the job are not just idle, as the term *leisure* may imply. They are doing something—using time to produce commodities to obtain utility; and it is useful to have this nonwork time brought into the analysis.

EXPLAINING LABOR FORCE PARTICIPATION RATES

At the start of this chapter we saw that labor force participation rates have been decreasing steadily for men but increasing for women. The largest changes have been for married women. Since World War II, their increase in labor force participation has been striking. In 1947, 22 percent of married women were in the labor force. By 1982 this figure had risen to 52 percent. Participation rates for married women are even higher in many European countries, reaching 70 percent in Sweden and 88 percent in the Soviet Union. In most developed economies, the labor force participation of women has been increasing, although often not as dramatically as in the United States.[6]

---

[6]See the special issue "Trends in Women's Work, Education, and Family Building," *Journal of Labor Economics* (January 1985), especially the article by Jacob Mincer, "Intercountry Comparisons of Labor Force Trends and Related Developments," pp. S1–32. Also see Constance Sorrentino, "International Comparisons of Labor Force Participation, 1960–81," *Monthly Labor Review* (February 1983), pp. 23–36.

Although most women now work in the labor market, 45 percent of married women in the United States are still not in the labor force. And some work more hours than others. About one-quarter of married women voluntarily work part-time schedules. What makes the difference? What factors influence the decision whether to work and how much to work? To what extent do the determinants of labor supply for women differ from those for men? Let us use the theory we have developed, together with empirical studies, to address these issues.

Significant Variables

Economists have done many studies of the determinants of labor supply. These studies look at variations in labor supply across different individuals, different labor markets, and over time. Various measures of labor supply have been used, although the most common are labor force participation and hours worked per year. Statistical techniques are used to investigate what measurable characteristics are related to the differences in labor supply. The theory that we have developed guides researchers in both the choice of explanatory variables and in the interpretation of results.

In this section we begin by summarizing the determinants of labor supply at a particular time. This *cross-section* approach looks at why some groups are working more than others. As we shall see, some of the major variables, in addition to gender, are age, family status, wage rates, and labor market conditions. Then we use this information to consider possible explanations for the diverging trends in labor force participation for women and for men.[7]

1. Age. For men the most important determinant of labor supply is the person's age. For those under twenty-five, labor force participation is low because many young men are devoting full time to schooling rather than holding a job. For older men, especially those over sixty-five, labor force participation is also low. In this case the primary explanation is the availability of pension income, although health limitations are also important for some of the elderly. Age has similar, though less dramatic, effects on the labor force participation of women. Differences in labor force participation by age are less pronounced for women than for men mainly because women aged twenty-five to fifty-five do not have as high participa-

---

[7]Our analysis is based on results from many studies, especially William G. Bowen and T. Aldrich Finegan, *The Economics of Labor Force Participation.* For married women, see also the pioneering studies by Jacob Mincer, "Labor Force Participation of Married Women," in *Aspects of Labor Economics,* A Conference of the Universities, National Bureau of Economic Research (Princeton, N.J.: Princeton University Press, 1962); and Glen G. Cain, *Married Women in the Labor Force* (Chicago: University of Chicago Press, 1966). For more recent contributions to the labor supply literature (including reviews of other studies), see Stanley H. Masters and Irwin Garfinkel, *Estimating the Labor Supply Effects of Income Maintenance Alternatives* (New York: Academic Press, 1977); James P. Smith, ed., *Female Labor Supply* (Princeton, N.J.: Princeton University Press, 1982); Michael C. Keeley, *Labor Supply and Public Policy;* Mark R. Killingsworth, *Labor Supply;* John Pencavel, "Labor Supply of Men," and Mark R. Killingsworth and James J. Heckman, "Female Labor Supply: A Survey," both in *Handbook of Labor Economics,* vol. 1, ed. Orley Ashenfelter and Richard Layard (Amsterdam: North-Holland, 1986), pp. 3–102 and pp. 103–204.

tion as men. In this age range, 95 percent of men are in the labor force compared with less than 75 percent of women.[8]

2. *Marital Status and the Presence of Children.*

Among those who have never married and have no children, there is little difference in the labor supply of men and women. However, for women marital status and the presence of young children are the primary determinants of labor force participation.

Married women work less than single women, especially when they have young children. Child care is an especially important component of home production for most families. Although much child care is performed by baby-sitters, day-care centers, and husbands, married women still provide most of such care. Since fertility decisions are made jointly with labor supply decisions, it is difficult to estimate whether the presence of young children significantly affects lifetime labor supply or whether the effect is mainly on the timing of employment decisions.

Another important determinant of a wife's labor force participation is the income of the husband. There are two reasons. First, families with higher income generally will be willing to devote more resources to rearing their children and to other home production activities. Traditionally, much more of this work has been done by wives than by husbands. Second, these traditional sex roles are reinforced whenever the wage rate available to the husband is greater than that available to the wife. The higher the relative market wage rate of the husband, the greater the economic incentive for a household division of labor where the husband devotes most of his time to market work and the wife devotes most of hers to home production, including child rearing.[9]

3. *Wage Rates.*

For men higher wage rates generally lead to reduced labor supply. In other words, the income effect of the wage increase outweighs the substitution effect. For married women the reverse is true. The substitution effect is greater than the income effect, so higher real wage rates lead to increased labor supply.

How can we account for this difference in the effect of wage rates on labor supply for husbands and wives? For those who are working, the income effect appears to be at least as large for women as for men. For those who are not working, however, an increase in the wage rate available in the labor market has no income effect. Since more women than men have not been in the labor force, especially in the past, more women than men will not have been subject to any income effect.

Differences in the average substitution effect between men and women also are part of the explanation. Traditionally, wives have had primary responsibility for home production, including child care, while husbands have had primary responsibil-

---

[8]It is in this middle age range, however, that the differences in labor force participation by gender have been diminishing the most as women have been increasing their lifetime labor supply.

[9]This argument assumes that the high-wage husband is more productive than the wife in market work but not in home production. Given differences in training and socialization, this is generally a realistic assumption.

ity for market work. The presence of home production as an important alternative to market work for wives will influence the magnitude of the substitution effect. Whenever good substitutes are available, the substitution effect will be large. Since in most families the home-production alternative is still more important for wives, the substitution effect of a wage increase will also be greater for wives than for husbands.

4. Labor Market Conditions. Labor force participation rates depend not only on whether people want to work but also on the amount and kinds of jobs that are available. For example, when unemployment rates are high and few employers are hiring, many who would like to work give up actively searching for jobs. As discussed earlier, a person is counted in the labor force only if he or she is employed (has a job) or is unemployed (without a job and actively searching for work). Therefore, if a person gives up searching for work, he or she is no longer counted as being in the labor force. This negative effect of high unemployment on labor force participation is called the *discouraged worker effect.*[10]

In some cases increased unemployment leads to higher labor force participation. If the primary earner in the family loses his or her job, other family members may have to seek jobs in order to reduce the family's income loss. This positive effect of unemployment on labor force participation is called the *added worker effect.*

During the 1950s and 1960s the discouraged worker effect was considerably larger than the added worker effect.[11] Thus high unemployment led to greater labor force participation. During the 1970s and 1980s, however, the discouraged worker effect was weaker, and changes in aggregate unemployment led to little change in the labor force.[12]

Other variables in addition to unemployment are related to labor supply, at least partly because they reflect differences in the availability of jobs. For example, labor supply generally is highest for those with the most schooling, in part because job opportunities are positively related to schooling. Labor markets with industries that traditionally have employed mainly males (Gary, Indiana, with its steel industry) have relatively high labor force participation rates for men and low rates for women.

TRENDS IN LABOR FORCE PARTICIPATION

In Table 3-3 we show changes in labor force participation rates by gender since 1890. For men there is little change prior to 1960, with a modest decline since then. For women there is a slow but steady increase from 1890 to 1940, a sharp increase

---

[10]If no jobs are available, the worker's wage rate on available jobs is zero. Consequently, the discouraged worker effect can be viewed as a substitution effect. Similarly, the added worker effect, discussed below, is largely an income effect.

[11]The classic study for this period is Bowen and Finegan, *Economics of Labor Force Participation.*

[12]See Olivia A. Mitchell, "The Cyclical Responses of Married Females' Labor Supply: Added and Discouraged Worker Effects," *Proceedings of the Industrial Relation Research Association* (1980), pp. 251–57. See also T. Aldrich Finegan, "Discouraged Workers and Economic Fluctuations," *Industrial and Labor Relations Review* (1981), pp. 88–102.

TABLE 3-3   Labor Force Participation Rates of Men and
Women, 1890–1989[a]

	PERCENT OF MEN IN THE LABOR FORCE	PERCENT OF WOMEN IN THE LABOR FORCE
1890	84.3	18.2
1900	85.7	20.0
1920	84.6	22.7
1930	82.1	23.6
1940	82.5	27.9
1945	87.6	35.8
1947	86.8	31.5
1950	86.8	33.9
1960	84.0	37.8
1970	80.6	43.4
1980	77.9	51.6
1985	76.3	54.5
1989	76.4	57.4

[a]Prior to 1947 based on population fourteen years of age and
over; thereafter sixteen years and over.
Sources: U.S. Department of Commerce, Bureau of the Census,
Historical Statistics of the United States, Colonial Times to 1970,
Bicentennial ed., part 1, 1975; U.S. Department of Labor, *Employ-
ment and Training Report of the President,* 1982, Table A-1, 48;
Employment and Earnings, January 1986 and January 1990.

during World War II, a brief decline after the war, and a large steady increase since 1950. To what extent can the determinants of labor supply we have discussed explain why the labor supply of women has been increasing while that of men has been decreasing? After a relatively brief discussion of the changes for men, we turn to a more extensive examination of why the labor force participation of women has been increasing so dramatically in recent years.

For men there have been declines in labor force participation among the young and the old but little change among those twenty-five to fifty-five. In this latter age group over 90 percent are in the labor force. In contrast, the labor force participation rate for those aged fourteen to nineteen has fallen from 62 percent in 1900 to 38 percent in 1980. For those sixty-five years of age and older the decline has been even more dramatic, from 63 percent in 1900 to 17 percent in 1989.

Among young men the downward trend in labor force participation has resulted mainly from an increase in school attendance. For older men the increased availability of pensions, especially Social Security, has enabled workers to retire earlier.

These declines in labor force participation among young and old men are mainly the result of income effects. As real (price-adjusted) wage rates have risen and families thus have higher incomes, it is easier for families to contribute to the support of their children. Children can stay in school longer because they are under less pressure to work to help support their families.

Clearly, the availability of Social Security and other pensions represents an income effect, reducing labor supply. In addition, the growth of real wage rates over the past century has made it easier to establish a generous Social Security system.

Increasing Market Work for Women

For women labor force participation rates have been increasing over the past century, despite the presence of the same income effects that have reduced the labor force participation of men. As we discussed earlier, the income effect of wage increases predominates for men while the substitution effect predominates for women, especially married women. Traditionally home production has been a more important alternative to market work for women than for men. Consequently, increases in the real wage rate have led mainly to more market work and less home production for women while leading to less market work and more leisure for men.[13] This argument, based on increasing real wage rates, can explain the diverging trends in labor supply for men and women until about 1970. But it cannot explain the continuing large increase in the labor supply of women once real wage rates stopped increasing in the 1970s.[14] Also real wage rates have been increasing in other countries, such as Japan and Germany, where the labor force participation of women has not increased.[15]

Other explanations for the long-term rise in the labor force participation of women (especially married women) include the substitution of capital for labor in home production as the prices of home appliances have risen less than wage rates. Probably of greater importance, there has been an increase in labor demand in the service industries and in clerical, sales, and other white-collar occupations, jobs that traditionally have employed a high percentage of women. Conversely, there has been a decline in demand for workers in many traditionally male blue-collar occupations.

Other factors are both cause and effect of the increasing labor supply of women. These include more schooling for women, greater age at first marriage, decreased fertility, more single-parent families, greater availability of day care, the rapid growth of fast-food establishments, and the increased availability of part-time jobs.

Because these trends either started much earlier or appear to be largely the result of the increasing labor force participation of women, none can adequately explain why the labor supply of married women has increased so dramatically during the past two decades. There seems to have been a change in attitudes about

---

[13]This argument was developed first by Jacob Mincer in his article, "Labor Force Participation of Married Women," in *Aspects of Labor Economics*.

[14]See James P. Smith and Michael P. Wood, "Time-Series Growth in the Female Labor Force," *Journal of Labor Economics* (January 1985), pp. S59–90. Over the period examined, 1950 to 1981, Smith and Wood conclude that 58 percent of the growth in the female labor force was due to increasing real wage rates, with about half of this effect working through the influence of wage rates on fertility and the effects of children on labor supply.

[15]See Constance Sorrentino, "International Comparisons of Labor Force Participation, 1960–81," *Monthly Labor Review* (February 1983), pp. 23–36.

sex roles, especially about whether women with children should work in the market-place or stay at home to provide child care and other forms of home production. The old convention that women vanish from the labor force after marriage has been replaced by expectations of a lifetime career, interrupted at most by very brief periods of child rearing. The greatest increases in labor force participation are for married women with very young children. For those with children under the age of two, for example, the labor force participation of married women with husband present has increased from 24 percent in 1970 to 49 percent in 1985.[16] There also has been a significant decline in the birthrate since the 1960s.[17] This decline and the current preference for small families should be interpreted not as a separate factor "causing" an increase in women's labor force participation but as the result of a joint decision, confirming a preference shift away from household activities and toward market activities.

Shifts in attitudes about sex roles and market work were influenced by World War II. The war effort and the associated very high demand for labor led to a large increase in labor force participation among married women. After the war many withdrew from the labor market. Still the notion of clearly defined sex roles had been weakened.

In the 1960s another change in attitudes began, one that continues strong today. This shift is associated with both the women's liberation movement and with campaigns to reduce sex discrimination, an issue discussed in Chapter 8. Not only have women's preferences shifted, but so have the attitudes of many husbands and most employers. The resulting increase in the percentage of women who are career oriented shows up most clearly in the increasing number of women who are pre-pared to spend many years preparing for careers in fields such as law, medicine, and university teaching.

Although a shift in attitudes about sex roles appears to be a major determi-nant of the increasing labor force participation of women over the past two decades, many women have been forced to work out of economic necessity. In some cases husbands have lost their jobs or have been employed in declining industries where wage rates have not kept up with increases in living costs. In such families wives often have had to work in order for the family to maintain its accustomed standard of living. In these cases an income effect clearly is at work.

Another important example of income effects increasing women's labor force participation is related to the dramatic increase in marital dissolutions over the past two decades.[18] After a marriage ends, many women have custody of the children but receive little child support from their former husbands. Although other alternatives such as welfare or moving in with relatives may be available, most single parents prefer to work if they can earn enough to support their families. The

---

[16]See Howard Hayghe, "Rise in Mothers' Labor Force Activity Includes Those with Infants," *Monthly Labor Review* (February 1986), pp. 43–45.

[17]For a discussion of changes in fertility rates, see Victor R. Fuchs, *How We Live* (Cambridge, Mass.: Harvard University Press, 1983), Chaps. 2 and 5.

[18]Ibid., Chap. 5.

possibility of a marital dissolution in the future also has provided an incentive for many married women to obtain a job so that they need not be so economically dependent on their husbands. Conversely the greater economic independence of women has been one factor increasing marital dissolutions, because fewer women are forced to maintain unsatisfactory marriages out of economic necessity.

Day Care for Children of Working Parents

The demand for day care has increased as more women with preschool-age children are working, or would be working, if adequate child care were available. With increased demand for child care, a debate has arisen over who should pay for such care. At present parents pay in most cases, although free (or subsidized) care also is provided by some firms, by the government, and by grandparents or other relatives. Employers can be expected to pay if and only if day care's costs are less than its gains in helping attract and retain workers. Government should provide day care to the extent that the benefits to those outside the family exceed its costs.

   As in the case of public education, one rationale for government subsidization of day care is the development of the child as a productive citizen. Another possible rationale is to reduce welfare costs by assisting low-income women with children to gain employment. Because the size of these benefits is not easy to establish, we have little good evidence on whether such benefits exceed the costs. Moreover, the answers may differ depending on the child, the child's family situation, and the quality and cost of the subsidized care.

CHANGES IN THE NORMAL WORKWEEK

The economic theory of labor supply is useful for explaining not only who will participate in the labor force but also how much those in the labor force will work. In the United States over the past century, rising wage rates and income levels have been accompanied by a marked decline in hours of work. The trend of weekly hours in manufacturing since 1890 is shown in Figure 3-6. Hours fell gradually until 1929, then more sharply during the Great Depression. The forty-hour workweek, in lieu of the previous forty-eight-hour norm, was promulgated in the National Recovery Administration codes of 1933 and 1934 and later in the Fair Labor Standards Act of 1938. The Fair Labor Standards Act does not prohibit work beyond forty hours, but the provision that such work must be compensated at 150 percent of the normal rate gives employers a strong incentive to avoid it. Hours averaged considerably fewer than forty during the 1930s because of depressed demand, rose well above forty during World War II under inflationary demand conditions, then settled back to an almost constant level after 1945. While there have been small cyclical variations around the forty-hour norm, the norm itself has not changed.

   Employers often find it profitable to pay overtime wage rates, despite the 50 percent overtime premium required by the Fair Labor Standards Act and despite the risk that fatigue will affect workers' output. By paying the overtime rate the

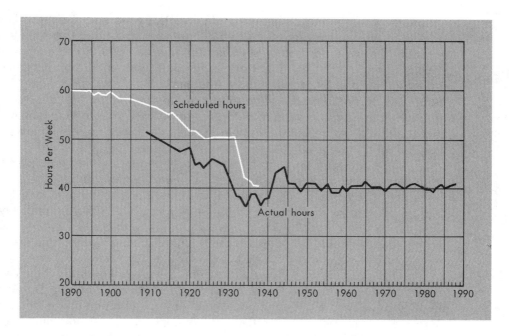

FIGURE 3-6   Average Weekly Hours in Manufacturing 1890–1988

employer avoids the cost of recruiting and training new workers and also avoids an increase in fringe benefits. Also overtime can be readily cut back when the demand for labor falls. In part because of the premium pay, some workers prefer to work overtime. In fact, overtime assignments often must be rationed, usually either by seniority or by rotating the opportunities among all workers.

Although there has been little change in the length of the full-time work-week since the 1940s, average hours worked per year have decreased because of the spread of paid vacations and holidays and because of the increase in part-time employment. Most workers now receive paid vacations of one to four weeks, and the length of service needed to qualify for these benefits has been steadily reduced. In addition, seven or eight holidays are usually paid for, and this list has grown longer over the years.

In the recession of the early 1980s may firms did negotiate a reduction in holidays or vacation days. This may mean that the long-term decline in hours worked per year is ending. On the other hand, the decrease in paid holidays and vacation time may be temporary, a more acceptable pay cut for many workers than an actual decline in take-home pay.

Although the workweek has not changed very much in recent decades for most full-time workers, the percentage of part-time workers has increased. About one-quarter of the work force now work fewer than thirty-five hours per week, while an additional 5 percent moonlight with a second part-time job in addition to their main employment. The two largest groups of part-time workers are students and mothers with young children. In addition, many older workers who have retired from their primary positions continue to work part time. Part-time workers generally receive lower hourly pay than full-time workers. Some employers are reluctant to invest in part-time workers, because the period for recouping such investment must be longer when the worker puts in fewer hours per week.[19] Nevertheless, many workers are willing to accept lower wage rates for shorter hours, especially those who have responsibilities for school work or for looking after young children. As more workers have sought such jobs, more employers have designed jobs to accommodate part-time workers.

One cannot be sure that hours actually worked at any time correspond precisely to what workers would prefer. It seems certain, however, that trends in workers' preferences and in actual hours have been similar. It is unlikely that many workers today would prefer the fifty-hour week of 1900; or, alternatively, that most workers would prefer only twenty-five hours, with the reduction of weekly income that this would necessarily entail. If either statement were true, one would expect more public outcry over the hours issue than there has been in recent years.

The prospect for the future is a continuing gradual decline in hours worked per year, as long as wage rates increase faster than the cost of living. But just how this decline will occur is less certain. There is some indication that workers prefer more time off in solid blocks rather than through shaving small amounts off the working day. An increase in length of vacations is naturally popular. The idea of an occasional "sabbatical" of several months for long-service workers, introduced some time ago in the steel industry, may grow in popularity. The three-day weekend is obviously attractive, as witness the legislative provision that standard national holidays *must* fall on a Monday. Some companies have experimented with a regular four-day week, without necessarily reducing weekly hours of work; and some workers have been willing to work as many as ten to twelve hours a day to achieve the longer weekend.

Another recent line of experimentation is "flexitime," which gives a worker more latitude in scheduling his or her working hours without altering total hours per week. These schemes typically provide a block of "core time," say 10:00 A.M. to 4:00 P.M., during which everyone is expected to be on the job. But arrival for work can be anywhere between, say, 8:00 and 10:00 A.M., and departure anywhere between 4:00 and 6:00 P.M., as each worker prefers. Total hours per day can also be varied by carrying over extra hours from one day to the next, provided the weekly or monthly total averages out correctly.

Such personal schedules are not feasible where workers' activities are highly interdependent, as on an auto assembly line. But where the work is largely independent, experience indicates that flexitime can increase job attractiveness without reducing productivity. Under such circumstances, we would expect a profit-maximizing firm to take advantage of flexitime, as an aid in the recruitment and retention of the firm's work force. Some firms have done so. Yet there are additional social gains that do not accrue directly to the individual employer. For

---

[19]See the discussion about investment by firms in workers in Chap. 6.

example, flexitime can ease child-care problems when both parents are working. It also can reduce traffic congestion during morning and evening rush hours. Thus there is a case for some government intervention to encourage flexitime; at least public employers should provide an example in their own employment policies.

Even greater benefits can occur, especially with regard to child care, if the employee can work in his or her own home. As communication technology has improved, working at home has become increasingly feasible. For example, it is quite easy for a worker to operate a computer terminal. The 1980 census showed that two million people, or 2.5 percent of the nonfarm work force, worked at home for money. This figure probably is a significant underestimate both because of underreporting and because work at home increased substantially during the 1980s.[20]

Because hours and work effort at home are difficult for the employer to monitor, frequently such work is paid for in terms of output produced (i.e., piece-work) rather than on an hourly basis. Opposition to home work has focused on the exploitation of such workers. Because no one is forced to work at home, the real issue is the competitive threat home work poses to the wage rates of those with regular jobs performed on the premises of the employer.

TAXES AND LABOR SUPPLY

We have shown how labor supply decisions are influenced by preferences for money income versus home production and by available economic opportunities, including both wage rates and nonwage income. Thus far in our discussion, we have said little about what causes wage rates and nonwage income to change. In the next two sections we focus on how taxes and income-maintenance programs affect labor supply by changing net wage rates and nonlabor income.

Any increase in taxes will reduce a person's income if all else is held constant. Consequently, a tax increase will have an income effect of increasing labor supply. We must qualify this, however, by noting that taxes are increased to accomplish certain objectives, such as financing government services. If taxes and government services are increased simultaneously and if the value of services equals the cost to the taxpayer, there need not be any net income effect.

Some taxes, including income and payroll taxes, are related to earnings. An increase in such tax rates will reduce the person's net wage rate after taxes are deducted. Thus the tax increase will have the same effect on labor supply as a decrease in the wage rate. In addition to the income effect, there will be a substitution effect reducing labor supply.

The income effect of a tax depends on the *average* tax rate (the total tax

---

[20]According to an estimate by the U.S. Chamber of Commerce and the American Telephone and Telegraph Company, ten million Americans do all their paid work at home, while another twelve million do some of their work there. See John Herbers, "Rising Cottage Industry Stirring Concern in U.S.," *New York Times,* May 13, 1986, p. A18.

payment divided by total income). In contrast, the substitution effect depends on the *marginal* tax rate (the extra tax payment that must be made on an extra dollar of income). If the tax rate is constant, the tax is called *proportional*. In this case the marginal and average tax rates are equal. On the other hand, if the tax rate increases with income, the marginal rate will exceed the average rate and the tax is called *progressive*.

Compare the labor supply effects of two taxes, one proportional and the other progressive. Assume that the average tax rate is the same in each case. Thus each will have the same income effect. Since the average taxpayer has a higher marginal tax rate under the progressive tax, the substitution effect will be larger for the progressive tax. Consequently, taxes are more likely to reduce labor supply if they are progressive than if they are proportional.

Any decision about changes in tax rates should be based not only on labor supply and other incentive effects of tax changes but also on value judgments concerning the equity of different ways of distributing the tax burden. For example, the degree of progressivity in our income tax should depend on value judgments about the desired distribution of aftertax income as well as on the work-incentive effects of high marginal tax rates on the well-to-do.

The relative size of the income and substitution effects of a change in tax rates (or of any other change in net wage rates) cannot be determined on theoretical grounds. Empirical studies are required. As discussed earlier, for the average man in the prime earnings years (about ages twenty-five to fifty-five), the empirical evidence suggests that the income effect is larger than the substitution effect.[21] Therefore, a decrease in tax rates will probably decrease labor supply.

The labor supply effect of any change in tax rates is measured by the wage elasticity of labor supply. This elasticity shows the percentage change in hours worked as a result of a 1 percent increase in the net wage rate. For "prime-aged" men the wage elasticity of labor supply is generally estimated to be in the range -0.2 to -0.1. Therefore, a tax cut that leads to a 10 percent increase in the net wage rate can be expected to *decrease* the average man's labor supply by 1 to 2 percent.

For women we showed earlier that the substitution effect of a wage (or tax) change is generally found to exceed the income effect. Thus a reduction in tax rates will increase the labor supply of the average woman and decrease her home production. Most economists believe that the wage effect is larger for women than for men, but there is little agreement on a precise numerical estimate.[22]

Tax rates affect not only hours of market work and home production but also many other labor supply decisions, including where to live and how much education to seek. These decisions are investment decisions. We analyze them in Chapter 4 when we discuss the concept of human capital.

---

[21]See the references in note 7. See also George Borjas and James Heckman, "Labor Supply Estimates for Public Policy Evaluation," *Proceedings of the Industrial Relations Research Association* (1978), pp. 320–31.

[22]For example, see the range of estimates in Keeley, *Labor Supply and Public Policy.*

INCOME MAINTENANCE AND WORK INCENTIVES

Work-incentive issues have played a major role in shaping our income-maintenance system. In this section we describe our current income-maintenance system and discuss how the economic theory of labor supply is helpful in analyzing policy issues in this area.

In Table 3-4 we show expenditures in 1985 for the principal income-maintenance programs in the United States. Several characteristics of the current system stand out. First, the system clearly differentiates among various groups of society. Most of this categorization is a response to the issue of work disincentives—an attempt to categorize those who are and are not expected to work and then to treat the latter more generously. For example, there are separate programs for veterans, single-parent families (Aid to Families with Dependent Children, AFDC), and the aged, blind, and disabled (Social Security, and Supplemental Security Income, SSI).

TABLE 3-4 Expenditures for Major Income-Maintenance Programs, Fiscal Year 1986

PROGRAM	EXPENDITURES (BILLIONS OF $)
Social insurance	390
Cash benefits	306
Social Security	196
Retirement and survivors' insurance	176
Disability insurance	20
Unemployment insurance	19
Public employee retirement	67
Workers' compensation	16
Other	8
In-kind benefits	84
Medicare	76
Other	8
Welfare	121
Cash benefits	29
Aid to Families with Dependent Children (AFDC)	15
Supplemental Security Income (SSI)	13
Other	1
In-kind benefits	92
Medicaid	48
Food stamps	12
Child nutrition[a]	6
Federal housing assistance for low-income families	12
Other	14
Total benefits	511
As a percent of GNP	12%

[a]Expenditures of the Food and Nutrition Service of the Department of Agriculture, except for food stamps. These food programs include school lunches and a Women, Infants, and Children's Program (WIC).

Source: *Budget of the United States Government* and *Social Security Bulletin* (January 1986).

Expenditures for social insurance programs are substantially larger than for welfare programs. Social insurance programs, such as Social Security, provide benefits to workers and their dependents who might otherwise suffer dramatic income losses because of old age or disability. Eligibility is not limited to the poor. Social insurance benefits are financed not out of the general revenues of government but rather from payroll taxes on employers and employees. Workers with higher earnings pay higher payroll taxes and generally obtain larger benefits. As earnings increase, however, taxes generally rise faster than benefits.

In contrast, welfare programs limit eligibility to those with low income and provide benefits that are unrelated to previous employment. Payments decrease as earnings or other sources of income increase. Finally, welfare programs are financed largely out of general tax revenues. Until the last two decades these welfare programs were designed to aid those not expected to work. Although many people identify the AFDC program with welfare, this program accounts for less than one-fourth of welfare expenditures. By far the most costly welfare program is Medicaid, which covers the medical expenses of most welfare recipients.

Assistance is given, both in cash, which can be spent as the beneficiary desires, and in direct aid for certain kinds of consumption, including food, housing, and medical care. Such noncash assistance is referred to as *in-kind benefits*. In Table 3-4 about two thirds of the total expenditures are for cash programs. Among welfare programs, however, the two in-kind programs, food stamps and Medicaid, account for a majority of expenditures. Moreover, there are many in-kind programs not listed in the table that provide benefits for the poor. These programs include subsidized housing; social services, such as day care and family counseling; employment and training programs; and a variety of educational programs. Although a great many programs have reducing poverty as one objective, some, such as many agricultural subsidies, mainly benefit those with relatively high incomes. Others, such as free public education, provide many benefits to the poor even though they are not generally considered part of our income-support system.

The achievements of our income-support system can be summarized in terms of the effects on the incidence of poverty in this country. Under the official definition of poverty, a family of four was poor if its income was less than $12,675 in 1989. If only market income was included in the income measure, then about 25 percent of all persons were poor, a figure virtually unchanged since the start of the poverty program in 1964. In contrast, after taking account of cash transfer payments and the monetary equivalent of in-kind transfers, only about 11 percent of the population were poor in 1988, down from 17 percent in 1964.[23] Thus the income-support system contributes significantly to the reduction in poverty. In addition, it also cushions income losses due to old age, disability, and unemployment, thereby not only reducing poverty but also reducing the economic burden on the relatives of those who cannot support themselves. On the other hand, our

---

[23]See Sheldon Danziger, Robert Haveman, and Robert Plotnick, "Antipoverty Policy: Effects on the Poor and the Nonpoor," in *Fighting Poverty: What Works and What Doesn't,* ed. Sheldon Danziger and Daniel Weinberg (Cambridge, Mass.: Harvard University Press, 1986).

income maintenance system may have contributed to the poverty problem by reducing the labor supply of beneficiaries and perhaps also by increasing the incidence of single-parent families.

The social insurance component of our income-maintenance system has enjoyed wide support, but the welfare programs have been very controversial. Much of the controversy relates to the effect of welfare on work incentives. Let us see how our analysis of income and substitution effects on labor supply can illuminate why welfare remains highly controversial, despite many efforts over the past twenty years to reform the welfare system.

Welfare payments are available to those who meet various eligibility requirements, including low family income and assets. Most programs have a *guarantee, G,* the amount a family can receive if it has no other income, and a benefit reduction (or marginal tax) rate, *r,* the reduction in benefits for each extra dollar of earnings. Together, the guarantee and benefit reduction rate determine the *break-even level,* the earnings level at which the family will no longer be eligible for benefits. For any earnings level, *E,* below the break-even level, the payments, *P,* can be calculated as

$$P = G - rE$$

Income-maintenance programs increase the income of the beneficiary and thus have an income effect reducing labor supply. The size of this income effect depends on the payment level, *P,* and thus varies positively with changes in the guarantee and negatively with changes in the benefit reduction rate. The benefit reduction rate also reduces the net wage. Thus in addition to the income effect of an income-maintenance program, there will be a substitution effect reducing labor supply. The combination of the guarantee and the benefit reduction rate leads to income and substitution effects that each reduce the labor supply of program beneficiaries.

The main reason why welfare is so controversial is an inherent conflict among several generally accepted goals. A successful welfare program should have at least the following three features: (1) It should provide adequate benefits to those in great need; (2) it should provide a strong incentive to work; and (3) it should not be too costly for taxpayers.

To provide generously for those in need, a large guarantee is necessary. Adequate work incentives require a low benefit-reduction rate. But if the guarantee, *G,* is high and the benefit reduction rate, *r,* is low, many families will be eligible for assistance. (The break-even level is G/r, since $P = G - rE$ becomes zero when $E = G/r$.) Moreover, with a high guarantee and a low benefit-reduction rate, benefits will be high for all program participants except those with high earnings. Thus if welfare is generous to those in need and also avoids strong work disincentives, it must be very costly to taxpayers.[24]

---

[24]Another conflict in objectives is between having a relatively simple income-maintenance system with strong work incentives or providing for particular needs, such as those for food, housing, and medical

There are several ways of dealing with the conflicting objectives of generosity, work incentives, and low cost. We shall discuss two—establishing different programs for different kinds of families and establishing work requirements instead of relying on work incentives.

In an effort to reduce work-disincentive effects, especially when the benefit reduction rate is very high, *work tests* have been established in many welfare programs. Under such work requirements, benefits are denied to those whom welfare administrators consider able but unwilling to work. This approach does provide a possible resolution to the conflicting goals of generosity, work incentives, and taxpayer costs. On the other hand, work requirements have several disadvantages. First, jobs must be available for welfare recipients. Especially during a recession, unsubsidized jobs are often very difficult to find. While the government can provide subsidized employment specially targeted for welfare recipients, this approach is often more expensive than cash assistance because of the costs of supervision and training. Second, under work requirements, administrators must be able to identify who should be forced to work. In the absence of clear guidelines it is easy for administrators to discriminate in favor of those they like and against those they dislike.

Another related response to the conflict in objectives is a *categorical* welfare system. Under this approach different programs are established by legislation for different categories of beneficiaries, depending on how much each is expected to work. For the disabled and others who are not expected to work, a high guarantee is appropriate, and a high benefit-reduction rate is of little concern. In contrast, for needy families who are expected to work, a low guarantee and low benefit reduction rate are more appropriate. The only welfare program that is available to all low-income families, regardless of other family characteristics, is food stamps, a program whose guarantee and benefit reduction rate are both low.

This categorical approach has been utilized extensively, but it does present some additional problems. First, it provides an incentive for people to alter their behavior to achieve eligibility for the more generous programs. In addition, the establishment of the categories depends on a societal consensus regarding who should be expected to work. This consensus no longer exists, especially concerning single mothers with young children, a fact that helps to explain why AFDC has been an especially controversial program.

The Case of AFDC

AFDC was developed in the 1930s as a program primarily for widows and their children. For the past several decades, however, most beneficiaries have received aid either because of a failed marriage or because of illegitimate births. Most

care. There appears to be more political support for food, housing, and health assistance than for cash benefits, even though a high percentage of cash payments are spent on food and housing. But providing assistance separately for food, housing, and other consumption items increases the cost and administrative complexity of welfare assistance. In addition, if benefits for each program decline with family income, the total benefit reduction rate for a family participating in several programs may be quite high—even if the benefit reduction rate is low for each individual program.

people agree that it is important to provide aid to poor children so that they can be healthy and have a good chance of growing up to be responsible, productive adults. On the other hand, few want to provide any incentive to marital dissolutions or illegitimate births. Because there is no simple way to accomplish the former without the latter, AFDC has been our most controversial welfare program.

In the 1960s an important issue was the incentive for a husband to desert his family, since in most cases the family would be eligible for assistance only if there was a single parent. To examine the effects of extending welfare eligibility to all two-parent families, a series of large *income-maintenance experiments* were established. These experiments are a valuable source of empirical estimates of labor supply effects. The experiments showed that among those eligible for the program a quite generous income-maintenance program would reduce hours worked by only about 5 percent for husbands but by about 20 percent for wives.[25] In addition, the cost of such a program would increase by over 30 percent as a result of these declines in labor supply.[26] (Recall that a decrease in labor supply decreases earnings, E, which increases payments since $P = G - rE$.)

To increase work incentives, in 1967 the benefit-reduction rate in AFDC was reduced to 67 percent. Because of deductions for work-related expenses and other factors, actual benefit reduction rates varied considerably from state to state, but averaged only 16 percent by 1971, down from 32 percent in 1967.[27] Partly as a result of the reduced benefit reduction rates and the corresponding increase in breakeven levels, there was a large increase in the number of families on AFDC.

In 1981 the official benefit reduction rate was increased to 100 percent for those who have been on aid for at least four months. Deductions also were tightened, leading to actual benefit reduction rates of about 70 percent, much higher than before the 1967 reforms.[28] Studies indicate that the labor-supply effects of this major increase in the benefit reduction rate have been relatively modest, perhaps because beneficiaries fear they will be terminated from welfare if they quit their jobs.[29]

---

[25]For a summary of the labor supply effects of these experiments, see Keeley, *Labor Supply and Public Policy,* and Robert Moffitt and Kenneth Kehrer, "The Effect of Tax and Transfer Programs on Labor Supply: The Evidence from the Income Maintenance Experiments," in *Research in Labor Economics,* Ronald G. Ehrenberg ed. (Greenwich, Conn.: JAI Press, Inc., 1981); and Philip K. Robins, "A Comparison of the Labor Supply Findings from the Four Negative Income Tax Experiments," *Journal of Human Resources* (Fall 1985), pp. 567–82.

[26]These figures are taken from Michael C. Keeley and others, "The Labor Supply Effects of Alternative Negative Income Tax Programs," *Journal of Human Resources* (Winter 1978), pp. 3–36. They apply to an income-maintenance program with a guarantee equal to the poverty line and a benefit reduction rate of 50 percent.

[27]See Thomas Fraker, Robert Moffitt, and Douglas Wolf, "Effective Tax Rates and Guarantees in the AFDC Program, 1967–1982," *Journal of Human Resources,* (Spring, 1985), pp. 251–63. Higher benefit reduction rates apply to those who are beneficiaries of additional programs, like Food Stamps, and thus subject to reductions in benefits from more than one program as earnings increase.

[28]Ibid. p. 257.

[29]For example, see Robert Hutchins, "Changing the AFDC programs: The Effects of the Omnibus Budget Reconciliation Act of 1981," Institute for Research on Poverty, discussion paper no. 764-84 (December 1984); and Robert Moffit, "Assessing the Effect of the 1981 Federal AFDC Legislation on

The Family Support Act of 1988

The Family Support Act of 1988 revised AFDC, increasing the self-sufficiency of single mothers on welfare and also increasing the financial responsibility of absent fathers for their children. Both steps were designed not only to strengthen families but also to reduce taxpayer costs.

The new program provides more education, job training, and day care than the old program did. Perhaps the most important provision as far as increasing child support from absent parents is concerned is the requirement that employers deduct such payments from parents' paychecks. Many families are on AFDC because of illegitimate births. In response to this problem, states are required to utilize paternity tests, which are now highly accurate. As a result of such tests, fathers will be required to pay child support, even if they have never been married to the mother.

Since the absent parent is at least partially responsible for the creation of the child, he (or occasionally she) should bear a significant portion of the costs of raising the child. Not only is this approach equitable, but it also creates better incentive effects. For example, by increasing the cost of becoming a father, it should make men more careful in their relations with women.

When a pregnancy does occur, the new welfare system reduces the incentive for the father to avoid financial responsibilities by not marrying the mother. Under the former system, the family might have lost its entire welfare eligibility if the parents married. Or if they did remain eligible for benefits, the father still became subject to a very high benefit-reduction rate on this earnings. Under the new system, these disincentives remain, but their net effect is smaller because even if the parents do not marry, the father is subject to a significant increase in his withholding payments to the government as his income rises. Not only do his taxes increase with income, but so do his child-support payments.

If the absent parent's income is relatively low, his child-support payments will also be low. In this case the government still needs to provide additional support to the caretaker parent and her children. As in the past such welfare payments will decline dollar for dollar as the father's child-support payments increase.

Let us consider the work-incentive effects of this mixture of child support and welfare. Assume that the absent father was not previously paying child support but must now do so and that his payments are proportional to his income. His new child-support payments represent a reduction in his net wage rate. This wage cut will increase or decrease his labor supply depending on whether the income or substitution effect dominates. Since the empirical evidence suggests that the income effect is larger than the substitution effect for the average man, there should be some increase in his labor supply.

If the minimum guarantee to the mother and children remains constant, the mother will lose less by working as her child support increases, since she will not

the Work Effort of Women Heading Households: A Framework for Analysis and the Evidence to Date," Institute for Research on Poverty, discussion paper no. 742A-84 (June 1984). For a somewhat different view, see Moffit, "Work Incentives in the AFDC System," *American Economic Review* (May 1986), pp. 219–23.

lose her support payments no matter how much she earns. When her support payments exceed her welfare guarantee, she will not be subject to any benefit reduction rate. As a result, the substitution effect should increase the mother's labor supply. Because the mother will be better off financially, there also will be an income effect leading her to work less. It is likely, but not certain, that the substitution effect will dominate. If so, the mother will work more as her net gains from working increase under the new system.

The increased emphasis on child support can potentially cost the taxpayer less, provide better work incentives, and still be more generous for those parents and children who are in greatest need. Such gains come at the expense of the absent parent, but it appears fair that he should bear more of the costs than he has in the past.

SUMMARY

1. A country's labor supply depends on its total population, on the age composition of this population, and on labor force participation rates. A person is counted as being in the labor force if he or she is able to work and either has a job or is "actively seeking" work. The labor force participation rate of any demographic group is the percentage of that group that is in the labor force at a particular time.

2. Labor force participation rates have been decreasing for men and increasing for women, especially for married women.

3. An individual's labor supply depends on his or her preference for market income versus leisure or home production. Labor supply decisions also are affected by income and substitution effects. As a person's income rises, he or she can afford to work fewer hours, an income effect. But as the person's wage rate rises, the opportunity cost of working fewer hours also increases, a substitution effect. Thus an increase in a person's wage rate leads to both an income effect, reducing labor supply, and a substitution effect, increasing labor supply.

4. For those who live in families, labor supply decisions usually are made on a family basis. There are advantages of specialization to be gained when one spouse concentrates primarily on market work, while the other concentrates on home production. Traditionally, husbands have specialized in market work and wives in child care and other aspects of home production, although differences in sex roles have been diminishing. The economic theory of labor supply is closely related to theories of marriage and of fertility.

5. Important determinants of labor force participation, in addition to gender, are age, marital status and presence of children, wage rates, and labor market conditions.

6. For those who are employed, there has been little change in the standard workweek since the 1940s. However, there has been a decrease in hours worked per year because the number of paid vacations and holidays have increased. There also has been an increase in part-time employment.

7. Tax rates lead to changes in labor supply through income and substitution effects. An increase in tax rates means a reduction in the after-tax wage. Thus there is a substitution effect reducing labor supply and an income effect increasing labor supply. The substitution effect depends on the marginal tax rate, while the income effect depends on the average tax rate.

8. Work-incentive issues have played a major role in shaping our income-maintenance system. Social insurance programs, such as Social Security, provide benefits to those who would otherwise suffer major income losses because of old age or disability. They are financed by payroll taxes. Welfare programs provide aid to families with low income, regardless of their employment history. The benefits are financed from general tax revenue.

9. Welfare programs have been very controversial because there is an inherent conflict among the following generally accepted goals: (a) welfare should provide adequate benefits to those in greatest need; (b) it should provide a strong incentive to work; and (c) it should not be too costly for taxpayers.

10. The work-incentive effects of welfare depend on the guarantee, the benefit-reduction rate, and the number of people eligible for benefits. The number eligible is related to the break-even level of income and to nonincome-related eligibility criteria such as age, disability, and the presence of young children in the family.

11. Welfare assistance is available to single-parent families through Aid to Families with Dependent Children (AFDC). The Family Support Act of 1988 revised AFDC to increase the self-sufficiency of single mothers and to increase the family responsibility of absent fathers for their children.

KEY CONCEPTS

LABOR FORCE
INCOME EFFECT, ON LABOR SUPPLY
SUBSTITUTION EFFECT, ON LABOR SUPPLY
MARGINAL RATE OF SUBSTITUTION
INDIFFERENCE CURVE
BUDGET CONSTRAINT
HOURS OF WORK, OPTIMAL
PERMANENT-INCOME HYPOTHESIS
INTERTEMPORAL SUBSTITUTION EFFECT
HOUSEHOLD PRODUCTION

FULL INCOME
DISCOURAGED-WORKER EFFECT
ADDED-WORKER EFFECT
FLEXITIME
TAX RATE, AVERAGE
TAX RATE, MARGINAL
TAX, PROPORTIONAL
TAX, PROGRESSIVE
BENEFIT REDUCTION RATE
INCOME MAINTENANCE PROGRAM

SOCIAL INSURANCE
WELFARE
IN-KIND BENEFITS
POVERTY LINE

GUARANTEE
BENEFIT-REDUCTION RATE
BREAK-EVEN LEVEL
WORK TEST

REVIEW QUESTIONS

1. "The new home economics, which views the family as engaged in rationally maximizing satisfactions, carries economic reasoning to a ridiculous extreme." Do you agree? Explain.

2. Can you account for the rapid increase in married women's labor force participation rate in recent decades? Would you expect this increase to continue over the next twenty years? Why or why not?

3. The text argues that as the real hourly wage rate rises, most workers will prefer to work fewer hours than before. Yet the standard workweek has remained "stuck" at forty hours since the 1940s, despite a large increase in real wage rates. Why?

4. "The idea that workers can freely choose how many hours to work is just an economist's pipe dream. In any business concern there is a standard workday and week, set by employer decision or union contract, and the worker can only take it or leave it." Discuss.

5. For the future is it reasonable to expect a decline in average hours worked per worker per year? If so, what form or forms would you expect this decline to take?

6. Discuss the effect of different types of taxes on labor supply. How would the effects of a property tax or a sales tax differ from those of an income tax?

7. Why do you think social insurance programs have been more politically popular than welfare programs for the poor?

8. Discuss the effect of each of the following on the work incentive effects of an income-maintenance program: (a) the guarantee, (b) the benefit reduction rate, (c) the break-even level, (d) categorical eligibility requirements, and (e) work requirements.

9. How would you recommend that the government deal with the issue of low-income single parents? How, if at all, would you modify the AFDC program? What are your views concerning the Family Support Act of 1988?

READINGS

Bowen, William G., and T. Aldrich Finegan, *The Economics of Labor Force Participation.* Princeton, N.J.: Princeton University Press, 1969.

Fields, Gary S., and Olivia S. Mitchell, *Retirement, Pensions, and Social Security.* Cambridge, Mass.: MIT Press, 1984.

Hausman, Jerry A., "Labor Supply," in *How Taxes Affect Economic Behavior,* ed. Henry J. Aaron and Joseph A. Pechman. Washington, D.C.: Brookings Institution, 1981, pp. 27–72.

Keeley, Michael C., *Labor Supply and Public Policy.* New York: Academic Press, 1981.

KILLINGSWORTH, MARK, *Labor Supply.* Cambridge: Cambridge University Press, 1983.

———, and JAMES J. HECKMAN, "Female Labor Supply: A Survey," in *Handbook of Labor Economics,* vol. 1, ed. Orley Ashenfelter and Richard Layard (Amsterdam: North Holland, 1986), pp. 103–204.

PENCAVEL, JOHN, "Labor Supply of Men: A Survey," in *Handbook of Labor Economics,* vol. 1, ed. Orley Ashenfelter and Richard Layard (Amsterdam: North-Holland, 1986), pp. 3–102.

SMITH, RALPH E., ed. *The Subtle Revolution: Women at Work.* Washington, D.C.: Urban Institute Press, 1979.

HUMAN CAPITAL:
EDUCATION
AND JOB TRAINING

Two centuries ago Adam Smith observed that the capital stock of a nation consists partly in

> the acquired and useful abilities of all the inhabitants or members of the society. The acquisition of such talents, by the maintenance of the acquirer during his education, study, or apprenticeship, always costing a real expence, which is a capital fixed and realized, as it were, in his person. Those talents, as they make a part of his fortune, so do they likewise of that of the society to which he belongs. The improved dexterity of a workman may be considered in the same light as a machine or instrument of trade which facilitates and abridges labour, and which, though it costs a certain expence, repays that expence with a profit.[1]

Smith's insight was forgotten by the economists who followed him, and the capital concept was narrowed to nonhuman instruments of production. Only in the 1950s did the concept of human capital reappear as an apparently fresh discovery. Since that time there has been a flood of research in this area. Who invests in education and job training and why? What are the benefits to the trained individual? What are the benefits to the economy? What conclusions can we draw about how much should be invested in education, and about who should bear the costs?

---

[1]Adam Smith, *The Wealth of Nations*, 1776, book 2, Chap. 1.

Chapter 3 was concerned with the quantity of labor supplied to the economy. In this chapter we turn to the quality of this labor, which clearly has improved over time. Americans today have, on the average, more than twice as many years of education as their grandparents. Their skills have also been substantially upgraded. About 50 percent of the labor force is now employed in professional, managerial, technical, and clerical occupations, compared with 25 percent in 1930. At the bottom of the ladder, the percentage of farmers, farm laborers, and other laborers has fallen from 33 percent in 1930 to about 7 percent today.

No one has ever seen a unit of human capital, so there is no way of measuring it directly. But if we assume that education and training are worth what they cost, we can use expenditures on them as an indirect estimate of the human capital stock. On this basis, it appears that the nation's stock of human capital is almost as large as its stock of physical capital.[2] And if we add other dimensions of human capital, such as investments in health, the stock of human capital probably exceeds that of physical capital and has been growing at a more rapid rate.[3] Relative to imports, the exports of the United States are often commodities that involve much human capital (for example, chemicals, computers, services) but not necessarily much physical capital.[4] This finding provides support for the view that in the United States human capital is more important than physical capital, at least relative to other countries.

Human capital clearly plays a large role in our economy. In this chapter we focus on one major aspect of human capital: investment in education and training by individuals and investment in education by government. Investment in workers by firms is discussed in Chapter 6, while government training programs are considered in Chapter 10.

Regardless of the type of capital or who is doing the investing, the same general principles apply to all investments. Each involves an initial cost, called the *investment,* and each yields an expected return in future years. From these figures, we can calculate a rate of return on the original investment, which helps in judging whether the investment is worthwhile. These principles apply to both physical and human capital. In the case of human capital, the investment is made in an individual and the main expected return is higher earnings in future years.

We will illustrate these principles by focusing on college and postgraduate training, which is both important and closest to your own experience. At the end of the chapter we raise a few questions about high school education and training on the job.

---

[2]See John W. Kendrick, *The Formation and Stocks of Total Capital* (New York: National Bureau of Economic Research, 1976); and Theodore W. Schultz, *Investing in People* (Berkeley, Calif.: University of California Press, 1981).

[3]From 1929 to 1969 the stock of human capital grew at 3.6 percent per year, with a 2.4 percent growth rate for the physical capital stock. See Kendrick. From 1969 to 1976 the contribution to growth of GNP per person was greater for education than for physical capital. See Edward F. Denison, *Accounting for Slower Economic Growth* (Washington, D.C.: Brookings Institution, 1977).

[4]For example, see Robert F. Lawrence, "Is Trade Deindustrializing America? A Medium-Term Perspective," *Brookings Papers on Economic Activity* (November 1983), p. 144.

THE EFFECT OF SCHOOLING ON EARNINGS

Schooling and other investments in human capital affect earnings in two important ways. First, during the period of schooling, earnings are reduced because the individual must devote time to education. In the absence of schooling, this time could have been used to work for pay. Thus, there is an *opportunity cost* of schooling. For public education this opportunity cost is the largest cost most individuals must pay.

While schooling reduces earnings during the period of education, it also increases earnings after the schooling is completed. Thus in the absence of on-the-job training and other forms of human capital that increase the earnings of older workers, the earnings profiles for those who do and do not attend college would look like those in Figure 4-1. While in school, the student earns an amount, *OA*, from part-time and summer jobs. But he or she could have earned *OB* by working full time throughout the year. Therefore, the opportunity cost of schooling is *AB*. In the absence of investment in schooling or other human capital, earnings would remain at *OB*. As a result of schooling, however, postschooling earnings will increase by *BC*, from *OB* to *OC*.

Schooling and other investments in human capital are usually made when the person is young. Any investment will have a greater payoff the longer the person can reap its benefits. The younger the student is when investing in schooling, the more years he or she can expect to be in the labor market after completing the education. While age may have some effect on the opportunity cost of schooling, *AB*, it usually will have more effect on the number of years the student can expect to achieve the postschooling earnings gain of *BC*.

Why does schooling increase earnings? The most generally accepted answer is that employers find workers with more schooling to be more productive workers. The more output a worker produces, the more the worker contributes to

FIGURE 4-1. Age-Earnings Profiles

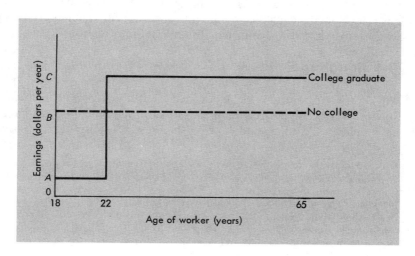

the firm's revenue, and thus the more the worker is worth to the firm. As long as a worker with more education is worth more to several firms, they will compete to employ this worker. If the wage is less than his or her value to each firm, employers will have an incentive to bid higher for the worker in order to increase the firm's profits. Only when the worker's wage equals the value of the extra revenue he or she can produce for the firm (the marginal revenue product) will the bidding stop and an equilibrium be reached.[5]

The Human Capital Model

Next let us consider why schooling increases the value of workers to firms. This issue is important, since the answer to this question influences how one views the desirability of additional investment in education to increase aggregate earnings and the growth of our economy.

The most obvious reason that firms prefer those with more education is the value firms place on the skills students learn in class. These skills include the ability to read critically, write effectively, solve mathematical problems, and learn the content of particular disciplines, such as economics. Many of these cognitive skills can be measured by objective tests. Yet the statistical evidence suggests that earnings are more closely related to years of schooling than to scores on such tests.[6] It is likely that the tests do not fully measure many important cognitive skills. It is also likely that schooling has effects on earnings that are independent of cognitive skills. For example, schooling may increase a person's self-discipline, willingness to accept authority, and ability to work with others.[7]

Thus far we have been describing what is often called the human capital model of investment in education. Students obtain education in order to learn skills that are valuable to employers and thus to earn higher wage rates. Students will invest in additional schooling until the costs of an extra unit exceed its benefits. This model assumes that it is reasonably easy (1) for students to identify which skills are valued by employers and (2) for employers to evaluate the extent to which students have developed such skills. While information is always imperfect, both firms and workers also invest in acquiring labor market information.

The Signaling Model

An alternative view of the labor market is the *signaling model,* developed by Spence, which emphasizes the uncertain information employers have about potential employees.[8] In this model, as we shall see, education serves as a sorting device,

---

[5]Chaps. 5 and 6 analyze the demand for workers by firms in much greater detail.

[6]For example, see Zvi Griliches and William M. Mason, "Education, Income, and Ability," *Journal of Political Economy* (May/June 1972), pp. 74–103; and John C. Hause, "Earnings Profile: Ability and Schooling," *Journal of Political Economy* (May/June 1972), pp. 104–38.

[7]See Herbert Gintis, "Education, Technology, and the Characteristics of Worker Productivity," *American Economic Review* (May 1971), pp. 266–79.

[8]See A. Michael Spence, "Job Market Signaling," *Quarterly Journal of Economics* (August 1973), pp. 355–74; and *Market Signaling.*

a device to help firms determine which workers will be most productive on the job. Education can fulfill this role even in the extreme case where it has no effect at all on the skills of any worker.

Spence emphasizes that for many positions the employer cannot determine very accurately how productive a new worker will be until the worker has been on the job for some time. As we shall see later in this chapter and in Chapter 6, most jobs involve considerable on-the-job training.

In evaluating job candidates, a firm must try to predict how easy workers will be to train, how productive they will be after training, and how long they are likely to stay with the firm after being trained. The amount and kind of schooling workers have attained often is used by a firm in making such predictions. Schooling thus signals information to the prospective employer.

Schooling will be an important signal in the labor model only if two conditions are met. First, its costs to the individual must be negatively related to the long-term value of the worker to the firm. Otherwise, those who would be poorer workers will have as much incentive as anyone else to invest in schooling. Thus schooling would cease to be a useful signal for employers.

A negative relationship between schooling cost and future productivity is plausible, since schooling will be most costly for those who either learn slowly or find schooling especially distasteful. Slow learners at school are likely to be slow learners on the job. And those who don't like school, say because of its discipline, are likely to have similar difficulty adjusting to the discipline of the work place.

The second condition for schooling to be an important signal in the labor market is that there cannot be any cheaper, more accurate, signals available. For cognitive skills, test scores are a cheap alternative that is probably more accurate than years of school. For attitudinal characteristics, the case is less clear-cut. Interviews and references are cheaper sources of such information but are not as accurate. Some attitudes, such as reliability and willingness to submit to discipline over a long period, require testing over several years.

It has proven very difficult to develop statistical tests to determine whether the human capital model or the signaling model is more accurate in our economy.[9] Intuitively, it seems clear that we learn some skills in school that are useful to employers, as postulated by the human capital theory. But to many it also appears plausible that schooling serves partly as a screening mechanism, as postulated by the signaling model. The distinction between the human capital and the signaling models is important mainly in estimating whether education is a good investment to society. Before addressing this question, we discuss how good an investment education is from the point of view of students.

---

[9]A good discussion of the difficulties is presented by John G. Riley, "Inflation, Screening, and Human Capital," *American Economic Review* (May 1976), pp. 254–60. For interesting attempts, see Richard Layard and George Psacharopoulos, "The Screening Hypothesis and the Returns to Education," *Journal of Political Economy* (Sept./Oct. 1974), pp. 985–98; John G. Riley, "Testing the Educational Screening Hypothesis," *Journal of Political Economy* (October 1979), pp. S227–52; Kenneth Wolpin, "Education and Screening," *American Economic Review* (December 1977), pp. 949–58; Dennis De Troy, "Veteran Status as a Screening Device," *American Economic Review* (March 1982), pp. 133–47; and Kevin Lang and David Kropp, "Human Capital versus Sorting: The Effects of Compulsory Attendance Laws," *Quarterly Journal of Economics* (August 1986), pp. 609–24.

IS SCHOOLING A GOOD INVESTMENT FOR STUDENTS?

Decisions about how much schooling to acquire are made by individuals, especially young people and their parents. These decisions are also influenced by government decisions, including how much and in what ways government is prepared to subsidize the costs of education.

In the previous section we discussed the benefits and costs of education in a qualitative fashion. In this section we discuss quantitative estimates. We seek to determine whether, on average, education is a good investment for the individual student. In the next section we look at whether education is a good investment for society as a whole. We focus most of our attention on the benefits and costs of a college education, since these estimates are most directly relevant to you. Our estimates are average values for all students. They show benefits to exceed costs by a considerable margin. As we discuss these estimates, make your own assessment of the benefits and costs for you, and compare your estimates with those we present for the average student.

The Benefits of Schooling to the Individual

Many people invest in education primarily to achieve higher earnings. Therefore, let us begin by looking at earnings differences by education. In Table 4-1 we present earnings by age and sex for workers in the United States in 1983, separately for those who have completed high school and college.

Those with a college degree have higher earnings. The effect of college is greater for males than for females for reasons we shall discuss in Chapter 8 when we examine labor market discrimination and its relation to inequality in the labor market. Earnings increase with age until a peak is reached, usually in the age range of forty-five to fifty-five. For college graduates, the increase with age is greater and the peak normally occurs at a later age. These increases in earnings by age result, at least in part, from effects of on-the-job training, which we consider at the end of this chapter.

Assuming that these earnings differentials in Table 4-1 will continue to hold in the future, how can we use this information to estimate the benefit to an individual of obtaining a college degree? We might just sum the earnings differences over all ages. To simplify the analysis, let us assume that the average difference in earnings between high school and college graduates is $10,000 per year and that the average college graduate works from ages twenty-two to sixty-one, a total of forty years. Summing the post-college earnings differentials gives us an earnings gain due to college of 40 × $10,000, or $400,000, a very sizable figure.

However, this estimate of $400,000 is too high for several reasons. First, since the benefits occur in the future, they must be discounted to their present value. Second, the earnings in Table 4-1 are total earnings, prior to taxes, yet benefits to the individual student will depend on the earnings he or she keeps after taxes. Third, those with more education are likely to have more native ability and thus probably

TABLE 4-1   Mean Earnings of Year-round Full-time
Workers by Age and Schooling, 1987

	SCHOOLING COMPLETED	
Age	High School (12 Years of School)	College (16 Years of School)
	Males	
18–24	$14,732	$22,255
25–29	21,143	29,233
30–34	24,145	33,831
35–39	26,573	39,087
40–44	28,498	42,855
45–49	29,838	46,378
50–54	28,944	50,215
55–59	29,481	44,686
60–64	28,528	48,719
65 +	27,010	35,815
Total	$24,745	$38,117
Age	Females	
18–24	$12,180	$17,584
25–29	15,247	21,800
30–34	16,317	25,205
35–39	16,902	24,229
40–44	17,504	25,528
45–49	18,221	27,495
50–54	17,135	24,578
55–59	17,138	22,746
Total	$16,223	$23,506

Source: *Current Population Reports,* series P-60 (Washington, D.C.: Government Printing Office, 1989).

would have earned more even if they had not received additional schooling. Fourth, in considering the net benefits of schooling, we must also consider its costs, including the earnings foregone while attending school. Let us consider how much of the $400,000 is likely to remain after adjusting for these considerations.

To begin, let us consider why it is not appropriate to count a dollar earned many years in the future the same as a dollar earned today. When prices are rising, a dollar in the future is worth less than a dollar today. With inflation, however, the earnings differentials in Table 4-1 are likely to grow. Since we are assuming that the earnings differentials in Table 4-1 remain constant, we are assuming that the analysis is done in *inflation-adjusted,* or real, dollars.

Aside from inflation, there is another reason why a dollar in the future is worth less than a dollar today. If you put money in the bank today, you can earn interest on that money. Some of this interest is an effort to adjust for the fact that with inflation the purchasing power of the original deposit declines. But some of this interest is a real return that exists, since the bank can lend your money to those with promising plans for investment in new plant and equipment or technology.

Since our analysis is net of inflation, let us assume that the inflation-adjusted, or real interest rate is 4 percent.

If the real interest rate is 4 percent and you put $96 in the bank today, the money will grow to a real (inflation-adjusted) value of about $100 a year from now. Thus $100 to be received a year from now is worth only about $96 today, even after adjusting for inflation. To be precise, it is worth $100/1.04, or $96.15. The *present value* of an income due one year hence is obtained by discounting that income by the rate of interest.

Income due two years from now must be discounted more heavily, since it is farther away. And we apply the same principle. If the rate of interest is 4 percent, $100 put out at interest today will in two years be worth $100 \times (1.04)^2$. To get the present value of income two years hence, we throw this into reverse. The $100 due two years from now is worth today $100/(1.04)^2$, or $92.46.

Now back to our college graduate. College training yields a *stream of future income* over a forty-year period. Recall that to keep things simple, we have assumed that a college degree increases earnings for men by $10,000 per year. Then by applying the reasoning above, we have the present value, *PV*, of the difference in income streams given by

$$PV = 10,000/1.04 + 10,000/(1.04)^2 + 10,000/(1.04)^3$$
$$+ \ldots + 10,000/(1.04)^{40}$$
$$= 9,615 + 9,246 + 8,890 + \ldots + 2083$$
$$= 197,928$$

Thus at a 4 percent real interest rate, the present value of the discounted income stream is less than half the value of $400,000.[10] At 2 percent, the present value would be $261,935, while at 6 percent it would be $150,462. Thus, the present value is very sensitive to the choice of an interest rate, which is unfortunate since the real interest rate varies from year to year and even from person to person. An alternate approach that partly avoids this difficulty and which we shall consider shortly is to calculate an *internal rate of return* to education.

Next let us look at the effects of taxes. The more income a person earns, the higher the taxes he or she must pay. In considering the return to the individual from a college education, the increase in income after taxes is of primary concern. Thus we must examine how much of the increased earnings because of college goes to higher taxes and how much remains as after-tax income for the individual.

Over a wide range of income, including that of most college graduates, the average tax rate for federal, state, and local taxes is about 25 percent.[11] More relevant, however, is the *marginal* tax rate—the tax paid on an extra dollar of

---

[10]Since the earnings differentials between college and high school graduates are greater for those over forty-five than for younger workers and since the discounting has more effect the longer the time period, a more precise analysis would show that the present value is even lower than indicated in the text.

[11]See Marilyn Moon and Isabel V. Sawhill, "Family Income: Gainers and Losers," in *The Reagan Record*, ed. John L. Palmer and Isabel V. Sawhill (Washington, D.C., Urban Institute Press, 1984), p. 328.

income, which is probably at least 33 percent for most college graduates.[12] Recall that we estimated the sum of all future earnings gains from college to be about $400,000. After discounting with a real interest rate of 4 percent, this gain dropped to about $200,000. After taking into account tax increases, the gain to the individual falls to perhaps $130,000.

The approach we have outlined gives us a quantitative measure of the benefits of a college degree. This approach, based on earnings figures such as those in Table 4-1, also enables economists to estimate the present value of anyone's expected lifetime earnings, after taxes. Such calculations are important in many legal cases, where a victim (or the victim's family) is due compensation for the earnings loss suffered as a result of an accident where someone else was at fault.

Next let us look at the various qualifications that must be made in considering our estimate of the value of a college education. First, we must take into account that those who complete college are not a representative sample of those who have previously completed high school. Those who have completed college, on average, come from higher-income families and have more ability, at least in terms of aptitude for college subjects. Those whose parents have more education and income may have more self-confidence, connections, and other advantages as well as greater opportunities to obtain more schooling. In addition, those with more ability for schoolwork might be expected to earn more in the labor market, even if they have not attended college.

A number of studies have tried to estimate how much of the higher earnings of those with more schooling is due to ability differences rather than to schooling effects per se. Most empirical studies have found that differences in years of school are more important than differences in ability or family background, even taking account of the fact that the data on schooling usually are more accurate than those on ability and family background.[13]

Of course, the effects of schooling on earnings will differ for those with different initial abilities. A good rock singer will not be able to increase his or her earnings very much by completing college. But someone with good mathematical ability and an interest in engineering will be able to earn much more if he or she goes to college and studies engineering.[14]

On balance it appears likely that an adjustment for ability would lower the earnings differentials in Table 4-1 slightly, on average. But there would also be

---

[12]See Charles R. Hulten and June A. O'Neill, "Tax Policy," in *The Reagan Experiment,* ed. John L. Palmer and Isabel V. Sawhill (Washington, D.C.: Urban Institute Press, 1982).

[13]For example, see Paul Taubman, "The Determinants of Earnings: Genetics, Family and Other Environment: A Study of Male Twins," *American Economic Review* (1976), pp. 858–70; Taubman, "Earnings, Education, Genetics, and Environment," *Journal of Human Resources* (Fall 1976), pp. 447–61; Zvi Griliches, "Sibling Models and Data in Economics: Beginnings of a Survey," *Journal of Political Economy* (October 1979), pp. 537–64; John H. Bishop, "Is the Test Score Decline Responsible for the Productivity Growth Decline?" *American Economic Review* (March 1989), pp. 178–97; and Richard B. Freeman, "Demand for Education," in *Handbook of Labor Economics,* vol. 1, ed. Orley Ashenfelter and Richard Layard, (Amsterdam: North-Holland, 1986).

[14]See Robert J. Willis and Sherwin Rosen, "Education and Self-Selection," *Journal of Political Economy* (October 1979), pp. 57–536.

considerable variation around the average, if we could adjust properly for all ability differences.

Next let us consider whether there are any reasons why our estimates of the benefits of a college degree, based on the data summarized in Table 4-1, might underestimate the total benefits of college. The data in Table 4-1 refer to money earnings. However, they leave out two potentially important benefits from education. First, additional schooling may pay off in terms of jobs that not only pay more but also are better in several other respects.

The managerial, professional, and technical jobs populated mainly by college graduates provide larger fringe benefits as well as higher annual earnings. They are also more creative, secure, prestigious, and generally satisfying. This impression was tested and confirmed in a study by Greg J. Duncan.[15] He had two data sets that enabled him to combine wage rates, fringe benefits, and several working-conditions variables.

> The principal finding is that education's well-documented pervasive importance for pecuniary benefits carries over to fringe and nonpecuniary benefits as well . . . when pecuniary and nonpecuniary variables are combined into a single composite earnings measure, the estimated coefficient on education is considerably greater (25 percent in one data set, 10 percent in the other) than when earnings are measured by the wage rate alone. [P. 481]

These nonpecuniary job benefits may outweigh the effects of any ability adjustment.

In addition to the benefits of schooling in terms of providing access to better jobs, schooling also has a number of other important benefits. For example, college helps broaden one's horizon and form new friendships. It can also increase enjoyment of leisure later in life and often helps sort out marital partners. Education can also increase one's productivity in home production (for example, shopping, child care), as well as on the job.[16]

Taking account of all these qualifications, our earlier figure of $130,000 is probably a conservative estimate of the economic benefits of college for the average male.[17] There is likely to be considerable variation around this average, however, for different individuals and possibly also for different schools. And we still must compare these benefits with the costs of college.

For women the earnings differentials in Table 4-1 are considerably lower than for men. Thus the estimate of lifetime earnings gain, after discounting at 4 percent and adjusting for taxes, is about $80,000 instead of $130,000. If a woman takes time off from work for child rearing or other household production, the earnings gain will be even lower. These low earnings effects for women are related to labor market discrimination and to the traditional division of labor within house-

---

[15]Duncan, "Earnings Functions and Nonpecuniary Benefits," *Journal of Human Resources* (Fall 1976), pp. 462–83.

[16]For an analysis of this possibility, see Robert T. Michael, "Education in Nonmarket Production," *Journal of Political Economy* (March/April 1973), pp. 306–27.

[17]The 4 percent real discount rate also is probably a high estimate, thus again leading to a conservative estimate of the economic gains from college.

holds, with men specializing in market work and women specializing in child care and other aspects of home production, discussed in Chapter 3. As discrimination in the labor market has declined and more women are taking vocationally oriented courses, the gender differential in the earnings effects of schooling should decline.[18] The issue of labor market discrimination is discussed in Chapter 15.

The Costs of Schooling to the Individual

Next we must estimate the costs of schooling and compare them to the benefits. For those attending state colleges or universities, including junior colleges, the average cost of tuition is about $2000. At private universities, tuition is much higher, over $10,000 at the most prestigious schools. Room and board cost $2,000 to $5,000 for those who live on campus, but these costs should be included only if the students would pay less for room and board if they were not at school. Books cost perhaps $400 per year. Thus the total out-of-pocket costs for four years of college range from about $5,000 to over $80,000.

As we emphasized earlier, the costs of college include not only the out-of-pocket expenses but also the earnings foregone by attending school. If a student attends school full time with no summer job or part-time job during the school year, the average foregone earnings would be about $13,000 for men and $10,000 for women. Adjustments to these figures have to be made both for taxes and for earnings of students. If we assume that the marginal tax rate for young people is about 25 percent (including Social Security, state and local taxes, and the federal income tax), and that the average student earns about $3,000 per year, then the foregone earnings each year will be about $7,500 for men and about $5,000 for women. Summing over four years gives us estimates of foregone earnings as $30,000 for men and $20,000 for women, which is much higher than the out-of-pocket costs of attending a state university.[19]

In addition to these monetary costs of schooling, one also needs to consider the consumption aspects of schooling. Many students greatly enjoy college and later in life look back fondly on their college days. For others, however, college can be a time of tension and very hard work. On balance, college appears to be a source of pleasure for most students, especially when it is compared with the alternative of working full time at an entry-level job open to those without a college degree. Thus in estimating the value of college as an investment, we make the fairly conservative assumption that college does not also have consumptive value.[20]

---

[18]See Solomon Polachek, "Sex Differences in College Major," *Industrial and Labor Relations Review* (July 1978), pp. 498–508; and Arthur E. Blakemore and Stuart A. Low, "Sex Differences in Occupational Selection: The Case of College Majors" *Review of Economics and Statistics* (February 1984), pp. 157–62.

[19]All the cost of college needs to be discounted up to age twenty-one, just as the future benefits were discounted back to this age. Since the cost is incurred over four years, at a discount rate of 4 percent, the cost estimates should be increased about 25 percent.

[20]One well-known study finds that education has negative consumption value for students. See Edward Lazear, "Education: Consumption or Production?" *Journal of Political Economy* (June 1977) pp. 569–97. However, this study suffers from some major biases, as pointed out in Joseph Da Boll-Lavoie, "An

Comparing Benefits and Costs

For the average young man going to a state-supported school, the total costs (including foregone earnings) of four years of college is generally less than $50,000. Even if he attends an expensive private university, the cost is not likely to exceed $100,000. Since we estimated the expected benefits to be substantially greater than $100,000, it appears that college is a good investment for the average man. The same thing is also true for women, except perhaps for those who plan to focus on home production rather than on careers in the labor market.

The conclusions stated above are consistent with the results in the economic literature. These studies generally present their findings in a slightly different manner, however. Instead of discounting by some real interest rate, an internal rate of return, *r,* is calculated. This rate of return is the discount rate at which the present value of the income stream yielded by the investment is equal to its cost. In other words, *r* must be such that the cost of education, *c,* equals the present value (*PV*) of the education to the student. Therefore, for a student who plans to work for forty years after college, *r* must satisfy the condition that

$$c = PV = \frac{\Delta E_1}{(1+r)} + \frac{\Delta E_2}{(1+r)^2} + \frac{\Delta E_3}{(1+r)^3} + \ldots + \frac{\Delta E_{40}}{(1+r)^{40}}$$

$$= \sum_{i=1}^{40} \frac{\Delta E_i}{(1+r)^i}$$

where ΔE_i is the effect of college on earnings in the ith year after graduation.[21]

Based on data for the 1950s and 1960s, the private rate of return for college education was generally estimated to be between 10 percent and 15 percent.[22] By 1974 Freeman estimated the rate of return for men had fallen to 8.5 percent.[23] Then, in the 1980s, the rate of return regained its previous level.[24] One explanation for these changes is the large size of the baby-boom cohort, many of whom attended college in the late 1960s and 1970s. If substitutability between young and old

Examination of Earnings Differences from Attending Private versus Public Colleges," Ph.D. dissertation at the State University of New York at Binghamton, 1988.

[21]If ΔE is constant, then $C = \sum_{i=1}^{40} \frac{\Delta E_i}{(1+r)^i} \cong \frac{\Delta E}{r}$, so $r \cong \frac{\Delta E}{C}$. If $\Delta E = \$10,000$ and $C = \$50,000$, then $r \cong 0.2$, or 20 percent.

[22]For example, see Gary S. Becker, *Human Capital;* Jacob Mincer, *Schooling, Experience, and Earnings;* Richard Raymond and Michael Sesnowitz, "The Return to Investment in Higher Education: Some New Evidence," *Journal of Human Resources* (Spring 1975), pp. 139–55; and Martin Carnoy and Dieter Marenbach, "The Return to Schooling in the United States, 1939–69," *Journal of Human Resources* (Summer 1975), pp. 312–32.

[23]See Richard B. Freeman, "Overinvestment in College Training?" *Journal of Human Resources* (Summer 1975), pp. 287–317.

[24]See J. Peter Mattila, "Determinants of Male School Enrollments: A Time Series Analysis," *Review of Economics and Statistics* (May 1982), pp. 242–51 and James P. Smith and Finis R. Welch, "Black Economic Progress After Myrdal," *Journal of Economic Literature* (June 1989), especially p. 559. Returns to education appear to have increased in recent years for women as well as for men. See Rachel Frieberg, Kevin Lang, and William T. Dickens, "The Changing Structure of the Female Labor Market, 1976–1984," *Proceedings of the Industrial Relations Research Association,* 1988, pp. 117–24.

workers diminishes with education, the rate of return to schooling will be low for a large cohort.[25] Another possible explanation for the recent increase in the rate of return is foreign competition. Increases in foreign competition have had their greatest effect on blue-collar jobs in manufacturing. Thus increased foreign competition in the 1980s quite likely reduced the relative earnings of men who were not college graduates.

Even if the rate of return should be as low as 7 or 8 percent, however, such a return is still very attractive. Because it needs no downward adjustment for taxes or inflation, it is a higher return than one can expect to earn on any bank account or than one can reasonably expect from the stock market. Thus college education appears to be a good investment, a conclusion that is quite consistent with our earlier discussion comparing the economic benefits of college to its costs. For those who do not have money to invest and have no collateral to secure a loan, it would not be possible to borrow to finance one's education, however, except for the existence of government assistance.

As we shall discuss shortly, the rate of return to a college education is likely to differ considerably from one individual to another. Although college appears to be a good investment for the average student, it is not a good investment for everyone. Thus when the average rate of return falls, as it did in the 1970s, it is not surprising that college becomes a poor investment for more potential students. In fact, the empirical evidence suggests that there is a strong negative relation between the average rate of return to a college education and the percent of high school graduates going on to college.[26]

The private rate of return for high school generally is estimated to be much higher than for college. As shown in Table 4-1, the earnings gains for completing high school is less than for college. This reduced earnings gain is more than offset, however, by no tuition and lower foregone earnings.

As shown in Table 4-2, school enrollment is very high at the high school level. Up until age sixteen, school attendance is compulsory. But even at ages sixteen and seventeen, when attendance is not compulsory and foregone earnings become a significant factor, well over 80 percent continue in school. At the college level, however, school becomes much more expensive, and at least for some, the rate of return may drop significantly. As a result, only 30 to 40 percent of all those in the college-age group are attending school. Until recently a higher percentage of men than women attended college. Now women have a slight edge over men, a change that reflects both the decline in labor market discrimination in top-paying jobs and the increased interest of many young women in competing for such positions.

Our discussion has focused on the high rate of return on college education for the average student. Despite this high rate of return, many young people do not

---

[25]See David C. Stapleton and Douglas J. Young, "Educational Attainment and Cohort Size," *Journal of Labor Economics* (July 1988), pp. 330–61.

[26]Mattila, "Male School Enrollments." Also see the evidence for the effects of relative salaries and of tuition on college attendance presented in Freeman, "Demand for Education."

TABLE 4-2   Percent Enrolled in School by Age and
            Sex, 1980

AGE	MALE	FEMALE
14	98.5	98.6
15	97.3	96.8
16	92.6	92.5
17	84.2	84.3
18	62.3	61.8
19	42.3	43.6
20	34.3	35.2
21	30.6	29.6
22	23.9	20.0
23	18.3	13.9

Source: *1980 Census of Population*, vol. 1, chap. D, pt. 1, United
States summary, table 260.

attend college. Let us examine why some people are more likely to attend college
than others.[27]

One consideration is differences in ability. The same investment in education will yield higher returns to more able people. Another consideration is access
to capital in order to finance educational costs. Children from poor families have
less access to finance or, what amounts to the same thing, will have to pay a higher
rate of interest on any money they can borrow. Even the cost of foregone earnings
may require borrowing if such earnings are needed to finance the living expenses of
the student.

The returns to additional schooling can be analyzed in the fashion explained earlier. The gain to a person with x years of schooling is the amount the
person will earn over and above what could be earned by a completely uneducated
individual. Let us call the latter amount the *earnings base*. The problem, then, is to
determine the *surplus* over the earnings base that can be attributed to education.

The horizontal axis in Figure 4-2 shows differing amounts that might be
invested in schooling, increasing from left to right in the usual way. The vertical axis
shows how much an additional dollar invested in schooling will yield in future
earnings, over and above the earnings base. Look, for example, at curve D_3, which
relates to a particular individual. The first bit of investment in schooling yields a
large return, indicated by G. As more and more money is devoted to education,
however, the returns gradually decline. D_3 slopes downward to the right. Human
capacities are limited, and hence successive units of investment yield diminishing
returns.

The fact that some people's D curves are higher than others—as illustrated
by D_1, D_2, and D_3—means that the same amount of investment in schooling yields
larger returns to some individuals than to others. This reflects *differences in ability*.

The D curves are *demand curves for schooling*. The S curves, on the other

[27]For detailed development of this line of analysis, see Jacob Mincer, "The Distribution of Labor
Incomes."

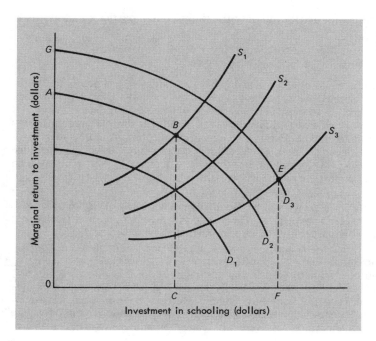

FIGURE 4-2. Effect of Ability and Cost of Funds on Schooling

hand, are supply curves, indicating the amount of financing available at each interest rate. To gain access to more money, higher interest rates must be paid. For example, a bank might charge more for a loan than a relative would.

The *S* curves differ because some people (or their parents) have more money or can borrow more readily than others. The *S* curves, then, can be interpreted as *opportunity curves,* while the *D* curves are *ability curves.*

A person's investment in schooling, and the earnings level that flows from this, is determined by the intersection of the specific *D* and *S* curves. Thus someone whose situation is indicated by D_2 and S_1 would settle at point *B*. One with the curves D_3 and S_3 would settle at point *E*.

We can also determine from Figure 4-2 how much each individual will earn over the earnings base. Consider the person whose equilibrium is at *B*. The first investment yields a return of *A*. Each additional unit of investment yields less than the previous one, as we travel down D_2. At the investment level *C* the total addition to earnings is the area *OABC*, that is, the *area under the returns curve.*[28] By the same reasoning the person whose equilibrium is at *E* will earn an amount *OGEF* over the earnings base.

There are millions of other intersection points like *B* and *E*, one for each labor force member. The degree of inequality in labor incomes depends on how

---

[28]Writing the earnings function as $E = f(I)$, the marginal return to investment is dE/dI. The total return to investment up to any level, *C*, is the integral of this function over the range in question. The reasoning is identical with that for the relation between marginal utility and total utility, or marginal cost and total cost.

these intersection points are distributed over the diagram in a particular economy at a particular time.

To illustrate, consider the following three hypothetical cases:

1. Suppose that one could establish *equality of opportunity*—equal access to finance for schooling and equal willingness to borrow in response to a given rate of return. In terms of Figure 4-2, all those in the market would then have the same *S* curve. (It will be useful to sketch a revised Figure 4-2 in order to visualize the consequences.) It is clear that this would not bring about equality of incomes. A more able individual, one with a higher *D* curve, would still invest more and achieve larger lifetime earnings than a less able individual. But the degree of inequality would be less than if differences of opportunity were also present.

2. Suppose, on the other hand, that all people are of equal *ability*—they have the same *D* curve (and again, a sketch will be useful). Here inequality of earnings depends solely on differences in opportunity. The people with greater opportunity will invest more; but the marginal return to their investment will be lower.

3. Suppose, finally, that the *D* and *S* curves are not independent of each other but are positively correlated—individuals with greater ability also have lower financing costs. It is not hard to find reasons why this might be so. Part of what appears as greater ability is doubtlessly not genetically determined but reflects greater motivation arising from a superior home environment. Here one has opportunity masquerading as ability. Parents with more education and larger incomes are more likely to encourage their children to persevere with education and are also better able to finance the necessary costs.

  • A diagram illustrating this possibility would show the people having the most favorable (highest) *D* curves as also having the most favorable (farthest to the right) *S* curves. The outcome would be a strong positive relation between ability, amount invested in schooling, and level of earnings, which would produce marked inequality in the distribution of labor incomes.

The differences that result from inequality of opportunity have been a major reason why government finances much of the cost of education. Before considering the case for such assistance and how such aid might be provided most effectively, we must first turn to investment in education from the point of view of the whole society. Instead of looking at the investment in schooling from only the student's point of view, we now need to consider the issue from a broader perspective. We need to consider not only the private rate of return to schooling but also the social rate of return.

IS SCHOOLING A GOOD INVESTMENT FOR SOCIETY?

Although the demand for education depends on private decisions, the supply of educational facilities depends mainly on government decisions. Thus the question of how much education should be produced depends on the benefits and costs to the whole society, not just to the individual student and his or her family. In this section we first look at whether additional schooling is a good investment from the point of view of the whole society. Then we look at who should pay for college. If the benefits accrue mainly to the individual student, then the student (or the student's family) should bear most of the cost. If the benefits accrue mainly to the rest of society, then college costs should be heavily subsidized by government.

The social return to education is the addition to national output arising from the worker's increased productivity. We assume for the moment that productivity is measured accurately by money earnings. (Everyone recognizes that because of labor market imperfections, earnings and productivity do not always correspond; but there is little agreement on the size of the discrepancy or how to adjust for it.) Note also that we should take gross income with no reduction for income tax, since the tax influences only the distribution of output gain and not its size. In estimating private returns, on the other hand, we take post-tax income, since that is what the individual actually receives.

On the cost side, the private calculation includes only costs borne by the student or his or her family. But in social calculations, we must count the full cost of buildings, teachers' time, and other inputs into education, regardless of how these costs are financed. At the elementary and high school levels, these costs come almost entirely out of public funds. Even at the college and graduate school levels, student tuition covers only a minor part of total educational costs.

The procedure for calculating social rates of return is exactly the same as that illustrated earlier for private rates. The internal rate of return is that which makes the future income stream, discounted to the present at that rate, exactly equal to the full cost of education. Because full cost is substantially *above* private cost, the social rate of return to education is considerably *below* the private rate— often by three or four percentage points, at the college level. If Freeman's estimates are still valid, the social rate of return to college education today is about 5 percent. The return to postgraduate training in the arts and sciences is even lower—very low indeed for Ph.D. programs in some areas.[29]

In evaluating such estimates, however, we must consider the possibility that higher education has *external effects,* that is, benefits to others in the economy that are not registered through the price systems. We saw earlier that education tends to raise women's labor force participation rates, with a consequent increase in labor supply and national output. Education may have important effects on the next generation. There is evidence that the amount of time mothers spend with their children varies directly with the mother's educational level.[30] Children of more educated parents receive more pre-school education in the home and more guidance and encouragement in the later school years. The fact that children of more educated parents typically score higher on IQ tests probably results from home environment as well as genetic endowment.

More scientists and engineers should accelerate research and invention, a

---

[29]See Freeman, "Overinvestment in College Training?"

[30]Arleen Leibowitz, "Education and the Allocation of Women's Time," in *Education, Income, and Human Behavior,* ed. F. Thomas Juster (New York: McGraw-Hill Book Co., for the Carnegie Commission on Higher Education, 1975).

major factor in productivity growth. More highly educated managers and supervisors add to the productivity of those working under them. More educated citizens should be more informed and active participants in public affairs. Education apparently reduces the propensity to engage in crime, partly by raising the prospective rewards from legal as against illegal activities.[31] Because most of these effects are not measurable, however, we cannot say how much they add to the social return to education.

Earlier we discussed two models for why schooling increases a worker's earnings: the human capital model and the signaling model. In the human capital model, schooling increases earnings because workers learn skills that make them more productive. The increased schooling increases total output in the economy.

In the signaling model, however, schooling is a sorting device. If a person obtains more schooling, then schooling leads to higher earnings for that person but not necessarily to greater productivity and output for the entire economy.

From the standpoint of the person deciding whether to go on to college, it does not matter why schooling increases earnings. The important point is that the employer is willing to pay more for the higher degree. Whether the person's schooling increases total productivity by as much as it increases his or her earnings has no effect on the private rate of return. But the effect of schooling on productivity does affect the social rate of return. While some upward adjustment to the social return must be made for the external effects of schooling discussed earlier, a downward adjustment must be made for the screening or signaling effect of schooling. Unfortunately, we have little good evidence on the size of either of these adjustments. In fact, we do not even have confidence in whether the net adjustment should be positive or negative.

Why does the estimate of social returns matter? First, we need it to judge whether too many or too few resources are being devoted to higher education. One can argue that resources should be allocated to producing human capital up to the point at which the marginal rate of returns equals that on physical capital, usually estimated in the range of 10 to 15 percent. By that test, if the social return to education is well below 10 percent, it would seem that the higher education industry is overexpanded. But to the extent that the true social return, including external effects, might be higher than the measurable return, this conclusion needs to be qualified.

Second, an estimate of social returns is necessary in judging how much of the cost of higher education should come from public funds. One school of thought regards higher education as essentially a private investment good, whose possession benefits the owner through higher lifetime income. So like any other investment good, it should be priced at cost. This would mean a tuition fee high enough to cover full educational costs. The counterargument for public subsidy of educational costs rests on a belief that the net external benefits are large enough to warrant substantial subsidy.

---

[31]Issac Ehrlich, "On the Relation between Education and Crime," in Juster, *Education, Income, and Human Behavior.*

WHO SHOULD PAY FOR HIGHER EDUCATION?

Who should go to college? As regards *how many* should go, the answer seems to be, as many as consider it worthwhile in terms of the costs and returns involved. As to *who* should go, the answer is those best qualified to benefit from higher education, regardless of family, sex, or race. The objective of opportunity based on merit is economically efficient as well as socially just.

But there is the question of cost. Higher education is expensive. Family ability to bear the cost differs widely. What scheme of educational finance is most compatible with the objectives just outlined?

One school of thought regards higher education as essentially a private investment good, whose possession benefits the owner through higher lifetime income. Why should this good be provided at public expense? Why shouldn't it be sold at cost, like any other capital good? The argument for pricing human capital at full cost is similar to that for pricing physical capital at full cost. Unless supply reflects all relevant costs, there cannot be the matching of costs and benefits required for efficient allocation of resources. Further, most of the higher earnings resulting from college education come as private benefits to the individual. So he or she, and not society, should bear the costs of the training.

Under the present system, most students in public institutions pay tuition covering only a small fraction of the cost of their education. They are thus receiving a substantial scholarship and—this is the main point—they receive it *without regard to financial need*. The scholarship benefits rich families in the suburbs along with poor families in the slums. Indeed, some studies indicate that students attending state-supported colleges and universities come from families whose average income is higher than that of the average taxpayer in the same state. Subsidizing of higher education may thus involve an income transfer in the "wrong" direction, from lower to higher brackets.

It is argued also that under the present system there is "unfair competition" between public and private institutions. The latter, having no direct access to tax funds, must charge relatively high tuition to survive. In order to admit students from low-income families, private colleges must "buy" them with scholarships, and their limited resources prevent doing much of this. Thus for students of modest means, the choice among institutions is unduly restricted. This limited choice is undesirable *per se,* and it also puts the public institutions under less pressure to do a good educational job. The problem could be corrected by setting tuition at a full-cost level in both public and private institutions while taking care of the ability-to-pay dilemma in other ways.

Another school of thought argues, however, that higher education should be priced below cost for all students on the ground that such education has large external effects on the community. This argument is used to support free elementary and high school education. Why stop at grade twelve? Why not extend the same reasoning through the college level? This is clearly the kind of argument in which no one can be proven right.

The closer education is priced to full cost, the more severe the problem of where students from low-income families can find the necessary funds. The family that wishes to buy an item of physical capital, such as a house, can wait until it has saved part of the purchase price and then borrow the remainder, putting up the house as collateral on the loan. But these options are much less feasible for investment in human capital. If students have to save the necessary funds, it takes time, during which they are growing older and passing beyond the normal college age group. It might mean entering college at the age of twenty-five instead of eighteen. If, on the other hand, they try to borrow for education, what can they put up as collateral? In a nonslave state individuals cannot mortgage themselves to guarantee repayment of the loan.

The private capital market, in short, is not well suited to financing educational investment. Any system of educational finance that implies heavy student borrowing must specify how borrowing facilities are to be provided.

There are numerous federal, state, university, and private loan schemes for students. Structuring a federal program involves several issues:

1. Should a federal agency lend directly to students, or should it merely guarantee loans made by others? (The main federal program at present is a guarantee program, which reinsures other lenders against risk of loss.)
2. Should students be allowed to borrow up to the full amount of direct educational expenses, including living costs? Or should there be a lower ceiling?
3. Should interest rates be at market levels or at some lower level? Loans below the market level would amount to a subsidy to higher education and, like any other form of subsidy, would have to be justified on the ground of external effects.
4. What are appropriate repayment arrangements? Some present programs have short repayment periods—say, ten to fifteen years beginning soon after graduation. This imposes a burden on the borrower at precisely the time when costs of buying and furnishing a house and rearing children are also high. Most families can repay with less effort at a later stage when child-rearing costs have declined. Repayment periods of twenty to thirty years, comparable to those for mortgage loans, would seem more efficient. The amount repaid might also be allowed to vary with the student's future income. This approach would reduce the risk to the student but at the cost of a greater risk to the lender.

What about outright scholarships, covering part or all of educational expenses, for children from low-income families? Subsidizing higher education through low-cost tuition, as we have seen, involves a substantial scholarship element *unrelated* to financial need, and can involve an upward redistribution of income. A more restricted system, limited to families in the lowest income brackets, would redistribute a smaller total amount of income, all in a downward direction.

There have been many sample surveys indicating that for students of equal academic ability the percentage graduating from college is much higher among those from high-income families. Some estimates from a recent study by Manski and Wise are presented in Table 4-3.

Holding the students' Scholastic Aptitude Test (SAT) scores and rank in

TABLE 4-3   Probabilities of Attendance and Completion at a Four-Year College, for High School Graduates, by Parental Education and Income

PARENTS' EDUCATION	PARENTS' ANNUAL INCOME	
	45% BELOW MEDIAN	60% ABOVE MEDIAN
	Probability of Attendance	
Less than high school	.11	.17
College degree or more	.33	.43
	Probability of Completion	
Less than high school	.04	.09
College degree or more	.17	.28

Source: Charles F. Manski and David A. Wise, *College Choice in America* (Cambridge, Mass.: Harvard University Press, 1983). The figures are calculated from those on page 13. The data are for 1972 and refer to those enrolling in a four-year college immediately after high school.

high school class constant, Manski and Wise find that who goes to college depends heavily on both parental education and income.[32]

Even among able students, very few from low-income families complete college. This clearly involves a substantial waste of talent. It seems both efficient and just to channel a larger proportion of talented people from low-income families into the higher-education system.

But would not an adequate loan fund system do the job? Why should anything more be required? A case for scholarships must rest on some combination of the following arguments: (1) that low-income families are more myopic, more risk averse, and/or poorly informed about education than high-income families; and that on this account they would underborrow from the loan fund; (2) that the present distribution of personal income is too unequal, and that in addition to redistributing cash to low-income families, we can reasonably redistribute goods such as educational benefits; (3) that subsidies to higher education are warranted by consumer benefits and external effects, and that this form of subsidization is preferable to others.

For students from low-income families, the most important scholarship program is the federal program of Pell grants, formerly called Basic Educational Opportunity Grants.[33] This program was established in 1972, primarily to increase the educational opportunities of students from poor families. It provides assistance of over $2 billion to students who attend universities, four-year colleges, community colleges, or vocational schools. The maximum grant is about $2,000 per year.

---

[32]While the effect of parents' education appears to be greater than the effect of their income, the results might be biased in this direction because of greater measurement error in the income variable.

[33]For more information on this program, see Sandra R. Baum and Saul Schwartz, "The Fairness Test for Student Aid Cuts."

TABLE 4-4   The Predicted Effect of Pell Grants on Post-High School
Enrollment, by Income Class

	% ENROLLED	
	With Grant	Without Grant
Lower income	47%	30%
Middle income	43%	38%
Upper income	54%	53%

Source: Manski and Wise, *College Choice in America*. The figures are calculated from
Tables 1.10 and 1.11 and are based on estimates for 1979. Low income is defined as
less than 86 percent of average family income while high income is more than 110
percent of average income.

Benefits are limited to 50 percent of costs and decline as family income rises. The
average grant is about $1,000 per year, which represents about one-quarter of the
out-of-pocket costs of college for those receiving grants. Federal assistance to students also is available in the form of guaranteed student loans and through the
work-study program, which makes payments to students in return for part-time
work at the college.

Federal policy in this area has varied over the years. During the late
1970s the tendency was to liberalize both the loan and scholarship programs. The
Reagan administration, on the other hand, tightened up the programs by lowering the family income level above which students become ineligible, by raising
interest rates, and by reducing the amounts budgeted for loan subsidies and
scholarships.

How effective have the Pell grants and other financial assistance programs
been in increasing the percentage of low-income students who go on to college?
Manski and Wise conclude that the effects of the Pell grants have been significant.[34]
Their estimates, presented in Table 4-4, show that the enrollment effects are quite
dramatic for those low-income families who receive most of the benefits. In years
when eligibility has been limited almost entirely to low-income families, as many as
40 percent of the beneficiaries might not otherwise have received post-high school
education. The enrollment effect of the Pell grants is heavily concentrated on two-
year community colleges and vocational schools. There is virtually no enrollment
effect on four-year colleges or universities.

Financial aid provided by colleges and universities from their own funds is
also based primarily on need. Such aid from colleges and universities probably has
had little impact on whether a student receives some education after high school but
may still be very important in influencing the type of school attended by students
from families of low and average income. Financial aid from schools also is likely to
have a significant effect on whether such students can continue in college and
obtain their degree.

---

[34]See Charles F. Manski and David A. Wise, *College Choice in America*.

THE MARKET FOR COLLEGE GRADUATES

We have been focusing on the decision to invest in a college education. For those who do go to college, the next important decision is the choice of occupation. As a student, you must decide on a major and then whether to continue on to a graduate or professional school. This decision is an investment decision, just like the decision of whether to go to college. As in the college case, the decision depends on both monetary and nonmonetary considerations. For example, a decision to prepare for a legal career will depend not only on expected earnings of a lawyer and the costs of law school but also on whether you would enjoy working as a lawyer.

Let us examine how markets work for the professional, technical, and managerial occupations entered by most college students. The labor market does operate slightly differently for these occupations than for those occupations that require less schooling.[35]

The market for occupations requiring a college education are similar to other labor markets on the demand side. Demand shifts are frequent and sometimes drastic. Notable examples are the sharp drop in demand for elementary and high school teachers in the 1960s and for college teachers in the 1970s. Defense industries employ a high proportion of scientists and engineers, and so do laboratories engaged in research and development (R&D) activity. So if the federal government increases or decreases its defense spending or support for R&D, there is a large impact on demand in these markets.

But high-level occupations differ in the supply response to demand shifts. The main reason is the length of the schooling period. If more freshmen enroll in engineering programs today, this will not add to supply until four years later. It takes six years to produce an M.B.A., seven years or more to produce a doctor or a college teacher.

When a student decides to study law or engineering, the decision is usually made on the basis of current job opportunities and relative salaries. If the demand for engineers is high today, jobs will be plentiful and salaries will rise. Thus many students will choose to become engineers. When these students graduate four years later, supply will increase. If demand has returned to its normal level, there will be severe competition for jobs and starting salaries will fall. Thus like the cycle in the production of beef cattle, the adjustment to equilibrium follows a lengthy cobweb pattern, as shown in Figure 4-3.

If college students could predict more accurately how starting salaries for various occupations were likely to differ by the time they graduated, then the market would operate more efficiently, and fewer students would end up disappointed. Although it is never possible to predict the future with great accuracy, it is possible to make some educated guesses. In particular, one can take some account of cobweb effects.

If starting salaries are an important concern to you, investigate the system-

---

[35]The leading student of these markets is Richard B. Freeman. See in particular his books *The Market for College-Trained Manpower* and *The Over-educated American*.

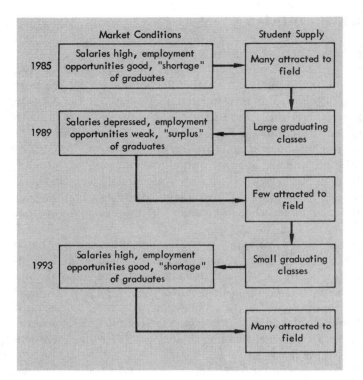

FIGURE 4-3. The Cobweb Model

atic highs and lows that recur every few years in some occupations, such as law and engineering.

Of course, career decisions should not be based only on starting salaries. Average earnings opportunities over a lifetime, ability to do well in the field, and nonpecuniary rewards are also important. While the cobweb mechanism has some effect on everyone in an occupation, those with appreciable experience usually are not in direct competition with new entrants, so cobweb effects have much less influence on the earnings of experienced workers.

EDUCATIONAL ISSUES AT THE PRECOLLEGE LEVEL

Elementary and secondary education involves problems of finance, curriculum, and quality. Responsibility for the public schools has traditionally been assigned to local governments, although higher levels of government provide increasing financial support.

The localities depend mainly on property taxes, and the amount of property subject to tax varies greatly between rich and poor communities. An identical tax rate yields several times as much revenue in a wealthy suburb as in a rundown inner-city district. As a result, school expenditure per student varies widely among school districts, even within the same state.

Quality of education is not easy to define, and we do not know much about the relation between spending per pupil and the quality of output. The most common quality measure—student performance on standardized tests—is influenced by parents' education and family income as well as by schooling. Still, there is considerable evidence that additional expenditure, particularly on better trained and more experienced teachers and on smaller class sizes, has a positive effect on student performance.[36] Thus the wide expenditure variation among school districts can be regarded as an effective denial of equal opportunity for education.[37]

In recent years there has been increasing concern about the average quality of public education, particularly at the high school level. For example, student test-score performance, which had been steadily increasing for many years, began to decline in the late 1960s and continued to decline until about 1980. This decrease in the educational performance of students appears to have contributed to the decline in productivity growth in recent years, an issue that we discuss in Chapter 9.[38] The educational attainment of a typical high school student in the United States is lower than in most other industrialized countries, perhaps in part because high school attendance is limited to more able students in many other countries.[39] Particularly in many central-city schools there is little doubt that the quality of education is low. Dropout rates are high, and many of those who "graduate" cannot do simple arithmetic or write a clear sentence. Many young people thus confront the labor market unqualified for anything but the most menial jobs, a handicap that may stay with them throughout life.

It is easier to criticize than to suggest effective remedies, especially since low educational attainment is closely related to factors outside the schools, particularly parental supervision of children. Some approaches, such as a longer school day and more extensive use of computer instruction, have been tried and found to be relatively ineffective.[40] Others that have been either tried or suggested by study commissions include (1) stiffer graduation requirements; (2) higher average salaries for teachers, to attract a better level of talent (at present, college seniors majoring

---

[36]See, for example, George E. Johnson and Frank P. Stafford, "Social Returns to Quantity and Quality of Schooling," *Journal of Human Resources* (Spring 1973), pp. 139–56; Anita A. Summers and Barbara L. Wolfe, "Do Schools Make a Difference?" *American Economic Review* (September 1977), pp. 634–52; and Ronald Rizzuto and Paul Wachtel, "Further Evidence on the Returns to School Quality," *Journal of Human Resources* (Winter 1980), pp. 246–54.

[37]Courts in some states have held that such wide differentials in school financing violate the guarantees of equal treatment embodied in state and federal constitutions, and have ordered remedial action. The remedies usually involve large state educational grants to local governments and a reorientation of these grants toward the lowest-income communities. A common principle is that districts that make the same tax effort on behalf of education will receive equivalent resources per student, regardless of differences in their tax base. Programs with such names as community power equalization, percentage equalizing, and guaranteed tax base all reflect this approach.

[38]See Bishop, "Test Score Decline."

[39]In a sixteen-nation survey, American high school students ranked third from the bottom in reading and science and lowest in math achievement among the industrialized countries. See Isabel V. Sawhill, "Human Resources," in *Regrowing the American Economy,* ed. G. William Miller (Englewood Cliffs, N. J.: Prentice-Hall, 1983), pp. 112–13.

[40]Richard J. Murnane, "Education and Productivity."

in education have lower SAT scores than those in any other specialty); (3) some differentiation of salaries by specialty, to enable schools to compete with industry for math and science teachers; (4) better teacher training, including extensive undergraduate training in the teacher's subject area and master's-level training in teaching skills; (5) national standards, based on ability in the classroom rather than courses taken, to certify who are the best teachers and to encourage school districts to compete for them; (6) greater autonomy (and accountability) for teachers in choosing instructional methods and allocating resources; and (7) evaluating and rewarding teachers and school administrators on the basis of how much students actually learn, instead of the current system where teachers are paid mainly on the basis of academic degrees and years of teaching experience.

It is also important to try to ensure that we have good tests of educational performance. To the extent that we are concerned with the relation between schooling and productivity in the workplace, Murnane argues that schools should focus more on teaching and testing

> the ability to understand directions . . . to ask questions, to assimilate and synthesize unfamiliar information, and to identify and solve problems that occur during the normal working day; in short, literacy and problem-solving skills in specific contexts.[41]

In the school-reform debate, the issue of merit pay has received considerable attention. Merit pay provides a financial reward to the most effective teachers and an incentive to others to try to achieve such raises in the future. Merit pay has been quite controversial, however, mainly because of the difficulty of judging who are the best teachers.[42] Another related approach that has received considerable attention recently is for school systems to provide significantly greater responsibility as well as significantly greater pay for the best teachers. Responsibilities could include working as mentors with other teachers and working with administrators to make major decisions at the level of the school rather than the school district.[43]

Another approach to improving the quality of schooling is to promote more competition. For example, we could reduce the differential cost of public and private schools by establishing tuition tax credits. A more extreme approach is the voucher system, proposed initially by Milton Friedman.[44] Under this system, parents of a school-age child would be given an education voucher, a cash grant usable only for school tuition and would then be allowed to buy education in any school of their choice. Public schools would cover their costs by tuition charges rather than

---

[41]Ibid., p. 233.

[42]For a good discussion of past experience with merit pay, see Richard J. Murnane and David K. Cohen, "Merit Pay and the Evaluation Problem: Why Most Merit Pay Plans Fail and a Few Survive," *Harvard Educational Review* (February 1986), pp. 1–17.

[43]This approach has been recommended by a national commission and is currently being implemented in Rochester, New York. See Robert E. Doherty and David B. Lipsky, "The Education Reform Movement and the Realities of Collective Bargaining," in *Proceedings of the Industrial Relations Research Association,* 1988, pp. 51–60.

[44]See Milton Friedman, *Capitalism and Freedom* (Chicago: University of Chicago Press, 1962).

budget allocations and would be in competition with private fee-charging schools. Supporters of the proposal argue that free choice among private and public schools would create a wider variety of educational institutions and would raise the average quality of schools by forcing all schools to compete for students. This approach would also be fairer, since families with high incomes already have the choice of sending their children to private schools or of moving to school districts that provide a high-quality education. Critics of the voucher plan contend that by encouraging private schools, the scheme would widen existing differences in school quality; that private schools would enroll the best students and bid away the better teachers; and that public schools would become a dumping ground for problem children.

Although there have been no tests of Friedman's idea of allowing much greater competition between public and private schools, in several states there have been experiments giving families a choice among public schools. In urban areas, where schools are close together, greater freedom of choice may create considerable competition among schools, even when the choice is restricted to the public sector. By not allowing private schools equal access to tax revenues, this approach reduces problems of job security for teachers and thus leads to less opposition from teacher's unions. On the other hand, it also makes it easier to impose centralized control over curriculum, teacher certification, and other issues that proponents of competition would like to see resolved through the market process rather than by political or bureaucratic forces. The idea of providing families with more choice seems sufficiently attractive for it to be tried out and evaluated carefully on an experimental basis.

The issues of educational choice and quality of instruction are important. One must recognize, however, that the problem of low educational attainment extends beyond the schools to broken homes, lax parental supervision, television, the drug industry, and other aspects of social structure.

What happens when the high school graduate hits the labor market? What features of the high school experience seem to affect labor market success? One study of a national sample of high school seniors traced them through the first four years of employment, measuring both the wage rate earned and the number of weeks employed during the year.[45] Interestingly, there was almost no relation between any measure of vocational training and later occupational success.

The two things most clearly related to success were (1) work while in high school (those who had worked sixteen to twenty hours a week in high school had substantially higher annual earnings later) and (2) academic achievement, as measured by class rank. The authors comment: "Combined with the results on hours worked in high school, this implies to us a substantial carryover to the labor market of individual attributes associated with or developed through work effort in and out of school. . . . Both high school academic performance and work experience seem to dominate specific vocational training as preparation for successful early experience in the labor market."

---

[45]Robert H. Meyer and David A. Wise, "High School Preparation and Early Labor Force Experience," in *The Youth Labor Market Problem,* ed. Richard B. Freeman and David A. Wise (Chicago: University of Chicago Press, for the National Bureau of Economic Research, 1982), pp. 277–347.

TRAINING ON THE JOB

Although formal education may provide background skills and enhance learning ability, much of the specific skill related to productivity is acquired after graduation. The medical graduate spends several years as an intern and resident. The young college teacher learns to teach by teaching. The skilled craftsperson often serves a three- to five-year apprenticeship. Semiskilled operatives and clerical workers usually go through a training period designed to familiarize them with the organization and to inculcate job skills.

Sometimes training by firms is rather formal, as with McDonald's Hamburger University. More often it is informal, provided by coworkers as well as by foremen and supervisors. Such informal training can continue for many years. As a result, most workers become more productive as they grow older, which helps explain why earnings generally rise with age (especially for younger workers), as we saw in Table 4-1.

The total cost of on-the-job training, including the opportunity cost of trainees' time is very substantial. Jacob Mincer estimates that for U.S. males the investment in on-the-job training by workers was more than half the investment in formal schooling.[46] His estimates do not include the large but not readily measurable costs of on-the-job training incurred by firms.

The skills acquired on the job are of two types: Some are specific to a particular employer, while others are transferable among employers.[47] The former is referred to as *firm-specific training* and the latter as *general training*. Carpenters or electricians can work for numerous building contractors or can set up repair businesses of their own; therefore, the skills learned are general. An illustration of firm-specific skills might be those of a worker engaged in fabricating a certain component of a Xerox machine. (There are several other producers of copiers, but they are not located nearby, and their machines are not identical.) In this case the worker can practice his or her acquired skills *only* with the present employer.

To the extent that workers and employers calculate economically, the costs of these two types of training will be distributed differently. The employer who provides general training cannot count on benefiting directly. Since the training also will be valuable at other firms, the workers will be able to command a higher wage at other firms once they have been trained. Therefore, if the firm tries to recapture the cost of training by paying the workers less than their marginal revenue product once they have been trained, the workers are likely to quit to seek a higher wage available from other employers. Because the employer will not reap the benefits of training, there is no reason the firm should bear its costs. In contrast, it is natural for the workers to bear the cost, since the "human capital" thus acquired is a personal possession they can carry to any job. Given full information and competitive conditions, then, the employer will pay the trainees a wage equal to their

---

[46]Jacob Mincer, "On-the-Job Training: Costs, Returns, and Some Implications," *Journal of Political Economy,* Supplement, *Investment in Human Beings* (October 1962), pp. 50–79.

[47]The reasoning in the next few paragraphs derives from Gary Becker, *Human Capital.*

productivity per time period *minus the cost of training them during that period*. The employer's total cost for wages plus training equals the workers' productivity, so the employer does not lose. The workers take a reduced wage during the training period, comparable to the reduced or zero earnings of college students; and they expect to be repaid in the form of higher earnings over their working life. Schooling can be regarded as an extreme case of general training, where the firm (the school) provides training as its primary output and charges tuition to cover its costs.

Firm-specific training is quite different. Here the workers' skills are not transferable. Therefore, after training, the workers will not command a higher wage at other firms. Thus the employer can expect to pay the workers less than their marginal revenue product once they have been trained. Since the firm can reap the benefits, the firm has an incentive to incur the costs.

When the firm pays all the costs, however, the workers have no incentive not to quit. If they do quit, then the employer loses the prospective benefits of the training. To reduce the chances of workers quitting after receiving firm-specific training, the firm may require the workers to share in both the benefits and cost of training. Then the firm and the workers will both lose if the workers quit or are laid off. Both the employer and the workers benefit if the workers remain with the firm for many years after being trained.

Since a significant proportion of the costs of firm-specific on-the-job training are borne by firms, we shall discuss the role of such training in more detail in Chapter 6, as part of our discussion on labor demand. Nevertheless, much firm-specific on-the-job training is paid for by workers. Jobs that offer such training, with large subsequent wage increases, may pay lower starting wage rates. Moreover, the workers are likely to lose the firm's contribution to their pension unless they remain with the firm for at least ten years.

There is doubtless some element of skill specificity in any job. Even the apparently transferable clothing cutter or steel-rolling-mill operator, once hired, learns to find his or her way to a particular workplace, learns the limits of the foreman's temper, the performance standards of the company, and minor differences in products, methods, and equipment. Similarly, in secretarial jobs, the worker must learn to understand the boss's quirks, how to read his or her handwriting, how the filing system works, and a host of other job-specific information.

The fact that the employer has an investment in a particular worker (including costs of recruitment and hiring as well as training) and the worker has an investment in his or her existing job makes the labor market operate much differently than it otherwise would, as we shall see in Chapter 6.

JOB SEARCH

Investment in human capital is not limited to the acquisition of skills. Consider the issue of job search, for example. A worker can be expected to search for job offers until the expected marginal return from additional search equals its marginal cost.

An investment in job search by a worker is as much an investment in human capital as is an investment in learning skills needed by employers. Job search costs the worker time and effort as well as out-of-pocket expenses, such as transportation costs for job interviews. If the worker gives up one job (or rejects a job offer) to devote more effort to finding a better position, the foregone earnings represent another cost of job search. For workers who have been laid off by a previous employer and are covered by unemployment insurance, unemployment benefits will reduce but not eliminate this cost of foregone earnings.

The benefits of extra search occur primarily in the future. As a result of greater search, the worker may be able to find a better job, one that may offer higher earnings and greater job satisfaction for many years in the future. Such benefits should be discounted to the present value, just like the benefits of schooling or on-the-job training.

For the worker who already has a job or a job offer, the benefits of additional search are the new job offers the worker hopes to receive, some of which may be superior to present alternatives. The worker probably has a vague idea of the range of wage rates available in the area but does not know which wage is offered at which place or which employers are hiring at the moment. Job search, then, is like drawing slips of paper from a black box, each with a wage rate written on it and a yes or no prospect of employment. As the worker continues to draw, there is always a chance that a high-wage job will pop out of the box.

The worker typically has only one job offer before him or her at a time, which must be accepted or rejected very quickly. So the worker needs a *decision criterion,* which will tell whether an offer should be accepted or rejected. This criterion is determined by weighing the costs of continued search against the expected benefits.

The decision criterion is most easily formulated as a minimum acceptable wage rate, the worker's *reservation wage,* although in practice other dimensions of the job will also be relevant. Let us suppose that the worker is unemployed while searching for a new job. Initially, her reservation wage will be framed mainly in terms of her past experience. If the worker has been earning $7 per hour, she may set it at $8 in order to improve herself. Her reservation wage will be influenced also by what she knows about the range of rates prevailing in the area and by whether jobs appear to be plentiful or scarce.

As she continues to search, her expectations of gains from further search are likely to fall. She will not apply entirely at random but will start with the places that she believes have the best jobs in the area. As she works down the roster from better to poorer employers, her estimate of the wage she can get will tend to fall. In a recession, no jobs may be available at anything approaching her former wage. If the cost of longer unemployment is high, the worker's reservation wage may fall drastically. On the other hand, if alternative sources of income are available (for example, from other family members or from income maintenance programs), the worker may become discouraged from further job search and simply drop out of the labor force.

This theory of job search has some interesting implications. As Stigler pointed out initially, it provides one reason for coexistence of different wage rates for the same skill in the same labor market.[48] Such differences would be eliminated only if workers continued to search the market as long as any wage differences remained. But workers will not continue because it does not pay them to do so. They will search only up to the point at which the marginal cost of further search equals the marginal benefit; and this is quite consistent with permanent wage differences.

Job search is an example of the economics of information. If information were perfect, there would be no need for costly search, since both the worker and employer would know which workers should be placed in which jobs. As Rees indicates,

> The search for information in any market has both an extensive and intensive margin. A buyer can search at the extensive margin by getting a quotation from one more seller. He can search at the intensive margin by getting additional information concerning an offer already received. When the goods and services sold are highly standardized, the extensive margin is the more important; when there is great variation in quality, the intensive margin moves to the forefront.[49]

Jobs differ in many characteristics other than wage rates, including effort required, safety, responsibility, and relations with coworkers. Workers also differ in terms of ability and expected willingness to stay with the firm. Thus in labor markets, the intensive margin generally is more important than the extensive margin. We shall return to the issue of job search, by both workers and employers, in Chapter 6.

MIGRATION

Most workers who change jobs remain within the same geographic labor market. Job changes that require moving to a new city generally are most costly. These costs are related to the distance of the move, to whether the migrant has family or friends at the destination, and to whether the migrant already has the promise of a job offer at his or her new location. If more than one family member is working, extra costs arise. For example, if a family moves to advance the husband in his career, the move may hurt the wife's advancement opportunities.[50]

Although the cost of migration can be very large, so can the benefits. A good example is the case of the immigrants to the United States from Europe in the nineteenth and early twentieth centuries. The trip was long, difficult, and expen-

---

[48]The economics of job search was first developed by George Stigler, "Information in the Labor Market," *Journal of Political Economy,* supplement (October 1962), pp. 94–105.

[49]Albert Rees, "Information Networks in Labor Markets," *American Economic Review* (May 1966), p. 560.

[50]See Solomon W. Polachek and Frances W. Horvath, "A Life-Cycle Approach to Migration: Analysis of the Perspicacious Peregrinator," *Research in Labor Economics,* ed. Ronald Ehrenberg (Greenwich, Conn.: JAI Press, 1977), pp. 128–29; and Steven Sandell, "Women and the Economics of Family Migration," *Review of Economics and Statistics* (November 1977), pp. 406–14.

sive, especially before the advent of steamships in the middle of the nineteenth century. As a result, most early immigrants to the United States left their native country permanently.

Since the 1920s we have established severe limitations on legal immigration. Over the past two decades, however, extensive illegal immigration has risen, primarily from Mexico. Our immigration policies and the effect of immigration, both legal and illegal, on labor markets in the United States is examined in Chapter 11, where we discuss the effects on American workers of living in a world economy.

Within the United States the most important migration across labor markets in the past twenty years has been from the Snowbelt to the Sunbelt,[51] that is, from the Northeast and Midwest to the South and Southwest. This migration has reflected not only the warmer climate of the South (an attraction now that air conditioning has become well established) but also its greater economic opportunities in the 1970s and 1980s. Partly because of this migration, the wage gap between the North and the South has narrowed.

Job-related migration is greatest among the young, especially those in their teens or twenties. This may be in part because young people are more adaptable. But much of the explanation lies in the economics of human capital. Migration is a costly investment. The younger the migrant and thus the more years he or she is likely to be in the labor force, the greater the expected return on the investment. The reasoning is the same as we have discussed in the case of education. Job-related investments in human capital, whether in schooling or migration, will usually have the greatest payoff if they are made when the worker still has many years of expected employment in which to recoup the benefits of his or her investment.

SUMMARY

1. Human capital represents an investment in people, with costs incurred initially in order to reap economic benefits in later periods. Such investments include education, on-the-job training, job search and migration. Although it is difficult to measure the stock of human capital, there probably is more human capital than physical capital in the United States.

2. Schooling decreases earnings initially because of the opportunity cost of students' time; time spent in school could have been spent working for pay instead. Postschool earnings generally increase either because skills learned at school increase workers' productivity (the human capital model) or because schooling serves as a convenient sorting mechanism for firms in selecting workers (the signaling model).

---

[51]For further discussion, see Peter Mieskowski, "Recent Trends in Urban and Regional Development," in *Current Issues in Urban Economics,* ed. Peter Mieskowski and Mahlon Straszheim (Baltimore: Johns Hopkins University Press, 1979).

3. To determine whether schooling is a good investment for the individual, one must compare the costs (foregone earnings, tuition, books) with the discounted present value of aftertax earnings gains. For the average student, college appears to be a good investment, one where the economic benefits exceed the costs. The returns do vary considerably, however, depending on the ability of the student and on his or her access to funds.

4. From the point of view of the entire society, we must also consider other benefits and costs of schooling. Additional benefits include the higher taxes paid by those with more schooling and the likely effects of education on such social benefits as technological change, the political process, and the raising of children. On the other hand, extra schooling by some will hurt others' job opportunities to the extent that the signaling model applies and schooling is a sorting device. At the elementary and secondary level, the out-of-pocket costs of public schools are paid for by taxpayers, not directly by the student or the student's family. Even at the college level, tuition covers only a small portion of the costs of instruction, especially at state schools.

5. If the benefits of schooling accrue mainly to the student, then the student or the student's family should pay most of the costs. For those who don't have access to the necessary funds, financial aid is appropriate, either through scholarships or through guaranteed loans. Providing tuition well below cost represents a subsidy to all students, regardless of need. This approach is appropriate only if there are substantial social benefits (external effects).

6. The market for college graduates operates a little differently from other labor markets because decisions about fields of study and occupation must be made based on predictions about labor market conditions some years in the future. Since most people expect the future to be like the present, there are oscillations in wage rates and the supply of students preparing for different occupations. These oscillations can be analyzed with the aid of the cobweb model.

7. Many proposals have been made to improve elementary and secondary schooling. Among the more controversial are proposals for more merit pay for teachers and for increasing competition among schools through education vouchers—or in more limited form, tuition tax credits.

8. Human capital includes not only education but also on-the-job training, job search, and migration. Of these probably the most important is on-the-job training. Such training can be either general or firm specific. Because the worker receives the benefits of general training, which is valuable in many firms, such training usually will be paid for by the worker. Since the benefits of firm-specific training, which is valuable only to one firm, will be shared between the worker and the firm, both will share the costs of such training.

KEY CONCEPTS

HUMAN CAPITAL
INVESTMENT IN EDUCATION
INVESTMENT IN EDUCATION, RETURN ON
OPPORTUNITY COST
SIGNALING MODEL OF SCHOOLING
COBWEB MODEL
PRESENT VALUE
INTERNAL RATE OF RETURN
RATE OF RETURN, PRIVATE
RATE OF RETURN, SOCIAL

OPPORTUNITY CURVE
ABILITY CURVE
EXTERNAL EFFECT
EDUCATION VOUCHER
FIRM-SPECIFIC TRAINING
GENERAL TRAINING
INTENSIVE MARGIN OF SEARCH
EXTENSIVE MARGIN OF SEARCH
DECISION CRITERIA FOR JOB SEARCH
RESERVATION WAGE

REVIEW QUESTIONS

1. In what respects is human capital similar to, and in what respects different from, physical capital?

2. Give all the reasons you can think of why conventional estimates of the private rate of return to education may be misleading.

3. What are the main reasons for a difference between private and social rates of return to education?

4. Suppose someone estimates that the social rate of return to four-year college education is 8 percent.
   (a) What are the possible sources of bias in such an estimate?
   (b) Assuming that you could get an accurate estimate, how would you use it in judging whether the allocation of resources to higher education is too large, too small, or about right?

5. To what extent is the distinction between the human capital and signaling models relevant in considering the rate of return to schooling?

6. To what extent, and using what information, did you and your parents make an estimate of prospective returns
   (a) in deciding to go to college?
   (b) in choosing a particular field of study?

7. There are large differences in individuals' stocks of human capital and, partly on this account, large differences in their money earnings. Support you think that these differences are undesirably large. What policy measures might serve to reduce the degree of inequality?

8. Explain and criticize the idea of pricing higher education at cost, accompanied by an adequate loan system for students.

9. College students can be subsidized in a variety of ways:
   (a) Below-cost tuition.
   (b) Loans at below-market interest rates.
   (c) Scholarship grants.
   Appraise the merits and limitations of each of these methods.

READINGS

BAUM, SANDRA B., and SAUL SCHWARTZ, "The Fairness Test for Student Aid Cuts." *Challenge* (May/June 1985), pp. 39–46.

BECKER, GARY, *Human Capital.* New York: National Bureau of Economic Research, 1975.

FREEMAN, RICHARD B., *Implications of the Changing U.S. Labor Market for Higher Education.* working paper no. 697. Cambridge, Mass.: National Bureau of Economic Research, June 1981.

———, *The Market for College-Trained Manpower.* Cambridge, Mass.: Harvard University Press, 1971.

———, *The Over-educated American.* New York: Academic Press, 1976.

———, "Overinvestment in College Training?" *Journal of Human Resources* (Summer 1975), pp. 287—317.

MANSKI, CHARLES F., and DAVID A. WISE, *College Choices in America.* Cambridge, Mass.: Harvard University Press, 1983.

MINCER, JACOB, "The Distribution of Labor Incomes: A Survey with Special Reference to the Human Capital Approach," *Journal of Economic Literature* (March 1970), pp. 1–26.

———, *Investment in Education: The Equity-Efficiency Quandary.* Special issue of *Journal of Political Economy* (May–June 1972), part 2.

———, *Schooling, Experience and Earnings.* New York: National Bureau of Economic Research, 1974.

MURNANE, RICHARD J., "Education and the Productivity of the Workforce," in *American Living Standards: Threats and Challenges,* ed. Robert E. Litan, Robert Z. Lawrence, and Charles L. Schultze (Washington: Brookings Institution, 1988), pp. 215–45.

SPENCE, A. MICHAEL, *Market Signaling.* Cambridge, Mass.: Harvard University Press, 1974.

DEMAND

In Chapters 3 and 4 we discussed the supply of labor. We have shown how individuals and their families decide how much to work in the marketplace and how much to invest in human capital. But we have said very little about the employer's demand for labor.

To understand labor markets, demand is just as important as supply. Without analyzing the demand for labor, we cannot know how many jobs will be available and thus how much of the labor force will be employed. Nor can we understand why some jobs pay more than other jobs, thereby providing workers with an incentive to invest in education and training as they seek these better-paid positions.

In Chapters 5 and 6 we investigate the demand for labor. Our primary theme in this chapter is the negative relation between the demand for labor and its cost, the wage rate. First we show why high wage rates have a negative effect on demand. Then we discuss what factors influence the size of this effect (or, more precisely, the elasticity of labor demand). For example, we show why the effect of wage changes is greater in the long run than in the short run.

In the latter part of the chapter we apply this theoretical analysis to two important issues in labor economics. First we show how the elasticity of labor demand affects the ability of unions to increase wage rates. Then we analyze the employment effects of minimum wage legislation.

Throughout this chapter we continue to use several simplifying assumptions, which were introduced in Chapter 2:

1. The cost of labor (and the attractiveness of jobs to employees) is measured by its hourly wage rate. Other job conditions are taken as given and constant. The wage is the sole variable that the employer can manipulate to attract additional labor.

2. All job vacancies are filled through the market. We ignore the fact that in practice many vacancies are filled through internal promotion.

3. Workers are interchangeable in the eyes of the employer and are of equal efficiency. We overlook the fact that in practice employers have hiring preferences based on sex, race, age, experience, and schooling; that workers differ in efficiency; and that to achieve full efficiency on a particular job usually requires a training period.[1] We also assume that each hour an employee works is equally productive, regardless of how many hours he or she has already worked that day or week and regardless of the worker's wage rate. Since we assume no costs of supervision and no fringe benefits, the employer's cost of labor is equal to the wage rate.

4. Employers are perfectly informed. For each wage rate, they know how many workers will be available to hire.

5. The primary objective of any firm is to maximize its profits.

The usefulness of these assumptions lies not in the fact that they correspond closely with reality but rather that they can be used to derive predictions that are often quite accurate. There is good reason for this accuracy. The economic forces that operate in these simple models are operative also in actual labor markets. As we show later in this chapter, a simple theory of labor demand can be developed from these assumptions. This theory helps explain why some unions have more ability than others to raise wage rates and why minimum wage legislation reduces the number of jobs available for teenagers.

For some problems, however, it is not wise to make these simplifications. In Chapter 6 we drop the assumptions of homogeneous labor, perfect information, and no internal promotion. Differences in the nonwage attractiveness of jobs (including both working conditions and fringe benefits, such as pensions and health insurance) are discussed in Chapter 7.

THE FIRM'S DEMAND FOR LABOR

In Chapter 2 we drew labor demand curves as sloping downward from right to left and explained briefly why that was a reasonable procedure. We must now give a more detailed explanation. Since firms are the basic employing unit, we begin with demand for labor by a single firm. Later we see how the demands of many firms can be added to obtain a *market demand schedule* for a particular kind of labor.

---

[1] In the discussion of empirical work at the end of the chapter, we do assume differences in worker efficiency across occupations and demographic groups. Even in this case, however, we assume no differences in efficiency among those in a particular occupation or demographic group.

Marginal Productivity Analysis

The concept of marginal productivity serves to explain why the demand curve for labor shown in Figure 5-1 has a negative downward slope. Other things equal, a firm will hire fewer workers at a higher wage than at a lower one.

To analyze the demand for labor, we start by asking why employers hire workers. They do so in order to produce output that can be sold at a profit. Thus the demand for any kind of labor is a *derived* demand, based on the demand for the product the labor produces. The product need not be a physical product, such as automobiles, but also includes services, such as those provided by hair stylists or doctors.

Consider an employer who is deciding whether to hire an additional worker. To maximize profits, how should the employer make this decision? First the employer should estimate the change in the firm's output if another worker is added.

> The change in output from an additional worker is called the marginal physical product of labor (*MPP*).

Next the employer will estimate the extra income gained from the sale of this additional output. If the extra output has no effect on the selling price, *P,* this extra revenue is the value of the marginal physical product, that is, *MPP* × *P.* Thus as long as the product price is fixed, the value of the marginal physical product is the firm's marginal revenue product of labor, where

> The marginal revenue product (*MRP*) is the additional revenue the firm gains by employing an extra worker.

To maximize its profits, the firm must set employment so that the marginal revenue product is equal to the marginal cost of hiring one more worker.

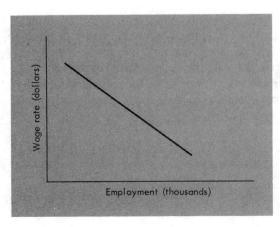

FIGURE 5-1   The Demand Curve for Labor

The marginal cost of labor (*MC*) is the extra cost the firm must pay in order to employ an additional worker.

As long as the wage rate is not affected by hiring another worker, the marginal cost of labor is equal to the worker's wage.

The general condition for profit maximization is that the firm should hire just enough workers so that

$$MRP = MC$$

The marginal revenue product of labor must equal its marginal cost. If *MRP* exceeds *MC*, the firm can increase its profit by hiring an additional worker. But if *MRP* is less than *MC*, the firm can increase its profit by hiring fewer workers. Only when *MRP = MC* will the firm not be able to increase its profits by changing its employment level.

In the special case where the product price is constant, we have shown that *MRP* = *MPP* × *P*. When the wage rate is constant, *MC* = *W*. Therefore, if both the product price and the wage rate are constant, the condition for profit maximization becomes

$$MPP \times P = W$$

The Law of Variable Proportions

To proceed further with the analysis, we must examine the technology of production. Without reviewing the whole of production economics, we can restate one of its central principles. This principle describes what happens as increasing quantities of labor are applied to a fixed quantity of capital goods—a plant. The principle is

> As increasing quantities of a variable factor are applied to a fixed factor of production, the resulting additions to output will eventually decrease.

The classical economists called this the *law of diminishing returns*. They derived it by applying more and more labor to a fixed acreage of land and thought of it as associated particularly with agriculture. But it is in fact a general principle, applicable to any kind of production. It is now usually called the *law of variable proportions*. It could also be called the *law of diminishing marginal productivity*.

The operation of the principle is illustrated in Figure 5-2. The *MPP* curve in Figure 5-2 shows marginal physical productivity rising in the early stages. One worker turned loose in a complicated plant will not produce much. The marginal product of a second worker will be higher, because the work can be subdivided more effectively. A third and a fourth worker will also add increasing amounts to the product. As more and more workers are added, however, the marginal produc-

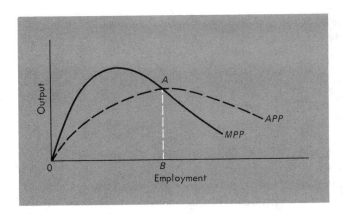

FIGURE 5-2   The Law of Variable Proportions

tivity of labor must eventually begin to decline, since each worker is working with less and less equipment. The *MPP* curve turns downward.

It is sometimes argued that the capital-labor ratio is fixed by technology (for example, one worker per machine), so that the marginal physical product of an extra worker will be zero. Usually, however, there are some other tasks that the worker can perform to help the firm. For example, some work, such as materials handling, can be done by hand if the items are not too heavy, even though machines are usually used when labor is expensive. Another example involves workers serving customers. An extra teller at a bank or clerk at a supermarket clearly improves the service whenever there are many customers waiting in line.

The average physical productivity curve, *APP*, which shows *average* output per worker at each level of employment, has a gentler upward and downward slope than the *MPP* curve. Note that *MPP* intersects *APP* at the point where *APP* is a maximum. This is no accident, as can be shown by a simple illustration. Take a football team averaging six feet in height, and add a player of six feet, six inches. The average of the group will now be higher than before. But if we had added a player of five feet, six inches, the average of the group would have fallen. The same principle holds here. So long as *MPP* is above *APP*—that is, so long as each new worker adds more than the average output of the workers previously employed—this keeps pulling the average *up*. But when *MPP* falls below *APP*, it begins pulling the average *down,* and *APP* begins to fall.

We can show also that it will never pay to operate this plant with fewer than *B* workers. Why? Because up to this point the average productivity of labor is still rising. This means that up to *B*, the fixed factor is not being fully utilized. So it cannot pay to operate to the left of *B*. Rather than do this, it would be preferable to abandon part of the plant and concentrate labor on the remainder, in order to reach the top of the *APP* curve. But that will rarely be necessary. The producer will normally operate the plant somewhere to the right of *B*, that is, somewhere on the declining section of the *MPP* schedule. *So only this part of the schedule will be shown in later diagrams.*

Marginal Revenue Product: Competitive Conditions

Suppose that the output of the firm is sold under conditions of pure competition. A producer under pure competition is by definition such a small part of total industry output that it can vary its rate of sales without affecting the market price. So there would be no point in setting the price below the market level. The company can sell as much as it wants to *without* doing that.

Think about what this means. It means that the *demand curve for the company's product is horizontal at the prevailing price.* It means also that under pure competition, *price and marginal revenue are equal,* where

> Marginal revenue (*MR*) is the amount that an extra unit of output adds to a firm's sales revenue.

If the firm can sell an additional unit with no reduction in price, its revenue is increased by the full price of that unit.

Labor's marginal revenue product curve, however, will still be downward sloping. Why? Because beyond a certain point the marginal physical product (*MPP*) of labor is declining. Since additional units of output are sold at an unchanged price, physical product and revenue product are strictly proportionate. As *MPP* falls, labor's *MRP* will fall at the same rate since $MRP = MPP \times P$ when the product market is competitive.

Marginal Revenue Product: Producers with Market Power

Pure competition is unusual. Most producers have some degree of *market power.* A seller has market power if able to influence the price of the product. In this case the seller must choose a price, and other things being equal, this price will determine how much can be sold. *The demand curve slopes downward to the right.*

Market power may exist for one of several reasons: (1) A company may be the only producer of a particular good. (2) There may be only a few producers, each with a sufficiently large output to affect the market price. (3) Each company's product may not be *quite* the same as that of others. Company *A* makes Wheaties, while Company *B* makes Krunchies. So company *A* sets the price of Wheaties and can set it higher or lower than the prices of competing brands.

In all these cases—monopoly, oligopoly, and monopolistic competition— the producer is faced with a downward-sloping demand curve. Having set the price, the producer can sell only the quantity demanded at that price, as shown by the demand curve. In order to sell more, the price must be lowered.

This has an important consequence: *Marginal revenue is no longer identical with price.* For a downward-sloping demand curve, *marginal revenue is always less than price.* Remember what marginal revenue is: the addition to revenue obtained by selling an additional unit of product. Why isn't this equal to the price obtained

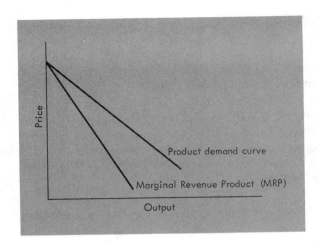

FIGURE 5-3   Marginal Revenue Product and the Firm's Product Demand Curve

for that additional unit? Because in order to sell an additional unit the producer must reduce the price not just for that unit but for all the goods being sold. The price cut on the goods that could have been sold anyway is a loss in revenue, which must be deducted from the sales price of the additional unit.

Thus at any point on the demand schedule, marginal revenue is less than price; that is, the *marginal revenue lies below the demand schedule* throughout its length and slopes downward more steeply, as shown in Figure 5-3.

What does this mean for labor's marginal revenue product? It means that as more and more workers are employed, their marginal revenue product (*MRP*) now falls for a double reason: (1) Each worker adds less to output—marginal *physical* output is falling; and (2) each additional unit of output adds less to sales revenue, because of the downward slope of the marginal revenue schedule. Thus labor's *MRP* schedule falls more sharply than its *MPP* schedule.

The Short-Run Labor Demand Curve

We conclude that for producers operating under pure competition as well as for those with market power, labor's *MRP* schedule will slope downward, as shown in Figure 5-4. Now how many workers will the employer hire? To determine the answer, we need additional information—namely, the rate of wages. If the firm can hire as many workers as it wants at the going wage rate, *W*, the marginal cost of labor is *W*, as we explained above. To maximize profits, the employer will observe the following rule:

> Increase employment up to the point at which the marginal revenue product of labor equals W, the marginal cost of labor.

Up to *E* in Figure 5-4, the additional revenue brought in by an additional worker is greater than his or her wage, so profit would be increased. Beyond *E*,

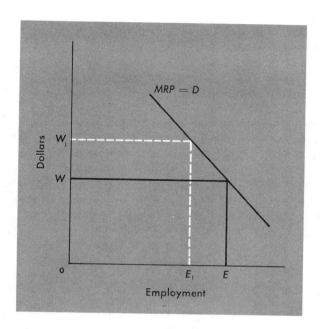

FIGURE 5-4 Labor's *MRP* Schedule Is Its Demand Schedule

however, an additional worker would bring in less than his or her wage, so profit would be reduced.

If instead of W, the wage were W_1, then the correct level of employment would be E_1. In fact, we can find the correct employment for any wage rate simply by moving along the *MRP* schedule. So we conclude that for a single employer who cannot affect the market wage rate:

> The demand schedule for labor is its marginal revenue product schedule.

This statement is sometimes wrongly called "the marginal productivity theory of wages." It is not a theory of wages because it does not specify how the wage rate is determined. The wage can be set by market competition, through collective bargaining, or by legal regulation. All it says is that once the wage is determined (by whatever means) the employer will try to adjust employment and output to maximize profit.[2] It is a theory of *labor demand*.

Up to this point our argument has assumed a profit-maximizing employer. A nonprofit employer, such as the government, will also have a negatively sloped demand curve. Instead of a marginal revenue product curve, it will have an analogous curve showing the extra value to the citizenry (or to elected officials) resulting from the output of additional government employees. The lower the wage rate of the government employees, the more tasks they can perform without their costs

---

[2]If the firm does not face a given wage rate and must pay a higher wage to obtain more labor, then for profit maximization, marginal revenue product will still equal marginal cost, but now marginal cost will exceed the wage rate. Employing an extra worker will require the employer to pay a higher wage rate for all workers as well as paying for the direct cost of the extra worker.

exceeding the value of the services provided. Thus the demand curve for government employees has a negative slope, the same as the demand curve for a profit-maximizing employer.

The Long-Run Labor Demand Curve

Thus far our argument applies only to the short run. It depends heavily on the law of variable proportions, which assumes that the stock of physical capital is fixed. In the long run, however, the firm can vary its capital stock as well as its level of employment.

In the long run, an increase in the wage rate will reduce the firm's employment for two reasons: a *scale effect* and a *factor-substitution effect.* In each case the crucial point is the effect of an increase in the wage rate *relative* to other prices, either the price of the firm's output or the price of other factors of production. Thus it is important to remember that the labor demand curve is based on the assumption that all other prices are constant. An increase in the wage rate when all other prices are increasing by the same percentage will have no effect on the firm's demand for labor.

First let us consider the scale effect. The argument here is similar to the one underlying the short-run labor demand curve. Recall that a profit-maximizing firm will hire more workers as long as their marginal revenue exceeds their marginal cost. If marginal cost exceeds marginal revenue, the firm will reduce its employment. An increase in the wage rate for an individual firm will not affect its marginal revenue but will increase its marginal cost. Therefore, if the firm was originally at equilibrium with marginal revenue equal to marginal cost, an increase in the wage will reduce employment. This decrease in labor demand is the *scale effect* of higher wage rates.

> The scale effect of a wage increase is the reduction in labor demand resulting from reduced output by the firm when labor becomes more expensive.

An analogous argument shows how a wage decrease will increase output and the demand for labor.

In the short run, the scale effect is derived from the law of variable proportions, assuming a fixed capital stock. But in the long run, the capital stock can be varied. As the wage rate increases, labor becomes more expensive relative to capital, and it becomes profitable for the firm to produce a given output with more capital and less labor. In other words, the firm will buy more labor-saving equipment and hire fewer workers as the wage rate increases. The resulting decline in labor demand is the factor-substitution effect of high wage rates.

> The factor-substitution effect of a wage increase is the reduction in labor demand resulting from the substitution of other factors of production when labor becomes more expensive.

Again an analogous argument applies to the effect of a wage reduction.

The effect of a given wage increase is likely to be greater in the long run than in the short run. The scale effect applies in both cases, but the firm can substitute capital for labor (or labor for capital) only in the long run.

MARKET DEMAND CURVES

The demand curve for a firm shows how much labor the firm will seek to employ at each wage rate, holding all other prices constant. The market demand curve shows how much labor *all* firms in the particular labor market will seek to employ at each wage rate, again holding all other prices constant. Recall that a labor market usually refers to a location and a skill (for example, unskilled labor in Chicago, human resource managers in the United States). In some cases the market may also correspond to an industry (such as the demand for steel workers), either because industry-specific skills are important or because of institutional factors, such as strong industrial unions.

Suppose there are many employers of a particular kind of labor in a particular market and we wish to add up their total demand in order to derive the market demand curve for labor. We do this by horizontal addition of the individual companies' demand schedules, just as we add individual customers' demand schedules to derive total demand for a product.[3] We now have an *aggregate demand schedule* for this kind of labor. It must slope downward, because the individual schedules from which it is derived slope downward.

The market demand curve shows how many workers will be hired in the labor market at each wage rate. If the wage rate is determined by collective bargaining or other institutional factors, the market demand curve provides us with a theory of employment. If the wage rate is determined by competitive forces, the market demand curve helps to determine the market wage.

If the labor market is competitive, the wage rate will be determined by the intersection of the market demand and market supply curves, as shown in Figure 5-5. We have just seen why the market demand curve will be negatively sloped. In contrast to the horizontal labor supply curve for the firm in a competitive labor market, the market supply curve will have a positive slope. More workers will be attracted to this labor market at higher wage rates. As explained in Chapter 4, at higher wage rates more workers will be willing to migrate to the geographic area or to invest in learning the necessary skills to enter the market.

Shifts in the Market Demand for Labor

We have shown how the amount of labor demanded depends on the wage rate. This relation is summarized in the downward-sloping demand curve. Other determinants of quantity demanded, such as changes in the demand for output, operate by shifting the market demand curve for labor. Let us see how this process works.

---

[3]One complication, however, should be noted. Suppose the companies are also producing the *same product.* Then a wage change, by changing employment and output, will also change the *price of the product,* which will shift each company's *MRP* schedule. We can still construct a labor demand schedule for each company and for the group; but in so doing, we must take the price effect into account.

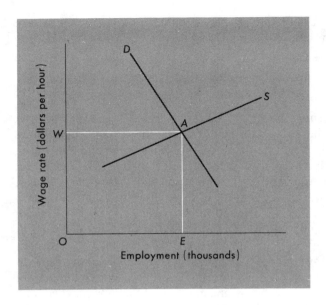

FIGURE 5-5 Equilibrium in a Competitive Labor Market

Assume that the demand for output in some industry declines, perhaps because of an increase in foreign competition. This decrease in demand for output either causes a reduction in output prices or a reduction in the amount of output sold. In either case the marginal revenue product of labor falls. Consequently, the demand curve for each type of labor used in the industry will shift to the left. At any initial wage rate fewer jobs will be available. The initial shift in the industry's product demand curve leads to a subsequent shift in its demand for workers.

If wage rates are determined entirely by institutional forces and do not change when demand falls, the decrease in demand will lead to an equal decline in employment. This can be see in Figure 5-6, where the wage is fixed at W. When demand decreases from D_0 to D_1, employment declines from E_0 to E_1. A similar argument applies to increases in labor demand as long as there are enough workers

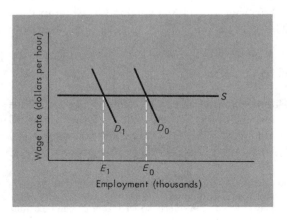

FIGURE 5-6 Demand Shifts with a Constant Wage Rate

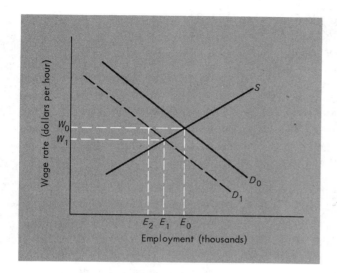

FIGURE 5-7   Demand Shifts with a Changing Wage Rate

available to hire. If there are not enough workers, an increase in demand also will lead to job vacancies.

If wage rates are determined by market forces and if the supply curve, S, is positively sloped, a shift in the market demand curve will lead to a change in the wage rate as well as in employment. As shown in Figure 5-7, in a competitive labor market the new equilibrium will be where the new demand curve intersects the labor supply curve.

Since the supply curve is positively sloped, the new equilibrium will be at both a lower level of employment and a lower wage rate. The decline in employment ($E_0 - E_1$) will be less than the shift in the demand curve ($E_0 - E_2$) except in the unlikely case that either the demand curve is completely vertical or the supply curve is completely horizontal. If the supply curve is flat, any shift in the labor demand curve will affect employment more than wage rates. On the other hand, if the supply curve is steep, a shift in demand will have a larger effect on wage rates than on employment.

Why Demand Curves Shift

Let us look more systematically at the reasons demand curves shift. Shifts in the demand for labor occur because of changes in demand for the product, changes in the nature of the production process, and changes in the price of other factors of production, including capital equipment and other kinds of labor.

Since the demand for labor is a derived demand, the most obvious determinant of the demand for auto workers is the demand for automobiles. If the demand for American-made autos declines (for example, because of increased foreign competition), the demand for auto workers will fall.

Changes in technology also affect the demand for labor. If a new robot is developed that can do the job a worker has been doing and can do it at less cost, the firm is likely to replace the worker with the robot. Thus the demand curve for this kind of worker shifts to the left as the technology of robots is improved.

The demand for labor will also shift because of changes in the price of other factors of production. Assume that the price of capital declines because of a decline in the real (price-adjusted) interest rate. As a result, firms will buy more capital equipment and *may* employ fewer workers. The shift in the long-run demand curve as a result of the decline in the price of capital depends on the relative size of the scale and the factor-substitution effects. The factor-substitution effect will decrease the demand for labor (shift the labor demand curve to the left), but there will also be a scale effect. Assume that the price falls for capital used in the automobile industry. Consequently, the auto industry can produce at lower cost, charge a lower price, and sell more automobiles. This scale effect will increase the demand for auto workers (shift the demand curve to the right). The net effect of the decrease in the price of capital on the demand for labor depends on whether the factor-substitution effect outweighs the scale effect.

In addition to changes in product demand and in the price of capital, the demand curve for particular types of labor (such as union versus nonunion, skilled versus unskilled) depends on the wage rates of other workers. For example, if we are considering the demand for union auto workers, we must take account of the possibility of a firm employing nonunion workers. If the wage is lower (relative to productivity) for the nonunion worker and if there are no legal constraints, we should expect employers to hire nonunion workers, at least in the long run. If the union wage is held constant, any decrease in the wage rate of nonunion workers (or any increase in their supply at a given wage rate) should reduce the demand for union labor.

Thus far we have treated different kinds of labor as substitutes in production. They can also be complements, however. For example, the availability of talented scientists and engineers in and around such universities as Stanford, Harvard, and the Massachusetts Institute of Technology has increased the demand for less skilled workers in the labor markets of Boston and the "Silicon Valley" of California.

CRITICISM OF THE MARGINAL PRODUCTIVITY THEORY

The marginal productivity theory of labor demand, which we have just presented, has played a major role in labor economics for many years. Nevertheless, it has been subject to frequent criticism.[4]

Some labor economists have argued that the theory is unrealistic, since employers do not usually think in terms of marginal revenue product. In most cases

---

[4]For a more extensive discussion of the history of marginal productivity theory and the criticisms of this theory, see Allan M. Cartter, *Theory of Wages and Employment*, Chaps. 2–4.

firms cannot even calculate the marginal revenue resulting from the employment of one additional worker.[5]

Nevertheless, firms do make judgments about whether a new employee is likely to be worth the cost. Fritz Machlup once suggested an interesting analogy. Imagine a driver deciding whether it is safe to pass a truck on a two-lane road with a car approaching in the other lane. This decision can be viewed as a mathematical problem involving the speed of each vehicle and the rate at which the driver can accelerate. But even if the driver is an engineer, he will not actually make such a calculation. Yet countless such decisions are made every day, with very few errors. In the same way, a businessperson can make a reasonable judgment about the effect of changes in employment on the profitability of his or her firm.

The behavior of businesspeople may be quite consistent with the marginal productivity theory, even if they describe their employment decisions in very different language. For example, employers often state that when the wage rate for their workers increases, the firm does not reduce the size of its work force. Instead, the firm increases its product price to cover the cost increase. But this price increase will reduce the output that the firm can sell.[6] When sales fall, the firm will reduce its output and employment. This behavior of the firm is quite consistent with the marginal productivity explanation of why the labor demand curve has a negative slope in the short run.

There is another, more general argument for the validity of the marginal productivity theory. Any firm that does not maximize its profits, as the theory predicts, will be at a competitive disadvantage. If markets are competitive, no firm can earn more than "normal" profits in the long run. If any firm has long-run profits much below the normal level, it will not have enough sales revenue to pay all its expenses. Thus the firm will be forced out of business and will not survive in the labor market. This *survival principle* ensures the validity of the marginal productivity theory, given the assumption of perfect competition.

In the real world the situation is more complex. Not all markets are competitive, especially in the short run. Uncertainty, based on imperfect information, plays an important role in the actual economy, although not in the idealized world of perfect competition. Because of imperfect information, firms can survive by being unusually competent at developing and marketing new products, even if they are not very sophisticated in their employment practices. In the language of the marginal productivity theory, the marginal revenue product of a worker depends not only on the amount of capital and on the number of other workers but also on

---

[5]For example, see Richard A. Lester, "Shortcomings of Marginal Analysis for Wage Employment Problems," *American Economic Review* (March 1946), pp. 63–82. See also the criticisms of Lester by Fritz Machlup, "Marginal Analysis and Empirical Research," *American Economic Review* (September 1946), pp. 519–54; and George Stigler, "Professor Lester and the Marginalists," *American Economic Review* (March 1947).

[6]The wage increase may also force some firms out of business. This event is most likely for firms whose labor costs are an unusually high percentage of total cost. Such firms will have to raise their price more than other firms to cover the cost of the higher wage. But at the higher price, they may not be able to sell enough to stay in business. Since the labor-intensive firms are most likely to go out of business, this effect of high wage rates is another reason the market demand for labor has a negative slope.

how successfully the firm can use its capital stock, adapt to changing technologies, and market its products.

Although the economic environment of firms is more uncertain and therefore more complex than the simple marginal productivity theory suggests, the theory is still highly useful. Firms may not be able to maximize profits with precision in determining their optimal employment levels. The attention of a firm's top executives is a scarce resource, so small differences in wage rates do not always influence important decisions.[7] Nevertheless, large differences in wage rates cannot be ignored without jeopardizing the firm's survival. In this sense the survival principle appears valid, even in a complex, uncertain, changing economy. Therefore, the conclusions of the marginal productivity theory have wide applicability, even if the reasoning that leads to them may appear oversimplified. Of particular importance, the demand curve for labor does have a negative slope.

ELASTICITY OF LABOR DEMAND

We have shown that the demand curve for labor has a negative slope. This conclusion applies whether the demand curve is for a firm or a market and whether the analysis is for the short run or the long run. For most practical issues we need to know not just that a wage increase will reduce the demand for labor but also how large such a reduction will be. For example, assume that a union is considering the employment effect of a wage increase. Would an increase of 10 percent in the industry's wage level (everything else in the economy remaining unchanged) reduce employment by 5 percent next year? Or by only 1 percent? The answer may have a considerable effect on the bargaining strategy of the union and of the employer. To obtain an answer we need to know the elasticity of the short-run demand for labor in the industry.

Recall from elementary economics that elasticity refers to the percentage change in one variable caused by a 1 percent increase in another variable. Thus the wage elasticity of labor demand shows the percentage effect on labor demand of a 1 percent increase in the wage rate. For example, if the wage elasticity is -0.5, a 10 percent increase in the wage rate will reduce the demand for labor by 5 percent. Algebraically, the elasticity of labor demand can be represented as

$$n = \frac{\%\Delta E}{\%\Delta W}$$

where $\%\Delta$ represents "percentage change in," E is employment, and W is the wage rate. For a given percentage change in the wage rate, the elasticity will be greater the larger the percentage change in employment. For example, Figure 5-8 presents two labor demand curves, a more elastic one in panel A and a less elastic one in

---

[7]For example, see Peter B. Doeringer and Michael J. Piore, *Internal Labor Markets and Manpower Analysis* (Lexington, Mass.: D. C. Heath & Company, 1971), especially Chap. 6.

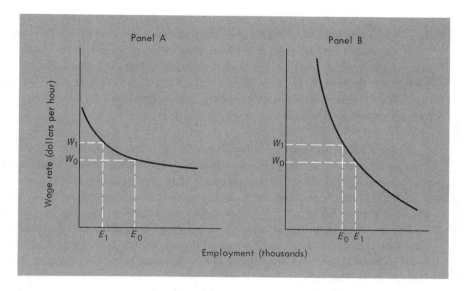

FIGURE 5-8   Elastic and Inelastic Demand Curves

panel B. The more elastic curve is flatter, which shows that a given change in the wage rate has a greater effect on labor demand.

Determinants of the Elasticity of Labor Demand

The wage elasticity of labor demand depends on:

1. Price Elasticity of Demand for the Product.   Suppose that a 10 percent wage increase raises total unit cost 5 percent and that product prices also rise 5 percent. If elasticity of demand for the product is low, say -0.5, sales will fall by only 2.5 percent (5×-0.5). But if elasticity were higher, say -2.0, sales would fall 10 percent (5×-2.0) because of the same wage increase. The larger the decline in sales, the more the firm will decrease employment. Thus the more elastic the demand for the product, the more elastic the demand for the labor used in making it. Note that the elasticity of product demand depends on the availability of effective substitutes for the product.

2. The Proportion that Labor Costs Form of Total Production Costs.   If labor is only 10 percent of the total, then a 10 percent wage increase will raise total unit costs only 1 percent. The effect on product prices, sales, and employment will be small. But if labor forms 80 percent of production costs, the impact will be greater. On this account a skilled craft union covering only a small part of an employer's labor force is in a stronger bargaining position than a plantwide union. The cost of buying off the craft group is small, and it lessens the employer's resistance; and the employment effect is too small to deter the union from an aggressive wage policy.

3. The Difficulty of Substituting Other Factors for Labor in Production. In some cases the existing technique of production may be the only known method, and the possibility of modifying it to save labor may be small. But in other cases there may be alternative methods involving greater mechanization. At a higher wage one or more of these methods will become profitable and will be brought into use. The greater the ability to substitute capital for labor, the greater the elasticity of demand for labor.

4. The Supply Curves of Productive Services Other Than Labor. (This is harder to grasp than the previous three points). Look at it this way: One reason for lower employment at a higher wage is that production costs rise, product prices rise, sales and output are reduced, and purchases of inputs are reduced. Suppose, however, that the industry uses some factor—say a specialized raw material with no other uses—with a supply curve that is highly inelastic. As the industry's demand for this material falls, its price will go down. This reduction in the industry's costs serves as an offset to the higher costs resulting from the wage increase. So the increase in total cost and price will be smaller, and the drop in sales and employment smaller, than they would be without this cushioning factor. In this case labor's gains are partly at the expense of the owners of this other factor.

To sum up: The demand for labor will be more inelastic—that is, a wage increase will produce a *smaller* drop in employment—in proportion as (1) demand for the product is inelastic; (2) labor costs form a small proportion of total costs; (3) the possibilities of substituting capital and other factors for labor are limited; and (4) the supply of one or more nonlabor factors is inelastic.

Empirical Evidence on Demand Elasticities

Many studies have tried to estimate wage elasticities of labor demand. Elasticities have been estimated for aggregate labor in the U.S. economy, labor in particular industries, different types of labor (for example, production and nonproduction workers) and for different demographic groups (for example, teenagers).

To make such elasticity estimates, one must be able to isolate the effects of wage differences on labor demand. To do so, one must hold constant all variables that shift the labor demand curve, notably shifts in product demand curves and changes in the prices (and availability) of other inputs, such as capital. In addition, one must adjust for the slope of the labor supply curve. These requirements are never satisfied completely and often are not even approximated. Thus it is not surprising that for each kind of labor there is at least moderate variability in the elasticity estimates.

Daniel Hamermesh has reviewed many such studies.[8] He concludes that for the economy as a whole and for most industries, the long-run labor demand elastic-

---

[8]See Hamermesh, "The Demand for Labor in the Long Run."

ity is in the range of −0.15 to −0.50. This range is for the effects of wage changes, holding output constant. Thus these estimates indicate the magnitude of the factor-substitution effect but do not include the scale effect. The scale effect may well be larger than the factor-substitution effect, especially when we are considering estimates for fairly narrowly defined industries.

In earlier work Hamermesh concluded that over a period of one year, the elasticity of demand for labor in the entire economy is about −0.3.[9] In this case the estimate is the sum of a −0.15 factor-substitution elasticity and a −0.15 scale elasticity. Over a longer period the elasticity should be somewhat larger. The longer the time period, the less costly it is for firms to substitute other factors of production or for consumers to shift their purchases to less labor-intensive commodities.

The elasticity of labor demand will be greater for a firm than for an industry, a labor market, or the entire economy. The lower the level of aggregation, the easier it is for the customer to purchase substitute goods or services. For example, when it is time to buy an automobile, it is relatively easy to shift from one's present car dealer to another in the same city. But it is more expensive to shift to reliance on taxis for one's transportation needs. Empirical studies have estimated that the long-run demand for labor in low-wage manufacturing is moderately elastic (slightly greater than 1.0 in absolute value).[10] The demand for labor by individual firms in these industries would be even more elastic.

In addition, the elasticity of demand normally will be greater for particular kinds of labor than for labor as a whole. It is usually easier to substitute one kind of labor for another than to substitute capital for labor. Certainly, this should be the case when we consider the elasticity of demand for workers of different age, race, or gender. Although there is no consensus in the empirical literature on the elasticity of demand for many demographic groups, the estimates do consistently show a highly elastic demand for young workers.[11] More generally the estimates indicate that the elasticity of demand is greater for unskilled than for skilled labor.[12]

To conclude this chapter, we discuss two applications of the theory of labor demand. First, we consider the implications of the theory for the ability of unions to raise the wage rates of their members. Then we discuss the employment effects of minimum wage legislation.

---

[9]Hamermesh, "Econometric Studies of Labor Demand and Their Application to Policy Analysis."

[10]See Albert Zucker, "Minimum Wages and the Long-Run Elasticity of Demand for Low-Wage Labor," *Quarterly Journal of Economics* (May 1973), pp. 267–77; and George E. Tauchen, "Some Evidence on Cross-section Effects of the Minimum Wage Rate," *Journal of Political Economy* (June 1981), pp. 529–47.

[11]See Daniel Hamermesh and James Grant, "Econometric Studies of Labor-Labor Substitution and Their Implications for Policy." They argue that the absolute value of the elasticity for young workers is clearly greater than unity.

[12]See Hamermesh, "The Demand for Labor in the Long Run." The evidence he reviews also indicates that human capital and physical capital are complements in production, while unskilled labor and physical capital are substitutes.

UNION WAGE GAINS AND ELASTICITY OF DEMAND FOR UNION LABOR

Most unions seek both high wages and secure jobs for their members. When a union increases the wage rate, however, it reduces the employment of union workers. This reduction follows from the negative slope of the labor demand curve. At higher wage rates, less labor will be demanded.

The employment effect of a wage increase will be of greatest concern when many union members are already unemployed. If employment is high and rising, a wage increase might only reduce new hiring by employers. In this case the union would not be very concerned, since its interest is mainly in the welfare of present union members. Because of high unemployment among many union members in the early 1980s, there was particular concern for the employment effects of union wage rates. High unemployment resulted partly from recession during 1982–83 and partly from special difficulties facing several highly unionized industries (for example, import competition in steel and automobiles).

If the demand for union labor is highly elastic (very responsive to changes in the wage rate), even a moderate increase in the union wage rate can cause all union members to lose their jobs. Obviously, a union will not try to raise wage rates under these conditions.

The elasticity of demand for union labor will be high in each of the following cases: (1) the partially organized industries, such as textiles, clothing, furniture, and in recent years, construction and coal mining; (2) industries where there is strong foreign competition, as in steel and automobiles; and (3) industries that have been deregulated (at least partially), including airlines and trucking. We shall discuss each of these cases in turn.

The elasticity of demand for union workers will be high when the union has not succeeded in organizing a large share of the workers (actual and potential) in an industry. In this case employers may be able to substitute nonunion for union labor.[13] Even where a particular employer is unable to do this, a union cannot raise wage rates very much if it has not succeeded in organizing the workers at all (or almost all) the firms in an industry. In this case the price elasticity of product demand will be very high for the unionized firms, since the output of nonunion firms is a good substitute. As explained earlier, the price elasticity of product demand is a major determinant of the wage elasticity of labor demand. Therefore, whenever nonunion firms are numerous enough to provide strong competition for firms that are unionized, the high elasticity of product demand will lead to a high elasticity of demand for union labor. Thus a union

---

[13]Under the National Labor Relations Act, private employers are allowed to hire strikebreakers. The employer need not rehire the strikers if they are no longer needed because they have been permanently replaced by the strikebreakers or because the jobs in question have been eliminated. For federal employees, strikes are illegal. When the air traffic controllers undertook an illegal strike in 1981, they were replaced by nonunion workers, thus ending the influence of the striking union, the Professional Air Traffic Controllers (PATCO).

must organize all competing workers and firms if it is to have much power to raise wage rates.

Next let us consider how a similar analysis can help explain why, during the early 1980s, several formerly powerful unions had to accept lower wage rates or make other concessions, a phenomenon called *concession bargaining*. During the period since World War II, both the United Automobile Workers (UAW) and the United Steelworkers of America have been among the largest, most powerful unions in the country. Each union was able to win high wage rates for its members.

In both steel and autos, all (or virtually all) of the industry in the United States is represented by the union. Product demand for each industry has not been very elastic, at least until recently. Both industries are capital intensive so that labor represents a relatively small portion of total costs. During most of the postwar period substitution of capital for labor did not occur rapidly enough to represent any significant threat to most union members. For these reasons the demand for union labor was quite inelastic, and unions were able to win high wage rates for their members.

For both the steel and automobile industries, increased foreign competition in recent years has reduced product demand and made it more price elastic. Since labor is a derived demand, the demand for labor has also declined and become more elastic, thus reducing the economic power of the UAW and the Steelworkers.

In Figure 5-9 we show how foreign competition or competition from non-union domestic firms makes the demand for union labor more elastic. If the union wage is no higher than the wage of foreign workers (and if the union does not reduce productivity, an issue discussed in Chapter 21), foreign competition will have little effect on the demand for union labor. On the other hand, if the wage rate for union labor is above that for equally productive foreign labor, the entry of foreign competitors will reduce the demand for union labor. Thus greater foreign competition makes the demand curve for union labor flatter (more elastic). In Figure 5-9 we show the extreme case where foreign competition makes the (long-run) demand curve for union labor completely elastic at the foreign wage rate, W. Because of transportation costs and other rigidities in the economy, the actual demand for labor is not likely to become perfectly elastic at W. Nevertheless, the demand curve for union labor will become more elastic above W because of the influence of foreign competition.

In the past competition from distant areas has led to increased emphasis on national rather than local unions, as discussed in Chapter 12. But it appears impossible to extend American unions to other cultures, for instance, to Japan. Instead, unions (together with the firms in their industry) have lobbied for the government to restrict imports. Such lobbying has had some success. But the cost of import restrictions is borne by consumers and by other industries. For example, the restriction of imported steel increases the price of steel to buyers in the United States. This increases the cost of producing automobiles in this country and thus contributes to the problem of foreign competition facing our automobile industry.

We do not mean to suggest that high wage rates (or any other effects of

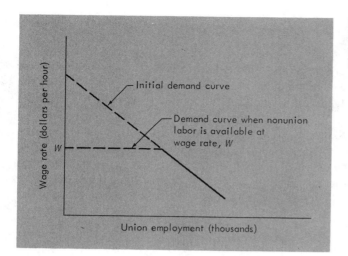

FIGURE 5-9   The Effect of
Nonunion Competition
on the Demand for
Union Labor

unions) are the only cause of the present problems facing the steel and automobile industries in the United States. Other problems may be much more important. For example, after the destruction during World War II, the United States had a virtual monopoly of the world steel market. But the development of steel mills in other countries (often with large government subsidies) and the failure of much of our domestic industry to convert to the latest technologies have greatly reduced our share of the world market.

While our steel industry has been declining since the 1950s, the problems of our automobile industry are more recent. The average car made in the United States is much larger than that in other countries, in part because the price of gasoline has been relatively low in this country. As gasoline became much more expensive in the 1970s, our automobile industry was vulnerable to competition from smaller foreign cars. High-quality small cars plus an extensive marketing effort enabled the Japanese to capture a sizable share of the market in the United States. As we shall discuss in Chapter 14, competition from abroad is not the only example of how greater product competition (and thus a more elastic labor demand) has reduced a union's power. Reduced government regulation of transportation has sharply curtailed the power of the Teamsters in the trucking industry and of many of the airline unions.

In this section we have shown how an analysis of the elasticity of labor demand can help explain some of the problems currently facing unions. Conversely, the analysis can help explain why some unions are still in a relatively strong position to obtain high wage rates for their members. Among such strong unions are many in the public sector including the American Federation of State, County, and Municipal Employees (AFS-CME), the American Federation of Teachers (AFT), and the National Education Association (NEA). The demand for union labor is relatively inelastic in each of these cases. Since local services are being provided, there is no threat of foreign competition. Although there could be a threat from nonunion workers willing to work for lower pay, political constraints—together with tenure and civil service regulations—generally prohibit governments from substituting non-union for union workers.

Some unions in the private sector have also been able to help protect themselves from nonunion competition through legislation. In construction, for example, the Davis-Bacon Act requires contractors working on federally funded projects to pay prevailing wage rates in the local labor market as determined by the Department of Labor. In practice this prevailing wage rate usually has been the union wage, thus protecting both union members and their employers from competition by nonunion firms employing workers at lower wage rates.

MINIMUM WAGES AND POVERTY

To reduce poverty among the working poor many people favor raising the minimum wage rate that employers must pay their workers. At least since the encyclical of Pope Leo XIII in 1891, there has been much discussion of the obligation of employers to pay a "living wage." In this country the first minimum wage law was passed by Massachusetts in 1912. A federal minimum wage was established as part of the Fair Labor Standards Act of 1938. The minimum was set at about 40 percent of the average hourly wage rate, and it applied to less than half of all nonsupervisory employees. Coverage was limited mainly to large firms in heavy industry (for example, manufacturing and mining). Since 1938 coverage has increased substantially and now includes over 80 percent of all nonsupervisory workers. Over time the minimum wage has been increased periodically as average wage rates have increased in the economy. Usually, the minimum wage has been between one-third and one-half the average manufacturing wage. In 1991 the minimum wage will be $4.25 per hour.

Economists generally have been critical of minimum wage legislation. The primary argument against such legislation is its effects on employment opportunities. As the wage rate is increased, employers' demand for labor will fall. There will be fewer job opportunities. Those who remain employed do gain a higher wage rate but at the expense of those who are no longer employed.

Labor Demand and Minimum Wage Rates

Let us examine the argument about employment effects more carefully. First we are assuming that wage rates and employment for unskilled labor are determined in a competitive labor market. As shown in Figure 5-10, the competitive equilibrium is at point A, where the wage rate is W_C and the employment level is E_C. If the legal minimum wage rate, W_M, is set higher than W_C, then establishing the minimum wage will reduce the employment of the unskilled. The economy moves to point B. The amount of the employment reduction, $E_C - E_M$, will depend on how much the wage rate is increased and on the elasticity of demand for unskilled labor.

The argument is generally accepted by economists. It does depend on a

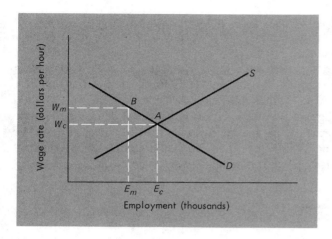

FIGURE 5-10   Employment Effect of
Minimum Wage Legislation

number of assumptions, however. First, we are assuming that employees comply with the legislation. In fact, the government allocates only limited resources to enforcement. Moreover, the penalties for first offenders who are caught paying less than the minimum wage are quite modest. Usually all the employer must do is compensate workers for the difference between what they were actually paid and what they would have earned at the minimum wage rate.

Given the weak incentives, it is not surprising that compliance is relatively low. Ashenfelter and Smith estimate that of all workers who would be earning less than the minimum in the absence of the legislation, only about 60 percent actually do earn the minimum wage.[14]

Employers who do comply with the minimum wage rate may still be able to reduce its impact by reducing nonwage compensation to offset the cost of the higher hourly wage. That is one reason minimum wage jobs often have poor working conditions and seldom offer much vacation time, health insurance, retirement benefits, or on-the-job training.[15]

Another assumption underlying the analysis is that all jobs are covered by the legislation. To the extent that some jobs are not covered (or that some covered employers do not comply with the legislation), those who can no longer obtain jobs at covered firms can still obtain jobs not covered by the legislation. The supply of labor available for uncovered jobs will increase, lowering the wages for such jobs. Therefore, such workers are worse off as a result of the minimum wage but not as badly off as if there were no jobs available. In recent years, however, most jobs have been covered by the minimum wage. So shifting to uncovered jobs is not a readily available option for most workers.

---

[14]See Orley Ashenfelter and Robert S. Smith, "Compliance with the Minimum Wage Law," *Journal of Political Economy* (April 1979), pp. 335–50.

[15]For example, see the discussion of these issues in Walter J. Wessels, *Minimum Wages, Fringe Benefits, and Working Conditions* (Washington, D.C.: American Enterprise Institute for Public Policy Research, 1980).

Because it is set well below the average wage rate in the economy, the minimum wage directly affects only a small portion of the workforce, probably between five and ten percent. Those most affected are teenagers and those with part-time jobs.[16]

Although most workers are not directly affected by the minimum wage, changes in the legal minimum still can have a significant effect on the whole economy. As we discuss in Chapter 6, employers seek to maintain customary wage differentials. Consequently, when an increase in the minimum wage forces an employer to raise the wages of her lowest paid workers, usually she will also raise the wages of other workers, especially those earning only a little more than the legal minimum. As a result, increases in the minimum wage have some inflationary effects, although there are many other more important determinants of inflation, as we shall see in Chapter 9.

Next let us consider some of the criticisms that have been raised against the standard economic argument that increases in the minimum wage will reduce employment. We have assumed that the labor market would be competitive except for the minimum-wage regulations. If the product market is not fully competitive, management may become lazy and inefficient. A forced increase in the wage rate may rouse management from its lethargy, leading to improvements in personnel and production management. Although the shock effect may raise labor's schedule of marginal physical productivity, employment will still decline unless product demand increases. As the physical productivity of labor increases, fewer workers will be needed to produce a given output.

In the case of monopsony, an increase in the minimum wage may increase employment. The argument is the same as that discussed in Chapter 2 when we showed how a union wage increase could increase employment. There are several important qualifications that must be made, however. First, if the minimum wage is set too high (for example, above the wage rate corresponding to a horizontal line through point *A*), the minimum wage will reduce employment. Second, the minimum wage needed to increase employment will vary from firm to firm and from occupation to occupation within firms. Third, there is little evidence to suggest that monopsony is important to our economy.[17] Most firms are located in urban areas where there are many firms in the labor market and relatively little collusion among employers.

The Magnitude of Employment Effects

Economists generally believe that the low-wage labor market is reasonably competitive and that increases in the minimum wage reduce employment opportunities. Still the size of the employment effect is an important issue. If the wage effect is larger (in percentage terms) than the employment effect, the net impact of the

---

[16]See Steven E. Haugen and Earl F. Miller, "Estimating the Number of Minimum Wage Workers," *Monthly Labor Review,* (January 1990), pp. 70–74.

[17]See E. G. West and Michael McKee, "Monopsony and 'Shock' Arguments for Minimum Wage Rates," *Southern Economics Journal* (January 1980), pp. 883–91.

minimum wage will be to increase the earnings of those whose wage rates were initially below the minimum. On the other hand, if the employment effect is larger, the net effect will be to reduce the earnings of low-wage workers. Thus the magnitude of the employment effect is directly related to the elasticity of labor demand. If the demand is inelastic ($-$elasticity<1.0), the wage effect predominates and earnings will increase. On the other hand, if the demand is elastic ($-$elasticity>1.0), the employment effect dominates and the earnings of low-wage workers will decline.

There are several ways of estimating the employment effects of minimum wage legislation. The simplest, most common approach is to relate changes in the level and coverage of the legislation to changes in employment, while attempting to hold constant the effects of other factors, such as changes in the level of aggregate demand in the economy. Such studies can be done for particular firms, industries, and demographic groups. In each case analysts focus on the low-wage groups that will be most affected by the legislation and for whom the most accurate estimates can be obtained.

The most thorough study of the effects of the minimum wage on a low-wage industry is Belton Fleisher's investigation of retail trade, an industry first covered by the federal minimum wage legislation in 1961.[18] Fleisher estimates that the elasticity of demand for low-wage labor in retail trade is about -2.0. If this estimate is accurate, a higher minimum wage will reduce the total earnings of those workers in retail trades who are directly affected by the legislation, since the percentage wage increase is only half that of the employment decline.

Many empirical studies have estimated the employment effects of minimum wage legislation on teenagers. A widely cited review article by Brown, Gilroy, and Kohen concludes that the best estimates show a 10 percent increase in the minimum wage causing a decrease of 1 to 3 percentage points in the total employment of teenagers.[19] Because some teenagers earn more than the minimum wage, or work on jobs not covered by the legislation, these results imply an elasticity estimate larger (in absolute value) than -0.1 to -0.3. Consequently, the estimates reviewed by Brown, Gilroy, and Kohen are not necessarily inconsistent with Fleisher's elasticity estimate for retail trade. Nevertheless, the demand for low-wage labor may be unusually elastic in retail trade. For example, the demand by customers for services, such as short checkout lines and assistance in carrying purchases, may be quite elastic. Recent estimates show a smaller effect for changes in the minimum wage. For example, Brown shows that a 20 percent decline in the effective minimum between 1980 and 1986 had little effect on either the employment to population ratio or the unemployment rate of teenagers.[20]

---

[18]Belton Fleisher, *Minimum Wage Regulation in Retail Trade* (Washington, D.C.: American Enterprise Institute for Public Policy Research, 1981).

[19]See Charles Brown, Curtis Gilroy, and Andrew Kohen, "The Effect of the Minimum Wage on Employment and Unemployment." See also the study by the same authors, "Time Series Evidence on the Effects of the Minimum Wage on Youth Employment and Unemployment," *Journal of Human Resources* (Winter 1983), pp. 3–31.

[20]Charles Brown, "Minimum Wage Laws: Are They Overrated?" *Journal of Economic Perspectives,* (Summer 1988), p.140.

The effects of the minimum wage legislation appear to be somewhat greater for black teenagers than for whites, although the findings on this point differ across studies. As we discuss in Chapter 10, there is a serious employment problem among black youths. John Cogan estimates that during the period from 1950 to 1970 this problem arose primarily for two reasons: (1) the decline in the demand for low-skilled agricultural labor as a result of the increased capital invested in agriculture and (2) limited availability of nonagricultural jobs for displaced black youths because of minimum wage legislation.[21]

Although there is good evidence that increases in the minimum wage have reduced the employment opportunities of teenagers, it is not clear that the minimum wage has led to a corresponding increase in youth unemployment. The labor force participation of youths is quite sensitive to job opportunities. Thus a decrease in job opportunities for teenagers may lead to a decrease in labor force participation rather than an increase in unemployment. According to estimates of Jacob Mincer, a 10 percent increase in the minimum wage decreases teenage employment by 2.1 percent for whites and 4.6 percent for blacks. These declines in employment are accompanied by declines in labor force participation of 1.6 percent for whites and 3.7 percent for blacks. The net increase in the teenage unemployment rate is much smaller, only 0.4 percent for whites and 0.8 percent for blacks.[22]

Because teenagers are the groups whose job opportunities have been most affected by the minimum wage, there have been numerous proposals to reduce the minimum wage for young workers. In 1989, Congress enacted a training wage whereby teenagers could be paid 85 percent of the minimum wage for the first three months of each youth's first job.

Any youth differential in the minimum wage should increase the employment of teenagers. Nevertheless, the idea of a lower minimum wage for youth has generated considerable opposition from those who believe that the job gains of teenagers would come mainly at the expense of fewer jobs for adults, as employers shift unskilled jobs from low-wage adults to teenagers, who could be paid even less. Reduced job opportunities for adults could be especially costly since more adults than teenagers are supporting other family members.[23]

The empirical evidence suggests that the minimum wage leads to a substantial loss in employment opportunities for teenagers but has little employment effect for other demographic groups. On balance, low-wage adults probably have been helped by minimum wage legislation, since some low-wage workers have obtained

---

[21]See Cogan, "The Decline in Black Teenage Employment: 1950–70," *American Economic Review* (September 1982), pp. 621–38.

[22]See Mincer, "Unemployment Effects of Minimum Wages," *Journal of Political Economy* (August 1976), pp. S87–105.

[23]There has been relatively little empirical work on the extent to which a youth differential in the minimum wage would decrease adult employment. One interesting study is Daniel S. Hamermesh, "Minimum Wages and the Demand for Labor," *Economic Inquiry* (July 1982), pp. 365–80. Hamermesh estimates that a youth differential would create at least four jobs for youths for every adult job that is lost. This finding is somewhat surprising, since unskilled adult labor should be a good substitute for unskilled teenage labor, in which case we might expect a greater decline in the demand for adult labor.

higher wage rates, while there have been few job losses. Teenagers who have been able to find jobs have also gained from the minimum wage. To what extent have these gains from the minimum wage led to reduced poverty, the major goal of the legislation? The evidence suggests that the minimum wage has had little net effect on poverty and the distribution of income.[24] First, as we have emphasized, there are employment losses as well as wage gains from the minimum wage. Second, the wage gains are small relative to the total income of the poor. Third, many of those who do gain from the minimum wage are children or other secondary earners in reasonably well-to-do families, families where the household head has a well-paying job. For these reasons minimum wage legislation does not appear to be a very effective antipoverty strategy.

On balance, both the benefits and costs of modest changes in the minimum wage appear to be rather small. As Brown writes:

> It is hard for me to see evidence that minimum wage increases have benefits which would overcome an economist's aversion to interfering with reasonably competitive markets. But the case against the minimum wage seems to me to rest more upon that aversion than on the demonstrated severity of any harm done to those directly affected.[25]

To reduce poverty among the working poor, an alternative to the minimum wage is to let employers pay the market wage and then for the government to subsidize the earnings of those with low incomes. An example of this approach is the earned income tax credit, which provides a 14 percent subsidy for the earnings of low-income parents. It does not reduce employers' demand for low-skilled workers. Also, it has little effect on either inflation or the structure of wage rates. The subsidy is limited to those in the most need and is not available to teenage children from middle-class families, the group most affected by the minimum wage. On the other hand, the earned-income tax credit does represent a cost to taxpayers. Also many of those most in need receive no benefits because they do not fill out a tax return.

SUMMARY

1. The marginal revenue product (*MRP*) is the additional revenue the firm gains by employing an extra worker. If the product market is competitive, then the marginal revenue product is equal to the product price times the worker's marginal physical product (MPP).

---

[24]See Edward Gramlich, "Impact of Minimum Wages on Other Wages, Employment, and Family Incomes," *Brookings Papers on Economic Activity* (1976), pp. 409–51; and William Johnson and Edgar Browning, "The Distribution and Efficiency Effects of Increasing the Minimum Wage," *American Economic Review* (March 1983), pp. 204–11.

[25]Brown, "Minimum Wage Laws," p. 144.

2. The marginal cost of labor (*MC*) is the extra cost the firm must pay in order to employ an additional worker.

3. In order to maximize its profits, the firm must have just enough workers so that *MRP = MC*.

4. The law of variable proportions states that as increasing quantities of a variable factor (such as labor) are applied to a fixed factor of production (such as physical capital), the resulting additions to output will eventually decrease.

5. Even if prices are fixed, as under perfect competition, the law of variable proportions ensures that *MRP* will decline as more labor is employed, at least past some employment level. The downward-sloping portion of the *MRP* schedule is the firm's short-run demand curve for labor, giving the amount of labor the firm will employ at any wage rate.

6. The firm's demand for labor will be more responsive to a change in wage rates (the labor demand curve will be flatter) in the long run than in the short. In both the short and the long run there is a scale effect, with high wage rates leading to less output and therefore to less employment. In the long run there is also a factor-substitution effect, as firms can then substitute capital for labor if the relative price of labor increases.

7. Market demand curves for labor are the horizontal sum of the labor demand curves for the individual firms in the market. Market demand curves shift because of changes in product demand, changes in technology, or changes in the prices of other factors of production.

8. The marginal productivity theory is a theory of labor demand, not of wage rates. It is useful in analyzing labor market issues whether wage rates are determined in competitive markets, through collective bargaining, or by government regulations.

9. The wage elasticity of labor demand is the percentage change in labor demand divided by the percentage change in the wage rate. The demand for labor will be more elastic, that is, a wage increase will produce a larger drop in employment (a) the more price elastic the demand for the product; (b) the larger labor costs are as a proportion of total costs; (c) the greater the ease with which capital or other factors of production can be substituted for labor; and (d) the more elastic the supply of the other factors of production.

10. Unions are concerned with job security as well as with wage gains. The ability of unions to win large wage increases for their members without decreasing employment opportunities significantly will be greater when the demand for union labor is inelastic. Unions will have little bargaining power over wage rates unless they have organized a whole industry. Because nonunion labor and output are good substitutes for union labor and the output of unionized firms, the elasticity of demand for union labor is high in a partially unionized industry. Increased foreign competition has increased the elasticity of demand for union labor in recent years in many industries, reducing union power to affect wage rates.

11. Increasing the legal minimum wage will reduce the demand for workers with little skill. The size of the employment loss depends on the elasticity of low-skilled labor. Since it is relatively easy to substitute more-skilled for less-skilled workers, the wage elasticity for low-skilled workers should be fairly high. Empirical estimates indicate that teenagers are the group whose employment is most affected by minimum wage legislation. For teenagers a 10 percent increase in the minimum wage causes employment to decrease by 1 to 3 percentage points.

KEY CONCEPTS

MARGINAL PRODUCTIVITY THEORY	MARKET DEMAND SCHEDULE
MARGINAL PHYSICAL PRODUCT	SCALE EFFECT
MARGINAL REVENUE PRODUCT	FACTOR-SUBSTITUTION EFFECT
MARGINAL COST OF LABOR	DEMAND FOR LABOR, ELASTICITY OF
VARIABLE PROPORTIONS, PRINCIPLE OF	DEMAND FOR UNION LABOR, ELASTICITY OF
DEMAND FOR LABOR, SHORT-RUN	MINIMUM WAGE
DEMAND FOR LABOR, LONG-RUN	EARNED INCOME TAX CREDIT

REVIEW QUESTIONS

1. What does it mean to say that a labor demand curve has a negative slope? Discuss how the negative slope of a labor demand curve is related to the law of variable proportions.

2. How and why does the labor demand curve for a firm differ in the short and the long run?

3. What is the difference between a labor demand curve for a firm and that for an entire labor market? How can the market demand curve be derived from the demand curves for the firms in the market?

4. What does it mean to say that there has been an increase in demand for a particular kind of labor? What factors cause shifts in labor demand?

5. In a competitive labor market, what effect will an increase in labor demand have on the wage rate and on employment? To what extent does the answer depend on the slopes of the supply and demand curves?

6. How realistic is the marginal productivity theory of labor demand? Discuss how the usefulness of the theory is related to the realism of its assumptions.

7. What determines the elasticity of demand for a particular kind of labor?

8. Why is the elasticity of labor demand greater for specific demographic or occupational groups than for labor as a whole?

9. Discuss the relation between the elasticity of labor demand and the ability of a union to win higher wage rates for its members. How does this analysis relate to the power of any unions with which you have had personal experience?

10. How does the elasticity of labor demand relate to the employment effects of minimum wage legislation? For what demographic groups are these employment effects likely to be especially large? Why?

READINGS

BROWN, CHARLES, CURTIS GILROY, and ANDREW KOHEN, "The Effect of the Minimum Wage on Employment and Unemployment." *Journal of Economic Literature* (June 1982), pp. 487–528.

CARTTER, ALLAN M., *The Theory of Wages and Employment.* Homewood, Ill.: Richard D. Irwin, 1959.

HAMERMESH, DANIEL S., "The Demand for Labor in the Long Run," in *Handbook of Labor Economics,* vol. 1, ed. Orley Ashenfelter and Richard Layard (Amsterdam: North-Holland, 1986), pp. 429–71.

———, "Econometric Studies of Labor Demand and Their Application to Policy Analysis." *Journal of Human Resources* (Fall 1976), pp. 507–42.

———, and JAMES GRANT, "Econometric Studies of Labor-Labor Substitution and Their Implications for Policy," *Journal of Human Resources* (Fall 1979), pp. 518–42.

MARSHALL, ALFRED, *Principles of Economics,* 8th ed. New York: Macmillan Publishing Co., 1920, pp. 383–86.

WELCH, FINIS, *Minimum Wages: Issues and Evidence.* Washington, D.C.: American Enterprise Institute, 1978.

INVESTMENTS BY FIRMS
IN WORKERS

In discussing the demand for labor in Chapter 5, we made an important simplification by assuming that all workers are equally productive. Given this assumption, employers need not be concerned with the quality of the workers they hire, their on-the-job training, how many hours they work, or how well motivated they are. In this chapter we focus on some of the policies that firms have developed to recruit, train, and motivate productive work forces. One of our primary themes will be the importance of on-the-job training for many jobs and its role in encouraging long-term relations between employers and their workers.

We begin by considering ability differences across workers. Such differences cause both firms and workers to invest in search as workers seek better jobs and employers seek better workers.

Next we examine the training costs of firms. We show how differences in such costs are related to many differences across labor markets, including promotion and pay policies and the length of time a worker normally works for a firm.

Heterogeneity among workers is not limited to skill differences and other forms of on-the-job training. Differences in work attitudes are also important. Next we discuss different policies of firms that influence the motivation of their employees. We will see that the policies a firm adopts depend on whether that firm invests heavily in its workers.

How firms react to changes in demand is the next topic. Here we emphasize how on-the-job training and long-term employment relations influence whether firms will respond to changing demand by varying wage rates, hours worked per employee, or employment levels. Such decisions of firms clearly are a factor in the effectiveness of macroeconomic policies to combat inflation and unemployment.

MATCHING WORKERS AND JOBS

Workers differ considerably in their abilities and aptitudes. In this section we discuss such differences and show how they lead to search in the labor market by both workers and firms. Just as a worker searches for the best available job, a firm seeks to recruit those workers who best fit its needs.

Ability Differences

At an abstract level economists can handle ability differences across workers by introducing the concept of an *efficiency unit of labor*. If worker *A* can produce 50 percent more than worker *B*, worker *A* represents 1.5 times as many efficiency units as worker *B*. A competitive labor market tends to equalize not the hourly wage received by each worker but the wage per efficiency unit. In this case worker *A* would earn 1.5 times as much as worker *B*. Similarly, once labor is viewed as heterogeneous, both the demand and supply curves should be viewed in terms of efficiency units of labor rather than hours of work.

The concept of efficiency units is all that would be necessary if workers differed in only one way. For example, if physical strength were necessary for most jobs and if variations in strength were the only important differences across workers, shifting from hours of labor to efficiency units would be sufficient for handling the effect of ability differences in the labor market.

But ability is not a single characteristic. People differ in mathematical ability, verbal skill, manual dexterity, physical health and energy, motivation and drive, dependability, creativity, and many other ways. Thus we should speak really of *abilities*. Moreover, the productivity of a particular kind of ability differs from job to job. Creativity may be highly necessary for a designer of theater costumes but not at all necessary for a milling-machine operator.

Since jobs differ in their ability requirements, and people differ in the abilities they have, there is an interesting problem of allocating people efficiently among jobs. In studying international trade, you may have learned about the theory of *comparative advantage*. This theory holds that world output is increased if each country specializes in producing goods in which it is *relatively* most efficient. Even if country *A* is absolutely less efficient than country *B* in everything, it will still have comparative advantage in goods for which its disadvantage is least.

In the same way we can reason that national output is increased if each worker is assigned to the job in which that worker is *relatively* most productive. Even if Ms. *A* is less productive than Ms. *B* on every job, there will be some job where her disadvantage is least. That is the job on which she has comparative advantage. Which job it is depends on her endowment of abilities, relative to the mix of abilities that various jobs require.

Job Search

In our economy no one actually assigns workers to jobs. The matching of jobs and workers is done by the labor market. Employers search for the workers who are best suited to their needs, and workers search for what they consider to be the best jobs. For both employers and workers the search is complicated because information is quite imperfect. It is difficult for the employer to know how productive new workers will be, especially if they must receive considerable training before reaching their full potential. Similarly, it is difficult for workers to know how well they will fit in and enjoy their new jobs.

The search for work goes on through many channels, differing somewhat with the skill involved. Skilled crafts people tend to work through the union office. White-collar workers make considerable use of private employment agencies. Branch offices of the state employment service, help-wanted advertising, and other media play their part. The commonest channel, however, is applying directly to the company or following up leads from friends and relatives.[1]

As we saw in Chapter 4, an investment in job search is as much an investment in human capital as an investment in education or on-the-job training. Just as workers invest by searching for a good job, employers invest by searching for good workers. The analogy can be taken a step further. Workers need to search not only for firms that are hiring but also for firms that will hire them. Similarly, firms must not only locate good workers but also persuade them to accept job offers. In other words, firms must recruit workers.

In developing a recruitment strategy, the firm must first determine the wage rate it will pay for each type of labor it needs. Wage costs are to some extent substitutable for recruitment costs. A company that is known to pay high wage rates to its workers can usually count on a stream of high-quality applicants for work. A company that pays much lower wage rates will have to spend more on advertising and other recruitment strategies. It is also likely to find its applicants are of inferior quality. We shall have more to say about this issue when we discus company wage policies in Chapter 7.

For firms that pay fairly good wages and are satisfied with the quality of their present work force, a frequent strategy is informal word-of-mouth recruitment. When a job opening occurs, the company passes the word first through present employees. It reasons that present employees will know what kinds of workers are needed. If the present employees are satisfactory, their friends and relatives are likely to be more satisfactory than a random sample from the labor market. In addition, people who already have friends in the company are more likely to accept jobs and settle down as permanent employees—an important consideration whenever jobs have high training costs, as we shall explain shortly. Although this informal approach is still important, it has become somewhat less prevalent in recent years because of employer concerns about discrimination. If the

---

[1]For statistical data, see Carl Rosenfeld, "Jobseeking Methods Used by American Workers," *Monthly Labor Review* (August 1975), pp. 39–42.

original workers at high-wage firms are almost all white men, word-of-mouth hiring is likely to restrict the job opportunities of women and minorities.[2]

Lower-wage employers are forced to rely more heavily on other approaches, especially at times of low unemployment. Some alternatives, such as help-wanted advertisements and private employment agencies, involve direct out-of-pocket costs. The Job Service, run by the state governments, will refer workers without requiring a fee. As we explain in Chapter 10, however, the Job Service often concentrates on finding jobs for disadvantaged workers rather than trying to find job applicants who meet employers' requirements. Thus the low-wage employer is faced with a choice of either paying a fee for the services of a private employment agency, incurring high interviewing costs by using the Job Service, or perhaps having both high interviewing costs and out-of-pocket expenses by using the help-wanted ads.

All expenses incurred by a firm in recruiting workers represent an investment in its work force. The firm incurs costs now in return for benefits expected in the future. In the next section we discuss how firms invest in training their workers.

TRAINING COSTS

Thus far we have discussed how the skills needed vary from one firm to another and how abilities vary among workers. This variety leads to search by both workers and firms as workers seek to achieve adequate earnings and firms seek to obtain satisfactory profits.

Some skills needed by employers usually must be learned before a worker will be hired. For example, most jobs require that a worker be able to read and write English. But many other skills, including how to operate the equipment and how to work effectively with the other employees, are learned on the job after the worker is hired. Thus in recruiting workers, the firm must be concerned not only with the present skills of the workers it hires but also with how easily they can learn new skills. It is also important to estimate how long the worker can be expected to continue working with the firm after being trained.

Hiring and Training Costs of Firms

In Chapter 4 we discussed how workers invest in skills needed by employers. Firms also invest heavily in their workers. By incurring costs of hiring and training workers, firms can develop a more productive work force. This investment will pay off as long as the present value of expected increases in productivity (relative to wage rates) exceeds the hiring and training costs.

Hiring costs for firms include costs of recruiting workers, evaluating the

---

[2] See the discussion of this issue in Chap. 8. For further analysis of the importance of informal sources of job information, from the point of view of the average worker as well as that of the firm, see Albert Rees, "Information Networks in Labor Markets."

qualifications of job applicants, and the paper work of putting successful applicants on the payroll. In addition to actual hiring costs, there are fixed costs of hiring new workers that result from the unemployment insurance program. If a firm hires a new worker and then lays the worker off, the firm's unemployment insurance tax increases. This experience rating of unemployment insurance is designed so that those firms that cause the most expenses under unemployment insurance will pay more of its cost than firms that seldom lay off workers.[3]

Once hired, new employees must be assigned to specific jobs. Sometimes there will be a costly period of trial and error before an employee is placed in a satisfactory position.

Upon being placed in any new position, an employee will usually receive training and orientation. For example, the worker may learn how to operate some machinery, either as part of a formal training program or informally with some assistance from coworkers using the same equipment. In addition, there will usually be orientation activities, ranging from elaborate lectures on company policies to simple information on whom to consult if any problems arise. Much of the training needed by new workers is not very technical in nature but rather involves learning how to interact effectively with coworkers, customers, and suppliers.

For many jobs, the extent of training will be rather limited. For others, however, particularly those where the employee must interact creatively with many other workers, the employee may still be learning his or her job for a long time. Long training periods are likely to be most important for top administrative jobs and among innovative firms, those providing new products or developing more efficient ways of producing existing goods and services.

In providing training to its workers, firms incur several kinds of costs. The most obvious costs are direct expenses of the firm, such as the salary costs of those providing the training and the costs of any materials consumed during training. In most cases, however, the *opportunity costs* of training will be greater than the direct costs. These opportunity costs include the extra output the trainees could have produced during the training period. Other opportunity costs include the use of capital equipment and the time of experienced workers. For example, much training is done informally by experienced workers showing new hires how to do the job. Although the process does not require the firm to employ special trainers, it normally does reduce the output of the experienced workers while they are teaching the new recruits. Partly for this reason, it is difficult to obtain accurate estimates of the cost of training for firms.

For the entire economy, there are no reliable estimates of the hiring and training costs incurred by firms. Studies have been done for some individual firms, however. In 1979, for example, an employers' group in Los Angeles surveyed its members and found recruitment and training costs to average $2,000 for clerical workers, $3,400 for production workers, and $9,100 for managers. Even higher figures were estimated in a study of the R. G. Barry Company. Although one needs to be cautious in generalizing from a few case studies, casual observation also

---

[3]See Chap. 10 for further discussion of the unemployment insurance program.

suggests that investment by firms in workers is quite extensive, especially for the more highly skilled jobs.[4]

Training Costs and Long-Term Employment Relations

If the firm has gone to considerable expense to train its present workers, the firm will want to keep these workers to recoup the returns from this investment. For example, employers will not be interested in hiring other workers who might be willing to work for a slightly lower wage. In addition, firms may be receptive to seniority rules that give preference to workers who have been longest with the company. Firms that have invested heavily in their workers will also interested in pension benefits that depend on length of service and need not be paid if the employee quits soon after being trained.[5] Each of these human resource practices should reduce quit rates, especially among workers who have been with the firm for several years and thus may have received considerable training at the firm's expense. The available data indicate that quit rates in the United States have been declining for many years.[6] This decline in quit rates is likely to have resulted from increased investment by firms in their workers. Of course, the causation can also go in the other direction. When expected quit rates are low, firms will be willing to invest more in their workers.

The training costs we have discussed so far are costs paid by firms. In addition, there are costs paid by workers. For example, a worker may be willing to take a lower starting wage if a job promises good training opportunities and prospects for higher wage rates in the future. Any difference in starting wage rates for jobs with and without such training opportunities is a training cost paid by the worker.

How are training costs split between the worker and the firm? In Chapter 4

[4]The Los Angeles study is cited by Daniel J.B. Mitchell and Larry J. Kimball, "Labor Market Contracts and Inflation" in *Workers, Jobs, and Inflation,* ed. Martin Neil Baily (Washington, D.C.: Brookings Institution, 1982), p. 216. The estimates for the R. G. Barry Company are discussed in Donald O. Parsons, "Specific Human Capital: An Application to Quit Rates and to Layoff Rates," *Journal of Political Economy* (Nov./Dec. 1972), pp. 1120–43. Also see the pioneering study by Walter Y. Oi, "Labor as a Quasi-Fixed Factor."

[5]The Employee Retirement Income Security Act (ERISA) of 1974 required that after a certain period of employment with the firm (typically ten years), the employee is entitled to the value of the employer's pension contribution on his behalf. The Tax Reform Act of 1986 requires such vesting after five years.

[6]Because of data limitations, studies of quit rates in the United States have been largely limited to manufacturing employment. These studies indicate that there has been a long-term decline in quit rates, at least once one corrects for changes in demand and in the demographic composition of employment. First there was a major decline in the 1920s, as shown by Arthur M. Ross, "Do We Have a New Industrial Feudalism?" *American Economic Review* (December 1958), pp. 903–20. More recent results show a decline for the period since 1950, a decline that is most pronounced for the period since 1958. See James F. Ragan, Jr., "Investigating the Decline in Manufacturing Quit Rates," *Journal of Human Resources* (Winter 1984), pp. 53–71. Both authors see increases in training and other fixed costs of employment as the primary explanations for the reduction in quit rates, although they recognize that related factors, including more generous pensions and the growth of seniority rules, have also played a role.

we showed that if the training is valuable in several firms and the labor market is reasonably competitive, the firm cannot pay less than the worker's marginal product after training, or else the worker will be bid away by competing employers. Consequently, the firm cannot gain by training the worker, and we expect the worker to bear the costs.

When training is useful mostly at a specific firm, the firm does have an incentive to provide training, since it receives some of the gains. Even in the case of firm-specific training, however, the worker is likely to pay some of the costs and receive some of the benefits. If both the firm and the worker share in the benefits and costs of training, each will have an incentive to continue the employment relationship. If either the worker quits or the firm terminates the worker, both will lose the investment they have made. Thus firms and workers must consider the future as well as the present in making employment decisions.[7]

Some mobility of labor is necessary for both an efficient allocation of labor in a changing economy and as a protection for any workers who believe they are being exploited by their present employers. On the other hand, high labor turnover reduces the incentive for firms and workers to invest in firm-specific human capital. Since such investment makes workers more productive, it can lead to significant benefits for both the firm and its workers.

The importance of firm-specific training is one factor explaining why some workers have long periods of employment with one employer. For example, Hall has estimated the eventual tenure (length of time with present employer) of all workers in the United States. His figures, presented in Table 6-1, show that most workers will hold their present jobs for a total of at least five years. Over one-fourth of all workers will hold their jobs for more than twenty years. Therefore, although there are many short-term jobs in our economy (one job in six lasts less than one year), long-term jobs are common. Such jobs appear to be highly valued by many workers and their employers.

In Japan long-term commitments between firms and workers are even stronger than in the United States, at least in large corporations. These Japanese employers provide a lifetime commitment to their workers. They also make a greater effort than most American employers to create a sense of community and good teamwork throughout the company. In return, the workers are exceptionally loyal and hardworking. These employment policies are cited frequently as one reason for the spectacular success of the Japanese economy during the period since World War II.[8] We shall discuss the Japanese employment system in more detail at the end of this chapter.

In the United States there are many different kinds of labor markets. How these markets operate depends partly on the amount and kind of training required for different kinds of jobs.

---

[7]To the extent that firms can borrow more easily than workers, firms can be expected to incur more of the cost of firm-specific training than their employees.

[8]For example, see Frank Gibney, *Miracle by Design* (New York: Quadrangle Books/The New York Times Book Co., 1982).

TABLE 6-1   Eventual Length of Present Jobs

	PERCENT WITH EVENTUAL TENURE	
	5+ Years	20+ Years
Total	57.8	27.9
Men	63.8	37.3
Women	49.6	15.1

Source: Robert E. Hall, "The Importance of Lifetime Jobs in the U.S. Economy," *American Economic Review* (September 1982), pp. 716–24.

TRAINING, MOBILITY, AND LABOR MARKETS

Some jobs require much more training than others. The amount of training, especially firm-specific training, helps explain why labor markets operate quite differently for different kinds of firms and workers.

When workers are all the same, as assumed in Chapter 5, an employer can hire any worker for any job. If a firm has invested heavily in recruiting and training its work force, however, many jobs can be performed best by those who are already in the firm. Such a firm will not be willing to hire replacements for its present work force, even if other workers would be willing to accept a slightly lower wage rate. In addition, the firm usually will fill many job vacancies by promoting its present employees rather than by hiring new workers from outside the firm.

Considerable differences exist across firms in their reliance on hiring from outside versus promotion from within. Let us consider three different strategies and how they relate to the training of the firm's workers.

For jobs that require little skill, a firm is likely to fill most vacancies with new hires and to have little internal promotion. If most of its jobs are of this type, a firm usually will pay low wages and have high turnover among its work force. Such firms are seldom unionized. High turnover of workers means that union organizers must spend more time recruiting workers, especially if there are long delays in holding the union representation election.[9] Even if the union does win the election, the low skill level of the work force makes it easier for the firm to try to replace its current workers if they strike. This type of market has been called an *open* or *secondary* labor market.[10]

Other firms have high turnover and fill most of their vacancies with new hires even though the jobs pay well and require considerable training. These *guild* labor markets are often unionized and generally occur when labor demand is quite

---

[9]See Chap. 14 for a discussion of union representation elections.

[10]See Clark Kerr, "The Balkanization of Labor Markets," and Peter B. Doeringer and Michael J. Piore, *Internal Labor Markets and Manpower Analysis*. For a more general analysis of internal labor markets, including historical, cross-country, and case-study approaches, see *Internal Labor Markets*, ed. Paul Osterman (Cambridge, Mass.: MIT Press, 1984).

variable across firms, but skills can be easily transferred from one employer to another. The worker's training may be *industry* specific, but it is not *firm* specific. The most important examples of guild labor markets are in construction. A member of one of the construction craft unions can move easily from one employer to another. Initial entrance into the craft may be quite difficult, however. In addition to learning the necessary skills, the worker must be able to gain entrance to the union.

The third type of labor market we consider is usually called either a *primary* or an *internal* labor market.

The Internal Labor Market

In a large, hierarchical organization there will usually be dozens or hundreds of different jobs.[11] Many of these are highly specialized, existing only within one industry or even one firm. The employer may not be able to find experienced workers in the outside market, but must provide the necessary training on the job. Much such training is firm specific. In these firms a worker will normally progress up a "job ladder" as he or she learns the necessary skills in lower-level jobs *and* as vacancies appear in the more skilled, higher-paying positions. Except for a few entry-level jobs, such firms fill most of their vacancies by promotion from within. Outsiders are considered only if no present employees are qualified and interested in the job.

Firms with internal labor markets are often organized by industrial unions. Typically, the union contract contains elaborate rules governing which employees are entitled to "bid" for a particular vacancy and how much weight shall be given to length of service, the ability of the worker, and other factors in selecting among bidders.

Internal labor markets have proved their worth to many employers, mainly in terms of reduced turnover costs and improved worker motivation. In the early years of industrialization, however, most employers emphasized the threat of firing as the chief motivation of workers. Then internal labor markets developed during World Wars I and II, in response to labor scarcity and government regulation, and during the 1930s, in response to union pressure.[12]

Even in the absence of unions, pressure from workers can lead to internal labor markets. As Osterman writes:

> Internal labor markets also develop from forces on the supply side. If a group of workers remains in the same firm for some time, then a set of expectations, or

---

[11]For an interesting, more theoretical discussion of internal labor markets, based on the perspective of exchange between parties when there are few participants in the market because of firm-specific human capital, see Oliver E. Williamson, Michael L. Wachter, and Jeffrey E. Harris, "Understanding the Employment Relation: An Analysis of Idiosyncratic Exchange," *Bell Journal of Economics* (Spring 1978), pp. 250–78.

[12]See Sanford M. Jacoby, "The Development of Internal Labor Markets in American Manufacturing Firms," in Osterman, *Internal Labor Markets*, pp. 23–69.

customs, will develop. These expectations, which can be enforced through noncooperation or even sabotage on the job, tend over time to be codified into a set of rules. The process of unionization speeds this up and formalizes it, and hence many internal labor markets emerge out of unionization drives. However, even in non-union situations, customizing rules and procedures and the force of group expectations can lead to internal labor markets. An example close to hand are the very structured rules and norms that govern hiring and promotion policies in academia.[13]

In internal labor markets the number of jobs that are open to outside hiring may be much smaller than the number of jobs in the plant. In each production department new workers may be hired as trainees at the bottom of the skill ladder. From that point they work their way up to more desirable and better-paid jobs as vacancies arise and in accordance with company policies or union contract rules. Jobs on these promotion ladders are open to outsiders only in the event that no insider wants the job.

Clerical workers and even executive personnel also tend to come in at the bottom and work up the ladder in a similar way. The main exceptions are professional, technical, and skilled jobs requiring extended training: doctors and nurses for the company's medical department, computer programmers in the office, skilled maintenance and repair people in the plant. Vacancies on such jobs will be filled by outside recruitment.

Dunlop has termed the jobs that are normally filled by outside recruitment the *ports of entry* into the company. He emphasizes that for many firms the number of such ports is limited but may change over time with changes in company organization and collective bargaining practices. The rules and procedures governing interjob movement within the company define how the firm's internal labor market operates. Direct linkage between the internal and external markets occurs only at the ports of entry.[14]

If total employment remains unchanged, a vacancy arising anywhere in the plant will still require recruitment of a worker from outside. But the point of hiring may be quite remote from the point at which the vacancy occurred. A vacancy on a skilled production job may lead to the hiring of an unskilled trainee, several insiders having meanwhile moved up the ladder.

This shift of many workers in order to fill one vacancy high up on a job ladder may be quite efficient for the firm. It assures that each worker has a good background for his or her new position. In addition, it provides an incentive for workers to stay with the firm in order to gain promotions in the future.

Problems do occur, however, when the firm faces declining demand and must lay off some of its workers. In an effort to keep its trained workers and to maintain their morale and productivity, a firm usually will lay off those workers with the least *seniority,* those with the fewest years of service with the firm. If the

---

[13]Paul Osterman, "Introduction: The Nature and Importance of Internal Labor Markets," in ibid., p. 12.

[14]For a good statement of these concepts, see John T. Dunlop, "Job Vacancy Measures and Economic Analysis," in *The Measurement and Interpretation of Job Vacancies* (New York: National Bureau of Economic Research, 1966), pp. 27–48.

decrease in labor demand is mainly for the jobs done by entry-level workers, no particular problems arise. But if the decrease in demand is for jobs filled by senior workers (workers who may be badly needed later when production demand increases), the situation is more complex. If the layoffs are made entirely on the basis of seniority in order to protect the most senior workers, many workers may have to be shifted to lower-level positions.

This process is called *bumping,* as each worker with more seniority bumps a less senior worker into a lower-paying job. Extensive bumping is costly to the firm for several reasons. First, the demotion, even if only temporary, can be demoralizing to the workers involved. Second, the workers who shift jobs may have to learn, or at least relearn, skills. This problem is particularly acute if layoffs are made on the basis of plantwide seniority, while skills are developed on a departmental basis. If on the other hand, layoffs are based only on seniority within each department, very valuable workers with considerable seniority may be lost in some departments, while entry-level workers can maintain their jobs elsewhere in the firm.

For jobs that are ports of entry for many companies, the concept of a general labor market makes sense. Workers can move from one company to similar jobs in other companies; and each company's terms of employment must be sufficiently in line with those of other companies to attract the number of recruits it needs. For jobs that are typically filled from within, the concepts of an areawide market and an equilibrium wage make considerably less sense. Such jobs are not fully insulated from the tides of labor demand and supply in the outside market; but they are a good deal more insulated than the port-of-entry jobs. Wage rates on them are not precisely determined by the market but are set by rule-of-thumb procedures that will be examined in Chapter 7.

The "Dual Labor Market" Hypothesis

Some economists have placed great emphasis on the distinction between firms that do and do not have internal labor markets. Firms with internal markets are said to be in the *primary* labor market, while those without are in the *secondary* labor market. The primary sector involves relatively large employers with well-defined internal promotion ladders. These firms offer stable employment, good promotion possibilities, and (usually) relatively good wages and working conditions. In the secondary market these features are absent. Jobs are short term, low skilled, low paid and offer little scope for promotion. The distinction is between an engineer employed by IBM and a dishwasher employed by Charlie's Quick Lunch.

Piore has characterized the two segments as follows:

> The basic hypothesis of the dual labor market was that the labor market is divided into two essentially distinct sectors, termed the *primary* and *secondary* sectors. The former offer jobs with relatively high wages, good working conditions, chances of advancement, equity and due process in the administration of work rules and, above all, employment stability. Jobs in the secondary sector, by contrast, tend to be low-paying, with poorer working conditions, little chance of advancement, a highly personalized relationship between workers and supervisors which leaves

wide latitude for favoritism and is conducive to harsh and capricious work discipline, and with considerable instability in jobs and a high turnover among the labor force. The hypothesis was designed to explain the problems of disadvantaged, particularly black, workers in urban areas, which had previously been diagnosed as one of unemployment.[15]

The concept of the dual labor market was developed by labor economists with first-hand knowledge of different labor markets rather than on the basis of statistical analysis. Nevertheless, there has been some statistical testing. Recently, for example, Dickens and Long have argued that schooling should have more effect on earnings in primary markets, where skills are important, than in secondary markets, where fewer skills are needed.[16] They find support for this hypothesis in their empirical work. Among those in their sample, which is limited to male heads of households, they conclude that the chances of being in the secondary market are greatest for blacks and for those who are over the age of sixty or under the age of twenty-five.

Some economists have questioned whether jobs can be sorted into the distinct boxes of "good" and "bad." Critics of the dual labor market theory argue that there is a continuum of jobs, from best to worst, with no clear-cut dividing line.[17] Workers in poorer jobs can advance to better ones, especially when the aggregate demand for labor is high.

There is little doubt that advocates of the dual labor market have made a contribution in emphasizing the negative feedback mechanisms operative in casual, low-wage employment. Employers in this market offer little stability of employment, opportunity for learning on the job, or prospect of advancement. Wages generally are low, and discipline can be harsh.

Workers employed on these jobs obtain a low yield on such human capital as they do possess. This gives them little incentive to invest in further education and training; and this reinforces the employer's conviction that they are unproductive and undeserving of better treatment. For other workers, especially women, the low yield on human capital provides little incentive to stay in the labor force continuously, thus reinforcing the view of some employers that women have a high turnover rate and shouldn't be hired for positions that require the firm to invest heavily in the workers' training. The lack of skill, work motivation, and continuous labor force participation, which makes it hard for low-wage workers to find better jobs,

---

[15]Michael J. Piore, "Notes for a Theory of Labor Market Stratification," working paper no. 95 (Cambridge, Mass.: Massachusetts Institute of Technology, 1972).

[16]See William T. Dickens and Kevin Long, "A Test of Dual Labor Market Theory," *American Economic Review* (September 1985), pp. 792–805.

[17]For a variety of views, see Glen G. Cain, "The Challenge of Dual and Radical Theories of the Labor Market to Orthodox Theory," *American Economic Review* (May 1975), pp. 16–22; Michael L. Wachter, "Primary and Secondary Labor Markets: A Critique of the Dual Approach," *Brookings Papers on Economic Activity*, no. 3 (1974), pp. 637–80; Paul Osterman, "An Empirical Study of Labor Market Segmentation," *Industrial and Labor Relations Review* (July 1975), pp. 508–23; Cain, "The Challenge of Segmented Labor Market Theories: A Survey," *Journal of Economic Literature* (December 1976), pp. 1215–57; David Gordon, *Theories of Poverty and Underemployment* (Lexington, Mass.: Lexington Books, 1972), and Paul Taubman and Michael L. Wachter, "Segmented Labor Markets."

cannot be taken as inherent characteristics of the workers themselves. In part, at least, these forces result from the feedback mechanism in which workers find themselves involved and from which it is not easy to escape.

Although some employers are mainly in the primary sector and others in the secondary sector, the two are by no means independent of each other. For example, large firms in the primary sector, such as IBM, will often subcontract some of their work. Then if demand falls, they can cut back on the subcontracting rather than lay off their own workers.

In the 1980s many primary-sector firms responded to greater competitive pressures, reduced union power, and a changing economic environment by increasing the flexibility of their work forces, including making greater use of secondary labor markets. As Belous emphasizes, firms have increased their labor flexibility in three ways: (1) by tying compensation more to the productivity, costs, and profits of the individual firm and less to industry patterns; (2) by establishing more flexible work rules; and (3) by reducing the number of *core workers* employed in internal labor markets and increasing the number of *contingent workers*.[18]

In this chapter our interest centers on the increasing use of contingent workers. They may be temporary workers hired directly by the employer or "rented" from a temporary-help agency. Or they may be workers employed by a subcontractor or a consulting firm. The contingent worker receives little on-the-job training, usually can be hired for less than the firm pays a core worker, and can be let go at little cost when not needed. On the other hand, because there is no long-term commitment on either side, contingent workers may not be available when they are most needed by the firm. Also the lack of on-the-job training limits the productivity of a contingent worker and offsets the advantage to the employer of the worker's low wage rate and limited benefits.

Hiring Standards and Job Competition

Although the number of contingent workers is increasing, most of the best jobs in our economy are held by core workers in internal labor markets. We have shown that these internal labor markets are characterized by promotion from within. But how does a worker move out of the secondary labor market and obtain an entry-level position in an internal labor market?

Not every applicant gets equal consideration. The employer with a good reputation for treating workers fairly and offering good promotion opportunities normally has many applicants for each entry-level job. To interview, test, and check references on every applicant would be very expensive. Screening devices reduce the flow to manageable proportions and thus hold down hiring costs. A variety of screening devices are sometimes used. Prior to antidiscrimination legislation, employers often used sex, race, and age. Now education is perhaps the most frequently used screening device. Testing for drug use also has become much more prevalent

---

[18]See. Richard S. Belous, "How Human Resource Systems Adjust to the Shift toward Contingent Workers." For the growing importance of the temporary-help industry, see Garth Mangum, Donald Mayall, and Kristen Nelson, "The Temporary Help Industry."

recently. There is considerable opposition to such testing, however, in part because the available tests are not highly accurate.

Judging an individual on the basis of the average characteristics of his or her group is obviously unfair to individuals of high ability who belong to groups that employers regard unfavorably. Such screening represents *statistical discrimination* by employers. The difficulties of dealing with this problem are discussed at some length in Chapter 8, where we examine labor market discrimination of various kinds.

Hiring preferences of employers, based mainly on employer opinions concerning the trainability and long-term potential of different workers, have other important consequences. First, "labor supply" to the firm includes only those workers whom the employer is willing to count as part of the supply; and this changes with the overall demand-supply situation. In a recession period, when many unemployed workers are available, an employer may be able to set high standards and get exactly the characteristics he or she prefers. But in a tight labor market the employer may have to reduce the requirements substantially.

A further consequence is that the pool of unemployed at any time is biased toward the least preferred members of the labor force. The unemployed can be regarded as arrayed in a queue, with employers hiring from the top of the queue and working downward. At the head of the queue are those workers whom most employers regard as the easiest to train and the most likely to remain with the firm after being trained. High school graduates, aged twenty to forty, with good school records generally receive first preference. For some jobs further education, satisfactory performance on aptitude tests, or experience with other employers may also be necessary. Toward the bottom of the queue for most employers come teenagers, those over sixty, the unskilled, and the illiterate.

For employers with significant training costs and with internal labor markets, Thurow has developed a *job competition model* that he contrasts with the usual *wage competition model* of the labor market. Instead of changes in wage rates, he emphasizes changes in hiring standards as the mechanism that equilibrates the labor market in response to changes in the supply and demand for workers. For workers who must change jobs, a change in hiring standards in the labor market is equivalent to a change in the market wage rate. For example, if hiring standards are increased, a worker seeking a new job will have to settle for a lower-paying position. For workers who do not change jobs, however, wage rates will change in response to changing labor market conditions under wage competition but not under job competition.

Thurow bases his theory on the following proposition:

> The key ingredient in the job-competition model is the observation that most cognitive job skills are not acquired before a worker enters the labor market, but after he has found employment through on-the-job training programs. Thus the labor market is not primarily a bidding market for selling existing skills, but a training market where training slots must be allocated to different workers.[19]

---

[19]See Lester Thurow, *Generating Inequality*, p. 76.

Much of this on-the-job training is done informally by established workers showing new employees how the job is done. If wage competition were prevalent, a senior worker would not provide such training since he would be training competitors for his job. After the new worker is trained, she might either take the senior worker's job or force him to take a lower wage rate in order to keep his position. To avoid such problems, most firms do not emphasize wage competition. Instead of cutting wage rates, firms usually lay off workers by seniority when demand falls and raise hiring standards when the supply of labor increases (e.g., when more workers apply for jobs). Consequently there is less threat to trained senior workers under job competition than under wage competition.

Thurow emphasizes that a worker's productivity depends not only on the amount of physical capital he or she has to work with but also on motivation, training, and on how well he or she fits together with coworkers as part of a smoothly functioning team. Consequently, it is important that workers perceive their wage rates to be fair. Most workers judge fairness mainly in terms of the wage differentials for various kinds of jobs. We discuss this topic further in Chapter 7 when we examine job evaluation procedures as part of our analysis of wage determination.

Both wage and job competition exist in the labor market. Job competition is most prevalent for firms with internal labor markets, especially where much teamwork and on-the-job training are necessary. It is most useful in explaining short-run responses to changes in the supply and demand for labor. Wage competition becomes more important in the long run when firms can enter an industry. For example, if an excess supply of labor develops at the going wage rate, then in the long run new firms can enter the industry, develop a skilled work force at a lower wage rate, and thus provide significant competition for established firms.

Employment at Will

The costs of losing one's job vary across different types of labor markets. In a secondary labor market it is usually easy for a worker to find alternative jobs that are almost as good as the one that has been lost. In a primary (internal) labor market, however, there is considerable on-the-job training and promotion by seniority within the firm. Thus an employee who has climbed some distance up a promotion ladder in one company and is then thrown out of employment by shifts in demand has suffered a real hardship. He is unlikely to be able to move horizontally to the same level of skill and earnings in another company. More probably, the worker will have to start near the bottom with a new employer and work up once more. A displaced worker may also lose accrued pension rights and other benefits earned by length of service.

Because senior workers in internal labor markets are likely to be seriously hurt if they lose their jobs, such workers are very concerned with job security. Partly because of this concern, layoffs for economic reasons are generally by seniority, thus providing greater protection for the senior workers who have the most to lose. But many employees are terminated for noneconomic reasons. Steiber estimates that three million workers per year lose their jobs because of "discharges for cause," including such factors as insubordination and excessive absenteeism.[20] Although many of these discharged workers are losing jobs in secondary labor markets where job turnover is usually high, all workers incur costs when they lose a job, especially when high unemployment makes new positions difficult to find.

In union firms discharges for cause are limited by terms spelled out in the union contract. If disagreements arise in applying the language of the contract to a specific case, then a grievance usually will be filed. Such a grievance is likely to be settled by outside arbitration.

For nonunion workers some protection from unjust discharge is available through legislation. For example, federal and state laws make it unlawful to discriminate in employment on the grounds of race, sex, religion, national origin, physical handicap, or age. Many government employees are also protected by civil service and teacher-tenure laws. All other employees are subject to the doctrine of *employment at will,* which Steiber describes in the following terms:

> This common law doctrine holds that an employment having no specific term may be terminated by either party with or without notice or cause. As one court put it 100 years ago, employment relations of an indefinite nature may be terminated at any time without notice "for good cause, for no cause, or even for cause morally wrong. . . ."[21]

In recent years courts in some states, especially California, have been placing restrictions on the doctrine of employment at will. In 1987 Montana passed the first state law overriding the doctrine of employment at will and protecting workers from discharge without adequate cause. Its provisions include an opportunity for the discharged worker either to receive a full trial or to take the dispute to arbitration, a quicker, less expensive procedure that has proved very useful in the union sector.

THE MOTIVATION OF WORKERS

There are many different determinants of worker productivity. The traditional theory of labor demand emphasizes differences in the amount of physical capital per worker. The human capital approach emphasizes differences in schooling and experience in the labor market. Thus far in this chapter we have concentrated on how the firm selects and trains its workers. Another important determinant of a worker's productivity is his or her work effort or motivation.

The work motivation of employees depends on many factors, including the compensation policies of the firm, its monitoring efforts, and the availability of good jobs with alternative employers.

One important consideration is whether the worker is paid by time or per

---

[20]See Jack Steiber, "Employment-at-Will: An Issue for the 1980s."
[21]Ibid., p. 2.

unit of output. It is likely that employees will work harder when they are paid on the basis of how much they produce rather than a fixed hour wage or monthly salary. In some jobs workers are paid on a piece-rate basis, with compensation closely tied to units of output produced. This approach is feasible, however, only when the output of the individual worker is readily observable and when no difficult judgments must be made about the quality of the work. In most jobs workers are paid per unit of time, not per unit of output. In Chapter 7 we will examine how the level and structure of a firm's compensation are likely to affect the work effort and productivity of its workers. When workers are paid by the hour, firms can and do try to maintain work effort and productivity standards by monitoring worker performance and then by terminating those who are not performing satisfactorily. This approach is useful on a wide scale only where firms have not invested much in worker training, since the firm loses its investment if it has to terminate a worker. It is also limited in its effectiveness, since monitoring is expensive and is only effective in maintaining minimal standards. Nevertheless, as both neoclassical and Marxist economists have emphasized, labor economics must be concerned with the distinction between labor time and work.[22]

Monitoring Worker Performance

In Bowles's model, for example, the firm's labor input is measured in terms of "work effort" rather than hours of work or wages. Work effort per hour of labor time depends on both the amount of time and money the firm spends on surveillance of its employees and on the workers' expected income loss if they lose their jobs. Thus, workers are expected to work harder the more the firm spends on supervisors and other methods of monitoring their performance.

If surveillance shows that a worker has been slacking, the ultimate sanction is for the firm to fire the worker. If other equally good jobs are readily available, the worker may not be significantly deterred by the threat of such sanction. On the other hand, if other jobs are not available, then such a threat is likely to be a major consideration in the worker's attitude toward his or her job. Thus, work attitudes are likely to vary with the state of aggregate demand in the economy and with whether the worker has been able to gain access to a reasonably secure well-paying job in the primary labor market.

This model can be applied to a wide variety of issues. For example, the choice of technology by a firm is likely to be influenced by surveillance considerations. Bowles indicates that the assembly line approach in manufacturing may have become popular partly because this technology makes it easy for the firm to see if anyone is not keeping up with the pace of the line. One goal of many recent

---

[22]For a Marxist approach, see Samuel Bowles, "The Production Process in a Competitive Economy." For a neoclassical approach, see Carl Shapiro and Joseph E. Stiglitz, "Equilibrium Unemployment as a Worker Discipline Device," *American Economic Review* (June 1984), pp. 433–44.

efforts to introduce computer-based technologies also has been to increase management's control over workers.[23]

Work motivation depends on the carrot as well as the stick. If the employer is perceived as treating the workers fairly, then the employees normally will work harder and, in general, be more accepting of the employer's goals.[24]

The Japanese Approach

In recent years much attention has been given to a management style that has been developed by the Japanese and appears to be quite successful in motivating employees. According to William Ouchi, the key ingredients of the Japanese system include:[25]

1. Lifetime Employment. About one-quarter of the Japanese labor force work for large firms and government agencies. Most of these workers are hired right out of school with the expectation that they will continue to work for the employer until age fifty-five.[26] The worker's primary loyalty is to the employer, not the occupation or profession. The rest of our analysis will focus on these long-term employees.[27]

Because the worker has an expected career of over thirty years with a single employer, management has an incentive to invest heavily in the worker, and the worker has an incentive to be concerned with the company's success. Educational credentials are very important in determining who gains access to the best jobs, which is consistent with the signaling model discussed in Chapter 4.

The large Japanese firms have been able to maintain the commitment to lifetime employment for many reasons. First, most of these firms have been very successful and so have been growing rapidly. Second, there are many satellite firms, providing supplies or other services to the primary firm. When demand falls, most of the adjustment costs are born by those smaller firms. Third, even large firms have many "temporary" workers, primarily women, who are not expected to stay

---

[23]See Harley Shaiken, *Work Transformed: Automation and Labor in the Computer Age* (New York: Holt, Rinehart, & Winston, 1984).

[24]For example, see George A. Akerlof, "Labor Contracts as Partial Gift Exchange."

[25]See William G. Ouchi. See also Frank Gibney, *Miracle by Design* (New York: New York Times Book Co., 1982); *The Management Challenge: Japanese Views,* ed. Lester C. Thurow (Cambridge Mass.: MIT Press, 1985); and Richard Tanner Pascale and Anthony G. Athos, *The Art of Japanese Management* (New York: Simon & Schuster, 1981). Another popular book on management, which is closely related to the work of Pascale and Athos, is Thomas J. Peters and Robert H. Waterman, *In Search of Excellence* (New York: Harper and Row, Publishers, 1982).

[26]At age fifty-five the retired worker is given a lump-sum separation payment, worth several years' salary. In addition, he or she usually will have a chance to work with some smaller firm that provides supplies or other services to his or her former employer.

[27]For an interesting discussion of how this system developed in Japan and why it was not adopted to the same extent in other industrialized countries, see Robert E. Cole, *Work, Mobility, and Participation* (Berkeley, Calif.: University of California Press, 1979).

with the firm for a lifetime and who can be laid off when times are hard. Gender inequality in the labor market appears to be even greater in Japan than in the United States.[28] Fourth, Japanese earnings are paid not only as fixed wages but also as semiannual bonuses. These bonuses often account for a third or more of the worker's earnings, with the size of the bonus depending on the economic performance of the entire company. If demand falls or the firm does poorly for some other reason, then the firm can cut its labor costs not by laying off permanent workers but by reducing the size of their bonuses. Despite these adjustments, occasionally firms have had to make layoffs or "request" early retirements.[29]

2. Evaluation and Promotion.   In personnel decisions, as in most other management decisions, Japanese companies generally take a long view. Workers are hired on the basis of their prospective contribution over many years. Pay increases and promotions are based mainly on length of service. Evaluations of individuals are made quite infrequently because of the belief that the success of a firm (or any work group) depends mainly on teamwork rather than on the ability of any one person.

3. Collective Decision Making.   In the United States most business decisions are made by a boss. Although the boss usually will consult his or her staff and work within guidelines set by superiors, the final decision is usually made by only one person, who is held accountable for its effects. In Japan decisions are made on a much more collective basis. All those affected by a decision are consulted. Every effort is made to achieve a consensus before any decision is reached. Such decisions, therefore, cannot be made quickly, but once a decision is reached it will be understood and accepted by everyone in the organization.

4. Nonspecialized Career Paths.   Workers in Japan typically learn many jobs within the firm. Moreover, no job is highly specialized. In the United States most jobs for production workers are quite simple and can be learned quite quickly. With low turnover in the work force, such speed is not essential, however. The Japanese worker expects to contribute as part of a team, working with coworkers and supervisors to improve production rather than be told, in detail, exactly how to perform the job. There is considerable emphasis on quality circles—small groups of workers that seek to improve product quality and reduce costs.

Wage rates are attached to individuals rather than to jobs, as in the United States. Thus Japanese firms can move a worker to a less demanding position with little opposition, since the worker will not suffer a pay cut or any loss of job

---

[28]See Jacob Mincer, "Intercountry Comparisons of Labor Force Trends and Related Development," *Journal of Labor Economics* (January 1985), pp. S1–32.

[29]See Koji Taira and Solomon B. Levine, "Japan's Industrial Relations: A Social Compact Emerges," *Industrial Relations in a Decade of Economic Change*, ed. Harvey Juris, Mark Thompson, and Wilbur Daniels (Madison, Wis.: Industrial Relations Research Association, 1986). See also Robert W. Bednarzik and Clinton R. Shiells, "Labor Market Changes and Adjustments: How Do the U.S. and Japan Compare?" *Monthly Labor Review* (February 1989), pp. 31–42.

security.[30] With nonspecialized career paths, it is possible for the firm to reassign workers easily as conditions change. This approach also reinforces the orientation of workers to the company as a whole rather than to the interests of any particular skill group. As a result, there is little resistance to technological change among Japanese workers. For example, Japanese workers generally have been enthusiastic about the introduction of robots.

> Japan uses more industrial robots than all other countries combined. Most of these robots were developed not by robot makers, but by users, such as automobile and transport companies, who wanted to minimize heavy labor. The robots are used for the simplest jobs, and nobody fears he will lose his job. Instead workers feel relieved that they are no longer required to do dirty work. Factory workers handling industrial robots give them pet names and regard them as subordinates. They believe that the robots help increase productivity, which will result in increasing their wages and contribute to the growth of their company, from which they can derive a sense of pride.[31]

5. Implicit Control Methods. Evaluation on the basis of explicit quantitative short-term targets, whether for a firm, a work group, or an individual, is much less common in Japan than in the United States. Since each worker in the Japanese firm knows and accepts the goals and style of the organization, there is less need to focus on short-term targets. In addition, the collective orientation of the Japanese provides important informal incentives for everyone to contribute to the welfare of the group. To quote Ouchi:

> The Japanese organization takes in only young people who are still in the formative stages of life, subjects them to multiple group memberships, and so inculcates in them the kind of devotion to co-workers that one sees in the United States Marines. It is not external evaluations or rewards that matter in such a setting. It is the intimate, subtle, and complex evaluation by one's peers—people who cannot be fooled—which is paramount. This central fact underlies much of the success of many organizations, not only in Japan but elsewhere.[32]

This Japanese style of management appears to be in some conflict with many American values, including cultural diversity, independence, individuality, and privacy. Nevertheless, many important features of this management style have been used by a number of our most successful firms, including IBM, Procter and Gamble, Hewlett-Packard, and Eastman-Kodak.

It is also important to remember that the Japanese style of management, with its emphasis on lifetime employment, applies only to a minority of the Japanese workers, mostly men working for successful large firms. Thus although there do appear to be important differences in management between the typical success-

---

[30]See Robert Cole, *Work, Mobility, and Participation: A Comparative Study of American and Japanese Industry* (Berkeley: University of California Press, 1979).

[31]From Hiroshi Takeuchi, "Motivation and Productivity," in *The Management Challenge: Japanese Views,* ed. Lester C. Thurow (Cambridge, Mass.: MIT Press, 1985), p. 28.

[32]Ouchi, *Theory Z*, p. 25.

ful firm in Japan and in the United States, focusing on the paradigm cases overstates the average difference between firms in the two economies.

We do not know how influential the Japanese management style has been in accounting for Japan's economic success. Even if its management style has played a significant role, there is still reason for us to be skeptical about how much firms in this country might profit from trying to adopt the Japanese style more extensively. Still we most likely do have something to learn. As Haruo Shimada writes:

> The single most important lesson we could extract from the Japanese experience, and one which is perhaps universally valid, is the effective development and utilization of human capital in corporate organizations, particularly human resource management strategies which include at least the following three elements: (1) systems of skill formation through both systematic training programs and continuous on-the-job training; (2) flexible allocation and reallocation of human resources through various forms of transfers across job lines; and (3) securing the workers' understanding of the constraints and priorities of corporate operations through joint problem-solving approaches.[33]

RESPONDING TO CHANGES IN DEMAND

Most firms would prefer to keep their present work forces rather than hire new employees at slightly lower wage rates. Employers are concerned not only for the welfare of their employees but also for hiring and training costs that they would have to incur in developing a new work force of equal productivity. If the firm tries to replace a few high-wage workers with new hires who are paid less, then there are likely to be adverse effects on the motivation of the existing workers, especially concerning their willingness to train and cooperate with the newcomers.

Since workers also value job security, many workers remain with the same employer for decades. Next let us consider the implications of this emphasis on long-term relations for how firms can be expected to respond to changes in the demand for labor.[34]

Increases in Demand

If the firm can consider its labor homogeneous (as assumed in Chapter 5), the firm can respond to an increase in demand either by hiring more workers or by increasing the hours of its present employees. Similarly, a decrease in demand could lead to either a decrease in employees or in hours worked per employee.

As we have emphasized in this chapter, only rarely can firms assume that

---

[33]Haruo Shimada, "Japan's Postwar Industrial Growth and Labor Management Relations," *Proceedings of the Annual Meeting of the Industrial Relations Research Association,* 1982, p. 248.

[34]Thurow's job competition model, discussed earlier, analyzes the effect on a firm's hiring standards of changes in demand and supply for the entire labor market, regardless of any changes in the firm's own demand for labor. By contrast, in this section we focus on changes in the demand for labor of the individual firm, regardless of any changes in the condition of the rest of the labor market.

labor is homogeneous. Adding new workers involves the cost of hiring and training these new employees. For some firms such costs are relatively minor. For many firms, however, substantial hiring and training costs are necessary for at least some kinds of workers. For such workers it may be more cost effective for the firm to respond to an increase in labor demand by increasing the workweek of present employees rather than by hiring additional workers.

First, let us look at the costs of increasing the workweek of the firm's employees. Since most employees already will be working at least forty hours per week, lengthening the workweek may cause fatigue that will lower productivity. A more clear-cut reason why increasing the workweek will increase labor cost per unit of output is the Fair Labor Standards Act (FLSA), which requires that all covered employees (most hourly-wage workers) receive a 50 percent premium whenever they work more than forty hours per week. In other words, overtime hours must be paid at a rate of "time and a half."

Thus far we have shown that the average cost of labor will increase whether the firm expands its labor input by increasing the size of its work force or by increasing the number of hours worked per employee. But the relative size of the cost increases will depend on whether the increase in demand is expected to be temporary or permanent. If the increase is expected to be temporary, a firm is more likely to increase hours, since overtime is relatively cheap if it does not need to be continued for very long. In contrast, the costs of hiring and training new employees are investments that are much more likely to be profitable if the new workers will be needed for a long time.

The size of the overtime premium sometimes exceeds 50 percent as a result of collective bargaining. In addition, there has been some discussion of amending the FLSA to increase the required premium in an effort to reduce unemployment by expanding job opportunities. Certainly, the size of the required overtime premium influences the employer's decision whether to hire new workers or increase the workweek when labor demand increases. If the fixed costs of employment per worker have increased over time, a higher overtime premium might appear appropriate simply to maintain the original disincentive for firms to rely heavily on overtime hours to meet their labor needs. For example, the required overtime premium might be increased from 50 percent to 100 percent (from time and a half to double time). There are several problems with such a proposal, however. First, if the cost of overtime labor increases, firms may substitute capital rather than hire new workers. Second, a higher overtime premium will make it more expensive for firms to increase output in response to an increase in product demand. Thus increases in aggregate demand probably would cause greater increases in inflation and smaller increases in output if the overtime premium were raised.

Decreases in Demand and Implicit Contracts

When a firm faces declining demand, it has choices available similar to those we have discussed for increases in demand. It can reduce some combination of wage rates, employment, and hours worked per employee. Although the factors discussed in connection with increases in demand are all relevant, some new ones must be introduced when discussing responses to declining demand.

A firm faces much more resistance to a wage cut than to a wage increase. First, there are costs to any change in wage rates, especially for unionized firms. Such firms have wage rates specified in union contracts. Although previously negotiated wage rates can sometimes be lowered through renegotiation when demand declines, the costs of doing so are high, as we shall see. Consequently, such alterations are rarely made.

Nonunion firms can change their wage rates unilaterally. Even in such cases, however, there may be an implicit contract between a firm and its workers, what Okun has called an invisible handshake.[35]

As we have emphasized in this chapter, when firms hire workers, usually both parties hope the employment relationship will last a long time. Whenever parties enter into any long-term relationship, each has expectations concerning how the other party will act. Although there are too many contingencies to put all the expectations in writing or even for each party to be certain that it understands all of its partner's expectations, nevertheless, such expectations are very important. If either party seriously violates the other's expectations, the relationship is not likely to last. This argument applies in a variety of contexts, including marital as well as employment relations.

In the employment relationship, a central expectation of most workers is that their wage rate will not decline in the future. Consequently, it can be quite costly for the firm if it violates this expectation. Quit rates will increase whenever other jobs are available; morale and productivity are likely to decline among those who remain; and it may be necessary to pay higher wage rates to hire workers of comparable quality in the future. Such problems exist for all firms, both union and nonunion. For union firms there is also the threat of a long, costly strike if the firm tries to cut its wage rates.

If the demand for its output falls substantially, a firm usually must reduce its labor costs. To reduce such costs, the firm must either reduce its employment, the average weekly hours worked by its employees, or their average hourly wage rate. We have argued that for many firms, it will be costly to reduce wage rates. If employees previously were working overtime, the firm is likely to reduce its average workweek, since overtime is especially expensive to the firm and is not part of normal expected pay for most workers. On the other hand, cuts in the workweek below normal levels, often called *work sharing*, do reduce take-home pay below normal expectations. Thus work sharing can cause the same turnover and morale problems as a cut in the workers' hourly wage.

Firms can reduce employment at modest cost through attrition resulting from quits and retirement.[36] No implicit contract need be broken when labor costs are reduced through attrition. Under normal circumstances, however, attrition will

---

[35]See Arthur M. Okun, *Prices and Quantities.*

[36]Even attrition can involve considerable costs, however, especially when many workers have to take on additional duties because of staff who have been lost.

lead to only small declines in employment. Firms where implicit contracts are important rarely have high turnover. Moreover, when demand falls during a recession, quit rates also decline because few jobs are available at other firms.

Because normal attrition results in only small employment declines for many firms, further cuts in labor costs often are necessary. One possibility is for the firm to provide greater incentives for early retirement, an approach that is most likely when the firm expects (1) the decline in demand to last a considerable time and (2) a highly elastic response to retirement incentives.

If normal attrition and extra incentives for early retirement are not sufficient, then the firm must either lay off workers or cut wage rates or average hours worked. In most cases the normal expectation is for firms to lay off those workers with the least seniority. At union firms this procedure usually will be included as part of the union contract.

There are several reasons why the average worker might prefer that there be some layoffs rather than a general cut in hours or wage rates. First, workers may not trust their employers. If the firm is allowed to reduce its wage rate whenever the firm is in severe financial difficulties, the firm has an incentive to exaggerate its financial problems to try to convince workers that pay cuts are necessary. If workers do not trust the firm (and do not have complete access to its books), they will be skeptical of all claims of the firm's financial distress. In contrast, any reduction in labor cost by reducing employment or hours of work ensures that the firm is not exploiting its workers, since the firm loses labor input in return for its reduction in total labor cost.

Second, unemployment insurance (UI) provides incentives to reduce employment rather than wage rates.[37] Unemployment benefits are available to most workers who are laid off but not to those who suffer wage reductions while remaining employed. In many states benefits are not available for those who suffer a decline in hours per week. If there were complete experience rating so that the firm's UI payments went up in proportion to the benefits paid to its former workers, UI would not encourage layoffs over wage reductions.[38] But since experience rating is not complete, a firm can reduce its labor costs at less expense to its employees if it lays workers off than if it reduces the wage rate.[39]

Third, the strategy of reducing labor costs by layoffs of the least senior workers has considerable support among workers.[40] Employees with the most seniority clearly benefit since they will retain their jobs and not suffer any cut in pay.

---

[37]See Martin Feldstein, "Temporary Layoffs in the Theory of Unemployment," *Journal of Political Economy* (October 1970), pp. 937–58.

[38]Experience rating refers to the increase in unemployment insurance tax that a firm must pay when it lays off additional workers and thus causes more benefits to be paid out under other programs. The extent of experience rating (and the details of how it works) differs considerably across states.

[39]For recent evidence on the importance of incomplete experience rating as a cause of layoffs and unemployment, see Robert H. Topel, "On Layoffs and Unemployment Insurance," *American Economic Review* (September 1983), pp. 541–59.

[40]Firms are seldom strongly opposed to basing layoffs on seniority, since firms will usually have invested less in their less-senior workers. However, an employer generally would prefer to base layoffs on how productive the worker is (relative to the wage rate) rather than simply on the worker's seniority position.

Those with low seniority are generally not so enthusiastic. They will lose their jobs, at least temporarily. If other jobs are not available and if UI benefits are not very high, workers with little seniority would be better off with a modest wage cut than being laid off.[41] Although wage rates could be reduced for junior workers but not for senior workers, the resulting pay differentials would violate the principle of equal pay for equal work, a basic tenet of many workers and most unions. Equal pay for equal work is advocated partly on equity grounds and partly because unequal pay for the same work leads to conflict among workers and creates an incentive for firms to try to shift work to those who are paid the least.

As long as the decline in demand is expected to be temporary, those laid off may not object too strenuously. Such workers expect to be recalled by the employer and to gain enough seniority so that eventually their risk of layoff will become very remote. The opposition to layoffs and the willingness to accept wage cuts to save jobs becomes much greater when the decline in demand threatens to be permanent so that workers cannot look forward to regaining their jobs and achieving future job security with the firm.

Union firms are more likely than nonunion firms to respond to a reduction in labor demand with layoffs rather than wage cuts or other adjustment mechanisms. In part, this may be because wage rates are set, usually for several years, by a union contract, which can be renegotiated only with considerable difficulty. As Medoff argues, however, the most basic explanation is the greater influence of senior workers under collective bargaining.[42]

In this section we have emphasized that wage rates do not decline readily in response to a decline in the demand for labor. This downward inflexibility of wage rates is not a new phenomenon. As Keynes emphasized, workers have long resisted reductions in *nominal wage rates,* wage rates measured in terms of dollars. When inflation increased in the 1970s, workers also became very concerned with declines in *real wage rates,* wage rates adjusted for changes in the average price level. Union contracts negotiated during this period frequently contained cost-of-living adjustments (COLAs) to compensate, though only partially, for expected increases in consumer prices during the term of the contract.[43] In addition, implicit contracts between workers and firms also began to emphasize protection for workers, not only from declines in nominal wage rates, but also from declines in real wages.

Once inflation has begun, the resistance of workers to real wage cuts (relative to layoffs) is one reason why it is difficult to reduce inflation without creating

---

[41]For a more extensive discussion of this point, see Mancur Olson, *The Rise and Decline of Nations* (New Haven, Conn.: Yale University Press, 1982), especially pp. 201–2.

[42]James Medoff, "Layoffs and Alternatives under Trade Unions in United States Manufacturing," *American Economic Review* (June 1979), pp. 380–95.

[43]COLA clauses do not provide for wage rates to increase by the full amount of any increase in consumer prices. Firms resist contracts that would protect workers completely from inflation because changes in a firm's product demand may not allow it to increase its prices as rapidly as the Consumer Price Index.

large-scale unemployment. This downward rigidity of wage rates is compounded by cost-plus pricing policies of many firms, which makes prices inflexible downward.[44] To the extent that nominal wage rates continue to increase during a recession, cost-plus pricing will lead to price increases even when demand is declining.

Although it would be better for the macroeconomy if firms would adjust to declines in aggregate demand primarily by reducing wage rates rather than by laying off workers, sticky wage rates do have important efficiency advantages for employers. Long-term relations between a firm and its workers would be soured by continual haggling over wage rates whenever there were short-term changes in a firm's demand or supply of labor. Rather than face productivity declines resulting from low morale among its workers, usually it is less costly for a firm to adjust to a temporary decline in demand by laying off junior workers rather than by reducing wage rates.[45]

SUMMARY

1. Workers differ considerably in their current abilities and in the ease with which they can learn new skills. Because information about such abilities is limited, firms must search for the best workers, just as workers search for the best jobs.

2. Many skills are needed by most employers. Such general skills as the ability to communicate effectively in English usually must be acquired by the worker before he or she will be hired by a firm.

3. Firms do invest heavily in their workers. Such investment includes hiring costs, the costs of training workers in the firm's procedures and equipment, and the costs of teaching new workers how to work effectively as part of a team. To protect such investments, firms can adopt many strategies, including (a) sharing both the benefits and costs of training and other investments with their workers, (b) recruiting workers who are likely to be willing to stay with the firm after being trained, (c) being receptive to union initiatives for seniority rules, and (d) providing pension benefits that depend heavily on length of service.

4. Investment in workers by firms is likely to be especially important when firms have internal labor markets and thus fill most jobs by promotion from within. Such a policy reduces turnover among employees and therefore increases the likelihood that the firm will be able to reap the benefits from its investment in its work force.

---

[44]See Okun, *Prices and Quantities*, Chap. 4.

[45]For further discussion of these issues, see Charles L. Schultze, "Microeconomic Efficiency and Nominal Wage Stickiness," *American Economic Review* (March 1985), pp. 1–15.

5. The dual-labor-market hypothesis emphasizes the distinction between jobs in the primary and the secondary labor markets. In the primary sector jobs are generally secure, pay is good, and there are well-defined promotion ladders. Such jobs usually involve internal labor markets. In the secondary labor market there is less job security, little chance for advancement, and relatively low pay.

6. For primary-sector jobs, with internal labor markets and significant training costs, Thurow has developed a job competition model of the labor market. In job competition, the labor market adjusts to changes in supply and demand by changes in the hiring standards of employers. In contrast, the traditional theory of labor markets, which Thurow calls the wage competition model and which we have discussed in Chapters 2 and 5, emphasizes changes in wage rates as the equilibrating mechanism when there are changes in supply or demand. One reason for the plausibility of job competition is that a firm's present employees will be reluctant to train new workers if providing such training will lead to a decrease in the firm's wages and a consequent decline in wage rates for those providing the training.

7. A worker's productivity depends not only on training and physical capital, but also on motivation, or how hard he or she is willing to work. One approach is to provide an incentive for hard work by paying workers in proportion to the output they produce. Another is for firms to monitor worker performance, where possible, and to fire those who are not producing.

8. The Japanese managerial style, based on lifetime employment of many workers, relatively broad training of workers by firms, and collective decision making and responsibility, appears to have been quite successful in increasing worker productivity and encouraging technological change.

9. Firms react to short-term changes in demand mainly by changing hours worked rather than wage rates. Temporary increases in demand are often met by increases in overtime, thus enabling firms to avoid the costs of hiring and training new workers.

When the demand for labor falls, firms usually reduce employment rather than wage rates. In contrast to reductions in wage rates, which many workers view as a violation of their implicit contract with the firm, employment cuts (a) ensure that the firm is not taking advantage of its workers; (b) enable the workers to obtain a net subsidy from unemployment insurance; and (c) are most responsive to the preferences of senior workers, who are not likely to be laid off but who would suffer from general wage cuts. Senior workers are in a powerful position because they are more valuable to the firm than inexperienced junior workers and because they play a large role in union affairs. Although junior workers lose their jobs through layoffs, such workers will be recalled by the firm if the decline in demand is temporary. Thus junior workers hope to gain the job security and other benefits of seniority in the future.

KEY CONCEPTS

EFFICIENCY UNIT OF LABOR	BUMPING
DECISION CRITERION, FOR JOB SEARCH	JOB COMPETITION MODEL
RESERVATION WAGE	CORE WORKER
FIRM INVESTMENT IN WORKERS	CONTINGENT WORKER
LABOR MARKET, SECONDARY	LIFETIME EMPLOYMENT
LABOR MARKET, PRIMARY	IMPLICIT CONTROL METHODS
LABOR MARKET, GUILD	IMPLICIT CONTRACT
LABOR MARKET, INTERNAL	WORK SHARING
PORTS OF ENTRY, TO A COMPANY	LAYOFF
SENIORITY PRINCIPLE	OVERTIME

REVIEW QUESTIONS

1. Under what circumstances will heterogeneity of labor lead to long-term relations between workers and firms?

2. After completing your schooling, do you expect to seek a long-term "career" job with one company? Why or why not?

3. Why do many firms rely heavily on informal word-of-mouth recruitment? Discuss how this recruitment strategy can lead to discrimination against women and minorities.

4. Explain the concept of the internal labor market. When will employers find it useful to fill a vacancy by internal rather than outside recruitment?

5. It has been argued that there are two distinct types of labor market, primary and secondary. What is meant by these terms? Is the distinction valid?

6. What is the difference between wage competition and job competition? Discuss under what circumstances each is most likely to occur.

7. Discuss alternative ways firms can try to motivate their employees. Which approaches do you believe are likely to be most successful? Why?

8. Compare the Japanese style of labor management with the approach of most firms in the United States. What do you see as the strengths and weaknesses of each approach?

9. Discuss the factors an employee should consider in deciding whether to respond to an increase in demand by hiring new workers or increasing the average workweek of present employees.

10. Why are firms more likely to respond to a decline in demand by laying off workers than by cutting wage rates?

READINGS

AKERLOF, GEORGE A., "Labor Contracts as Partial Gift Exchange," *Quarterly Journal of Economics* (November 1982), pp. 543–69.

BELOUS, RICHARD S., "How Human Resource Systems Adjust to the Shift toward Contingent Workers," *Monthly Labor Review* (March 1989), pp. 7–12.

BOWLES, SAMUEL, "The Production Process in a Competitive Economy: Walrasian, Neo-Hobbesian, and Marxian Models." *American Economic Review* (March 1985), pp. 16–36.

DOERINGER, PETER B., AND MICHAEL J. PIORE, *Internal Labor Markets and Manpower Analysis.* Lexington, Mass.: D. C. Heath & Company, 1971.

KERR, CLARK, "The Balkanization of Labor Markets," in *Labor Mobility and Economic Opportunities,* ed. E. Wight Bakke. Cambridge, Mass.: MIT Press, 1954.

MANGUM, GARTH; DONALD MAYALL; and KRISTEN NELSON, "The Temporary Help Industry: A Response to the Dual Internal Labor Market," *Industrial and Labor Relations* Review (July 1985), pp. 599–611.

OI, WALTER Y., "Labor as a Quasi-Fixed Factor," *Journal of Political Economy* (December 1962), pp. 538–55.

OKUN, ARTHUR M., *Prices and Quantities.* Washington, D.C.: Brookings Institution, 1981.

OUCHI, WILLIAM G., *Theory Z.* New York: Addison-Wesley Publishing Co., 1981.

REES, ALBERT, "Information Networks in Labor Markets," *American Economic Review* (May 1966), pp. 559–66.

STEIBER, JACK, "Employment-at-Will: An Issue for the 1980s," presidential address, *Proceedings of the Annual Meeting of the Industrial Relations Research Association,* 1983.

STIGLER, GEORGE J., "Information in the Labor Market," *Journal of Political Economy,* supplement (October 1962), pp. 94–105.

TAUBMAN, PAUL, and MICHAEL L. WACHTER, "Segmented Labor Markets," in *Handbook of Labor Economics,* vol. 2, ed. Orley Ashenfelter and Richard Layard, pp. 1187–1217. Amsterdam: North-Holland, 1986.

THUROW, LESTER. *Generating Inequality.* New York: Basic Books, 1975.

WAGE DETERMINATION

In Chapter 2 we explained how wages would be determined in the simplest possible labor market: All workers are of equal ability and regarded as interchangeable; workers and employers have full information about market conditions; the wage rate is the only measure of job attractiveness; employment relations are transient, and terms of employment are renegotiable from day to day.

The discussion in Chapter 6 has shown how far these assumptions are from reality. Now we must consider wage determination when the labor market is more complex. We begin by discussing the meaning of wage rates.

Next we consider wage differentials in a competitive labor market where wage rate differentials are only one of the factors workers consider in choosing among jobs. Then we discuss issues of monopoly power, especially those involved in occupational licensing.

The theory of wage determination usually assumes that wages should depend on the characteristics of the worker and of the job, not on those of the employer. In practice, however, a firm does appear to have some choice over its wage rates. We consider how this choice is exercised, why some employers choose to pay high wages while others do not.

In most companies many job vacancies are filled not by hiring in an outside market but by promotion within the firm. We examine how the employer determines the appropriate wage for a job when there is no outside market to provide guidance.

Next we consider how imperfect information and the difficulty of monitoring worker performance affects wage differentials within a firm. Here we discuss why most but not all workers are paid per unit of time rather than per unit of output. We examine the issues surrounding merit pay and profit sharing. We also consider how employer concerns about worker performance affect the time path of earnings over an employee's career with the firm.

A worker's compensation includes not only the wage rate but also pension rights, health insurance, vacation time, and a variety of other benefits. We discuss why benefits have been steadily increasing as a percentage of total compensation and why benefits are more important at some firms than others.

WAGES: MEANING AND MEASUREMENT

We can gain some appreciation for the complexity of wage rates by considering the various possible meanings of *wages*. Some of the disagreement that arises in discussing wage rates is due to the fact that people are talking about different things.

Most wage earners have an hourly rate of pay, usually referred to as the *base rate,* but this is not necessarily the amount that the worker actually receives. Many people work on a piecework or incentive basis, under which the amount they receive depends on how much they produce. Under an incentive system a worker is expected to earn a good deal more than the base rate—indeed, it is this expectation that provides the incentive to maintain a high rate of output. For jobs above the unskilled level, there is usually a *rate range* rather than a single rate, and workers move up within this range on the basis of seniority and merit. A worker may work overtime, which is usually compensated at one and one-half times the regular wage, or may work on a second or third shift and receive a premium for this.

For these and other reasons, a worker's *average hourly earnings* may be considerably above his base rate of pay. The distinction is important, because the wage statistics collected and published regularly by the U.S. Bureau of Labor Statistics relate to earnings rather than to wage rates.

A still higher figure is *total hourly compensation,* which includes a variety of fringe benefits paid for by the employer: paid vacations, paid holidays, other payments for time not worked, payments for medical and hospital insurance, payments into pension funds, employer contributions under the Social Security and unemployment compensation system, and other possible items. The total is what an hour of labor actually costs the employer and what the worker receives, in cash or in benefit rights, per hour worked. This figure, in short, corresponds most closely to the concept of wages in theoretical labor market analysis. It is also what unions and employers bargain about—a total "package," including improvements in benefits as well as in wage scales, but which can be reduced to a cents-per-hour equivalent. In later sections, when we use the term *wages* without qualification, we mean total hourly compensation.

While this total is the key figure, certain other calculations are important to employers and workers. The company is interested in two things: how much it costs to hire an hour of labor and how much is produced during this hour. It is not wages as such that matter but wages in relation to productivity.

Hourly compensation divided by hourly output yields *labor cost per unit of output*. This figure, and its movement over time, is very significant in business calculations. If compensation rises faster than productivity, labor cost per unit will be rising, and it is a reasonable prediction that the product price will rise to cover the higher costs. For the economy as a whole, an index of commodity prices parallels quite closely the index of unit labor costs.

The worker is interested in how much is in the pay envelope and in how much this money will buy. Weekly *take-home pay* is influenced not only by total hourly compensation, but also by how much comes in the form of cash rather than benefits; by the number of hours worked per week; and by the size of deductions for Social Security, personal income tax, and other purposes. Because of these additional factors, take-home pay can change considerably even without any change in hourly compensation.

How much the paycheck will buy—*real* wages, as distinct from *money* wages—depends on the movement of consumer prices. Historically, money wages have risen more rapidly than retail prices, so that real wages have also risen. Since 1973 there has been little increase in real wages, however, an issue we discuss in Chapter 9.

COMPENSATING DIFFERENCES IN WAGES

In seeking to explain why some wage rates are higher than others, we begin by asking what could happen in a competitive labor market. Remember the requirements for competition: many employers and workers, no organization on either side of the market and no government intervention, full information about job vacancies and workers' abilities, freedom to enter or leave the market at will. It is important in this connection that workers have not only equal opportunity for employment but also equal opportunity to obtain the education that is a prerequisite for entrance to many occupations.

The operation of such a market has been explored by economists for more than two centuries.[1] Adam Smith was the first to note that jobs differ widely in their intrinsic characteristics. Some can be learned in a week, while others require long and expensive education. Some offer steady work throughout the year, others only seasonal or intermittent work. Some jobs require much more responsibility than others. Some involve disagreeable working conditions—dust, noise, extremes of heat or cold, risk of injury, heavy physical effort—while others have light, clean, and pleasant surroundings. Smith reasoned that a job that involved training costs or disagreeable conditions would have to pay a wage sufficient to induce workers to

---

[1] For an extensive discussion of the theory, including applications to numerous issues, see Sherwin Rosen, "The Theory of Equalizing Differences," in *Handbook of Labor Economics,* vol. 1. Ed. Orley Ashenfelter and Richard Layard (Amsterdam: North-Holland, 1986), pp. 641–92.

bear the costs or put up with the conditions. The wage premium needed for this purpose is called a *compensating difference,* since it serves to compensate for differences in the nonpecuniary attractiveness of different jobs to workers on the margin in deciding which job to take. If the labor market is fully competitive, this premium will be *the only reason for long-term wage differences among jobs.*

Undoubtedly the most important single factor is differences in the length and cost of the education required for an occupation. The higher earnings of people in technical, professional, and managerial occupations are due mainly to this factor. The concept of returns to education was discussed in Chapter 4, and no more need be said at this point.

The effect of irregular employment is also obvious and well confirmed by evidence. Construction workers earn hourly rates that appear high relative to those in manufacturing and service industries. One reason is that most construction workers cannot work a full two-thousand-hour year. In the northern states, at least, construction activity falls off during the winter months. A high hourly rate is needed to offset intermittent employment and to bring annual earnings up to a competitive level. This is also a factor for harvest labor on farms, longshoring, merchant shipping, and other seasonal or casual occupations.

We limit ourselves here to the question of how far wage differences serve to offset differences in physical conditions of labor. We start from the fact that jobs do differ widely in physical conditions: indoor or outdoor work, conditions of heat or cold, risk of illness or accident, heavy or light physical effort, monotony or variety, speed of work, and many other things. Workers also have differing preferences regarding working conditions. Tastes differ in "buying" jobs, just as they do in buying consumer goods. Most workers would regard outdoor work in Alaska or Siberia as disagreeable. But some might actually be exhilarated by the cold, others would mind it only a little, while still others would mind it a lot.

A competitive labor market produces a pattern of relative wage rates and an allocation of workers among the available jobs. We can show that this allocation satisfies two conditions:

1. Stability. Each worker is in the job that best suits his or her preferences. Equalizing differences in wages are just sufficient to offset other job characteristics for workers at the margin of decision, leaving no incentive to change jobs.

2. Efficiency. The allocation maximizes utility derived directly from work; or, to put the point in reverse, it minimizes the total dissatisfaction associated with work. Jobs that have some disagreeable feature will be held by people to whom that feature is least disagreeable.

An Example of Job Choice

These points can be illustrated by a simple example involving only one company and one disagreeable job characteristic. The market wage in a community for a particular kind of labor is shown by *W* in Figure 7-1. One company, however, differs from the others in using machinery that involves a higher risk of accidents. The line *WS* shows the supply curve of labor to this company. The flat section *WA* means that some workers in the community aren't concerned about accidents and would accept jobs in the company at the standard wage. Beyond *A*, however, the supply curve begins to rise, indicating that some workers find the accident risk mildly distasteful and others find it highly distasteful. These workers will accept jobs only at higher wage rates, which will offset the risk involved.

The wage this company will have to pay depends on its demand for labor. Two possibilities are shown in Figure 7-1. If the demand curve intersects the supply curve within its horizontal section, the company need pay only the standard wage. For example, with a demand curve *D*, it can hire *N* workers at a wage of *W*. But if the demand curve is high enough to intersect the supply curve in its rising section, then a higher wage will be needed. For example, with a demand schedule D_1, the company will hire N_1 workers at a wage of W_1. The distance WW_1 is a *compensating difference* in wages, just sufficient to attract the marginal worker at point *B*. Most companies are probably in this second situation, which is why compensating differences are important.

What conclusions can we draw from this case?

1. The size of the compensating difference in wages is governed by the preferences of the *marginal* worker. If this company needed still more labor, it would have to move up the supply curve, paying a higher wage to attract workers to whom risk is still more disagreeable.
2. The assignment of workers to jobs in this company is efficient in the sense defined above. Those who are employed are those to whom risk of accident is *least* disagreeable. Others to whom risk is more disagreeable, distributed along the supply curve to the right of *B*, are not employed by this company.

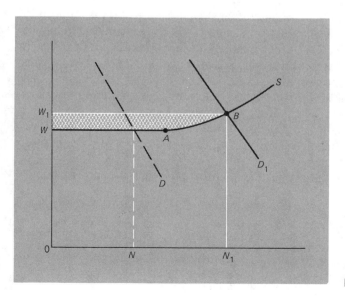

FIGURE 7-1 An Example of Compensating Wage Differences

3. The shaded area WBW_1 is significant in two ways. From the standpoint of the workers, it is a windfall, usually called a *rent*. Everyone except the marginal person would have been willing to work for less than W_1. But everyone gets W_1. A system of competitive labor markets serves to maximize such rents.

4. From the company's standpoint, the area represents the extra cost of operating with unusually dangerous equipment. If it could remove the excess risk by installing safety devices, and if that would cost less than WBW_1, then it would be profitable to do so. Thus there is an economic incentive to reduce disagreeable conditions of work—up to a point.

While this illustration involved only one company and one working condition, the logic can readily be extended to many companies and many conditions. To the extent that workers are informed and mobile, they will sort themselves out as described above.

Evidence on Compensating Differences

Although the theory of compensating differences goes back more than two centuries, efforts at statistical testing are quite recent. Testing is difficult because while theorizing always proceeds on the assumption of "other things equal," in the real world other things are never equal. The employment relation has so many dimensions that it is hard to isolate the influence of only one working condition. Still, fragments of information are becoming available.[2]

Outdoor work in cold climates is disagreeable to most people. It is not surprising, then, that wage rates in Alaska are considerably above those in the "lower forty-eight." Especially high rates were paid during construction of the Alaska pipeline, which involved work in all seasons as far north as the Arctic. Another well-known illustration comes from the Soviet Union where wage rates are centrally determined. But workers are largely free to choose where to work, and most would prefer to work in the Ukraine rather than in Siberia. So the authorities pay a substantially higher wage rate, as well as generous fringe benefits, to induce workers to move to Siberia in sufficient numbers to meet the demand for labor.

There has recently been considerable research on the relation of wage rates to risk of death on the job.[3] Nine studies, using different data sets, all conclude that (other things equal) there is a positive relation between wage rates and the risk of fatal accidents. The studies suggest that workers receive between $20 and $300 per year for every one-in-ten-thousand increase in the risk of being killed. Who says you can't set a value on a human life? Workers apparently do this every day in their job choices.

Research on nonfatal accidents and health impairment due to work condi-

---

[2]A dozen studies are listed and summarized in Charles Brown, "Equalizing Differences in the Labor Market," *Quarterly Journal of Economics* (February 1980), pp. 113–34. See also Greg J. Duncan and Bertil Holmlund, "Was Adam Smith Right after All? Another Test of the Theory of Compensating Wage Differentials," *Journal of Labor Economics* (October 1983), pp. 366–79.

[3]See a survey in Robert S. Smith, "Compensating Wage Differentials and Public Policy: A Review," *Industrial and Labor Relations Review* (April 1979), pp. 339–52.

tions is less conclusive. Here, too, most studies find a positive relation between wage rates and unsafe working conditions.[4] The relation is not as strong as for the risk of death, however, probably in part because workers' compensation also compensates for some of the costs of work-related accidents.

For high-risk jobs, each worker has to evaluate whether the wage premium for the extra risk is sufficient compensation. Moreover, these risk premiums provide an economic incentive for each employer to reduce risks. Whenever the cost of a new technique to reduce risk is less than the expected savings from lower wages, the employer can be expected to introduce the technique in order to increase the firm's profits. If workers had sufficient information on the risks of different jobs, there would be little need for the government to regulate occupational health and safety as it currently does through the Occupational Health and Safety Administration (OSHA). Unfortunately, workers seldom have accurate information on the risks of different jobs, especially at the time of hiring. As workers continue with the employer, they obtain better information, but the costs of mobility also rise. In addition, even scientists cannot agree on many risks, especially the long-term effects on health of various levels of such substances as asbestos, coal dust, vinyl chloride, and benzene. Thus there is a case for OSHA regulations, especially with regard to substances that have long-term effects on health, effects where workers are not likely to be well informed.

While the theory of compensating differences can explain many differences in wage rates, there are many that it cannot explain. For example, even in competitive labor markets there can be long lags in adjustment. That is true especially of occupations with long training periods, such as engineering or medicine. In addition, labor markets often are not competitive. Unions represent one important noncompetitive aspect of many labor markets. Their effects will be discussed at some length in the latter part of the book. Next we examine the influence of another important barrier to competition and the free mobility of labor from one job to another.

OCCUPATIONAL LICENSING

An important example of noncompetitive labor markets occurs when entry into an occupation requires a license from the government.[5] The number of licensed occupations has increased from well under one hundred in the 1950s to over five hun-

---

[4]For example, a study of chemical companies found that when workers are informed about risks through hazard warnings posted in the plant, they react in the expected direction: There is (1) a demand for a wage premium to offset the risk and (2) an increase in quit rates. See W. Kip Viscusi and Charles J. O'Connor, "Adaptive Responses to Chemical Labeling: Are Workers Bayesian Decision Makers?" *American Economic Review* (December 1984), pp. 942–56. Also see Viscusi and Michael J. Moore, "Workers' Compensation: Wage Effects, Benefit Inadequacies, and the Value of Health Losses," *Review of Economics and Statistics,* (May 1987), pp. 249–61.

[5]For analysis of this issue, see Alex Maurizi, "Occupational Licensing and the Public Interest," *Journal of Political Economy* (March–April 1974), pp. 399–413 and Simon Rottenberg, "The Economics of Occpational Licensing," in *Aspects of Labor Economics,* ed. H. Gregg Lewis (Princeton, N.J.: Princeton University Press, 1962).

dred.[6] By requiring a license before one can practice an occupation, the government restricts entry into occupations ranging from medicine to hairdressing. To the extent that licensing shifts the labor supply curve to the left for these occupations, it will also increase the relative earnings in these fields.

The rationale for occupational licensing is to protect the consumer. It is difficult for the consumer to judge the competence of many specialists. If we have to undergo surgery, for example, we feel more secure if we know that the surgeon has gone through extensive training and, on this basis, has been licensed by the state.

In practice, however, licensing, by restricting the supply of practitioners, often does more to protect the economic position of incumbents in the profession than it does to protect the consumer. While licensing requirements and procedures differ from occupation to occupation and from state to state, certain practices are widely prevalent, all of which are easier to understand if we look at licensing as providing protection to incumbents.

First, the political pressure for licensing generally comes from those in the profession, not from consumers.

Second, the licensing board that determines competence consists of members already in the occupation. While such people are the most knowledgeable and thus in the best position to judge the competence of those seeking to enter the field, present practitioners also have an incentive to be strict in the admission of newcomers in order to limit the supply of practitioners and thus increase their earnings. For example, despite the flight of many well-qualified physicians from Germany to the United States in the 1930s, there was no increase in the number of foreign doctors licensed to practice in this country.[7]

Third, occupational licensing generally raises the standards for new entrants to the occupation, for example by increasing educational requirements. By increasing the cost of entering the profession, such requirements will reduce the supply of applicants. On the other hand, there seldom is any testing of incumbents. Those who are in the field prior to the initiation of licensing requirements are exempt as a result of a "grandfather clause." Once newcomers have their license they are seldom tested to see if they have kept up with advances in the field. Even if the incumbent has become senile, it is rare that his or her license will ever be revoked.

Fourth, in some cases, such as medicine, the profession can restrict entry by controlling the schools that applicants must attend in order to become licensed. If both the number of schools and the number of admissions per school can be regulated, then members of a profession can have a dramatic impact on the number of new entrants.

Fifth, most licensing is done at the state level. If the professional is already licensed in one state but must incur significant costs to become licensed in another,

---

[6]Morris Kleiner, Robert Gay, and Karen Greene, "Barriers to Labor Migration: The Case of Occupational Licensing," *Industrial Relations* (Fall 1982), pp. 383–91.

[7]See S. David Young, *The Rule of Experts.*

then interstate mobility is reduced. In some cases, such as law, it really may be necessary to incur new training to be qualified to practice in a new state. But in many fields there is no apparent need for different requirements in different states.

Sixth, licensing requirements often require skills that are not very relevant for job performance. As Young writes,

> For example, occupations such as plumbing and barbering rely on written exams devised by state licensing boards that test little more than the ability to memorize irrelevant facts. Another example is the California licensing exam for architects, in which candidates are expected to discuss the tomb of Queen Hatsheput and the Temple of Apollo.[8]

Seventh, licensing occurs for many occupations, such as barbers and beauticians, where consumers are perfectly capable of judging quality for themselves.

The effects of licensing on earnings vary from occupation to occupation, from state to state, and from one time period to another.[9] For those who meet costly licensing requirements, the net gain in lifetime earnings is offset by the costs of meeting the requirements, such as attending extra years of school. Thus the benefits of licensing are restricted to those who were in the profession before the licensing began and have been "grandfathered in" rather than having to meet the requirements. The costs to society recur each year, however, at least to the extent that newcomers must take unnecessary schooling and consumers must pay the higher costs that result from restricted entry.

From the perspective of the consumer, it appears that the government can often play a useful role by providing information. For example, the government could develop competency tests and indicate what these tests are, who has passed them, and how recently. Then consumers could judge for themselves whether they wished to restrict their purchases to those who had passed such tests.

WAGE DIFFERENCES AMONG EMPLOYERS

We have discussed differences in wage rates across occupations. Such differences are important in determining the occupational choice of individuals but do not require much decision making by employers. In any simple model of the labor market, competition will force each employer to pay similar wage rates for workers with the same skill in the same geographical labor market. Yet there is considerable evidence that employers in the same labor market do pay different wages for similar work.

---

[8]Ibid. p. 38.

[9]For example, the effect on licensing on the earnings of physicians appears to have declined since the 1930s as the power of the American Medical Association (AMA) has declined. See Milton Friedman and Simon Kuznets, *Income From Independent Professional Practice* (New York: National Bureau of Economic Research, 1945); and Keith B. Leffler, "Physicians' Licenses: Competition and Monopoly in American Medicine," *Journal of Law and Economics* (April 1978), pp. 165–86. Friedman and Kuznets found an earnings effect of 16.5 percent for the 1930s while Leffler found little effect for the 1970s.

At a qualitative level, there is the testimony of practitioners and informed observers of wage determination. Anyone who has discussed wage setting with company executives has encountered such statements as "We pay the highest wages in town," or "We keep up with the average of rates in our area," or "We try not to fall more than ten cents an hour below the area average." Executives take it as obvious that they have some room for maneuver and can usually give a reasoned account of their wage strategy. Again, anyone who has engaged in arbitration of labor disputes has been presented with tables showing the rates paid by different employers for supposedly similar work. Intercompany equity is usually taken as one of the more compelling arguments in wage negotiations, and evidence of inter-company differences is used to document claims of inequity.

There is also a large amount of statistical evidence. The U.S. Bureau of Statistics has made many citywide wage surveys, aimed at analyzing the rates paid by different employers for the same occupational title. These commonly show a rate range of the order of 20 to 30 percent.

A serious difficulty in such studies is lack of full comparability in the data. Even though different plants use the same job title, the work may differ considerably. *Welding* is not the same in an aircraft plant and a shipyard, and even *common labor* is not as standardized as the term implies. Particularly troublesome is the question of worker quality, which is undoubtedly important but difficult to measure, and in any event, not measured in most wage comparisons. Studies that have tried to get at this problem typically conclude that higher-wage companies do get a somewhat higher quality of labor. The Rees-Shultz study of a number of occupations in the Chicago labor market found a positive relation between workers' earnings and such proxies for quality as years of schooling, years of work experience, and (for typists and accountants) scores on performance tests.[10]

But are the differences in quality as large as the differences in wages? Do the higher-wage employers get as much as they pay for? Most scholars, including Rees and Shultz, have concluded that the answer is probably negative.

Several studies have also concluded that there are substantial long-term wage differences across industries, even after controlling for a wide variety of worker and job characteristics, including unionization.[11]

What are the characteristics of firms and industries that pay relatively high wage rates?[12]

---

[10]Albert Rees and George P. Shultz, *Workers and Wages in an Urban Labor Market* (Chicago: University of Chicago Press, 1970), p. 219.

[11]See F. Bloch and M. Kuskin, "Wage Determination in the Union and Nonunion Sectors," *Industrial and Labor Relations Review* (January 1978), pp. 183–92; and Lawrence F. Katz, "Efficiency Wage Theories: A Partial Evaluation."

[12]For example, see Sumner H. Slichter, "Notes on the Structure of Wages," *Review of Economics and Statistics* (February 1950), pp. 81–92; Melvin W. Reder, "Wage Differentials: Theory and Measurement," in *Aspects of Labor Economics* (Princeton, N.J.: Princeton University Press, 1962), pp. 257–311; Leonard W. Weiss, "Concentration and Labor Earnings," *American Economic Review* (March 1966), pp. 96–117; Stanley H. Masters, "Wages and Plant Size: An Interindustry Analysis," *Review of Economics and Statistics* (August 1969), pp. 341–45, and Katz, "Efficiency Wage Theories."

1. Size of Establishment. Other things being equal, larger plants tend to pay higher wages than smaller ones.

2. Profitability of the Company. Where profits are high, wage decisions are likely to be more generous than where profits are low.

3. Ratio of Labor Costs to Total Costs. A low ratio, so that wages are not a major factor in management's profit calculations, makes for a relatively high wage level. Oil refining is a notable example.

4. Degree of Industrial Concentration. While the evidence is not entirely clear, it appears that tight oligopolies with "cooperative" pricing arrangements pay higher wages than companies in more competitive industries.

5. Degree of Unionization. A difficulty here is that large plant size, a high concentration ratio (as indicated by the percentage of industry output produced by, say, the four largest companies), and strong unionization tend to go together. Thus it takes careful statistical analysis to separate the effect of each factor. The indications, however, are that unionization by itself is significant, and so is concentration by itself.

For these reasons there appears to be a wage hierarchy among companies, related partly to the industry to which they belong; and this ranking seems to remain rather stable over long periods of time.

Granted that employers have some latitude in choosing a wage level, how do they choose? Why do some prefer to be high-wage companies and others low-wage companies? How is wage level related to hiring strategy, and how does strategy change over the course of the business cycle?

The High-Wage Employer

Occupying a high rank in the local wage hierarchy is not always a matter of choice. If the plant is part of a national organization, major wage decisions will be made at headquarters and will be influenced by company policy as well as by local labor market circumstances. If the company is unionized, the union will usually try to achieve a uniform wage scale in all the company's plants, wherever located. Thus a steel mill in Birmingham, Alabama, may find itself paying wages that while only average for Pittsburgh, are well above the average in Birmingham. Even in the absence of unions or any threat of unionization, for most firms there will be some wage rate, above the market-clearing level, where profits are maximized. This profit-maximizing wage is called the *efficiency wage.*

Next let us consider the various economic gains to a firm from a high-wage position, gains that up to some point may fully offset the higher wage costs.

1. The probable gain in worker quality has already been noted. The high-wage plant, with an ample supply of applicants, can impose stricter hiring standards. Its recruit-

ment costs will also be lower, since workers come to it instead of the company's having to search the market.

2. The high-wage company can also demand superior performance after employment—regular attendance, consistent effort, high output standards. Workers who know that they have a job above the area level will be anxious to keep it and will be willing to put in a good day's work in return for good pay. Workers are likely to work harder, require less monitoring, and take more initiative when they believe they are being paid well and treated fairly.

3. Quit rates will be lower, since the worker's estimate of the probability of finding a better job will be lower if the wage is already high. Quits are expensive because of the cost of recruiting and screening a replacement, training the new worker, and bringing him or her up to full proficiency. Reduced turnover, then, is a substantial offset to higher wage costs.

4. The extra elbow room resulting from a high-wage position means that the company does not have to reconsider its wage level at frequent intervals. If the labor market tightens, it will have to adjust eventually, but not immediately. This situation economizes the time of management officials.

5. In the case of a nonunion company, a high-wage policy may be regarded partly as insurance against unionization. The argument that "the union can't get you any more than you're getting now" is more effective when backed by high wages.

6. In a unionized company, a high-wage policy may reduce losses from labor disputes and work stoppages.

7. If we interpret *economic* broadly to include psychological satisfaction of executives as well as company profits, there are other gains from a liberal wage policy, such as prestige in the community and popularity with employees.

The Low-Wage Employer

How does a company judge whether it is close to "the prevailing wage" for the area? One source of information is area wage surveys conducted by the local Manufacturers' Association or Chamber of Commerce. The surveys reveal, among other things, the average straight-time hourly earnings (ASTHE) of each company of significant size. These can be ranked from top to bottom, and any company can see where it stands in the ranking. Average hourly earnings is a fallible standard, however, because it depends partly on the skill mix of the establishment. A plant in which the work requires a large portion of low-skilled workers could reasonably be expected to have ASTHE below the area average.

For this reason employers also pay attention to hourly rates for specific jobs for which there is an active "outside market." Maintenance electricians, carpenters, and other crafts people, as well as watchmen, guards, janitors, and elevator operators, are jobs of this sort. So are bookkeepers, cashiers, typists, stenographers, and secretaries. In manufacturing the starting rate for new production workers is especially important.

Since this survey information is available only at intervals and is not entirely easy to interpret, employers tend to attach special importance to the highest-wage companies in the area. They are the largest and most visible competitors for labor, and it is their rates that are most likely to be known and gossiped about by workers. A lower-wage company, then, may gauge its wage position partly by how far it is below the top of the ladder.

How low can an employer sink in the wage structure? A prime consideration is the level of employment needed to meet production requirements in, say, the six months immediately ahead. Even if this is the same as present employment, some hiring will be necessary to replace losses through quits and retirements. The minimum feasible wage can be defined as the wage that will produce just enough applicants (or, more correctly, enough acceptances of job offers) to maintain the desired employment level. This wage will be related to the rate of change of desired employment—higher if employment is rising than if it is stable or falling. It will be related also to nonwage characteristics of the jobs.

This minimum wage, however, will not necessarily be the most *economic* wage for the company, for reasons already suggested. The workers who would accept jobs at this wage would be of relatively low quality, and they would have little motivation to perform effectively. Moreover, the lower the wage, the higher will be the quit rate and the resulting costs of recruitment, screening, and training.

A wage somewhat above the bare minimum, therefore, may actually lower labor costs per unit of output. To maximize profit, the employer should raise wages as long as the gain from improved labor quality and reduced turnover exceeds the addition to the wage bill. When marginal wage costs and benefits are exactly equal, the employer has reached the economic wage.

Even the low-wage employer, then, has to choose a wage level; and the economic wage will differ from one employer to the next. Companies will differ in rates of desired employment expansion, in nonwage characteristics of jobs, in susceptibility to quits, and in efficiency in recruitment and training. They will differ also in their appraisal of the imperfect information available. For these reasons one should expect dispersion of company wage levels, rather than the identity that would occur in a simplified market model.

The characteristics of low-wage employers are the reverse of those of high-wage employers. They tend to be nonunion and relatively small, to sell their products in competitive markets, and to have low profit margins. They are to be found mainly in light manufacturing, trade, and the service industries. They are not low-wage employers because they prefer to be—indeed, a position near the bottom of the area wage structure is precarious and uncomfortable. The situation is rather that their wage-paying ability is severely constrained by product market conditions.

Over the course of years, there is turnover of employers as well as workers. Many low-wage companies are companies en route to elimination from their respective industries. Their profit margins are declining because of falling product demand, poor management, antiquated equipment, or locational disadvantages. As downward pressure from the product market continues, they sink gradually lower in the area wage structure (not by cutting wages, which is a rare occurrence, but by giving smaller increases than other employers). They are forced to test how low they can sink and still maintain a work force. Eventually, they find out. They are forced through the floor of the area wage structure or squeezed against the union scale or the legal minimum wage. At this point the game is over.

Response to Cyclical Fluctuations

A major feature of actual labor markets is fluctuation of aggregate demand for labor. These upswings and downswings of demand affect employers' wage strategy and the size of intercompany wage differences.

The strategy of high-wage employers is relatively deliberate, sluggish, acyclical. They are far enough above the area level so that they are not constrained by short-run changes in the labor market. They count on making wage increases year after year. They are usually monopolists or oligopolists and tend to set prices by a percentage markup over average unit cost of production. An orderly and predictable upward movement of wages contributes to orderly, controlled price adjustments. When a trade union is in the picture, wage schedules will usually be adjusted only once a year; and union leaders, like employers, prefer a regular pace of increases. This arrangement serves as a demonstration to the members that the union officers are "delivering the goods" and deserve to be kept in office.

Fluctuations in labor demand, then, show up mainly in the distance by which low-wage firms find it feasible to lag behind the leaders. During an upswing of demand the high-wage firms will not only be raising wages according to usual practice but will also be increasing employment. They will be encouraging applications for work and accepting a higher proportion of applicants than usual. Firms toward the bottom of the wage structure will find their applications declining in numbers and quality. They will also find their quit rates rising because of the increased opportunities for job-hopping to the higher-wage firms. To hold down turnover costs and achieve *their* desired rate of employment, they will have to raise wages by *more* than the high-wage firms are doing, thus narrowing the gap between them. During periods of nearly full employment, then, the area wage structure tends to contract like a squeezed accordion.

During a downswing the reverse tendencies come into play. The higher-wage firms will be laying off workers or at any rate ceasing to hire. Laid-off workers and new entrants will be forced lower down in the wage structure in the search for work. The low-wage firms will find their queue of applicants growing longer and improving in quality, while at the same time their quit rate is falling. They will thus find it feasible to lag further behind the wage leaders. They need not cut wages to achieve this result. Since the leaders are raising wages year in and year out, all the low-wage firms need do is give smaller increases. Thus the wage structure expands again in response to a general decline of employment.

This cyclical compression and expansion of the wage structure is confirmed by a number of statistical studies.[13] Reduction of intercompany differences is particularly noticeable under war conditions (1942–45, 1950–53, 1966–69). During World War II and the Korean War the compression was intensified by wage controls, which operated to allow low wages to move up faster than high ones. If American labor markets were consistently as tight as they have been during these

---

[13]Michael L. Wachter, "Cyclical Variation in the Interindustry Wage Structure," *American Economic Review* (March 1970), pp. 75–84.

periods of peak demand, we would move toward a narrower band of intercompany differences than has prevailed in the past. But most labor markets have been rather loose most of the time, with the number of unemployed workers considerably exceeding the number of job vacancies. This is a major reason why intercompany wage differences have remained large.

The other major effect of cyclical fluctuation is on employers' hiring standards. We noted earlier that employers use a variety of screening criteria to determine acceptability for employment. If a company finds its pool of acceptable applicants running down, the pool can be enlarged in either of two ways: by raising its relative wage rate to draw in more applicants or by lowering its hiring standards so that a larger proportion of applicants are rated as "acceptable." To the extent that the lowering of standards means accepting workers of lower productivity, it amounts to an increase in the wage *per efficiency unit of labor.* This tendency, plus increased use of overtime and rising quit rates, is one reason why unit labor costs of production tend to rise toward the top of an economic upswing.

Pressure to reduce hiring standards during an upswing impinges in the first instance on the low-wage firms, which are the first to feel the pinch of labor shortages. In a strong upswing, however, the tendency will extend eventually to most employers. During a downswing the tendency goes into reverse. As labor supplies become more ample, hiring standards are raised again, and only members of preferred groups of workers are kept in or added to the work force. The fact that adjustment of hiring standards is so rapidly reversible may cause employers to prefer it over wage increases as a means of attracting labor in a tight market. Wage increases are seldom reversible. Thus they are more likely to cause a permanent escalation of labor costs.

The variety of adjustments open to the employer have been well described by Hildebrand:

> For instance, suppose that the local labor market becomes progressively tighter. To avoid raising wage rates, the employer may intensify his recruiting efforts, perhaps improving nonpecuniary conditions as well. In some cases he may be able to simplify certain jobs, breaking them up into multiples requiring a lower grade of labor. If necessary, he may reduce his standards for hiring and for promotion, deliberately accepting candidates of lower efficiency on the premise that the enforced rise in unit labor costs will be temporary, that poorer workers can later be laid off or demoted. For the same underlying reasons, he may tolerate some rise in costs of turnover, and some fall of efficiency among the already employed, the second expressed by increases in absenteeism, tardiness, and bad work, and possibly by slow-down tactics.
>
> Together, these responses serve as expansion joints for absorbing the shock of a change in market forces, one that enables the employer to put off raising wage rates, mainly by tolerating a decline in labor efficiency and a rise in indirect employment costs. Although unit labor cost will still rise, to some extent its course will be reversible when the market loosens up. By contrast, a rise in wage rates for practical purposes is irreversible.[14]

---

[14]George H. Hildebrand, "External Influence and the Determination of the Internal Wage Structure," in *Internal Wage Structure,* ed. L. J. Meij (Amsterdam: North-Holland 1963), pp. 277–78.

A corollary of this mechanism is that the fate of the less-preferred groups in the market—young workers, the relatively unskilled, uneducated, and unproductive—depends on maintenance of high aggregate demand for labor. In a very tight market employers will follow the maxim, "If the body is warm, hire it." The less-preferred groups will have a chance to be hired and to get training and work experience. In a slack market, on the other hand, many will be ruled out of employment by conventional hiring criteria. Thus high labor demand is an important complement to antidiscrimination policies.

THE INTERNAL WAGE STRUCTURE: JOB EVALUATION

So far we have concentrated on the *average wage* level of a company. Most companies, however, hire dozens or hundreds of different types of skill. Each of these jobs has its own wage, varying from the entrance rate, or common labor rate, to the highest-skilled jobs in the plant. How does management determine proper relative wage rates for these many kinds of work? And how does the presence of a union alter the process?

Some kinds of labor may be in general demand throughout the area and hence may have an *outside market*. This is likely to be true for jobs at the bottom and top of the skill ladder, for unskilled labor, on the one hand, and for skilled maintenance crafts people, on the other. It seems also to be true of standard office occupations.

But the outside market impinges only at certain points in the company wage structure. There are a great array of semiskilled and skilled production jobs that are specific to a particular industry or even a particular company. Workers are usually not hired into these jobs from the outside but work up from within the company on a seniority basis. It is not easy for them to transfer to other companies, since the same job may not exist elsewhere, and since other companies also prefer to promote from within. Thus there is an *inside market* for these jobs but no outside market. The precise ranking of jobs and the determination of proper wage differences between them become matters for administrative discretion and collective bargaining.

A pattern of job rates develops in the first instance through shop custom. Certain jobs come to be regarded as related to each other on the basis of physical contiguity, sequence of production operations, or a learning sequence in which workers progress from lower to higher rank in a work team. Workers and foremen develop ideas about how much more one of these jobs should pay than another. Once established, these wage relationships tend to persist through custom. When asked to explain why their wage schedule looks as it does, most plant managers will say, "We have always done it that way," or "It just grew up that way."

Reliance on custom alone, however, is not always satisfactory. It is particularly unsatisfactory as an answer to workers or union officials who contend that a particular rate is too low and should be raised. Management has thus turned increasingly to systems of *job rating* or *job evaluation* that purport to provide a scientific basis for determining the relative worth of different jobs. There are several reasons for the popularity of these systems. Some managers believe they provide an absolutely fair and incontrovertible basis for determining relative wage rates. Even those who recognize that no wage scale can presume to have absolute justice seek the definite standards provided by job evaluation, because they make for administrative uniformity and simplicity in handling wage matters. Job evaluation provides a yardstick by which management can judge the merit of complaints by workers or the union; at least, it enables management to answer these complaints and to provide a rational explanation of its wage decisions.

Job Evaluation Procedures

Job evaluation procedures are complex and vary from case to case. In general, however, the procedure is as follows:

One must first select a set of *factors,* or criteria, to be used in rating jobs and set a maximum point score for each factor. An example is the widely used rating scale of the National Metal Trades Association. The factors used and the maximum possible score for each are as follows: education (70), experience (110), initiative and ingenuity (70), physical effort (50), mental and visual effort (25), responsibility for equipment and processes (25), responsibility for material or product (25), responsibility for safety of others (25), responsibility for work of others (25), working conditions (50), and work hazards (25). More briefly, these factors may be summarized as education, experience, and skill (250), responsibility (100), effort (75), and working conditions (75). Note that these factors are the same ones that Adam Smith discussed many years ago in his analysis of wage differentials in competitive labor markets.

The next step is to make a careful description of each job in the plant and to rate each job in terms of the selected factors. The rating applies to *the job itself,* not to the workers who happen to be doing the job at the time. The result is a total point score for each job, which enables one to rank all jobs in the plant in order of importance. These scores are not precise measurements but contain a large element of judgment.

The next step is usually to group the different jobs into a limited number of brackets, or *labor grades*. Thus jobs with a score of 450 to 500 may be put in labor grade 1, jobs with a score of 400 to 450 in labor grade 2, and so on down. In some systems the numbering is the other way round, so that the *lowest* jobs are in labor grade 1.

Next it is necessary to decide what shall be the highest and lowest wage rates in the plant. What rate shall be paid for, say, class 1 toolmakers, and what shall be paid for sweepers, laborers, and janitors? In a nonunion plant this decision is usually made on a comparative basis, that is, by surveying the rates currently paid for class 1 toolmakers and laborers by other plants in the area or industry. Under trade unionism, of course, determination of the high and low rates becomes a matter of bargaining, though rates in other plants will probably still be used as data for bargaining purposes.

It must be decided, finally, how rapidly the rates for intermediate labor grades shall rise; that is, what the shape of the *rate curve* shall be. Two very different rate curves are shown in Figure 7-2. Employers tend to favor a schedule similar to curve *B*, under which rates rise rather slowly for the first few labor grades in which the bulk of the labor force is concentrated, and then more rapidly in the higher labor grades, where there are few workers.

As a practical matter, the decision will be influenced a good deal by the shape of the existing wage schedule of the plant. At some stage in the procedure, it is usual to take the existing rate for each job, chart it against the point score for the job, and fit a curve to the scatter diagram thus obtained. The rate curve finally adopted under the job evaluation system will not necessarily have exactly the same shape as this empirical curve, but it is likely to resemble it rather closely. Custom and established wage relationships provide a powerful argument; and if the present wage structure of the plant resembles curve *B*, management is unlikely to agree to a new schedule resembling curve *A*.

It is clear from this brief description that rate setting based on job evaluation is not scientific in the sense of mathematical precision. Judgment must be exercised at each step in the procedure—the choice of rating factors, the assignment of the point weights to each factor, the actual description and rating of jobs, the determination of the top and bottom of the wage structure, and the determination of the shape of the rate curve between these points. The judgments of different individuals on each point are bound to differ somewhat, and the final outcome is a working compromise. Job evaluation does, however, make the exercise of judgment more deliberate and systematic than it might be without definite rules of procedure. We shall say more about this point in Chapter 8 when we discuss the issue of comparable worth (pay equity).

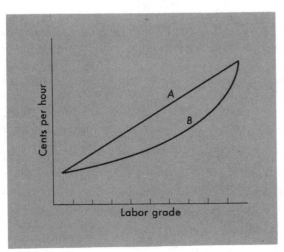

FIGURE 7-2   Occupational-Rate Curves for a Plant

Although the wage rates on many jobs are determined by a job evaluation system, there need not be a unique wage for each job. Often those with more seniority will get a higher wage. Merit raises are also common. Both of these issues are discussed in the next section as we consider the relation of earnings to productivity and work incentives. Yet another approach is called *payment for knowledge* and occurs most frequently when production is organized by flexible work teams rather than by narrowly defined job classifications. This approach stresses worker flexibility. By paying a worker more the more tasks he or she can perform, payment for knowledge provides workers with an incentive to master more tasks and thus to contribute to the flexibility of the work team.[15]

ADJUSTING EARNINGS TO PRODUCTIVITY

A major simplification in Chapter 2 was that we assumed all workers to be of equal ability. This idea is clearly untrue, and we must now consider how differences in ability affect wage rates.

Pay on the Same Job: Time Payment

Any manager knows that a hundred workers assigned to the same job will produce different amounts per hour, especially on jobs that are not machine controlled and where the worker has some choice of work speed and work methods. In the models of Chapter 2 all workers on the same job are paid the same wage. But here is Mr. A turning out 100 widgets an hour, while Mr. B turns out 150. Should the two be paid the same hourly wage? Will the market yield them the same wage?

As we discussed in Chapter 6, economists usually handle this problem by the concept of an *efficiency unit of labor,* a worker of standard or average efficiency. If Mr. A in our example is an average worker providing 1.0 efficiency units, then Mr. B is providing 1.5 efficiency units. The competitive market tends to equalize not the hourly wage received by each worker but the *wage per efficiency unit.* In this case Mr. B would tend to earn 1.5 times as much as Mr. A. Thus by using wages per efficiency unit, we can reconcile differences in wage rates for workers of different training or strength with the conclusion that wage rates per unit of labor should be equal in a competitive equilibrium and generally should be tending toward equality.

But what about the problem faced by the employer, who cannot very well set a different wage rate for each worker on a job? In practice this apparently insoluble problem is eased in several ways. First, productivity differences on the same job will rarely be as wide as in our example. In screening applicants for the job, the employer will set some minimum standard of performance, and this cuts off the lower end of the productivity distribution. After hiring, the foreman will set some minimum pace of work expected of everyone in the group. If a worker's

---

[15]For example, see Thomas A. Kochan, Harry C. Katz, and Robert B. McKersie, *The Transformation of American Industrial Relations* (New York: Basic Books, 1986), Chap. 4.

output is below average, the supervisor can resort to instruction, admonition, example, sarcasm, cajolery, and the ultimate threat of discharge. The workers themselves will establish a consensus on how much work is expected of them, and this standard will be observed even by workers of superior ability. Mr. B will deliberately slow down his speed so as not to show up his good friend Mr. A.

Such productivity differences as remain can be handled partly by setting not a single hourly rate for the job but a rate range of, say, $10 to $12 per hour. Workers with superior productivity can be given merit increases that move them up toward the top of the range, while poor performers remain near the bottom. This is common practice not only for blue-collar jobs but also for higher occupational levels. Universities and colleges usually maintain a wide range of salaries for full professors, say, from $50,000 to $70,000 a year. Where a particular faculty member stands in this scale depends partly on his or her specialty—the outside market for teachers of engineering or computer science is stronger than for teachers of classics or philosophy. But within a specialty salary depends heavily on individual productivity in teaching and research.

Although merit pay is quite common, it is controversial. For many jobs it is difficult to measure performance objectively. One response is for employers to give everyone similar raises, even though it may still be called a merit plan.[16] The alternative is for employers to base merit decisions on the subjective views of supervisors. When this is done, workers are likely to be disappointed, since the average worker generally believes that his performance is above average.[17] Also some workers are concerned that supervisors will reward their favorites, those who are unusually cooperative toward their supervisor rather than those who are doing the most to promote the well-being of the company. Unions, in particular, have been wary of merit pay, not only because many workers see it as inequitable but also because union leaders often see merit pay as a device that can be used by management to emphasize differences among employees and thus to undermine worker solidarity.

While short-run differences in productivity are inevitable among workers doing the same job, one of the most common ways of minimizing this problem in the longer run is for the firm to promote the most productive workers to a better job with a higher salary. Because such promotions are subject to many of the same problems as merit raises, unions usually push for seniority as the main determinant of promotion. Nevertheless, most promotion decisions are based on ability as well as seniority.

Pay on the Same Job: Payment by Results

There may seem to be an even simpler way of relating earnings directly to individual productivity. Why not pay workers according to how much they produce? Then the wage is not so much per hour of time but so much per unit of output. This approach might seem also to provide maximum incentive to work effort. The

---

[16]See Fred K. Foulkes, *Personnel Policies in Large Nonunion Companies* (Englewood Cliffs, N.J.: Prentice-Hall, 1980), Chap. 9.

[17]For example, see Herbert H. Meyer, "The Pay-for-Performance Dilemma," *Organizational Dynamics* (Winter 1975), pp. 41–46.

workers will drive themselves, with no need for driving by supervisors; and the more they produce, the more they will earn. But this approach is not as simple as it sounds. A look at how piece-rate systems operate will explain why.

Suppose a plant is operating under the simplest type of piecework system, in which a worker's earnings vary directly and proportionately with output. And suppose it has been determined, on the basis of market comparisons or job evaluation, that a particular job should pay $8 per hour. Next it is necessary to make a work-speed decision. How many units of output should the worker be required to produce per hour in order to receive $8? If it is reasonable to require twenty pieces in an hour, the piece rate will be 40¢; if the worker should turn out twenty-five pieces the piece rate will be 32¢. Thus the question amounts to asking how many seconds or minutes should reasonably be allowed for the worker to produce a unit of output. At this point the time-study manager and the stopwatch enter the picture.

Ideal time-study procedure, not always adhered to in practice, is as follows: The first step is to standardize conditions on the job and determine the best way of doing it through a methods analysis, including a study of workers' motions on the job. Operators on the job are then trained to use the proper methods until they do so naturally and automatically. This first step is essential to accurate time study and can often by itself yield large increases in productivity. The next step is to select an operator who appears to be of average speed and ability and to time her production over a long enough period so that variations in her speed of work can be averaged out. The worker will hardly ever take exactly the same time for two successive units of output. The only way to eliminate these irregular fluctuations in work speed is to time a considerable number of units and take an average.

The actual work of timing jobs is a good deal more complex than this brief statement suggests. The timer does not simply measure the time required for the whole process of turning out a unit of output. He breaks the production process down into each separate movement of the worker's hands and body. The time required for each of these movements is recorded separately. This enables the observer to determine whether the worker is using the proper methods, whether certain motions are taking more time than they should normally take, and even whether the worker is deliberately holding back during the time study.

After time study has determined the average time required to turn out a unit of product, certain adjustments must be made in this result. If it seems that the operator was above or below "normal" ability or was working above or below "normal" speed during the study, an adjustment must be made on this account. In addition, allowances are usually added for fatigue, unavoidable delays, necessary personal time, and other possible interruptions to production. At the end of the process, one obtains a total of, say, three minutes per unit. This indicates a normal hourly output, or "task," of twenty units. If expected hourly earnings on the job are $8, the piece rate must be 40¢.

It is clear that this process is not mathematically precise and that it involves numerous judgments by the time-study observer. Was the worker timed actually of average ability? Was the worker using the best methods available? Was she working at the right rate of speed? There is an almost unavoidable tendency for workers to slow down while being timed, even if unintentionally, and the time-study manager must correct for this as well as possible. Again, what allowance should reasonably be made in the circumstances for fatigue, personal time, unavoidable stoppages of production, and other factors?

The upshot is that time study does not resolve all controversy over work speeds. If workers feel that the required pace of work is excessive, they will resent and resist it. If a union is involved, it will usually insist on a voice in the setting of time standards and piece rates on individual jobs, and rates that appear out of line will be protested through the grievance procedure.

A further fact of life is that incentive systems usually do not induce workers to produce at full capacity. Workers rightly fear that if they work too hard, management will conclude that they are earning "too much" and will respond by retiming the job and cutting the piece rate. Thus there is a tendency for incentive workers to hold down their production at all times, and for different workers on a job to maintain about the same rate of output. Workers who rise much above the accepted rate are called speed artists, rate busters, and other uncomplimentary names. Unless they desist from their high rate of production, they are likely to find that things happen to their machines, that wrenches fall accidentally on their heads, and that they are ostracized by their fellows. The result is that incentive systems usually fail to obtain maximum effort from the faster workers; their rate of production is limited by social pressures exerted by their fellow workers. And an incentive system requires completely individualistic behavior to maximize its effects.

The agreed rate of output on a job is usually set slightly below the level the workers think would cause management to retime the job and cut the piece rate. Workers with long experience under incentive systems develop a keen sense of what is a "safe" amount to earn on a particular job, and they are careful not to exceed this amount. If too much work is done one day, part of it is hidden overnight and turned in the next day, during which the worker takes it easy. Some workers prefer to work rapidly for several hours, produce their "quota," then take it easy for the rest of the day. The most serious aspect of these output standards is that they become fixed by custom and persist even after improved methods have made a higher level of output appropriate. When this happens, the main effect of improvements in methods is to increase the amount of leisure that the workers have on the job rather than to increase their output.

Similar, but more difficult, problems occur in setting rates for sales commissions. Setting a commission rate is more complex, since it is difficult to know how many sales a particular territory should generate. Because there is a larger random element in sales than in production, there is also less reason for workers to set group norms and enforce them by social pressures.

INCENTIVE PAY VERSUS TIME PAYMENT

About 85 percent of wage and salary earners are paid on a time basis and 15 percent on an output basis. Incentive systems are used most widely in manufacturing, but their use varies from industry to industry.

Why is incentive payment used in some situations and time payment in others? The choice must result from interaction of employer and worker preferences. One might expect that employers would generally prefer incentive payment. Worker output varies considerably among workers and even for the same worker at different times. Under time payment the employer bears the risk of these fluctuations, while under incentive payment the risk is shifted to the worker. Piece-rate payment provides certainty about labor cost per unit of output. Even if it does not induce maximum worker output, it might be expected to stimulate a higher rate of output than time work with the consequent reduction in unit overhead costs. It also reduces the burden on supervisors, who no longer have to police work speeds from hour to hour.

On the other hand, incentive systems do require a good deal of administration. While they reduce foreman-worker bickering over work speeds, they can lead to much bickering over the setting and changing of piece rates. In addition, because of workers' reactions to time study and their effort to control output rates, the stimulus to higher output may be less than expected.

Perhaps more important, the feasibility of incentive payment is limited by the nature of the product and the production process. It works best where output consists of small, discrete units that can be identified with an individual worker or a small group. Where work is machine paced, as on an assembly line, work speed is no longer a matter of individual choice, and so incentive payment is inappropriate. Nor is it feasible in continuous-flow processes such as petroleum refining or chemical production.

From the employer perspective there are some additional problems with using piece rates. This system emphasizes the quantity rather than the quality of output. For goods and services where quality is important, the firm may have to devote considerable resources to quality control. If the worker is paid only on the basis of production that meets quality standards, then the piece-rate approach is likely to increase worker-management conflict over how such standards are set and enforced. Similarly tying payment directly to output creates an incentive for the workers to maximize output without being concerned about maintaining capital equipment. Although employees may lose pay from downtime, such pay losses are fair only if the worker is, in fact, responsible for the maintenance problem, another cause of potential dispute. In some firms this set of problems is mitigated by requiring that workers provide their own tools.

These quality problems are much less serious for salespeople being paid on commission. For such workers a problem is the incentive to make sales that the consumer doesn't need, such as repair services fixing what is not broken. To the extent that salespeople need to develop good, long-term relations with their customers, such problems are considerably reduced.

What about worker preferences? Faced with two jobs expected to yield the same earnings per hour, one of which is paid on a time basis and the other on a piece-rate or commission basis, workers might be expected to prefer the greater certainty of time payment. They realize that their output will fluctuate, sometimes because of machine breakdowns, and that sales will almost always vary, since they depend on the changing needs of customers. True, incentive systems try to meet this problem by providing a guaranteed hourly rate regardless of output or sales. But this guaranteed minimum is set well below the worker's normal hourly earnings and so does not remove the risk of subnormal earnings from time to time.

If this view of worker preferences is correct, we can predict that hourly earnings under incentive payment will be higher than on comparable jobs under time payment. An employer choosing incentive payment will have to offer higher wages to induce workers to accept the risk involved. In addition, the workers who choose such jobs will be those who are naturally faster and who prefer a high tempo of work rewarded by higher earnings. Research studies appear to support this hypothesis. One study of punch-press operators in Chicago found that piece-rate workers earned about 9 percent more per hour than those paid on an hourly basis.[18] Another study of auto-repair workers found that those paid on an incentive basis earned 20 to 50 percent more than hourly workers.[19] A third study of over 100,000 employees in the footwear and men's clothing industries found that the earnings premium for incentive workers averaged 14 percent.[20]

Group Incentives

When output is produced by a team rather than an individual, as for example, on an assembly line, then incentive pay for an individual makes little sense, since each worker has little control over his or her output. In such cases group incentives often make sense. For example, a group of workers may receive a periodic bonus that is related to the net revenue they have generated or to the company's overall profits.

An approach that has become increasingly prevalent in recent years is called *gain sharing,* where the firm shares a portion of the gains in productivity, cost reduction, sales, or other measures of group performance with the work group that has created the gains.[21] This gain-sharing approach is attractive to both firms and workers, especially when the demand for labor is low. In this case the firm may cut the wage rate, thereby reducing its costs. To reassure its employees, however, it can establish profit sharing or some other form of gain sharing, so the workers are guaranteed higher earnings once the firm improves its performance.

Gain sharing also serves an important purpose in emphasizing that workers and management have a common interest in achieving a good rate of profits. If many workers are included as part of one gain-sharing group, however, the extra effort of each individual worker will have little effect on his or her earnings. Thus

---

[18]John Pencavel, "Work Effort, On-the-Job Screening, and Alternative Methods of Remuneration," in *Research in Labor Economics,* vol. 1, ed. Ronald Ehrenberg (Greenwich, Conn.: JAI Press, 1977), pp. 225–58.

[19]Sandra King, "Incentive and Time Pay in Auto Dealer Repair Shops," *Monthly Labor Review* (September 1975), pp. 45–48.

[20]Eric Seiler, "Piece Rate vs. Time Rate."

[21]See Carla O'Dell and Jery McAdams, "The Revolution in Employee Rewards," *Management Review* (March 1987), p. 31, and *Paying for Productivity,* ed. Alan S. Blinder, (Washington: The Brookings Institution, 1990).

the individual incentive effect of such gainsharing is likely to be modest unless the approach can create a different atmosphere and generate positive social pressures within the group. Empirical evidence supports this view.[22] For example, profit-sharing is most effective at increasing productivity when firms also create a cooperative team spirit and encourage workers to participate in all important decisions.

Another type of compensation, related to company performance, has become increasingly important in the United States in recent years. Partly as a result of increased tax benefits, employee stock ownership plans (ESOPs) have grown rapidly since the mid-1970s.[23] Under these plans the firm contributes shares of the company's stock to the employee in addition to a regular pay check. Since the value of the firm's stock is related to its profits, especially in the long run, an ESOP provides an extra incentive for workers to be productive. ESOPs also can be used as a source of capital to the firm. For example, employee ownership has sometimes been instituted to avert the closing of a plant and the loss of jobs by employees.

Most ESOPs are similar to pension plans, since the worker cannot cash in the contributed stock immediately. They are quite risky as a retirement plan, however, since the retirement income is tied entirely to the future performance of one company.

Earnings and Length of Service

Up to this point we have focused on production workers who are paid either an hourly wage or a piece rate. Many workers, including almost all white collar employees, are paid salaries, which do not vary with hours of work. As Goldfarb indicates,[24] salaries are most likely when the employer is more concerned about the quality of job performance than the hours devoted to the job.

Next let us consider how both wage rates and salaries vary with length of service. Especially in large firms with well-developed internal labor markets, earnings rise markedly with length of tenure with the same firm. This effect, moreover, is independent of total length of labor market experience. A recent analysis of workers in firms with a thousand or more employees found that fifteen years of service accounted for an increase of 26.1 percent in earnings, while thirty years of service meant an increase of 52.6 percent.[25]

There are several possible reasons for this relation, which are not mutually exclusive. An obvious reason, discussed in Chapter 6, is employer investment in firm-specific training. As the worker's human capital grows through training and continued work experience, his or her productivity and value to the employer also increases. There is some question, however, whether this can be the whole explana-

---

[22]See Blinder, *Paying for Productivity,* especially page 13.

[23]For a more extensive discussion, see Corey Rosen, Katherine J. Klein, and Karen M. Young, *Employer Ownership in America: The Equity Solution* (Lexington, Mass.: D. C. Heath & Company, 1986).

[24]See Robert S. Goldfarb, "The Employer's Choice of Paying Wages or Salaries," *1987 Proceedings of the Industrial Relations Research Association,"* pp. 241–47.

[25]M. Hashimoto and J. Raisian, "Employment Tenure and Earnings Profiles in Japan and the United States," *American Economic Review* (September 1985), pp. 721–35.

tion.[26] The tenure-earnings profile is quite steep, while one might expect the productivity gain from experience to be only moderate. Moreover, the productivity gain should taper off in time, and beyond a certain age productivity might actually fall. But the earnings profile rises steadily and, while it seems to plateau after thirty years of service, it does not decline.

A related consideration is that the employer, having invested in the worker, tries to discourage quitting, which would mean loss of some human capital. The expectation of an increase in earnings with continued service provides an incentive to stay with the job. A long-service worker who changes employers will have to start over at the bottom of the tenure-earnings ladder and may suffer a large earnings loss. This situation is reinforced by the fact that increasing seniority also raises one's entitlement to vacation pay, pension rights, and other benefits.

Another possible explanation, based on work-effort incentives, has been developed by Edward Lazear.[27] If a firm hires workers for jobs that are expected to last many years, then both the firm and its workers will be interested not only in present wage rates but also in the wages paid over the workers' entire career with the firm. In equilibrium the present value of all future wages must equal the present value of the marginal output produced by the worker during his or her entire career with the firm. But in any one time period, the wage need not equal the worker's marginal product.

If productivity and the present value of wage payments are held constant, neither the workers nor the firm should have any strong interest in how the wage rate changes as the workers' length of service with the company increases. But the timing of wage payments may affect the workers' productivity. If wage rates initially are set below productivity levels but then increase faster than productivity over time, the worker has a greater incentive to perform well on the job because she will suffer a greater loss if fired for shirking. Yet this particular incentive effect should not be overemphasized. In the primary labor market, senior workers seldom lose their jobs, in part because termination for any but the most egregious offenses is likely to have a significant adverse effect on the morale of the remaining workers.

If workers are paid less than their productivity when they are young and more than their productivity when they are older, firms need to ensure that senior workers don't stay on the job for too many years. Yet it is difficult to terminate older workers for cause. As a result, firms often used to establish compulsory retirement rules, usually at an age when the worker was eligible for Social Security and/or a company pension. In 1986 the Age Discrimination in Employment Act was amended to make such compulsory retirement illegal. Now employers must either try to ensure that wages do not exceed productivity for older workers, or they must

---

[26]James L. Medoff and Katharine G. Abraham, "Are Those Paid More Really More Productive? The Case of Experience," *Journal of Human Resources,* Spring 1981, pp. 186–216, and by the same authors, "Experience, Performance, and Earnings," *Quarterly Journal of Economics,* Dec. 1980, pp. 703–736.

[27]This argument is developed by Lazear in "Why Is There Mandatory Retirement?" *Journal of Political Economy* (December 1979), pp. 1261–84; and, "Agency, Earnings Profiles, Productivity, and Hours Restriction," *American Economic Review* (September 1981), pp. 606–20.

structure their pension plans so that most older workers will continue to retire at the previous retirement age.

We have discussed some of the incentive effects that occur in long-term employment relations where wage rates do not have to equal productivity in each time period. Next let us consider another example. In this case the rewards for long service to the firm come primarily in the form of promotions to high-paying jobs for those who have been the best workers. This approach is unusual in most occupations but is common for executives. Lazear and Rosen offer the following analysis of this kind of reward system.

> Consider the salary structure for executives. It appears as though the salary of, say, the vice-president of a particular corporation is substantially below that of the president of the same corporation. Yet presidents are often chosen from the ranks of vice-presidents. On the day that a given individual is promoted from vice-president to president, his salary may triple. It is difficult to argue that his skills have tripled in that 1-day period, presenting difficulties for standard theory where supply factors should keep wages in those two occupations approximately equal. It is not a puzzle, however, when interpreted in the context of a prize. The president of a corporation is viewed as the winner of a contest in which he receives the higher prize, W_1. His wage is settled on not necessarily because it reflects his current productivity as president, but rather because it induces that individual and all other individuals to perform appropriately when they are in more junior positions. This interpretation suggests that presidents of large corporations do not necessarily earn high wages because they are more productive as presidents but because this particular type of payment structure makes them more productive over their entire working lives. A contest provides the proper incentives for skill acquisition prior to coming into the position.[28]

Such contests are one reason why promotions to top jobs yield large wage increases even if there are several almost equally qualified candidates competing for the promotion.

THE COMPENSATION PACKAGE: WAGES AND BENEFITS

Benefits now constitute a large and growing proportion of workers' incomes and employers' payroll costs. A survey of 910 companies by the U.S. Chamber of Commerce reports that in 1987 employee benefits averaged 37 percent of payroll, or $5.13 per payroll hour, or $10,718 per year per employee.[29] There was substantial variation, however, among companies. While 10 percent of companies had benefits of less than 25 percent of payroll, another 10 percent had benefits of 46 percent or more. In interpreting these figures, one must remember that the sample

---

[28]Edward P. Lazear and Sherwin Rosen, "Rank-Order Tournaments as Optimum Labor Contracts," *Journal of Political Economy* (October 1981), pp. 841–64. The quote is from page 849.

[29]*Employee Benefits*, U.S. Chamber of Commerce (Washington, D.C.: 1988). A similar survey is published each year.

consisted primarily of large companies and the benefits are positively related to size of company. An average for all companies in the country would be somewhat lower, probably about 20 percent of payroll.

The trend in benefit costs has been strongly upward. The Chamber of Commerce survey reports that benefit payments increased from 15 percent of payroll in 1951 to 26 percent in 1971 and 37 percent in 1987.

Quantitatively most important are

1. Retirement Pensions. Virtually all wage and salary earners are now covered by the Social Security system, which levies an equal percentage tax on employer and employee. In addition, about 75 percent of plant workers and 80 percent of office workers are covered by company pension programs.

2. Paid Vacations and Holidays. These are now enjoyed by more than 80 percent of plant employees and 90 percent of office employees. Vacations are normally linked to length of service. A common formula at present is one week after one year of service, two weeks after five years, three weeks after ten years, and four weeks after twenty years. Paid holidays per year have increased from four or five some years ago to ten or more at present. In addition to the standard national holidays, some employers provide a *floating holiday*—for example, a holiday on the worker's birthday.

3. Insurance and Health Programs. More than 90 percent of both plant and office employers have company-financed life insurance, hospitalization insurance, and surgical insurance. A majority also have illness and accident insurance. About one-third of plant employees and two-thirds of office employees have specified periods of sick leave on part or full pay.

While those are the most expensive items, they by no means exhaust the list. Other benefits enjoyed by a substantial minority of workers include free or discounted merchandise or meals, dental benefits, maternity leave with pay, child care, optical care, work-clothing allowance, legal aid, paid education, and company stock or stock options.

These facts raise several questions: Why do benefits exist? Are they an addition to, or a substitute for, cash wages? How can we explain their rapid growth over the past several decades?

The Rationale of Benefits

Benefits introduce a substantial gap between *current money wages* and *total compensation*. In earlier chapters we tended to speak of employers competing for labor on the basis of wage rates. It is more accurate to regard them as competing in terms of total compensation. In choosing among alternative jobs, workers can make a rough calculation of the dollar value of benefits and add this amount to each employer's wage offer.

The labor market places constraints on the employer. An employer who wants to attract a certain quantity and quality of labor must offer a certain level of total compensation. But the division of the compensation package between wages and benefits can vary, and different companies obviously make different choices. These choices result from the interplay of demand and supply and of employer and worker preferences.

The simplest assumption about employers is that they regard a dollar as a dollar. They are concerned about total compensation, since it affects production costs and profits. But the division of compensation between wages and benefits is a matter of indifference. A company that behaves in this way will be prepared to offer workers the alternatives charted in Figure 7-3. Total compensation, determined by the labor markets, is OC. If all of this is put into current wages, the company will be operating at point C on the vertical axis. If it is all put into benefits (overlooking the fact that this would not be possible in practice), the company will be operating at C on the horizontal axis. The solid line connecting these points shows other possible wage-benefit combinations, all of which would cost the employer the same amount.

There might be reasons, however, why an employer would consider a dollar spent on benefits as more useful (less costly) than a dollar spent on wages. One possible reason is tax advantages. Extra money put into wages will raise the company's Social Security and unemployment compensation taxes, which are based on payroll. The same money put into pensions or health services will not be taxed. Another possibility is that benefits may have a productivity effect. Benefits that increase with length of service, such as paid vacations and pension rights, tend to attach the worker more firmly to the company. This reduces the company's turnover and hence its hiring and training costs. Also, long-service workers should be more productive than short-service workers, because of accumulated job experi-

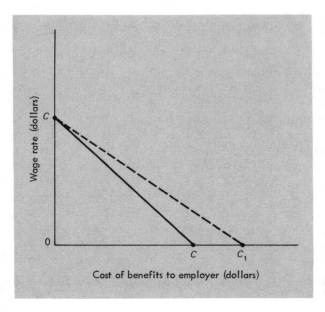

FIGURE 7-3   The Trade-off between Wage Rates and Benefits

ence. Paying benefits that are tied to length of service not only increases the job tenure of present workers but also makes it easier for the firm to recruit workers who expect to stay with the firm for a long time, since the benefits will have a higher expected value for such workers.

Such considerations might lead a company to offer the tradeoff shown by CC_1 rather than CC. Note that along CC_1 the company is offering *more* than a dollar increase in benefits in return for a dollar reduction in wages. One could also chart the opposite possibility, where a company considers a dollar in benefits *less* useful than a dollar in wages. For example, benefits such as sick leave may increase absenteeism. Also many benefits are the same for all workers. Thus a firm that wants to maintain significant earnings differentials for different kinds of workers can do so more easily if it has high wage rates and low benefits.

What about worker preferences? Is a dollar in benefits as desirable as a dollar in wages? One's first inclination would be to say no. There are two main kinds of benefits:

1. Payment in Goods. This means a certain amount of vacation time (leisure) or a certain amount of health care. Here receipt of the compensation is tied to the consumption of these particular goods. It is a general principle, which you may recall from your elementary course, that a person will always prefer a thousand dollars of cash to a bundle of goods with the same value. The reason is that the cash can be spent on anything one wishes, so that the person can buy an assortment of goods that best suits her preferences. Some firms have adopted *cafeteria plans,* which allow workers to elect the benefits they prefer, up to some dollar limit. This approach increases the complexity and thus the administrative cost of a benefit package, but it reduces the problem of workers' receiving benefits that they find to be of little value. With a cafeteria plan, for example, there is no danger that a worker will receive a medical benefit that is completely redundant with that received by his spouse.

2. Deferred Compensation. Pension rights are the leading example of this. Here the worker is giving up present income in exchange for a promise of future income but with no option as to the amount. Some workers might prefer to save more than this amount, and others less. Again, it would seem that cash payment is preferable, since it allows the savings decision to be geared to individual preferences.

The main alternative consideration is that cash wages are taxed, while benefits are not. Workers' wages are subject to both Social Security and income taxes. Payments in goods are generally not taxed. And deferred benefits are not taxed until the person begins to draw pension payments. The sharp increase in the marginal tax on earned income since 1940 has no doubt led workers to look more kindly on untaxed benefits.

The few research studies of worker preferences suggest that workers do recognize the tradeoff between wages and benefits.[30] Moreover, some studies sug-

---

[30]See Stephen Woodbury, "Substitution between Wage and Non-wage Benefits," *American Economic Review* (March 1983), pp. 166–82.

gest that the average tradeoff is close to one-for-one. There is, however, a wide range of variation in individual preferences, related to age, income level, education, family circumstances, and other matters.

How does all this work out in the labor market? We can visualize individual company offer curves, such as those shown in Figure 7-3, as consolidated into a market offer curve. This shows the terms on which all employers in the market are willing to trade off wages for benefits. In Figure 7-4 we assume a one-for-one tradeoff.

Each worker in the market will have a personal indifference curve, showing alternative wage-benefit combinations that would be equally acceptable. Ms. A in Figure 7-4 is strongly wage oriented and will seek out an employer offering the combination shown by W_a and F_a, with benefits about 20 percent of total compensation. Ms. B, on the other hand, has a strong interest in benefits and will look for an employer offering the combination W_b and F_b, with benefits about 40 percent of total compensation.

There are several implications in this analysis:

1. Different companies will offer different wage-benefit combinations, a fact that is confirmed by the data cited earlier. To some extent this will determine the kind of job applicant they attract. The combination W_bF_b may appeal more strongly to mature workers who have family responsibilities and are closer to retirement age.
2. The *average* wage-benefit mix in the market will depend on *average* worker preferences—whether more people are like Ms. A or like Ms. B.
3. Workers pay for their own benefits through an equivalent reduction in their current wage.

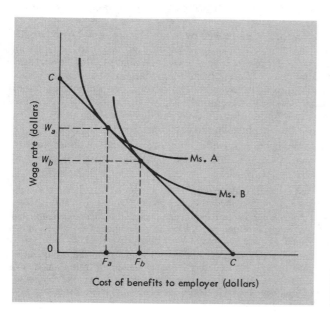

FIGURE 7-4 Employer and Worker Preferences Determine the Wage-Benefit Mix

4. In a labor market that is reasonably competitive and where information is adequate, the market should respond to worker preferences for benefits. If legislation is passed to override the market and require that firms provide benefits without any reduction in pay, there is a danger that firms will become less willing to hire people who are eligible for such benefits. For instance they might not hire women who are eligible for maternity benefits. Similarly, the requirement in the Tax Reform Act of 1986 that employer pension plans be vested after five years costs a firm money and is likely to lead to either less generous pensions, reduced wage rates, or some other long-run adjustment in the compensation policy of any firm that did not previously vest its pension benefits this soon.[31]

The Rise in Benefits

How can we explain the strong upward trend in the benefit share of total compensation over the past half century? Several factors have contributed to this trend.

1. The increase has not been entirely voluntary. Social Security taxes have been raised sharply by legislative action. Another large item, surgical and hospital insurance, is only semivoluntary. A company can decide whether to provide this insurance to employees. However, once the decision has been made, it has proven difficult for employers either to reduce the level of benefits or to keep the cost of existing insurance coverage from increasing rapidly.

2. The marked rise in marginal tax rates on wage income has already been noted. This rise has made benefits increasingly attractive as a way of reducing tax payments by both employer and employee.[32]

3. Personal incomes have more than doubled, in real terms. This has raised demand for almost every kind of consumer good, including goods provided as part of employer compensation packages: leisure time through paid vacations and holidays, health care, insurance against illness and accident, pension rights as an alternative to individual saving. The demand for most benefits is likely to be income elastic.

4. A growing share of the labor force is employed by relatively large employers, public and private. There are economies of scale in providing group insurance, health care, and pension benefits. So large employers have been able to offer these benefits at lower cost than smaller employers. In addition, large employers are especially apt to emphasize long-term employment relationships and the internal labor market and to value benefits related to seniority as a way of attaching workers to the firm. It is no accident that large firms not only pay higher wages but also show larger benefits and a higher benefit share in the compensation package.[33]

5. In the unionized sector of the economy, trade union pressure has been important. In Chapter 20 we'll present evidence that benefits are substantially larger and

---

[31]When pension is vested after five years, it means that a worker is eligible for pension benefits even if she quits or is terminated by the employer, so long as she has been with the firm for at least five years.

[32]Sloan and Adamache estimate that each 1 percent increase in the marginal tax rate increases health and life insurance benefits by 1.7 percent. See Frank A. Sloan and Killard W. Adamache, "Taxation and the Growth of Nonwage Compensation," *Public Finance Quarterly* (April 1986), pp. 115–37.

[33]The fact that wage rates and benefits both increase with size of firm may seem to contradict our earlier statement that workers pay for their own benefits by accepting lower wages. But a little thought will show that there is no contradiction. The situation is that large employers (1) *offer higher total compensation,* and (2) choose to allocate more of total compensation to benefits. These policies presumably have some payoff in terms of quality and stability of the labor force.

form a higher percentage of the compensation package in union than in nonunion establishments.

The growth in benefits as a percentage of total compensation slowed in the 1970's and had largely ended by the mid 1980's. The decline in the growth of benefits can be explained by changes in those factors that previously had led to rapid growth.[34] As we shall see in Chapter 9, real wages have grown very little in the 1970's or 80's. Also the influence of unions has declined sharply, especially in the private sector, a topic we discuss in Chapter 14. Two other considerations may be even more important. One is the substantial decline in marginal tax rates in the late 1980's, and the other is the increased importance of temporary workers. Temporaries usually receive much lower benefits than the permanent employees of large firms.

The health insurance component of benefits has become an especially important issue as the rise in health costs has led many firms to cut back on their health benefits, often despite strong opposition by employees. Cost-cutting measures include increasing deductibles and coinsurance, requiring third-party reviews for many procedures, and establishing incentives for employers to utilize relatively low-cost preferred providers.[35]

Although most families have access to health insurance that is either partially or entirely subsidized by an employer, some do not. Federal programs are available to the elderly (Medicare) and for many of the poor (Medicaid). Still, some are not eligible for health benefits from either an employer or the government. Such people are often unemployed or working for a small, low-wage employer who does not provide such benefits. While private health insurance can be purchased by individuals, it is quite expensive. Thus many who have low income but do not qualify for Medicaid take the chance that they will remain healthy rather than incur the high cost of individual coverage. When those not covered by any health insurance become seriously ill, it is a major problem. Other developed economies avoid this problem by having health benefits provided to everyone through the government.

SUMMARY

1. In a competitive labor market wage differences would be *compensating differences,* serving to equalize the attractiveness of different jobs to workers on the margin of decision. Jobs differ widely in the conditions they offer, and workers differ in their preference for different job characteristics. In a competitive labor market, workers will sort themselves out among jobs in such a way that (a) each worker is in the job that best suits his or her preferences; and (b) the allocation minimizes the total dissatisfaction associated with work, that is, jobs with some

---

[34]See Stephen A. Woodbury, "Economic Issues in Employee Benefits," unpublished manuscript, W.E. Upjohn Institute for Employment Research, 1990.

[35]See Sean Sullivan, "News Directions to Managing Health Care Costs," *1988 Proceedings of the Industrial Relations Research Association,* pp. 94–101.

disagreeable feature will be held by people to whom that feature is least disagreeable.

2. Labor markets are not all competitive. One important example is restricted entry to some occupations because of occupational licensing. Such licensing is intended to protect the consumer, but often it does more to protect the economic position of those already in the occupation.

3. There is considerable variation in the wage rate offered by different employers for the same job in the same labor market. High-wage employers do attract high-quality workers; but the difference in quality appears to be less than the difference in wages.

4. A common technique for determining relative wage rates for specialized jobs that may have no equivalent in the outside market is *job evaluation*. This procedure involves a considerable element of judgment. But it makes determining the relative worth of different jobs more explicit, systematic, and negotiable.

5. Under time payment workers' earnings are adjusted to their individual productivity through devices that *reduce* the productivity spread—employer selection, day-to-day supervision, observance of customary output norms by the work group; and by devices that *recognize* the remaining productivity spread, such as rate ranges and more rapid promotion.

6. Payment by results would appear to both stimulate and reward maximum individual effort. But in many situations it is not feasible; its administration is controversial; and its actual motivating effect falls short of potential.

7. Large employers usually have workers with long tenure whose earnings rise substantially with tenure. This is advantageous to the employer in reducing costs of turnover. It is also an important consideration for workers in choosing and changing jobs.

8. The division of the compensation package between direct wage payments and benefits can be regarded as determined in the market, where workers with differing preferences find their way to employers offering different wage-benefit combinations. The long-term increase in the share of compensation going to benefits has been influenced by many factors, including changes in real income, marginal tax rates, and federal legislation.

KEY CONCEPTS

BASE RATE
AVERAGE HOURLY EARNINGS
TOTAL HOURLY COMPENSATION

LABOR COST PER UNIT OF OUTPUT
TAKE-HOME PAY
WAGE RATE, REAL

WAGE RATE, MONEY
COMPENSATING DIFFERENCES
OCCUPATIONAL LICENSING
EFFICIENCY UNIT OF LABOR
JOB EVALUATION
LABOR GRADE
RATE CURVE
TIME WORK
INCENTIVE WORK

TIME STUDY
GAIN SHARING
TENURE-EARNINGS PROFILE
BENEFITS
PAYMENT IN GOODS
DEFERRED COMPENSATION
COMPANY OFFER CURVE
MARKET OFFER CURVE

REVIEW QUESTIONS

1. Why are compensating wage differences necessary? To whom are they necessary? To whom are they paid?

2. What are the structural features of a competitive labor market?

3. Explain the reasoning behind the proposition that in a competitive labor market workers are allocated to jobs in a way that maximizes job satisfaction (or minimizes dissatisfaction) for the labor force.

4. "There are many wage differences in the United States that the theory of compensating differences cannot explain." Do you agree? Give some examples.

5. Discuss the arguments for and against occupational licensing. For which occupations is the case for licensing strongest? For which occupations is it weakest?

6. (a) Explain the main alternative concepts of *wages*. (b) When we talk about *company wage policy,* which concept are we using?

7. As human resources director of a company, you are responsible for recommending to top management how large a wage increase should be made for the year ahead. What kinds of information would you need to prepare your recommendation?

8. What characteristics of actual labor markets permit companies to pay different wage rates for the same job in the same market?

9. What company characteristics are likely to put a company in the low-wage rather than the high-wage category?

10. Over the course of a business cycle, how will the wage-employment strategy of a high-wage company differ from that of a low-wage company?

11. "Job evaluation provides a firm scientific basis for determining correct wage rates for each job in the plant and removes any need for judgment or bargaining on this issue." Discuss.

12. "Time study is a scientific procedure that leaves no room for argument or bargaining over work speeds." Do you agree? Explain.

13. Why may some workers have a stronger interest in benefits than others?

14. On the surface, it appears that benefits are an *addition* to cash wages. But the text argues that they are really a substitute for cash wages. Can you reconcile the apparent conflict?

READINGS

BLINDER, ALAN S., ed., *Paying for Productivity,* Washington, D.C.: The Brookings Institution, 1990.

KATZ, LAWRENCE F., "Efficiency Wage Theories: A Partial Evaluation," in *NBER Macroeconomics Annual 1986,* ed. S. Fisher, pp. 235–76. Cambridge, Mass.: MIT Press.

SEILER, ERIC, "Piece Rate vs. Time Rate: The Effect of Incentives on Earnings," *Review of Economics and Statistics* (August 1984), pp. 363–76.

SMITH, ADAM, *Wealth of Nations,* book 1. New York: Modern Library, 1937.

VISCUSI, W. KIP, *Employment Hazards: An Investigation of Market Performance.* Cambridge, Mass.: Harvard University Press, 1979.

YOUNG, S. DAVID, *The Rule of Experts: Occupational Licensing in America.* Washington, D.C.: Cato Institute, 1987.

DISCRIMINATION

As we have seen in the last several chapters, earnings differ across workers for many reasons. Some workers are more productive than others, often because they have invested more in education or on-the-job training. Some workers prefer to work many hours of overtime, whereas others prefer part-time work. Wage differentials can compensate for differences in the nonmonetary attractiveness of jobs. Some workers have the ability or luck to be employed in expanding firms or occupations, whereas others are in declining ones. Barriers to entry and union bargaining power also affect earnings opportunities.

In this chapter we consider another source of earnings differentials—discrimination in the labor market. First we examine differences in earnings by race and sex. It is not a simple matter to determine how much of these differences is the result of labor market discrimination. We investigate the controversies that surround the relation between earnings differences and discrimination. Next we consider alternative theories of discrimination and how these theories differ in their assessment of the role of firms, workers, and the government in maintaining discrimination. We conclude with a discussion of government antidiscrimination policies, with particular attention to the controversies surrounding affirmative action and comparable worth.

EARNINGS DIFFERENTIALS BY RACE AND SEX

In this section we look at income and occupational differences by race and then by sex.

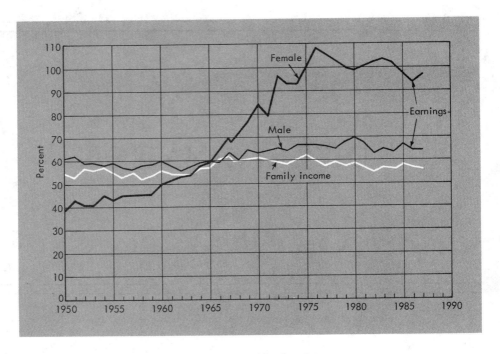

FIGURE 8-1 Black Income as a Percentage of White Income.

Source: U.S. Bureau of the Census, *Current Population Reports*, series P-60

Racial Inequality

We look first at differences in income between blacks and whites. Then we briefly consider the income of Hispanics. Black income as a percentage of white income is shown in Figure 8-1.[1] Since 1950 the average family income of blacks usually has been between 50 and 60 percent of whites. During the 1950s there was little change in the income of blacks relative to whites, despite large-scale migration of blacks out of the south, where racial discrimination was most overt and blacks' relative income was especially low. During the 1960s some improvement did occur in the relative income of blacks, partly as a result of civil rights legislation (especially Title VII of the Civil Rights Act of 1964, which outlawed discrimination in employment) and partly because of the high demand for labor, which historically had aided blacks more than whites. Since the mid-1970s, the relative family income of blacks has declined modestly, primarily because of the large increase in black, female-headed families with low incomes. As a result, income inequality among blacks has increased and is now considerably greater than among whites.

---

[1] Prior to 1967 data are not available for blacks but only for nonwhites, which also include Indians, Japanese, and Chinese.

In addition to relative family income, Figure 8-1 also shows the relative wage and salary earnings of blacks separately for men and women. The most dramatic change is the increase in the relative earnings of black women. In 1950 the average black woman earned less than 40 percent of the earnings of the average white. Since the mid-1970s, however, there has been no appreciable racial difference in the women's earnings.

Among men a sizable racial earnings differential remains, a differential that is almost as great as the one for family income.[2] The improvements in the relative earnings of black men that did occur in the 1960s and 1970s were mainly among young men, especially among those with more education and from relatively prosperous families. Among young men entering the labor market, the relative earnings of blacks increased. But as these new entrants achieved greater experience in the labor market, the racial earnings gap widened somewhat. In the 1980s this pattern changed, and now, at the beginning of the 1990s, the racial income gap is narrowing among older workers. But it is no longer diminishing much for those who are younger, perhaps because of declines in the relative quality of black schooling.[3] If so, these new findings suggest that racial inequality may increase rather than decrease in coming years.

The wage and salary data in Figure 8-1 are for all workers. Many employees work full time, full year, but because of unemployment or other reasons, some only work part time or part of the year. For both men and women the black unemployment rate is about double the white rate. On the other hand, among women more whites than blacks voluntarily work part time. If we adjust for these differences, the black-white earnings ratio increases slightly for males and decreases to about 90 percent for females. Still, the general pattern of results does not change dramatically. Differences in wage rates rather than in hours worked are the primary determinant of black-white earnings differentials, especially for males.

We can learn more about the relative labor market position of blacks and how it has been changing over time by looking at the kinds of jobs held by blacks and whites. In Table 8-1 we look at occupational changes by race, for both women and men, since 1960.

Black women have gained clerical jobs and left positions as private household workers. These changes are much larger than any changes in the occupational distribution of white workers. Since secretaries and typists generally are paid much more than maids, this change in the occupational distribution is a major reason for the increase in the relative earnings of black women. Although black women now earn approximately as much as white women, they work longer hours. In addition, as we shall see shortly, women of both races earn much less than their male counterparts.

---

[2]See Saul D. Hoffman, "Black-White Life Cycle Earnings Differences and the Vintage Hypothesis: A Longitudinal Analysis," *American Economic Review* (December 1979), pp. 855–67; Edward Lazear, "The Narrowing of the Black-White Wage Differential Is Illusory," *American Economic Review* (September 1979), pp. 553–64; and Richard Freeman, "Black Economic Progress Post-1964: Who Gained and Why?" in *Studies in Labor Markets*, ed. Sherwin Rosen (Chicago: University of Chicago Press, 1980).
[3]See James P. Smith and Finis R. Welch, "Black Economic Progress after Myrdal," pp. 557–61.

TABLE 8-1   Changes in the Occupational Distribution of Workers, by Race and Sex, 1960 and 1989

| | MALE | | | | FEMALE | | | |
| | WHITE | | NONWHITE | | WHITE | | NONWHITE | |
	1960	1989	1960	1989	1960	1989	1960	1989
Professional and technical workers	11.4	15.3	3.8	8.5	13.1	18.5	6.0	14.4
Managers and administrators	14.5	14.7	3.0	6.7	5.4	11.6	1.8	7.4
Sales workers	6.5	11.7	1.7	5.8	8.5	13.6	1.5	9.4
Clerical workers	7.2	5.3	5.8	9.0	32.4	28.2	9.3	25.9
Precision production, craft, and repair workers	19.7	20.2	9.5	15.9	1.1	2.2	0.5	2.4
Operatives	19.0	13.8	24.2	21.5	15.1	6.6	14.1	10.6
Nonfarm laborers	6.5	5.8	22.6	11.2	0.3	1.6	0.6	2.3
Private household workers	0.1	0.1	0.4	0.1	6.1	1.3	35.1	3.5
Other service workers	5.6	8.5	14.8	18.2	13.7	15.0	21.4	23.7
Farmers and farm laborers	9.4	4.6	14.3	3.1	3.8	1.2	9.6	0.4

Source: U.S. Bureau of Labor Statistics, *Employment and Earnings* (January 1990 and November 1961). The data are not fully compatible for two reasons. The occupational definitions differ across the two periods (see Table 2-2), and the data for 1960 are for all nonwhites, not just blacks. Of these two problems the first is probably the more important. In particular, the increase in salesworkers for all demographic groups is due mainly to the change in definitions.

Among black men there has been a significant decrease in jobs as laborers (both farm and nonfarm) and a sizable increase in professionals, managers, craft workers, and foremen. As in the case of women, these occupational shifts to higher-paid occupations have been much greater among blacks than among whites. Yet there has been little gain in the relative earnings of black males since 1960. The reduction in racial inequalities by occupation has been less dramatic for men than for women. In addition, white men continue to be more successful than any other demographic group in competing for the top jobs within each occupation. Next let us look at the economic position of other racial and ethnic groups. Asian men earn, on average, about the same as whites, and Asian women earn a little more.

Aside from blacks, Hispanics are the largest, most visible ethnic-racial minority group in the United States. In 1987 employment among those of Hispanic origin was not far below that of blacks. Hispanics accounted for 7 percent of total employment and blacks for 10 percent. The Hispanic population is increasing more rapidly than that of either whites, Anglos, or blacks as a result of both immigration and high fertility.

Since a considerable part of this immigration has been illegal, and since illegal aliens seldom appear in census data, one must take income data for Hispanics with a grain of salt. The employment data are likely to be underestimates and the income data, overestimates. Income data on Hispanics have been collected on an annual basis only since 1975. Since that time, Hispanic family income and the earnings of Hispanic males have been about 70 percent of the corresponding white values, both slightly higher than for blacks. Among women, Hispanic earnings are about 90 percent that of whites. There are several important subgroups of Hispanics. Average earnings are highest for Cubans, lowest for Mexican-Americans, and intermediate for Puerto Ricans.

Gender Inequality

In addition to income and occupation inequalities by race and ethnicity, inequalities by gender have been the focus of much attention in recent years. First note that the gender inequalities in occupational status shown in Table 8-1 are considerably greater than the racial inequalities. Women are underrepresented as managers, craft workers, foremen, operatives, and laborers, while overrepresented among clerical and service workers. In fact, occupational segregation by sex is even greater than is suggested by the figures in Table 8-1. If we define occupations more narrowly, sex segregation usually increases. For example, the figures in Table 8-1 show that the percentage of women in professional jobs is slightly larger than that for men. Yet as can be seen in Table 8-2, there is enormous sex segregation within professional occupations. Professionals in relatively high-paying fields, such as physicians, lawyers, judges, architects, and engineers, are more than 90 percent male, while those in low-paying positions, such as librarians, elementary school teachers, dieticians, and nurses, are over 90 percent female. As the labor force participation of women has increased, both absolutely and relative to men, a higher percentage of women are now employed in most occupations. These increases have been

TABLE 8-2   Sex Distribution of Employment in Selected Professional Occupations, 1960 and 1989

Occupation	WOMEN AS A PERCENTAGE OF TOTAL EMPLOYED		PERCENTAGE OF ALL WORKERS EMPLOYED IN THE OCCUPATION IN 1989	
	1960	1989	Female	Male
Engineers	0.8	7.6	0.3	2.6
Architects	2.0	20.6	0.1	0.2
Lawyers and judges	3.4	22.3	0.3	0.9
Physicians	6.9	17.9	0.2	0.7
Pharmacists	7.5	32.3	0.1	0.2
Natural scientists	8.3	26.9	0.2	0.6
Accountants	16.4	48.6	1.3	1.1
Teachers, college and university	23.7	38.7	0.5	0.7
Computer programmers	29.8	35.2	0.4	0.6
Vocational and educational counselors	41.0	60.4	0.2	0.1
Secondary school teachers	49.3	52.6	1.2	0.9
Librarians	83.2	87.3	0.3	0.0
Elementary school teachers	85.8	84.7	2.4	0.4
Dieticians	92.8	90.8	0.6	0.0
Registered nurses	97.5	94.2	2.8	0.1

Source: For 1989, U.S. Bureau of Labor Statistics. *Employment and Earnings* (January 1989). For 1960, Victor R. Fuchs, "A Note on Sex Segregation in Professional Occupations," *Explorations in Economics Research* (NBER), 2 (Winter 1975).

greatest in predominantly male occupations such as law, science, and accounting. Still, only an extremely small percentage of women are employed in such occupations, as can be seen from the figures in column 3 to Table 8-2. Although occupational segregation by gender does appear to be decreasing, such declines are very small.[4] While some occupational segregation by race still exists, it is much smaller and has been decreasing much faster than the sex segregation of occupations. From 1960 to 1980 occupational segregation by race declined by 40 to 50 percent, while by gender it declined only about 10 percent.[5] By 1980 most occupations were pretty well integrated by race but were still largely segregated by gender. Even when

[4]Using an index where 100 represents complete segregation and zero represents none, Beller finds that occupational segregation by sex declined from 68 to 1972 to 63 in 1981. Thus we are still much closer to complete segregation than to equal representation in all occupations. Even among young workers, occupational segregation remains about 60 percent. See Andrea H. Beller, "Trends in Occupational Segregation by Sex and Race: 1960–1981," in *Sex Segregation in the Work Place: Trends, Explanations, and Remedies,* ed. Barbara E. Reskin (Washington, D.C.: National Academy Press, 1984). The decline in sex segregation in the 1970s was much greater than in the 1950s or 1960s. See also Francine D. Blau and Wallace E. Hendricks, "Occupational Segregation by Sex: Trends and Prospects," *Journal of Human Resources* (Spring 1979), pp. 197–210; and V. Burris and A. Wharton, "Sex Segregation in the U.S. Labor Force," *Review of Radical Political Economy* (Fall 1982), pp. 49–50.

[5]See Victor R. Fuchs, "Women's Quest for Economic Equality."

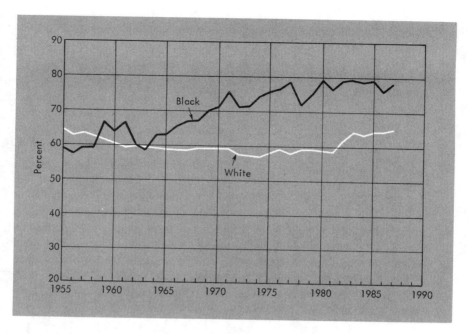

FIGURE 8-2   Median Earnings of Females as a Percentage of Males for Full-time,
Full-year Workers

Source: U.S. Bureau of the Census, *Current Population Reports,* series P-60.

occupations are gender integrated, it is common for occupations within individual firms to be highly segregated.[6]

Next let us consider the earnings of women relative to men. Since a higher percentage of women prefer part-time jobs, the most appropriate measure of gender earnings inequality is the relative earnings of full-time, full-year workers. Such figures are presented in Figure 8-2. Since the early 1960s there has been a fairly steady rise in the earnings of black women relative to black men. For blacks the earnings ratio is now about 80 percent. Among whites there was little change in the relative earnings of women in the several decades prior to 1980. Since 1980 the earnings ratio has increased, from just under 60 percent to about 65 percent.

There is a sharp difference between men and women in how earnings vary over the life cycle. As shown in Figure 8-3, male earnings increase sharply during the twenties and thirties, while the earnings profile of women is much flatter. Thus among workers in their forties, the average woman earns only 54 percent of the average man's salary.

Of course, the ratio of female to male wage rates is not a complete measure of economic inequality among men and women. Other important issues include both the relative influence over economic decisions by husbands and wives and the

[6]See Francine Blau, *Equal Pay in the Office,* (Lexington, Mass.: D. C. Heath, 1977); and William T. Bielby and James N. Baron, "A Woman's Place Is with Other Women: Sex Segregation within Organizations," in *Sex Segregation,* pp. 27–55.

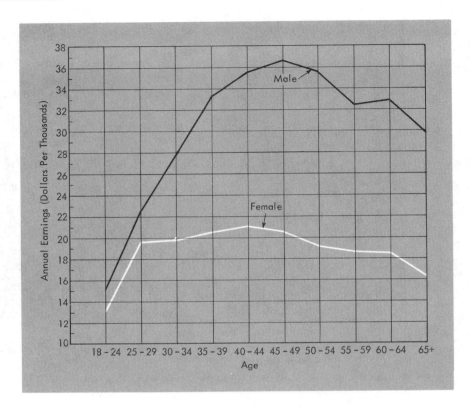

FIGURE 8-3 Life-cycle Earning Profile of Men and Women for Full-time, Full-
            year Workers, 1987

increasing importance of single-parent families, most of which are headed by
women. Unless women are gaining significantly more control over economic resources in husband-wife families, they probably have relatively fewer economic
resources at their command now than they did several decades ago.[7]

Inequality and Discrimination

We have seen the labor market inequality that exists between blacks and whites,
between Hispanics and Anglos, and between men and women. In this section we
consider how much of such inequality is attributable directly to discrimination in the
labor market.

First, we need a definition of discrimination. *Discrimination* occurs whenever someone's opportunities are not based on his or her individual capabilities but
are limited because of membership in a group. Discrimination can occur in many
areas, including housing and education as well as in the labor market. *Labor market*

---

[7]For an analysis of this issue, see Victor R. Fuchs, *Women's Quest for Economic Equality,* especially
Chap. 5; and his article, "His and Hers: Gender Differences in Work and Income, 1959–79," *Journal of
Labor Economics* (July 1986), pp. S245–72.

discrimination occurs when members of one group have lower earnings than another and when those earnings differentials cannot be attributed to any productivity differences between the two groups.

Next, let us contrast discrimination with two other concepts with which it is sometimes confused: prejudice and segregation. *Prejudice* occurs when a person dislikes those in another group. Prejudice is an attitude. A person who says "I can't stand blacks," or "Women are too emotional to think rationally" is demonstrating prejudice. If the person takes no action based on these prejudiced attitudes and beliefs, discrimination need not occur. Usually, however, a prejudiced attitude will lead to acts of discrimination. For example, an employer may refuse to hire blacks because the employer believes that blacks are not trustworthy.

A related concept is that of *segregation*. Segregation exists when there is physical separation between groups. If most blacks attend one school and most whites another, there is racial segregation in these schools. Similarly, when most secretaries are women and most plumbers are men, there is sex segregation of occupations.

Since segregation is defined in terms of physical separation, it is easier to measure than discrimination. Clearly, segregation can result from prejudice and discrimination. On the other hand, it can result from voluntary choice, as when those who prefer Italian food and those who prefer Mexican food usually patronize different restaurants.

In this chapter our primary focus is on discrimination in the labor market. Such discrimination occurs whenever someone's job opportunities are not based solely on the individual's productivity, his or her ability to do the job, but also depend on group membership, such as race or sex. Thus if a black woman earns less than a white man but is identical to him in all respects except for race and sex, she is the victim of discrimination in the labor market. This definition of labor market discrimination seems clear, but it is difficult to measure how much of the earnings inequality by race or gender is due to such discrimination and how much is due to productivity differences.

Racial Discrimination in the Labor Market

Let us look first at the relation between earnings inequality and racial discrimination in the labor market. Not all of the earnings differential between blacks and whites is due to labor market discrimination. The average black in the labor market is younger and has less schooling than the average white, although racial differences in schooling have narrowed considerably in recent years. Since earnings increase with age and schooling, some of the black-white earnings differential is due to differences in age and schooling rather than to labor market discrimination. To measure labor market discrimination, the researcher must try to estimate what the black-white earnings differential would be if blacks and whites did not differ in age, schooling, or any other individual characteristic that affects a worker's productivity in employment. Any differential in earnings that remains after controlling for the effects of differences in productivity can be attributed to current discrimination in the labor market. In contrast, differences in productivity are caused by differences in schooling, family background, and on-the-job training. Such productivity differences may be closely related to prior labor discrimination, which affects family income and the ability to provide good educational opportunities, but they do not represent current discrimination by employers.

Most empirical studies have attempted to divide the black-white earnings differential into a portion attributable to productivity differences and a residual, attributable to labor market discrimination. These studies have generally focused on differences in the earnings of males, partly because racial differences in female earnings have become very small.

A study by Corcoran and Duncan was able to control for an exceptionally large number of productivity-related characteristics, including training, absenteeism, and several measures of work experience as well as years of school.[8] On the basis of their analysis, Corcoran and Duncan conclude that these productivity differences account for 53 percent of the earnings differential between black and white men. The most important productivity differences are greater schooling and on-the-job training of whites.[9] Almost all of the earnings differential between Hispanic and Anglo men can be attributed to differences in proficiency in the English language.[10]

If current discrimination in the labor market does account for about half the lower earnings of black males, then despite governmental policies to eliminate discrimination by employers, such discrimination still plays a major role in our economy. The statistical estimates of the extent of labor market discrimination all suffer from a significant limitation, however. No researcher has complete data on the productivity characteristics of workers. Researchers can measure age, years of school, and work experience fairly accurately, but they rarely have reliable data on school quality, work habits, motivation, or skills learned on the job. These unmeasured productivity characteristics may vary by race (or sex) because of societal attitudes, the socioeconomic status of one's parents, or cultural background. If the unmeasured productivity characteristics are lower, on average, for blacks than for whites, productivity differences may really account for much more than half the black-white earnings differential for males. Thus current labor market discrimination may account for little of the racial differential in earnings.

As we mentioned earlier, however, these studies seek to measure only the magnitude of present discrimination in the labor market. The effects of past discrimination are very difficult to estimate. But past labor market discrimination affects productivity characteristics, such as school attainment. As a result of such discrimination, black families have fewer resources to devote to their children's education.[11] In

---

[8]See Mary Corcoran and Greg J. Duncan, "Work History, Labor Force Amendment, and Earnings: Differences between the Races and Sexes," *Journal of Human Resources* (Winter 1979), pp. 3–20.

[9]Other studies are reviewed by Glen Cain in his article, "The Economic Analysis of Labor Market Discrimination: A Survey," in *Handbook of Labor Economics,* vol. 1, ed. Orley Ashenfelter and Richard Layard (Amsterdam: North-Holland, 1986), pp. 693–785. These studies estimate that for national samples 18 to 60 percent of the wage gap between black and white males can be attributed to differences in measures of productivity, such as years of school.

[10]See Walter S. McManus, William Gould, and Finis R. Welch, "Earnings of Hispanic Men: The Role of Proficiency in the English Language," *Journal of Labor Economics* (April 1983), pp. 110–30.

[11]See Barry R. Chiswick, "Differences in Education and Earnings across Racial and Ethnic Groups: Tastes, Discrimination, and Investments in Child Quality," *Quarterly Journal of Economics* (August 1988), pp. 571–97.

addition, past discrimination will affect past employment, which affects both on-the-job training and work attitudes.[12]

Gender Discrimination in the Labor Market

Earnings differentials by gender are larger than by race. How much of the sex differential in earnings can be attributed to productivity differences and how much to labor market discrimination? Corcoran and Duncan estimate that productivity differences account for 44 percent of the male-female earnings gap. In contrast to race, where the main productivity difference is less schooling for blacks, for women the main differences are less on-the-job training and tenure with the present employer.

As in the racial case, however, these estimates must be treated cautiously. First, differences in productivity measures by gender may result from the labor market discrimination.[13] Differences in on-the-job training, for example, may result directly from discrimination by employers rather than from voluntary choices by women. Also differences in tenure are cause as well as effect of differences in wage rates. Among those with equally well paying jobs, there is no appreciable difference in quit rates among men and women.[14]

On the other hand, there are likely to be important productivity effects that are not captured in the analyses of Corcoran and Duncan and of other researchers because the necessary data are not available. For example, fewer wives than husbands may seek higher-paying jobs when such jobs involve longer hours, rotating shifts, and more responsibility.[15] Since many wives devote more time to home production and less time and effort to the labor market than their husbands do, such wives also have less incentive to develop career-oriented human capital.[16] It is not clear, however, whether the average woman has been less career oriented than the average man in her schooling decisions because many women plan to devote less time to the labor market (the *human capital* model) or because of other factors, including women's perception of discriminatory barriers in many occupations.

A basic prediction of the human capital approach is that expected continuity of employment should be more important than gender in determining earnings and occupational status. In contrast, the empirical evidence indicates that continu-

---

[12]See Michael J. Piore, "Jobs and Training," in *The State and the Poor,* ed. S. H. Beer (Cambridge, Mass.: Winthrop Press, 1970), pp. 53–83.

[13]See Cain, "Labor Market Discrimination," for a review of the many studies of the male-female earnings gap.

[14]See Barbara R. Bergmann, "Does the Market for Women's Labor Need Fixing?" *Journal of Economic Perspectives* (Winter 1989), pp. 43–60.

[15]For a study arguing this point of view based on an analysis of one large firm, see Carl Hoffman and John Shelton Reed, "Sex Discrimination—The XYZ Affair," *The Public Interest* (Winter 1981), pp. 21–40.

[16]See Jacob Mincer and Solomon W. Polachek, "Family Investments in Human Capital: Earnings of Women," *Journal of Political Economy,* part 2 (March–April 1974), pp. S76–108. For some related analysis, see also Mincer, "Family Migration Decisions," *Journal of Political Economy* (October 1978), pp. 749–74. See also Polachek and Frances W. Horvath, "A Life-Cycle Approach to Migration: Analysis of the Perspicacious Peregrinator," in *Research in Labor Economics,* vol. 1, ed. Ronald G. Ehrenberg (Greenwich, Conn.: JAI Press, 1977). These studies show that among families that move, the husband's earnings are likely to increase and the wife's to decline, findings that are consistent with a household division of labor emphasizing male earnings and a migration decision made to increase total family income.

ity of employment does not affect whether a woman will be employed in a predominantly female occupation. Women with more continuous employment histories are just as likely to be in traditionally female occupations as are those with very intermittent employment.[17] If women's expectations of future employment are reasonably accurate, this finding is strong evidence against the human capital approach. Other evidence is presented by Groneau. He shows that much of the difference in wages between women and men results from men having jobs that require more on-the-job training, but that women do not gain access to such jobs nearly as often as men even if they have a similar schooling, labor market experience, and tenure with their present employer.[18] These studies do not suggest that differences in schooling and labor market experience have no effect on male-female earnings ratio, but they do imply that such differences in human capital are by no means the complete explanation for the lower earnings of women.

If differences in human capital cannot fully explain why women do not gain ready access to the jobs that require the most training and responsibility, then the most likely alternative explanation is discrimination by employers. Support for this hypothesis is provided by the differences in earnings between men and women in narrowly defined occupational categories and by the many court cases in which firms have been found guilty of discriminating against women.[19]

With this background in mind, how might we explain the recent increase in the relative earnings of women, after a long period of little change? Part of the explanation involves changes in relative human capital. In the 1960s and 1970s many housewives with little previous experience in the labor market were entering the labor force. Since their wage rates were low, they had a negative effect on the relative earnings of women. Given high occupational segregation by gender, this increase in labor supply of women may also have decreased the relative earnings of those in predominantly female occupations. These negative effects on relative earnings counterbalanced the positive effects of reduced discrimination by employers and more career-oriented schooling by many young women.

In the 1980s fewer women entered the labor force with little human capital. On the contrary, the education and work experience of working women have increased relative to that of working men. These changes probably account for part of the recent increase in the relative earnings of women.[20] Another possibility is an accelerating decline in discrimination by employers. These two factors should reinforce each other. As employers provide more opportunities, women devote more effort to preparing for careers, and they stay in the labor force more continuously. Then as more women obtain jobs in nontraditional areas, societal attitudes change,

---

[17]See Paula England, "The Failure of Human Capital to Explain Occupational Sex Segregation," *Journal of Human Resources* (Summer 1982), pp. 358–70. Evidence against the human capital view also is presented by William T. Bielby and James N. Baron, "Sex Segregation within Occupations," *American Economic Review* (May 1986), pp. 43–47.

[18]See Reuben Gronau, "Sex-related Wage Differentials and Women's Interrupted Careers—The Chicken or the Egg?" *Journal of Labor Economics* (July 1988), pp. 277–301.

[19]See Bergmann, "Does the Market for Women's Labor Need Fixing?"

[20]See James P. Smith and Michael Ward, "Women in the Labor Market and in the Family," *Journal of Economic Perspectives* (Winter 1989), pp. 9–23.

and it becomes easier for male employers and coworkers to accept women in jobs traditionally reserved for men. This process can be expected to continue. Reductions in discrimination will encourage women to invest in more human capital, and more women in top jobs will lead to changes in societal attitudes about appropriate sex roles. The result will be further reduction in discriminatin as well as preparation for nontraditional jobs by larger numbers of women. Thus in contrast to racial inequality, there is reason to believe that inequality by gender will diminish in coming years. There are still significant limits to this process, however, as long as sex roles remain somewhat distinct and women continue to have most of the responsibility for home work and child rearing.[21]

THEORIES OF DISCRIMINATION

Three general sources of labor market discrimination have been analyzed by economists. We shall discuss each in turn. The first is *personal preferences* or *prejudice,* where employers, workers, or customers dislike associating with workers of a particular race or sex. The second source is *imperfect information,* where employers judge potential job candidates on the basis of average characteristics of their group rather than solely on their individual characteristics. Finally, there is discrimination based on *market power.* Market (or monopoly) power usually involves the ability to exclude potential competitors. If white male workers are able to increase their opportunities by excluding minorities and women, the exercise of monopoly power by white males results in discrimination against women and minorities. We shall refer to discrimination resulting from each of these sources as *preference discrimination, statistical discrimination,* and *monopoly discrimination.*

Preference Discrimination

The theory of preference discrimination has been developed extensively in a pioneering book by Gary Becker.[22] This theory starts with the assumption that white men have a "taste for discrimination." This "taste" means that white men have a preference for associating with other white men rather than with blacks or women. More specifically, if white men have a taste for discrimination, they are willing to pay a price to avoid contact with blacks or women. Such tastes for discrimination may exist for certain types of contact but not for others. For example, a white male may have a strong preference not to have a black woman as his boss but may not be concerned if the black woman serves as a subordinate. For example, even when overt racial discrimination was common, few whites objected to having black maids. In general, tastes for discrimination are most likely to be important for economic and social situations where the white male is not clearly in a superior situation. As Thurow has emphasized, white tastes for discriminatin involve a pref-

---

[21]See Nancy S. Barrett, "Obstacles to Economic Parity for Women," *American Economic Review* (May 1982), pp. 160–65.
[22]See Becker, *The Economics of Discrimination.*

erence for social rather than physical distance from blacks.[23] The same argument is even more obvious in considering the relations between men and women.

The theory of preference discrimination developed by Becker does not explain how tastes for discrimination are formed. Such tastes are assumed to be determined entirely by noneconomic considerations. Instead, the theory shows how tastes for discrimination affect economic decisions. The effects differ depending on who is assumed to have such discriminatory tastes. We shall look in turn at discrimination by employers, customers, and employees. Then we shall return to the issue of differences in tastes for discrimination for different types of contact between the races and sexes and its implication for the crowding of women and minorities into low-paying occupations.

1. Employer Discrimination. To simplify the analysis of tastes for discrimination by employers, let us assume that there are no differences in productivity by race or gender and no tastes for discrimination by either employers or customers. Under these circumstances an employer shows a taste for discrimination if, and only if, that employer is unwilling to employ blacks or women in the same jobs and at the same wages as white men. This taste for discrimination may be based on the personal preference of the employer, especially if the firm is small and there is considerable personal interaction between employer and workers. Or the taste for discrimination may be based on the community norms or political pressures, in which case the employer may expect to pay a social or political cost if he or she deviates from such norms.

If there is no discrimination, all workers are equally productive, and the labor market is competitive, an employer will hire a worker if and only if the worker's marginal revenue product, MRP, is at least as great as the worker's wage, W. In equilibrium, the employer will hire until $MRP = W$. Thus if there is no discrimination against men, $MRP_m = W_m$. On the other hand, if the employer has a taste for discrimination against women, the employer will hire a woman only if the firm can make an extra profit to compensate for the employer's discriminatory tastes. Therefore, in equilibrium, $MRP_f = W_f + d_f$ when d_f is the premium that the employer adds to compensate for his taste for discrimination. Since $MRP_f = MRP_m$ we see that $W_m - W_f = d_f$. If the employer hires women, it will only be at a lower wage than men. The difference in wage rates by sex equals the employer's premium for hiring women, d_f. If the employer is not allowed to pay women less than men but can control whom he hires, no women will be employed.

Next consider the more realistic case where there are differences in productivity across workers. If the wage rate is held constant at W, exceptionally productive women may be hired, since for such women MRP_f will exceed $W_f + d_f$. When there are productivity differences across workers, it is clear that the discriminatory employer is reducing profits by reducing the pool of qualified applicants from which he can recruit. Some women are being turned down in favor of men when the

[23]See Lester C. Thurow, *Poverty and Discrimination* (Washington, D.C.: Brookings Institution, 1969), especially Chap. 7.

women would be more productive. Such discrimination by employers is just as inconsistent with profit maximization as refusing to sell to certain customers (based on race or sex) even though the customer has the money and wants to buy.

As long as the firm is in a competitive product market, then, in the long run, firms must maximize profits in order to survive. If a firm does not maximize profits, it will obtain a lower return on its assets than those that do. Thus the profit-maximizing firm will be better able to compete for scarce resources and will expand at the expense of those that discriminate, eventually putting them out of business. This argument implies that as long as there are some employers who do not discriminate, competitive forces should act to eliminate discriminatory employers and thus to eliminate labor market discrimination.

Since Becker's work, economists have emphasized that competition reduces discrimination and when competition exists, there will be little discrimination by employers. This argument is important. Firms in competitive industries are more subject to economic pressures and perhaps relatively less subject to social and political pressures that may act outside the labor market. In the past, when discrimination was the social norm, discrimination appears to have been greater in less competitive industries.[24] On the other hand, political pressure to eliminate discrimination against women and minorities now may be greatest in noncompetitive industries and, of course, also in the government itself.[25]

Although competition is likely to reduce current discrimination in the labor market, it is not likely to eliminate it for several reasons. First, in a dynamic economy, with both technology and consumer tastes constantly changing, firms can survive by excelling in how they adapt to (or control) change in technology or tastes, even if they do not maximize profits in all other respects. Second, if there are differences in average productivity by sex or race, and if it is difficult to measure individual productivity, discrimination by firms may be perfectly consistent with profit maximization. We shall examine this case when we discuss the issue of statistical discrimination. Third, discrimination may exist in the labor market, despite competitive forces, if there are tastes for discrimination by workers or customers.

2. Customer Discrimination. Employers may discriminate against women and minorities not because the employer has a taste for discrimination but rather because the firm's customers have such discriminatory tastes. For production-oriented jobs, this argument is not very relevant. It is important, however, for sales

---

[24]For racial discrimination, see William G. Shepherd, *Market Power and Economic Welfare* (New York: Random House, 1970); William S. Comanor, "Racial Discrimination in American Industry," *Economica* (November 1973), pp. 363–78; Walter Haessel and John Palmer, "Market Power and Employment Discrimination," *Journal of Human Resources* (Fall 1978), pp. 545–60; and William R. Johnson, "Racial Wage Discrimination and Industrial Structure," *The Bell Journal of Economics* (Spring 1978), pp. 70–81. For sex discrimination, see the article by Haessel and Palmer, "Market Power and Employment Discrimination"; Sharon Oster, "Industry Differences in the Level of Discrimination against Women," *Quarterly Journal of Economics* (1975), pp. 214–29; and Orley Ashenfelter and Timothy Hannon, "Sex Discrimination and Product Market Competition: The Case of the Banking Industry," *Quarterly Journal of Economics* (February 1986), pp. 149–73.

[25]For example, see Thomas Sowell, *Race and Economics* (New York: David McKay Co., 1975), Chap. 6.

positions. Firms selling in predominantly white areas usually will prefer white sales-people, and those in predominantly black areas usually will prefer blacks—on the assumption that potential customers are generally more comfortable dealing with someone of their own race.

3. *Employee Discrimination.*

If white male workers have a taste for dis-crimination, they will be willing to forgo some job opportunities to avoid working alongside women or blacks. Employers who wish to retain present white male employees will hesitate to hire blacks and women for fear that their present employ-ees will quit or that their morale and productivity will decline. In addition, white males may be unwilling to train blacks and women to prepare them for better-paying jobs.

When employees have a taste for discrimination, there need not be overall discrimination in the labor market, however. If some firms discriminate in order to avoid dissention among white male employees, other firms can concentrate their hiring among women or blacks. These nondiscriminating firms will be able to compete successfully, assuming that there are no average productivity differences by race or sex and no tastes for discrimination by customers. Thus some segregation of firms by race and sex will result from tastes for discrimination by employees, but there is no reason why wage rates or job opportunities of women and minorities must be affected. Jobs not available for women and minorities in some firms should be fully balanced by jobs available with other employers.

4. *Occupational Crowding.*

As we discussed earlier, tastes for discrimina-tion are likely to vary with circumstances. White males do not mind giving orders to blacks or women but are more likely to object to receiving orders from them or being treated as equals. Consequently, we should expect greater barriers to women and minorities for top jobs, at least in the absence of government policies to combat discrimination in the labor market. Conversely, blacks and women will be "crowded" into the lower-paying occupations.[26] To the extent that blacks and women are ex-cluded from the better-paying jobs and forced to settle for lower-paying positions, the total supply of labor is reduced for top jobs. This reduction in supply will increase the pay of those who can gain access. Similarly, crowding in the lower-status occupa-tions decreases the wage for such jobs for all who hold them—white men as well as women and minorities. Thus discrimination that applies mainly to the best jobs is likely to increase the inequality of earnings for white men as the inequality between the races and between the sexes. The main effect of occupational crowding, however, is to lower the wage rate of women, since as we have seen, occupational segregation is mainly a matter of segregation by gender.

---

[26]See Barbara Bergmann, "The Effect on White Incomes of Discrimination in Employment," *Journal of Political Economy* (March–April 1971), pp. 294–313; and "Occupational Segregation, Wages, and Prof-its When Employers Discriminate by Race or Sex," *Eastern Economic Journal* (April–July 1974), pp. 103–10.

Statistical Discrimination

In the preceding section we have shown that competition can be expected to reduce preference discrimination, since such discrimination is costly to firms, workers, and customers. In this section we show that as a result of imperfect information, statistical discrimination is not costly to firms. It can be an effective way to maximize profits even though such discrimination reduces the job opportunities of women and minorities. In fact, we shall show that such discrimination reinforces stereotypes by race and sex.[27]

Employers do not know how productive a worker will be until the worker is hired and actually on the job. For some jobs this is not much of a problem. If hiring and training costs are low and if it is feasible for the employer to discharge workers who do not meet initial expectations, any mistakes the firm makes in its hiring decisions will not be very costly. Consequently, imperfect information is not likely to have much effect on the firm's hiring decisions.

For many jobs, however, including most high-paying positions, imperfect information plays a much greater role. Many jobs require much on-the-job training. Such training can involve specific technical skills but also often consists of learning how to interact effectively with coworkers and customers. Some jobs also entail considerable recruitment costs, especially for professional positions where there is a national market. Whenever such training and hiring costs are borne by the firm, employers have an incentive to be very careful whom they hire. In such cases the firm must try to predict how easy job applicants will be to train, how productive they will be after training, and how long they will stay with the firm once training is completed.

The readily available information on which a firm can base its predictions includes race and sex. Since these characteristics are not based on individual choices, decisions based on race and sex are not likely to be very accurate for individuals. Yet information on race and sex can be obtained at virtually no cost. Consequently, even though employers usually also pay attention to characteristics of job applicants that involve individual choice, such as schooling and employment history, employers are likely to interpret such characteristics differently depending on the sex and race of the job applicant.

If most employers believe the average woman will not stay on the job as long as the average man, women will receive few job offers for positions that involve extensive training paid for by the firm. Especially for young women, employers may discount a previous history of steady employment on the grounds that the woman's circumstances may change. For example, if she is single, the employer may believe that she is likely to marry and relocate if her husband works in a

---

[27]The analysis in this section is based on A. Michael Spence, *Market Signaling.* See also Edmund Phelps, "The Statistical Theory of Racism and Sexism," *American Economic Review* (September 1982), pp. 659–61; and Dennis J. Aigner and Glen G. Cain, "Statistical Theories of Discrimination in the Labor Market," *Industrial and Labor Relations Review* (April 1977), pp. 175–87.

different city or is transferred. If the young woman is married but childless, the employer may fear that she will have children and drop out of the labor force for a period. Even if these perceptions are valid, on average, they still create unfair barriers for those women who would not relocate and who do plan to work continuously. The effect of such perceptions on job opportunities is referred to as statistical discrimination. Similar arguments apply to racial discrimination, although in this case employers are more likely to be skeptical of the applicant's ability to do the job than of his willingness to stay with the firm.

Statistical discrimination also affects human capital decisions. For example, if employers are reluctant to hire women for jobs when the firm must invest in considerable on-the-job training, the lack of such job opportunities will encourage women to prepare mainly for less skilled, intermittent jobs (for example, retail sales versus managerial positions) and to devote more time to child care and home production. Similarly, if employers discount the quality of schooling for blacks, blacks have less incentive to acquire a good education. Thus statistical discrimination by employers can often be a self-fulfilling prophecy, leading to the reinforcement of initial stereotypes. In this sense competition in the marketplace may actually strengthen statistical discrimination by increasing the risk to firms that do not act on the basis of societal stereotypes.

Societal stereotypes are difficult to overcome not only because they are reinforced by competitive pressures but also because of pressures from white male workers, who often feel threatened by women and minorities. Newly hired blacks and women may be socially ostracized by the work force, which was previously limited to white males. Sexual harassment may also be prevalant against women. As Barrett indicates:

> Overt sex harassment is common when blue-collar women try to do traditionally masculine work. Pornographic material is sometimes displayed to embarrass women and show them "their place."
>
> The male buddy system also operates. In many factory environments, teamwork is essential for effective completion of jobs, and men often refuse to cooperate with a woman who dares to invade male territory, particularly if she refuses to exchange sexual favors.[28]

Social pressures on women to avoid nontraditional jobs are not limited to harassment by male workers. Bergmann writes:

> Working in an occupation that is typed as appropriate to a woman has served, until very recently, to show and confirm a woman's "femininity," just as wearing makeup and high heels does. Belonging to an occupation that is identified as male has been a part of a man's display of "masculinity." People who fail to behave in ways considered appropriate to their sex let themselves in for social penalties, ranging from being stared at, to ridicule and ostracism. As a result, displaying behavior exhibiting "masculinity" or "femininity" amounts to a compulsion in most people.

---

[28]See Nancy Barrett, "Occupations, Economics, and Career Opportunities," in *The Subtle Revolution: Women at Work,* ed. Ralph E. Smith (Washington, D.C.: Urban Institute Press, 1979), p. 48.

Many of the differences between the sexes in conventional behavior involve hardships for women, with high heels presenting an obvious example. Most women, however, choose to stick to the conventions, disabling as they are, to avoid the greater pain of the label "unfeminine." . . .

However, men's and women's jobs differ so greatly in advantages that unless there is an explicit and outright prohibition against their doing so, some women do want to breach the walls. . . .

If more women were allowed to enter all-male jobs, the idea that these jobs are off-limits to women and unfeminine would change. Thus the preservation of occupational segregation requires that virtually all women be kept out of the men's preserve. Defenses against women interlopers must be constantly in readiness.[29]

Since statistical discrimination reinforces the stereotypes on which it is based, such discrimination can be very difficult to overcome. Once some initial progress is made, however, each advance makes further progress easier. For example, as more women desire careers and are willing to work full time without significant interruption, for child rearing or any other cause, gender becomes a less useful predictor of job commitment for employers. The resulting increase in job opportunities has encouraged more women to aspire to high-paying careers, thus further reducing the usefulness of sex as a predictor of job commitment. On the other hand, attitudes about sex roles in the family do not appear to be changing very rapidly.[30] But without major changes in such sex roles, gender distinctions are likely to remain important in the labor market.

Statistical discrimination based on race appears to have become considerably more complex over the last generation or two. Employers are now quite willing to hire blacks who are clearly well educated, even though prejudices may remain against lower-class blacks with less schooling. As blacks improve their economic status, there is more willingness to look at blacks as individuals. Although this process has reduced statistical discrimination based solely on race, it has not been of much help to blacks who are either unable or unwilling to adapt to white conventions. Statistical discrimination now appears to be based on such criteria as schooling, clothing, and speech as well as skin color. Differences among workers in the ability to communicate, including cultural differences, speech dialects, body language, and so forth, can also reduce the productivity of a work group, thereby providing an incentive for a profit-maximizing employer to hire all workers from one subculture, an approach that handicaps those from minority groups.[31] Al-

---

[29]Barbara R. Bergmann, *The Economic Emergence of Women,* pp. 94–95

[30]Although the market work of women has increased dramatically in recent years, there has not been any sizable increase the amount of time husbands devote to home production. Even when both spouses work full time, the wife does most of the housework. Total hours of work, for pay plus work in the home, used to be greater for the average husband than for the average wife. Now the reverse is true. See Clair Vickery, "Women's Economic Contribution to the Family," in *The Subtle Revolution.* Nevertheless, there is some recent evidence that husbands of working wives are doing a little more housework, especially among young families. For example, see Francine P. Blau and Marianne A. Ferber, "Women in the Labor Market: The Last Twenty Years," in *Women and Work,* vol. 1, 1985.

[31]See Kevin Lang, "A Language Theory of Discrimination," *Quarterly Journal of Economics* (May 1986), pp. 363–82. Also see Robert Axelrod, *The Evolution of Cooperation* (New York: Basic Books, 1984), especially pp. 145–50.

though this approach is similar to statistical discrimination in some respects, it depends on current productivity differences rather than on expected differences in the employer's returns to on-the-job training.

As barriers have fallen for blacks who are well educated and willing to adopt white styles and conventions, the problem of disadvantaged workers in the labor market appears to be more one of class, or more accurately, of class and race together, rather than just a racial problem.[32] Moreover, the labor market problems of blacks are compounded by racial discrimination in housing, which together with schools that are frequently inferior in black neighborhoods, reduce both the educational and employment opportunities of many blacks.

Discrimination in Noncompetitive Markets

We have analyzed discrimination in the context of competitive markets. But not all markets are competitive with freedom of entry and flexible wages and prices. Direct entry restrictions exist through such devices as occupational licensing requirements and the control of entry to some occupations by craft unions. Wages can be set above competitive levels by collective bargaining or by government regulations (for example, minimum wage legislation).

All these examples involve some kind of monopoly power, the power to benefit certain individuals at the expense of others. For example, let us assume that in the absence of unionization, all markets were competitive. Then the establishment of unions and collective bargaining usually would result in higher wage rates and better job security for the unionized workers at the expense of job opportunities for nonunion members. Similarly, as we saw in Chapter 7, occupational licensing requirements, although sold politically on the basis of protection to consumers, are generally administered by those already in the occupation for their own advantage but at a cost of higher prices for consumers and reduced job opportunities for those who cannot pass the licensing requirements. Minimum wage legislation also benefits some low-wage workers at the expense of reduced job opportunities for others. In this section we consider how unions and other noncompetitive elements in the labor market affect discrimination against blacks and women.

First, consider the case where wage rates are set by collective bargaining or government regulation. If the wage is set above the competitive level, there will be an excess supply of qualified workers seeking employment. If there are skill differentials among workers, employers will seek to hire the most skilled. But if skill differences are small, other criteria must be used. Discrimination against some workers must occur. If there is any prejudice against them, women and minorities will be among the victims. Since discrimination is costless to the firm under such circumstances, competitive pressures will not act to reduce discrimination. Moreover, as Thurow has emphasized, statistical discrimination is likely to be much more extensive when wage rates are rigid. Small differences in employer perceptions of

---

[32]For an interesting analysis along these lines, see William Julius Wilson, *The Declining Significance of Race,* 2d ed. (Chicago: University of Chicago Press, 1980).

ability across race or sex groups can lead to large differences in job opportunities when wage rates are above the competitive level, at least if there are no legal constraints on discrimination.[33]

Next, consider the case where a group of workers can exercise power by directly excluding other workers from competing for jobs. This situation exists in the case of some craft unions. While industrial unions rely mainly on the strike weapon to achieve wage gains, craft unions, such as those in construction, often achieve high wage rates and job security partly through controlling entry into the occupation. When there are many small firms in the industry, each with a highly variable demand for skilled labor, union hiring halls and apprenticeship programs can be valuable for employers. In this case the union, representing present workers, has an incentive to limit the entry of new workers. Proverbially, such entry can sometimes be limited to close relatives of present union members. When the workers control entry, any plausible excuse to exclude groups of potential new entrants will be useful to the union and its incumbent workers. Thus unions that control entry to an occupation are likely to exclude women and minorities.

Although antagonisms between the races or sexes can conceivably strengthen a union's position if there is much prejudice in the society, in most cases such antagonisms are likely to hurt the union. As we saw in Chapter 5, a union must represent all workers in an occupation within the product market of the employer in order to raise wage rates without suffering large losses in employment. But if there are sharp divisions among the workers, organizing a union will be more difficult, as will effective bargaining once the union is formed. Consequently, employers may be able to exploit divisions by race and sex in order to reduce the collective influence of workers. According to this view, discrimination benefits owners and managers while hurting all workers, white men as well as women and minorities.[34] Conversely, we should expect unions to try to reduce such divisions in order to create and maintain union power.

The analysis in this section leads to two very different hypotheses about the effects of unions on discrimination against minorities and women. The first predicts that unions will increase such discrimination. At least in the past, craft unions have directly excluded women and minorities.[35] Moreover, when collective bargaining increases wage rates above competitive levels, the resulting excess supply of labor

---

[33]See Lester C. Thurow, *Generating Inequality* (New York: Basic Books, 1975), Chap. 7.

[34]For example, see David M. Gordon, *Theories of Poverty and Underemployment* (Lexington, Mass.: D. C. Heath & Company, 1972), Chap. 5; Richard C. Edwards et al., eds., *Labor Market Segmentation* (Lexington, Mass.: D. C. Heath & Co., 1975); David M. Gordon, Richard Edwards, and Michael Reich, *Segmented Work, Divided Workers* (Cambridge: Cambridge University Press, 1982); and Michael Reich, *Racial Inequality—A Political-Economic Analysis* (Princeton, N.J.: Princeton University Press, 1981). For a critique of such views, see Glen G. Cain, "The Challenge of Segmental Labor Market Theories to Orthodox Theory: A Survey," *Journal of Economic Literature* (December 1976), pp. 1215–57.

[35]For example, see Ray Marshall, *The Negro Worker* (New York: Random House, 1967); and *The Negro and Organized Labor* (New York: John Wiley & Sons, 1965); and William B. Gould, *Black Workers in White Unions: Job Discrimination in the United States* (Ithaca, N.Y.: Cornell University Press, 1977).

makes it less costly for firms to discriminate. On the other hand, unions may reduce discrimination against women and minorities. In particular, unions have an incentive to avoid discrimination in order to unionize all workers in an industry and to avoid dissention among union members. Thus there may be less discrimination in labor markets that are highly unionized than in those where unions have little influence.

The empirical evidence indicates that unionization reduces racial inequality in earnings but increases sexual inequality. Unions raise the wage rates of blacks a little more than those of whites and a higher percentage of black workers are union members.[36] Moreover, the black-white earnings ratio is highest in states, metropolitan areas, and industries where unionization is high.[37] These results are average effects for the economy as a whole. In contrast, the craft unions in construction have increased racial inequality since the percentage of construction workers who are unionized is much lower among blacks than among whites.[38] Thus the empirical results are consistent with the hypothesis that most unions (especially industrial unions) have narrowed racial inequality, probably in an effort to increase worker solidarity and the bargaining power of the unions.

The effect of unions on sexual inequality in the labor market is quite different. Unions have increased the earnings differentials between men and women. There is little difference in the union wage effect by gender, but unionization is lower among women than among men, although the difference has been diminishing in recent years.

In this section we have outlined three different theories of labor market discrimination. These theories are not mutually exclusive. Each can account for certain aspects of discrimination. In examining discrimination in a labor market with little on-the-job training or unionization, such as the market for workers in fast-food restaurants, the preference theory of discrimination appears most useful. In markets where on-the-job training is important, such as management positions, we expect statistical discrimination to be the most relevant theory. Both of these theories predict occupational crowding, which is especially important in the case of women. In unionized labor markets, consideration of bargaining power becomes relevant. Disagreements over the relative importance of the alternative theories of discrimination is one reason for the controversies concerning the desirability of governmental policies for equal employment opportunity (EEO). We turn next to an examination of these policies.

---

[36]See Orley Ashenfelter, "Discrimination and Trade Unions," in *Discrimination in Labor Markets,* ed. Ashenfelter and Albert Rees (Princeton, N.J.: Princeton University Press, 1973); Ashenfelter, "Union Relative Wage Effects: New Evidence," in *Econometric Contribution to Public Policy,* ed. Richard Stone and William Peterson (New York: St. Martin's Press, 1979); and Richard B. Freeman and James L. Medoff, *What Do Unions Do?* (New York: Basic Books, 1984).

[37]See Ashenfelter, "Racial Discrimination and Trade Unionism," *Journal of Political Economy* (May–June 1972); and Reich, *Racial Inequality.*

[38]See Ashenfelter, "Discrimination and Trade Unions."

ANTIDISCRIMINATION POLICIES

Federal efforts to check discrimination in employment go back at least to the 1940s but were intensified from the early 1960s onward. Nondiscrimination in employment is official policy in the federal government, and there has been a serious effort to move women and black workers up the ladder to senior positions. Although women and blacks are still underrepresented at the cabinet and subcabinet levels, they occupy a growing number of positions at the level of bureau chief, division chief, and senior staff adviser.

Since the early 1960s the federal government has established two sets of rules in an attempt to eliminate discrimination in private employment. The first is a *nondiscrimination* requirement that applies to all except very small firms. The second is a requirement that most federal contractors engage in *affirmative action* to actively seek out minorities and women when these groups are underrepresented in the employer's work force. Both sets of rules are generally referred to as *equal employment opportunity* (EEO) policies.

Combating Discrimination

Prior to the federal legislation of the 1960s, most states outside the South enacted *fair-employment-practice* laws, prohibiting discrimination in employment on the basis of race, color, religion, and national origin. Such laws generally did not prohibit sex discrimination. The first federal legislation outlawing labor market discrimination was the Equal Pay Act of 1963. This legislation prohibits an employer from paying any employee wages "less than the rate at which he pays wages to employees of the opposite sex . . . for equal work in jobs the performance of which requires equal skill, effort, and responsibility, and which are performed under similar working conditions." Jobs need only be substantially equal—not identical in all respects. Given the prevalence of occupational segregation, there is now much debate about broadening this legislation so that women will receive the same pay as men who perform jobs of *comparable worth,* an issue we shall discuss shortly.

The Civil Rights Act of 1964: Title VII

The most comprehensive federal statute prohibiting employment discrimination is the Civil Rights Act of 1964. Title VII of this act makes it unlawful for an employer "to refuse to hire or to discharge any individual, or otherwise to discriminate against any individual with respect to his compensation, terms, conditions, or privileges of employment, because of such individual's race, color, religion, sex, or national origin" and also "to limit, segregate, or classify his employees in any way which would deprive or tend to deprive any individual of employment opportunities."[39] Similar prohibitions apply to employment agencies, unions, or joint labor-

---

[39]Discrimination Act of 1968, as amended, prohibits employers from discriminating against workers over the age of forty and makes mandatory retirement illegal.

management committees in charge of apprenticeship or other training programs. Title VII applies to all employers in interstate commerce with twenty-five or more employees and to unions with more than twenty-five members.

Individuals who believe they have been the victims of discrimination can sue the employer directly. In addition, the Equal Employment Opportunity Commission (EEOC) was set up to try to resolve complaints. Since 1972 it has also been empowered to bring suits. The successful plaintiff in a Title VII action is entitled to be "made whole" for any wage loss due to discrimination. In the case of a class action suit, such back pay can be substantial. In an out-of-court settlement with the American Telephone and Telegraph Company in 1973, for example, AT&T agreed to provide $45 million in back pay.

While the influence of the EEOC expanded during the 1970s, it has become less active during the 1980s. Under the Reagan administration, the EEOC has been one of the government agencies affected by a general policy of trying to reduce the federal government's role in regulating the private company.[40]

The philosophy of Title VII is that blacks and women are no longer to be discriminated against but instead are to be judged by objective standards, standards that are color blind and sex neutral. In the words of the *Harvard Law Review,*

> Employers could continue to set rigorous qualifications for these job openings and test for worker productivity as long as they did so fairly. The act thus includes an antipreferential provision (e.g., no quotas are necessary), affirms the legality of professionally developed ability tests, and protects bona fide seniority systems.[41]

In some cases discrimination is easy to identify. It obviously occurs if an employer refuses even to consider any women or blacks who apply for a job, no matter how strong their apparent qualifications. The only case where an employer may limit a search to those of one gender or race is where there is a bona fide occupational qualification (bfoq), as in casting for some parts in a drama.

Unfortunately, in many other situations it is not easy to develop the objective standards on which Title VII is predicated. Consequently, Title VII has led to considerable litigation. Two of the major issues have been hiring standards and seniority rules.

The Supreme Court addressed the issue of hiring standards in the case of *Griggs* v. *Duke Power Company* in 1971. The *Griggs* case was a class action by black employees against a North Carolina employer with a long history of employment discrimination where blacks had been limited to the lowest-paying jobs. On July 2, 1965, the day Title VII became effective, the employer added a requirement for its previously white jobs that all successful applicants must have a high school diploma

---

[40]For example, see George C. Eads and Michael Fix, "Regulatory Policy," in *The Reagan Experiment,* ed. John L. Palmer and Isabel V. Sawhill (Washington, D.C.: Urban Institute Press, 1982), pp. 129–53; and D. Lee Bawden and John L. Palmer, "Social Policy," in *The Reagan Record,* ed. Palmer and Sawhill (Washington, D.C.: Urban Institute Press, 1984), pp. 177–215.

[41]"Employment Discrimination and Title VII of the Civil Rights Act of 1964," a lengthy unsigned note in the *Harvard Law Review* (March 1971); the quote is from p. 1114.

and achieve satisfactory scores on two standard aptitude tests. The plaintiffs could not prove discriminatory intent, but they did show that 34 percent of whites in North Carolina had completed high school but only 12 percent of blacks and that 58 percent of whites could pass similar tests but only 6 percent of blacks. Thus the effect of the new requirement was to exclude a much higher percentage of blacks than whites. Consequently, the Court ruled that the burden of proof was on the employer to show that the new hiring standards were good predictors of success in the jobs for which they were required. This the employer could not do. In fact, the Court found that "the white employees hired before the company's requirement went into effect who have not completed high school or taken the tests have continued to perform satisfactorily and make progress in departments for which the high school and test criteria are now used."

In this case there appears to have been strong evidence that the Duke Power Company continued to discriminate after 1965, and the Supreme Court found the company guilty of violating Title VII. Of greater importance, this case established the precedent that if test scores, educational degrees, and other screening devices were used by employers as hiring requirements, and if they had an adverse effect on the hiring of minorities or women, then the burden of proof is on the employer to show that there was a legitimate nondiscriminatory reason for such hiring. For many years an employer who could not do so was liable to be sued and found guilty of discrimination. Rather than face this risk, most firms made a major effort to increase their hiring of women and minorities and to avoid any screening devices that would disproportionately exclude these groups.[42]

In 1989, however, in the case of *Wards Cove Packing Co.* v. *Atonio* a more conservative Supreme Court reversed the principle established in the Griggs decision. Now, anyone charging an employer with discrimination bears the complete burden of proving such discrimination, even if the employer's policies result in disproportionately few women or minorities being hired or promoted to top jobs. This decision is likely to reduce substantially the effectiveness of federal anti-discrimination policy. Consequently it has led to proposed legislation aimed at overturning the decision.

AFFIRMATIVE ACTION

The Civil Rights Act of 1964 prohibits discriminatory action by employers. Its focus is entirely on the employment process: the recruitment, hiring, promotion, and discharge of workers. Under this landmark legislation no preference is to be given to minorities or women. If the employment process is nondiscriminatory, so should

---

[42]Another example of the difficulty of avoiding discrimination without focusing on the effects of employer policies is word-of-mouth recruitment. This recruitment policy can be useful for both employers and employees, since it provides reliable information to both parties at low cost. If the initial work force consists of white males, however, such recruitment will result in the hiring of few women or minorities, even though the employer has a good business reason for such a recruitment strategy and is not deliberately discriminating.

be the results. Thus, to identify discrimination, one should focus on the employment process, not on how many women and minorities are employed, the results of the process. In practice, it may be necessary to look at the results as well, as the *Griggs* case and its doctrine of disparate impact demonstrate. Still, the primary emphasis under Title VII is on the employment process, not on the resulting composition of employment by race and sex.

Affirmative action represents a different approach to combating discrimination in employment. It puts more emphasis on the results than on the employment process. If women and minorities are underrepresented in certain kinds of jobs relative to their availability in the employer's labor market, advocates of affirmative action believe that the employer is under an obligation to make an extra effort to increase their representation in such jobs. There are several arguments in favor of affirmative action. First, as we have seen, it is a difficult matter for the courts to determine when an employment process is discriminatory. Thus focusing on results may be simpler and more practical than focusing primarily on the process. Second, affirmative action may act to break down stereotypes about women and minority workers—those stereotypes that underlie statistical discrimination. By providing more opportunities in top jobs, it enables more women and minorities to show their capabilities. Third, low representation of women and minorities in certain jobs may be the result of past discrimination. Many advocates of affirmative action believe society must overcome the effects of such past discrimination if it is to provide true equality of opportunity.

Opponents of affirmative action emphasize that when affirmative action leads to any preference for women and minorities, it represents reverse discrimination against white males. Such reverse discrimination is seen as unfair to present white males, who as individuals, may never have discriminated against a woman or a black.[43] Especially in the case of race, affirmative action in the labor market may provide benefits mainly to better-educated blacks, those who need little assistance, while providing little help to blacks with less education, those who are in the greatest need.[44]

The issue of stereotypes depends crucially on the nature of the affirmative action. If a firm makes an extra effort to recruit, hire, and promote qualified women and minorities for positions in which they previously have been underrepresented, and the firm provides sufficient training to these new workers, the women and minority workers are likely to perform well. Consequently, their success should break down any stereotypes indicating that women and minorities do not want or cannot do various jobs. On the other hand, if enough preference is given to hiring and promoting women and minorities that unqualified applicants are taken while qualified white males are passed over, and if little training is given to the new workers, the women and minorities are not likely to succeed. In this case their

---

[43]For example, see Nathan Glazier, *Affirmative Discrimination, Ethnic Inequality, and Public Policy* (New York: Basic Books, 1975).

[44]For example, see Wilson, *Declining Significance of Race,* especially pp. 178–79; and Glenn C. Loury, "The Moral Quandry of the Black Community," *The Public Interest* (Spring 1985), pp. 9–22.

failure will reinforce the stereotypes that women and minorities are poor workers for certain kinds of jobs.

Affirmative action policies have been undertaken voluntarily by many employers. In addition, government contractors are required to have affirmative action plans. In 1965 the Office of Federal Contract Compliance Program (OFCCP) was established by executive order of the president to monitor the labor market policies of firms with federal contracts. Under executive order 11246, as amended, the OFCCP requires all firms with sizable federal contracts to analyze their employment of women and minorities relative to their availability in the labor market.[45]

Then the employer must develop a detailed *affirmative action plan* indicating how such underutilization will be corrected. This plan must include specific numerical goals and timetables indicating what will be accomplished each year for each occupation. Failure to develop and implement an affirmative action plan can lead to the loss of government contracts.[46] Although rarely invoked, this sanction is sufficiently powerful so that contractors have devoted considerable effort to affirmative action issues.

Once the employer and the OFCCP have agreed on an affirmative action plan, the employer must attempt to implement it. If the employer makes a good faith effort but fails to meet the goals and timetables, the firm will not be judged in noncompliance and thus in danger of losing government contracts.

The resources of the OFCCP have been very limited. Enforcement was particularly weak during the Reagan administration, which was openly hostile to affirmative action.[47] Because the OFCCP program is based on an executive order, Reagan could have abolished it on his own authority, without any congressional action. Largely because of political pressure from large employers, Reagan decided to maintain the program and not to make any significant changes in its formal requirements.[48]

Title VII of the Civil Rights Act of 1964 explicitly outlaws the use of any quota system. Although an employer is required only to make a good-faith effort, some opponents of affirmative action consider the goals-and-timetables approach to involve quotas and thus be illegal under Title VII. As recently as 1987 in *Johnson v. Transportation Agency,* the Supreme Court upheld the legality of the OFCCP pro-

---

[45]For a discussion of the availability issue, see Ronald G. Ehrenberg and Robert S. Smith, "Economic and Statistical Analysis of Discrimination in Hiring," *Proceedings of the Industrial Relations Research Association,* 1983.

[46]One criticism of the OFCCP affirmative action program has been the amount of paperwork required, especially in developing affirmative action plans. Such paperwork is necessary both in determining the need for and in monitoring the success of affirmative action programs. Reporting requirements are only a tool, however, and will be effective only to the extent that these requirements actually influence decision making. Later we shall examine estimates of the OFCCP program's effect on the employment of women and minorities.

[47]See Jonathan S. Leonard, "Women and Affirmative Action," *Journal of Economic Perspectives* (Winter 1989), pp. 61–75.

[48]See Marilyn Power, "The Reagan Administration and the Regulation of Labor: The Curious Case of Affirmative Action," in *The State and the Labor Market,* ed. Samuel Rosenberg (New York: Plenum Press, 1989), pp.197–206.

gram. Now, however, a more conservative Court appears hostile to the principles of affirmative action. Until there are either further judical rulings or new legislation, the long-run legal status of many affirmative action programs remains unclear.

Pay Equity

As we showed in the first section of this chapter, women earn much less than men, and there has been little change in the relative earnings of the two sexes. Moreover, there is great occupational segregation by sex. Many argue that because of sex discrimination, the jobs held primarily by women pay much less than jobs typically held by men. If jobs were paid in accordance with what the employees are worth to the employer and to society, the pay differential between men and women would narrow dramatically—at least this is the view of those who would require employers to provide equal pay for jobs of comparable worth, a concept originally called comparable worth and now referred to mainly as pay equity, especially by its supporters.[49]

We have seen that under both the Equal Pay Act and the Civil Rights Act of 1964, employers must pay equal wage rates to men and women doing the same (or even very similar) work. For jobs that are dissimilar, however, the courts have not required that employers attempt to pay comparable wages for comparable jobs. Nevertheless, a number of cities and states have implemented this approach for their own employees either voluntarily or through collective bargaining.[50] Generally, they have done so by increasing the wage rates for predominantly female jobs faster than for those held predominantly by males. Usually the relative earnings of women have increased by 5 to 10 percent where employers have adopted pay equity.[51]

Let us look more carefully at the arguments for pay equity. First, as we have seen earlier, there is considerable evidence of sex discrimination in the labor market, even though there is dispute over what proportion of the sex differential in earnings is attributable to discrimination. Reduction in discrimination that opens up new job opportunities will mainly help younger women. For older women workers the main hope for a fairer economic reward is to force employers to redesign their pay schedules.

As we discussed in Chapter 7, many firms already use job evaluation plans to set wage rates by comparing the value of different kinds of jobs. Although the

---

[49]For a good discussion of the arguments for and against comparable worth, see Michael Evan Gold, *A Dialogue on Comparable Worth.* For a favorable analysis of comparable worth, see Donald J. Treiman and Heidi I. Hartmann, *Women, Work, and Wages: Equal Pay for Jobs of Equal Value.* For critical views, see E. Robert Livernash, ed., *Comparable Worth.*

[50]In the province of Ontario, Canada, a comparable worth policy affecting private as well as public sector employers was established by legislation in 1989. In the United States, Minnesota and Iowa are two states that appear to have been especially active in implementing comparable worth for public-sector employees.

[51]See Mark R. Killingsworth, *The Economics of Comparable Worth* (Kalamazoo, MI: W.E. Upjohn Institute, 1990), especially p. 277.

labor market is the primary determinant of entry-level wages, for jobs that are filled by promotion from within, the relative wage rates are frequently determined by a formal job evaluation process. Under job evaluation each job is rated according to a set of factors, such as effort, working conditions, skills required, and responsibility. Once scores are assigned to each factor for each job, these scores must be weighted by a quantitative measure of the importance assigned to each factor. Obviously, many value judgments must be made as part of this job evaluation process. Advocates of comparable worth argue, however, that such value judgments can lead to a much more equitable wage structure than arises from market competition, at least with regard to differences in pay between predominantly male and female jobs. Although biases against women exist in many job evaluation schemes, advocates of pay equity argue such biases are easier to correct than discrimination in the market determination of wage rates.

The pay-equity approach would reduce pay differentials between men and women who work for the same employer. Thus it would have no effect on pay differentials that occur because women are more likely than men to work for low-wage employers in low-wage industries. Partly for this reason, even if occupations that were predominantly female paid as much as those that were predominantly male (holding constant skill, responsibility, and other factors on which job evaluation ratings are based), there would still be significant pay differentials between men and women. Thus movements toward pay equity can reduce only a very small part of gender inequality in the labor market.[52]

Critics of comparable worth emphasize that this doctrine runs counter to the principles of supply and demand on which our market economy is based. Job evaluation schemes may be useful in setting wage rates for jobs in the internal labor market filled by promotion from within. But for jobs filled through the external labor market, an employer must set wage rates comparable to those of other employers. If the wage rate for predominantly male jobs is set too low, then the employer will not be able to recruit qualified job applicants. If the wage rate for predominantly female jobs is set above the market level, the employer will be at a competitive disadvantage.

If all employers follow the comparable worth principle, a different set of problems arise. Since an employer's demand curve for each kind of labor is negatively sloped, as discussed in Chapter 5, an increase in the wage rate for predominantly female jobs will lead to fewer such jobs being offered by employers. A higher wage is not likely to have any dramatic short-run effect on employment, although it will increase the costs to employers if there is no effect on wages for jobs held mainly by men. In the long run, the elasticity of demand for traditionally female jobs is likely to be greater, however, as employers have time to make greater substitutions, both among occupations and between labor and capital. If jobs in traditionally female occupations decline faster than women can obtain nontraditional jobs, women will suffer more frequent or longer spells of unemployment.

---

[52]See George Johnson and Gary Solon, "Estimates of the Direct Effects of Comparable Worth," *American Economic Review* (December 1986), pp. 1117–25.

Few, if any, women are likely to lose their jobs when a pay equity plan is implemented. Wage adjustments have been modest and have been phased in over several years, providing enough time for employment adjustments through attrition. After several years, the effects on the relative employment of men and women typically have been under 10 percent.[53]

An illustration may help emphasize the conflict between market forces and the doctrine of comparable worth. Michael Gold relates the following:

> I was talking to Ronald Ehrenberg the other day, and he said he estimated that the price in town for a youngster to mow a lawn is about $4.00 an hour, but the price for a baby-sitter is about $1.50. And then, Ehrenberg, who is a respected economist, added, "It's strange, when you think about it, because your children are a lot more important to you than your lawn." He knew I was interested in comparable worth, so I suspect he was teasing me. But who could disagree that children are more important than lawns? Once again, the way we talk obscures the simple facts that there are plenty of baby-sitters available for $1.50 an hour, but a youngster will not cut your grass for less than $4.00 an hour.[54]

To increase the relative earnings of women, the main alternative to pay equity is to reduce the sex segregation of jobs. If more women seek out and obtain jobs not traditionally held by women, the relative earnings of women will increase for two reasons. First, nontraditional jobs generally pay higher wage rates. In the short run, this consideration will dominate. In the long run, however, as more women obtain nontraditional jobs, the supply of labor will decrease in traditional jobs. This reduction in supply should increase wage rates in jobs traditionally held by women, thus further diminishing the wage gap between men's and women's jobs. But such desegregation of jobs is occurring slowly and thus will not provide any substantial benefits to most women who are presently working in traditional jobs.

How are more women to obtain nontraditional jobs? First, all discriminatory barriers to such jobs must be removed. As a result of the Civil Rights Act of 1964, considerable progress already has been made in this regard. Second, affirmative action is relevant in filling jobs where there now are few women. Because of such factors as educational preparation, on-the-job training, and seniority, such policies have a much greater impact on the opportunities of new entrants to the labor force than on the opportunities of those who have been working for many years. For women now employed in traditional jobs, pay equity is the most effective way to reduce unfair pay differentials between men and women.

Effect of Antidiscrimination Policies

As we have seen, since 1964 the federal government has made a major effort to reduce discrimination in the labor market. We conclude with a brief discussion of the effectiveness of such policies.[55]

---

[53]See Killingsworth, *Economics of Comparable Worth*, especially p. 281.

[54]Gold, *Dialogue on Comparable Worth*, p. 66.

[55]For a review of the literature focusing on the effects of policies to reduce the wage gap between women and men, see Morley Gunderson, "Male-Female Wage Differentials and Policy Responses."

First let us look at the effects of EEOC enforcement activities. Beller evaluates the effect of EEOC by relating the extent of EEOC enforcement in different states to the employment and earnings of blacks and women. She finds little effect for blacks, but a 3 to 10 percent reduction in the female-male earnings differential as a result of EEOC activities.[56] Although Beller's approach is useful, it does not explain the effects of the legislation on social norms, effects that are likely to be unrelated to the extent of enforcement in different states.

Many studies have been made of the OFCCP program. Such studies usually compare the experience of government contractors, who are directly affected by the program, with noncontractors, who are not. Such comparisons include several possible difficulties. For example, government contractors might bid blacks or women away from noncontractors, thus leading to an overestimate of the program's effect. Nevertheless, initial estimates showed only small effects of the OFCCP program, probably because enforcement of the program was rather limited.[57] More recent studies show considerably larger effects for the 1970s, especially for blacks, but little effect in the 1980s, when enforcement declined.[58]

Our primary interest is the total effect of antidiscrimination policies on the earnings and employment opportunities of women and minorities. To evaluate the effects of federal antidiscrimination programs on these changes, we must try to compare the present economic position of blacks and women with what their position would have been if the Civil Rights Act of 1964 had not been passed and there were no affirmative action programs like OFCCP. Making accurate estimates is difficult, if not impossible. For example, changes in the demand and supply of labor by occupation, industry, and geographic area can lead to changes in the relative earnings of women and minorities, even if there is no change in discrimination.

Let us look first at changes over time in the relative earnings of women. As we saw in the introduction, the earnings of women relative to men did not change very much from the mid-fifties to about 1980. At first glance this finding suggests that there was little reduction in discrimination against women during this period, despite the Civil Rights Act of 1964 and affirmative action. On the other hand, the relative supply of women in the labor market increased greatly over this period,

---

[56]Andrea H. Beller, "The Effect of Economic Conditions on the Success of Equal Employment Opportunity Laws: An Application to the Sex Differential in Earnings," *Review of Economics and Statistics* (August 1980), pp. 379–87; and "The Economics of Enforcement of an Antidiscrimination Law: Title VII of the Civil Rights Act of 1964," *Journal of Law and Economics* (October 1978), pp. 359–80.

[57]For example, see Orley Ashenfelter and James J. Heckman, "Measuring the Effect of an Antidiscrimination Program," in *Evaluating the Labor Market Effect of Social Programs,* ed. Ashenfelter and James Blum (Princeton, N.J.: Industrial Relations Section, Princeton University, 1976); For a review of this and other early studies, see Charles Brown, "The Federal Attack on Labor Market Discrimination: The Mouse that Roared?" in *Research in Labor Economics,* ed. Ronald G. Ehrenberg (New York: JAI Press, 1984).

[58]For example, see studies by Jonathan Leonard, "The Impact of Affirmative Action on Employment," *Journal of Labor Economics* (October 1984), pp. 439–63; "Employment and Occupational Advance under Affirmative Action," *Review of Economics and Statistics* (August 1984), pp. 377–85; and "What Was Affirmative Action?" *American Economic Review* (May 1986), pp. 359–63, and "Women and Affirmative Action," *Journal of Economic Perspectives,* (Winter 1989), pp. 61–75. 1986), pp. 359–63. Also see two studies by James P. Smith and Finis R. Welch: "Affirmative Action and Labor Markets," *Journal of Labor Economics* (April 1984), pp. 269–301, and "Black Economic Progress after Myrdal."

apparently without an equally large increase in the demand for traditionally female jobs. Thus in the absence of any reduction in labor market segregation and discrimination against women, the market forces of supply and demand probably would have led to a reduction in the relative wage rate for women. The stability of women's earnings relative to men's during the sixties and seventies also reflects the offsetting influence of two other conflicting trends: (1) more continuous labor force participation by many women, leading to more work experience and training; and (2) increasing numbers of women who are new entrants or reentrants to the labor force and who thus have below-average work experiences and on-the-job training. Since 1980 the relative earnings of women have increased. Over this period, women's labor force participation has continued to increase, but there have been fewer new entrants to the labor force who lacked human capital. Instead, a higher percentage of the female labor force have attained advanced schooling and have prepared for the careers that have opened up for women as a result of both government antidiscrimination policies and changes in attitudes. It appears that we now are seeing the long-run effects of reduced labor-market discrimination against women.

As we saw in Figure 8-1, since 1964 the black-white earnings ratio has increased substantially for women and modestly for men. Reductions in discrimination clearly have contributed to the improvement in the relative economic position of black women. The source of the gains for black males has been the subject of considerable controversy, however.[59] Freeman has emphasized the role of antidiscrimination policy. In contrast Smith and Welch emphasize improvement in the quality of black schooling.[60] They also stress that this improvement in the relative quality of black schooling, which has resulted largely from the migration of blacks from the rural South to the urban North, now depends mainly on changes in black schools in urban areas, where there is little sign of significant improvement.[61]

Instead of focusing on economywide changes, another approach is to examine careful case studies of particular industries. An excellent example is the study of

---

[59]Some claim that the increase in the relative earnings of black males is largely spurious, since the increased generosity of transfer benefits may have caused a disproportionate number of black men with low earnings to drop out of the labor force and thus not be included in the earnings data. See Butler and Heckman, "Government Impact on the Labor Market Status of Black Americans." See also the supporting evidence in Donald O. Parsons, "Racial Trends in Male Labor Force Participation," *American Economic Review* (December 1980), pp. 911–20.

Recent studies by Brown and by Vroman indicate that contrary to the hypothesis of Butler and Heckman, earnings improvements have occurred since 1964, even after adjusting for the decreased labor force participation of blacks. See Charles Brown, "Black-White Earnings Ratios Since the Civil Rights Act of 1964: The Importance of Labor Market Dropouts," *Quarterly Journal of Economics* (February 1984), pp. 31–47; and Wayne Vroman, "Transfer Payments, Sample Selection, and Male Black-White Earnings Differences," *American Economic Review* (May 1986), pp. 351–54.

[60]For example, see Richard B. Freeman, "Black Economic Progress after 1964: Who Has Gained and Why?" in *Studies in Labor Markets,* ed. Sherwin Rosen (Chicago: University of Chicago Press, 1981); and "Changes in the Labor Market for Black Americans, 1948–72," *Brookings Papers on Economic Activity* (1973).

[61]James P. Smith and Finis Welch, "Black/White Wage Ratios: 1960–1970," *American Economic Review* (June 1977), pp. 323–38; and "Black Economic Progress after Myrdal."

the textile industry in South Carolina by Heckman and Payner.[62] They find that in the mid-sixties employment opportunities for blacks in textiles increased dramatically, with federal antidiscrimination policies playing an important role. Tight labor markets were also a contributing factor. Heckman and Paynor point out that, in fact, "what seems quite plausible is that in 1965 entrepreneurs seized on the new federal legislation and decrees to do what they wanted to do anyway."[63] Tight labor markets cannot be the whole story, however. When labor demand was equally high during World War II, employers responded by hiring more white women, not blacks.

Since 1964 efforts to increase the opportunities of women and minorities appear to have been made by most employers. In part such efforts are the result of changes in societal attitudes. In part they are the direct effect of enforcement activities of Title VII and the affirmative action requirements of the OFCCP. Since changes in societal attitudes have led to, and were affected by, federal antidiscrimination policies, it is very difficult to separate out the precise effects of these policies. The important point is that discrimination against women and blacks appears to have been reduced, and federal policies have contributed to its reduction.

It is also important to keep in mind, however, that the relative employment and earnings of women and minorities are affected by other government policies as well as by those aimed directly at reducing discrimination. For example, monetary and fiscal policies affect aggregate demand in the economy. When aggregate demand is high relative to supply, few workers are available, so employers cannot be choosy about whom they hire. Hiring standards are lowered whether such standards are explicit, as in the case of skill or educational requirements, or implicit, as in the case of discrimination against women or minorities.[64] Recessions have had an especially adverse impact on blacks, since many blacks hold cyclically sensitive jobs in durable goods industries, such as steel and autos.

SUMMARY

1. Since 1950 the average income of black families has been between 50 and 60 percent that of whites, with the peak occurring from the late 1960s to the early 1970s. For black men earnings have averaged about 55 to 70 percent of whites, with the peak in the late 1970s. For black women earnings have risen rapidly since 1950 and are now roughly equal with the average earnings of white

---

[62]See James J. Heckman and Brook S. Payner, "Determining the Impact of Federal Antidiscrimination Policy on the Economic Status of Blacks: A Study of South Carolina," *American Economic Review* (March 1989), pp. 138–77.

[63]Ibid., p. 174.

[64]Low aggregate demand for labor has also had an adverse effect on affirmative action. Affirmative action plans will not increase the employment of women and minorities unless firms are hiring. Also, the opposition of white males to affirmative action is weaker when overall job opportunities are good. Thus the increasing opposition to affirmative action over the past decade probably has resulted, in part, from the generally weak labor market during this period.

women. The relative economic position of Hispanics is approximately the same as that of blacks.

2. For full-time workers the average earnings of women was approximately 60 percent that of men for many years. Recently it has increased to about 65 percent.

3. Inequality in earnings by race or gender can result either from productivity differences or from labor market discrimination. On average, blacks have less schooling than whites, while women have less on-the-job training and seniority with their present employer. Such differences in readily measurable characteristics, related to productivity, account for perhaps half the differences in earnings between blacks and whites, a little less than half the earnings differential between women and men. It is impossible to precisely determine the relative importance of productivity differences and labor market discrimination, however, since many productivity traits cannot be measured accurately (for example, the quality of schooling and training), and because discrimination can also affect access to schooling and training opportunities.

4. Economists have several theories of labor market discrimination. The best known, developed by Gary Becker, is called *preference discrimination*. It starts with the assumption that white males have a "taste for discrimination," which means they are willing to pay a price to avoid contact with blacks and women. Such tastes for discrimination are most plausible when white men are dealing with blacks or women who are in a position of authority. There is little evidence to support the view that white males object to having blacks or women as subordinates. Thus in the absence of government policies, blacks and women are likely to be crowded into the most subordinate, lowest-paying jobs.

5. In Becker's theory, a white male must pay a price to discriminate. Given imperfect information, however, race and gender may be useful proxies for employers. For example, firms may avoid hiring blacks because they are viewed as having poorer schooling and thus as being more difficult to train. Similarly, employers may worry that women will leave the firm should they marry or have children. Discrimination based on such stereotypes is called *statistical discrimination*. Such discrimination can maximize the firm's profits if the stereotype bears some relation to reality and if information on race and gender is much easier to ascertain than is reliable information on trainability or expected quit rates. Statistical discrimination reinforces stereotypes against blacks and women. It can reduce the incentive to invest in education or other forms of human capital. If women are excluded from jobs that offer much training by firms, such exclusion also provides little incentive for women to remain with the firm should their home responsibilities increase.

6. Rigid wage rates and monopoly power are likely to increase discrimination in the labor market. Unions appear to have decreased racial inequality in most cases, perhaps because of the need for worker solidarity if unions are to be effective. On the other hand, unions probably have increased sexual inequality.

7. Title VII of the Civil Rights Act of 1964 outlawed labor market discrimination on the basis of race, color, religion, sex, or national origin. Under this legislation blacks and women should be judged by objective standards that are color blind and sex neutral. Unfortunately, it has been difficult to develop such standards.

8. Affirmative action is required of most government contractors. Under affirmative action, if women and minorities are underrepresented in certain kinds of jobs, relative to their availability in the employer's labor market, then the employer is under an obligation to make an extra effort to increase their representation in such jobs.

9. The average woman earns a considerably lower wage than the average man. In addition, there is great occupational segregation by sex. Advocates of pay equity argue that because of discrimination, jobs held primarily by women are not paid as much as they should be. Critics reply that increasing the wage rate for such jobs would lead to many unfortunate results, including fewer job opportunities for women, increased costs for firms, and higher prices for consumers.

10. There is little consensus as to the effectiveness of government policies in reducing labor market discrimination. The relative position of women and minorities in the labor market is affected, not only by antidiscrimination policies but also by other policies, especially monetary and fiscal policies that influence the aggregate demand for labor.

KEY CONCEPTS

DISCRIMINATION, LABOR MARKET
JOB SEGREGATION
DISCRIMINATION, PREFERENCE
DISCRIMINATION, STATISTICAL
DISCRIMINATION, MONOPOLY

NONDISCRIMINATION REQUIREMENT
DISPARATE IMPACT
AFFIRMATIVE ACTION
PAY EQUITY

REVIEW QUESTIONS

1. What does *employment discrimination* mean? How does it differ from total discrimination? From job segregation?

2. What evidence would you examine to determine whether an employer has engaged in discrimination against women workers or black workers?

3. The earnings of married women are considerably lower as a percentage of married men's earnings than the earnings of single women as a percentage of single men's earnings. How could you account for this?

4. "Equal pay for equal work is not necessarily in the long-run interest in working women. Willingness to work for less is one way that women can outcompete men and take over additional areas of employment." Discuss.

5. "The fact that women usually earn less than men on the same job arises mainly from differences in continuity of employment and on-the-job training. Since these characteristics are unlikely to change, the wage differential is unlikely to change either." Do you agree? Explain.

6. Would you expect earnings of black men to become equal to those of white men with the same personal characteristics? Why or why not?

7. Affirmative action programs have been criticized as involving reverse discrimination against white males. Do you agree with this criticism? Why or why not?

8. Do you favor efforts to pay women equal pay for jobs of comparable worth? Defend your position.

9. Discuss the effectiveness of federal policies to eliminate discrimination in the labor market.

READINGS

BECKER, GARY S. *The Economics of Discrimination*, 2d. ed. Chicago: University of Chicago Press, 1971.

BERGMANN, BARBARA R., *The Economic Emergence of Women*. New York: Basic Books, 1986.

FUCHS, VICTOR R., *Women's Quest for Economic Equality*. Cambridge, Mass.: Harvard University Press, 1988.

GOLD, MICHAEL EVANS, *A Dialogue on Comparable Worth*. Ithaca, N.Y.: Industrial and Labor Relations Press, Cornell University, 1983.

GUNDERSON, MORLEY, "Male-Female Wage Differentials and Policy Responses." *Journal of Economic Literature* (March 1989), pp. 46–72.

LIVERNASH, E. ROBERT, ed., *Comparable Worth: Issues and Alternatives*. Washington, D.C.: Equal Employment Advisory Council, 1980.

LLOYD, CYNTHIA B., and BETH T. NIEMI, *The Economics of Sex Differentials*. New York: Columbia University Press, 1979.

MASTERS, STANLEY M., *Black-White Income Differentials*. New York: Academic Press, 1975.

REICH, MICHAEL, *Racial Inequality—A Political–Economic Analysis*. Princeton, N.J.: Princeton University Press, 1981.

SMITH, JAMES P., and FINIS R. WELCH, "Black Economic Progress after Myrdal," *Journal of Economic Literature* (June 1989), pp. 519–64.

SMITH, RALPH E., ed., *The Subtle Revolution: Women at Work*. Washington, D.C.: Urban Institute Press, 1979.

SPENCE, A. MICHAEL, *Market Signaling*. Cambridge, Mass.: Harvard University Press, 1974.

TREIMAN, DONALD J., and HEIDI I. HARTMANN, *Women, Work, and Wages: Equal Pay for Jobs of Equal Value*. Washington, D.C.: National Academy Press, 1977.

WILSON, WILLIAM JULIUS, *The Truly Disadvantaged*. Chicago: University of Chicago Press, 1987.

———, *The Declining Significance of Race*, 2d. ed. Chicago: University of Chicago Press, 1980.

REAL WAGE RATES, PRODUCTIVITY, AND INFLATION

In this chapter we focus primarily on the determinants of real wage rates and on how the average level of wages has been changing over time. At the end of the chapter we also discuss inflation and how changes in aggregate demand affect money wage rates.

Wage rates usually rise year after year, and since World War II the increase has been unusually rapid. In 1947 workers in private nonagricultural industries averaged $1.13 per hour. In 1988 they averaged $9.29 per hour, more than an eightfold increase.

What matters, however, is how much these wages will buy. The increase in money wages must be adjusted for increases in the Consumer Price Index (CPI). This adjustment shows the increase in *real wages*, or wages in dollars of constant purchasing power.

The record of money wages, consumer prices, and real wages since 1860 is summarized in Table 9-1, and year-to-year changes since 1947 are shown in Figure 9-1. The trend of money wages is strongly upward. This trend is no recent development, but goes back as far as our records exist. However, the rate of increase in real wages, shown in the last column of Table 9-1, bears little relation to the increase in money wages. Real wages have risen rapidly at times when money wages were also rising rapidly (1910–22, 1940–50); but real wages have also risen rapidly when money wages were moving upward slowly (1880–90, 1930–40).

The years since World War II differ from earlier periods in that the upward movement of prices has been unusually rapid. Prices have risen during business

TABLE 9-1 Money Wages, Consumer Prices, and Real Wages in Manufacturing, United States, 1860–1988

	PERCENTAGE CHANGE		
	Money Hourly Wages	Consumer Prices	Real Hourly Wages
1860–70	+ 53	+ 41	+ 8
1870–80	− 10	− 22	+11
1880–90	+ 18	− 11	+32
1890–00	+ 3	− 8	+12
1900–10	+ 29	+ 16	+14
1910–22	+141	+ 78	+37
1922–30	+ 12	0	+13
1930–40	+ 26	− 16	+50
1940–50	+131	+ 72	+34
1950–60	+ 57	+ 23	+28
1960–70	+ 49	+ 31	+13
1970–80	+117	+113	+ 4
1980–85	+ 27	+ 28	− 1
1985–88	+ 8	+ 10	− 2

Sources: 1860–1929: Clarence D. Long. "The Illusion of Wage Rigidity: Long and Short Cycles in Wages and Labor," *Review of Economics and Statistics* (May 1960). This study draws on basic research by the author and by Albert Rees at the National Bureau of Economic Research
1929–57: Albert Rees, *New Measures of Wage Earner Compensation in Manufacturing, 1914–57,* occasional paper 75 (New York: National Bureau of Economic Research, 1960).
1957–88: Standard Bureau of Labor Statistics series, as published in *Economic Indicators* and *Economic Report of the President, 1990.*

cycle upswings but have not fallen on the downswing as they used to do. Money wages have also risen rapidly, managing in most years to outrace the price level. But despite this, real wages have not risen unusually fast, and the rate of increase has in fact declined since the 1940s. It is clear from Figure 9-1 that the rise of real wages slowed down in the late 1960s and came to a complete halt after 1973. The reasons for this slowdown, and the question of whether it will continue in future, are central issues for this chapter.

DETERMINING THE REAL WAGE LEVEL

If changes in real wages do not depend on changes in money wages, what do they depend on? Logically, real wages can rise because of these factors:

1. Output per worker (the productivity of labor) is rising. Part of this output, of course, goes to the owners of capital. But if labor's share of output produced remains unchanged, then real wages will rise at the same rate as labor productivity.

2. Labor's share of output produced is increasing. Even with no increase in productivity, that could produce some increase in real wages.

In American experience, and for that matter in other industrialized countries, the first factor has been the most important. So most of this chapter will be devoted to it. But there has also been a modest increase in labor's share of national output, which will be noted shortly.

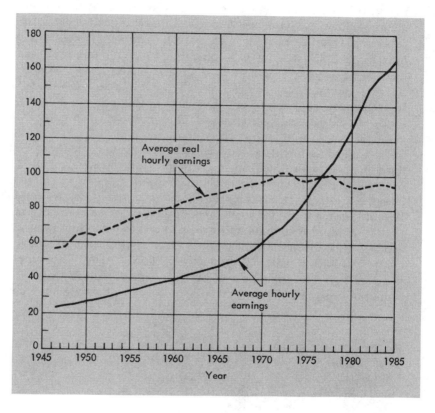

FIGURE 9-1   Hourly Earnings and Real Hourly Earnings for the Private Nonagricultural Economy (1977=100)

The Productivity Schedule

It will be useful here to introduce a diagram developed originally by John Bates Clark of Columbia University.[1] Clark assumed a simplified economic system with the following characteristics: (1) Free competition prevails throughout the econ-

---

[1]Clark, *The Distribution of Wealth* (New York: Macmillan Publishing Co., 1899).

omy, in both product markets and factor markets. Prices and wages are not manipulated by collusive agreements or government regulation. (2) The quantity of each productive resource is assumed to be given. Moreover, no changes occur in the tastes of consumers or the state of the industrial arts. The same goods therefore continue to be produced year after year in the same quantities and by the same methods. (3) The *quantity* of capital equipment is regarded as fixed, but it is assumed that the *form* of this equipment can be altered to cooperate most effectively with whatever quantity of labor is available. Although this seems at first glance a queer and unreal assumption, it makes a good deal of sense for long-term problems. Over a period of decades plants *can* be adapted as they wear out and have to be replaced. If labor becomes more plentiful relative to capital, plants and machines can be redesigned to use greater quantities of labor. If labor becomes scarcer, equipment can be redesigned to use less labor. (4) Workers are assumed to be interchangeable and of equal efficiency. This assumption means complete absence of occupational specialization. The result is a single wage rate rather than a variety of rates for different occupations.

    Clark summarized the operation of such an economy in a diagram, reproduced here as Figure 9-2. The line *AB* represents the marginal physical productivity of labor, that is, the amount added to the national product by the employment of additional workers. Clark showed this curve as falling steadily from the beginning. Actually, it might rise for some time, but this point is not important.

    E represents the number of workers available for employment, which we assume to be given and constant. If all these people are employed, the last one added will have a marginal productivity of *EC* = *OW*. The wage rate cannot be more than *OW*, for then it would not pay to employ the last worker. The wage rate cannot be less than *OW*, for in this event some employer, seeing a chance to make a

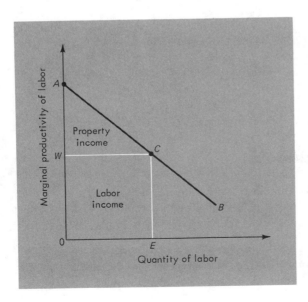

FIGURE 9-2   Determination of the General Level of Real Wages

profit by hiring the worker for less than her marginal productivity, would try to lure the worker away from her present employer. Competition among employers for labor will ensure that the worker receives the full marginal product OW but no more.

It follows next that no other worker in the system can receive a wage higher than OW. It may seem that those workers above the margin—that is, those to the left of E on the diagram—are being cheated by this arrangement. They seem to be producing more than they are getting. Actually, however, under the assumption of perfect interchangeability of workers, no worker is more valuable than any other. If one worker doing a particularly important job were to drop out, someone could be taken from the margin to replace him. Hence, one cannot earn more than another. If this were not so, and if each worker were paid his or her specific productivity, nothing would be left over for the other factors of production. As it is, however, the workers as a group receive as wages the area $OECW$, that is, the number of workers multiplied by the wage rate. The triangular area ACW goes to the owners of land and capital.

The fact that there are thousands or millions of employers in the economy makes no difference to the argument. In a purely competitive labor market, each employer will be obliged to pay the market wage, OW. The employer will then adjust hiring of labor so that the marginal productivity of the last worker hired is also OW. Thus both the wage of labor and the marginal productivity of labor will be equal in all employing units; and it will not be possible to raise national output by transferring workers from one unit to another. Labor is ideally allocated.

Nor does it make any basic difference that there are in fact many skill levels in the economy. The assumption of a single skill level and a single wage rate is merely a convenient simplification. We could assume instead that there are several occupational levels, in which wages at any time bear a fixed relation to each other and move up and down together. We could then regard OW as an average of these occupational rates. The conclusion would remain the same. The level of the average wage depends on the height of the productivity schedule and on the supply of labor.

Clark's diagram shows the situation at a particular time—say, in 1990. Total national output in this year is shown by the area $OACE$. Labor's share of this output is the rectangle $OECW$, and the area ACW shows the income received by property owners.

The main use of the diagram, however, is to analyze events over time. Over the course of years and decades, two things are happening: (1) The productivity schedule AB is moving upward to the right; and (2) the supply of labor, shown by E, is also increasing. These shifts are illustrated in Figure 9-3. As they occur, the marginal productivity of labor rises from C to C_1 to C_2, and the average real wage rate rises accordingly from OW to OW_1 to OW_2.

This looks too simple to be true, and you may think of some possible objections. First, not all of the labor force is employed. So a 10 percent increase in the labor force does not necessarily mean a 10 percent increase in employment. If we were discussing year-to-year shifts, this point would be important. But over a period of decades, it is only a minor qualification. The average unemployment rate

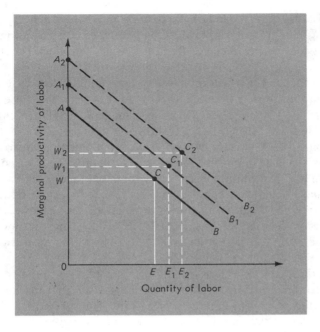

FIGURE 9-3   Movement of the Real Wage Level over Time

does vary from decade to decade, but not by a great amount. It is growth of the labor force that dominates the rightward shift of *E*.

Second, you may say that the real wage rises in Figure 9-3 only because we drew the lines so as to *make* it rise. This is quite true, as you can verify with pencil and paper. When *E* rises to E_1, you could easily raise A_1B_1 by *less* than we have done in the diagram. If the shift were small enough, the new intersection point, C_1, might lie horizontally to the right of *C*, so that there would be *no rise in real wages*. Something similar seems to have happened in the United States in the years 1970–90. And there are countries in other parts of the world where the real wage level has not risen for generations.

All one can say, then, is that Figure 9-3 shows *typical* behavior in a progressive, growing economy. A rising real wage level is normal not only for the richer industrialized countries but also for most Third World countries as well.

Third, you may note that we have constructed Figure 9-3 in such a way that the relative size of the labor and property shares does not change much over the years. This is not a necessary fact of life. It would be possible to draw diagrams showing the labor share either rising or falling over the course of time. Again, we can say only that Figure 9-3 is a reasonable representation of experience in the United States. There has been a modest increase in labor's share of national income since 1900, and this increase has contributed slightly to the increase of real wages. But the overwhelming source of the increase has been the upward shift of the productivity schedule *AB* and the great increase in output per worker.

This point is illustrated in Figure 9-4, which shows indexes of output per hour and real compensation per hour in the private nonfarm economy since 1947.

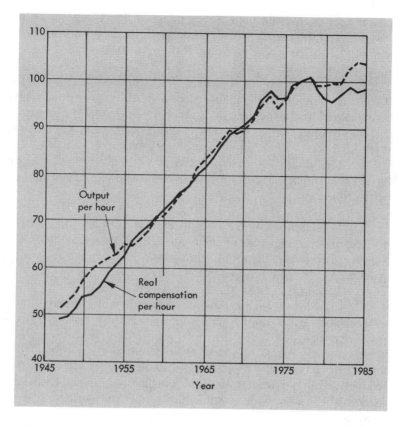

FIGURE 9-4   Indexes of Output per Hour and Real Compensation per
Hour, Nonfarm Business Sector, 1947–1985
(1977=100)

Note that the two measures move very closely together—so closely that it is often
hard to distinguish them on the diagram. For example, the rise of both worker
productivity and worker compensation leveled off after 1973. This parallel movement is no accident but rather reflects a close economic relation.

These facts suggest several questions: Why does the productivity schedule
normally shift upward over time? Why did this shift slow down in the late 1960s and
virtually cease after 1970? And what is it reasonable to expect in the future?

SOURCES OF PRODUCTIVITY GROWTH

The most obvious source of a rising marginal productivity of labor schedule is an
increase in the capital goods that labor uses in production. Here we should not
think just of factories and assembly lines but also of strip-mining equipment, combine harvesters, airplanes, supermarkets, office buildings, computers, telecommuni-

cation equipment, and many other things. If labor supply is growing at 1 percent per year and the capital stock at 3 percent, then each worker has more machinery and other capital goods to work with, year after year. Thus output per worker should also be rising.

Statistical studies, however, have turned up a startling fact: Usually less than half, sometimes only a quarter or less, of the growth in output per worker can be explained by the increase in capital per worker. Most of the growth in productivity remains unexplained. This unexplained portion has been labeled "the residual." It has also been called "a measure of our ignorance."

This discovery, now twenty-five years old, set off a search for additional factors that might account for the residual. The most important of these appear to be the following:

1. Technical Change   As the capital stock and the labor force grow, we do not just produce more of the same goods by the same methods. Rather, we seek to discover and apply techniques that produce either a new product, an improved product, or the same product at lower cost.

Technical change comes from several sources:

(a) *Basic scientific research,* which lays the foundation for new products and techniques, is done mainly in universities. But in agriculture, medicine, atomic energy, and space research, government laboratories are important; and some large companies also do basic research. (b) *Applied research,* aimed at converting general knowledge to specific uses. (c) *Development,* which includes product design and operation of pilot production units, is done mainly by business concerns. The lone-wolf inventor also remains important. One study of sixty-one major twentieth-century inventions found that more than half were the product of individual inventors.

Research and development, usually shortened to *R&D,* is one of the fastest-growing activities in the economy. Expenditure on R&D has risen more than twenty-fold since 1940. The federal government sponsors basic research through the National Science Foundation and its own laboratories, and also provides more than half the money for company research labs.

2. Improvements in Capital Quality   This is closely related to the previous point. Invention leads not only to more machines but also to different and better machines. As old equipment wears out, it is replaced by equipment with greater productive capacity per dollar of cost.

Recognition of this fact has led to the concept of *vintage capital.* Each part of the nation's capital stock is dated by its year of origin, and it is assumed that each year's capital is x percent more productive than that of the year before. (This is the reverse of what happens with vintage wine, which gets better with age!). For example, if capital is improving in quality at 3 percent per year, then capital of 1990 vintage will be more than twice as productive as capital of 1970 vintage and will get more than twice as much weight in the total capital stock. When you add up the nation's capital stock year by year on this basis, you get a faster rate of increase than you would get otherwise.

3. Improvements in Labor Quality Labor as well as capital has improved over time in the American economy. Indeed, this improvement can be viewed as a different kind of capital formation, an increase in the stock of human capital discussed in Chapter 4. Americans today, on the average, have more than twice as many years of education as their grandparents. Their level of skill and experience has risen. A much larger proportion of the labor force today consists of skilled crafts people, white-collar workers, executives, and professional people.

One way to adjust for this improvement in the quality of the labor force is to use relative earnings as an indicator. If supervisors earn twice as much as laborers, their hours can be given double weight in the national total, and professional people might receive a weight of four or five. Thus one can develop vintage measures of labor supply comparable to the vintage capital measures. Total labor supply, adjusted for quality in this way, rises a good deal faster than the crude total of hours worked.

4. Intangibles Other possible sources of productivity growth are harder to capture statistically. An illustration is improvements in business management. As of 1900, most business managers had at most finished high school and then learned to manage by doing it. Today managers are almost always college trained, and in addition, most have M.B.A.s or other graduate training. The scientific management movement which set in around 1900 brought major advances in production and human resource management, and the movement later spread to marketing, finance, and other areas. Developments in organization theory have improved the overall coordination of large enterprises. Recently, mathematical methods (operations research, econometrics, linear programming) have been used with increasing success in management decision making; and the growth of computer technology permits elaborate calculations that were quite impossible earlier. Nor are organizational improvements confined to the enterprise. Improvement of economic information and of product and factor markets can lead to better overall coordination of the economy, with a consequent rise in productivity.

THE PRODUCTIVITY SLOWDOWN

We have noted at several points the leveling off of growth in output per worker and in real hourly wages after 1973.[2] The sources of this slowdown are still being studied and debated. There are several plausible suspects.

---

[2]This section draws heavily on the analysis of Martin N. Baily, "What Has Happened to Productivity Growth?" Also see William J. Baumol, Sue Ann Batey Blackman, and Edward N. Wolff, *Productivity, and American Leadership: The Long View* (Cambridge, MA: MIT Press, 1989).

First, the period since 1973 was characterized by slack demand and a low GNP growth rate. From 1960 to 1973 U.S. GNP grew at an average rate of 4.1 percent per year. From 1973 to 1988 this growth dropped to 2.7 percent. The rate of productivity growth declined even more dramatically. From 1960 to 1973 output per hour of work in the private sector grew at an average annual rate of 2.9 percent. From 1973 to 1988 it grew by an average of only 1.1 percent. The recessions of 1973–75 and 1981–82, associated partly with the two oil price explosions, were the most severe of the postwar period. In periods of slack demand workers are not laid off as rapidly as output falls, so that productivity growth is often negative. Thus recessions account for part of the decline in output and output her hour.

Second, this period saw an unusual influx of new and inexperienced workers to the labor force. You will recall from Chapter 3 that from 1945 to 1965 the labor force was growing at little more than 1 percent per year. In the late 1960s, however, the growth rate rose above 2 percent and remained at that level through the 1970s, reaching a remarkable 3.3 percent in 1978. This growth resulted partly from the growing up of those born in the postwar baby boom and partly from the sharp increase in women's labor force participation. It might be expected that these new workers were less productive in the first instance than more experienced workers; and their growing importance in the labor force probably slowed overall productivity growth. During the 1980s labor force growth slowed somewhat as the number of teenagers declined. Still the labor force continued to grow by about 1.5 percent each year, mainly because of the increasing labor force participation of women.

Third, while the growth rate of labor supply was rising, the growth of the capital stock was falling somewhat. The two recessions cut into business profits, reducing both the inducement to invest and the funds available for investment. Also important was a considerable increase in uncertainty about the future and thus about what kinds of investment might be most profitable. Such uncertainty resulted, among other things, from sharp changes in oil prices, variable rates of inflation, and changes in the extent of foreign competition as the value of the dollar rose and then fell. In the face of such uncertainty a risk-averse investor will only commit to a new undertaking if the expected rate of return is very high. As a result, the growth of physical capital per hour of labor fell sharply, from about 2.6 percent per year from 1959 to 1973 to 1.2 percent from 1973 to 1979. Since productivity depends partly on the amount of such capital that labor has to work with, one would expect as a result a lower rate of productivity growth. Since 1979 there has been a faster growth in physical capital per worker, almost back to the rate of the 1960s; but there has been only a modest increase in the growth of labor productivity during the 1980s.

Fourth, of the capital that was created a good part was diverted to special purposes. The oil-price shocks led to substantial investment in energy-saving equipment, that is, equipment that enabled oil to be replaced by coal and other fuels or which reduced total energy use per unit of output. Further, the environmental legislation that peaked around 1970 led to a burst of investment in pollution-control equipment. This investment does indeed produce a product—cleaner air or water—but this product is not counted in measured GNP.

Fifth, the rate of growth of technology and innovation appears to have slowed down. For example, spending on research and development (R&D) has declined, and so have the number of patents granted to U.S. inventors. Because spending for R&D is a long-term investment by firms, it will be affected by the same factors that have led to the decline in physical investment per worker. It is surprising, however, that technological change appears to be declining at the same time that we are going through a computer revolution.[3] There is no strong empirical evidence that changes in R & D are a major cause of the productivity slowdown. In the words of one leading scholar,

> While R & D is probably not the major culprit in the recent productivity slowdown and the associated erosion of our international competitiveness, it is hard to overestimate its importance for the long-run growth of the world economy.[4]

Government is responsible for much research and development, either directly through government spending or indirectly through policies in areas such as patents. But much responsibility for innovation also rests with the managers of firms in the private sector. Managers in the U.S. have been charged with being too concerned with short-run profits and not enough with long-run growth and productivity. There is evidence that the United States has been lagging in this area, especially compared to Japan.[5]

Sixth, there has been a decline in the school performance of American youth, as measured by a variety of standardized tests. This decline, which started in the late 1960s has been sizable, more than the equivalent of a grade in school. Bishop shows that this decline is likely to have had an appreciable effect on the productivity of American workers.[6] It cannot account for the majority of the decline in output, however, because many workers currently in the labor force were educated before school performance began to deteriorate. But because workers remain in the labor force for many years after completing school, the decline in school performance will continue to have a depressing effect on productivity for well into the twenty-first century.

Finally, it is worth noting that the productivity slowdown was not confined to the United States. In almost all the industralized countries the growth rate of

---

[3]One possible explanation for this paradox runs as follows. Although computers have had a major impact in many areas, the biggest changes in recent years have been in office automation. In contrast to other areas, such as production, increases in office productivity seldom lead directly to extra output that can be sold. Instead, the extra output may be an extra report to an executive, an extra draft of a regular report, or the maintenance of more extensive records. Such increased paperwork may be necessary for bureaucratic or legal purposes, but so far there is little evidence that there has been any corresponding increase in the amount or quality of final goods and services produced in the economy.

[4]See Zvi Griliches, "Productivity Puzzles and R & D: Another Nonexplanation," *Journal of Economic Perspectives* (Fall 1988), p. 19.

[5]See Martin Neil Baily and Margaret M. Blair, "Productivity and American Management," in *American Living Standards: Threats and Challenges* (Washington: Brookings Institution, 1988), pp. 178–214.

[6]See John H. Bishop, "Is the Test Score Decline Responsible for the Productivity Growth Decline?" *American Economic Review* (March 1989), pp. 178–97.

output per worker was cut to half its previous level. Even in Japan it fell from 8.5 percent per year in 1960–73 to 3.0 percent in 1973–81. Of course, the oil price shocks adversely affected all countries. In addition, some of the factors responsible for the world economic boom of 1945–73—the rebuilding of Europe and Japan, the catching up by other countries with U.S. technology, rapid growth of world trade through lowering of trade barriers, reduction of transport and communications costs, and creation of the European Common Market—were factors that could not continue at the same pace forever. As the effects of these uniquely favorable circumstances faded, some slowdown in world economic growth was to be expected and was bound to react on the United States.

Since 1980 there has been a substantial improvement in productivity in the manufacturing sector. Output per labor hour increased at an annual rate of 3.4 percent from 1979 to 1988 compared to 1.4 percent from 1973 to 1979. In many cases management has responded to increased foreign and domestic competition by laying off employees, both blue and white collar, in order to increase productivity and reduce costs. Also less efficient plants have had to close because of competitive pressures.

On the other hand, there has been a much smaller increase in productivity for the economy as a whole. For the entire private sector, output per labor hour only increased at an annual rate of 1.4 percent from 1979 to 1988, larger than the 0.8 percent average for 1973–79 but well below the 2.9 percent average for 1959–73. Thus while foreign competition has reduced employment and profits in much of manufacturing, it does appear to have been responsible for greater gains in productivity in the part of the economy that is most vulnerable to such competition.

What is likely to happen to productivity changes in the United States economy over the next couple of decades? On the favorable side, those in the baby-boom generation are now reaching their peak productivity, and there are relatively few unskilled teenagers entering the market or about to enter in the near future. As women's labor force participation continues to increase, now more women are entering the labor market with considerable human capital. These labor force changes are likely to continue and should improve the productivity outlook, other things being equal.

There is stronger evidence on the negative side. As we have seen, despite these labor force developments, the productivity of labor has been increasing only a little over 1 percent per year in the 1980s. There are several possible reasons for this low growth. First, there does not appear to have been any increase in the rate of technological change. Second, the amount of physical capital per worker has been growing very slowly since 1982. In addition, when firms do invest in either physical or human capital, they are often emphasizing more flexibility and less specialization, as a result of the increased variability of both product demand and input (especially energy) prices.[7] While less specialization reduces long-term risks, it also

---

[7]See Michael J. Piore and Charles F. Sabel, *The Second Industrial Divide* (New York: Basic Books, 1984).

may result in lower productivity gains than would occur with increasing specialization in a economy with steady stable growth.

Changes in productivity will be affected by the policies of both firms and governments. Thus far we have focused primarily on the decision making of firms. Next let us look at what government can do to increase productivity growth and thus to increase the real incomes of its constituents. First, the federal government needs to try to maintain a stable economic environment, thereby encouraging private investment by reducing uncertainty. In addition, government at all levels can increase productivity by funding basic and applied research; by disseminating both the results of this research and information on technological developments in other countries; by strengthening public education, especially in the areas of science and technology; and by strengthening competitive forces throughout the economy.

Although changes in productivity are the main determinant of changes in real wage rates, we should note that they are not the only determinant of changes in the standard of living. While the growth of productivity and real wage rates have slowed dramatically, average living standards appear to have been somewhat less affected. Living standards are also related to changes in per capita income, which has grown at a considerably faster rate than real wage rates over the past two decades because of a declining birth rate and because of the increasing labor force participation of women.[8] Borrowing from abroad has also enabled us to maintain private consumption and investment, while significantly increasing the federal deficit. As we look toward the future, however, birth rates are no longer declining, and it is unclear for how long we can continue to borrow large sums from abroad. Thus it seems likely that living standards will increase less rapidly, or at least no more rapidly, than real wage rates and productivity in coming years.

PRODUCTIVITY AND WAGES: A QUALIFICATION

The notion that in the long run the rise of real wages is linked to the rise of productivity seems so obvious that it is in danger of being misunderstood. Wage changes show a good correspondence with the movement of output per worker hour. This correspondence holds, however, only *over considerable periods of time and for the economy as a whole.* One cannot expect that wage movements and productivity movements will correspond within particular companies or industries.

The reason is that productivity trends vary widely from one branch of production to another. For the private economy as a whole, Kendrick's measure of total factor productivity rose at an average rate of 1.7 percent per year over the period 1899–1953. The rate of increase was 0.7 percent, however, in anthracite coal mining, 1.1 percent in farming, 2.0 percent in manufacturing, 3.2 percent in trans-

---

[8]For example, see Frank Levy, "Incomes, Families, and Living Standards," in *American Living Standards: Threats and Challenges,* ed. Robert E. Litan, Robert Z. Lawrence, and Charles L. Schultze (Washington: Brookings Institution, 1988), pp. 108–55.

portation, and 5.5 percent in electric utilities. Within manufacturing the productivity increase averaged only 1.0 percent in lumber products but was 4.1 percent for rubber products.[9] When one considers that these rates of increase are compounded annually, it is obvious that productivity levels had pulled very far apart by the end of the period. Taking 1899 as 100, the productivity index for anthracite coal had risen by 1953 to only 147, whereas for electric utilities it has risen to 1,764.

If, then, wage changes in each industry were geared to productivity changes *in that industry,* the wage structure would rapidly be pulled apart. Wages of workers in electric power companies would rise to fantastic heights, while miners' wagers would stagnate. Because of the transferability of labor on the supply side of the market, such extreme divergence of wages is unnecessary and unfeasible. In fact, Kendrick's calculations for thirty-three industry groups over the period 1899–1953 show no significant relation between rate of increase in factor productivity and rate of wage increase in the same industry.

What happens is, rather, that the wage level rises more or less evenly in all companies and industries (though not *entirely* evenly). The rate at which the wage tide rises is geared to the *average* rate of productivity increase in the economy. The impact of this rising tide on a particular industry depends on how its own rate of productivity increase compares with the general average.

An industry in which productivity rises faster than the wage level will experience a fall in unit labor costs and, probably, in unit total production costs. Under competitive conditions, this would mean a drop in prices—not necessarily in absolute terms but relative to prices of goods in general. Even for a monopolist a decline in unit cost will lower the profit-maximizing price. Research studies show that industries with an above-average productivity increase do in fact show a decline in relative prices. Recent examples include electric power and such manufactured products as plastics, radio and television sets, household appliances, tires and tubes, and synthetic fibers. Partly because of these relatively low prices, output and employment in such industries rise faster than in other industries. There is a marked relation over long periods between an industry's rate of productivity increase and its rate of output increase.

Industries in which output per worker-hour rises more slowly than the wage level are in a less happy position. Their unit labor costs and probably unit total costs will be rising. That will force a relative rise in their selling prices, which in turn will tend to reduce sales, output, and employment. This seems to be the situation in many of the service industries. Barbers' productivity has not increased very much over the years; and so as the general wage level has risen, the price of a haircut has gone up within living memory from fifty cents to over ten dollers—much more than the general price level. Longer hair and less frequent haircuts are a rational consumer response. In the case of products to which consumers are not strongly attached, the steady rise of costs and prices may gradually extinguish the industry. The long decline of the "legitimate theater" is a case in point.

---

[9]John W. Kendrick, *Productivity Trends in the United States* (Princeton, N.J.: Princeton University Press, 1961), pp. 136–37.

CHANGES IN FACTOR SHARES

We have argued that *in the long run* the movement of real wage rates has been dominated by upward shifts in the productivity schedule. But we have not said much about why productivity change is not a major determinant of short-run changes in real wage rates.

Average real wage rates are determined by labor's share of total income as well as by productivity. In the long run there has been little change in labor's share. During the last half of the nineteenth and the first half of the twentieth century, there was a modest increase in labor's share and a corresponding decline in capital's share of total income. Since 1950, however, there has been little long-term change. In the United States and also in much of Europe labor's share has settled down in the range of of 75 to 85 percent of total income.

Although there is no longer any appreciable long-term trend in labor's share, there is considerable variation over the business cycle. Labor's share of income produced in the private economy varies countercyclically. As output rises during an upswing, profits rise faster than output, and labor's share declines. This is usually attributed to the *capacity effect;* that is, a decline in average fixed cost and average total cost as output rises.[10] Even if the product price does not rise, this capacity effect permits a wider profit margin per unit. It is sometimes explained also by a presumed lag of wages behind prices during cycle upswings; but such a lag, if it exists at all, seems too small to make much contribution to profits.

During a decline in output these tendencies are reversed. The profit share falls and the labor share of income rises. This is noticeable in Figure 9-5 for the recession years of 1938, 1946, 1949, 1954, 1958, 1970, 1974 and 1982. One moral is that conclusions about long-run changes in labor's share should be based on averages for a period of years rather than one single-year comparison. For example, a comparison of the boom year 1966 with the recession year 1974 would seem to show a marked rise in labor's share. But that may be due entirely to differences in utilization of plant capacity.

One reason that labor's share of total income rises during a recession is the reluctance of employers to layoff workers in whom they have made a considerable investment. Layoffs obviously do occur, but only when a firm believes they are essential to reduce costs. Partly because of this reluctance and partly because the firm often cannot use its physical capital as effectively at lower levels of output, productivity falls when demand declines during a recession. Typically, however, there is little change in real wage rates during a recession, so labor's share increases. As a result there is no short-term relation between productivity changes and wage rates. Thus we need to focus on long-term productivity changes in examining the effect of productivity on wage rates.

---

[10]The underlying assumption is that in recession years many firms are operating to the left of the minimum point on their average total cost curves. For manufacturing, at least, there seems good warrant for this assumption. The minimum point on the average total cost (*ATC*) curve is usually estimated at about 90 percent of physical plant capacity. During recession years since 1945, output rates have typically been in the range of 80 percent to 85 percent of capacity.

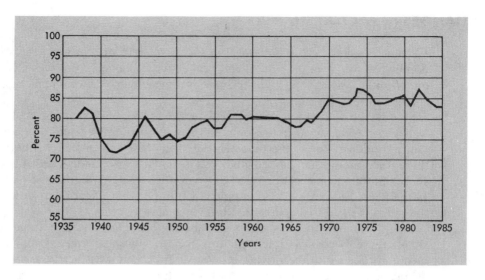

FIGURE 9-5 Employee Compensation as a Percentage of Income Produced, 1937–
85, for All Corporate Business

In part, the productivity slowdown since 1970 has resulted from weak demand in the economy over much of this period. The slowdown has lasted long enough, however, for it to have had a significant effect on the growth of real wage rates, as we showed in Table 9-1.

In the past economists focused much attention on changes in labor's share of income, more so than we do today. Now economists look primarily at the size distribution of income.

CHANGES IN THE DISTRIBUTION OF WAGES

As interest in factor shares has diminished, economists now focus more attention on the size distribution of incomes. This is an important complicated topic, about which we can only say a few words here.

From the viewpoint of labor economics, probably the most noteworthy finding has been an increase in the inequality of earnings in recent years.[11] Results for 1963–86 for one measure of earnings inequality are presented in Figure 9-6. These figures show a decrease in inequality from the early 1960s to the mid-1970s, followed by an increase in inequality since then. Others, using different data, have

---

[11]For example, see Bennett Harrison and Barry Bluestone, *The Great U-Turn* (New York: Basic Books, 1988), Chap. 5, and Michael W. Horrigan and Steven Haugen, "The Declining Middle-Class Thesis: A Sensitivity Analysis," *Monthly Labor Review* (May 1988), pp. 3–14, and *A Future of Lousy Jobs?* ed. Gary Burtless (Washington: The Brookings Institution, 1990).

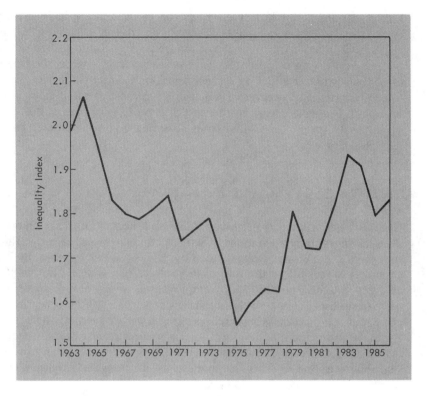

FIGURE 9-6   Inequality in Annual Wages and Salaries, 1963–86
(decycled)

Note: The data reflect the variance in the logarithm of annual wages and salaries of all U.S. workers aged sixteen and over. The raw data on the variance in wages drawn directly from computer analysis of the data from *CPS* have been adjusted for variations in the business cycle so that the figure represents underlying trends rather than simply the fluctuations associated with years of expansion and recession. This economic decycling was accomplished in a two-stage regression: the logarithm of GNP was first regressed against a straight time trend, and the resulting residuals were then used to decycle the earnings data.

Source: Special tabulations from the March issues of the U.S. Census Bureau, *Current Population Survey*, 1964–1987. Adapted from Bennett Harrison and Barry Bluestone, *The Great U-Turn* (New York: Basic Books, Inc., 1988), p. 119.

found an increasing inequality throughout the period.[12] The increase in earnings inequality is quite pronounced among men but not among women.

The causes of the recent increase in earnings inequality are not well understood. Part of the explanation is an increase in the percentage of part-time workers. Still, there has been a significant increase in inequality even if we focus entirely on

---

[12]See W. Norton Grubb and Robert H. Wilson, "Sources of Increasing Inequality in Wages and Salaries, 1960–1980," *Monthly Labor Review* (April 1989), pp. 3–13.

hourly earnings. For hourly earnings the main increase in inequality appears to come from increasing inequality of earnings across industries, especially from differences in productivity growth across industries.[13] As indicated earlier, in a competitive economy long-run differences in productivity growth across industries should have their primary effect on the distribution of employment not wage rates. Over the course of many years, this conclusion is almost certainly applicable to the U.S. economy. Over the course of the past fifteen or twenty years, however, changes in productivity growth across industries do appear to have increased earnings inequality significantly.

THE MONEY WAGE LEVEL AND INFLATION

Next we discuss changes in money wages and their relation to inflation. As we have seen, changes in living standards depend on changes in real wage rates, where the real wage is the money wage divided by the cost of living. Does the rate of increase of money wages affect the rate of increase of real wages and thus lead directly to changes in living standards? For employees as a whole, the answer is no. A faster increase in the average level of money wages will be about offset by a faster rate of price increases. Real wage increases depend on productivity increases. Increases in the money rate and inflation introduce more uncertainty into the economy and, as a result, may decrease productivity and real wage rates. In any event, there is no reason why a long-run increase in money wage rates and inflation will increase real wages.

Why, then, is there so much conflict over money wage increases? The reason is that these increases affect the *relative* position of different groups of workers. A group that wins increases larger than the average for all workers can improve its real wage position. A group that obtains below-average increases will lose in real wages. The struggle over money wages is a struggle for relative advantage.[14]

The average rate of increase in money wages mainly affects the rate of price increase—the *inflation rate;* and both rates are related to the level of economic activity. During an economic upswing, growing tightness of labor markets eventually leads to a faster rise in money wages, which is accompanied by a higher inflation rate. During a recession the inflation rate falls but only moderately and with considerable lag. Overall, the years since 1945 show a marked uptrend in both money wage and price levels. The economy seems now to have a strong inflationary bias.

We cannot go into depth about the causes and consequences of inflation;

---

[13]See Linda A. Bell and Richard B. Freeman, "The Facts about Rising Industrial Wage Dispersion in the U.S.", *Industrial Relations Research Association Proceedings,* December 1986, pp. 331–37; Chris Tilly, Barry Bluestone, and Bennett Harrison, "What is Making American Wages More Unequal?" ibid., pp. 338–48; and Grubb and Wilson, "Sources of Increasing Inequality."

[14]This struggle over money wages and relative position is related to unionization. In this chapter we focus on the issue of average wage rates and their relation to inflation. In Chap. 20 we consider the effect of unions on wage rates, including the inflationary impact of unions.

but we can offer some comments, focused mainly on the role of wages in inflationary movements.

The traditional explanation of inflation attributes it to excessive aggregate demand for goods and labor. Inflation occurs, it is argued, when demand rises above the productive capacity of the economy, when there is "too much money chasing too few goods." In this model one has *either* unemployment, when aggregate demand is below capacity, *or* inflation, when aggregate demand exceeds capacity, but never both at the same time. The policy moral is clear: Use monetary and fiscal instruments to hold aggregate demand just a bit below output capacity, in which case the price level will remain stable.

This rather comfortable model, unfortunately, does not correspond with experience in recent decades. Experience contradicts it in three respects: (1) Inflation is a normal fact of life, not an unusual occurrence. In no year since 1949 has the general price level remained stable. (2) During an economic upswing, the inflation rate begins to rise well before the economy reaches capacity operation. (3) During a downswing, when the economy is operating below capacity, prices do not fall as they would in the traditional model. On the contrary, they continue to rise, though generally more slowly. We have both excessive unemployment *and* inflation. These are the awkward facts we must try to explain.

The Underlying Rate of Inflation

The rate of inflation at any time is related to the rate of increase in production costs and in money demand, both of which depend mainly on the rate of wage increase. On the cost side, the arithmetic is as follows: Suppose the annual rate of increase in labor productivity is 1 percent. If, then, the hourly cost of labor to employers (including fringe benefits as well as direct wage payments) is also rising at 1 percent, *labor cost per unit* of output will remain unchanged. But if labor costs rise faster than productivity, unit labor cost will increase. If labor cost per worker-hour in a particular year rises by 5 percent, while output per worker-hour rises only 1 percent, then unit labor cost will rise by 4 percent. It is a good guess that non-agricultural prices will also rise by 4 percent.

Leaving aside farm prices, in which movements are somewhat different, the *prices of nonagricultural products move very closely with unit labor costs*. Figure 9-7 shows an index of unit labor costs and of prices from 1947 to 1985. The close parallelism of the two series is evident.

Why should prices behave in this way? The behavior is compatible with the hypothesis that industrial prices are set by a percentage markup over unit labor cost and that this percentage is relatively stable.[15] Many companies, particularly oligopolists with market power, seem to behave in this way. But we do not assert that all prices are determined by such a markup—simply that the price level behaves *as if* the principle were widely followed.

---

[15]For an example of such a model, see Oliver J. Blanchard, "The Wage Price Spiral," *Quarterly Journal of Economics* (August 1986), pp. 543–65.

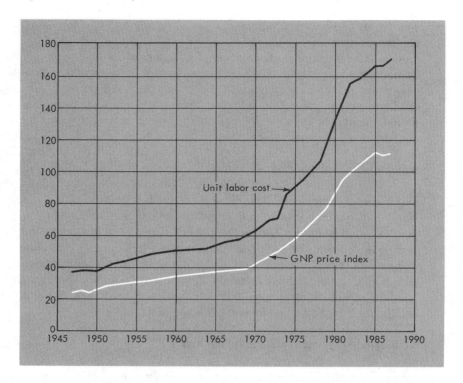

FIGURE 9-7   Unit Labor Costs and GNP Price Index for the Private Nonfarm
Economy, 1947–87 (1977=100)

Source: Data are from *Economic Report of the President*, 1990 (Washington, D.C.: Government Printing Office).

To round out the picture, the rate of increase in prices—specifically, retail prices to consumers—feeds back into the rate of wage increase. If prices have been rising at 6 percent a year and are expected to continue rising at this rate in the year ahead, then workers will expect larger wage increases than if prices had remained stable, in order to "stay ahead of the cost of living." They may expect increases of, say, 6 percent. If they get these increases, and if productivity rises at the normal 2 percent, then prices will indeed rise at the expected 4 percent. The expectation is self-fulfilling. The 4 percent increase will produce demands for another 6 percent wage increase next year, and so on. This is what is meant by the phrase "wage-price-wage spiral." The 4 percent used in this illustration is also called the *underlying rate of inflation.*

All this clearly has monetary implications. The faster the rate of price increase, the faster the rise of GNP measured in current dollars. Since demand for money depends heavily on money GNP, the demand for money will be rising. So a persistent inflationary movement implies willingness of the monetary authorities to satisfy this demand by raising the money supply.

A rising price level can always be ascribed to monetary causes in the sense that the monetary authorities *could,* by curbing the rate of increase in money supply and raising interest rates, bring on a recession that would decelerate the wage-price increase but at the cost of rising unemployment. This approach has serious costs, both economically and politically. If inflation is rising and perceived to be an especially serious problem, however, then the Federal Reserve System (the Fed) may pursue such a strategy, as it did from 1979 to 1982.

Acceleration on the Upswing

When a business cycle upswing carries beyond a certain point, the inflation rate begins to rise. There are several reasons for this, including the behavior of raw material prices and supply bottlenecks in particular industries. But the most important reason is an accelerated rise in labor costs.

As the unemployed pool shrinks during an upswing, employers are forced increasingly to bid against each other for workers of acceptable quality. Pressure to raise wages will impinge initially on the lowest-wage companies, as described in Chapter 7; and for a while the higher-wage companies may be content to see their wage premium narrow. Eventually, however, they too will raise wages to restore something like their customary advantage, thereby restoring the pressure on the low-wage employers.

In addition to bidding up hourly rates, employers will tend to relax their hiring standards and accept workers of lower productivity, which again will raise unit labor costs. There will also be an increase in overtime work, which must be paid for at premium rates.

There have been numerous efforts to estimate the unemployment rate below which inflation will tend to accelerate. This rate is called the *nonaccelerating inflationary rate of unemployment* (NAIRU), or the natural rate of unemployment, and is currently considered to be approximately 6 percent.

Recent structural changes in the economy have changed the unemployment-inflation dilemma in several ways. First, increases in the proportion of the labor force represented by young people and by women with little human capital increased the nonacceleration rate of unemployment in the seventies, but declines in the number of young workers reduced it in the eighties. Second, the decline in productivity growth has narrowed the gap between the rate of increase in wages and prices. With 3 percent productivity growth, a 5 percent annual rate of wage increase would mean an underlying inflation rate of 2 percent. But with 1 percent productivity growth, the same rate of wage increase will mean an underlying inflation rate of 4 percent.

Slow Deceleration on the Downswing

It is not hard to explain why inflation accelerates toward the peak of a business cycle. Such behavior has been characteristic of cyclical upswings before and after 1940. What is harder to explain is wage-price behavior on the downswing. Before 1940 prices normally fell on the downswing, offsetting the rise on the upswing and maintaining rough stability of prices over the long run. Now that no longer happens. Wages and prices continue to rise during recession, though typically at a lower rate than before. When there is a large surplus of unemployed workers, why don't wages fall or, at any rate, stop rising?

One reason, underlined in Chapters 6 and 7, is the continuity of the employment relation. It is not worthwhile for a company to always drive the hardest possible wage bargain or to continually replace higher-paid labor with lower-paid labor. Rather, the company wants to protect its investment in its present labor force and to keep employees contented and productive by meeting their wage expectations. These expectations now call for a sizable annual increase in money wages, partly to offset cost-of-living increases, partly in the hope of getting ahead of these increases and winning improved living standards. Such expectations can be reduced, as they were for many workers during the recession of 1982–83, but only at the cost of high unemployment.

COPING WITH INFLATION

Unlike unemployment, inflation involves no direct loss of output or income. But inflation, or more correctly *unanticipated inflation,* does redistribute income among groups in the economy. Borrowers benefit at the expense of lenders, since they are able to repay their loans in depreciated dollars. Any group whose money income rises less rapidly than the price level suffers a loss in real income. This is true particularly of people living on fixed incomes. Groups whose incomes rise faster than prices are winners in the inflation lottery.

Inflation has other undesirable side effects. It undermines people's belief in the stability of money values and discourages saving. It distorts business calculations, typically leading to understatement of depreciation requirements and hence an overstatement of profits. Since the corporate income tax is based on reported (money) profits, businesses are overtaxed. So were individuals, before the indexing of income tax brackets that took effect in 1985. Inflation increases tension and bickering among economic groups, each fearing that it will be left behind in the inflation race.

For all these reasons people just do not like inflation. Economists, too, would agree that an economy with low or zero inflation is preferable to one with chronic high inflation. Differences of opinion relate mainly to methods of inflation control. We shall look briefly at three approaches: *creating economic slack,* attention to *supply and production costs,* and direct government pressure on wages and prices, usually called *incomes policy.* These are not necessarily alternatives but in principle can be used together to work down the inflation rate.

Creating Economic Slack

This remedy is the traditional one, on which policy makers still mainly rely. If inflation is high and accelerating, the Fed can always apply the monetary brakes. By reducing the growth rate of money supply and raising interest rates, the Fed can slow the growth of aggregate demand and even bring on a recession. To a considerable extent, recessions are now deliberate, aimed at reducing the inflation rate.[16] This remedy is unpopular, since it involves a substantial increase in unemployment. When recession sets in, there is strong pressure to shift back to an expansionist course—lower interest rates, tax cuts, and so on.

But suppose the brakes were kept on. Could the inflation rate be reduced as much as we wish? The answer (ignoring external supply shocks) appears to be yes—but only gradually and at considerable cost in lost output and employment. The period of 1980–83 is usually cited as a case in point. The Federal Reserve System followed a generally restrictive policy, involving unusually high rates of interest. This policy helped to bring on a short recession in 1980 and a more severe recession in 1982–83, during which the full-time unemployment rate reached a peak of 11 percent. The inflation rate did respond. The Consumer Price Index had risen by 13.3 percent in 1979 and by 12.2 percent in 1980. In the years 1982–85, the rate of increase was only about 4 percent.

This deceleration in the rate of price increases was accompanied by a parallel deceleration in the rate of wage increases. As the surplus of unemployed workers grew, and as employers' profits were trimmed by recession, the rate of wage increases fell sharply. In the years 1981–83 many workers, and even many union workers, experienced either a wage freeze or an actual cut in wage rates. For the private nonagricultural economy the rate of increase in average hourly earnings fell from 9 percent in 1980 to 4.6 percent in 1983. Rather surprisingly, it continued to fall to 2.4 percent in 1987, even though output was rising and unemployment was falling. Why was this? a continuing aftershock from the recession? the effect of declining union influence? Whatever the reason, the rate of wage increases did not start to go back up until unemployment fell below 6 percent in 1988. Even then there was only a very modest acceleration of money wages. The moderate pace of wage increases helps to explain why inflation did not re-ignite during the upswing in the economy during the latter 1980s.

There is general agreement that it is impossible to make a transition from a higher to a lower level of inflation without macroeconomic restraint. The cost of such a transition is the loss of output and employment during a policy-induced recession. There have been several attempts to estimate the *sacrifice ratio,* that is, the percentage loss of potential output required to lower the inflation rate by 1 percent. On reasonable assumptions it comes out around 3 percent, though some estimates are even higher. The policy issue at any time is whether the inflation rate is high enough so that the price of reducing it is worth paying.

---

[16]An interesting concept that has surfaced in this connection is that of the *political business cycle.* The idea is that if a newly elected president wants to attack inflation, he or she should bring on a recession *early* in the administration. Then, after applying the medicine for a year or so, the president can reverse course and raise aggregate demand, so that employment is moving briskly upward by the time of the next election. Models of voting behavior suggest that voters are strongly influenced by the *rate of change* in output and employment during the year before that vote. President Carter mistimed his recession for 1980, just before the election, and suffered accordingly. President Reagan's recession hit bottom in December 1982, and the vigorous recovery in 1983 and 1984 helped keep him in office for a second term.

A further policy issue is whether the pain involved in the transition to a lower inflation rate—the length and severity of recession—can be reduced by using auxiliary devices *in support* of macroeconomic restraint. The two devices commonly suggested are measures affecting supply and costs of production and wage-price restraint or incomes policy.

Supply and Production Costs

As we have seen, productivity growth is highly important. If aggregate demand is rising at 5 percent yer year, the inflation rate will be lower if aggregate supply is rising at 4 percent than if it is rising at only 2 percent.

Government can do a variety of things to encourage research and development, stimulate business investment, increase the human capital stock, and otherwise raise the growth rate of output capacity. But we should realize that these measures are slow moving. Over ten or twenty years it might raise output capacity considerably, but it will not do much to lower the inflation rate this year or next year.

Other policies also need to be considered. During an economic upswing some industries hit capacity earlier than others. Price increases in these bottleneck industries—which are often industries producing raw materials, machine tools, or other producers' goods—then become cost increases for other industries, intensifying upward pressure on the price level. It is mainly the responsibility of the companies involved to foresee such capacity bottlenecks and to avert them by building new capacity in anticipation of future increases in demand. But government can play a useful monitoring and advisory role and can sometimes provide incentives for capacity increases that would not otherwise be undertaken. (French experience with "indicative planning" since the 1940s suggests the usefulness of systematic consultation between government and industry experts in comparing demand and supply estimates for some years ahead and in considering the amount of investment needed to avert supply bottlenecks.)

Government itself is the most important price fixer in the economy. It sets minimum wages, whose impact ramifies up through the lower levels of the wage structure. It sets minimum prices for many farm products through the price support system; tariff rates and import quotas, which raise the price of many manufactured goods; minimum rates for rail, air, and truck transportation; and maximum prices for electric power and telephone service.

Pressure on government to adjust these prices comes mainly from producer groups and is consistently in one direction—upward. Thus, on the one hand, political leaders denounce inflation as a national evil, while at the same time their microeconomic actions contribute to inflation. This paradox cannot be removed entirely. But it could be ameliorated by anything that would reduce the political influence of producers, would build up counterpressure from consumers, or would permit systematic intervention by agencies concerned with macroeconomic objectives in making microdecisions. The recent progress of deregulation is encouraging and has lowered transportation prices.

The logic of the approach suggested in this section has been well summarized by Lindbeck:[17]

> It is important to stress that there are at least two different kinds of "fine tuning." *One* type is that the government tries continuously to keep aggregate demand very close to the capacity ceiling of the economy, which tends to create a situation with excess demand ["bottlenecks"] in many sectors simultaneously with excess supply ["slack"] in others. It was this type of fine tuning which ran into severe difficulties in the late 1960s and early 1970s.
>
> A *different* type of fine tuning . . . is to be very "modest" with expansions of aggregate demand after a rather high, but not quite "full" level of capacity utilization has already been reached, and instead try to achieve full employment by way of factor mobility policies and selective demand and supply management. [p. 9]

Incomes Policy

But isn't there another way out? Why can't we, like King Canute, wave our arms at the incoming tide of wage and price increases and say "Stop." Efforts to impose direct restraint on wage and price increases, by various combinations of persuasion and coercion, are usually called *incomes policy*.

The central idea is to convince the different groups in the economy who are contending for larger incomes that there is only so much to go around. People's *real* incomes can increase year by year only by as much as the *real* output of the economy rises. Efforts to get more than this by raising *money* incomes are bound, for society as a whole, to be self-defeating. Inflation can be regarded, indeed, as a process of adjustment of the economy to a set of inconsistent claims, with some groups being disappointed at each point. Somebody *has* to be disappointed if money claims add up to more than the economy can produce.

The policy dilemma is this: At one extreme, mere coaxing of companies and unions to "be reasonable" cannot have much effect. Everyone will pay lip service to the desirability of avoiding inflation but then will go ahead and do whatever self-interest dictates in the circumstances. At the other extreme, a comprehensive system of legal controls over wages and prices, like those used during World War II and again during the Korean War, is unfeasible under peacetime conditions.

The obvious political objection to comprehensive wage and price control is that business and labor leaders are resolutely opposed to it, and so it cannot win either congressional approval or the degree of voluntary compliance needed to supplement legal procedures. But equally serious, from an economic standpoint alone, such a system would have undesirable side effects. The reason is that in a market economy *specific* wages and prices typically change at different rates, depending on supply and demand shifts in particular markets. These diverse movements serve the function of balancing the quantities supplied and demanded in each market in the short run and of reallocating productive resources in the long run. A

---

[17]Assar Lindbeck, "Stabilization Policy in Open Economics with Endogenous Politicians," *American Economic Review* (May 1976), pp. 1–19.

control system, which tends to impose uniform rules based on "fairness," retards these desirable adjustments and may even prevent them.

There are many reasons why wages for a particular kind of labor may rise more (or less) rapidly than wages in general. For example, it is natural and desirable for wages in a particular occupation to rise faster than other wages if (1) demand for this kind of labor is rising rapidly, so that higher wages are needed to recruit additional workers; (2) there has been a change in the nature of the job—it has become harder or more unpleasant, or it has become more skilled, requiring a longer period of training; or (3) there has been a shift in workers' tastes away from the kind of work in question—fewer people want to be coal miners or domestic servants. One would expect wages for these jobs to rise faster than wages in general because of the shrinkage of supply.

Now suppose a control board lays down the principle that no wage shall rise by more than 4 percent a year, and suppose market conditions for a particular job call for a 6 percent increase. The fact that the wage rate is pegged *below* the market level will lead to a shortage of labor for that job. The free flow of labor in response to market conditions has been blocked.

The same reasoning applies to product prices, which are typically changing at quite different rates. If the Consumer Price Index (CPI) is rising at 4 percent per year, some prices will be falling, others rising at 2 percent, others at 6 percent or 8 percent. The basic reason, over the long run, is differing behavior of production costs. Some industries are more successful than others in raising productivity and reducing cost through technological progress.

These differential price movements serve a valuable economic function. Industries that manage to reduce their selling prices relative to other industries can increase their sales to consumers, expand their production facilities, and make still further gains in productivity in a continuing "virtuous circle." Conversely, products whose costs and prices remain relatively high will find their market shrinking. Thus productive resources flow toward those sectors of the economy in which technical progress is most rapid. A price control system need not permanently block such adjustments, but it does tend to retard them.

There is the further difficulty that a price fixed below the equilibrium level creates a shortage of the good in question. The quantity demanded exceeds the quantity supplied. So whose demands will be satisfied and whose will not? Unless a rationing system is introduced, this question will be decided by informal, haphazard methods—for example, by motorists lining up at the gas pumps. There will also be a strong incentive for sellers to charge black market prices above the legal maximum, or to evade controls by reducing product quality. To prevent such actions will require a substantial enforcement staff. War conditions apart, it seems doubtful that the benefits are worth the administrative costs plus the disruption of the market mechanism.

Inflation generates additional conflict and uncertainty, thus hurting the economy. As we have stressed in this chapter, however, a more important issue is the behavior of real wage rates. Increased inflation in the 1970s may have contributed to the low growth rate of productivity and real wage rates in the 1970s and 80s. Yet many other factors also have contributed to the productivity slowdown.

SUMMARY

1. Labor's real wage depends mainly on the national productivity schedule and the quantity of labor employed. The productivity schedule normally moves upward over time, and the real wage level rises at roughly the same rate.

2. The rate of productivity increase depends not only on investment in physical capital but also on technical change, which makes capital more productive; on accumulation of human capital; on improvements in economic management; and on other intangible factors.

3. The rate of productivity increase slowed dramatically after 1973 and has remained low in the 1980s. Reasons for the initial slowdown include two unusually severe recessions, a large influx of inexperienced workers into the labor force, a lower rate of investment, diversion of considerable investment to environmental protection and to energy conservation in response to higher oil prices, a lower rate of technological change and innovation, and a decline in school performance. Some, but not all, of these factors have continued to the present time.

4. There has been little change in labor's share of national income since about 1950. The inequality of labor income has increased in recent years owing partly to an increase in earnings inequality across industries.

5. The inflation rate at any time is closely related to the rate of increase in labor costs per unit of output, that is, the rate of increase in money wages minus the rate of increase in productivity. This is usually called the *underlying rate of inflation.*

6. During a business cycle upswing, when output rises above a certain level and unemployment falls below a certain level, the inflation rate will begin to rise. The point at which this happens is called the *nonaccelerating inflationary (or natural) rate of unemployment,* currently estimated at about 6 percent. During a business cycle downswing the rate of increase in wages and prices falls, but with considerable lag, and never to zero.

7. The traditional method of reducing the inflation rate is to bring on a recession through monetary restriction; but this is very costly in terms of output and employment. Other approaches include incomes policies and reducing bottlenecks in supply.

KEY CONCEPTS

REAL WAGE RATE
MARGINAL PRODUCTIVITY SCHEDULE, NATIONAL
TECHNOLOGICAL CHANGE

THE PRODUCTIVITY SLOWDOWN
INCOME, LABOR SHARE
EARNINGS INEQUALITY

INFLATION	UNEMPLOYMENT, NONACCELERATING INFLA-
INFLATION, UNANTICIPATED	TIONARY RATE OF (NAIRU)
INFLATION, UNDERLYING RATE OF	INCOMES POLICY

REVIEW QUESTIONS

1. How can the real wage per worker-hour rise even in years when national output is falling?

2. In neoclassical or marginal productivity theory, what determines the level of real wages at a particular time? What assumptions underlie the reasoning?

3. "Wages depend basically on productivity. So to determine how much wages should be raised this year in a particular company or industry, one need look only at the increase in output per hour." Discuss.

4. How might one expect wages, prices, output, and employment to change over the course of time in an industry with zero productivity increase?

5. Why has productivity growth slowed in recent years? Why is this productivity slowdown an important issue?

6. Is the rate of productivity increase during the 1980s likely to recover from the low level of the 1970s? Why or why not?

7. Does an increase in money wages necessarily mean an increase in real wages:
   (a) in a single industry?
   (b) in the economy as a whole?

8. What is meant by the *underlying rate of inflation?* What information would you need to estimate this rate for the year ahead?

9. Do you think that incomes policy can contribute to control of inflation? If not, why not? If so, what features would you build into an incomes policy?

READINGS

BAILY, MARTIN NEIL, "What Has Happened to Productivity Growth?" *Science,* October 24, 1986, pp. 443–51.

BAUMOL, WILLIAM J., SUE ANN BATEY BLACKMAN, and EDWARD N. WOLFF, *Productivity and American Leadership: The Long View.* Cambridge, MA: MIT Press, 1989.

FLANAGAN, ROBERT, DAVID SOSKICE, and LLOYD ULMAN, *Unionism, Economic Stabilization, and Incomes Policy.* Washington, D.C.: Brookings Institution, 1983.

HICKS, SIR JOHN, *The Theory of Wages,* 2d ed. New York: St. Martin's Press, 1966.

LITAN, ROBERT E., ROBERT Z. LAWRENCE, and CHARLES L. SCHULTZE, eds., *American Living Standards: Threats and Challenges.* Washington, D.C.: Brookings Institution, 1988.

OKUN, ARTHUR M., and GEORGE L. PERRY, eds., *Curing Chronic Inflation.* Washington, D.C.: Brookings Institution, 1978.

10

UNEMPLOYMENT

High unemployment, together with inflation, has been a major problem of our economy in recent years. In this chapter we begin by defining unemployment and discussing how the unemployment rate is used as a measure of economic performance. Next we analyze different kinds of unemployment: frictional, structural, and deficient demand. Although interrelated, each has its own causes and costs. With this conceptual material as background, we discuss how unemployment varies for different demographic groups and how it has been changing over time. We also discuss the issue of deindustrialization and the problem of displaced workers, who after losing a long-term job, have to take a much lower paying position. We conclude with a discussion of policy issues including unemployment insurance, job search assistance, public employment programs, and policies to reduce deficient-demand unemployment by making wage rates more flexible.

UNEMPLOYMENT: MEANING AND MEASUREMENT

To be unemployed means to be without a job but looking for work. Since the national unemployment rate receives so much attention, let us look more carefully at the source of these figures. Every month in the Current Population Survey the federal government interviews a sample of about seventy thousand households. The interviewer asks what each household member was doing in the previous week. People who did any work for pay, part time or full time, are counted as employed.

People who had a job but were not working because of a temporary layoff or because they had not yet started on a new job are counted as unemployed. For a person without a job, the interviewer asks: "Has he [or she] been looking for work in the last four weeks?" Those looking for work are considered unemployed. Those not looking are classified as not in the labor force.

On closer examination, however, the line between unemployment and not being in the labor force is quite fuzzy. The concept of "looking for work" is ambiguous. Looking, but how hard? If not, why not? If you ask those not looking for work whether they would like a regular job, a sizable number will answer yes.[1] A common reason for not seeking work is a belief that there are no jobs for which the person could qualify. People who would like a job but who have stopped looking because of a belief that no jobs are available are usually called *discouraged workers.* Unfortunately, it is difficult to obtain reliable information on the number of discouraged workers.

The official unemployment rate is the unemployed as a percentage of all those in the labor force (those working or unemployed). Although the official unemployment rate receives by far the most attention, there are many other measures that are of some interest. Some of these are presented in Table 10-1. In 1989, when the official unemployment rate was 5.2 percent, the alternative measures range from 1.1 percent who were long-term unemployed (over fifteen weeks) to 7.2 percent when unemployment is adjusted for part-time employment and job seeking. As we shall see shortly, the unemployment rate is especially useful as a measure of changes in economic performance. In general, the different unemployment rates presented in Table 10-1 all increase or decrease when aggregate demand changes in the economy, although the first two measures (long-term unemployment and unemployed job losers) increase in relative magnitude during recession periods.

Uses of Unemployment Rates

Unemployment figures come in for much criticism. One reason is that people have different purposes in mind, and no one measure can serve all purposes. So it is worthwhile to ask: What are the various questions we might ask about the economy, and what measure of unemployment is relevant in each case?

1. A Business-Cycle Indicator. Here the crude full-time unemployment rate performs well. It typically begins to shoot up when economic activity turns down and continues to rise throughout the recession. Indeed, the unemployment rate may go on rising for some months after an economic upswing has begun. (The reason is that the labor force is rising month by month. Only when the economy has built up enough steam so that the number of new jobs created exceeds the increase in the labor force will the unemployment rate begin to drop.) With some lag,

---

[1]See evidence on this point in Kim B. Clark and Lawrence H. Summers, "Labor and Unemployment: A Reconsideration," *Brookings Papers on Economic Activity* (1979), pp. 13–66.

TABLE 10-1   Different Unemployment Rates

UNEMPLOYMENT RATE CONCEPT	PERCENT, 1989
Total unemployed, as percent of the labor force (standard official measure)	5.2
Persons unemployed 15 weeks or longer as a percent of the civilian labor force	1.1
Unemployed job losers as a percent of the civilian labor force	2.4
Unemployed married men as a percent of the married male labor force	3.0
Unemployed full-time job seekers, as percent of full-time labor force	5.4
Unemployed full-time job seekers plus half unemployed part-time job seekers plus half those involuntarily on part time because of economic reasons as a percent of the labor force minus half of part-time labor force	7.2

Source: *Employment and Earnings*, January 1990.

however, the unemployment rate does turn down and continues to fall throughout the upswing.

2. A Hardship Indicator.   When one reads in the newspaper that seven million Americans are without work, one is apt to conclude that this many people are suffering. The term *unemployed* conjures up a picture of a person with a family of five who has been out of work for months and who has no other source of income. There are such people, but they are a distinct minority of the unemployed. A more frequent case, at least when the economy is not in recession, is an unemployed teenager, enrolled in school, living with his or her parents, and seeking part-time work.

A person unemployed for a month or so between jobs, as many millions are each year, does not suffer serious hardship. Workers on temporary layoff from jobs to which they will return in a few weeks or months are not really out on the street. Sources of income support during longer spells of unemployment are much larger than they were in earlier times: state unemployment compensation payments, which during recessions are usually extended to thirty-nine or even fifty-two weeks; supplementary unemployment benefits negotiated by unions in some industries; earnings of a second wage earner in the family; publicly financed food stamp and medical-care programs.

Much unemployment does cause serious hardship. Certainly, during a recession the amount of hardship increases substantially. But to determine how much, one must look below the totals to just who is unemployed, for how long, and with what other sources of support.

Unemployment is not the best measure of economic hardship. For most purposes a better measure of hardship is whether a person is living in *poverty*. The official definition of poverty is based on family income relative to family size. A family may be poor even though no one in it is unemployed. Age or disability may keep family members from working even if jobs are available. Or the family may be poor even if all adults are working throughout the year. This situation is likely when skill levels are low, family size large and especially when only one parent is present.

3. A Measure of Economic Performance. In addition to the hardship that it causes for many individuals, unemployment is also important as a measure of the overall performance of the economy. When the unemployment rate is high, output is low. When unemployment rises, profits decline more dramatically than labor earnings. Investment also falls. Thus labor will have less, and older, capital to work with in the future. Thus the costs of unemployment in terms of lost output and income, both now and in the future, are much larger than the output that could have been produced by the unemployed workers themselves. Even if we limit ourselves to the short-run relation between unemployment and total output (GNP), each one-percentage-point increase in the unemployment rate is associated with a decrease of more than 2 percent in GNP in the economy.[2]

4. A Target for Macroeconomic Policy. The federal government has monetary and fiscal instruments that can be used either to stimulate or to restrain economic activity; and an important policy issue at any time is what degree of stimulus or restraint is desirable. Although unemployment rates alone cannot answer this question, they can provide useful information.

An important concept is NAIRU, the nonaccelerating inflationary rate of unemployment, discussed on page 263. This rate is generally considered to be about 6 percent. Of course, an unemployment rate of 6 percent need not be accepted as a policy target. As we shall see, economic policy can reduce this rate to some extent. In addition, policymakers must balance a variety of economic objectives. The extra output that can be gained by temporarily reducing unemployment below its natural rate may be judged as worth the cost. But the costs in terms of building more inflation into the economy must also be considered. From a long-run perspective, avoiding inflation is generally preferred, since it is much more costly to reduce inflation once it has begun than to keep inflation from starting.

FLOWS THROUGH THE LABOR MARKET

It is perhaps natural to think of the employed and the unemployed as separate, stationary groups. The employed are working away at their regular jobs month after month. The unemployed are surplus labor, sitting on the side in a stagnant

---

[2]The relation between unemployment and GNP was first studied by Arthur Okun, who estimated a relation of 3 percent change in GNP for each one-percentage-point increase in the unemployment rate. More recent estimates are somewhat smaller but still greater than two to one. See Robert J. Gordon and Robert E. Hall, "Arthur M. Okun 1928–80," *Brookings Papers on Economic Activity,* 1980–81, pp. 1–5.

pool. This is by no means the case. In any month of the year millions of people are losing jobs, while other millions are finding new jobs. There is a large back-and-forth movement between the employed and unemployed groups. There are also large flows into and out of the labor force.

The size of these flows is suggested in Figure 10-1. The number of manufacturing workers losing jobs (*separations*) and the number of workers being hired (*accessions*) are typically 4 to 5 percent of total manufacturing employment *per month*. The main reason for permanent separation from a job is quitting. Workers may also be laid off, but half or more of these workers eventually return to work with the same employer. In the case of unionized establishments, the union contract usually provides that laid-off employees must be recalled to work before new employees are hired.

Layoffs and quits fluctuate in opposite directions with the swings of the business cycle. Quits rise in prosperous years when job opportunities are plentiful, such as 1950–53, 1964–69, 1973–73, 1976–79, and 1988–89; and they fall in recession years when jobs are harder to find, such as 1954, 1958, 1961, 1971, 1974–75, and 1981–83. Layoff rates move in the opposite direction, rising in recession, falling during economic upswings.

A more complete view of labor market flows is provided in Figure 10-2. At

FIGURE 10-1   Accessions, Separations, Quits, and Layoffs: Annual Average of Monthly Rates, U.S. Manufacturing

Source: *Employment and Earnings*, 1980. The data are not available after 1979.

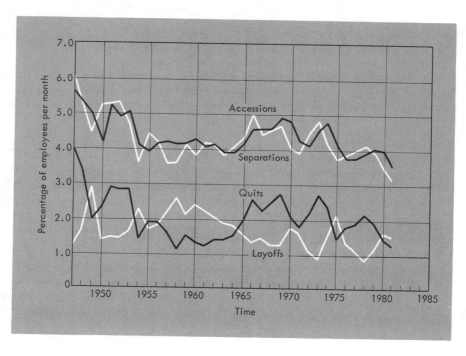

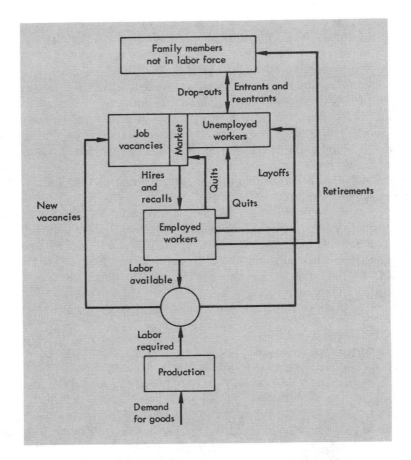

FIGURE 10-2 Flows and Stocks of Workers and Jobs

Source: Adapted from Charles C. Holt, "Improving the Labor Market Trade-Off Between Inflation and Unemployment," *American Economic Review* (May 1969), pp. 135–46.

the bottom of the diagram is the production apparatus of the economy. Total demand for output rises at an erratic pace over the course of time, generating demand for additional workers. Rising demand for labor creates job vacancies, which appear on the left side of the diagram. Vacancies are also created continuously through quits and retirements.

On the supply side, people come into the market from several sources. The most obvious source is the unemployed. But many people find new jobs and quit their old ones without ever being unemployed. A large proportion of new jobs are found through friends and relatives, classified ads, and other channels available to those who already have a job. Similarly, people just entering or reentering the labor market may go directly into a job or may spend some time in unemployment.

The unemployed pool, then, consists of those who have been discharged, those who have been laid off (and who may or may not be available for other jobs), those who have quit without already having found a new job, and part (but not all) of the new entrants or reentrants to the labor force.

The families at the top of the diagram are the ultimate source of labor supply. Here there is a continuous two-way movement of people into and out of the labor force. The size of these flows is not commonly recognized. In a typical month there are several million entering the labor force and several million leaving it.[3] Another surprising fact is that almost half of people's spells of unemployment are ended not by finding jobs but by withdrawal from the labor force. But this withdrawal may be quite temporary—almost half of those reentering the labor force have been out of it for less than two months.

While the structure outlined in Figure 10-2 is easily understood, several features of its operation should be underlined. First, unemployed workers and vacant jobs normally coexist, and in large numbers. One tends to think of the unemployed as a surplus, as people "left over" after all vacancies have been filled. It is more accurate to think of them as people in motion through the market, people in the course of being fitted into vacancies that are thus destroyed, although the supply of vacancies is constantly being renewed. The relative sizes of the "vacancies box" and the "unemployed box" vary, of course, with fluctuations in aggregate demand. During an economic upswing, the vacancies box expands and the unemployed box shrinks; and conversely in recession.

Second, the flows in the diagram are not independent of each other but are strongly interrelated. More specifically, the system exhibits *negative feedback;* that is, a change that by itself would raise (or lower) the level of unemployment produces other changes that tend to move unemployment back toward the initial level. For example, an increase in vacancies resulting from a general increase in labor demand tends to reduce the unemployed pool. But an increase in vacancies also tends to increase the quit rate and the flow of new workers into the labor force, which tends to replenish the pool. Again, an increase in layoffs during recession raises the number of unemployed; but this lowers the quit rate and increases the number of discouraged workers dropping out of the labor force, which brakes the increase in unemployment.

Third, and partly because of this negative feedback, the net change in the *stocks* of vacancies and unemployed workers is small relative to the gross *flows* of people through the market. The year-to-year change in the number of unemployed is typically less than a million. The flow through the market, however, is of the order of thirty million per year. Interestingly enough, the size of the flow during prosperity does not vary much from its size during recession. During recession the layoff rate rises, but the quit rate falls; and conversely during expansion. These opposite fluctuations, which stand out clearly in Figure 10-1, roughly offset each other, so that the "total separations" line is less bumpy than the line for quits or for layoffs.

---

[3]Clark and Summers, "Labor and Unemployment."

SOURCES OF UNEMPLOYMENT

Unemployment in the economy at any time can be attributed to three main sources: (1) *frictional unemployment,* arising from normal turnover in the labor market and the fact that finding new jobs takes time; (2) *structural unemployment,* associated with a mismatch between workers' qualifications and the qualifications required for vacant jobs; and (3) *deficient-demand unemployment,* arising from inadequate total demand for labor. While these categories are not entirely independent, they provide a useful framework for our discussion.

Frictional Unemployment

Frictional unemployment arises partly from short-term irregularities in the demand for labor by particular industries and enterprises, which occur apart from general cyclical fluctuations. In such industries as merchant shipping and longshoring, the number of workers needed in a particular port varies from day to day. Orders coming into a manufacturing plant in a particular month may be larger or smaller than expected. Although employment fluctuations can be smoothed out by use of inventories, overtime work, and other buffers, they cannot be avoided entirely.

Seasonality of operations is a familiar phenomenon, especially in agriculture and building construction. In the colder regions of the country building activity tapers off during the winter months. In crop raising there is a peak of activity during the harvest season. The men's and women's clothing industries work hard while getting out the spring and fall styles but slacken off in between. Seasonal industries tend to attract enough labor to meet their peak requirements during the rush seasons, which means that some of these people are unemployed in the slack seasons. In a competitive labor market this failure to obtain a full year's work would be compensated by a higher hourly rate. Unemployment insurance also reduces the cost of unemployment to those working in seasonal industries. But the idle time is still wasteful from a social standpoint.

Even if seasonal and irregular fluctuations were absent, the large flows of workers through the labor market would involve some unemployment between jobs. Workers need time to inquire of friends and relatives, visit the state employment service, apply directly to companies, weed out acceptable from unacceptable jobs; and the employer needs time to interview applicants, administer preemployment tests, and decide whom to hire.[4]

The level of frictional unemployment depends partly on the efficiency of the labor market. If the average job-hunting period could be cut from four weeks to two weeks through improvements in information and clearinghouse facilities, fric-

---

[4]Suppose, for example, that 30 percent of the labor force must find new jobs each year. Assume that job hunting requires an average of one month and that no job hunting is done while holding a job. This would produce an average unemployment rate throughout the year of $^{30}/_{100} \times ^1/_{12} = ^1/_{40}$, or 2.5 percent of the labor force.

tional unemployment would be cut in half. How much can actually be done in this direction will be discussed later.

But the level of frictional unemployment is also affected by the state of demand, by the relative number of job vacancies and unemployed workers. It makes a great difference whether the number of vacancies equals the number of unemployed or whether it is only one-half or one-fourth that number.

Frictional unemployment occurs even when labor markets are in equilibrium, with demand equal to supply. It occurs because of imperfect information and the associated search costs of firms and workers. Some frictional unemployment is necessary in a growing dynamic economy, where employers' needs for workers with specialized skills frequently change.

Structural Unemployment

Structural unemployment is a more serious problem. It occurs because instead of a single labor market, we have a great number of submarkets for particular jobs with specialized skills and qualifications. Most of the interaction between workers and vacancies occurs within these submarkets. The walls between submarkets are rather impermeable in the short run, and they are not easy to penetrate even in the longer run. Thus it is possible, even normal, to have an excess of vacancies over unemployed workers in some markets coexisting with an excess of workers over vacancies in others. Vacancies and unemployed cannot get together and cancel out, but simply coexist. Unemployment arising in this way is usually called *structural*.

To take an extreme example: Suppose all the new jobs becoming available in a particular year are professional jobs requiring college training, while all the new workers becoming available are high school dropouts. Then the vacancies would presumably continue unfilled, and the workers would continue unemployed. Such structural unemployment is likely to last longer than frictional unemployment, and its reduction requires greater effort and expense.

Long-term structural unemployment usually occurs because the wage rate for a certain kind of labor (for example, dishwashers or steelworkers) is set above the equilibrium level where demand is equal to supply. As shown in Figure 10-3, at a wage rate of W_0, supply equals demand. At a higher wage, like W_1, supply exceeds demand. When the wage is W_1, employment is E_1, the number of workers that firms are willing to employ at this wage. But at W_1, E_2 workers want such work. $E_2 - E_1$, the difference between the supply and demand for labor at the going wage rate, represents structural unemployment.

Structural unemployment may exist for several reasons. For example, the government may require that the wage rate be above the equilibrium level, as with minimum wage legislation, an issue discussed in Chapter 5. Perhaps the most common cause of structural unemployment is changes in the composition of labor demand. Such shifts can create an excess supply of workers in some occupations and geographic areas and an excess demand in others. *If* wage rates were very flexible or *if* costs of mobility were low so that workers could easily shift skills or

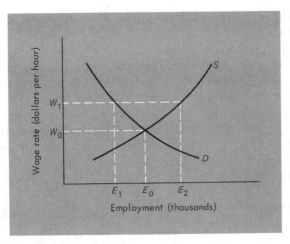

FIGURE 10-3   Structural Unemployment

locations, structural unemployment would be little different from frictional unemployment. These assumptions are generally not true, however. Consequently, structural unemployment is important in our economy.

Structural unemployment may have increased during the past decade as a result of such factors as increased foreign competition in certain industries and the shift of industry from the Snowbelt to the Sunbelt. Automation is often cited as another major cause of structural unemployment. Although technological change certainly does cause some workers to lose their jobs and become structurally unemployed, there is little evidence to suggest that this problem has been increasing. In fact, the slowdown in the growth of productivity, discussed in Chapter 9, suggests that technological change may have been declining rather than increasing.

Although technological change is unlikely to create massive unemployment, structural unemployment is a serious problem facing some workers. Such unemployment occurs mainly because of shifts in the demand for labor, together with inflexible wage rates and immobile workers. To analyze the effects of a demand shift graphically, consider two diagrams, as in Figure 10-4. Assume that the first market is for computer programmers and that in this market wages are flexible upward. The second market is for steelworkers, and wages are inflexible downward in this market, at least for a considerable period of time. The initial equilibrium in each market occurs at wage W_0 and employment level E_0, when the demand curves are given by D_{0c} and D_{0s}. Now assume that demand shifts, so that there is more demand for computer programmers (for example, because of reductions in the cost of computers) and less demand for steelworkers (for example, because of increased foreign competition). Thus the demand curve for programmers shifts to the right to D_{1c}, while that for steelworkers shifts to the left to D_{1s}. Since the wage rate for computer programmers is flexible upward, after some moderate adjustment period, the wage will increase from W_0 to W_1, and employ-

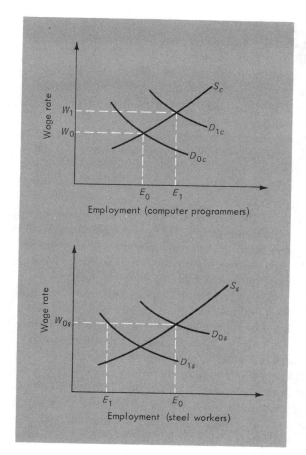

FIGURE 10-4 Shifts in the Demand for Labor and Structural Unemployment

ment will increase from E_0 to E_1.[5] If the wage rate for steelworkers is inflexible downward (for reasons discussed in Chapter 6), employment declines from E_0 to E_1. If the laid-off steelworkers remain in the labor force but do not find other jobs, they represent structural unemployment.

The extent of structural unemployment depends on how many of the laid-off steelworkers obtain jobs in other industries. Both supply and demand factors play a role here. Obviously, it makes an important difference whether other employers are hiring workers. Thus structural unemployment will be much greater when aggregate demand is low, as it was during the early 1980s. For this reason one

---

[5]If the wage rate is not flexible upward, the increase in demand will lead to an excess demand for computer programmers. This excess demand means that employers will have many job vacancies they are unable to fill. Except in the very short run, however, wage rates are generally flexible upward. Even if they are not, employers can adjust to the excess demand by lowering their hiring standards, as discussed in Chap. 6.

cannot completely separate structural from deficient demand unemployment. Nevertheless, the analytical distinction is a useful one, in part because the two types of unemployment suggest different policy responses.

Usually there are some jobs available someplace. Even in the Great Depression of the 1930s, it was said that one could always try to sell apples or shine shoes. Therefore, in considering why laid-off workers often do not obtain alternative jobs, one must analyze supply as well as demand.

As we discussed in Chapter 3, income and substitution effects influence labor supply decisions. If an unemployed worker lives in a family with other earners or has any other source of income, such resources will enable the worker to search longer for a good job. The worker will not be forced to take any job offer that comes along, even if the pay is very low. In addition to this income effect, there may also be a substitution effect. If the jobless worker is covered by unemployment insurance, he will receive benefits until he finds a new job. In this case both the income and substitution effect provide an incentive for further job search, so that the worker, is not forced to accept employment at a low wage rate. We shall discuss the labor supply effects of unemployment insurance later in this chapter.

If the worker has no other means of support (no assets, no other family income, no capacity to borrow, and no available income maintenance benefits), he has little choice. The worker must either take any available job or else turn to crime. In other words, those with no other resources cannot afford to be unemployed. In this sense poverty is a more serious problem than unemployment. Although unemployment probably could be reduced by lowering unemployment insurance benefits and thus putting workers under greater economic pressure to find jobs quickly, there are strong arguments against this approach. Much unemployment is due to changes in demand and in technology that are beyond the worker's control. Thus it is only fair that society offers some protection to the worker against the cost of job loss.[6] Assistance is available through unemployment insurance and also to some extent through training programs and other aids to mobility. These policy alternatives are discussed later in this chapter.

Deficient-Demand Unemployment

Deficient-demand (or cyclical) unemployment arises from inadequate aggregate demand in the economy. Since labor is a derived demand, low aggregate demand for output leads directly to low demand for labor. As discussed in Chapter 6, declining demand for labor is more likely to lead to layoffs and unemployment than to reductions in wage rates, especially when the decline in demand is expected to be temporary.

---

[6]In addition to equity consideration, unemployment insurance may make the economy more efficient. If a skilled worker is forced to take an unskilled job, her skills are not utilized. As long as the worker's skills are needed somewhere and the worker can search for a better job more effectively while unemployed, it may be more efficient for the entire economy if the worker continues searching for a better job.

Declines in demand resulting in high unemployment are called *recessions*. Such recessions occurred in 1954, 1958, 1961, 1971, 1974–75, and 1981–83. During recessions the full-time unemployment rate usually rises three or four points, adding some four million workers to the unemployed. Other workers are reduced to part-time work. Many people become discouraged about the prospects of finding work and leave the labor force, so that the amount of "hidden unemployment" increases. Thus the amount of slack capacity in the economy at the bottom of a recession is considerably larger than the unemployment rate might suggest. As we mentioned at the beginning of this chapter, it appears that each one-percentage-point increase in the unemployment rate is associated with a decrease of more than 2 percent in GNP in the economy. (See page 274.)

The costs of recessions are very high, including not only lost income and output but also increases in alcoholism, other illnesses, and crime, as many workers and their families have great difficulty adjusting to job losses and prolonged unemployment.

Decreases in demand generally have their greatest effect on those with little skill. Workers without much education or experience who do not already have a job will find it difficult to find one as firms either stop hiring or tighten their hiring standards. Workers with little experience and training are also the most likely to lose their jobs during a recession. Layoffs by seniority give an advantage to those who have been with a firm the longest. Even when layoffs are not based strictly on seniority, firms have an incentive to concentrate their layoffs among those workers in whom the firm has invested the least training expenses.

High aggregate demand not only can eliminate deficient-demand unemployment, but by making more jobs available, it can also reduce unemployment due to frictional and structural causes. At high levels of aggregate demand, however, inflation will accelerate (the rate of inflation will increase). As indicated previously, the minimum unemployment rate that does not lead to accelerating inflation is called the nonaccelerating inflationary rate of unemployment (NAIRU). It is also called the natural rate of unemployment. There is nothing really natural about this unemployment rate since it depends on the levels of frictional and structural unemployment, both of which can be influenced by government policies, as we shall see shortly. Nevertheless, the natural unemployment rate is an important concept. Most economists believe that in the long run, it is impossible to use aggregate demand to reduce unemployment below the natural rate without ever accelerating inflation.

Deficient-demand unemployment is usually defined as unemployment that exceeds the natural rate. Let us examine the concept of the natural rate of unemployment more carefully. If the natural rate is 6 percent and if the economy were at this point, then "by definition," inflation would continue at a steady rate—neither increasing nor decreasing. Does this mean that there would be enough jobs for all workers? At 6 percent would the unemployment problem simply be one of matching workers and jobs rather than expanding the total number of jobs available? Probably not, according to evidence presented by Katharine

Abraham.[7] She looks at the relation between the number of vacant jobs that firms are trying to fill and the number of unemployed workers seeking jobs. Clearly, there is an inverse relation between unemployment and job vacancies. As aggregate demand increases, unemployment declines and vacancies increase. But except at very low unemployment levels (for example, about 3 percent), the unemployment rate always exceeds the vacancy rate. Abraham's analysis suggests that policy proposals to reduce unemployment by devising ways to improve the matching of workers to jobs cannot lead to a dramatic reduction in total unemployment, although they may still be quite valuable in lessening unemployment that is frictional or structural.

The most effective way to reduce most unemployment in the short run is to increase aggregate demand in the economy. During World War II, for example, the overall unemployment rate fell to 1 percent, even though it had been 15 percent in 1940. We have not increased aggregate demand to very high levels in recent years for fear of increasing inflation. However, the high unemployment of 1982–83 resulted largely from efforts to reduce the rate of inflation.

Why Wage Rates Are Not More Flexible

When aggregate demand declines, why does unemployment increase significantly while there is little initial decline in wage rates and prices?

First, wage rates are often set for several years through collective bargaining. Even firms that are nonunion seldom change their wage rates more than once a year. There are considerable transaction costs involved in deciding how to change wage rates, especially if such decisions involve collective bargaining and the possibility of a strike.

In Chapter 6 we discussed several other reasons why a decline in a firm's demand for labor usually has a greater effect on employment than on wage rates. For example, unemployment resulting from lost jobs is subsidized by the unemployment insurance system. The most important reason, however, is the support by senior workers of the principle that declines in demand should be met primarily by layoffs among those with the least seniority. This approach protects senior workers from the effects of all but the most cataclysmic declines. Senior workers have a disproportionate influence on shaping union policy. Firms also are responsive to the desires of senior workers, especially when employers have invested heavily in their training. Even junior workers are not too opposed to layoffs by seniority, since most junior workers hope to become senior workers and thus gain future job security from this principle.

Next let us consider a firm with a steady demand for labor that faces an increasing number of job applicants because of higher unemployment in the local labor market. Let us assume that many of these workers have considerable experience on similar jobs and are willing to work for less than the firm's present wage

---

[7]See Katharine G. Abraham, "Structural/Frictional vs. Deficient-Demand Unemployment: Some New Evidence," *American Economic Review* (September 1983), pp. 708–24.

scale. Why doesn't the firm either reduce the wage rate of its present employees or replace many of them with new workers at a lower wage?[8]

Lowering the wages of present workers (insiders) will have adverse effects on their morale, which is likely to reduce present productivity. In addition, it may lead to a higher quit rate in the future when alternative jobs are more readily available. If the firm is unionized, lowering wage rates would often require a costly strike. If it is not unionized, then cutting wage rates is likely to increase the chances of future unionization.

Replacing the insiders with lower-paid newcomers (outsiders) would lead to a different, probably more severe, set of problems for the firm. First there are the direct costs of hiring and firing workers. Second, and more important, the incumbent workers are likely to be very hostile to the newcomers. By refusing to cooperate with them, these insiders can greatly reduce the productivity of the outsiders. In addition, harassment by the incumbents will make the job unpleasant for the new hires and may cause many to quit. While these problems of noncooperation and harassment can be reduced by the firm's efforts to supervise and monitor the workers, such efforts can never be completely successful and can be quite costly. Thus most firms are at least partially dependent on the voluntary cooperation of their workers, especially the more senior workers who will train and socialize the new hires.

Next let us consider what happens when aggregate demand increases. In this case, the initial effects are on employment rather than on wage rates. Most firms can expand their employment rather easily without increasing their wage rates. If many workers are to be hired, then the quality of a firm's new hires may decline. Although a decrease in the quality of workers represents a cost to employers, this cost must be paid only for the new workers. In contrast, a wage increase usually would have to be paid for all existing workers as well as for the new hires. Thus wage rates will be raised only if either the quality of available applicants becomes very low or, more likely, in response from pressure by present workers to share in the firm's prosperity. If the increase in demand is economywide, workers will also seek compensation for the effects of any accompanying inflation.

As we have seen, there are good reasons why changes in aggregate demand lead mainly to changes in employment, at least in the short run. From a macro-perspective, however, it would be better for the economy if employment could stay relatively steady at the full employment level, with changes in demand mainly affecting wages and prices. Obviously, a decline in aggregate demand will have a less adverse effect on the economy if it leads to wage and price declines rather than to increases in unemployment. In the case of increases in aggregate demand, the argument is more subtle. In the short run, the economy benefits from high output and employment when aggregate demand increases. But in the long run, the effect of high demand will be mainly on wages and prices. Thus the short-run gains from

---

[8]The discussion in the next two paragraphs draws on Assar Lindbeck and Dennis J. Snower, "Wage Setting, Unemployment, and Insider-Outsider Relations," *American Economic Review* (May 1986), pp. 235–39. See also by the same authors, *The Insider-Outsider Theory of Employment and Unemployment.*

high aggregate demand come at the cost of higher long-run inflation. With wages and prices relatively inflexible downward, the costs of reducing such inflation later on are very substantial.

Wage rates appear to have been much more flexible prior to the 1930s than they have been since then. Wage rates became less flexible downward in the 1930s and 1940s for a variety of reasons, including increases in unionization, greater influence of personnel departments, and the establishment of unemployment insurance.[9] In addition, a social ethic developed during the Great Depression that "good" employers should not cut wage rates. This view found support in Keynesian economics but actually originated earlier than Keynesian theory. It was expressed in legislation including the Davis-Bacon Act of 1931, which regulated wage rates on federal construction projects; the National Industrial Recovery Act of 1931, which was later declared unconstitutional; the Wagner Act of 1935, which encouraged unionization; and the Fair Labor Standards Act of 1938, which included the first federal minimum wage rate.

To maintain the advantages of long-term contracts while introducing more flexibility into the wage system, Mitchell has proposed that more contracts should include *profit sharing* or other gain-sharing provisions where wages automatically increase when the firm's product demand increases, and decrease when demand falls.[10] If compensation were tied to some easily measurable variable, such as a firm's total sales, this approach could also counter workers' suspicion that an employer will try to exaggerate its economic plight in order to force concessions from its employees.

Tying compensation directly to a firm's sales or profits could make wage rates more flexible. The main problem with this approach is the preference most workers have for a fixed wage. By knowing their future earnings, they can plan their finances with less risk. Of course, junior workers face the risk of layoffs. But senior workers are at relatively low risk, unless they are in industries with high structural unemployment.

Regardless of the future of gain sharing, we should remember that policies to reduce unemployment need not focus just on programs to provide direct assistance to those currently unemployed. Broader issues, including the effect of compensation policies on the demand for labor, also need to be considered.

THE DIFFERENTIAL IMPACT OF UNEMPLOYMENT

Unemployment is distributed very unevenly over the labor force. Laborers experience much more unemployment than skilled manual workers, and the latter have substantially higher rates than clerical workers do. There are also important differences by sex, race, and age.

---

[9]This paragraph is based on Daniel J. B. Mitchell, "Wage Flexibility in the United States: Lessons from the Past," *American Economic Review* (May 1985), pp. 36–40.

[10]See Mitchell, "Gain-Sharing: An Anti-Inflation Reform," *Challenge* (July–August 1982), pp. 18–25.

TABLE 10-2   Unemployment Rates, 1989, 1985, 1982, 1979

DEMOGRAPHIC GROUPS	1989	1985	1982	1979
Total population	5.2	7.1	9.7	5.8
Whites	4.5	6.2	8.6	5.1
Males	4.5	6.1	8.8	4.5
16–19 years	13.7	16.5	21.7	13.9
20+ years	3.9	5.4	7.8	3.6
Females	4.5	6.4	8.3	5.9
16–19 years	11.5	14.8	19.0	14.0
20+ years	4.0	5.7	7.3	5.0
Black and other races	11.4	15.1	17.3	11.3
Males	11.5	15.3	18.2	10.4
16–19 years	31.9	41.0	44.0	31.3
20+ years	10.0	13.2	16.2	8.5
Females	11.4	14.9	16.4	12.3
16–19 years	33.0	39.2	43.8	35.6
20+ years	9.8	13.1	14.3	10.2

Source: *Economic Report of the President, 1990.*

In Table 10-2 we show unemployment rates by race, sex, and age for 1989, 1985, 1982, and 1979. Although the overall unemployment rate was much greater in 1982, the relative unemployment rates for the different demographic groups do not change greatly from year to year. Those with generally high unemployment, such as young blacks, suffer the greatest increases in recessions.

There is relatively little difference in unemployment between men and women. The unemployment rate for men does vary more with economic conditions, so the male rate is higher in a recession year like 1982. A higher percentage of men are employed in relatively high-paying cyclically sensitive jobs, as in the production of durable goods, while women are disproportionately employed in less cyclically sensitive positions, including clerical jobs.

The unemployment rate for all blacks is more than double the rate for whites. As discussed in Chapter 8, racial differences in the labor market reflect some combination of differences in skill levels, differences in work attitudes, and the effect of labor market discrimination.

The biggest differences in unemployment are by age, with the rate for teenagers about three times that for adults. Much youth unemployment is frictional, associated with high mobility of many young workers from job to job. About half the teenagers classified as unemployed are also in school. Most are looking for part-time work only, and most are living at home. Thus in terms either of welfare or of potential labor supply, the figures on teenage unemployment have a different meaning from those on adult unemployment. In addition, the magnitude of the youth unemployment problem is diminishing as overall unemployment declines and as the percentage of the population who are teenagers declines.

Still there is a youth employment problem. For example, unemployment among youth reduces future wage rates, either because the unemployed miss out on valuable work experience and on-the-job training or because they come to be viewed as poor risks by employers.[11] High youth unemployment is also a problem because it is heavily concentrated among a small group who lack work for extended periods of time. Freeman and Wise note that "over half of the male teenage unemployment is among those who are out of work for over six months, a group constituting less than 10 percent of the youth labor force and only 7 percent of the youth population.[12] Other youth have left the labor force because they could not find jobs, an especially serious problem for those who are not in school and who are from families who are too poor to provide any appreciable financial support.

The unemployment rate is much higher among black than white youths, and blacks account for a disproportionate share of long-term unemployment among youths. Why is that so? In the 1950s there was virtually no difference by race in teenage unemployment. Thus we need to consider why the unemployment rate has increased much faster for blacks than for whites over the past several decades. First, there has been a significant migration of blacks from rural areas to central cities, especially in the 1950s and early 1960s. Between 1950 and 1970, for example, the percentage of black youths working on farms declined from 34 to 2 percent, while the corresponding decline for whites was 23 to 5 percent. Many farm youths earn very little, but they seldom show up in our unemployment figures. Thus, as Cogan has demonstrated, much of this increase in black youth unemployment can be attributed to the shift from rural to urban areas, a shift precipitated by the decline in demand for unskilled labor in agriculture.[13]

The unemployment rate among central-city black youths is considerably higher than for all young blacks.[14] The high unemployment and low labor force participation of central-city blacks result from a surplus of unskilled labor at the going wage. This surplus may have been caused more by minimum wage legislation than by market forces.

Why does there appear to be a much greater differential between supply and demand for black than for white youths? On the demand side youths have been hurt by increased competition from other groups, including women and immigrants and, at times, by low aggregate demand in the economy. Although all youths are affected by these factors, young blacks may be especially affected since they are often at the end of the job queue, as discussed in Chapters 6 and 7. Racial discrimination by employers is also a factor, although such discrimination is less overt than in the past.

Much of the problem of inner-city black youth employment appears to be

---

[11]See David Ellwood, "Teenage Unemployment: Permanent Scars or Temporary Blemishes," in *The Youth Labor Market Problem*, pp. 349–85.

[12]Richard B. Freeman and David A. Wise, "The Youth Labor Market Problem: Its Nature, Causes, and Consequences," in *The Youth Labor Market Problem*, pp. 1–16.

[13]See John Cogan, "The Decline in Black Teenage Employment, 1950–70," *American Economic Review* (September 1982), pp. 621–39.

[14]See Richard B. Freeman and Harry J. Holzer, "Young Blacks and Jobs—What We Now Know," *The Public Interest* (Winter 1985), pp. 18–31. The subsequent discussion of central-city black youth unemployment draws heavily on results of the NBER study, summarized by Freeman and Holzer.

on the supply side. The skills and attitudes of youths are affected by the quality of the schools they attend. Freeman and Holzer stress the importance of family characteristics. They found that youths from welfare families or who live in public housing fare far worse in the labor market than other youths from similar neighborhoods who have stable family lives. Conversely, young blacks are more likely to hold jobs if other family members are working. When others are working, the young people may have better information about jobs and better connections for getting employed. Or the results may reflect differences in attitudes toward work across families. Given similar job opportunities, black youths appear at least as willing to work as white youths.[15] But because of lower average skill levels, blacks have fewer opportunities. Those with relatively low skills generally must accept low-wage rates in order to gain employment. But the effectiveness of this strategy is limited both by minimum wage restrictions and by the reluctance of many blacks to accept low-paying dead-end jobs. This reluctance is reinforced to the extent that other alternatives, such as criminal activity, are viewed as attractive possibilities.

UNEMPLOYMENT AND JOB LOSSES

When we think of the problems of unemployment, we are more likely to think of a middle-aged steelworker in the Monongahela Valley than a black teenager in New York City. The problems of job loss (or displacement) are related to, but by no means identical to, the probems of unemployment. In nonrecession times close to half the unemployed are first-time job seekers or have been out of the labor force for some time. Many of the rest are on temporary layoff from a permanent job. In contrast, the most severe unemployment problems are those that result from the permanent loss of a long-term job. Such displacement is of particular concern to older workers. Since such workers generally will have accumulated considerable seniority with their employers, they are the least likely to be laid off. When older senior workers are laid off, however, owing to the permanent closing of their plant, for example, they face especially great displacement costs since they can seldom obtain new jobs as good as those they have lost.

Older workers are at a disadvantage competing for jobs for several reasons. Employers may believe that older workers are more difficult to train. For those nearing retirement age, there is only a short period in which the employer can recoup investment costs, and pension costs may be high. Even in the absence of these difficulties, an older worker seeking a new job most likely will have to take a

---

[15]For example, in an experimental program that offered minimum wage jobs to all 16- to 19-year-olds from low-income households in certain geographic areas, a much higher percentage of eligible black youths took advantage of such jobs than whites. The jobs were part time during the school year and full time during the summer and were available only to those who were still in school but had not graduated from high school. See George Farkas and others, *Impacts from the Youth Incentive Entitlement Pilot Projects: Participation, Work, and Schooling over the Full Program Period* (New York: Manpower Research Demonstration Corporation, 1982). Also see Harry J. Holzer, "Reservation Wages and Their Labor Market Effects for Black and White Male Youth," *Journal of Human Resources* (Spring 1986), pp. 157–77.

pay cut, since the firm-specific skills learned on his or her former job will not be valuable to the new employer. If the worker also has to relocate in order to find employment, such mobility costs often will be greater for the older worker, who may have to cut valued ties to home, family, and neighborhood.

A displaced worker is likely to be unemployed initially while searching for a new job. Within a few months, however, most displaced workers will either find some acceptable new job or give up searching. If the worker has considerable savings or is eligible for either Social Security or a private pension, then he or she may choose to retire. If such retirement income is not available, then the worker may be supported by a spouse or other family member. Unemployment insurance, which we shall discuss in more detail shortly, can help cushion the initial income effects of a job loss, but such benefits are available only for a limited time. If none of these alternatives is available, then a displaced worker has little choice but to accept whatever job may be available, even if the job pays much less than the former job. The average drop in earnings for displaced workers varies depending on the general availability of jobs in the local labor market and on the occupation and industry of the displaced worker. Jacobson estimated that in the 1970s among permanently displaced male workers, those in high wage industries such as steel and autos suffered annual earnings losses of about 50 percent over the first two years and 12 to 16 percent over the next four years.[16] In contrast, among low-wage industries, such as shoes and apparel, the earnings losses from displacement are much smaller, only about 10 percent in the first two years and virtually nothing thereafter.

In the early 1980s job losses were even greater, especially among blue-collar workers. From 1979 to 1983 nearly 5.8 million such workers were displaced. As of early 1984, 64 percent of the men were reemployed, with an average wage loss of 10 percent. For women the effects are more dramatic. Among blue-collar women only 50 percent were reemployed by 1984, and the average wage loss for these workers was 26 percent.[17]

Job loss by workers can lead not only to economic difficulties but also to serious health problems. Brenner has estimated a significant effect of changes in aggregate unemployment on aggregate mortality and on admission to mental hospi-

---

[16]See Louis S. Jacobson, "Earnings Losses of Workers Displaced from Manufacturing Industries," in *The Impact of International Trade and Investment in Employment,* ed. William C. Dewald, a conference of the U.S. Department of Labor (Printing Office, 1978); and "Earnings Loss Due to Displacement," working paper CRC-385 (Public Research Institute of the Center for Naval Analysis, April 1974). See also the discussion by Barry Bluestone and Bennett Harrison, *The Deindustrialization of America* (New York: Basic Books, 1982).

[17]See Michael Podgursky and Paul Swaim, "Job Displacement and Earnings Loss: Evidence from the Displaced Worker Survey," *Industrial and Labor Relations Review* (October 1987), pp. 17–29. Among white-collar workers the reemployment rate was 75 percent for men and 62 percent for women, with wage losses of 4 and 16 percent, respectively. For all displaced workers those with the most general education appear to suffer the fewest losses, while those with the most specific training suffer the most. A later survey in January 1986 found somewhat higher reemployment rates, probably because of lower aggregate unemployment. See Francis W. Horvath, "The Pulse of Economic Change: Displaced Workers of 1981–85," *Monthly Labor Review* (June 1987), pp. 3–12.

tals.[18] Case studies have also emphasized the psychological costs of job loss and unemployment, especially for those who see their role in the family and community primarily as that of earner or "breadwinner." When such workers lose their jobs, they can easily lose their self-confidence, become depressed, feel useless, and turn to drink.[19]

As Bluestone and Harrison indicate,

> Loss of a work network removes an important source of human support. Psychosomatic illnesses, anxiety, worry, tension, impaired interpersonal relationships, and an increased sense of powerlessness arise. As self-esteem decreases, problems of alcoholism, child and spouse abuse, and aggression increase.[20]

In considering the desirability of policies to reduce unemployment and job losses, these social-psychological costs of job loss must be considered as well as the income costs.

LABOR MARKET POLICIES TO REDUCE UNEMPLOYMENT

In this section we consider government policies to reduce unemployment and to help workers who lose their jobs. We begin with a discussion of information and placement services provided by the Job Service—activities designed to reduce frictional unemployment.

Structural unemployment has increased considerably in recent years, partly as a result of foreign competition. In Chapter 11 we discuss why economists are generally hostile to import restrictions, preferring other policies such as retraining and relocation programs to assist displaced workers. Here we examine public employment and training programs to aid the unemployed.

Some unemployment is unavoidable in a dynamic economy. Therefore, we conclude with a discussion of unemployment insurance, the primary program designed to provide income assistance to unemployed workers who have lost their jobs because of a decline in the demand for their labor.

---

[18]See M. Harvey Brenner, *Mental Illness and the Economy* (Cambridge, Mass.: Harvard University Press, 1973); and "Estimating the Social Costs of National Economic Policy: Implications for Mental and Physical Health and Clinical Aggression," a report prepared for the Joint Economic Committee, U.S. Congress (Washington, D.C.: Government Printing Office, 1971).

[19]See Sidney Cobb and Stanislav V. Kasl, *Termination: The Consequences of Job Loss,* Public Health Service, Center for Disease Control, National Institutes for Occupational Safety and Health, U.S. Department of Health, Education, and Welfare (Washington, D.C.: Government Printing Office, June 1977). See also E. Wight Bakke, *The Unemployed Man* (New York: E. P. Dutton & Co., 1934); Richard Wilcock and Walter Frank, *Unwanted Workers: Permanent Layoff and Long-Term Unemployment* (New York: Glenco Free Press, 1963); Joanne Preal Gordus, Paul Jarley, and Louis A. Ferman, *Plant Closings and Economic Dislocation* (Kalamazoo, Mich.: W. E. Upjohn Institute, 1981), Chap. 6; and Bluestone and Harrison, *Deindustrialization of America,* Chap. 3.

[20]Bluestone and Harrison, *Deindustrialization of America,* p. 66.

Information and Placement: The Job Service

The job search process is costly, since it takes time for firms and workers to locate each other. Information in the labor market is far from perfect. With better information, job search might be less time consuming. In addition, there might be less mismatching of workers and jobs. Employers could hire workers better suited to their requirements, and workers could find jobs offering better pay or working conditions.

To what extent can the government ensure that better information is available, thereby improving the job search process? First, the government might require that firms provide adequate notice to workers who are to be laid off so that such workers can have time to search for new positions before losing their jobs. Such measures have existed in other countries for many years. In the United States plant-closing legislation, passed in 1988, requires firms to give sixty days' notice to employees before a plant is closed or before large-scale layoffs that will last for at least six months. Many employers vigorously opposed the legislation, partly out of general opposition to government regulation and partly out of fear that workers would become less productive as they worry about finding a new job.

Second, government can develop and publicize projections of the future demand for different occupations. Such information is especially valuable for students as they decide upon careers. A good deal of occupational information is available. The Department of Labor projects demand for a large number of occupations and prepares occupational handbooks for use by employment service staff, school counselors, and others. These projections, however, are subject to a considerable margin of error. Trends may differ across local labor markets, while the Bureau of Labor Statistics (BLS) projections are average national figures. In addition, technological change can alter the skill proportions required for any type of production. The size of such shifts is hard to predict. Further, there is usually some substitutability among skills. If skilled crafts people become scarce, jobs can often be redesigned to be done by less-skilled workers. Finally, demand is not independent of relative wage rates, a fact that tends to be overlooked in many manpower projections.

For those who are out of school and already in the job market, the Job Service provides assistance. The Job Service was established by the Wagner-Peyser Act of 1933, which granted federal matching funds to each state that set up an employment service to help workers find jobs.

The function of an employment service is to provide a meeting place for buyers and sellers of labor. Any employer with a vacant job may place an order at the Job Service, specifying the nature of the work, the qualifications required, the starting wage, and other relevant facts. Any unemployed worker may register for work at the Job Service, and workers who have applied for unemployment compensation are required to register. The registration form, usually filled out with the aid of a trained interviewer, contains key facts about the worker and about his or her last few jobs.

The problem facing the Job Service official is to match orders and registrations as effectively as possible. When an order is received, the official looks through the active file of registrants for workers who appear qualified for the job in question. She makes a tentative selection, talks with the worker to find out whether he is interested in the job, and if he is interested, passes him on to the employer. The employer need not hire workers sent out by the Job Service, nor need workers accept the jobs to which they are sent, although there may be some pressure on workers drawing unemployment insurance benefits.

Only a small proportion of all job vacancies are filled through the Job Service. Moreover, most of these are for short-term jobs requiring little skill. Why is the Job Service not more widely used? The main reason is that employers can usually fill a good vacancy quickly without resorting to the Job Service. Word of the vacancy gets passed on to friends and relatives of people already in the plant, the foreman remembers someone who used to work on that job and looks that person up, or the union has a suggestion to make. Thus a worker with good contacts can usually locate a job through the grapevine so feels little need for the Job Service. Where employer and worker are able to locate each other directly, there is no need for the Job Service to intervene. It exists to supplement other methods of work seeking, not to supplant them.

The Job Service is hampered by the inherent complexity of the placement job. It is hard to become familiar enough with all the jobs in a area and with the idiosyncrasies of each employer so that one can tell whether a particular worker will be acceptable for a particular job. It is difficult also to gauge accurately the experience and abilities of each registrant. When a worker says that he is a toolmaker, is he really a toolmaker or only a grade B machinist? A failure to judge accurately both the worker and the job leads not merely to a lost placement but also to a loss of prestige with the employer and worker involved. For many jobs private employment agencies appear to be more successful in meeting this challenge.

Ironically, one reason why the Job Service is not more widely used stems directly from its mission to help workers who are having trouble finding jobs. The Job Service is widely regarded as a social welfare agency whose task is to find work for the unfortunate. It is put under pressure to give priority in referrals to disadvantaged groups in the labor force—the long-term unemployed, members of minority groups, people with physical or mental disabilities. But the Job Service cannot push such people into employment in the face of employers' natural desire to find the most efficient candidate for each job. Ill-conceived efforts to do so may sacrifice the respect and cooperation of employers on whose job orders the Job Service ultimately depends.

Considering these difficulties, the efficiency of Job Service operations in most states is surprisingly high. But the gap between performance and potential remains wide. There is need for clearer recognition of the service as an *economic* agency rather than a *welfare* agency. Its task should be to serve all members of the labor force rather than merely the hard to place, to reflect employer requirements accurately and objectively, to locate the person most suited to a particular job rather than the person who needs work most. It cannot hope to correct the distress resulting from inadequate demand for labor or from personal handicaps or from mistaken hiring preferences. It can hope to reduce frictional unemployment, to cut employers' hiring and training costs, and to secure a more efficient matching of individual capacities and job requirements.[21]

Employment and Training Programs

The Job Service can reduce frictional unemployment but not high unemployment due to inadequate aggregate demand for labor. When unemployment is high, many favor government employment programs to provide jobs for the unemployed. Examples of such programs include the Public Works Administration (PWA) and the Works Progress Administration (WPA), both established in response to the depression of the 1930s, the Public Employment Program (PEP), established in response to the recession of 1970–71, and CETA, a set of employment and training programs established by the Comprehensive Employment and Training Act of 1973.

These programs have had a variety of goals in addition to reducing unusually high rates of unemployment. Some, such as the PWA, have focused on the construction of long-term capital improvements. Others, such as CETA, have emphasized the provision of local government services, such as day care and the maintenance of parks.

If the jobs are mainly for long-term public works, considerable lead time is needed to plan and execute projects of lasting value. But by the time the projects can be implemented there may no longer be a large surplus of workers, especially for the skilled workers who form an essential part of most large-scale construction efforts. Services and short-term repairs are easier to set up quickly, but the output from such programs is less visible. Consequently, this approach has often been vulnerable to charges of "make work" and "leaf raking." The Reagan administration terminated the subsidized jobs component of CETA partly because of skepticism about the value of the output they produced.

In addition to the type of work to be done, another issue is which level of government can best administer a program of subsidized employment. Since most such programs involve some income redistribution, they can be financed most effectively at the federal level. If any state establishes a major program to redistribute income from the rich to the poor, it will tend to drive out the rich and attract the poor, thus making the program more expensive. Because of barriers to international migration, this problem is much less acute for the federal government.

But if the federal government administers all aspects of a jobs program, a new bureaucracy must be set up. Moreover, it may be difficult to ensure that local preferences receive sufficient attention, both concerning which workers are to be hired and what jobs they are to do. Therefore, in recent years most public employment programs have been administered by state and local governments. On the other hand, when the programs are federally financed but administered mostly at the state and local level, other problems arise. For example, are all of the new,

---

[21]For an eloquent statement of this view, see E. Wight Bakke, *A Positive Labor Market Policy* (Columbus, Ohio: Charles C. Merrill Publishing Co., 1963).

federally subsidized jobs a net addition to employment? Or do they in part replace "regular" state and local employees? When subsidized workers are "free" in the sense of being paid from federal funds while regular workers have to be paid from the state or local budget, there is a strong incentive to substitute the former for the latter. Such substitution is called the *fiscal substitution effect*. Programs can have rules prohibiting this practice, but such rules are not easy to enforce, especially where state or local government employment is expanding so that unsubsidized employees are not being laid off.

An important issue is whether a program of subsidized employment should be considered temporary or permanent. It is usually justified on countercyclical grounds as a way of coping with high aggregate-demand unemployment during a recession. The rationale is that as the private economy recovers, people will move off the public employment rolls and into private-sector jobs. But it takes time to set up productive jobs, so it is difficult to create such jobs so that they are available just when they are needed.

One could justify a permanent program on grounds of structural unemployment. It could be argued that government should serve as "employer of last resort" for people whose characteristics make it unlikely that they can get and hold regular jobs. But this is a different justification from the usual countercyclical justification. Further, a continuing structurally oriented program would need to be designed differently from a temporary countercyclical program. For example, a structurally oriented program should be concerned especially with hiring disadvantaged workers who have little chance of employment in unsubsidized jobs even when the overall unemployment rate is at normal levels. In contrast, when a program is federally funded but locally administered, local officials have an incentive to hire the most qualified workers (often called creaming) in order to produce the most output with the available financing.

For workers who cannot find and hold adequate jobs without a government subsidy, it may be preferable for the government to provide training for a better job. The federal government has been heavily involved in training activities for the structurally unemployed, especially among the young, ever since the Manpower Development Training Act (MDTA) of 1962. Such training was also an important component of the CETA programs. In 1982 CETA was replaced by the Jobs Training Partnership Act (JTPA), which emphasizes job training in close consultation with the private sector. Considerable money for retraining workers is also available through the Omnibus Trade Bill of 1988. Part of this legislation is the Economically Dislocated Workers Adjustment Assistance Act (EDWAAA), which provides subsidized training and placement assistance to dislocated workers formerly served by Title III of JTPA as well as to those losing their jobs as a result of foreign competition.

Most training programs have offered either institutional training provided by government agencies or on-the-job training provided by private firms.

1. Institutional Training. This involves some combination of classroom instruction and practice work, often using the facilities of local vocational schools, but sometimes involving construction of new training facilities. Courses offered include such things as *welding skills* (welder, auto-body worker, sheet-metal workers); *machinery skills* (machinist, auto mechanic, electronic technician, customer-service repair person); *clerical skills* (keypunch worker, accounting clerk, typist, receptionist, computer operator); *food skills* (food-preparation worker); and *medical skills* (nurse's aid, medical transcriber, operating-room technician).

2. On-the-Job Training (OJT).   This involves contracting with an employer to train workers in the plant, with a guarantee to hire those who successfully complete the training period. Government typically pays half the worker's wage during training. OJT has the advantage that people who show good ability during the training period can go directly into regular jobs, so there is no placement problem. But under OJT, the company usually screens and selects the trainees, and it will naturally select the most trainable and resist the seriously disadvantaged. Also the company will provide training only when demand is increasing.

Other important types of training include prevocational classroom programs for those with serious educational or language problems and work-experience programs for those who need assistance in developing good work habits or who need to establish credentials as dependable workers. Another major component of most training programs is job search assistance, such as coaching in how to interview for a job. Evaluation studies have generally found only modest effects on the postprogram earnings of male participants, but sizable earnings gains for females.[22]

Unemployment Insurance

In our economy unemployment is likely to remain at relatively high levels. Structural unemployment remains a serious problem, and the aggregate demand for labor is constrained by fear that higher demand will lead to accelerating inflation.

To help reduce the cost of unemployment to workers who lose their jobs, the Unemployment Insurance (UI) program was established as part of the Social Security Act of 1935. Unemployment insurance consists of fifty state programs, each meeting minimal federal standards. There is no uniformity in coverage, eligibility, benefits, or financing across states. Nevertheless, the purpose of the program and its general methods of operation are similar throughout the country.

The primary objective of the unemployment insurance program is to provide cash payments to those who are involuntarily unemployed in order to help them maintain a close-to-normal standard of living. Other important objectives are

---

[22]For example, see the studies reviewed by Michael E. Borus, "Assessing the Impact of Training Programs," in *Employing the Unemployed*, Eli Ginzberg, ed. (New York: Basic Books, 1980); and Laurie J. Bassi and Orley Ashenfelter, "The Effect of Direct Job Creation and Training Programs on Low-Skilled Workers," in *Fighting Poverty: What Works and What Doesn't*, ed. Sheldon Danziger and Daniel Weinberg (Cambridge, Mass.: Harvard University Press, 1986). The greater effects for women may occur because the women participants in employment and training programs have usually had less work experience than the men and may need more assistance gaining access to entry-level jobs.

to enable workers to find employment consistent with their work skills and experience, to stabilize the economy, and to shift some of the cost of unemployment to those firms that lay off many workers.

Almost all workers are covered by unemployment insurance. To be eligible for benefits, however, a worker must meet the following three conditions: (1) The worker must have sufficient employment in the recent past. Often the requirement is that the worker have earned a minimum amount (for example, $1,000) during the past year. This requirement eliminates all new entrants to the labor force from eligibility. (2) The worker must be able to work and be actively seeking a job. The UI claimant must register with the Job Service, must be available for referral to job openings, and may not refuse an offer of suitable employment. (3) Workers may have to wait longer to start receiving benefits (or may receive none at all) if they were not laid off but left their previous job for some other reason, such as voluntarily quitting, being discharged for misconduct, or going on strike. These requirements are designed to ensure that benefits go to those with a previous commitment to work, who are making a good-faith effort to find new employment, and who have lost a job through no fault of their own.

The benefits available from unemployment insurance vary considerably by state. Generally, the benefit level depends on the worker's previous earnings but is subject to both a minimum and a maximum weekly benefit. For many workers the weekly benefit is approximately half the take-home pay lost to unemployment. For such workers the *replacement rate* is 50 percent. A higher rate would be of greater assistance to the unemployed but would increase the program's cost. In addition, it would reduce the incentive for the worker to find a new job, thus increasing unemployment.

Benefits are available for only a limited time. They are designed as a cushion to support a worker until he or she can find a new job. When the economy is not in a recession, the maximum duration of benefits in most states is twenty-six weeks. During a recession this maximum is usually extended, generally to about a year. For those who still cannot find work and do not have family members who are working, some assistance from food stamps and other welfare programs will frequently be available when UI benefits are exhausted.

Like all other income maintenance programs UI has an income effect reducing labor supply. The replacement rate creates a substitution effect, also reducing labor supply. Workers who lose their jobs and are receiving UI benefits must continue searching for work and must accept suitable jobs that turn up. These work requirements are designed to reduce the work disincentive effects of UI but are difficult to enforce effectively. When jobs are scarce and unemployment is high, good jobs are very difficult to find regardless of how hard one looks. But even when jobs are readily available, some workers will only go through the motions of searching for work, since they prefer to receive UI benefits, at least for a while. Most of the empirical evidence focuses on the labor supply effects of relatively small changes in the parameters of the UI program, especially the replacement rate. From such studies, for example, we learn that increasing the replacement rate from

0.4 to 0.5 of previous earnings probably increases the average spell of unemployment by about three to five days.[23]

The unemployment insurance program is financed by a payroll tax on employers. In a typical state the maximum tax rate is about 5 percent, and only the first $7,000 of annual earnings is taxed. By not taxing total earnings, the UI system provides a disincentive for hiring either part-time workers or those with little skill. Usually the tax rate is much lower for firms with few layoffs whose workers seldom receive benefits. This variability in the tax rate, called *experience rating,* is designed to penalize employers who lay off many workers. Thus experience rating creates an incentive for such firms to stabilize their employment. Since most states have minimum and maximum tax rates that are applicable for many firms, this incentive effect of experience rating is not as extensive as it might be, however. Because experience rating is quite incomplete, UI provides a net subsidy to a firm's workers who are laid off that would not be available should the firm adjust to declining labor demand in other ways, such as by reducing wage rates. Thus, as discussed in Chapter 6, UI provides an incentive for firms to lay off workers rather than to lower wages. The increase in unemployment resulting from this dimension of unemployment insurance may be larger than that resulting from its effect on the labor supply of recipients. This component of unemployment could be reduced, at little cost, by improving the experience rating of UI tax rates.[24]

Unemployment insurance plays a valuable role in cushioning the income losses of many workers who lose their jobs. It is far from a complete solution to the hardship of unemployment, however. Because of concern for both cost and work-incentive effects, eligibility is limited, the replacement rate is seldom much above 50 percent, and benefits are only temporary.

When the economy is performing well and many jobs are available, most unemployment is frictional. The present unemployment insurance system is quite effective in reducing the cost of such unemployment for eligible workers. Under these economic conditions most workers can find a job within a few months. For those who cannot, work experience and other training programs are likely to be more appropriate than more generous UI benefits.

During a recession unemployment insurance provides less adequate protection. When jobs are not available, the low replacement rate creates considerable hardship. Although benefits are available for a longer period during a recession, many still exhaust their benefits as the number of long-term unemployed increases. Also unemployment insurance is of no help to those who have not had enough previous employment to qualify for benefits. It would be possible to

---

[23]For example, see Ronald G. Ehrenberg and Ronald Oaxaca, "Unemployment Insurance, Duration of Unemployment, and Subsequent Wage Gain," *American Economic Review* (December 1976), pp. 754–66; the special issue of *Industrial and Labor Relations Review* (July 1977); and Gary Solon, "Work Incentive Effects of Taxing Unemployment Insurance Benefits," *Econometrica.* (March 1985), pp. 295–306.

[24]See Martin Feldstein, "The Effect of Unemployment Insurance on Temporary Layoff Unemployment," *American Economic Review* (December 1978), pp. 834–45; and Robert H. Topol, "On Layoffs and Unemployment Insurance," *American Economic Review* (September 1983), pp. 541–49.

modify the program to reduce these problems but not without increasing the program's cost. There really is no substitute for an economy with adequate job opportunities.

SUMMARY

1. Workers are counted as being unemployed if they are not employed but are actively searching for work or if they are on temporary layoff from a job. The unemployment rate is the number unemployed divided by the number in the labor force, where the labor force is all those who are either employed or unemployed. Although the unemployment rate receives much attention, the dividing line between those who are unemployed and those who are not in the labor force is often rather fuzzy.

2. The unemployment rate is used as a business-cycle indicator, as a hardship indicator, and as a target for macroeconomic policy.

3. The employed and unemployed are not separate, distinct groups. Each month millions of people shift back and forth between employment and unemployment and also in and out of the labor force.

4. Frictional unemployment arises from normal turnover in the labor market because finding a new job often takes time. Structural unemployment refers to long-term unemployment resulting from a mismatch between workers' skills and the need of employers. For example, there is much structural unemployment in the steel industry because of a decline in the demand for steelworkers, even though jobs may be available in other industries for computer programmers or engineers. Deficient-demand unemployment arises from an inadequate demand for all kinds of labor.

5. Wage rates that are relatively inflexible downward are an important cause of both structural and demand-deficient unemployment. Wage rates are inflexible downward for several reasons, probably the most important being the influence of senior workers who are hurt by wage cuts but not by layoffs of junior workers. Long-term contracts also reduce the short-term flexibility of wage rates, both up and down.

6. Unemployment rates differ dramatically for different kinds of workers. The highest rates are for black teenagers in central cities. Racial discrimination and minimum wage legislation probably contribute to the high unemployment of these young blacks, but much of the problem appears to lie in poor work attitudes and inadequate skills.

7. The loss of a job is an especially serious problem for older workers. A displaced worker usually will be unemployed initially. Within a few months, however, most will either have found a new job or have given up searching and thus have left the labor force. Workers with no other means of support—such as savings, unemployment insurance, or income from other family members—are under great pressure to take a new job even if it pays much less than the job that was lost. Thus the problem of job loss is much broader than the problem of unemployment. Job loss by workers can lead not only to serious economic difficulties but also to serious health problems.

8. The Job Service helps workers find jobs, thus reducing frictional unemployment. Only a very small percentage of all job vacancies are filled through the Job Service, however.

9. Policies to reduce unemployment through retraining, relocation, or better labor market information are not likely to be very successful unless there is sufficient demand for labor in the economy. One way to increase the demand for workers, especially those with high unemployment rates, is through public employment. To be successful, however, such programs must solve several difficult administrative issues. Previous public employment programs in the United States have had limited success. Such programs were terminated by the Reagan administration.

10. To help reduce the cost of unemployment to workers who lose their jobs, an unemployment insurance (UI) program was established as part of the Social Security Act of 1935. Although the primary objective of the program is to help the unemployed maintain their standard of living, other important objectives are to help workers find good jobs, to stabilize the economy, and to shift some of the cost of unemployment to those firms that lay off workers.

KEY CONCEPTS

UNEMPLOYMENT, FULL TIME
UNEMPLOYMENT, PART TIME
UNEMPLOYMENT, RATE OF
SEPARATION RATE
ACCESSION RATE
QUIT RATE
LAYOFF RATE
UNEMPLOYMENT, FRICTIONAL
UNEMPLOYMENT, STRUCTURAL

UNEMPLOYMENT, DEFICIENT-DEMAND
JOB SERVICE
ADJUSTMENT ASSISTANCE
EMPLOYMENT AND TRAINING PROGRAMS
FISCAL SUBSTITUTION EFFECT
UNEMPLOYMENT INSURANCE
REPLACEMENT RATE
EXPERIENCE RATING

REVIEW QUESTIONS

1. What are the main purposes for the unemployment rate? Discuss which you believe is most important. Are there any changes you would suggest in the way unemployment is measured?

2. "Because the line between being in the labor force but unemployed and being out of the labor force is so unclear, the official unemployment figures seriously understate the economy's potential labor reserve." Discuss.

3. Explain the main interactions among labor market flows that occur
   (a) during a decline in the aggregate demand for labor
   (b) during an upswing in the aggregate demand for labor

4. Distinguish clearly between frictional, structural, and deficient-demand unemployment.

5. Discuss why wage rates are inflexible downward and how this wage rigidity affects unemployment.

6. Why is it impossible to determine how much of the unemployment in existence at a particular time is attributable to frictional, structural, and demand factors?

7. Compare the costs of frictional, structural, and deficient-demand unemployment. To what extent are different policies required to deal with each? Are some policies appropriate for each kind of unemployment?

8. What is the appropriate role of the Job Service in the labor market? Discuss the problems that arise if the Job Service puts its primary emphasis on providing placement assistance to those workers who have the most difficulty finding jobs.

9. What role should employment and training programs play in combating demand-deficient unemployment? structural unemployment?

10. Discuss the major economic issues involved in both the benefit structure and the financing of unemployment insurance.

READINGS

ABRAHAM, KATHARINE G., "Structural/Frictional vs. Deficient-Demand Unemployment: Some New Evidence." *American Economic Review* (September 1983), pp. 708–24.

FREEMAN, RICHARD B., and HARRY J. HOLZER, eds., *The Black Youth Employment Crisis.* Chicago: University of Chicago Press, 1986.

————, and DAVID A. WISE, eds., *The Youth Labor Market Problem: Its Nature, Causes, and Consequences.* Chicago: University of Chicago Press, 1982.

FRIEDMAN, MILTON, "Inflation and Unemployment." *Journal of Political Economy* (June 1977).

GUNDERSON, MORLEY, NOAH M. MELTZ, and SYLVIA OSTRY, *Unemployment: International Perspectives.* Toronto: University of Toronto Press, 1987.

LINDBECK, ASSAR, and DENNIS J. SNOWER, *The Insider-Outsider Theory of Employment and Unemployment.* Cambridge, Mass.: MIT Press, 1989.

NATIONAL COMMISSION ON EMPLOYMENT AND UNEMPLOYMENT STATISTICS, *Counting the Labor Force*. Washington, D.C.: Government Printing Office, 1979.

REES, ALBERT, "An Essay on Youth Joblessness," *Journal of Economic Literature* (June 1986).

SINCLAIR, PETER, *Unemployment: Economic Theory and Evidence*. New York: Basil Blackwell, 1987.

AMERICAN WORKERS
IN A WORLD ECONOMY

We live in a world economy. As transportation and communication have improved, long distances have become less important. Because the United States is a large, diverse country, international trade plays a lesser role in our economy than in that of many other countries. In recent years, however, both trade and immigration have become increasingly important for our economy. Exports and imports each account for over 10 percent of our GNP, up from about 5 percent twenty years ago. In addition, immigrants and refugees have accounted for about half our population growth since 1970.

We begin this chapter by discussing the effect of international trade on employment, output, and consumption. Next we consider various government policies formulated to deal with foreign competition, including tariffs, quotas, and other forms of import protection; industrial policies intended to increase the competitiveness of our most essential industries; and income maintenance and retraining programs designed to assist workers who have lost their jobs because of foreign competition.

Foreign competition in product markets has become more pronounced, causing serious problems for many American workers. Increased mobility of workers has also made labor markets more international in scope. Wage levels in the United States are high, and enforcement of our immigration laws is lax, especially across our long borders with Mexico and Canada. Consequently, many immigrants have come to this country, either legally or illegally, to seek greater economic opportunity. Many refugees also have come seeking greater political freedom. In the concluding section of this chapter we discuss recent immigration to the United States, our immigration policies, how these policies have evolved over time, and the difficult problem of how to respond to the large-scale illegal immigration of the past quarter century.

EMPLOYMENT, PRODUCTIVITY CHANGE, AND FOREIGN COMPETITION

To examine the effect of international trade on employment in the United States, it is useful to begin with a discussion of long-term employment trends. Then we can examine how these trends have been affected by the recent increase in foreign competition.

Throughout the world economic development has been associated with a shift in employment from agriculture to manufacturing. Since World War II, however, the percentage of the American labor force employed in manufacturing has been falling steadily, as we saw in Chapter 2. As manufacturing employment has become less important, employment in the service industries has risen. Shifts out of farming no longer play a major role because only a small percentage of the labor force remains in agriculture.

Productivity Change

If the productivity of labor increases unusually fast in one industry, then its costs and prices should fall. With falling prices, demand and output will rise. Thus an unusually high growth in labor productivity will lead to greater output. The effect on the industry's employment is ambiguous, however. The greater output will lead to higher employment, other things being equal. On the other hand, the original increase in labor productivity means that less labor is needed per unit of output. As in the case of a wage change, there is both a scale effect and a factor-substitution effect. Because we do not know which of these effects is larger, we do not know whether an increase in labor productivity will increase or decrease an industry's labor demand and employment.

In the United States since World War II labor productivity has risen very rapidly in agriculture. Although agricultural output has increased, employment has fallen. Labor per unit of agricultural output has fallen substantially. But output has risen slowly because the demand for food is relatively inelastic and because food prices have not fallen very much relative to other prices.

Labor productivity in manufacturing and other goods-producing industries, such as mining and construction, has increased less than in agriculture but more than in most services. The number of manufacturing workers has remained relatively constant while the number of service workers has risen dramatically. Because of productivity increases in manufacturing, its share of total output (GNP) has remained relatively constant since 1950, despite a sharp decline in the percentage of all workers employed in manufacturing.

Foreign Competition

We have seen that productivity increases can either increase or decrease employment in an industry or a sector of the economy. These conclusions apply to an economy that is sheltered from foreign competition, perhaps because of transportation costs or import quotas, or if productivity increases occur uniformly in all countries. If productivity increases are greater in other countries than in the United States, the price of imports will fall relative to the price of U.S. goods. If there are no import restrictions, then imports will increase. Exports will decline. Output and employment in the American industry will fall.

Average productivity in the United States remains higher than in most other countries, including Japan. But the rate of growth of productivity has been much lower in America than in Japan, especially in industries such as steel, electronics, and automobiles. Consider the automobile industry. Japanese attempts to sell automobiles in the United States failed abysmally in the 1950s. Although the cars were inexpensive, they were of poor quality. By the 1970s the Japanese could produce small cars that not only sold for less than American cars but also were of higher quality. According to the estimates of Abernathy, Clark, and Kantrow, by 1981 the average cost advantage of the Japanese on a small car was about 20 percent.[1] About half this advantage represents lower labor costs per hour of labor and the other half represents superior productivity of the Japanese auto industry.

The automobile industry is a good example of a high-wage industry suffering from foreign competition from the developed economies, especially Japan. Much of the foreign competition facing the United States comes from less-developed countries, including Mexico, Brazil, Korea, Taiwan, Singapore, and Hong Kong. Competition from these markets has created serious problems for many of our low-wage industries, especially textiles, apparel, and shoes.

Such industries are *labor intensive.* They do not require any very complex capital equipment, and there is relatively little technological change. Although some skill is required of the workers, such skills do not require either lengthy training periods or extensive teamwork. Because relatively unskilled labor represents a high proportion of total cost in these industries, it is difficult for the United States to compete against countries with much lower wage rates. Instead, it makes sense for the United States to concentrate on producing goods and services that are more *capital intensive,* especially those that require more human capital and thus pay higher wage rates. We shall discuss policy responses to increased foreign competition shortly.

The Value of the Dollar

Competition is based heavily on relative prices. As we have seen, changes in relative productivities affect differentials in costs and in prices. In considering an individual industry, such as automobiles or textiles, the rate of productivity growth

---

[1] William J. Abernathy, Kim B. Clark, and Alan M. Kantrow, *Industrial Renaissance* (New York: Basic Books, 1983), Chap. 5.

in the United States, relative to other countries, is a prime determinant of changes in the competitiveness of our industry, especially in the long run.

For short-run changes in the economy as a whole, foreign competition is determined mainly by the value of the dollar relative to other currencies. If the dollar is high relative to other currencies, such as the Japanese yen, then a dollar will buy an unusually large number of yen. Because the cost of a Japanese auto is set in terms of yen, a high value of the dollar will decrease the cost of the car in dollars, which enables the Japanese to sell more cheaply to American consumers. By the same reasoning, a high value of the dollar makes American products more expensive for the Japanese.

From the end of World War II to 1973 countries tried to maintain fixed exchange rates. Under the Bretton Woods agreement of 1944 the major industrial countries agreed to use fiscal and monetary policies to keep the value of their currencies from changing, relative to each other and to gold. While countries needed to revalue their currencies occasionally, such changes were relatively infrequent.

Since 1973 exchange rates have been flexible, which means that the relative value of different currencies has been free to vary with changes in supply and demand. Instead of using fiscal and monetary policies to keep the value of its currency in line, each country has been free to use such policies to meet domestic objectives.

From 1973 to 1980 the value of the dollar fell relative to most other currencies. As a result, our exports increased and our imports declined. From 1980 to 1985 the value of the dollar increased by over 50 percent, causing a corresponding price increase for American products relative to their foreign competitors. This increase in the value of the dollar led to serious problems for our export industries, such as agriculture, and for industries that compete with imports, such as automobiles. Since 1985 the value of the dollar has declined, helping our export and import-competing industries. Not all the economic effects of the dollar's lower value have been positive, however. When the dollar has less value, the price of foreign goods for Americans is greater, and American firms that are no longer subject to as much foreign competition can charge higher prices. Although diminished, foreign competition remains intense for many industries, especially those where productivity has been increasing faster abroad than in the United States.

ADJUSTING TO INCREASED FOREIGN COMPETITION

In this section we discuss policies to help industries and workers adversely affected by foreign competition. First, we discuss import-protection policies. Then we consider industrial policies to help industries respond to the challenge of increased competition. We conclude with a discussion of retraining, relocation, and income maintenance policies to help workers who have lost their jobs.

Import Protection

To assist industries having problems with foreign competition, various policies have been established to restrain imports. The AFL-CIO, the unions directly affected, and the employers suffering from severe foreign competition all agree that import restrictions are essential, especially when other countries are either subsidizing their export industries or placing major restrictions on their own imports.

Historically, the main import barrier has been a *tariff*, a tax on imports. Since World War II the United States has led efforts to reduce tariffs in all countries. Nontariff protection, such as *import quotas* on steel and textiles, has now replaced tariffs as the main barrier to imports.

To evaluate the arguments for protection from foreign competition, let us begin with the case for free trade. Most economists favor free trade because it allows each country to specialize in those activities in which it is most productive relative to other countries. This is the *principle of comparative advantage*.

Let us develop an example to see how this principle works. The United States can produce many agricultural and some high-technology commodities more efficiently than Japan (that is, the United States can produce a given level of output with fewer inputs), but Japan can produce many manufactured goods more efficiently than the United States. Consequently, the United States should concentrate primarily on agricultural and high-technology goods and Japan on mass-production manufacturing, with the United States exporting food and computers to Japan for automobiles and other manufactured goods. If each country specializes in what it does best, such specialization will yield greater output and thus greater possibilities for both consumption and investment than if both countries tried to be economically self-sufficient. What counts is the *relative* efficiency of each country in producing different goods. For example, if the United States could produce both grain and automobiles more efficiently than Japan, but its efficiency advantage was greater in grain, then the United States should specialize in grain and Japan in cars even though the United States could make cars less expensively than Japan.

Advocates of high tariffs, import quotas, or other protectionist measures often argue that such measures are needed for a short period while an industry modernizes its production in order to meet the challenge of foreign competition. In fact, however, protection against imports usually reduces the competitive pressure on firms to become more efficient.[2]

Another argument for protection, especially for the steel industry, is national defense. Yet steel is a durable good where stockpiling is relatively easy. Also a war large enough to seriously disrupt imports is unlikely to spare our domestic steel industry.

---

[2]For a discussion of the steel industry, see Robert W. Crandall, "Trade Restrictions as a Barrier to Structural Adjustment in the International Steel Industry," a paper presented at the annual meeting of the American Economic Association (New York, December 1985). For the case of shoes, see Stephen D. Cohen and Ronald J. Meltzer, *United States International Economic Policy in Action* (New York: Praeger Publishers, 1982), Chap. 4.

The primary argument stressed by most protectionists is unfair competition from abroad. Many other countries are providing an unfair advantage to their export industries, though below-cost export pricing by government producers, through special tax advantages to private sector export producers, or through export subsidies such as cheap credit to foreign buyers. As long as other countries are pursuing such policies, we should retaliate, which may lead to freer trade in the long run.

There are important weaknesses in this argument for protection as a retaliatory measure. First, any additional trade barrier, regardless of who imposes it, reduces the gains available to both economies from trade. Second, retaliation by the United States may not lead other countries to reduce their trade barriers but instead may lead them to retaliate against us. Retaliation by the United States is only likely to work if there are norms, generally accepted in the international community, that are being violated by our competitors. On many issues such norms have been established as part of the General Agreement on Tariffs and Trade (GATT), but there are other important topics on which no such norms exist.[3]

Although import restrictions or other forms of retaliation are likely to hurt the economy as a whole, they will help the industries and workers who are suffering directly from foreign competition. Import restrictions on foreign steel do help steelworkers in the United States, but by making steel more expensive in this country such quotas hurt those who use our steel, including our automobile industry and its workers. If other countries retaliate by restricting their imports from the United States (for example, by restricting grain imports), our farmers are hurt. Thus there is a basic equity issue as to whether efforts should be made, through protectionist or other measures, to aid victims of foreign competition at the expense of other economic sectors.

In our market economy we expect firms and workers to look out for their own interests and to pay a price if they do not do so successfully. On the other hand, we restrict some business practices, such as selling output below cost in order to drive competitors out of business and obtain a monopoly position. Similarly, the United States imposes an "antidumping" import duty equal to the difference between the export price a country charges in the United States and the price charged in its domestic market.

Workers and firms generally are aware that they can achieve sizable gains if effective import restrictions are established for their industry. Quotas generally are preferable to tariffs for those seeking protection. Although tariffs would generate revenue for the federal government, quotas have generally been preferred by those

---

[3]For further discussion of the issue of unfair competition and how the United States should respond, see Robert E. Baldwin and T. Scott Thompson, "Responding to Trade-Distorting Policies of Other Countries," *American Economic Review* (May 1984), pp. 271–76; and Judith L. Goldstein and Stephen D. Krasner, "Unfair Trade Practices: The Case for a Differential Response," *American Economic Review* (May 1984), pp. 282–87.

seeking protection.[4] From the perspective of a threatened industry, a quota is better, since it is less likely to be offset by a continuing decline in the cost competitiveness of the affected industry and because the effect on product prices is less visible to the consumer. Because import quotas can provide large gains for a small percentage of the electorate, workers and firms in the affected industry have a strong incentive to become well informed and to lobby to increase their influence in the political process. The losses to consumers (and to those producing for export) from import quotas generally exceed the gains to the protected industries. But since the individual consumer pays only a small cost, consumers have little incentive to become well informed and to lobby.

Nevertheless, the gains to free trade are apparent to many, including exporters. Thus some trade barriers have been falling. For example, in 1988 the United States and Canada negotiated a free-trade agreement, which will phase out all tariffs between the two countries over a ten year period. The twelve nations of the European Economic Community, with a combined GNP about equal to that of the United States, have agreed to unify their economies and to remove all internal trade barriers by 1992. Although these agreements may be difficult to fully implement, they will result in some significant reduction in barriers to trade.

As competition in international trade intensifies, three large trading blocks are developing; the United States and Canada, Europe, and Japan. It is not yet clear whether trade barriers among these three blocks will increase or decrease in the future.

Industrial Policy

Many industries are suffering long-term structural problems, at least partly as a result of increased competition from imports. Among the industries affected are steel and automobiles, industries that have long been associated with the industrial strength of the United States. Competition from the Japanese has also been very strong in many relatively new, technologically advanced industries. Such competition is now beginning in silicon chips and advanced computers.

The reasons for the success of the Japanese economy are complex. One factor is the Japanese system of labor relations, discussed in Chapter 6. Another possible reason is the close cooperation between business leaders, bankers, and the Ministry of International Trade and Industry (MITI). With this Japanese experience in mind some in the United States have advocated that this country establish an industrial policy to improve the productivity of our economy. For example, Magaziner and Reich

suggest that U.S. companies and the government develop a coherent and coordinated industrial policy whose aim is to raise the real income of our citizens by

---

[4]Quotas can either be set unilaterally or be negotiated with our trading partners under the threat of more severe unilateral action if no agreement is reached. Such negotiated restrictions are referred to as voluntary restraint agreements.

improving the patterns of our investments, rather than by focusing only on aggregate investment levels.[5]

As Schultze indicates in his critique of industrial policy, such a policy is based on the premise that

government [should] deliberately set out to plan and create an industrial structure, and a pattern of output and investment, significantly different from what the market would have produced. . . .

Industrial policy thus aims to channel the flow of private investment towards some firms and industries—and necessarily, therefore, away from others. The government develops, at least in broad outline, an explicit conception of the direction in which industrial structure ought to be evolving, and then adopts a set of tax, loan, trade, regulatory, and other policies to lead economic activity along the desired path.[6]

In Japan and some other countries an important component of industrial policy has been protection from foreign competition until a fledgling industry was in a position to compete successfully in the world economy.

In the United States more emphasis has been given to industrial policy as a way to help declining industries, especially those suffering from increased foreign competition. In the automobile industry, for example, the federal government provided loan guarantees to the Chrysler Corporation as part of a financial package that enabled the company to modernize its production and ultimately become competitive once more. In return for government assistance, workers had to agree to wage cuts, suppliers and bankers had to wait longer to receive payments due, and stockholders had to forego normal dividends.

Although the Chrysler "bailout" succeeded, other government efforts have not worked out as well. Despite considerable import protection, for example, the steel industry shows little sign of modernizing sufficiently to regain its competitive position in the world market, except perhaps for certain specialty items.

There are several reasons to be skeptical about the wisdom of an industrial policy to revitalize industries having difficulties because of foreign competition. First, as the steel industry illustrates, it is difficult to ensure that import protection or other subsidies to such industries will lead to greater modernization rather than simply allow firms to continue in their previous ways now that they are subject to less competitive pressure from the marketplace. Second, it is very doubtful that the government has the knowledge to do better than the market in determining which industries should receive the most capital and other resources. Third, even if the government could develop such knowledge, it is unlikely that the American political system would allocate resources across firms, industries, or regions on the basis of economic criteria rather than political pressure. Markets generally are more

---

[5]Ira Magaziner and Robert Reich, *Modernizing America's Business* (San Diego, Calif.: Harcourt Brace Jovanovich, 1982), p. 4.

[6]Schultze, "Industrial Policy: A Dissent," p. 4. Much of our discussion of industrial policy is based on Schultze's analysis.

efficient than governments in allocating resources because profit opportunities provide investors with an especially powerful incentive to seek out those industries where their capital will be most productive.

Our political system is more decentralized than the Japanese and our traditions are more individualistic. Thus an industrial policy is less likely to be effective in the United States than in Japan. In addition, it is not clear that industrial policy has played any substantial role in the economic success of the Japanese. Hugh Patrick, professor of Far Eastern economics at Yale comments:

> Indeed, looking at Japanese industrial development as a whole in the post-war period, I think the predominant source of its success was the entrepreneurial vigor of private enterprises that invested a good deal and took a lot of risks. The main role of the government was to provide an accommodating and supportive environment for the market, rather than providing leadership or direction. Unquestionably, government planning bodies were important in a few industrial sectors, but not in many others, which flourished on their own.[7]

Although industrial policy has many weaknesses, the United States government should play some role in helping industries to compete internationally. First, the government should help support basic research where results are difficult for firms to patent. Second, the government has primary responsibility for education in the United States. Thus it needs to ensure that an adequate supply of engineers, scientists, and other educated workers are available for firms. Third, the government has responsibility to assist workers who have lost their jobs because of foreign competition, technological change, or other structural changes in the economy.

Assisting Dislocated Workers

When an industry is suffering from foreign competition and many workers are losing their jobs, it is generally better for the economy if the government tries to help the workers find new jobs rather than try to save jobs by restricting imports. The benefits from unrestricted trade can finance considerable subsidies to displaced workers for retraining, relocation, and income support. Many European countries have more extensive programs than the United States in these areas, perhaps in part because foreign trade has been more important for their economies.

Workers who lose their jobs as a result of foreign competition and cannot find new jobs are structurally unemployed. Thus our discussion in chapter 10 of policies, such as employment and training programs, for the structurally unemployed also applies to this special case. In fact, there is little economic reason to have programs aimed at those who have been hurt by foreign competition but that are not open to those who have lost their jobs for other reasons, including technological change, shifts in consumer tastes, and firms going out of business for any other reason. Politically, however, foreign competition does present a special case

---

[7]Interview in *Manhattan Report on Economic Policy,* Manhattan Institute for Policy Research, vol. 2, no. 7 (October 1982). Quoted in Schultze, "Industrial Policy."

because the threat comes from another country and because assisting workers may reduce the danger of import restrictions.

The Trade Adjustment Assistance (TAA) program was first established as part of the Trade Expansion Act of 1962, was significantly expanded under the United States Trade Act of 1974, and then cut back in 1985. TAA was designed to provide job search, retraining, and relocation assistance to displaced workers as well as extra income support. Prior to 1985 the program mainly provided income support, a form of supplementary unemployment insurance.[8] TAA was designed with both equity and efficiency goals in mind. The equity goal of cushioning income loss was reasonably well achieved for those who receive benefits.[9] But the efficiency goal was more elusive. By providing generous support to recipients, TAA reduced the incentive for workers to find new jobs. Thus Richardson found that three out of four workers receiving TAA benefits returned to their former employers. Of those who did lose their jobs permanently, TAA recipients were more likley to end up with lower-paying new jobs than those who received only UI, perhaps because TAA recipients waited too long in hopes of returning to their former employers.

In 1986 the TAA program was modified. Now participation in job search activities is required as a condition for receiving allowances. The revised program also provides more retraining.

Another approach has been proposed by Robert Lawrence.[10] He suggests that workers who have been displaced as a result of foreign competition should be given a subsidy equal to perhaps 50 percent of the difference between the worker's hourly pay on the new job and that on the job lost. The subsidy would not be permanent but might last for several years. This approach, which Lawrence calls *trade adjustment compensation,* would be especially valuable for older workers with high seniority and many firm-specific skills. Such workers seldom can obtain new jobs that pay nearly as well as those they have lost. This approach also provides a strong work incentive, since the value of the subsidy would increase the more hours the person worked. While Lawrence's proposal for trade adjustment compensation is designed primarily to aid workers who have lost their jobs because of foreign competition, his proposal also deserves attention for dealing with other structural dislocations, including workers who have lost their jobs because of technological change.

---

[8]According to Richardson, for example, from 1975 to 1979 only 1 out of 30 TAA recipients entered training, only 2 out of 200 received a job search allowance, and only 1 of 350 received a relocation allowance. See J. David Richardson, "Trade Adjustment Assistance and the United States Trade Act of 1974: An Analytical Examination and Worker Survey," in *Import Competition and Response,* ed. Jagdish N. Bhagwati (Chicago: University of Chicago Press for the National Bureau of Economic Research, 1982). The empirical evidence of TAA cited in the next two paragraphs is also taken from this source.

[9]Together with Unemployment Insurance (UI), TAA replaced an average of 76 percent of workers' after-tax income, although the TAA payments often did not come until more than a year after the workers lost their jobs. TAA benefits were heavily concentrated in a few industries. Between 1975 and 1980, for example, one-third of all recipients were in either the footwear or the automobile industries, while these two industries accounted for less than one-sixth of UI recipients.

[10]See Lawrence, *Can American Compete?* pp. 131–33. A variant of this approach is being tried out as a pilot project under the Omnibus Trade and Competitiveness Act of 1988.

IMMIGRATION POLICY

Foreign competition has become an important issue for many American workers. Although this competition often arises in the product market, American workers are also subject to another kind of foreign competition. In the absence of legal restrictions labor as well as output is mobile across countries. For example, U.S. wage rates are much higher than those in Mexico and most other Latin American countries. Consequently, many Mexican workers desire to work in the United States, either temporarily or permanently. American firms also have an incentive to encourage such migration in order to obtain a larger supply of hard-working low-wage labor.

Our nation is one of immigrants. As recently as the early twentieth century the annual rate of immigration was about one million people per year, more than 1 percent of the total population of the United States. In the early years of the country many people came either for religious freedom or as slaves. Since the legal prohibition of the slave trade in the early nineteenth century, most immigrants have come voluntarily to improve their economic opportunities.

In Chapter 4 we discussed how the decision to migrate depends on whether the expected benefits (for example, higher earnings at the destination) exceed the expected costs (for example, severing ties to family and friends, learning a new language and culture). In addition, the extent of migration across countries also depends very heavily on government restrictions.

The United States has never restricted emigration to other countries. However, because of good opportunities in this country, we have never experienced any significant out-migration.

Prior to 1924 the United States also placed little restriction on immigration.[11] Since 1924 legal immigration has been severely restricted, partly because of concern that competition by immigrants was reducing the wage rates and job opportunities of American workers. Since the mid-1960s, however, there has been considerable illegal immigration into the United States. After outlining the history of our immigration policies, we consider the effects of immigration on our economy.[12]

The History of Immigration Policy in the United States

In the nineteenth century most immigration was from western and northern Europe. The majority of the U.S. population lived on farms, and new land was available on the frontier. Immigration could help develop the country and expand its boundaries. It could also provide cheap labor for employers, an important political force in the period after the Civil War.

---

[11]Restricted immigration by nationality began with the exclusion of Chinese in 1882.

[12]For a more detailed discussion of this history, see Vernon M. Briggs, *Immigration Policy and the American Labor Force.* For a recent brief account, see also *The Economic Report of the President* (Washington, D.C.: Government Printing Office, 1986), Chap. 7.

By the beginning of the twentieth century opposition to immigration was developing for several reasons. First, the majority of the immigrants were now coming from southern and eastern Europe, population groups that were seen as both alien and "inferior" by many Americans whose ancestry was from western Europe. Second, organized labor now had somewhat greater political influence. The AFL was strongly opposed to continued large-scale immigration. New immigrants sometimes were imported as strikebreakers and were often willing to work below the union rate. Third, by the time of World War I some employers were opposed to immigration on the grounds that too many of the new immigrants were socialists and unionists.

Employers in the United States managed quite well during World War I, despite both a high demand for labor and a significant drop in immigration. After the war the possibility of greatly increased immigration scared many people and led to much more stringent restrictions. As a result, Congress passed the Immigration Act of 1924, limiting immigration from Europe, Asia, and Africa to fewer than 400,000 people per year, with the majority to come from the countries of northern and western Europe. Immigration from southern and eastern Europe was limited to about 155,000, far below the numbers that had been coming from these countries. Within these limits preference was given to those with skills "urgently needed" by employers. The legislation was enforced with reasonable success. Because emigration from Europe was costly, the threat of deportation provided a significant deterrent to illegal immigration.

Immigration fell dramatically in the 1920s. Yet employers still desired the cheap labor that immigrants had previously provided. As a result, beginning with World War II, opportunities for blacks in the North increased substantially. In contrast to the migrants from Europe, blacks could return home easily. Thus temporary migration was more common than among immigrants from Europe. Temporary migration also has been common among those entering the U.S. illegally from Mexico in recent years.

Although there was relatively little change in our laws restricting immigration from other countries from the 1920s to the 1960s, since then there have been several important changes. First, a preference system was established, putting primary emphasis on the reunification of families rather than on skills needed in the labor market. Second, restrictions have been applied to the Western as well as the Eastern Hemisphere, a change instituted in 1968 as the primary demand for immigration to the United States shifted from Europe to Latin America. An annual limit of 270,000 was established, with no further restrictions by continent, except for a limit of 20,000 from any individual country. This quota system does not include immediate relatives (spouses, minor children, and parents of adult citizens). Each year there are almost as many immigrants who are relatives as there are entering under the quota system. Refugees are also not included in the quota. Under the Refugee Act of 1980 nearly 100,000 political refugees have been admitted to the U.S. each year. With refugees and immediate family members (spouses, minor children, and parents of U.S. citizens) included, total legal immigration is over half a million per year. Return migration is about 100,000, leading to net legal immigration of slightly under 500,000 annually.

The quotas set are much lower than the number wishing to immigrate, especially from Mexico. Policing the long border is difficult and the penalties for being caught are small (usually just being sent back to Mexico). Obviously, it is impossible to obtain accurate estimates of the number of illegal immigrants. Total immigration, both legal and illegal, has probably accounted for about half the population increase in the United States since 1970. Between 1970 and 1980, the proportion of the population who are foreign born increased from 4.8 to 6.2 percent.

The average legal immigrant is much more highly skilled than the average illegal immigrant. Both groups usually settle in one of six states. Almost half the immigrants go either to New York or to California while about one quarter go to Texas, Florida, Illinois, or New Jersey. Thus the effects of immigration, both legal and illegal, are heavily concentrated in a few parts of the country. Within each state the majority of the immigrants tend to settle in large cities.

Illegal Immigration

In the United States enforcement of the immigration laws is not very effective. Ever since the United States began to restrict immigrants there has been some illegal immigration.[13] But widespread illegal immigration is a relatively recent phenomenon. Most illegal immigration is from Mexico and other countries of Latin America. Prior to 1968 it was relatively easy for anyone from the Western Hemisphere to immigrate legally.

Starting in the late 1960s illegal immigration increased dramatically. Although it is difficult to make accurate estimates of illegal activities, many researchers believe that current illegal immigration is at least equal in numbers to legal immigration. One reason for the increase in illegal immigration in the late 1960s was the very high demand for labor as a result of the Vietnam War. This high demand encouraged employers to seek cheap foreign labor for jobs that Americans were not willing to take. In addition, the population of Mexico has increased dramatically. Although Mexico has developed its economy, there have been few gains for the majority of the population. With a large, growing surplus of workers in Mexico, an increasing number are seeking jobs in the United States. It is estimated that about 60 percent of illegal immigrants to the United States come from Mexico, with another 20 percent from the countries of the Caribbean where low income and high population growth are also common.

As we shall discuss in more detail shortly, illegal immigration has some advantages for the United States. Cheap labor is available, helping both employers and their customers. The pressure to restrict immigration in recent years has come

---

[13]For more information, see Briggs, *Immigration Policy and American Labor Force;* Michael J. Piore, *Birds of Passage* (Cambridge: Cambridge University Press, 1979); and Walter Fogel "Illegal Alien Workers in the United States," *Industrial Relations* (October 1977), pp. 243–63.

mainly from those concerned with its effects on the employment and earnings of American citizens. Those favoring restrictions have had enough strength to get legislation passed but not enough to have it effectively enforced.

Approximately one million illegal immigrants were apprehended each year during the early 1980s, an impressive total considering that the Immigration and Naturalization Service (INS) had only about two thousand border patrol officers and fewer than two thousand other immigration inspectors. Processing one million illegal immigrants through our criminal justice system would be very expensive. In addition, there is little support for large penalties to those whose only crime is seeking better opportunities in the United States. Thus the only penalty for most illegal immigrants who are apprehended is being sent back to their homeland. For many of those apprehended, this simply means being sent from one side of the Mexican-U.S. border to the other, where they can return again with only relatively minor difficulty. Crossing the border is sufficiently difficult that families with young children are largely excluded, but most able-bodied single adults can make it—if not initially, then on a subsequent try.

Prior to the late 1980s the only way the government could enforce the immigration laws was to apprehend and penalize the immigrants themselves, primarily by deportation. As a result of increased concern over the effects of large illegal immigration, in 1986 Congress passed the Immigration Reform and Control Act (IRCA), also known as the Simpson-Rodino bill. In an attempt to reduce the job opportunities for illegal immigrants, the IRCA established penalties (sanctions) for employers who knowingly hired illegal aliens. At the same time it granted amnesty to illegal immigrants who had lived continuously in the United States during the five years prior to the date the legislation took effect in 1987.

As Chiswick points out, there are several reasons why this legislation is not likely to be very effective in reducing illegal immigration.[14] First, even before the IRCA was passed, many employers thought it was against the law to employ illegal immigrants. Second, although under IRCA an employer must check a worker's documents (e.g., birth certificate, driver's license) before hiring to ensure that the worker is not an illegal alien, the employer need only certify that the documents appear genuine. More elaborate checking would have been even more costly for employers than the present certification procedures. Yet the current approach provides a significant incentive for illegal aliens to obtain counterfeit documents or to use the legal documents of other people. Third, the responsibility for checking on employers rests with the wage and hours inspectors of the Department of Labor. There are not a large number of such inspectors, however, and the number has not been increased, despite the major new responsibilities they have been given under the IRCA.[15]

The amnesty provisions of the IRCA were designed to protect illegal aliens

---

[14]See Barry R. Chiswick, "Illegal Immigration and Immigration Control," *Journal of Economic Perspectives.*

[15]These inspectors also enforce other legislation, such as the Fair Labor Standards Act, with its provisions for minimum wage rates and a 50 percent premium for overtime hours.

already well established in the United States from the consequences of employer sanctions. In the long run, however, these provisions may do more to increase the supply of low-wage labor in this country than the employer sanctions do to decrease the supply of such labor.[16] First, legal aliens can more readily apply for unemployment insurance and thus are less likely to leave the U.S. at the end of a seasonal or other short-term job. Second, families of those granted amnesty are likely to immigrate. Many such family members are likely to become unskilled workers in the United States. Third, this amnesty is likely to encourage some potential migrants to believe that additional amnesties will be established in the future, thus increasing the incentive to become an illegal alien. Large-scale immigration is all the more likely in the future, since so many have already come. Many potential immigrants have family and friends living here who can provide information about opportunities and also be of assistance to new immigrants, thus reducing the adjustment costs of immigration.

Although the IRCA may not have been very effective in reducing illegal immigration, it may have increased discrimination against Hispanics. If employers fear they will be penalized for hiring anyone who turns out to have been an illegal immigrant, then one way they can reduce this perceived risk is to avoid hiring anyone who they suspect might be in this country illegally. Because illegal immigration is more common among Hispanics than among Anglos, some employers have avoided hiring Hispanics as a consequence of the IRCA.

THE EFFECTS OF IMMIGRATION

Since the 1960s the United States has experienced a second peak wave of immigration, one comparable to that of the 1890–1911 period. During both periods immigration of all kinds has amounted to about 40 percent of the annual growth in the U.S. population. Because of increased immigration and the decline in domestic fertility rates, the proportion of the population who are foreign born increased from 4.8 to 6.2 percent between 1970 and 1980.

As we discussed in Chapter 4, immigration can be expected to improve the economic position of most migrants. But what effect does immigration have on the host country? This issue has played a major role in shaping the immigration policy of the United States. As we have seen, a major motivation for restricting immigration has been concern for possible adverse effects of such immigration on those already here. Let us consider the validity of that concern.

Skilled Immigrants

Twenty-two percent of legal immigrants have completed four or more years of college, compared with only 16 percent of the native born.[17] These highly educated immigrants will have already received their education at their own expense or at the

---

[16]Ibid. p. 111.

[17]See *Economic Report of the President* (Washington, D.C.: Government Printing Office, 1986), p. 220.

expense of their country of origin. Because of their education and other skills, such immigrants usually have high earnings. Initially, there are some adjustment costs, so the immigrants earn less than U.S. workers of comparable skill for the first few years in this country. After a decade or two, the average immigrant actually earns more than a native-born worker of comparable education and experience.[18]

Our society gains from skilled immigrants in several ways. After the initial adjustment period, immigrants may earn more than equally skilled nonmigrants because migrants are typically very hard working and ambitious. Without such personality traits, people are less likely to migrate to a new country. Because their earnings are high, the skilled immigrants will pay considerable taxes. There will be higher demand for workers with complementary skills. We may also gain from the externalities associated with higher education, especially in the case of new discoveries by immigrant scientists. The main group in this country that is likely to lose are those with similar skills. The large-scale immigration of foreign physicians, for example, reduces the demand for American doctors, thereby reducing their incomes. There is also likely to be a loss for the country of origin, which has borne the cost of educating the worker. This problem, often referred to as the *brain drain,* is a legitimate concern of countries that are losing many highly educated workers, who emigrate for better opportunities abroad. But such immigration is generally a plus from the perspective of the United States economy. Although the United States places restrictions even on the immigration of the highly educated, this group does receive some preference in filling the immigration quotas.

Unskilled Immigrants

The concern with immigration in recent years has focused on the effects of large-scale illegal immigration. Most such immigrants are unskilled. Many are not able to speak English. Let us examine the effect of such immigrants, starting with the effect on unskilled American workers and then shifting to the effects on the entire American economy.

Most illegal immigrants come seeking jobs and are successful in finding them. Those arguing for tighter enforcement of immigration policies often argue that each job obtained by an immigrant results in one less job for an American citizen. In contrast, advocates of the status quo argue that illegal immigrants take jobs that American workers are not willing to accept, jobs with low pay and poor working conditions.

As can be seen with the aid of Figure 11-1, neither of these views is likely to be correct. With the present illegal immigration the wage rate is W_0 and total employment is E_0. At this low wage rate almost all the jobs go to illegal immigrants, but there are E_2 native-born workers.

If the supply of illegal immigrants were eliminated, the supply curve for unskilled workers would shift from S_0 to S_1, and the employment of unskilled

---

[18]See Barry R. Chiswick, "The Effect of Americanization on the Earnings of Foreign-Born Men," *Journal of Political Economy* (October 1978), pp. 897–921.

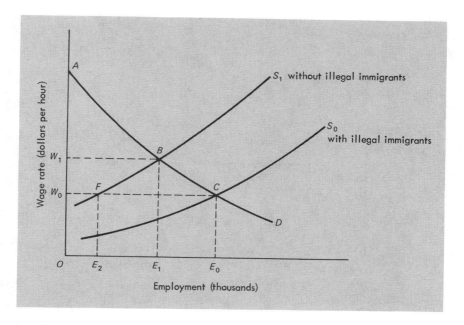

FIGURE 11-1   Demand and Supply of Unskilled Labor with Competitive Labor
Market

American workers would increase from E_2 to E_1 while the wage would rise from W_0 to W_1. The higher wage rate would increase the number of Americans willing to take the jobs previously held mostly by illegal immigrants. On the other hand, the higher wage rate would also reduce the total number of jobs available.

The negatively sloped demand curve for unskilled labor results from both scale and factor-substitution effects, as discussed in Chapter 5. If employers can substitute other factors of production fairly easily in the long run, as is likely to be true in some manufacturing industries, then the demand curve in Figure 11-1 will be relatively flat. In this case, eliminating illegal immigrants from the labor market would lead to little increase in the wage rate and little increase in the employment of American workers. On the other hand, if it is not possible to substitute other factors of production, as may be true for some services, then the demand curve will be less elastic and there will be greater increases in both the wage rate and in jobs for the native born.

Thus far we have assumed that the labor market is competitive. Since the jobs are low-wage positions, they should be subject to minimum wage legislation. So we would have the situation shown in Figure 11-2.

With the minimum wage rate the elimination of illegal immigrants from the labor market need not increase the market wage and could lead to an extra job for the native born for each illegal immigrant eliminated from the market. Although minimum wage legislation is not always enforced effectively, most illegal immigrants do earn approximately the minimum wage. Because of wage rigidities, illegal

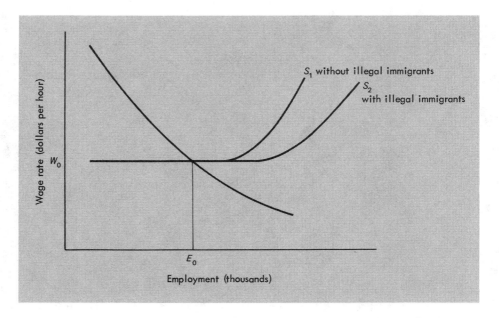

FIGURE 11-2   Demand and Supply of Unskilled Labor with Minimum Wage Rate

immigration may significantly decrease the job opportunities of unskilled American workers. For example, illegal immigration may have led to an appreciable increase in youth unemployment.

The empirical evidence, though limited, suggests that legal immigration has only a small effect on the employment and earnings of the native born.[19] There has been less empirical work on the effects of illegal immigration. Perhaps the best evidence that illegal immigrants have an appreciable impact on at least some parts of the country comes from Smith and Newman, who found that real wage rates are lower for areas near the Mexican border, where the influence of illegal immigrants is likely to be greatest.[20]

We have seen that immigration of unskilled workers hurts the economic position of unskilled native-born workers. Other Americans gain from immigration of unskilled workers. Lower wage rates as a result of the illegal immigration of unskilled workers should result in lower prices for consumers and in higher profits for employers. Greater profits for employers provide an incentive for firms to encourage such immigration. As long as the labor and product markets are reasonably competitive, however, the availability of cheap labor from illegal immigrants

---

[19]See Jean Baldwin Grossman, "The Substitutability of Natives and Immigrants in Production," *Review of Economics and Statistics* (November 1982), pp. 596–603.

[20]See Barton Smith and Robert Newman, "Depressed Wages along the Mexican-U.S. Border: An Empirical Analysis," *Economic Inquiry* (January 1977), pp. 51–61.

should lead to increases in the number (and size) of employers of unskilled labor, thus reducing profits to the normal competitive level. In the long run, the main effect of increased immigration should be lower prices for the output they produce; therefore, the main long-run beneficiaries of illegal immigration are the consumers of their output.

For the economy as a whole let us consider whether the economic gains to the United States from illegal immigration are likely to exceed the costs. If wages are rigid downward, then immigrants gain at the expense of increased unemployment among American workers. Total output and income remain constant while the share going to U.S. citizens declines. On the other hand, if the economy is competitive, with flexible wages and prices, then immigration will increase total income and output. In Figure 11-1 the value of total output (and income) increases for $OABE_1$ to $OACE_0$ as a result of illegal immigration. The net increase in total income is E_1BCE_0. Since the income of the immigrants is E_2FCE_0, the income of Americans will increase or decrease depending on whether E_1BCE_0 is greater or less than E_2FCE_0, which in turn depends on the slopes of the supply and demand curves. If the supply and demand curves are reasonably steep (inelastic), then the presence of illegal immigrants in the labor market may increase the aggregate income of the native born.

Illegal immigrants receive very few public services.[21] Many are here temporarily, with no children to be educated. Because they are here illegally, most such immigrants seek to avoid all contact with the authorities and seldom claim benefits from Unemployment Insurance, Social Security, or other income maintenance programs. Yet most have Social Security and income taxes withheld from their paychecks. Thus illegal immigrants probably provide a net subsidy to the native born by paying more in taxes than they receive in government services.

Many people gain from illegal immigration, including employers, consumers, and taxpayers. Some native-born workers lose, but others gain. When the immigrants are unskilled, the economic gains may well be greater from illegal than legal immigration, since illegal immigrants are less likely to use government services. Because many of the effects of illegal immigration are positive, it perhaps should not be surprising that we have not devoted extensive resources to enforcing our immigration laws.

In the long run, however, illegal immigration may be costly, as increasing numbers of immigrants settle down and raise families. Second-generation immigrants are often less willing to work hard at low-wage jobs and more willing to use government services.[22]

---

[21]See *The Economic Report of the President* (Washington, D.C.: Government Printing Office, 1986), pp. 213–34. The use of transfer payments is low even when legal immigrants are included in the analysis; see Francine D. Blau, "The Use of Transfer Payments by Immigrants," *Industrial and Labor Relations Review* (January 1984), pp. 222–39.

[22]See Piore, *Birds of Passage*.

SUMMARY

1. The economy of the United States has become increasingly affected by developments in other countries. Imports and exports have both increased significantly. American workers in many industries have suffered from the effects of foreign competition.

2. In an economy that is sheltered from foreign competition an unusually large increase in an industry's labor productivity can either increase or decrease its employment depending on whether the reduced labor needed per unit of output is more than offset by the increased total output that results from lower costs and prices.

3. If productivity in an industry is increasing faster in other countries, and if there are no restrictions on international trade, then output and employment in that industry in the United States will fall as other countries increase their share of the world market. Although average productivity in the United States remains high relative to most other countries, the rate of productivity growth has been much higher in Japan. This increase in Japanese productivity has led to employment losses in many industries in the United States, including automobiles, steel, and electronics.

4. Import protection through either quotas or tariffs helps protect the jobs of some workers, at least temporarily. However, import protection also results in higher prices for American consumers and can lead to fewer jobs in other industries.

5. An industrial policy, where the government helps provide more capital to certain industries, is not likely to improve the economy because the government is not apt to do better than the market in determining which industries should receive more capital and other resources.

6. For workers who lose their jobs because of foreign competition, government can provide retraining and job search assistance. Some temporary income support is also desirable, although care must be taken that such support not be so generous that workers have little incentive to seek new positions.

7. Labor as well as output is mobile across countries. Thus U.S. workers are affected directly by labor market competition from immigrants as well as indirectly by product market competition from imported goods.

8. Since 1924 immigration into the United States has been severely restricted, partly in an effort to improve the job opportunities of American workers.

9. In recent decades illegal immigration has become common. The majority of illegal immigrants are unskilled workers from Mexico. As long as the wage differential between the United States and Mexico remains high and the Mexican population continues to increase rapidly, there is an incentive for Mexican workers to immigrate to the United States.

10. Reducing illegal immigration would reduce the supply of unskilled workers, thus increasing wage rates and job opportunities for unskilled Americans. For each illegal immigrant excluded, there would not be an additional job available for the native born, however, because the higher wage rate would reduce the demand for unskilled labor. High wage rates would also increase firms' costs, thus leading to higher prices for consumers.

KEY CONCEPTS

COMPARATIVE ADVANTAGE	IMMIGRATION QUOTA
VALUE OF THE DOLLAR	BRACERO
IMPORT QUOTA	GUEST WORKER
TARIFF	EMPLOYER SANCTIONS
INDUSTRIAL POLICY	AMNESTY
TRADE ADJUSTMENT COMPENSATION	BRAIN DRAIN
IMMIGRANTS	

REVIEW QUESTIONS

1. Discuss why foreign competition has increased in recent years.
2. Do you believe you have gained or lost as a result of foreign competition? Why? Do you believe your answer will be different twenty years from now?
3. Discuss the arguments for and against import quotas and other trade restrictions as a response to foreign competition.
4. To what extent is foreign competition influenced by fiscal and monetary policies?
5. Discuss the case for using industrial policy to increase the ability of the U.S. economy to compete with other countries, especially Japan.
6. Should there be special programs to aid workers who have been displaced by foreign competition—programs in addition to those available to help other unemployed workers?
7. Should the United States continue to severely restrict legal immigration? If so, which of the following groups should be given the most preference for admission?
   (a) political refugees
   (b) highly skilled workers, such as physicians and scientists
   (c) close relatives of U.S. citizens

324 American Workers in a World Economy

8.   What should be done about the problem of illegal immigration? Discuss the value judgments underlying your proposal. Also discuss the economic effects of illegal immigration and how these effects are related to the political feasibility of your proposal.

READINGS

BALDWIN, ROBERT E., and ANNE O. KRUGER, eds., *The Structure and Evolution of Recent U.S. Trade Policy.* Chicago: University of Chicago Press, 1985.

BRIGGS, VERNON M., JR., *Immigration Policy and the American Labor Force.* Baltimore: Johns Hopkins University Press, 1984.

CHISWICK, BARRY R., "Illegal Immigration and Immigration Control," *Journal of Economic Perspectives* (Summer 1988), pp. 101–15.

FOGEL, WALTER, "Illegal Alien Workers in the United States," *Industrial Relations* (October 1977), pp. 243–63.

LAWRENCE, ROBERT Z., *Can America Compete?* Washington, D.C.: Brookings Institution, 1984.

PIORE, MICHAEL J., *Birds of Passage.* Cambridge: Cambridge University Press, 1979.

SCHULTZE, CHARLES L., "Industrial Policy: A Dissent," *Brookings Review* (Fall 1983), pp. 3–12.

THE EVOLUTION
OF AMERICAN UNIONS

Sidney and Beatrice Webb defined a trade union as "a continuous association of wage earners for the purpose of maintaining or improving the conditions of their working lives." This chapter examines the development of such associations in the United States.

We begin with a brief discussion of the benefits and costs of unions to their members and then show how this framework of analysis can be used to help explain the history of American unions. This chapter serves as an introduction to the labor relations section of the book. Therefore we also consider the trade union world of today and how unions and collective bargaining in the United States differ from the experience in other countries, especially Japan. Important aspects of labor history are also examined in Chapter 13, where we consider the effects of changing public policies, and in Chapter 14, where we discuss in more detail the decline of unions in the private sector, especially since the 1970s.

UNION MEMBERSHIP: COLLECTIVE BENEFIT
AND INDIVIDUAL COST

By acting collectively as a union, workers can increase the cost to employers of resisting their demands.[1] Because it is easier for an employer to replace an individ-

---

[1]This section is based largely on Mancur Olson, *The Logic of Collective Action*.

ual employee than a large group of workers, unionized workers can usually obtain higher wages and better working conditions than if they were not organized.

The costs of joining a union vary greatly depending on the response of employers to unions. If employer opposition is strong and if there are no legal constraints, then the employer may fire any worker it suspects to be a union member.

Since 1932 it has been illegal to discharge an employee for union membership or activities. For most workers today the principle costs of union membership are union dues and any wages lost while on strike. These costs are usually rather modest. For example, many unions charge dues equal to about two hours' pay per month plus an initiation fee that seldom exceeds one hundred dollars. Strikes account for less than 1 percent of the working time of the average union member.

Even if the costs of joining a union are small relative to the benefits the union can provide, it may still be very difficult to organize a union. The problem is that most union benefits are collective, while costs are not.

A union must negotiate comparable wages for all equally productive workers employed by the same firm. If the union negotiated higher wages for its members, then the employer would have a strong incentive to replace the union workers with cheaper nonunion labor. When the union provides equal benefits to union and nonunion workers, there is no economic incentive for an individual worker to pay the costs of union membership. Such collective benefits generate the problem of *free riders,* as each worker has an incentive to let others bear the costs of obtaining the collective benefits.

Once a union is established, it may be able to negotiate a dues checkoff, where the employer agrees to deduct union dues from the paychecks of all workers in the bargaining unit. No such compulsion is possible to solve the free-rider problem when the union is first being organized, however. In this case workers have to have sufficient regard for each other and enough social interaction, on or off the job, so that social pressures will cause workers to act in the group interest rather than just in their individual self-interest. Those who are able and willing to take a leadership role win additional respect from their peers. In contrast, those who would undercut the union wage or work as strikebreakers face the threat of ostracism. Violence is also possible, especially in the case of strikebreakers. The importance of a group perspective, reinforced by social pressures, underlies the concept of worker solidarity.

The costs and benefits of union membership depend on many factors, including legislation and community attitudes as well as on the nature of both labor and product markets. We shall see their influence as we discuss the historical development of unions in the United States.

THE FIRST AMERICAN UNIONS

This history of American unionism is frequently dated from 1792, when a local union was formed by the journeymen cordwainers (shoemakers) of Philadelphia. Within the next ten years unions of shoemakers, carpenters, and printers were founded in Baltimore, Philadelphia, Boston, New York, and several other cities.

What accounts for the appearance of these associations? They cannot be traced to particular oppression of workers at that time. On the contrary, most workers were better off in 1800 than they had been in 1780. It is significant also that unions did not appear at first among the most exploited groups—the cotton-mill workers and home workers on piece rates—but among skilled tradesmen, such as the printers, carpenters, and shoemakers. In the United States as in most other industrial countries the relatively skilled and prosperous workers organized first. The first unions in Great Britain, for example, consisted of building- and printing-trades workers, who were followed shortly afterward by unions of tailors and wool combers. In Sweden the first unions were formed by the printers, the next by the carpenters, and the next by the skilled metal-trade workers.

Unions have arisen as local organizations of workers who shared a particular skill. Such workers are a relatively small group with strong social as well as vocational ties, a situation in which social pressures can be especially effective. It is also more difficult for an employer to combat a union of skilled workers because there will be fewer potential strikebreakers available to import from other areas. Skilled workers are scarcer, usually are less desperate for jobs, and may have a greater feeling of solidarity with others possessing similar skills.

Threats to an established position in the larger community can be effective in causing skilled workers to see a need to organize to protect their position. None of the industries organized during the period 1790–1830 had been significantly affected by machine methods. An important stimulus to union organization in some industries, however, was the broadening of the domestic market for manufacturers, which resulted from the improvement of transportation facilities. This expansion meant intensified competition in the sale of goods—shoes made in Philadelphia competed increasingly with shoes made in New York, Baltimore, and other cities. The merchant capitalist appeared, playing off small masters against each other and forcing them to cut wages in order to survive, thereby causing the workers to unite in opposition.

The growth of the market also fostered division of labor and development of larger production units. Even without mechanization of production, this meant that it took more capital to set oneself up in business and that it was increasingly difficult for journeymen to rise to the master class. The gulf between worker and employer widened. For the first time there appeared a group of permanent wage earners, who had little expectation of becoming masters in the future. Moreover, greater specialization of tasks reduced the element of skill in the production process. The semiskilled operative appeared, and the need for fully skilled workers diminished. This threat to the skilled worker's skill was unpleasant in itself and also threatened his earning power.

The extension of the market for manufacturers can scarcely explain the rise of unionism in industries such as printing and building construction, which continued to cater to purely local markets. While product markets in these industries remained local, however, the labor market broadened steadily as improved transportation increased the mobility of labor. Printers, carpenters, and bricklayers began to move about the country in considerable numbers and were sometimes used by employers to undercut local wage scales. Some means had to be found for controlling this competition.

Until after the Civil War almost all unions were local unions of workers in a particular trade or industry, and they were confined largely to a few cities along the Atlantic seaboard. These early unions were strikingly modern in objectives and methods. From the beginning regulation of wages was the main issue, and the strike was the main weapon. There was little, it is true, that could be termed *collective bargaining* during this period. In the beginning the union simply decided on its "price" (i.e., wage rate), and the members pledged themselves not to work below this price. A little later it became customary for a union committee to visit each employer and request his adherence to the union rate. Those who refused to agree were struck. There was still no written agreement with employers, and the procedure could scarcely be called bargaining. The wage scale was determined unilaterally by the union, and employers were given the choice of conforming or not conforming. When nonconforming employers were struck, the *walking delegate,* who at first was an unpaid worker but later became a paid official, went from shop to shop to make sure that all union members were out. Strikebreakers were called *rats,* and later *scabs.* The locals of the same trade in different cities exchanged lists of scabs and agreed not to admit them to membership. This activity was almost the only contact between local unions in the early days. Strikes were financed by levies on the membership. They were relatively peaceful, and except in depression periods, most of them were successful.

Another policy of the earliest trade unions was not to work with nonunion men. The union shop, like the union wage scale, was enforced directly through a pledge by unionists "not to work for anybody who does not pay the rate nor beside anyone who does not get the rate." Nonunionists were also boycotted socially; union men would not live in the same boarding houses or eat at the same places as nonunion men.

Apprenticeship regulations were another major concern of the early unions. Their main purpose was to prevent employers from replacing journeymen with learners, runaway apprentices, and women at wage rates below the union scale. The number of apprentices an employer might train was usually limited to a certain proportion of the number of journeymen employed. They were required to serve a specified period of apprenticeship, and only journeymen who had completed this apprenticeship were admitted to the union and allowed to work in union shops.

These unions, though few in number, were sufficiently strong and aggressive to arouse consternation among employers. Editorial writers denounced unionism; employers' associations were formed to combat it; and conspiracy cases were launched against the unions in the courts. The antiunion arguments, like the union tactics of the day, have a surprisingly modern ring.[2] Time has brought little change

---

[2]The master carpenters of Boston, for example, when confronted in 1825 with a demand for a ten-hour day, replied that they could not believe "this project to have originated with any of the faithful and industrious sons of New England, but are compelled to consider it an evil of foreign growth, and one

in the issues at stake and the arguments advanced on either side. Many of the arguments put forward today might easily have been copied from newspapers and speeches of a hundred years ago.

An important characteristic of these early unions was their inability to withstand business depression. They sprang up and flourished in good years but were nearly all wiped out during depression periods. During recessions there is a surplus of skilled as well as unskilled workers, often including immigrants from other depressed areas searching for work in a new location. Under such circumstances worker solidarity is much more difficult to maintain.

In order for a union to maintain its strength during recession, special circumstances are necessary. For example, the social bonds may be unusually strong among the union members so that no one is willing to take another's job by working below the union wage. Alternatively, outsiders must be excluded from the labor market, by legal restrictions or perhaps by illegal threats of violence. Because these conditions are difficult to meet, it is not surprising that for many years union strength declined dramatically in recessions. In boom periods it was much easier to form and maintain a strong union.

After the Civil War the situation began to change. The depression of the years 1873 to 1878 reduced union membership from about 300,000 to 50,000; but it did not wipe out unionism completely as earlier depressions had done. With this development and with the foundation of the American Federation of Labor (AFL) in 1886, we enter a new period of trade union history.

THE EVOLUTION OF UNION STRUCTURE

There are four main organization units in the trade union world: local unions of workers in a particular trade or industry; citywide and statewide federations of local unions, regardless of industry; national unions of workers in the same trade or industry; and peak federations of these national unions, such as the AFL-CIO.

The organizational structure may be visualized more readily by looking at a particular union. The printers' local number 6 in New York City is a branch of the International Typographical Union, and holds its charter and authority only from the international union. At the same time Local Number 6 is a member of the New York City Federation of Labor and the New York State Federation of Labor. At the national level the Typographical Union is affiliated with the AFL-CIO.

These organizational units did not develop overnight, nor did they develop simultaneously. They represent successive stages of development, comparable to strata in a geological formation. The first local union was the Philadelphia shoemakers' union, founded in 1792. Next in order of development came the city federations

---

which we hope and trust will not take root in the favored soil of Massachusetts. . . . And especially that our city, the early rising and industry of whose inhabitants are universally proverbial, may not be infected with the unnatural production." John R. Commons et al., *History of Labor in the United States,* vol. 1, p. 160.

of local unions, the first of which were founded in New York, Philadelphia, and Baltimore in 1833. The first national union that has had a continuous existence up to the present day was the International Typographical Union, founded in 1850. The first federation of national unions that has had a continuous history to date was the American Federation of Labor, founded in 1886.

Other forms of organization have also been tried during the past 150 years. There have been attempts to combine people from different trades and industries into a single local union and to combine these "mixed locals" into an all-inclusive national organization. The outstanding example of this type of organization was the Knights of Labor, which flourished briefly during the 1880s. There have also been attempts to merge federations of local trade unions, local labor political clubs, and miscellaneous labor groups into a federation such as the National Labor Union, which flourished during the late 1860s. These movements suffered from a lack of homogeneity of interest among the membership. Because of diversity of the membership, a chronic shortage of funds, an absence of systematic organizing tactics, and a lack of interest in continuous bargaining with employers, they made only slight headway on the economic front. Their activities were oriented mainly toward politics, and here they tended to dissipate their energies in broad middle-class reform movements of little immediate interest to wage earners. The organizational forms that we find in existence today are the survivors, which have proved their ability to survive by the concrete functions they perform.

These different organizational units are not of equal importance in the labor world. The key unit around which all else revolves is the national union of workers in a particular trade or industry. The national union is more important than the locals of which it is composed, and it is also more important than the federation with which it is affiliated. This has not always been the case, and we need to ask how the national union has come to occupy its present key position.

The Dominance of the National Union

The beginnings of local unionism around the year 1800 have already been described. These isolated locals soon found that they were in a relatively weak position compared with that of a strong employer. Consisting of workers in only one trade, with limited funds and no outside support, they often crumbled when forced to strike against a large employer or employers' association. The need for some kind of defensive alliance with other unions was felt almost from the beginning.

Such an alliance can be formed on either of two bases. The local may join with local unions of other trades in the same *area* to form a citywide or statewide organization; or it may join with other local unions in the same *trade or industry* to form a national trade union. The first efforts were in the former direction. Citywide federations, called at the time *trade assemblies,* sprang up in Philadelphia, New York, and Baltimore in 1833, as we have noted, and in ten other cities during the next two years. The main function of these groups was mutual aid in strikes. Funds were obtained by taxing each local so many cents per member per month, and the tax was sometimes raised to meet emergency situations. A local that wished to go on strike usually had to secure approval either by a majority or by two-thirds of the member locals in order to draw strike benefits from the common fund. The trade assemblies also functioned as boycott organizations, lobbyists, propaganda bureaus, and publishers of labor newspapers. In some cities they sponsored an independent labor party. The usefulness of the city federation is proved by the fact that it has persisted, with some change of functions, to the present day.

Why did the local unions find it necessary to go beyond this and to establish national unions of their respective trades and industries? One important reason was the nationalization of the market for many goods. Hoxie has laid down the principle that union organization tends to parallel the organization of the industry. In an industry in which employers compete on a national basis the isolated local soon finds itself competing with local unions in other plants of the industry. In this sort of competition wages tend to be leveled down to the lowest rates prevailing anywhere in the country. If a local in one area obtained a higher wage than elsewhere, then the cost to its employers would be above average, and firms in that area would be at a competitive disadvantage. As a result, there would be fewer, if any, jobs for the workers in the high-wage local union.[3]

Another reason for national unions was the migration of journeymen from one city to another. The local unions of printers, for example, began to exchange lists of scabs, to regulate the conditions under which printers from one area might secure work in another area, and to provide "tramping benefits" to support the brother in the trade during his journeys in search of employment. A permanent national organization facilitated these exchanges and made it possible to enforce uniform apprenticeship and membership rules. With the passage of time improved transportation facilities made it easier for delegates to assemble at national conventions and for organizers from the national office to travel throughout the country.

National unions date for all practical purposes from the Civil War. Two so-called national unions of shoemakers and printers were formed in 1835 and 1836, but they were confined to the Atlantic Coast and were wiped out almost immediately by depression. Three permanent organizations appeared during the 1850s: the printers (1850), molders (1859), and machinists and blacksmiths (1859). The first period of intensive national organization, however, was from 1863 to 1873. During these years some twenty-six new national unions were formed, many of which have survived to the present day. The present unions of locomotive engineers, locomotive firemen, carpenters, cigar makers, bricklayers, and painters date from this period.

The national unions showed much greater resistance to depression than the earlier local unions. The depression of 1873 to 1878 caused a great decline in union membership, but at least eleven nationals are known to have survived these years, and eight new nationals were founded during the depression. The reasons for the greater permanence of a national union are not difficult to see. Even though many of its local unions are wiped out during a depression, the national headquarters can

---

[3]In other words, the elasticity of labor demand for the workers in any one local is quite high as long as there is a national product market. Recall the discussion of the elasticity of labor demand in Chap. 5.

continue on a reduced scale and serve as a center for reviving the lost locals when prosperity returns. Moreover, a national union tends to expand constantly to the limits of its trade or industry. Its officers have the duty of organizing the unorganized; their prestige and even their continuance in office depend on successful performance of their function.

The national unions did not merely survive but gradually took over more and more functions from the local unions and city federations. They early began to build up war chests to aid in financing strikes. To prevent dissipation of these funds it was necessary to forbid local unions to call strikes without the sanction of the national union. The national officers thus became involved in disputes between local unions and employers, with a view to preventing strikes except when absolutely necessary. From this point it was a natural step for national officers to begin participating in the negotiation of new contracts with employers. This significant involvement of national leaders in the affairs of local unions was also desirable in order to keep some reasonable relation among the wage schedules and other contract terms secured by the various locals. These tendencies, to be sure, have been strongest in industries with a national product market. In industries where competition is confined to a locality, such as building construction, the local unions have retained a large measure of autonomy.

It was natural also that national officers with an intimate knowledge of the trade or industry should take over the work of organizing new locals. The great majority of full-time union organizers now draw their pay from the treasuries of the national unions. The benefit functions of the unions also become centralized increasingly in the national office. Uniform rules for sickness benefits, death benefits, strike benefits, and other types of payment were established throughout the union, and funds were paid to the national treasurer and were disbursed by him.

The expanding functions of the national unions tended to transfer the loyalty of local unions from the city federations to the national union of the trade. Most workers naturally have a sense of closer solidarity with others in their own trade or industry. This feeling was now reinforced by the material benefits received from the national organizations. Dues payments to the national organization and cash benefits received from it soon amounted to many times the amounts paid to the city federations. The national unions benefited by the truth expressed in the maxim, "Where your treasure is, there will your heart be also."

The predominance of the national union was strengthened also by the turn that the labor movement took in the 1880s away from political action and toward direct bargaining with employers on the economic front. Had the labor movement taken a strong political turn, the outcome might well have been different. The city, state, and national federations are the natural units for political action. For reasons to be discussed below, however, political action has played a minor role in the labor movement over the past century. The state and city federations have accordingly fallen to a subordinate position. They continue to meet regularly, give a certain amount of support to member locals in strikes and organizing campaigns, approve legislative demands of member locals and lobby for them in city councils and state legislatures, conduct educational and propaganda activities, and in some cases support candidates for public office. The local union's real loyalty, however, is to the national union of its trade or industry. It is to the national union that it looks for support, and in any conflict of principles or policies it is the policies of the national union that will prevail.

The American Federation of Labor (AFL)

In the United States national unions are more powerful than any federation based on them. The first successful federation dates from the 1880s, although several attempts at national federation were made in earlier days, notably by the ill-fated Knights of Labor established in 1869. This heterogeneous organization cut across industry lines and included large numbers of low-skilled workers, who joined enthusiastically but were easily discouraged and quick to drop out.

The national unions of skilled craftsmen eventually concluded that they would do better to form their own federation. The American Federation of Labor, founded in 1886, quickly assumed a leading role in the trade union movement. It was a hard-hitting organization, led by Samuel Gompers and other energetic men in their thirties, who almost immediately launched the first successful strikes for the eight-hour day. The AFL also had a distinctive philosophy of unionism that appealed strongly to most organized workers.

What were the cardinal points of this trade union philosophy? The first element that may be noted is group consciousness. Earlier workers had not distinguished their interest from those of farmers and middle-class people. They had joined in political reform movements that also drew support from these other groups. All this was changed by Gompers and his followers, most of whom had been reared as Marxian socialists. Although they later abandoned most of the tenets of Marxism, they retained a conviction that the interests of workers were distinct from those of other groups. Gompers argued that the workers must defend their own interests and must refuse to be drawn into middle-class reform movements. He asserted also that there is little hope of the workers' climbing out of their class through producers' cooperatives, antimonopoly campaigns, or other methods.

A second principle was that of organization by trades. Gompers believed that to lump together different trades, as the Knights of Labor had done, reduced the cohesiveness of the union. Greatest solidarity was obtained when each craft had its own union. The desirability of strong national unions, buttressed by large treasuries and extensive benefit systems, was stressed from the beginning. The Cigar Makers' Union, under Gompers's leadership, showed the way in this direction in 1879 by adopting a high scale of dues and benefits and by giving the national officers complete control over the local unions. The Cigar Makers' organization was used as a model by most other national unions during the next ten years, and its prestige contributed to the election of Gompers to the AFL presidency. The marked success of British craft unions cut on this same pattern and the influence of British immigrants in American unions also helped to shape AFL thinking in these formative years.

Early AFL leaders insisted also that each national union must be autonomous within its own field of operation. The federation entered the scene only to define and enforce the jurisdictions of the member unions, and to perform certain political and educational functions. The federation, in short, was a confederation of sovereign bodies. Its chief power was that of granting jurisdiction over particular trades or industries: jurisdiction granted to one union must be observed by others, and dual unionism must be suppressed at all costs. This attitude toward dualism sprang partly from the unfortunate experience of the national unions in competition with the Knights of Labor during the 1880s. It sprang also from the fact that the AFL had to contend with strong and determined employer opposition. The existence of two unions in an industry gave the employer a chance to play each against the other, and the labor movement therefore has a strong practical interest in preventing dual organization. The bitterness of the rivalry between the AFL and CIO from 1935 to 1955 can be understood only in terms of this long-standing taboo on dual unionism.

The third cardinal principle was that labor's objectives should be pursued mainly on the economic front through collective bargaining with employers. In spite of the socialist training of its founders, the AFL soon came to accept the main outlines of the capitalist order. Gompers believed that unions should not try to overthrow capitalism but should try to get as much as possible for the workers by collective bargaining within the confines of the existing system. When someone asked Gompers what the aims of the federation were, he is reported to have answered, "More, more, more—now!" When another AFL leader was called before a congressional committee in 1883 and asked about the ultimate objectives of trade unionism, he replied as follows: "We have no ultimate ends. We are going on from day to day. We are fighting only for immediate objects. . . . We are opposed to theorists. . . . We are all practical men."[4] There has never been a better summary of the traditional AFL position.

The device of the union contract or collective agreement, which had been used by a few unions in the 1880s, became during the 1890s the accepted method of dealing with employers. The AFL hammered out and wrote into union contracts a new conception of the union as a continuously operating organization rather than as a sporadic protest and strike movement. The union was to be a partner, though perhaps only a junior partner, in the conduct of industry. It was to be active every day in the year, representing the interests of its members on all fronts, winning small gains that would eventually mount up to an impressive total.

A corollary of the AFL's emphasis on collective bargaining was the avoidance of political organization or at least of anything approaching an independent labor party. The labor movement had experimented with labor parties and political action since at least 1830. Gompers and his group felt that these activities had not gotten anywhere in the past and had served mainly to split the unions and divert them from their real business. They believed that the unions could get what they wanted through pressure on the established political parties—voting for candidates

---

[4]J. B. S. Hardman, *American Labor Dynamics*, (New York: Harcourt, Brace, and World, 1928), p. 79.

who had shown themselves to be "friends of labor," getting union demands written into party platforms, lobbying in Congress and the state legislatures, and so on.

UNION GROWTH IN MODERN TIMES

The growth of unionism in the twentieth century is shown in Figure 12-1 and Table 12-1. Figure 12-1 shows the estimated number of union members year by year since 1897. The black line includes Canadian members of American unions, who have numbered about one million in recent years. The white line for recent years includes only members within the United States.

Table 12-1 shows union membership as a percentage of nonagricultural employment for selected years since 1880. Note that union membership grew rapidly during the New Deal and World War II years, 1933–45, and has decreased since then.

FIGURE 12-1   Trade Union Membership in the United States, 1897–1989.

Source: Data for 1897–1960 are from the Bureau of Labor Statistics, *Handbook of Labor Statistics,* 1950, p. 139; and Bureau of the Census, *Statistical Abstract of the United States,* 1962. Data for 1956–80 are from the Bureau of Labor Statistics, *Directory of National and International Labor Unions in the United States,* 1982–83. For the years since 1983 the data are from the January issues of *Employment and Earnings.* All are published by the Government Printing Office, Washington, D.C.

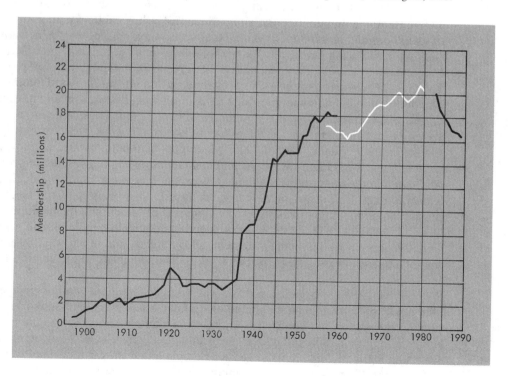

TABLE 12-1   Union Membership as a Percentage of Nonagricultural Employment, Selected Years, 1880–1989

	AVERAGE ANNUAL UNION MEMBERSHIP			AVERAGE ANNUAL UNION MEMBERSHIP	
Year	Thousands	Percent of Nonagricultural Employment	Year	Thousands	Percent of Nonagricultural Employment
1880	200.0	2.3	1939	8,980	28.9
1890	372.0	2.7	1945	14,796	35.8
1900	865.5	4.8	1956	17,490	30.4
1910	2,140.5	8.4	1966	17,940	28.1
1920	5,047.8	16.3	1972	19,435	26.4
1930	3,392.8	8.8	1980	20,095	23.0
1933	2,857	11.5	1985	16,926	18.0
			1989	16,960	16.4

Source: Data through 1945 are from Lloyd Ulman, "American Trade Unionism—Past and Present," in *American Economic History*, ed. Seymour E. Harris (New York: McGraw-Hill Book Co., 1961), pp. 393, 421. Data from 1956 to 1980 are from Bureau of Labor Statistics, *Directory of National International Labor Unions in the United States, 1982–83* (Washington, D.C.: Government Printing Office). Data for 1985 and 1989 are from *Employment and Earnings*.

From 1880 until the early 1930s union membership rose gradually and intermittently, going up in prosperity periods and falling back in depression. Unionism was confined largely to the skilled crafts and did not succeed in penetrating the basic manufacturing industries. Except for a brief spurt during and after World War I, union membership never rose above 10 percent of nonagricultural employment. The Great Depression of the 1930s brought a shift in attitudes toward unionization. The depression led many to question the assumptions of capitalism and its emphasis on individual competition. Consequently, various approaches, utilizing collection action, were tried during the New Deal. For our purposes the primary policy change was the Wagner Act of 1935, which put the federal government on record for the first time as favoring unions and included a variety of substantive provisions (discussed in the next chapter) aimed at reducing the costs of union organizing. This legislation resulted in major new organizing drives, especially in the large mass-production industries, drives led by the Congress of Industrial Organization (CIO).

Between 1933 and 1939 union membership tripled, and unions for the first time became firmly established in steel, automobiles, and most other branches of manufacturing. Organization spread from the skilled crafts to the semiskilled and unskilled.

By 1939 the organizing drive was losing momentum, and union membership might once more have stagnated or declined had it not been for World War II. During the war years administration policy remained favorable to unionism, and union leaders were enlisted both in the production drive and in the effort to stablize wages and prices. The sharp increase of employment in war industries was favorable to enrolling more union members. Employers were more concerned with recruiting labor and getting out production than with fighting the union, and employer resistance to organization subsided for the time being. So another five million union members were added. Unions came to include more than a third of the nonagricultural labor force and about 60 percent of all manual workers in the economy.

In retrospect, 1953 appears as a high watermark in union penetration of the economy. The percentage of nonagricultural workers who are union members has been falling since then. We shall discuss the decline and the reasons for it in some detail in Chapter 14. In this chapter we focus on the development of unionization from the late nineteenth century through the period of relative stability from the 1950s until the early 70s.

The Congress of Industrial Organizations (CIO)

While the AFL was quite successful in organizing skilled workers, it made little progress in the mass-production manufacturing industries, where the bulk of the plant labor force was semiskilled or unskilled. This posed a strategic choice between organization by occupation or *crafts,* under which carpenters employed by U.S. Steel would join the Carpenters' Union, toolmakers would join the Machinists' Union, and so on; and *industrial* unionism, under which everyone in a steel mill would belong to a single Steelworkers' Union.

The AFL leadership, dominated by craft unions that wished to preserve their right to enroll members of their craft who worked in manufacturing plants, favored the craft basis of organization while failing to implement it effectively. But this view was challenged in the early thirties by a group led by John L. Lewis of the Mine Workers, Sidney Hillman of the Clothing Workers, and David Dubinsky of the Ladies' Garment Workers, unions which themselves were industrial in form. After being outvoted at the 1935 AFL convention, six of these unions nevertheless set up a Committee for Industrial Organization (CIO) devoted to organizing industrial unions in the basic manufacturing industries and then bringing these new unions into the AFL. The AFL Executive Council, however, scenting a threat of dual unionism, first suspended and then expelled the unions that had formed the CIO. These unions then banded together in 1938, along with the new unions that they had fathered in the meantime, to form a rival federation—the Congress of Industrial Organizations.

The success of the CIO organizing drives is now a matter of history. During the late thirties one antiunion citadel after another capitulated. The list of employers organized by the CIO between 1936 and 1941 reads like a Who's Who of American industry: Ford, General Motors, Chrysler, General Electric, Westinghouse, United States Steel, Bethlehem Steel, Republic Steel, Youngstown Sheet and Tube, Goodyear, Firestone, Goodrich, the major oil companies, the larger radio and electrical equipment manufacturers, the "big four" meat-packing companies, and so on.

An important factor in this success was a favorable government attitude toward unionism throughout the Roosevelt era. Unions that formerly had to strike to win union recognition could now use the election procedures of the National Labor Relations Board, and the board also protected them against harassing tactics by the employer, which were now forbidden as "unfair labor practices." A second factor was the prolonged rise in business activity after 1933. Except for the relapse of 1937 and 1938, employment and production rose steadily from 1933 to 1945. This provided a favorable setting for union organization. Yet another factor was the closing of our borders to large-scale immigration, which occurred in the 1920s. Without the immigrants it was much more difficult for employers to replace union with nonunion labor, especially during times of low unemployment.

The new industrial unions of the CIO shared many of the views of the AFL, including the emphasis on economic objectives (e.g., wages, hours, and working conditions) and on achieving such objectives primarily through collective bargaining rather than political action. In contrast to the craft unions of the AFL, however, collective bargaining with the new industrial unions led to increasingly lengthy, detailed union contracts. Management retained the right to make such basic decisions as what output to produce, where it would be produced, and at what price it would be sold. But jobs, and the access of different employees to such jobs, were defined in much greater detail than in the older craft unions.

The New Deal System of Industrial Relations

Let us see how such differences developed. Typically the initial contract between an employer and any union is relatively short and written in rather general language. Such generally worded contracts then lead to disagreements as to how to apply the language to specific cases. For the construction crafts such disputes are usually resolved informally between the firm's owner and the business agent of the union. Because a firm's demand for labor varies markedly from project to project, workers normally move from firm to firm. In this fluid context both sides have an incentive to resolve conflicts of interpretation quickly.

In contrast, in the case of industrial unions workers often stay with a single employer for thirty years or more. Although they shift positions within the firm, still they will normally stay several years on any one job. In this context there is more at stake in disputes over (1) how to define a particular job, (2) whether a worker's conduct on the job warrants his or her dismissal, (3) who should be offered the job if it becomes vacant, and (4) who should be laid off when demand declines. Because more is at stake when a job is expected to last many years, generally worded contract language tends over time to become lengthier and more detailed as both sides bargain over conflicts of interpretation.[5]

---

[5]No matter how detailed the language, however, no contract can anticipate all contingencies. Thus disputes over contract interpretation often lead to grievances. Such grievances usually originate on the shop floor and can often be resolved between higher levels of the union and the employer. If no resolution can be reached between the parties, then the dispute is usually sent to an outside arbitrator for a decision. The arbitrator's decision is binding for the life of the contract, but either the union or the firm can seek to reverse the arbitrator's decision when the next contract is negotiated. If this effort is successful, then the contract will have established more detailed rules for the workplace.

With industrial unions jobs are normally described in considerable detail. Workers are expected to do only those tasks that are in their job descriptions. The union contract defines the pay scale for each job. Jobs are grouped into promotion "ladders." The union contract spells out the emphasis to be placed on various promotion criteria for workers who seek to move up the ladder. Industrial unions have sought to make seniority the primary criterion, while employers favor ability to do the job. Unions fear that ability to do the job is subjective and that use of this criterion by managers leads to favoritism, often on behalf of the more submissive workers.

This system, sometimes called the New Deal system of industrial relations, can be quite rigid. It is a more detailed, legalistic system than exists in most other countries or in American craft unions. It did not originate entirely with unions, however, but grew out of American management practices in the early twentieth century. At that time the dominant approach was "scientific management," or *Taylorism,* which emphasized time and motion studies for defining and evaluating jobs.[6]

Although it is still very important today, the New Deal industrial relations system has been placed under considerable stress as a result of changes in the economy in the 1980s. Increased foreign competition; deregulation of airlines, trucking, and other industries; and the recession of the early eighties have reduced the size and strength of many important unions in the private sector. Those unions that remain strong often have shifted, to at least some degree, to new approaches, often emphasizing broader job descriptions and greater input of workers into shop-floor decisions throughout the life of the union contract. We shall discuss these developments in more detail in later chapters.

The AFL-CIO

The industrial unions of the CIO still play a large role in our economy. So do the craft unions of the old AFL.

The division between the AFL and the CIO weakened the labor movement both at the bargaining table and in the political arena. Negotiations between the two groups finally led to a merger in 1955, with the formation of the AFL-CIO.

The old AFL had quite limited power over its affiliated unions, and that remains true of the AFL-CIO. Its constitution does go further than its predecessors in prescribing standards of conduct for its members. For example, no union that is dominated by Communists or racketeers may remain in the federation. But the threat of expulsion has proven ineffective against the more powerful unions. The outstanding example is the Teamsters' Union, which simply ignored federation orders to eliminate corruption and in 1957 accepted expulsion with equanimity. The union flourished on its own for many years, depriving the AFL-CIO of valuable revenues and support. After thirty years it rejoined the AFL-CIO in 1987 as both organizations sought to rebuild their political influence.

---

[6]See Thomas A. Kochan, Harry C. Katz, and Robert B. McKersie, *The Transformation of American Industrial Relations.* p. 29.

The national unions, then, remain largely autonomous in managing their internal affairs and continue to be the real power centers of the labor movement. The national unions are not members of the AFL-CIO in the sense that Minnesota is part of the United States. Their position is more like that of countries within the United Nations, which by threatening to withdraw can veto actions contrary to their interests. They confer power on the federation much more than they draw power from it.

THE TRADE UNION WORLD TODAY

Table 12-2 shows how the largest national unions changed in size between 1980 and 1987. Most unions that bargain with private-sector employers declined substantially in membership during the 1980s. Some of these declines were substantial, for instance, the Steelworkers, who lost more then half their members between 1980

TABLE 12-2   Unions with 200,000 or More Members, 1987

	MEMBERSHIP (1,000s)	
ORGANIZATION	1987	1980
National Education Association (NEA)	1,829	1,684
Teamsters	1,700	1,891
State, County, and Municipal (AFSCME)	1,032	1,098
Food and Commercial Workers	1,000	1,300
Automobile Workers (UAW)	998	1,357
Electrical Workers (IBEW)	765	1,041
Service Employees	762	650
Teachers (AFT)	651	551
Carpenters	609	784
Communications Workers	515	551
Machinists	509	754
Steelworkers	494	1,238
Laborers	371	551
Operating Engineers	330	423
Hotel and Restaurant Workers	293	400
Postal Workers	230	251
Paperworkers	221	275
Plumbers and Pipefitters	220	352
Letter Carriers	200	230

All of these unions are members of the AFL-CIO except the NEA.

Source: The figures are from the *Statistical Abstract of the United States* for 1984 and 1989. For the NEA and AFT the 1987 figures are from Sar A. Levitan and Frank Gallo, "Can Employee Associations Negotiate New Growth?" *Monthly Labor Review* (July 1987), pp. 5–14. For the Teamsters the 1987 figure is from George Reuben, "A Review of Collective Bargaining in 1987," *Monthly Labor Review* (January 1988), p. 36. All figures exclude Canadian members.

and 1987. In contrast, the public-sector unions have not changed very much in size in recent years, although the teachers unions have made some sizable gains.

Union membership is concentrated in a few large unions, and the degree of concentration is increasing. In 1948–50 the five largest unions had 25 percent of all union members. By 1974 this had risen to 34 percent and by 1987 to 38 percent. Concentration has grown partly as a result of union mergers. A union in financial difficulties, like a company in financial trouble, often tries to save itself by seeking a strong partner. About half the unions in the United States have fewer than fifty thousand members. Except for a few highly skilled craft groups like airline pilots and professional football players, these small unions have difficulty raising enough money for organizing activity, strike benefits, lobbying, and maintaining a national office.

Since the AFL-CIO reunion in 1955, there have been well over fifty mergers of unions within the federation. Although the merger movement peaked during the lean years of 1980–83, several new mergers are occurring each year. Some of the merged groups have a long history. In 1983 the boilermakers' union, 103 years old, merged with the cement workers' union, 45 years old. In most cases the merged union remains relatively small. In a few, however, it is very large. The Food and Commercial Workers, formed from the Retail Clerks and the Meat Cutters, is one of the largest in the country.

Partly through mergers, some unions confined originally to a single industry have spread out to become union conglomerates. The most notable example is the Teamsters, which by a willingness to organize anybody in any field, has become the largest union in the country. It includes not only truckers, who are now a minority, but also grocery clerks, brewers, nurses, clerical workers, launderers, circus workers, police, public works employees, and many others. About two-thirds of the Steelworkers' members work outside steel. The United Automobile Workers has members in twenty manufacturing industries; and the Machinists, in eighteen. The concept of a clear-cut and limited jurisdiction is in decline.

The Unevenness of Union Coverage

The coverage of trade unionism is uneven—by occupation, by industry, by region of the country. Several different measures of the extent of unionization are useful: the percentage of production workers who are union members; the percent unionized among workers covered by the NLRA or eligible for public-sector unions; and the percent of workers who are covered by a collective bargaining agreement, whether or not they actually belong to a union. We present figures from Kokkelenberg and Sockell, who exclude managers in the private sector from their analysis, since such managers are not covered by the NLRA. According to their estimate, the percentage of workers who are union members is relatively high in metal mining (64 percent), coal mining (66 percent), construction (34 percent), railroads (87 percent), bus lines (43 percent), trucking (48 percent), air transportation (45 percent), water transportation (50 percent), telephone service (64 percent), electric light and power (47 percent). In manufacturing the overall percentage is 36 percent, but it is higher than this in some major industries: glass products (65 percent), steel works and rolling mills (69 percent), aluminum (56 percent), farm machinery (50 percent), motor vehicles (66 percent), aircraft (44 percent), pulp and paper (67 percent), oil refining (39 percent), and rubber products (45 percent).[7]

In other manufacturing industries, however, the union percentage is low. Examples are electrical computing equipment (6 percent), mobile homes (16 percent), photographic supplies (10 percent), textile mills (23 percent), printing and publishing (22 percent), footwear (22 percent). There are also many intermediate industries in which the percentage unionized runs close to the 36 percent average for all manufacturing. In industries employing mainly white-collar sales and service workers the unionized percentage is low: wholesale and retail trade (11 percent), finance, insurance, and real estate (5 percent), business and repair services (9 percent), personal services (7 percent), entertainment and recreation services (15 percent), professional and related services (23 percent).

The estimates of union membership by occupation confirm the heavily blue-collar character of American trade unionism. Thus 39 percent of skilled craftspersons, 42 percent of semiskilled operatives, and 32 percent of nonfarm laborers are union members. But many other main occupational groups are essentially nonunion: sales workers (4 percent), clerical and kindred workers (16 percent), farm workers (2 percent), service workers (17 percent). Unionization is 22 percent among professional and clerical workers.

In geographic terms unionism is strongest in the belt of industrial states running from New York to Chicago. New York, New Jersey, Pennsylvania, Ohio, Indiana, Michigan, and Illinois all show union membership as a proportion of production workers in the 25–33 percent range. The figures are slightly lower for the Pacific Coast, Hawaii, and Alaska but drop to 10–25 percent for most of the New England, North Central, and Mountain states. In the South and Southwest a few states show unionized percentages as high as 20 percent, but most states are below this. Examples are Georgia (9 percent), Florida (11 percent), North Carolina (8 percent), Texas (8 percent).

These regional differences to some extent reflect differences in the composition of employment. States that have many workers in manufacturing, construction, and transportation also have many union members. But the weakness of unionism in the South is not just a matter of the industry mix. The same industries are less unionized there than in other parts of the country.

It is useful to look also at the coverage of trade unionism by sex and race (Table 12-3). Women workers, particularly blue-collar women workers, are substantially less unionized than men. This does not appear to be due to stronger antiunion sentiment among women than among men. In a quality-of-employment survey conducted in 1977 by the Institute of Social Research of the University of Michigan, a sample of nonunion workers were asked: "If an election were held with secret

---

[7]See Edward C. Kokkelenberg and Donna R. Sockell, "Union Membership in the United States, 1973–81," *Industrial and Labor Relations Review* (July 1985), pp. 497–543.

TABLE 12-3   Percentage of Private-Sector Wage and Salary Employees Who Belong to a Union or a Union-like Association

	ALL WORKERS (%)	BLUE-COLLAR WORKERS (%)	WHITE-COLLAR WORKERS (%)
All employees	20	30	9
Sex			
Male	27	37	10
Female	11	17	8
Race			
White	20	30	8
Nonwhite	27	31	17

Source: Richard B. Freeman and James L. Medoff, *What Do Unions Do?* (New York: Basic Books, 1984), p. 27. Data are from the Bureau of Labor Statistics, *Current Population Survey*, May 1977.

ballot, would you vote for or against having a union or employees' association represent you?" Of the women in the sample, 41 percent said they would vote for a union, compared with only 27 percent of the men. This is consistent with behavior in NLRB elections, where postelection surveys show women at least as likely to vote union as men in the same unit.

The main reason for the difference in coverage, then, is a difference in the kind of work done. Heavy manufacturing, mining, transportation, and construction, which are relatively highly unionized, employ mainly men. Women work mainly in trade, finance, and service industries, which are little unionized. Within manufacturing, they work mainly in clothing, textiles, and other light manufacturing industries, where the unionized ratio is also low.

Unionization is much higher among women in the public sector than in the private sector. With public-sector unions accounting for an increasing percentage of all union members, the differences between men and women in the percent unionized have declined a little. By 1988 only 20 percent of male workers were union members, while unionization among women had increased slightly to 13 percent.

Nonwhite workers are somewhat more likely to be unionized than white workers. That is partly a matter of preference and may stem from a perception that black workers have more to gain from union organization.[8] This perception is correct. We shall see in Chapter 20 that the wage-raising effect of unionism is considerably larger for black workers than for whites.

Despite large differences in the extent of unionization across different groups of workers, industrial relations in the United States were fairly stable throughout the fifties, sixties, and early seventies. The extent of unionization has declined considerably in the private sector since that time, a topic we discuss in some detail in

---

[8]In the opinion survey described earlier, 70 percent of nonwhite blue-collar workers said they would vote for a union, compared with 34 percent of white blue-collar workers. Among white-collar workers, 67 percent of nonwhite workers expressed preference for a union, compared with 26 percent of white workers.

Chapter 14. First let us complete this overview by comparing unionization and collective bargaining in the United States with that in other countries.

COMPARISONS WITH OTHER COUNTRIES

There are substantial differences in union strength across countries. Most strongly unionized is Sweden, where about 85 percent of potential union members are in unions. In the United Kingdom and Australia the proportion is about 50 percent, in West Germany about 40 percent. The United States, with less than 20 percent, is at the low end of the scale. The most strongly unionized group in every country is government employees, with private blue collar workers next, and white-collar workers least well organized. A typical pattern would be 75 percent of government employees in unions, compared with 50 percent of private blue-collar workers and 20 to 25 percent of private white-collar workers.

When we look more closely at what unions do, we find three kinds of situations: (1) countries in which politics prevails, notably France and Italy; (2) countries in which collective bargaining prevails—Germany, the United Kingdom, Scandinavia, U.S., Canada, Australia; and (3) Japan, where the system of employment gives a quite different twist to industrial relations.

Unions in Countries Where Politics Prevail

In France and Italy the largest union federations have close links with the Communist parties of those countries (though there are smaller socialist-oriented and Catholic-oriented federations). In both countries class lines are firmly drawn, and class antagonism is strong. Employers typically look down on their workers and are strongly opposed to dealing with trade unions. The unions are weakly organized and poorly financed, and members' attachment to them is loose. A union can call workers out for a mass meeting or a one-day strike, but it cannot get them to pay dues or come to regular union meetings. Apparently blocked from advancing through collective bargaining, unions turn instead to political activity. Economic and social reforms in these countries have been achieved almost entirely through legislation rather than through bargaining with employers.

Unions in Countries where Collective Bargaining Prevails

In the other market economies, too, the trade union federation is usually allied with a Labor or Socialist political party. The American labor movement is unique in its refusal to ally itself permanently with either of the major political parties. Unions pick and choose among candidates from one election to the next, the choice depending mainly on an individual's voting record. Labor functions as a pressure group, while in other countries it often participates in forming the government.

While politics is always important, the main union technique is collective bargaining with employers. The bargaining system varies from country to country, often differing substantially from U.S. practice. Consider, for example, the case of the United Kingdom. Traditionally, British unions have been strictly private associations, operating with little support or restraint from government. Collective bargaining agreements are short and simple, usually specifying only minimum rates of pay, with employers free to pay more if market conditions warrant. Agreements are of indefinite duration, with either party free to demand changes at any time. There is usually no established grievance procedure, and grievances that cannot be adjusted by informal discussion often lead to walkouts by employees. Shop stewards and other local union officials have a rather free hand in calling such walkouts, and there is little control by national union officers. Contrast this with U.S. practice: detailed regulation of union-management relations by government; detailed collective agreements for a specified period, with strikes forbidden during this period; employers usually forbidden to do either more or less than the contract prescribes; elaborate grievance procedures culminating in arbitration, which largely eliminates wildcat strikes; a generally businesslike relation between unions and management, without the overtones of class antagonism, which colors relations in the United Kingdom and other European countries.

In Britain craft unions predominate, while German unions are organized on an industrial basis to an even greater degree than in the United States. Although socialism was strong among the German working class in the late nineteenth and early twentieth century, now the labor movement is an important supporter of capitalism. Jacobi writes:

> Unions have not exercised their potential for disruption or veto power to attack capitalism, but, on the contrary, have accepted responsibility for promoting the political and economic development of a capitalist democracy. During the long period of prosperity in the 1960s and 1970s their role . . . was to secure social peace by continuously improving the living conditions of the working population without endangering stability and growth. In view of the current modernization and technological change, the trade unions' . . . function is to mitigate the social consequences of this process and to provide a high level of acceptance among the employees.[9]

Because unions play a constructive role supporting the economic system, they are not opposed by employers the way they generally are in the United States.

In Germany collective bargaining focuses on issues of wage rates and job security. Collective agreements automatically apply to all firms in the industry, unless the employer and the union reach a separate agreement. Thus there is no nonunion domestic competition.

In addition to collective bargaining, German workers also influence workplace decisions through a system of *codetermination*. Legislation requires that workers be represented on the board of directors of all large companies. Since the

---

[9]Otto Jacobi, "World Economic Changes and Industrial Relations in the Federal Republic of Germany," in *Industrial Relations in a Decade of Economic Change,* ed. Hervey Juris et al. (Madison, Wis.: Industrial Relation Research Association, 1985), p. 231.)

workers' representatives are in a minority, they have little real power. On the other hand, they do have an excellent opportunity to both receive early information on company policies and make decision makers aware of worker views. In addition, worker representation has major symbolic significance.

More real power for workers exists on works councils, established at each plant through national legislation. Here representatives elected by the workers have the same number of votes as the management representatives. Works councils must be consulted about any changes in working conditions, including plant shutdowns, and must consent to many changes, including the transfer or disciplining of workers. Although works councils cannot call a strike, they can take an unresolved dispute to a labor court. Also the union members of a works council can encourage the union to strike if a dispute with management becomes sufficiently important. Thus works councils have considerable influence.

Because workers and management are both equally represented, the structure of the works councils encourages cooperation rather than confrontational approaches. In contrast, local unions in the United States are responsive mainly to their membership, which often encourages a more confrontational emphasis. The German codetermination approach appears to have weathered the economic disruptions of the late seventies and early eighties with less change than many other industrial relations systems, including those of both Britain and the United States.

Unions in Japan

Japanese industrial relations differ from those in any other country, reflecting aspects of Japanese culture and a distinctive system of employment. Lifetime employment is the general rule in the larger companies, though less common in small companies. Manual and clerical workers enter the company after school graduation, and managerial employees after graduation from college, and they normally stay with the company until retirement. Turnover rates are very low by U.S. standards. Wages rise with age and length of service—sometimes strictly on the basis of age, sometimes with modifications to recognize unusual merit. In the larger companies as much as 25 percent of total compensation takes the form of bonuses, paid in midyear and at year-end. Bonuses vary somewhat from year to year, depending on the company's profit showing, and can be viewed as a form of profit sharing.

This system produces considerable loyalty to the company and a concern with the company's economic performance. The loyalty is further strengthened by the fact that Japanese managers do not stand aloof from workers at lower levels but spend a lot of time mingling with them both at work and on social occasions. The feeling of class division and even confrontation often found in the West is largely absent. The atmosphere is rather that of a family or at least a club.

Not surprisingly, then, the dominant feature of the Japanese trade union world is the local union of workers in a particular company. The local includes manual and white-collar employees, without regard to occupation, and also includes the first few layers of supervision below the rank of section chief. The local collects dues, which are often checked off by the employer in the usual way. But the bulk of this money stays with the local, whereas in the United States half or more is usually passed on to the national union. Many Japanese locals do not even belong to a national union; and even in industries that have a national union, this body plays only a limited role in local collective bargaining. The three top labor federations are essentially political bodies. Two of them are allied with political parties, and all act as lobbyists on labor issues.

The local union and the company are so intertwined that it is hard to distinguish between them. Since top managers are drawn from the ranks of lower management, almost all have been union members in earlier years. Local union officers, including the full-time officials found in larger locals, are drawn disproportionately from the supervisory ranks. When they leave union office, they go back to their regular jobs in the company, on which their status and security really depend. There is no separate career ladder for union officers, independent of the company ladder, as there is in the United States. A study of a large steel company local concluded: "The labor union is operated by the company's key employees. As a result, the union is not free to function separately and independently of company policy, but rather might be described as 'cohesive' with the company."[10]

Given this structure, collective bargaining is necessarily company by company. Each year, to be sure, there is a "spring wage offensive." The top labor federations announce a target for general wage increases, which is supported by publicity and one-day street demonstrations. Then bargaining goes on at the local level. It invariably turns out that the average actual wage increase for the year is considerably below the announced target, and there is much variation even among companies in the same industry. The individual company's ability to pay is clearly a major consideration.

Contrary to U.S. practice in which collective bargaining agreements are detailed and legalistic documents, Japanese agreements are usually brief statements of general principles. They say, in effect, that the company and the union recognize each others' existence and are prepared to get along together. There is usually no specified procedure for handling individual grievances, and even where a formal procedure is specified, it does not seem to be used very much. If an employee complains of unfair treatment, the Japanese reaction is, "Let's have a meeting." Everyone concerned sits down to talk, and the discussion goes on until some solution is reached.

Strikes are unusual and, where they occur are almost always of the one-day variety. They are a way of saying to management, "Look, we really care about this issue." They are not a lengthy test of economic strength, as in most other countries.

In the Japanese context this system has apparently been conducive to high worker morale and productivity and to a rapid rise in living standards based on this productivity. But this is not to say that the system is readily transferable to other countries. The advice sometimes given to American managers—do like the Japanese—is overly simplistic.

---

[10]See Walter Galenson, "The Japanese Labor Market," in *Asia's New Giant,* ed Hugh Patrick and Henry Rosovsky (Washington, D.C.: Brookings Institution, 1976), pp. 587–672.

Because the Japanese system has been quite successful and has received considerable attention in the United States, we shall conclude by making a few comparisons between the industrial relations systems of the two countries.

INDUSTRIAL RELATIONS IN THE UNITED STATES

Industrial relations and collective bargaining in the United States differ considerably from the Japanese system:

1. In large organizations there is an implication of continuing employment conditional on good performance. But this falls considerably short of the lifetime employment system. New employees may be hired at any age and released at any age. The sense of attachment to a single company is weaker than in Japan; and turnover is considerably higher, among managers as well as workers.

2. The tradition of union-management relations is adversarial rather than cooperative. Most managements regard the union as an unnecessary outside intruder in the plant, to be resisted and contained wherever possible. Most unionists assume that management is mainly interested in low production costs rather than employee welfare, which can be protected only by union vigilance and ultimate resort to the strike. While personal relations may be polite and even friendly, the organizational relation is one of armed truce.

3. Organization along occupational lines is important, often leading to several unions in the company. At most, the local may include all blue-collar workers. White-collar workers, where they are organized at all, are almost always organized separately. Supervisory workers are almost always excluded from the union.

4. Any identification of a local union with the company is weakened in two additional ways. First, the national union is much more powerful here than in Japan. Indeed, the local derives its charter from the national and is subordinate to its rules and procedures. The national union usually sends staff members to advise and assist the local in bargaining with employers, and in many industries (automobiles, basic steel, coal mining, trucking) the national union bears the brunt of the negotiations. It has a large war chest and is the main source of financial support in strikes.

   Second, while most local union officers are also company employees, national union officers and salaried union representatives are not identified with any company. Working for the union is a separate career, and people who perform well at a lower level can expect to move up to higher levels of responsibility and pay. An ambitious worker thus has a choice of working up the company ladder *or* the union ladder. You work up the union ladder partly by demonstrated ability to resist and outwit the employer.

5. Union-employer agreements are long and complex, setting forth the rights and duties of the parties in detail. They cover virtually all personnel practices as well as production practices with a significant impact on employees. A worker who believes that management has violated the contract can file a grievance. If this dispute cannot be settled by the foreman and the union shop steward, it goes up to higher levels of union-management negotiation, and if still unsettled goes to binding arbitration by a neutral umpire. The procedure ensures final settlement

without a strike, and hundreds of thousands of such cases are decided every year.

6. Contracts are normally for three years, with wage increases for the second and third years specified in advance. Failure to agree on the terms of a new contract before the old one expires normally means a stoppage of production. The strike is open ended and may go on for weeks or months. It is a process by which the parties inflict costs on each other in order to secure concessions leading to an eventual settlement. Japanese unions, on the other hand, are apparently willing to accept the most they can get by persuasion, without wielding the strike weapon.

7. Government regulation of industrial relations is unusually detailed and complex. The root cause is perhaps that unions and employers are so suspicious of each other that they have resorted to law wherever it seemed this might strengthen their position. How a union can be organized, how it must manage its affairs, the subjects that unions and employers may bargain about, the economic weapons they can wield against each other, are all regulated in detail. Industrial relations, like many other areas of American life, has become a lawyer's paradise. In Japan, on the other hand, it appears that labor lawyers are rare.

   While union-management relations are generally adversarial, American unions are not necessarily impervious to considerations of productivity and efficiency. Particularly where a company is doing badly and may even be threatened with failure, the union will often cooperate in programs to tighten efficiency and reduce costs. It does usually insist, however, that such programs be operated through the union rather than alongside it. Any effort by management to appeal *directly* to employees through workshop meetings, "quality circles," or whatever, is viewed with suspicion as an effort to circumvent and weaken the union.

Once more, pluses and minuses. U.S. managers clearly have less freedom to maneuver than their Japanese counterparts do. Efforts to raise productivity are more severely constrained. But perhaps U.S. unions are able to drive a tougher wage bargain. Perhaps workers are better protected by adherence to a formal grievance procedure. Whatever the answers to such questions, it seems likely that unions in each country will continue to work along accustomed lines.

SUMMARY

1. A union must negotiate similar wage rates for all workers who are equally productive. Otherwise the employer will have an incentive to employ only the least expensive workers. As a result, many of the benefits of unionization are collective benefits. This creates a free-rider problem that union organizers must overcome.

2. The first unions in the United States were local organizations of workers sharing a particular skill. They developed in the late eighteenth and early nineteenth centuries, often in response to threats to the economic position of skilled workers as wider markets led to greater competition and to greater division of labor. These unions were short-lived and could not withstand a business depression.

3. After the Civil War national unions arose in several occupations. Such unions could usually survive a depression, at least in skeletal form, and the national office could help organize new locals when conditions improved. For a union to have much influence over wage rates, it must organize all the workers within a product market. Otherwise competition from firms in unorganized areas will serve as a significant check on prices and thus also on wage rates for the unionized firms. Consequently, for industries with a national market, a union is under strong pressure to become national in scope.

4. The American Federation of Labor (AFL) arose to help deal with jurisdictional disputes and political lobbying, but power in the labor movement remained centered in the national unions. The AFL emphasized economic objectives, such as higher wages, reduced hours, and better working conditions. It did not seek to overthrow the capitalist system but rather to win greater gains for workers within the system through collective bargaining.

5. Unionization increased significantly during the 1930s and 1940s as a result of the Wagner Act and the high demand for labor during World War II. During this period the mass-production industries, like steel and automobiles, were organized successfully for the first time. In many cases this was accomplished by new industrial unions. Such unions formed the Congress of Industrial Organization (CIO). For many years there was bitter rivalry between the craft unions of the AFL and the industrial unions of the CIO, a rivalry that weakened the labor movement. By 1955 the two groups were able to reconcile their differences and merge.

6. Industrial unions often negotiate long contracts, with detailed descriptions of jobs and of the rules by which workers can move from one job to another. Usually seniority is a major criterion. Wage rates are attached to jobs rather than to the characteristics of the worker who holds the job. This approach is called the New Deal industrial relations system.

7. Since the 1960s unions in the public sector have become an important part of the labor movement. There has been a significant decline in unionization in the private sector, beginning in the 1970s. Both of these topics are addressed in detail in later chapters.

8. The extent of unionization in the United States varies considerably by occupation, industry, geographic region, and gender.

9. There are substantial differences in the labor movement and in collective bargaining across countries. In Italy and France political action is more important than collective bargaining. In Britain craft unions dominate, while industrial unions are the norm in Germany. In Germany many decisions, including plant closings, must be approved by works councils, where labor and management are equally represented. In Japan unions at the company level predominate. Many workers have lifetime employment with the firm. Strikes usually are short. Union and management are closely related, with officials moving back and forth from one side to the other. There is considerable conflict, especially during the annual spring offensive but also much cooperation.

KEY CONCEPTS

COLLECTIVE BENEFIT

FREE RIDER

SCAB

UNION, LOCAL

UNION, NATIONAL

UNION, CRAFT

UNION, INDUSTRIAL

STATE FEDERATION

NATIONAL FEDERATION

CODETERMINATION

REVIEW QUESTIONS

1. What is the free-rider problem? Why is it a concern of unions? How can unions deal with this issue?

2. To what factors can one attribute the beginnings of modern trade unionism around 1800?

3. In a depression workers would seem to need special protection against wage cuts and loss of jobs. Why, in spite of this, has union membership usually declined in depression periods?

4. Explain why skilled workers have usually been the first to form stable trade unions.

5. What explains the dominance of the national union over the other forms of trade union organization in the United States?

6. The rise of the CIO was pictured at the time as a victory of *industrial unionism* over *craft unionism*. What do these terms mean? Is this a correct interpretation of CIO development?

7. Why are fewer women than men union members? How and why has this differential been changing?

8. How do unions in other countries differ from those in the United States? To what extent do you think the United States might draw on the experience of other countries to improve industrial relations and collective bargaining in this country?

READINGS

BERNSTEIN, IRVING, *The Turbulent Years: A History of the American Worker, 1933–41.* Boston: Houghton Mifflin, 1970.

COMMONS, JOHN R., et al., *History of the Labor Movement in the United States,* New York: Macmillan Co., 1918.

DUNLOP, JOHN T. and WALTER GALENSON, *Labor in the Twentieth Century*. New York: Academic Press, 1978.

KOCHAN, THOMAS A., HARRY C. KATZ, and ROBERT B. MCKERSIE, *The Transformation of American Industrial Relations*. New York: Basic Books, 1986.

OLSON, MANCUR, *The Logic of Collective Action*. Cambridge, Mass.: Harvard University Press, 1971.

PERLMAN, SELIG, *A History of Trade Unionism in the United States*. New York: Macmillan Co., 1937.

TAFT, PHILIP, *Organized Labor in American History*. New York: Harper & Row, Publishers, 1964.

ULMAN, LLOYD, *The Rise of the National Trade Union*. Cambridge, Mass.: Harvard University Press, 1955.

UNIONS, POLITICS, AND THE LAW

We have seen that unions in the United States have been concerned primarily with economic issues. Yet the effectiveness of unions depends on the legal and political environment in which they operate. Through statutes, administrative regulations, and judicial decisions the larger community enforces its will in *public policy*. First we discuss different views about the value of unions, not just to their members but to society as a whole. Then we demonstrate how public policy toward unions has changed, largely as a result of changes in such views. We also consider how unions attempt to influence public policy and with what success. Unions themselves are political organizations. Thus we conclude by looking at the government of unions and considering how responsive unions are to the preferences of rank-and-file union members.

THE VALUE OF UNIONS TO SOCIETY

Public policy toward unions is affected by how the general public views unions. In Chapter 12 we focused on the benefits and costs of unions to their members. In the public policy context, however, we need to be concerned with the benefits and costs of unions to the whole society.

The Conservative View

If the economy were sufficiently competitive, with adequate information, flexible wage rates, and full employment, no significant costs of moving from job to job, and no concentration of power among employees, then competition would provide adequate protection to workers. In this world if a worker is dissatisfied with a job, he or she can quit and find a better one. If no better job is available, then the worker should either increase his or her skills or lower his or her expectations. In this competitive world unions can improve the wages and working conditions of their members but only at the expense of other workers as well as employers and consumers. Such monopoly gains on the part of unionized workers (or any other group) are considered socially undesirable by economists and by most citizens. The main exception would be if unionized workers would otherwise have had very low incomes. In this case there could be an income redistribution argument for unionization. But as we discussed in Chapter 12, unions generally have been stronger among workers with considerable skill than among those with the least skill and earnings potential.

How close does our actual economy come to the assumptions of the competitive model? Conservatives generally argue that it comes reasonably close, close enough to support the conclusion that unions have a negative net effect on the economy and thus should not be encouraged by public policies.[1] As we shall see, conservative views dominated public policy toward unions in this country until the 1930s.

The Radical View

Radicals also have been frequently critical of unions. In their view our capitalist system needs to be overthrown by a socialist revolution. Workers are likely candidates to lead such a revolution, but most unions act to ameliorate the conditions of workers under capitalism, thus forestalling the necessary revolution. Although some of the CIO unions were led by Communists until they were expelled in the late 1940s, Communists and Socialists have never been a dominant influence in the American labor movement. They have influenced public policy toward unions mainly by helping to energize conservative opposition.

The Liberal View

Since the 1930s public policy has supported unions whenever workers have voted in their favor. This approach is consistent with the liberal view that capitalism provides a good foundation for the economy but generates too much inequality and too much power for the well-to-do. To counter these flaws in capitalism, liberals generally favor considerable governmental regulation of the economy as well as organization of workers into unions as a counterbalance to the power of large employers.[2]

---

[1]For example, see Milton and Rose Friedman, *Free to Choose* (New York: Harcourt, Brace, Jovanovich, 1980), chapt. 8. Also see Dan C. Heldman and James T. Bennet, *Deregulating Labor Relations* (Dallas: Fisher Institute, 1981).

[2]For example, see John Kenneth Galbraith, *American Capitalism, The Concept of Countervailing Power* (Boston: Houghton Mifflin, 1952). Because, as we shall see, the liberal approach has underlain most of our labor policy for the last fifty years and because it is less consistent with simple microeconomic theory than the conservative approach, we shall discuss liberal views in greater detail.

Liberal labor economists often have emphasized imperfections in labor markets, such as imperfect information, costs of mobility, and monopsony. As we shall see, public policy first became favorable toward unions during the 1930s, largely in response to the high unemployment of the Great Depression. During the thirties and in the following years many liberal economists saw the union emphasis on high wage rates as helping the economy avoid mass unemployment by contributing to aggregate demand in the economy.[3]

Today most economists see the monetary and fiscal policy of the federal government, rather than union wage rates, as the key to stabilizing aggregate demand at sufficiently high levels to avoid a depression. But there are other reasons why it may be appropriate to support the union goal of taking wage rates out of competition. For example, Piore and Sabel suggest that firms are more likely to compete in terms of technological innovation if they cannot compete by each trying to pay a lower wage.[4] In the same vein Wright argues that the economic development of the South in recent decades has resulted, in part, from protective legislation of the federal government established during the 1930s, legislation (such as minimum wage rates) that made it more difficult for southern employers to compete with those in the North on the basis of lower wage rages.[5] Efficiency-wage theory, as discussed in Chapter 6, also shows how high wage rates, above the market-clearing level, may lead to gains for employers and the total economy as well as for workers.

Today the most prominent liberal view on unions, at least within the economics profession, is that of Freeman and Medoff.[6] They emphasize that in addition to the market mechanism of exit from one job to another, workers can also seek to improve their position by voicing complaints and making suggestions for change. If an individual worker complains about conditions on the job (e.g., unfair treatment by the foreman), however, that complaint may lead to the worker's being fired for being a troublemaker. Thus workers need to develop a collective voice. By acting collectively workers can greatly increase the costs to the employer of firing workers for complaining about wages or working conditions. Such collective action is especially needed when the cost of mobility is high, so that exit to another employer is not an easy option for the workers. Collective action is also important

---

[3]The conservative approach to reducing unemployment during the depression was to advocate lower wage rates, so that firms would want to hire more workers. As we discussed in Chapter 10, cutting wage rates can help reduce structural unemployment. But as Keynes demonstrated, cutting wage rates is not likely to solve the problem of demand-deficient unemployemt because a lower wage rate for all firms not only decreases the cost of labor to firms but also decreases workers' incomes, thus reducing the demand for the products firms sell and their demand for labor. This Keynesian argument implies that it is not only humane but also good for the economy to avoid wage competition, at least during a depression. In the terminology of the labor movement, we should "take wage rates out of competition."

[4]See Michel J. Piore and Charles F. Sabel, *The Second Industrial Divide* (New York: Basic Books, 1984), especially pp. 270–72.

[5]See Gavin Wright, *Old South, New South: Revolution in the Southern Economy Since the Civil War* (New York: Basic Books, 1984), especially chaps. 7 and 8. By the same author, also see "The Economic Revolution in the American South," *Journal of Economic Perspectives* (Summer 1987), pp. 161–78.

[6]Richard B. Freeman and James M. Medoff, *What Do Unions Do?* (New York: Basic Books, 1984).

when many items of concern (e.g., safety conditions, the speed of a production line) cannot be changed for one worker without also being changed for many coworkers. Freeman and Medoff agree with conservatives that unions have some bad economic effects, because a union does have monopoly power. Nevertheless, they conclude that the benefits of an effective collective voice for workers often exceed the monopoly costs of unions.

In summary, liberals do not share the conservatives' faith that markets and individual competition can solve most labor problems. Nor do they reject capitalism, as do most radicals. Instead, using a variety of arguments, most liberals see a useful role for unions in the economy and favor public policies to support unions.

We shall examine the impact of unions on the economy in more detail in Chapters 20 and 21, where we shall present empirical evidence to help assess the relative importance of the monopoly and collective-voice aspects of unions. In this chapter we focus on how differences in attitudes toward unions have led to quite different public policies toward organized labor. We also consider the influence of unions on public policy. Unions have been active supporters of many issues, ranging from labor-law reform, to import protection and restrictive immigration, to civil rights and Social Security.

PUBLIC POLICY TOWARD UNIONS

Historically, American public policy has moved from a position of complete freedom of action and absence of direct government controls to one of increasingly detailed regulation of union activities. As the American continent was settled and developed, legal institutions inherited from the English system altered as they adjusted to the problems of governing on a continental scale. Unions learned how to develop and exercise political power. They engaged in a continuing conflict with employers on the political level no less than in collective bargaining. Each side adopted in turn the weapons and tactics of the other. The prize was control over the rules of the game, for these rules affected the growth, power, and operation of organized labor. The relative fortunes of each side fluctuated, and the balance of power tilted with changes in the external environment.

Two elements of consistency can be identified amid the zigzags of policy. First, there was a consistent assertion of the public interest—the two sides could not be left completely free to fight out their differences. Second, in the U.S. there has been a basic approval of conflict, as a healthy and creative force, which should be curbed only as it becomes disruptive.

Major shifts in labor policy are marked by acts of Congress and the state legislatures. The legislature is the proper body for defining social policy; but under the American Constitution the judicial and executive branches of government have elements of independent authority. American courts, through judicial review, have a considerable power of veto. The courts say that they merely interpret the law and the Constitution; but as one student of labor law has said, this only means that they are reserving the freedom to change their minds. Landmarks of policy change thus appear in Supreme Court decisions. The tremendous power of the American President, and to a lesser extent of the state governors, means that the executive branch also has a powerful voice in labor policy. The National Labor Relations Board, the National Mediation Board, and other agencies charged with administering the statute law of industrial relations have elements of independent power, and some of their major decisions stand for a long time.

This fragmentation of power and rivalry between separate units of government, which could happen in few other countries, have made it possible for the contest between labor and management to be shifted from one arena to another, as one side saw some advantage to be gained. Loss of ground at the bargaining table may be regained by an appeal to the government. *Law* becomes a weapon in the struggle for power.[7] The intrusion of government ever deeper into industrial relations has created an increasingly large, complex, and often contradictory body of rules.

Judicial Control of Union Activities

A review of the turning points in American labor policy begins with a long period of a century or more when the power of the judiciary was unchallenged. Trade unions have been subject to comprehensive government control through the courts from the very beginnings of union organization.

There are two main types of legal rule: statutory rules enacted by the legislature and common law rules, which are unwritten and are based on consistent lines of previous court decisions. The courts have the final word in administering both types of rules. Statutory law is applied first by administrative agencies, such as the National Labor Relations Board, but decisions can be appealed by the losing party to the lower courts and eventually to the Supreme Court. Thus the practical effect of a law is tested in a series of hearings, first administrative and then judicial, and in the end the judges often decide what the statute means.

Common law rules, on the other hand, are rules that have developed solely or primarily through the accumulation of judicial decisions. Instead of interpreting the language of a statute, the court decides a dispute on the basis of a line of precedents, a logical sequence of decisions in previous cases where the court finds elements of similarity. In the absence of statutory law, judicial application of common law principles shaped the growth of unionism for almost a century.

To enforce their decisions, the courts have three types of legal remedies. The first of these is criminal prosecution. If it can be shown that union members have broken laws concerning theft, trespass, assault and battery, arson, and other crimes, or even that they have violated local ordinances prohibiting loitering, obstructing traffic, or disturbing the peace, they may be subject to fine and imprisonment. The number of workers who have been punished for real or alleged misdemeanors runs into the hundreds of thousands. The second type of remedy is civil

---

[7]Archibald Cox, "The Role of Law in Labor Disputes," *Cornell Law Quarterly*, 39 (1954), p. 592.

suit for damages. If union members cause damage to an employer's property, suit can be brought against the workers and in some circumstances against the union. The third and perhaps most important type of remedy is the injunction. This is a court order restraining the party against whom it is issued from doing specified acts. If the person goes ahead and does these things anyway, he may be ruled in contempt of court and punished by fine or imprisonment. The speedy and powerful character of this procedure has caused it to be widely used in labor cases.

The long period of judicial control was repressive and negative in character. Judges for the most part concluded that unionism was an undesirable activity that if it could not be prevented altogether, should be held within narrow limits. This view was due partly to the nature of law itself and partly to the personal predilections of the judges. Law is necessarily a conservative force. It exists to protect established rights. The common law of Great Britain, carried over in large part into American practice, gives special weight to rights connected with property ownership. Unionism, however, attacks the rights of the owners of industrial enterprises to manage them as they see fit. It seeks to curb property rights in order to establish new rights of workers in their jobs. The common law also regards freedom of contract and freedom of trade as desirable social objectives. The union, however, exists to restrict competition and establish a quasi-monopolistic position for its members. Unionism thus seemed contrary to the spirit of the common law, and it was easy for judges to find rules and precedents that would repress the activities of organized labor.

The judges' legal training in common law principles was buttressed by their political preferences. They came mainly from the propertied class, mingled more freely with employers than with workers, and tended naturally to sympathize with the interests of property owners. Their political thinking was influenced also by classical and neoclassical economics, which could find no useful place for joint action by wage earners.

The Doctrine of Criminal Conspiracy

In the early nineteenth century a number of court cases declared union activity of any sort illegal as a criminal conspiracy under the common law, punishable by fine or imprisonment. In other cases it was held that union actions designed to raise wages or reduce hours were lawful but that other objectives, such as the closed shop, were unlawful. The basic legality of trade unionism was not settled until the case of *Commonwealth* v. *Hunt*, decided in 1842. In this case Chief Justice Shaw of Massachusetts held that union activities were not *per se* unlawful, their legality depending rather on the objectives they sought to attain. Workers who were powerless as individuals could, he said, combine lawfully for mutual assistance. They might increase their control over their own livelihood by bargaining as a group with their employer. He held further that the closed shop was a legitimate union objective and that a strike to obtain it was not illegal. The case was not appealed to the Supreme Court of the United States, perhaps because it was recognized as a policy that would reduce labor violence and thereby benefit the expanding industries of

Massachusetts. Labor peace required some show of equal treatment before the law. At any rate, the doctrine of criminal conspiracy disappeared from American labor policy after this decision.

Trade Unions "Lawful" for What?

Unions thus came to be regarded as lawful associations, but the question remained open as to what kinds of activity a labor union could legally pursue and what actions were forbidden to it. To this question the courts applied the common law rule that harm intentionally inflicted on another is actionable unless it can be shown that the harm was justifiable. This idea arose out of business disputes, where the courts developed a line of precedents ruling that pursuit of economic self-interest by normal business methods is sufficient justification for harm done incidentally and without malice to the interests of others.

A strike or boycott clearly harms the employer and frequently other groups and individuals as well. This provides a ground for finding such activity unlawful unless the union can justify it as necessary to promote the economic interests of the workers. A judgment of fact must be made as to what tactics really advance the economic interests of the workers and under what conditions their claims are strong enough to justify the damage inflicted on the employer and on third parties. In the absence of a legislative statement of policy, the courts decided these questions case by case.

During this period the common law of labor relations developed somewhat differently in the different states. The courts of New York, for example, allowed considerably more scope for union activities than did the courts of Massachusetts or Pennsylvania. But in most states legitimate union activity was narrowly confined to peaceable strikes for improved wages, hours, or working conditions. Strikes for the closed shop, sympathetic strikes in aid of workers in related industries or trades, strikes against one employer to compel him to bring pressure on another employer (secondary boycotts), and many other types of activity were held unlawful. Once the objective of a strike had been ruled illegal, even peaceable actions in support of the strike came under the ban. And when the object of the strike was lawful, a court might nevertheless find that the tactics used were unduly coercive or injurious.

In the efforts of employers to seek court protection against strikes and boycotts, the favored weapons were criminal prosecution of union leaders and suits for damages. But in the 1880s a speedier and more effective instrument was developed—the labor injunction, which spread rapidly and continued unchecked until the 1930s.

Government by Injunction

The injunction was originally a court order designed to prevent threatened physical damage to property, under circumstances in which later action through regular court processes would be too slow. This device also came from English law.[8] The injunction was presumed to be a temporary restraining action to prevent irreparable damage to tangible property interests. It "froze" the relative position of two antagonists until the dispute could be settled in court. But once it was applied to *economic* damage and to *intangible* property, in practice the necessity of later legal action was forestalled. The injunction is one of the speediest of legal remedies. Requiring only the judge's signature and backed by the court's full authority of fine and imprisonment, it could close down a picket line and bring a strike to a halt within a matter of hours.

When American courts extended the idea of safeguarding property interests to such intangibles as "justifiable expectation of profit" from the continuous operation of a business, the entire strategy of the union was undercut. Under such an interpretation, it could be shown that any strike was *ipso facto* injurious to property. American courts also tended to accept unsubstantiated allegations that the strikers were threatening physical damage and to take affidavits from only one side of the controversy. This was a clear abuse of the equity procedure, which should obviously be applied without favoring one antagonist over the other. Yet the existence of many such cases has been well documented.

The injunction procedure usually operated as follows:[9] The company would go to a judge, usually one already known to be antiunion, and present a written complaint, stating that the union was threatening imminent damage to the employer's property and that this damage could be prevented only by issuing an order restraining the union from certain specified actions. Many injunctions were actually drawn up by a company attorney and simply signed by the judge. Even if the judge decided to take evidence from the union, this evidence would be limited to an affidavit replying to the employer's charges; the union could not call witnesses or present oral testimony. After considering the employer's and possibly the union's statements, the judge decided whether to issue the injunction.

The temporary injunction, or *restraining order,* was usually drawn in sweeping terms, restraining anyone from interfering with the employer's business in any way. Judges occasionally went into detail, specifying that there must be only one picket at each plant entrance, that he must be standing so many feet from the gate, and so on. But the general vice of injunctions was their vagueness. They were drawn in broad terms. Anyone who supported the strike in any way could be held guilty of a violation, tried without a jury for contempt of court, and severely punished.

In theory there was a later hearing by the court, at which witnesses were heard, after which the temporary injunction was either vacated or made permanent. But the strike was usually won or lost in the intervening months. Even when

---

[8]The injunction developed as one of the remedies in *courts of equity,* which in England are separate courts with separate judges and a body of precedents different from the *courts of law,* where disputes between two adversaries are tested in open trials with judge and jury. But American courts sit simultaneously as trial courts and equity courts, the judge applying the different bodies of precedent according to the type of action taken by the plaintiff.

[9]The classic study is Felix Frankfurter and Nathan Greene, *The Labor Injunction* (New York: Macmillan Co., 1930).

the injunction was not strictly enforced, its application to a labor dispute brought the weight of law down against the strikers. With the union stigmatized before the public, its members became demoralized and intimidated, its treasury melted away, and its drive was weakened. In the more usual case where the injunction was broadly drawn and vigorously enforced by the police, it was an almost unbeatable method of strikebreaking.

An indirect result of the injunction procedure was to stimulate union interest in political activity. Many state judges were elected, and the others were appointed by elected officials. Unions saw the point of taking an active role in this process. They also appealed repeatedly to Congress and the state legislatures to pass statutes legalizing trade union activities and forbidding the courts to interfere with them. These efforts were largely unsuccessful. Few laws were passed, and even these were unfavorably interpreted in hostile court decisions.

The Norris-LaGuardia Act and the Railway Labor Act

Labor's long-standing demand that government cease repressing union activities and adopt a neutral stance finally came to fruition with the passage of the Norris-LaGuardia act of 1932. The legislation set up for the first time a national policy in labor relations. Carefully drafted, its provisions specifically removed the judicially built obstacles to union organization and peaceable union activities.

The act, which is still in effect, declares that as a matter of sound public policy the individual worker would "have full freedom of association, self-organization, and designation of representatives of his own choosing, to negotiate the terms and conditions of his employment, and that they shall be free from the interference, restraint, or coercion of employers of labor, or their agents, in the designation of such representatives or in self-organization or in other concerted activities for the purpose of collective bargaining or other mutual aid or protection." Activities that the courts are forbidden to enjoin are listed: (1) a concerted refusal to work; (2) membership in, or support of, a labor organization; (3) peaceable urging of others to leave work; (4) publicizing a trade dispute by any method not involving fraud or violence; (5) peaceable assembly; and (6) payment of strike benefits and aid to anyone interested in a labor dispute who is party to a lawsuit. Moreover, yellow-dog contracts, where workers promise not to join unions, were made unenforceable in the courts.

The issuance of labor injunctions by the federal courts was further controlled by procedural requirements. The employer was required to prove that the regular police force was either unwilling or unable to protect his property. He also had to be innocent of violating any labor law. The judge, in issuing a temporary injunction, had to hear witnesses from both sides and could not rely solely on affidavits. A jury trial was permitted if contempt-of-court proceedings followed issuance of an injunction.

The provisions were essentially negative and neutral. The intent and effect of the law was to remove certain legal restraints by which trade union action had been controlled and to leave the unions free to exert their full economic power against the employer.

The other early federal labor legislation was the Railway Labor Act of 1926. The railroad unions were quite strong and eager to stabilize labor relations in their industry. Since a railroad strike could paralyze the economy, special provisions were established so mediators, appointed by the government, might help to avoid such strikes. Airlines are also covered by amendments to this legislation, rather than by the National Labor Relations Act, which is the major law covering most employers in the private sector. We turn next to this legislation.

PROTECTIVE LEGISLATION: THE WAGNER ACT

A major change in direction came only three years after Norris-LaGuardia, with the passage of the National Labor Relations Act of 1935, commonly known as the Wagner Act from its principal sponsor, Senator Wagner of New York. From this date onward, government was to take an active part in labor relations.[10] Passage of the Wagner Act and its subsequent approval by the Supreme Court marked a change in direction so revolutionary that it can only be understood by recalling the atmosphere of the early 1930s, when worldwide depression had brought stagnation to the American economy. Underlying the provisions of the act was a belief that unionization would bring higher wages and greater purchasing power, which would contribute to economic recovery.

The philosophy of the Wagner Act was essentially as follows: it is desirable that terms and conditions of employment be regulated by collective bargaining. It is also desirable, therefore, that workers should organize strong and stable unions as rapidly as possible, without the crippling effects of bitter organizational strikes. This objective will not be accomplished if government follows a hands-off policy, since employers have many effective methods of resisting union organization. It is necessary, therefore, that government should restrain the use of certain types of coercion by employers for a long enough period to allow unions to be formed throughout industry.

Workers were not required to join unions, but the union organizer was to be given full freedom in presenting his case to them, while the employer was required to remain silent and inactive. The act took the position that a worker's decision concerning union membership is none of the employer's business. The role of government, through the National Labor Relations Board, was to ensure that union organization was not hindered by employer action. It was assumed that if employer pressure were removed, most workers would choose to join unions. The growth of union membership from about four million in 1933 to fifteen million in 1948 seemed to confirm the accuracy of this forecast, although it must be remem-

---

[10]The National Labor Relations Act of 1935 can be found in 49 Stat. 449; the Taft-Hartley amendments are in 61 Stat. 136 (1947), and the Landrum-Griffin amendments in 73 Stat. 519 (1959). The full text of the act with amendments is found in 28 U.S.C. 151 *et seq.*

bered that high employment and excess demand for labor during and after World War II also did much to promote unionization.

The Wagner Act gave employees the right to organize unions, to bargain collectively through representatives of their own choosing, and to engage in other concerted activities for the purpose of mutual protection. Employers were prohibited from engaging in *unfair labor practices,* which included: (1) interference with, restraint of, or coercion of employees in the exercise of their rights under the act; (2) domination of, interference with, or financial support of a union organization; (3) discrimination to encourage or discourage union membership, except where a closed union shop was established by agreement with a majority of the employees; (4) discrimination against an employee for filing charges or giving testimony under the act; and (5) refusal to bargain "in good faith" with the legal representative of the employees.

The act provided that where doubt existed as to the majority status of a union, the matter could be decided by a secret ballot of the workers involved, a *represention election,* or some other suitable method. Such elections and other fact-finding aspects of the act were to be administered by the National Labor Relations Board, which was also given responsibility for prosecuting unfair labor practices by employers.

The Supreme Court's long record of antilabor decisions created expectations that the Wagner Act would be declared unconstitutional. But the Court had finally decided to accept the authority of Congress and the president in determining national economic policy. The great popularity of President Roosevelt and his unprecedented landslide victory in 1936 were doubtless factors in the Court's change of attitude.

The constitutionality of the Wagner Act was upheld by the Supreme Court in 1937 in the case of *National Labor Relations Board* v. *Jones and Laughlin Steel Corporation,* by a vote of five to four, a decision based on Congress's right to regulate interstate commerce.[11] For a decade thereafter, the Wagner Act was the unchallenged law of the land. It was still not generally accepted by employers, however, and in the early years there were serious difficulties in administering the act. The NLRB staff was inadequate and inexperienced for handling the flood of unfair labor practice charges that came in 1937 and 1938. But the board developed informal and increasingly effective administrative procedures and by concentrating its effort on key cases was able to bring about widespread observance of the act. In the twelve years from 1935 to 1947, over 45,000 unfair labor practice cases and over 59,000 representation cases were handled either formally or informally. Collective bargaining became the accepted method of conducting industrial relations.

Acceptance of the Wagner Act soon led to passage of "little Wagner Acts" in many of the industrial states. State labor relations acts were enacted by Utah, Wisconsin, New York, Pennsylvania, and Massachusetts in 1937, Rhode Island in 1941, and Connecticut in 1945. These state laws are important, because the Wagner Act (and its successors) cover only establishments engaged in interstate commerce.

---

[11]*National Labor Relations Board* v. *Jones and Laughlin Steel Corp.,* 301 U.S. 1 (1937).

A third or so of the nonagricultural workers in the country are subject primarily to state regulation.

Government protection of union-organizing activities, combined with the rising level of employment after 1933, led to a rapid increase in union membership. The CIO, which was not in existence when the Wagner Act was passed, quickly unionized most workers in the mass-production industries. This was not accomplished, however, without a number of large and bitter strikes, culminating in the wave of sit-down strikes during 1937. Regardless of the reason for these strikes, middle-class opinion tended to label the sit-down as a sign of "radicalism" in the new unions. Instances of violence or irresponsibility during strikes and occasional malfeasance by union officials were publicized by newspaper editors, columnists, and commentators. Public opinion, particularly in small towns and rural areas, became increasingly critical of union objectives and tactics.

The strongest criticism of the Wagner Act, if one ignores the attacks of those who rejected it altogether, was that its treatment of unions vis-à-vis management was inequitable. Employer tactics were severely restricted, but no comparable restrictions were imposed on the union. There was also criticism that the rights of individual employees were not sufficiently protected under the act. This objection is not surprising, since the purpose of the act was to favor collective action in all cases in which a majority had voted for it.

RESTRICTIVE LEGISLATION

The unfavorable public reaction did not lead to repeal of the federal and state labor relations acts, though repeal was the hope of many employers. It resulted rather in the passage of additional laws intended to control certain types of union activity. In an effort to achieve a workable balance of power between unions and employers, government was projected ever further into the labor relations scene.

The Taft-Hartley Act of 1947

During World War II labor disputes were handled under special emergency provisions by the national War Labor Board. When government control of wages ended with the war, there was no accepted plan for resolving the difficult issues of wages and hours in the reconversion period. Unions demanded higher wage rates to compensate for reduced earnings caused by shorter workweeks and less overtime pay. Serious strikes over this issue occurred in the steel, coal, and automobile industries in 1946, and there was also a nationwide railroad strike. Public alarm over the large number of strikes was partly responsible for election of a Republican majority to Congress in 1946. In 1947 Congress passed the National Labor Management Relations Act of 1947, commonly known as the Taft-Hartley Act after its two principal sponsors.

The new law was in form an amendment of the Wagner Act, most of the provisions of the earlier law being carried over intact. As the appendix to this chapter shows, the explicit philosophy of the legislation is still very favorable to collective bargaining. But the Taft-Hartley amendments do introduce many new provisions, and the total effect is to establish a rather different philosophy of labor relations. The Wagner Act assumed that most workers prefer to join unions; that the interests of unions and their members are identical; that restricting certain employer tactics will ensure sufficient equality of bargaining power between unions and management; and that once the parties have been brought to the bargaining table, they should be left free to write whatever contract provisions they choose. Government should not try to shape the content of collective agreements.

In contrast, the Taft-Hartley Act reflects a distrust of collective action, regardless of majority sanction. Its outlook may be summarized as follows: (1) Workers may or may not wish to join unions. Their right to stay out should be protected against coercion from any quarter, including the unions; and workers already in unions should be given reasonable opportunity to get out if they so desire. (2) The interests of members and of the union organization are not necessarily identical. Workers need protection against the union as well as against the employer. Government may have to regulate internal union affairs for this purpose. (3) Unions are not necessarily the weaker party in collective bargaining. In some areas of the economy the employer may be the underdog. To ensure true equality of bargaining power, the law must restrain unfair tactics of unions as well as of employers. (4) There is a public interest in the terms of union contracts. It may be necessary to prohibit some contract provisions; government is entitled to scrutinize bargaining results as well as bargaining procedures. (5) The public also requires protection against crippling stikes in essential industries, and special procedures are needed to deal with such strikes. (6) Union political power should be specially controlled; it is necessary to prohibit unions from contributing to federal election campaigns.

The Taft-Hartley Act thus moved away from the policy of protecting unions and toward a policy of protecting employers, individual workers, and the general public. A variety of restrictions were imposed on union operations. The unions strongly opposed the act and later worked energetically to secure its repeal. These efforts were unsuccessful, however, and the Taft-Hartley Act continues as the main federal legislation governing labor relations.

Most provisions of the act can be related to three professed objectives:

1. To equalize bargaining power by restraining certain tactics of both unions and employers. To this end the act lists certain unfair practices on the part of unions, parelleling the list of unfair employer practices that was carried over intact from the Wagner Act. Unions may not interfere with the individual employee's right not to participate in collective bargaining. They may not attempt to cause employers to discriminate against nonunionists, except as may be required by a valid union-shop agreement. They may not refuse to bargain collectively with an employer. They may not engage in secondary boycotts or jurisdictional strikes, or in strikes to force recognition of one union when another has already been certified as bargaining

representative. They may not extract money from an employer for work not needed or not actually performed.

2. Second, the act attempts to protect individual employees against the union in a variety of ways. Union contracts may no longer establish a closed shop or any other system of preferential hiring. A union may not charge excessive dues or initiation fees. Although it remains free to discipline and expel members, it cannot cause the employer to discharge a worker under a union-shop contract if the worker was denied membership or dropped from membership for any reason other than non-payment of dues and initiation fees. In addition, employees are given a way of getting rid of a union that they no longer wish to represent them. If 30 percent of the employees in a bargaining unit file a petition requesting decertification of the union representing them, the National Labor Relations Board must conduct a secret ballot to determine the wishes of the majority.

   The checkoff system of collecting union dues is regulated by a proviso that dues can be deducted from the paycheck only with the written consent of the individual employee. Employer payments to union welfare funds are permitted only if certain conditions are observed, such as separation of the welfare funds from general union funds and joint union-management administration. The act provides further that union funds may not be used for political purposes.

3. A third professed objective is to protect innocent bystanders against the consequences of interunion or union-management strife. The innocent party may in some cases be the employer. Under the Wagner Act an employer sometimes found himself caught in the crossfire of two rival unions, each seeking to organize his plant and each threatening to shut it down, unless granted recognition. Since the employer could not petition for a National Labor Relations Board election to settle the issue, his hands were tied. The Taft-Hartley Act accordingly provides that employers as well as unions may petition the National Labor Relations Board for a representation election. A similar situation often arises in jurisdictional disputes where two unions—say, the carpenters and machinists—each demand that the employer assign a certain type of work to its members under penalty of shutdown. The Taft-Hartley Act forbids strikes in such situations and provides that they be decided by the National Labor Relations Board unless the rival unions work out their own arrangements for settlement. This provision has stimulated the growth of private settlement machinery, notably as between the various building-trades unions.

We have already noted the act's restrictions on the secondary boycott, an old union device of putting pressure on one employer so that he will exert pressure on another employer whom the union is really after. Strikes often cause inconvenience to another neutral party, the consuming public. The Taft-Hartley Act contains no limitations on strikes in general, but it does provide a procedure for use in "national emergency" disputes. Strikes that in the opinion of the President imperil the national health or safety are made subject to injunction for a maximum period of eighty days. The President is authorized to appoint a special board of inquiry, which makes a preliminary investigation prior to the time an injunction is sought and must turn in a final report when the injunction has been in effect for sixty days. If the parties, with the aid of the Federal Mediation and Conciliation Service, have not been able to settle the dispute by this time, the National Labor Relations Board is required to poll the employees as to whether they are willing to accept the employer's last offer. After this step the injunction is dissolved, and the President may, if he wishes, refer the dispute to Congress and recommend a course of action.

The board of inquiry is specifically prohibited from recommending terms for settlement of the dispute. These provisions do not apply to government employees, who are prohibited by the act from striking; nor do they apply to railroad workers, for whom a special procedure is provided by the Railway Labor Act.

The Landrum-Griffin Act of 1959

In the decade from 1947 to 1957 there was continued complaint of corruption and high-handed procedures in trade union government. Such practices may not have been widespread in the sense of involving large numbers of union members; but the complaints were genuine, they had high publicity value, and they were sometimes supported by sensational testimony.

The Landrum-Griffin Act (also called the Labor-Management Reporting and Disclosure Act) undertook to protect union members in several ways against arbitrary action by union officials:

1. It provides a "bill of rights" for union members. They are guaranteed the right of free speech in union meetings, the right to run for union office, and the right to vote equally with other members in union elections. Dues, initiation fees, and assessments must be approved by membership vote. In any disciplinary proceeding against a member, the union must observe due process. The member must be served with specific written charges, given a reasonable time to prepare his defense, and assured of a full and fair hearing. A member has the right to sue the union for infringement of his rights, and the union cannot prevent the member from going to court.

2. Every labor organization must adopt a constitution and bylaws and file a copy with the secretary of labor. In addition, every local as well as national union must file an annual financial report, listing its assets, receipts and expenditures, salary payments to officers, and related data. It must also report direct or indirect loans to any business, and any other loan in excess of $250. Union officers must report any holdings of securities and any financial transactions with the union or with companies with which the union has bargaining relations. These provisions are intended to check embezzlement, bribery and extortion, and other ways of profiting from union office.

3. The act regulates the use of the trusteeship device. This device is normally used for legitimate purposes, such as phasing out a defunct local or correcting local mismanagement; but it has also been used on occasion to perpetuate a national union machine or to milk funds from local treasuries. Landrum-Griffin prohibits transfers of funds, requires that any trusteeship be authorized by a proper tribunal after fair hearing, and provides that it automatically becomes invalid after eighteen months unless the union can make a case for its continuance.

4. The act provides standards and safeguards for the conduct of local and national union elections. Complaints of election irregularities can be filed with the secretary of labor. If investigation shows the complaint to be justified, the secretary may ask the courts to set aside the election results and order a new election under the supervision of the Labor Department.

5. The act establishes a fiduciary relationship between the union officer and the union, enabling members to bring suit for improper monetary management or conflict-of-interest situations. A union officer cannot acquire personal interests that conflict

with those of the union and, in the event of a conflict, must act in the union's interest rather than in his own. The act puts the union official in the legal position of a bank trust officer managing the estate of a client.

Recent Developments

Labor law is a living and changing thing. The books are not closed. Some features of present laws and the ways they are administered are displeasing to unions, while others are objectionable to employers. So almost every session of Congress sees proposals for amendment of existing statutes. Some proposals are passed. For example, the National Labor Relations Act was amended in 1974 to include hospital workers and others in the health industry. Most frequently the proposals are not enacted because of a standoff between business and union lobbyists.

The most notable example is the Labor Law Reform Bill of 1977–78, introduced at the urging of the AFL-CIO with a view to curbing the activities of strongly antiunion firms such as J. P. Stevens and Company. A relatively mild bill, it aimed to facilitate union organizing drives by streamlining the NLRB election procedures, by penalizing employers' unfair labor practices more severely, and by providing equal time for the union to address employees on company time before an election. With Democratic majorities in the House and Senate, and with President Carter favoring the bill, passage seemed assured. The bill did pass the House by a substantial majority. But business groups then mounted a strong lobbying campaign against it. In the Senate two senators led a successful filibuster, and the bill never came to a vote. We shall discuss this bill in more detail in Chapter 14. In that chapter we also discuss how the National Labor Relations Act works, especially its provisions for certification elections to determine if workers wish to be represented by a union.

UNIONS AND POLITICS

Unions are strongly affected by public policy. We have already discussed the major changes in legislation and the judicial decisions that have affected union power during the past century.[12] Next we will consider how unions have attempted to influence public policy and look at some of the legislation passed with the support of the labor movement.

---

[12]Unions are also affected by the way the laws are administered by the executive branch. In Chapter 14 we shall discuss changes in the administration of the National Labor Relations Act. But executive action is also important at the state and local levels. Let us consider one dramatic example. Assume that in trying to break a strike, an employer hires strikebreakers to replace those who are on strike, and violence is anticipated as the strikebreakers attempt to cross the strikers' picket line. Clearly the police must prevent the violence. But do they do so by escorting the strikebreakers through the picket line or by discouraging the strikebreakers from crossing the line. For an important strike, this decision will be made by elected officials to whom the police report. The decision will be based, in considerable part, on community attitudes and on the relative political power of the union and the employer.

The AFL

Prior to the New Deal of the 1930s unions had relatively little political power. Under Gompers the AFL restricted its political agenda to issues directly affecting unions, for instance, efforts to combat the power of injunction against strikers. In part, the AFL had to focus its limited political capital where it was most needed. But also Gompers was distrustful of government. If unions came to be too dependent on government aid, then they would lose their freedom of independent action. And if the government created programs, such as unemployment compensation, to aid workers directly, then workers might come to rely too heavily on government (a fickle ally) and not enough on unions.

In contrast to the close association between unions and labor political parties that developed in Europe, where organized labor represented a much higher proportion of the working class, Gompers emphasized that labor should be free of any long-term alliances with one party. Instead, labor should "reward its friends and punish its enemies" regardless of their political party.

Because of strong employer opposition and generally conservative social attitudes prior to the 1930s, the AFL had quite limited success with its political agenda. With the New Deal and the rise of the CIO, labor's political clout increased considerably. Over the past half-century organized labor has become involved in a much wider range of political issues and has developed strong ties with the Democratic party.

The New Deal

The primary labor legislation of the New Deal was the Wagner Act of 1935. But the Great Depression of the 1930s also led to many other important laws affecting workers. Some of the most important legislation, for instance, the Social Security Act of 1935, was in the field of income maintenance. Other legislation passed during this period dealt with the regulation of wage rates and hours worked.

In 1931 Congress passed the Davis-Bacon Act, prohibiting the federal government from paying less than the prevailing wage on its construction projects. Under this legislation, which remains important today, the prevailing wage has almost always been interpreted to mean the union wage. The act is based on the assumption that construction firms should not compete on the basis of wage rates.

The Fair Labor Standards Act (FLSA) of 1938 set a minimum wage of twenty-five cents per hour and required employers to pay a 50 percent premium for any hours in excess of forty that an employee worked each week. Coverage of the legislation initially was quite limited, but it has been expanded over time by a series of amendments. Such amendments have also raised the minimum wage, which was $3.35 in 1989. Almost all union members earn more than the minimum wage. Still, the minimum wage has become an important issue for unions. One reason is that organized labor seeks gains for all workers, but another reason is that high-wage union labor will be under less competitive pressure from firms employing low-wage nonunion workers as the legal minimum rises and the coverage of the legislation expands. Unions have also been interested in the overtime-hours provisions of the FLSA. Requiring a premium for overtime hours does more than increase the compensation of those who work overtime. It may also reduce unemployment by creating an incentive for employers to respond to increases in demand by hiring more workers rather than by increasing overtime.

The 1940s and 1950s

During the early 1940s the economy expanded rapidly, responding to the high demand of World War II. Unemployment fell from 19 percent in 1938 to 1 percent in 1944. During World War II the federal government imposed controls on wage rates to combat inflation. Unions did not provide much resistance to such controls, partly because of concern for the war effort and partly because many unions won recognition in return for no-strike pledges.[13]

Although organized labor has developed a broader political agenda since World War II, its first priority has been to maintain its legislative gains of the thirties and early forties in the face of more conservative times. The political conflicts leading to, and resulting from, the Taft-Hartley amendments to the National Labor Relations Act are the leading example.

The Sixties and Seventies: Public Interest Labor Law

In the sixties and early seventies unions played a leading role in much new legislation, sometimes referred to as public interest labor law.[14] The main statutes here are the Employees Retirement Income Security Act (ERISA), which regulates the administration of employer pension plans; the Occupational Safety and Health Act of 1970, administered by the Occupational Safety and Health Administration (OSHA); and employment-discrimination laws, especially Title VII of the Civil Rights Act of 1964, administered by the Equal Employment Opportunity Commission (EEOC). Although these laws do not bear directly on union-management relations, they have important indirect effects.

A union that considered working conditions unsafe or unhealthy could always protest to the employer, seek appropriate clauses in the union contract, and process individual cases through the grievance procedure. But now in addition it can seek an investigation by OSHA, present evidence, and follow up on the results. The union organization is in a better position to seek legal remedies than is the individual employee in a nonunion plant. If the employer fails to implement OSHA orders and continues to maintain unsafe conditions, the workers can walk out and

---

[13]In addition, firms and unions found ways to get around the controls. For example, unions could gain more for their workers by focusing on benefits, such as vacations, holidays, health insurance, and pensions—none of which were subject to much regulation.

[14]William B. Gould, *A Primer of American Labor Law*, chap. 11.

shut down the plant (which OSHA itself is forbidden to do). The courts have held that such a walkout does not violate the no-strike clause in a union contract.

Hiring, promotion, layoff, and other personnel decisions are usually regulated in detail by the union contract. So here the antidiscrimination statutes, and EEOC activities in enforcing them, have had a substantial impact. Unions as well as employers are forbidden to discriminate, either by colluding with an employer in discriminatory employment policies, or unilaterally—for example, by restricting minority admission to apprenticeship programs, which are the normal admission channel to some of the skilled trades. Discrimination in admission to union membership is of course forbidden. Unions in construction, railroading, and a number of other industries have traditionally practiced racial discrimination, and their policies have been modified only by continuing government pressure. Especially in the public sector, some difficult problems have arisen as a result of conflict between the goals of affirmative action and the seniority rules in union contracts.

The AFL-CIO was a leader in helping to enact the Civil Rights Act of 1964, the Occupational Safety and Health Act of 1970, and the Employee Retirement Income Security Act of 1974.

UNION POLITICAL POWER

Unions seek to influence legislation and the way it is administered by helping to elect officials who are sympathetic to the goals of organized labor and by lobbying officials, both elected and appointed, to show them why they should support labor's position on particular issues. Organized labor has considerable money available to spend in support of these activities. But employers usually have more money and often, though not always, advocate positions opposed to those of labor. On the other hand, unions have some advantages over employers in the political arena. For example, unions may be able to recruit more volunteer workers. Only rarely, however, can unions bring out a large vote of their members for a particular candidate. Union members consider many factors in addition to the views of their leaders in deciding whom to vote for. A particularly dramatic example occurred in 1984 when despite very strong support for Walter Mondale by the AFL-CIO and most of its affiliated unions, Ronald Reagan received 45 percent of the vote from union households.[15]

How effective have unions been in the political arena? Clearly the answer differs from issue to issue and from one time period to another. As we have seen, unions were much more successful in the 1930s and in the late sixties and early seventies than in most other periods. Especially in the 1930s organized labor was seen by many as the spearhead of a broad, progressive coalition, concerned with the welfare of all workers.[16] In recent years, however, labor's political influence has

[15]See A. H. Raskin, "Labor: A Movement in Search of a Mission," in *Unions in Transition*, Seymour Martin Lipset (San Francisco: ICS Press, 1986), p. 31.

[16]See Michael J. Piore, "Can the American Labor Movement Survive Re-Gomperization?" *Proceedings of the Thirty-Fifth Annual Meeting, Industrial Relations Research Association*, Madison, Wis.: 1983.

declined as it has come to be seen more as a special-interest group, looking out primarily for the self-interest of its members.

In most periods and on most issues labor's political influence has been relatively limited. On broad political issues like those discussed above labor is only one of many important actors in the political arena. Moreover, labor often speaks with a divided voice on such issues, with some unions taking positions opposite to those of the AFL-CIO. On narrower issues, for instance, labor law reform, there is much greater agreement among unions but fewer allies and more powerful enemies, especially among employers. Union have sometimes been successful in uniting with employers to obtain legislation benefiting particular industries, such as import protection for automobiles in the early 1980s, but such efforts have often failed. An important example is the unsuccessful opposition of the Teamsters and the trucking industry in the late 1970s to any deregulation of the industry.

The legislation most favorable to unions was passed in the 1930s, a period when unions had little organized political power but when bad economic conditions led to broad public support for efforts to modify our economic system. Since that time the political power of unions has been rather limited but by no means completely inconsequential.

Freeman and Medoff conclude:

> In short, while unions would like to pass laws that enhance union strength, they represent too small a proportion of the population and engender too great business opposition to succeed. Through no virtue of their own, their main political success is as the voice of workers and the lower income segments of society, not as a special interest group enhancing its own position.[17]

A similar conclusion was reached two decades ago by Bok and Dunlop:

> The record suggests that organized labor has not been able to achieve important legislative goals unless its objectives have corresponded with the sentiments of the electorate or the prevailing convictions in Congress.
>
> Despite these limitations, it would be wrong to assume that labor's political power has been negligible. Without union efforts, workers and low-income groups would have little organized political support, and their interests would be more vulnerable to the pressure of other powerful groups. Through constant lobbying and political campaigning, unions have doubtless helped to give birth to Medicare and to enlarge social security and unemployment and workmen's compensation benefits.[18]

As we disscussed in the introduction, a major economic argument for unions is their ability to give a greater voice to their members. This voice is important in the political arena as well as the workplace. In the labor market the gains from unions as a collective voice of the workers must be balanced against the costs

---

[17]Freeman and Medoff, *What Do Unions Do?*, p. 202.
[18]Derek C. Bok and John T. Dunlop, *Labor and the American Community* (New York: Simon & Schuster, 1970), p. 424.

of their monopoly power. In political competition, however, most potential excesses that might result from the organized power of workers are fully offset by the political power of employers, which usually exceeds that of unions.

UNION GOVERNMENT: THE INTERNAL POLITICS OF UNIONS

We have described the role of unions in governmental politics. Next let us consider the internal politics and decision making of unions. Our primary interest is in seeing how responsive unions are to the preferences of their members. This issue is important in evaluating the desirability of unions, in considering government policies to protect unions or to limit their influence and, as we shall see in Chapter 15, in modeling the economic objectives of unions.

The government of a local union is relatively simple, while management of the national organization is more complex. The business of a local union is carried on in weekly or monthly meetings of the membership. When plants are very large, as in the automobile industry, some locals are so large that it is physically impossible to have a single meeting; then a delegate system has to be used. The typical local union, however, has at most a few hundred members, who can be brought together in a single meeting and can take a direct hand in union affairs if they wish to do so.

Only a small proportion of union members actually take an active and continuous interest in union affairs. On important occasions—the election of officers for the coming year, the formulation of demands to be presented to the employer, the ratification of a new contract, or the taking of a strike vote—a large percentage of the membership will appear at the meeting. Between crises, however, attendance shrinks to perhaps 5 to 10 percent of the membership. The day-to-day work of the union is carried on by a few "wheelhorses" who are willing to put in the necessary time. These are the professional politicians of the labor movement, corresponding to the ward and precinct leaders in a political machine. This active minority, however, is in close touch with the remainder of the membership. Even though only two workers from a certain department of the plant show up at the meeting, they probably have a good idea of what the other workers in the department are thinking. They also carry back and explain to their fellow workers the decisions made at the meeting. There is thus a great deal of informal representation of the inert majority, and the government of the union is more democratic than might appear at first glance.

The officers of the local union usually work in the plant along with the rest and receive no pay for their union activities. Exceptions are sometimes found in large locals, where union office may become a full-time job. The local officers carry on the day-to-day work of keeping the union running, persuading new workers to join, collecting dues, and handling grievances arising in the plant. On major problems, such as the negotiation of a new contract or the handling of a strike, they are usually advised and assisted by a field representative of the national union.

Because a national leader cannot be in close touch with most rank-and-file members, a different leadership style is necessary. National leaders tend to be more autocratic than those at the local level. There are two main constraints, however, on the ability of national leaders to set their own course. The first is the union's constitution, which is much more detailed than the charters of business corporations, often running to forty or fifty printed pages. The duties and powers of union officers, the rights and duties of union members, and the procedures for conduct of union business are all set forth at length in the constitution.

The second constraint is the national convention, the supreme governing body of the union. Most unions hold their conventions every year or two years, though sometimes conventions are held three or four years apart. The convention consists of delegates from the affiliated local unions. Each local is usually represented in proportion to its dues-paying membership, which means that the larger locals have a dominant voice. The convention listens to reports by the national officers on developments since the last convention, discusses these reports, and approves or disapproves them. It elects officers to serve until the next convention. The present officers naturally try to stage manage the convention so as to put their performance in the best light and to win reelection. Usually they succeed, but not always. The convention is free to debate any question of union policy or organization and has the power to amend the union constitution.

Complaints about lack of democratic control are more apt to occur at the national level than at the local level. The Landrum-Griffin Act requires that local officers be elected at least once every three years, and annual elections are common. Local officers are drawn from the general membership, and turnover is quite high. The proportion of local offices changing hands is usually at least 20 percent and in some unions as high as 50 percent. So while "boss control" can occur, it is not widespread.

National union presidents and other officers tend to stay in office for longer periods. Union officers—like officeholders in industry, government, and elsewhere—become attached to their jobs and spend part of their energies on staying in office. The methods used to do so are those of machine politics anywhere. The union leader makes friends with as many members as possible, performs various services for them, distributes salaries and jobs in the right quarters, and stage manages the national convention to keep the spotlight on himself or herself and away from critics. All this is done in perfectly good faith. The officer becomes convinced after a few years that he or she can run the union better than anyone else and is often right. Indeed, unless the officer is able to "deliver the goods" year in and year out, no amount of political machination will suffice to keep him or her in office.

Where a national union president has remained in office for a long time, he will usually be an unusually able person with a good grasp of the industry's problems, who has kept in close touch with membership opinion. Continuity and experience in the top union offices clearly has advantages to the union, along with possible disadvantages.

Conclusions about union democracy depend somewhat on the meaning one gives to this term. If one asks, "Are the forms of democracy observed?" the answer must be yes. Union constitutions are thoroughly democratic. The system of government is normally a one-party rather than a multiple-party system, but this is characteristic of virtually all private associations.[19]

If one asks, "Do the members determine union policy?" the answer is usually no. Policy is determined by the national leaders and to a lesser extent by local leaders, within rather wide limits set by the members' interests and attitudes.

If one asks, "Are unions by and large operated in the interest of the members?" the answer is predominantly yes. Most union officers are honest and people of good will. They would rather do a good job for their members than not, and this is sensible also from a political point of view. It helps to keep the machine popular and reelection easy.

If one asks, "Can the members get rid of their leaders and install new ones whenever they wish?"—perhaps the most searching test of democratic control—the answer is yes and no. As we have indicated, contests over local office are frequent, and the turnover of local officers is high. At the national level it is possible to revolt against and overthrow an entrenched machine, but it is certainly not easy. It requires organization and hard work and involves a good deal of personal risk for leaders of the insurgent faction.

The most damaging criticism of union government in the United States is that it fails to recognize the right of legitimate opposition and to provide adequate protection for the dissenting member. A salaried union official who ends up on the losing side of an internal power struggle is almost certain to be out of a job. A member who opposes the leadership will in some unions be exposed to physical violence. In others the member will be expelled, with possible loss of employment. As regards determination of union policy, the key questions are, Do the demands that unions present to employers generally represent the preferences of union members? Or are union officers sufficiently secure and self-interested to override members' preferences in important respects? Do union officers behave more like candidates for political office in the United States? Or do they behave more like authoritarian political leaders in some other countries?

As a general rule, the assumption of membership control is surely more plausible. Union officers normally campaign for reelection by keeping an ear to the ground and responding to perceived wishes of the membership. Those who seriously misjudge membership sentiment usually do lose office sooner or later. The occasional cases of boss rule, accompanied by severe membership dissatisfaction, stand out just because they are exceptions.[20] Racketeering is also relatively rare, although flagrant cases have occurred in some unions, including the Teamsters, Longshoremen, Hotel and Restaurant Workers, and some of the unions in the building trades. Despite these exceptions, in the chapters that follow we shall

---

[19]The only two-party system that has operated over a long period of time is found in the International Typographical Union. This is an unusual situation that is scarcely likely to develop in other unions. For a good analysis of the International Typographical Union case, see Seymour M. Lipset, J. S. Coleman, and M. Trow, *Union Democracy in the International Typographical Union* (New York: Free Press, 1956).

[20]Worker views of unions are discussed in Chap. 14, where we analyze the decline of private-sector unions in recent years.

generally assume that union leaders act in the best interests of their members. The interests of all workers are not identical, however. In later chapters we shall show why unions, as political organizations, tend to favor the interests of their more senior members, while market competition among employers for workers favors the interests of younger, more mobile workers.

SUMMARY

1. Public policy toward unions is affected by how people view the benefits and costs of unions to society. Conservatives argue that unions are a monopoly, harmful to society and to nonunion workers. Competitive markets are good for the economy, including workers. When markets are competitive, the worker who is unfairly treated by one employer can quit and obtain a job with another firm at a wage equal to the value of his or her marginal product.

2. Liberals are less confident than conservatives that the economy is highly competitive and that a market distribution of income is basically fair. Recently Freeman and Medoff have emphasized that unions may improve a competitive economy by providing workers with a collective voice. Such a voice can be quite important for those workers for whom the costs of quitting are high. A collective voice is necessary, since employers may retaliate effectively against workers who complain as individuals, without the backing of a powerful group.

3. Public policy toward unions was developed initially by the courts, under the common law. For the most part judges held conservative views, concluding that union activity was undesirable and should be kept within narrow limits, if not prevented altogether.

4. With the depression of the 1930s, public attitudes became less favorable to competition and more supportive of collective action, including unions. The National Labor Relations Act of 1935 (the Wagner Act) actively encouraged workers to form unions. Employers were prohibited from engaging in a number of *unfair labor practices* to combat unions.

5. The Taft-Hartley Act of 1947 represents a set of amendments to the Wagner Act, putting restrictions on the activities of unions as well as employers in an effort to equalize the bargaining power of unions and management and to protect the general public.

6. The Landrum-Griffin Act of 1959 attempts to protect union members from corrupt or dictatorial leaders by requiring that unions be run quite democratically. No major labor legislation has been passed since 1959, although there have been some unsuccessful attempts, especially the labor law reform bill of 1977–78.

7. In part because they are so heavily affected by public policy, unions often have been active in politics. Prior to the 1930s, the AFL had a limited political agenda. It sought mainly to limit the influence of the courts on collective bargaining, especially by limiting the ability of employers to break strikes by obtaining antistrike injunctions. Since the 1930s unions have been active in a much wider array of political issues. Although unions often have had considerable political power, employers usually have had greater power, especially in recent years. The influence of unions is greatest when they are seen as representing most workers, whether or not they are union members, and is weakest when they are seen as a special-interest group seeking special gains for workers who are already reasonably well off.

8. Unions appear to be reasonably democratic, especially at the local level. Although there is corruption in some unions, most union officials are honest people of good will, and most unions are operated in the interests of the membership. Since the interests of different union members differ, union leaders must decide how to balance the demands of different constituencies. In comparison with market forces, most unions put relatively greater emphasis on the preferences of senior workers, who are less mobile and likely to be more active in the union.

KEY CONCEPTS

EXIT
COLLECTIVE VOICE
STATUTORY RULES
INJUNCTION, LABOR
CONSPIRACY DOCTRINE

SECONDARY BOYCOTT
LOCKOUT
UNFAIR LABOR PRACTICE
REPRESENTATION ELECTION
PUBLIC-INTEREST LABOR LAW

REVIEW QUESTIONS

1. How do the views of conservatives and liberals about how the economy operates affect their views concerning the desirability of unions?

2. Explain why union organization was easier after the passage of the Wagner Act.

3. Compare the philosophy and objectives of the Taft-Hartley Act and those of the Wagner Act. To what extent does the Taft-Hartley legislation move toward or away from the public-policy approach that prevailed before the 1930s?

4. Does it make sense to have a special set of rules for industrial relations in the railroad and airline industries? Explain.

5. The major purpose of unions is to bargain with employers. They must have the ability to wage a successful strike if the initial negotiations are unsuccessful. Secrecy is necessary in most bargaining, and strikes require the unity and discipline of an army. In this context, how democratic should we expect unions to be? In practice,

do unions appear to be democratic enough? too democratic? How useful does legislation such as the Landrum-Griffin Act appear to be in regulating union democracy? Discuss.

6. Unions affect the economic position of workers through the political process as well as through collective bargaining. Discuss union efforts in this regard, and compare such efforts to those of European unions.

READINGS

GETMAN, JULIUS G., *Labor Relations: Law, Practice, and Policy.* Mineola, N.Y.: Foundation Press, 1978.

GOULD, WILLIAM B., *A Primer of American Labor Law.* Cambridge, Mass.: MIT Press, 1982.

GREGORY, CHARLES V. and HAROLD A. KATZ, *Labor and the Law.* 3d rev. ed. New York: W. W. Norton, 1979.

WELLINGTON, HARRY H., *Labor and the Legal Process.* New Haven, Conn.: Yale University Press, 1968.

APPENDIX

Excerpt from the introduction to the National Labor Management Relations Act, as amended.

Declaration of Policy

Industrial strife which interferes with the normal flow of commerce and with the full production of articles and commodities for commerce, can be avoided or substantially minimized if employers, employees, and labor organizations each recognize under law one another's legitimate rights in their relations with each other, and above all recognize under law that neither party has any right in its relations with any other to engage in acts or practices which jeopardize the public health, safety, or interest.

It is the purpose and policy of this Act, in order to promote the full flow of commerce, to prescribe the legitimate rights of both employees and employers in their relations affecting commerce, to provide orderly and peaceful procedures for preventing the interference by either with the legitimate rights of the other, to protect the rights of individual employees in their relations with labor organizations whose activities affect commerce, to define and proscribe practices on the part of labor and management which affect commerce and are inimical to the general welfare, and to protect the rights of the public in connection with labor disputes affecting commerce.

Findings and Policies

The denial by some employers of the right of employees to organize and the refusal by some employers to accept the procedure of collective bargaining lead to strikes and other forms of industrial strife or unrest, which leave the intent or the necessary effect of burdening or obstructing commerce by (a) impairing the efficiency, safety, or operation of the instrumentalities of commerce; (b) occurring in the current of commerce; (c) materially affecting, restraining, or controlling the flow of raw materials or manufactured or processed goods from or into the channels of commerce, or the prices of such materials or goods in commerce; or (d) causing diminution of employment and wages in such volume as substantially to impair or disrupt the market for goods flowing from or into the channels of commerce.

The inequality of bargaining power between employees who do not possess full freedom of association or actual liberty of contract, and employers who are organized in the corporate or other forms of ownership association substantially burdens and affects the flow of commerce, and tends to aggravate recurrent business depressions, by depressing wage rates and the purchasing power of wage earners in industry and by preventing the stabilization of competitive wage rates and working conditions within and between industries.

Experience has proved that protection by law of the right of employees to organize and bargain collectively safeguards commerce from injury, impairment, or interruption, and promotes the flow of commerce by removing certain recognized sources of industrial strife and unrest, by encouraging practices fundamental to the friendly adjustment of industrial disputes arising out of differences as to wages, hours, or other working conditions, and by restoring equality of bargaining power between employers and employees.

Experience has further demonstrated that certain practices by some labor organizations, their officers, and members have the intent or the necessary effect of burdening or obstructing commerce by preventing the free flow of goods in such commerce through strikes and other forms of industrial unrest or through concerted activities which impair the interest of the public in the free flow of such commerce. The elimination of such practices is a necessary condition to the assurance of the rights herein guaranteed.

It is hereby declared to be the policy of the United States to eliminate the causes of certain substantial obstructions to the free flow of commerce and to mitigate and eliminate these obstructions when they have occurred by encouraging the practice and procedure of collective bargaining and by protecting the exercise by workers of full freedom of association, self-organization, and designation of representatives of their own choosing, for the purpose of negotiating the terms and conditions of their employment or other mutual aid or protection.

THE DECLINE OF
PRIVATE-SECTOR UNIONS

There have been many sharp changes in the importance of unions in the United States. When the Wagner Act was passed in 1935, unions represented only 7 percent of the total labor force and 14 percent of the labor force outside of agriculture. For the period since World War II the changes are shown in Figure 14-1. Unionization peaked in 1953 at 33 percent of nonagricultural employment. Since then the percent unionized has declined, slowly from 1953 to 1975 and more rapidly since the mid-seventies. By 1988 only 17 percent of wage and salary workers were represented by a union.

In the past two chapters we have discussed the major factors accounting for the increase in unionization in the 1930s and 1940s including changing attitudes toward workers as a result of the depression of the 1930s, the Wagner Act of 1935, and the great demand for labor during World War II. In this chapter we focus on the subsequent decline in unionization, especially during the period since 1975. We discuss the effect of changes in the economy, in managerial opposition to unions, in the operation of the legal system, and in public attitudes. We also make some very brief international comparisons, especially with Canada, and examine the response of unions in the United States to the increasingly hostile environment in which they operate.

In discussing changes in unionization since the 1950s, it is important to distinguish between changes in the private and the public sectors. Members of private-sector unions work for profit-making firms, while those in public-sector unions work for the government. Despite the overall decline in unionization, Figure

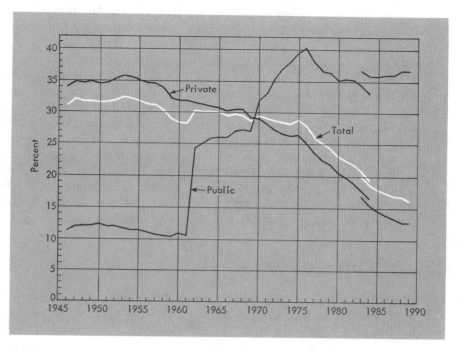

FIGURE 14-1 Changes in the Percent of Workers Who Are Union Members

Note: Data for the period 1946–84 are from Leo Troy and Neil Sheflin, *U.S. Union Sourcebook* (West Orange, N.J.: Industrial Relations Data and Information Services, 1985.) These data are for dues-paying union members. The data for the period 1983–88 are from the January issues of *Employment and Earnings*. These figures, based on household-survey data from the CPS, are for all wage and salary workers, including the small number who are in agriculture.

14-1 also shows that there has been a significant increase in unionization in the public sector since 1960. Thus the decline in private-sector unionization has been even more dramatic than that for the economy as a whole. Before considering the reasons for the decline in unionization in the private sector, let us briefly discuss the increase in public-sector unions.

If we include bargaining associations that function much like unions, such as the National Education Association, then 37 percent of all government employees are currently organized, almost three times the percent organized in the private sector.

Between 1960 and 1976 the number of government workers in unions increased from under one million to almost six million. Since 1976 public-sector unions have grown very little. Nevertheless, because of the decline in private-sector unions, the proportion of union members in the public sector has continued to increase, from 6 percent in 1960 to 27 percent in 1976 to 36 percent in 1989. We shall return to the issue of public-sector unions in Chapter 19.

Between the mid-fifties and the late eighties the proportion of all private nonagricultural workers who were union members declined from 35 percent to 12 percent. There was a steady downward trend throughout the period, although the magnitude of the decline accelerated in the late seventies and early eighties. For example, the percent unionized declined from 21 to 12 percent from 1975 to 1989. There has been a sharp decline in almost all occupations and industries.

How can we account for this dramatic decline? A number of hypotheses have been developed, including (1) changes in the composition of employment, by industry, occupation, and demography (e.g., gender and age); (2) other changes in the economy, including increased foreign competition and deregulation of some industries; (3) increased opposition to unions by management; (4) changes in the legal environment; (5) changes in public attitudes toward unions; and (6) declining effectiveness of unions in appealing to workers and in responding to changes in the economy. We shall consider each of these explanations in turn.

CHANGES IN THE ECONOMY

We look first at some long-term trends in the economy that appear to have had an adverse effect on unionization. Then we consider a number of reasons why there has been a decline in the demand for union labor since the mid-1970s.

Changes in the Composition of Employment

As we saw in Chapter 2, there have been a number of important long-run trends in the composition of employment. Over the past thirty to forty years the most important trends for our purposes have been the following: an increase in the proportion of white-collar jobs; a decrease in the proportion of jobs in heavy industry (manufacturing, mining, and construction) and in transportation; an increase in the proportion of jobs in the South and in metropolitan areas; an increase in the average education of the labor force; and an increase in the proportion of jobs held by women. Except for the increased employment in metropolitan areas, all of these changes have acted to reduce the percentage of private-sector workers who are unionized. Unionization is quite low among white-collar workers, in jobs outside heavy industry (except in the public sector), in the South, among those with schooling beyond the high school level, and among women.

For the period 1954 to 1979 Freeman and Medoff have calculated the effect on the decline in private-sector unionization of these trends in the work force, assuming there were no changes in the rate of unionization within each subgroup over this period. Their results, which are presented in Table 14-1, show that over this period these changes in the composition of the work force can account for about 70 percent of the decline in unionization in the private sector and that the most important change appears to be the increase in white-collar workers. Moreover, one reason why unionization has fallen in the private sector but not in the public sector is the greater unionization of white-collar workers in the public sector.

TABLE 14-1   Estimates of the Impact of Structural Changes in the Work Force on the Decline in Unionism, 1954—79

CHARACTERISTIC	RELATION TO UNIONISM	ESTIMATED IMPACT ON PERCENTAGE ORGANIZED
Personal		
Age	Younger workers less likely to be union	−0.4
Education	Better educated less likely to be union	−0.7
Sex	Women less likely to be union	−0.8
Total Personal		−1.9
Job		
Occupation	White-collar less likely to be union	−3.0
Industry	Manufacturing, construction, mining, transport more likely to be union than services, trade, finance	−1.9
Total job		−4.9
Geography	South less likely to be union; SMSAs more likely to be union	−1.4
Total related to structural changes		−8.2
Total change		−11.3

Note: SMSA stands for Standard Metropolitan Statistical Area.
Source: Richard B. Freeman and James L. Medoff, *What Do Unions Do?* (New York: Basic Books, 1984), p. 225. Reprinted by permission.

As Freeman and Medoff themselves emphasize, there are a number of reasons to view these results very cautiously. First, it is not clear why we should assume that the percentage unionized will stay constant for each subgroup. For example, we have seen that the percent unionized has increased very sharply among public-sector workers during this period. Why didn't a similar increase occur among any groups of private-sector workers?

Second, some of the trends represented in Table 14-1 may have been the result rather than the cause of declining unionization. For example, the increase in the proportion of jobs in the South probably has resulted, at least in part, from efforts of employers to expand their nonunion plants relative to their union operations.[1]

Third, employment trends by industry, occupation, schooling, and gender have been quite similar in all the developed economies. Yet only the United States has experienced a dramatic decline in the percentage of the work force who are union members. For example, Canada is subject to all the same trends as the United States (except for increasing employment in the Sunbelt) but has not experienced any decline in the percentage of private-sector workers who are unionized.[2] We shall discuss the Canadian experience in more detail shortly.

---

[1]For example, see Thomas A. Kochan, Harry C. Katz, and Robert McKersie, *The Transformation of American Industrial Relations,* (New York: Basic Books, 1986), Chap. 3.

[2]For example, see Noah M. Meltz, "Labor Movements in Canada and the United States," in *Challenges and Choices Facing American Labor,* ed. Thomas A. Kochan (Cambridge, Mass.: MIT Press, 1985), pp. 315–34.

Finally, the long-term trends emphasized in Table 14-1 cannot explain why there has been a particularly sharp decline in unionization in recent years in the United States, even within industries and occupation that traditionally have been highly unionized.[3]

In summary, changes in the composition of the work force are not a full explanation for the decline of private-sector unions in the United States since the early 1950s. Nevertheless, these changes in the work force do represent one important change in the environment facing unions in recent decades. We turn next to other important changes in the economic environment affecting unions.

We indicated earlier that the decline in the percent unionized among private-sector unions has accelerated since 1975. During this period there have also been a number of important changes in the economy, each of which is likely to have reduced the demand for union labor. Let us examine the effect of (1) increases in foreign competition, (2) increases in domestic competition from the South and other areas where unions are weak; (3) increased domestic competition resulting from the partial deregulation of our transportation and communication industries, (4) the severe recession of 1982–83, and (5) increases in the wage differential between union and nonunion workers.

Foreign Competition

One of the most important changes in the economy in recent years has been an increase in foreign competition. In 1970 imports and exports each represented 4 percent of GNP. By 1988 imports had risen to 13 percent of GNP and exports to 11 percent. Instead of being primarily a national economy, the United States now was much more affected by events in the global economy. Major industries, including steel and automobiles, suffered important losses as a result of increased competition from other countries, especially Japan. Such losses were greatest in the early 1980s and contributed significantly to the recession of 1982–83. As the value of the dollar rose sharply (about 50 percent) relative to other countries from 1980 to 1983, the price of American goods rose relative to those of other countries. With the higher prices, exports fell to 5 percent of GNP.

The increase in foreign competition put great pressure on our export and import–competing industries. (See the discussion in Chap. 11.) Unionized firms, such as those in the auto industry, had been able to pay high wages, in part because all domestic firms were unionized and thus subject to similar labor costs. Now, with the increase in foreign competition, such firms are under much greater pressure to hold prices down. Many unionized firms are particularly vulnerable to such pressures because of high wage rates and also because union work rules often reduced

---

[3]For example, Farber shows that only about one-fifth of the decline in unionization between 1977 and 1984 can be accounted for by changes in the composition of the labor force with regard to gender, race, region, industry, and occupation. Henry S. Farber, "The Recent Decline of Unionization in the United States," *Science,* November 13, 1987, pp. 915–20.

the flexibility of management to respond to shifts in demand and other changes in the economy.

Firms responded to increased foreign competition in many ways, including shifting work from union to nonunion plants, subcontracting to nonunion suppliers, and seeking wage and work-rule concessions from unions.[4]

Foreign competition is important in most manufacturing industries. In services, on the other hand, the market is usually local rather than international. Over the past two decades the increase in foreign competition for production goods has contributed to the declining importance of unionization in heavy industry and the increasing relative importance of service workers, especially government employees, in the labor movement of the United States.

Increased Domestic Competition: The South

In the United States unionization has always been much stronger in urban than in rural areas and in the North than in the South. The development of improved communication and transportation, especially the interstate highway system, has made both areas more accessible and has reduced the advantage of better rail and water transportation in much of the urban North. In addition, the South has become more attractive to northern firms (and their managers) for a variety of reasons, including the development of air conditioning, better schools, and improvements in race relations. Since the civil-rights revolution of the 1960s many southern governments have courted northern capital more aggressively, with the low-wage relatively nonunion environment as one of the selling points.[5]

Increased Domestic Competition: Deregulation

In addition to increased competition from abroad and from areas of the United States where unions are weak, greater domestic competition has also occurred in some industries as a result of reduced government regulation.

The most dramatic deregulation occurred with the Airline Deregulation Act of 1978, which phased out all regulation of the major domestic routes. The purpose of this legislation was to improve performance and lower prices by relying on market forces rather than government regulation to control the industry. Deregulation led not only to greater competition among existing carriers but also to the entry of new, nonunion airlines, offering much cheaper fares, partly as a result of lower labor costs. New nonunion carriers had lower labor costs because of both lower wage rates and fewer restrictive work rules on issues like the size of crews and maximum monthly flight hours for pilots. Increased competition has led to some

---

[4]For example, see Kochan et al., *American Industrial Relations*, especially Chaps. 3 and 4.

[5]James C. Cobb, *The Selling of the South: The Southern Crusade for Economic Development, 1936–80* (Baton Rouge: Louisiana State University Press, 1982).

decline in employment but mainly to less generous union contracts. Labor costs fell 20 to 40 percent.[6]

The deregulation of the airline industry helped lead to the partial deregulation of the trucking industry, established under the Motor Carrier Act of 1980. This legislation, passed despite strong opposition from both the American Trucking Industry and the International Brotherhood of Teamsters, made it easier for new, nonunion firms to enter the industry and to compete by charging lower prices. Except for political constraints, trucking is an easy industry for new firms to enter. Consequently, reduced legislation has had considerable effect. The percentage of truck drivers who are Teamsters has declined considerably, and there have been significant reductions in wage rates and prices. Because entry has been easier for nonunion firms, more union jobs have been lost in trucking than in airlines. As of 1985 truck drivers represented only 9 percent of the total membership of the Teamsters, a union that has moved out from its base in trucking and organized workers in many different industries and occupations.[7]

The Recession of 1982–83

The early 1980s were a time of major recession in the economy. The low demand for output led to reduced profits and further pressure on firms to reduce costs. For many industries, such as steel, automobiles, airlines, and trucking, the recession reinforced the economic pressure of foreign competition and of deregulation. But the recession had some effect on all industries, even those not affected by other changes in the economy. The recession caused employers to be more concerned with reducing costs and less concerned with maintaining production. As a result, employers were often more aggressive in their bargaining. High unemployment also made it easier for firms to recruit strikebreakers, often in an effort to break the union. Some of the employer policies developed during the recession carried over into the more prosperous period of the late eighties, thereby contributing to the continuing low rate of unionization in the private sector.

Increases in the Union Wage Differential

The wage differential between union and nonunion workers appears to have been higher in the 1970s and early 1980s than previously. During the 1970s inflation was high, but there was no growth in productivity or real wage rates. During the fifties and sixties when productivity was increasing, workers had become used to real (inflation-adjusted) wage increases of 2 to 3 percent a year. Now many nonunion workers had to adjust to declines in real wage rates. In contrast, most unions were

---

[6]See Peter Capelli, "Airlines," in *Collective Bargaining in American Industry,* ed. David B. Lipsky and Clifford B. Dorn (Lexington, Mass.: D. C. Heath, 1987); and Kirsten Ruth Wever, "Changing Union Structure and the Changing Structure of Unions in the Post-Deregulation Airline Industry," *Proceedings of the Industrial Relations Research Association,* 1986, pp. 119–36).

[7]For a more extensive discussion of changes in collective bargaining in the trucking industry, see Chap. 18.

able to continue to provide modest increases in real wages for their members during the seventies. As a result, the wage differential between union and nonunion workers widened.[8] Despite the union concessions of the early eighties, estimates of this union wage differential have remained high.[9]

This larger union wage differential reduced union membership in two ways. First, by increasing the relative cost of union producers it put such producers at a competitive disadvantage, thereby reducing their sales and their employment. Second, the larger differential was most likely a factor contributing to the stronger opposition of management to unions. We shall discuss this opposition shortly.[10]

Changes Since the Mid-Eighties

We have seen that long-term trends in the economy, such as the declining proportion of blue-collar jobs, have contributed to the decline in the percentages of the work force that is unionized. These long-term trends are continuing and will create further difficulties for the labor movement, unless it can find better ways to organize workers in expanding industries and occupations.

Although the long-term trends continue to show a relative decline in the kinds of jobs where unionization has been high, the short-term trends are more favorable to unionization. Let us consider in turn changes in international competition, government deregulation, and the aggregate demand for labor.

The value of the dollar was much lower in the late eighties than in the first half of the decade, which has eased the pressure of foreign competition somewhat. Firms that compete in international markets no longer need to be closing as many plants. And multinational firms are less likely to build new plants outside the United States.

Although the decreased value of the dollar has reduced foreign competition and thus helped unions in the United States, shifting exchange rates and the internationalization of the economy have hurt unions by increasing uncertainty about the future. As a result of increased uncertainty, firms are less willing to invest large amounts of capital in highly specialized production methods that can be changed only at great cost when demand shifts. Especially with the increased avail-

---

[8]See George E. Johnson, "Changes over Time in the Union-Nonunion Wage Differential in the United States," in *The Economics of Trade Unions: New Directions,* ed. Jean-Jacques Rosa (Boston: Kluwer Nijhoff, 1984).

[9]See Daniel J. B. Mitchell, "Recent Union Contract Concessions," *Brookings Papers on Economic Activity,* no. 1 (1982), pp. 165–201; see also Richard Freeman, "In Search of Union Wage Concessions in Standard Data Sets," *Industrial Relations* (Spring 1986), pp. 131–4; and two articles in the May 1986 *American Economic Review,* Richard Edwards and Paul Swaim, "Union-Nonunion Earnings Differentials and the Decline of Private-Sector Unionism, pp. 97–102, and Peter Linneman and Michael L. Wachter, "Rising Union Premiums and the Declining Boundaries among Noncompetition Groups," pp. 103–8.

[10]Although this widening differential should also have made unions more attractive to workers, probably the effect on managerial opposition was more important. For example, see Richard B. Freeman, "The Effect of the Union Wage Differential on Management Opposition and Union Organizing Success," *American Economic Review* (May 1986), pp. 92–96.

ability of computers, firms can invest in less specialized equipment.[11] On the other hand, for many unions the essence of the union contract is the detailed specification of narrowly defined jobs and of rules indicating how workers are to be allocated to these jobs. Although firms can respond to their need for greater flexibility by negotiating such flexibility into their union contracts, they can also respond by trying to operate without a union. Equally important, greater uncertainty also leads to an increase in the use of temporary workers, who are harder to unionize because of their short-term interest in the job.[12]

On balance, foreign competition continues to hurt unions and unionization but not as badly as in the early eighties. Deregulation also continues to hurt some unions. Many union jobs were lost, especially in trucking, to lower-cost nonunion firms who were able to enter markets as a result of deregulation. Although these jobs are unlikely to be won back, unions are not likely to lose many more jobs, as there has been no additional deregulation since the early 1980s.

All unions were adversely affected by the recessions of 1975–76 and 1982–83. Since 1983 aggregate demand has increased considerably, with unemployment falling from 9.6 percent in 1983 to 5.2 percent in 1989. High aggregate demand for labor has increased the number of jobs available for union members, decreased the pressure on firms to reduce costs, and reduced the availability of strikebreakers.

INTERNATIONAL COMPARISONS

As we have seen, there are many plausible reasons why changes in the economy might have contributed to the decline in unionization in the United States, especially during the 1970s and 1980s. Most of these changes will have affected many countries. Thus if economic factors are a complete explanation, we should see fairly similar declines in unionization across countries. As we see in Table 14-2, however, this is not the case. Since 1970 the rate of unionization has fallen much more in the United States than in any other country. In many countries unionization has actually risen over this period. As a result, it seems unlikely that economic changes can be the major reason why a smaller percentage of the U.S. work force is now unionized. As we shall see, economic factors have most likely interacted with specific legal, political, and attitudinal considerations to lead to the major decline in unionization in the United States.

The Canadian experience provides a particularly instructive comparison with the United States. The two economies are closely interrelated. Many of the same unions operate in both countries.[13] Yet since the mid-1960s the percent of the

---

[11]For a discussion of this issue and its effects on organized labor, see Michael J. Piore and Charles F. Sabel, *The Second Industrial Divide*.

[12]See Garth Mangum, Donald Mayall, and Kristen Nelson, "The Temporary Help Industry: A Response to the Dual Internal Labor Market," *Industrial and Labor Relations Review* (July 1985), pp. 599–611.

[13]Many unions in the United States emphasize that they are "internationals," which usually means that they have locals in Canada as well as in the United States.

TABLE 14-2   Union Membership as a Percent of Nonagricultural Wage and Salary Employees Across Countries 1970–86

	1970	1979	1985/86	1970–79	1979–86
			FOR THE YEARS		
Countries with sharp rises in density					
Denmark	66	86	95	+20	+9
Finland	56	84	85	+28	+1
Sweden	79	89	96	+10	+7
Belgium	66	77	—	+11	—
Countries w/moderate rises in density					
Italy	39	51	45	+12	−6
Germany	37	42	43	+5	+1
France	22	28	—	+6	—
Switzerland	31	34	33	+3	−1
Canada	32	36	36	+4	0
Australia	52	58	56	+6	−1
New Zealand	43	46	—	+3	—
Ireland	44	49	51	+5	+2
Countries w/stability or decline in density					
Norway	59	60	61	+1	+1
United Kingdom	51	58	51	+7	−7
Austria	64	59	61	−5	+2
Japan	35	32	28	−3	−4
Netherlands	39	43	35	+4	−8
United States	31	25	17	−6	−8

From Richard B. Freeman, "The Changing Status of Unionism around the World: Some Emerging Patterns," in *Organized Labor at the Crossroads*, ed. Wei-Chiao Huang (Kalamazoo, Mich.: W. E. Upjohn Institute for Employment Research, 1989), p. 130.

labor force that is unionized has increased substantially in Canada and decreased in the United States. Although the rate of unionization in both countries was similar in the 1950s, now it is about twice as high in Canada.[14]

There do not appear to be any significant differences in economic trends that can explain the difference between the trends in private-sector unionization in the United States and in Canada. Instead, we need to look at differences in the political arena, including both the legal system and public attitudes. Here we can give only an extremely brief historical overview.[15]

---

[14]Meltz shows that if the industrial structure were similar in the two countries, the rate of unionization in Canada would be even larger, relative to that in the United States. See Noah M. Meltz "Labor Movements in Canada and the United States," in *Challenges and Choices Facing American Labor*, ed. Thomas A. Kochan (Cambridge, Mass.: MIT Press, 1985).

[15]This discussion is based on ibid.; Seymour Martin Lipset, "North American Labor Movements: A Comparative Perspective," and Christopher Huxley et al., "Is Canada's Experience 'Especially Constructive'?" both in *Unions in Transition*, ed. Lipset (San Francisco: Institute for Contemporary Studies, 1986); Joseph B. Rose and Gary N. Chaison, "The State of the Unions: United States and Canada," *Journal of Labor Research* (Winter 1987); and Anil Verma and Mark Thompson, "Managerial Strategies in Canada and the U.S. in the 1980s," *Proceedings of the Industrial Relations Research Association*, 1988, pp. 257–64.

The major increase in unionization occurred a little later in Canada than in the United States. Until World War II the Canadian legal system was quite hostile to unions, contributing to a low rate of unionization. The percentage of the work force represented by unions increased dramatically in the 1940s as a result of changes in legislation as well as the high demand for labor during World War II.

After a period of little change from the late 1940s to the late 1960s, Canadian unionization increased again in the 1970s and remained high in the 1980s. Much but not all of the most recent increase in unionization has been in the public sector. Labor became stronger politically in the sixties and seventies for various reasons, including the rise of the New Democratic Party (NDP), a third party formed in 1961 with the assistance of organized labor. Increased Canadian nationalism and the rise of French separatism in Quebec both served to strengthen the political position of the Canadian labor movement. The economic difficulties of the seventies and eighties did not lead to any Canadian attempt to eliminate New Deal collectivist approaches, as occurred in the Reagan administration in the United States.

Industrial relations is subject mainly to provincial law in Canada, in contrast to the United States where federal legislation (the NLRA) is dominant. There are no Canadian provinces where unions are weak, as they are in most of the southern states in the U.S. Thus there is no place where Canadian firms can establish new plants and be optimistic that these plants will remain nonunion. Canadian managers have generally accepted unions, either because the managers are less hostile to unions than their counterparts in the United States or because Canadian unions are stronger.

In summary, political developments and shifts in public opinion appear to have led to increased support for unions in Canada at the same time that they have led to increased opposition to unions in the United States.

THE ROLE OF MANAGEMENT POLICIES

In this section we consider the role of increased managerial opposition as a possible explanation for the decline in private-sector unions in the United States in recent years. The changes in the economy, discussed previously, have encouraged managers to make greater efforts to avoid unionization. In addition, many other factors are involved. Before looking at how management has become more aggressive in combating unionization, we look first at how industrial relations practice differs in union and in nonunion firms.

Industrial Relations Policies of Nonunion Firms

In order to understand the environment in which unions operate and the ability of many nonunion employers to resist unionization, it is necessary to look more carefully at the practice of industrial relations by nonunion employers.

There are many different kinds of nonunion firms. At the risk of considerable oversimplification, we can divide them into two general categories. First, there are many low-wage firms that are nonunion. The paradigm case is a small firm in a competitive industry. Often the firm's management is not particularly good, which together with the competitiveness of the industry, means that profits are low. The firm simply cannot afford to pay its workers well or to develop good working conditions. Turnover in the firm's work force is high, as workers quit to obtain better jobs elsewhere. In terms of the dual-labor-market theory (see Chapter 6), this type of firm is part of the secondary labor market.

Because of low wage rates, few (if any) benefits, and poor working conditions, one might expect such firms to be prime candidates for unionization. Such is not the case, however. If a union did organize the firm and establish higher wages and better working conditions, then the firm could attract better workers and establish better morale among its work force. But because the firm's management is weak, it is unlikely to make the most effective use of better workers. Thus any resulting gains in productivity from higher wage rates would be unlikely to offset the higher cost of labor. Consequently, profits would decline from their previous low level, forcing the firm out of business. Unless unionization led to improvements in management and a substantial increase in worker productivity, a union would not be able to gain much for the firm's workers.

There are two other reasons why the typical small, low-wage firm is not likely to be organized by a union. First, any employee with the ability to organize a union probably could improve his or her situation more easily by finding a better job with a different employer. Second, organizers on the payroll of an existing union would view the firm as a low-priority target because of its small size and the high turnover of its work force as well as its inability to pay high wage rates.

At the other extreme, there are a significant number of large nonunion firms that pay high wage rates and earn good profits. These firms are in the primary labor market. Because of their size, profitability, and resulting visibility in the community, they would appear to be prime candidates for professional union organizers. How do such firms avoid unionization?[16]

Any large, profitable firm that wants to remain nonunion must pay at least as well as a comparable unionized firm.[17] But good pay, including benefits, may not be sufficient to keep a firm nonunion. Workers also need to feel that management is

---

[16]The following discussion relies heavily on Fred K. Foulkes, *Personnel Policies in Large Nonunion Companies,* a study of twenty-six large, profitable nonunion firms, all in industries that are fairly heavily unionized.

[17]Clearly the same arguments apply to a partly organized firm that wants to keep the union out of its nonunion plants.

concerned with their welfare, not just with profits. An egalitarian philosophy often helps, as symbolized by a cafeteria where all employees including top management eat and a parking lot where all have equal access to the best parking places. Even more important, top management must be careful in its selection, training, and evaluation of supervisors and other managers. Supervisors must have the respect of the workers. They must be in charge but must not be overly authoritarian or play favorites. Rather than just give orders and enforce discipline through punishment, they must establish effective teamwork and be good listeners. Top management must also develop good communication mechanisms, so that it can be aware of complaints and can make its decisions understandable to the workers.

Firms that are especially concerned about employee relations, whether primarily to forestall unionization or for other purposes, typically place great emphasis on job security and on promotion from within the company. In his study of nonunion companies, for example, Foulkes concludes:

> The companies studied utilize a remarkable number of techniques to provide full or nearly-full employment, or to delay layoffs as long as possible. Among the techniques used are: hiring freezes, reliance on attrition to reduce the work force, use of temporary or former employees for specified periods of time, inventory buildups, use and disuse of subcontractors, voluntary leaves of absence, vacation banking, special voluntary early-retirement programs, moving work to people, moving people to work, training, and work sharing. . . .
> The significance of employment security can not be overestimated. Eliminating employees' feelings of job insecurity and fear of layoff can be an important cornerstone of a company's employee-relations program.[18]

Treating employees well, providing job security, good pay, and frequent promotion opportunities are easiest when the firm is highly profitable and expanding. Although high profitability and generous human-resource policies often go together, it is not clear whether this is primarily because good treatment of workers leads to high productivity and profits or because high profits make it easier for the firm to treat its employees more generously.

The Attitudes of Managers toward Unions

Almost all managers of nonunion firms seek to remain nonunion. Many although not all managers in firms that are unionized would rather the firm did not have a union (or unions). Why are most managers opposed to unions? As Mills emphasizes, often managers' "opposition to unions seems to be a matter of general doctrine rather than of analysis of the specific situation involved."[19] But where does this general doctrine come from? In part, there is an inherent conflict of interest between managers and workers over how much of the firm's revenues should be

---

[18]Foulkes, *Personnel Policies,* p. 332.
[19]D. Quinn Mills, "Management Performance," in *U.S. Industrial Relations 1950–80: A Critical Assessment,* ed. Jack Steiber et al. (Madison, Wis.: Industrial Relations Research Association, 1981), p. 115.

allocated to unionized workers versus managerial salaries and perquisites. Similarly, there is a conflict between management's desire to run the firm with as few constraints as possible and the desire of most workers to have a say in the rules and, in particular, to be able to reduce management's opportunity to reward its favorites and punish those who stand up for workers' rights.

But the issue is not simply a power struggle over issues of self-interest to management and workers. To see why, let us look briefly at the function of management. Top managers often feel that the essence of their job lies in adjusting the conflicting pressures placed on the company by competitors, customers, suppliers, stockholders, bankers, wage earners, and others. The conflicting nature of these pressures means that management cannot afford to be fully responsive to any one of them. For example, it will often have to resist certain demands of workers in order to ensure competitive prices for customers and reasonable values for stockholders. If the firm has a vigorous union, however, it will be more costly to resist the workers' demands, thus complicating the task of management and increasing the chance of failure. Of course, a union will seldom, if ever, press demands to the point where the union expects the firm to go out of business, thus costing the workers their jobs. But managers are likely to make more conservative assumptions than the union (and its workers) about the need for the firm to protect itself against various contingencies. And even though the union seeks the survival of the firm, it need not seek the survival of the firm's managers in their present jobs. Thus there is much room for legitimate conflict between union and management, without seeing the issue simply as too much greed on either side.

Another view, which has been prominent in recent years is for managers to see unions as resulting from a failure of management.[20] Advocates of this view assert that when managers are sensitive to the needs and desires of their workers (for recognition and voice as well as for monetary rewards), then employees will not want a union to intervene and thus complicate the relationship between the worker and his or her managers. In the words of one manager,

> A union creates a bad atmosphere. It creates an adversary kind of relationship. Where a union exists it pits people against the manager and this is not healthy for the company, for the manager, or for the people.[21]

Although most managers prefer to deal with a nonunion work force, not all actively oppose unions. Even among those who detest unions, managers often try to get along rather than suffer the costs of a continuing war with the union. For managers of a firm that is already unionized, it is risky to try to abolish the union. If the workers are committed to the union, as is likely to be the case, then efforts to defeat the union, either by breaking a strike or through a decertification election, are almost certain to antagonize many workers. If the workers quit (or are replaced by strikebreakers), then the firm must incur the expense of recruiting and training

---

[20]For example see ibid., p. 112.
[21]Foulkes, *Personnel Policies,* p. 53.

their replacements. If the workers are upset with the firm but do not quit, then their productivity is likely to decline, as discussed in Chapter 6.

If the firm is not already unionized, then its managers can oppose a union organizing drive without nearly as much concern for the impact of such efforts on the morale of their workers. In this case the main constraint on efforts of the employer to combat unionization is the National Labor Relations Act (NLRA) discussed below.

Although most small firms are either nonunion or else entirely unionized (at least for blue-collar workers), many large firms operate some plants that are unionized and others that are not. In recent years many multiplant firms have expanded their nonunion operations at the expense of their union plant. Unions typically are well established in the older plants but are not powerful enough to keep the company from expanding the relative size of its nonunion operations.[22]

In all time periods most managers have had a negative view of unions. To evaluate managerial opposition to unions as a cause of the recent decline in the extent of unionization in the private sector, we must examine changes in managerial policies toward unions.

Prior to the 1930s firms faced fewer constraints on their antiunion activities. The Wagner Act of 1936 greatly aided union-organizing efforts. The success in the late thirties of the organizing drives in such key industries as steel and automobiles, plus the high demand for labor during World War II, led to the grudging acceptance of unions by most major corporations.

By the 1970s top management no longer saw unionization as inevitable and often established new plants in areas where unionization was least likely, like the South. In most cases management now was prepared to contest vigorously all efforts to organize nonunion operations. During the 1970s and 1980s firms also became more sophisticated in combating union-organizing campaigns. As we shall discuss next, union efforts to win recognition through National Labor Relations Board (NLRB) elections were fought through delays and other manipulation of NLRB procedures as well as through long-term efforts to develop and maintain good relations between workers and management.

UNION ORGANIZING AND THE NLRB

A decline in union membership can occur either because unions are losing too many former members or because they are not organizing enough new ones. Increased foreign competition and the recession of 1982 caused many union members to lose their jobs. Those without a job usually stop paying union dues and are no longer counted as union members.[23]

---

[22]For example, see Kochan et al., *American Industrial Relations*, chap. 3; and Anil Verma and Thomas A. Kochan, "The Growth and Nature of the Nonunion Sector within a Firm," in *Challenges and Choices Facing American Labor,* ed. Kochan, (Cambridge, Mass.: MIT Press, 1985).

[23]Empirical estimates show that changes in the economy were responsible for much of the decline in unionization in the 1970s, a conclusion that probably applies with even more force to the early 1980s. See William T. Dickens and Jonathan S. Leonard, "Accounting for the Decline in Union Membership, 1950–1980," *Industrial and Labor Relations Review* (April 1985), pp. 323–34.

Changes in the economy have contributed to increased opposition to unions on the part of management. This increased opposition has taken several forms. In a few cases unionized firms have sought to eliminate the union either through an NLRB decertification election or by breaking a strike. More frequently, partially unionized firms have expanded their nonunion operations, or firms that had been fully unionized have added new nonunion plants. In all such cases employers are making greater efforts to keep unions from organizing the nonunion workers.

Unions need to organize new plants and new firms in order to avoid a continual loss of members. Each year many plants close, and many firms go out of business. At the same time, old firms open new plants, and new firms start up. Of those that are closing, some are unionized and some are not. But almost all new ones initially are nonunion. Thus normal turnover of business establishments will reduce union membership unless unions can organize new workers.

Freeman and Medoff estimate that under normal economic conditions, unions would lose about 3 percent of their membership each year if they did not organize any new workers through NLRB elections.[24] With union membership at slightly under 13 percent of the private-sector work force, the percent unionized would decline by about 0.4 percentage points ($0.13 \times 0.03 \times 100$) each year if there were no new organization of workers. Conversely, union membership would remain stable at 13 percent of the work force if 0.4 percent of all workers were newly organized each year. Yet in recent years only about 0.3 percent of the work force has been organized each year through NLRB elections.[25] If this rate of organization continues, Freeman and Medoff indicate, unionization among workers in the private sector will continue to decline for some time and eventually will stabilize at 10 percent of the work force.

The NLRB Election Process

Let us look next at how a union tries to organize a nonunion firm or plant, how a firm resists such organizational attempts, and the role of the federal government in the process. An organizing campaign typically proceeds through a number of well-defined stages:

1. There is an initial meeting between the union organizer and a group of workers, leading to formation of an employee or "inside" organizing committee. The respect enjoyed by members of this committee is important to the success of the organizing drive.

2. Union supporters then try to persuade other employees to sign cards authorizing the union to act as their bargaining agent. The success of this effort is critically important. The union must get cards from 30 percent of the employees to petition for an election. Usually the union will want authorization cards for over 50 percent

---

[24]See Richard B. Freeman and James L. Medoff, *What Do Unions Do?* p. 241.

[25]Even this low figure does not account for the cases where a union wins a certification election but never really functions as a union because it fails to win a contract with the employer. For example, see William N. Cooke, *Union Organizing and Public Policy: Failure to Secure First Contracts* (Kalamazoo, Mich.: W. E. Upjohn Institute, 1985).

of the workers before considering it has enough chance of success to justify calling for an election.

3. Once the union has enough authorization cards, the union will write a formal letter to the employer, asserting its majority status and asking the employer to enter into collective bargaining.

4. In most cases the company will reject the union's claim.[26] Some workers may have signed cards under social pressure and can be expected to vote differently in a secret ballot. In addition, the employer can seek to influence the vote by presenting to the workers management's case against the union and by other tactics, such as obtaining a more favorable election unit from the NLRB or delaying the election until union sentiment may have died down.

5. If the company rejects the union claim to represent a majority of the workers, the union will file an election petition with the NLRB. The stakes in the *certification election* are high. If the union loses, there can be no new election in that bargaining unit for at least one year.[27]

If the union wins the election, it becomes the *exclusive bargaining representative* of the workers in the election unit.[28] By law the union must give equal representation to all those in the unit, even those who do not join the union and thus pay no dues to support its activities. Management must also deal similarly with all workers, in accordance with the union contract. For example, it cannot strike a separate bargain with any individual or group of workers. Thus management cannot reward what it regards as good performance by a worker unless such a reward is allowed in the union contract.

Although such limitations on unions and management may seem unfair, they are designed to lessen conflict among the workers and to strengthen the position of the union, as long as it is supported by a majority of the workers. Except in right-to-work states, unions can generally solve the problem of free riders who don't want to pay dues by negotiating with management so that all workers in the bargaining must join the union or at least pay dues.

The Role of the NLRB

In directing and supervising an election, the NLRB has two main responsibilities:

1. To win certification a union must demonstrate that it is the choice of a majority of employees "in an appropriate bargaining unit." But what is an appropriate unit? There is often disagreement on this point between the employer and the union, and there may also be disagreement within the labor force. The board must resolve this issue before an election can be held.

---

[26]The percentage of cases where management offers no resistance to the claim of the union that it represents a majority of those in the bargaining unit decreased from 42.6 percent in 1955 to 7.9 percent in 1978. See Ronald L. Seeber and William N. Cooke, "The Decline in Union Success in NLRB Representation Elections," *Industrial Relations* (Winter 1983), pp. 34–44.)

[27]If two unions are contesting the election, workers can vote for either one or for no union. If none of the three choices receives a majority, a runoff election will be held.

[28]The union remains the bargaining representative unless it loses a decertification election or fails to negotiate a contract within a year.

2. The board is responsible for policing the campaign tactics of the parties. The stakes are high; feelings on both sides run high; and tactics can easily go beyond sweet reason to deception, intimidation, and coercion. The board must decide whether either or both sides have used tactics constituting an "unfair labor practice." In this case the board may set aside the election result and order a new election.

Among the most troublesome issues concerning the size of bargaining units are the following: (1) Should the unit include all of the companies plants, stores, or other units? and (2) Should the unit include all categories of employees (except for supervisors and managers, who are not covered by the NLRA)?

The positions of the parties on these issues reflect the underlying power struggle between them. Usually the incipient union will have won more recruits in some plants, or among some categories of employee, than among others. It may argue for an election district including only those areas in which the union is strongest. In this event the company may argue for a larger district, including employee groups in which the union is weak, to reduce the union's chance of getting an overall majority.

When the employer and union cannot agree on a bargaining unit, the board uses such criteria as "(1) similarities in skills, duties, and working conditions; (2) the nature of an employer's organization (e.g., the organizational and supervisory structure, the integration of various operational functions, and physical proximity); and (3) the employees' preferences."[29]

The timing of the board's decision is also important.[30] For example, considerable delay in defining the bargaining unit will often give an advantage to the employer, especially if the union's organizational drive grew out of some particular employer action that upset the workers. Delays also cause problems for the union if there is high turnover among the work force, thus requiring the union to convince a continuing stream of new hires about the advantage of union membership.

Rules Regarding Campaign Tactics

Concerning election campaigns, there is hardly any imaginable tactic that has not been used and challenged during the many thousands of union elections. This has led to a large number of rules and precedents governing election conduct. Some of the key issues follow.

1. Misrepresentation. The parties enjoy the usual right of free speech. But can they say anything? How truthful must they be, especially in what they say about each other? Between 1970 and 1982 the board reversed itself three times on this issue. The board's current position is that

---

[29]Cooke, "Decliine in Union Success," p. 29.

[30]See Myron Roomkin and Richard N. Bloch, "Case Processing Time and the Outcome of Representation Elections: Some Empirical Evidence," *University of Illinois Law Review* (1981), pp. 75–97.

We will no longer probe into the truth or falsity of the parties' campaign statements, and . . . we will not set elections aside on the basis of misleading campaign statements. We will, however, intervene in cases where a party has used forged documents which render the voters unable to recognize propaganda for what it is.[31]

The board is concerned, however, with threats or promises that would interfere with a free choice by workers.

2. Campaign Promises and Predictions. Charges on this score are almost invariably against the employer. Union statements about the great gains they will win for employees are dismissed as mere puffery; but the board reasons that the company has the power to make its predictions come true. The result is that employers have to be careful. As the Supreme Court said in the Gissel case: "The prediction must be *carefully phrased* on the basis of *objective fact* to convey an employer's belief as to *demonstrably probable* consequences *beyond his control.*"[32] If there is any implication that the employer will take action on his own for reasons unrelated to economic necessities, this is no longer a *prediction* but a *threat.* To say, "If we are organized, we will shut down," is clearly a threat. But to say, "Paying the union scale will put us out of business" may be permissible, given adequate documentation.

3. Offers and Inducements. A company is suspect if it grants an increase in wages or other benefits during the election period. The board presumes that this constitutes "interference" with the election. The burden of proof is on the company to rebut this presumption by showing that the increase was in accord with a regular schedule, or was in accord with past practice, or was decided on before the election had been set.

The same general principles apply to an *offer* of improved benefits, direct or implied, or to a *postponement* of benefit increases until after the election. If there is any implication that workers will not receive the improved benefits unless they vote the right way, it will be held to constitute interference.

4. Reprisals. Firing union sympathizers or any other actual or threatened reprisal against union activists is illegal and is grounds for setting aside an election. An employer must reinstate the fired worker and provide back pay, net of what the worker earned (or could reasonably have been expected to earn) since being fired. Such a weak penalty is consistent with Supreme Court decisions that, in the absence of any clear congressional intent, the authority of the board is limited to remedial, not punitive, remedies. Because the remedy is uncertain and likely to be long delayed, the threat of firing can have a chilling effect on the activities of union supporters. On the other hand, the employer can expect a light penalty, especially if

---

[31]Cited by Robert E. Williams, *NLRB Regulation of Election Conduct* (Philadelphia: Industrial Research Unit, Wharton School, University of Pennsylvania, Labor Relations and Public Policy Series, no. 8, rev. ed., 1985) p. 59.

[32]Ibid., p. 69, with emphasis by the author.

the company believes there are plausible grounds other than union activity for which the worker can be terminated. Thus it is not too surprising that there have been many cases where workers appear to have been fired illegally for supporting union-organizing efforts.[33] As we shall discuss shortly, unions have been unsuccessful in their efforts to amend the NLRA to increase the penalties to an employer who illegally fires workers for union activities.

From an Election to a Contract

We have seen that unions are now winning many fewer NLRB certifications. Where the union does win, however, one might expect this to be the end of the matter. But it is not the end. Company executives may continue to believe that the workers were misled and that collective bargaining is not really in their interest. Certainly, it will not be considered in the company's interest. So executives may continue to resist the signed agreement that would solidify the union's position.

Once a union wins a certification election, the NLRA does require the employer (and the union) to bargain in good faith. Refusal to bargain may be remedied by an affirmative order of the NLRB. If the board's order to bargain has been properly issued, the United States Court of Appeals is required to compel enforcement under contempt-of-court penalties. Moreover, certain kinds of bargaining behavior may be held to constitute an unfair labor practice.

But what does this duty actually mean? Does it mean going through the motions, or does it mean serious bargaining? And what is "serious" bargaining? In congressional debate on the Wagner Act, it is stated that this provision "only leads the employees to the door of the employer . . . what happens behind those doors is not inquired into." But this view turned out to be untenable. As one party or the other did not like what was going on behind the doors and complained to the board, the duty to bargain began to be defined in depth by board and court decisions.

To avoid reaching an agreement with the union, the main legal technique is simply prolonged hard bargaining. Company representatives can appear regularly at the bargaining table, defending proposals the union regards as unacceptable and giving reasons for refusing to accept the union proposals. This can go on for quite a long time without violating the good-faith requirement described above.

What can the union do? If it thinks the company has violated the good-faith rule, it can file an unfair labor charge with the NLRB. But final disposition of this charge may take years. Alternatively, the union may call a strike. But a strike is definitely a two-edged weapon. The employer is entitled to replace the strikers with new employees, which will shift the composition of the labor force in a nonunion direction. Moreover, at any time after one year from the original election, another election may be held to decertify the union. This time the union may very well lose.

As a practical matter, then, a union with a large and solid election majority is likely to secure a contract. But if its victory is only marginal and if it is up against

---

[33]Paul Weiler, "Promises to Keep," pp. 1769–1827.

a determined employer, it may well fail to do so. There is a substantial leakage between the elections stage and the contract stage.[34]

Changes in the Legal Environment

We have discussed the procedures and the legal issues involved in certification elections, the main mechanism that labor law provides to unions as they try to organize nonunion firms or the nonunion plants of a firm that is partially organized. Our primary objective in this chapter is to explain the decline of private-sector unionization, especially since the mid-seventies. There have been no changes in the basic law, the NLRA, since 1974 and no major changes affecting the ease or difficulty of organizing workers since the Taft-Hartley amendments of 1947. Thus changes in the legislation cannot explain the decline in unionization.

As we have seen, however, there has been an increase in employer opposition to union organizing. Since the 1970s firms have been spending heavily on labor-management consultants to combat union-organizing campaigns.[35] There has also been a dramatic increase in the number of unfair labor practice charges brought against employers, from under fourteen thousand in 1960 to over thirty-one thousand in 1980, with little change in the portion of such charges that the NLRB has found to have merit.[36]

The large increase in union charges of unfair labor practices during the 1970s led to significant delays in the NLRB's processing of charges. Within a few years the average time required for a decision on a charge of unfair labor practice was over a year and a half. If the firm appealed the board's decision, then the delay in the courts was typically another year and a half.

Such delays have increased the incentive for firms to engage in practices that are borderline (or worse) legally.[37] For example, consider delays in reinstating workers the NLRB determines to have been fired for union activities, despite the employer's claim that the firing was for some other cause. The longer the delay in reinstatement, the greater the damage to the fired workers and to the union. The delay typically hurts the union's organizing campaign if reinstatement is not announced until after the certification election. Although delay will also increase the cost of back payments to the firm, most firms regard the cost of such back payments to a few workers as small compared to the gains of remaining nonunion.

---

[34]For unions winning certification elections in 1979–80, only about three-quarters succeed in negotiating a contract within three years. In other words, the leakage rate is about one-quarter. See Cooke, "Decline in Union Success." One major determinant of whether the union will be successful is whether it already represents other workers employed by the firm. For those that do not, the leakage rate increases to about one third.

[35]In 1985 the AFL-CIO estimated that firms were spending $100 million annually on such consultants.

[36]During the 1980s the number of charges declined, probably in part because unions have realized that filing charges often was not a very useful strategy.

[37]For empirical evidence, see Robert J. Flanagan, *Labor Relations and the Litigation Explosion* (Washington,: D.C. Brookings Institution, 1987), Chap. 5.

Labor Law Reform

As firms have become more aggressively antiunion, union leaders have sought amendments to the NLRA so that firms can not so easily delay certification elections or influence such elections illegally without having to pay any substantial penalties. The labor reform bill of 1978 was designed to deal with these issues. First, it included several provisions to speed up the decision-making processes of the NLRB. Since some delays are unavoidable, the legislation also would have required the NLRB to seek temporary injunctions so that firms could be forced to reinstate immediately any workers who the NLRB and the courts suspected were fired for union activities. As a result of the injunction, such workers would remain on the job until a final decision was made on the merits of the charge against the employer.

In addition, the labor reform bill would have increased the penalties against firms that violated the law. For example, the House version of the bill would have provided double back pay, with no deduction for interim earnings, if the firm was found to have discharged a worker for union activities. Firms found to have willfully violated orders of the NLRB would have been barred from receiving any federal contracts for a three-year period. And firms would have been required to pay compensation to the workers if after the union had won a certification election, the employer was found to have refused to bargain.

The bill appeared to have the support not only of President Carter but also of majorities in the House and the Senate, both of which were controlled by the Democrats. The bill died in the Senate as a result of a filibuster. No other legislation has been forthcoming, in part because labor's political power, which was low during the Carter administration, declined even further under Reagan and Bush. In fact, Reagan's breaking of a strike by the air-traffic-controllers' union symbolized the weak political position of labor and may have helped legitimate union opposition among many private-sector employers.

UNION ORGANIZING AND PUBLIC OPINION

Unions may have been less successful in NLRB elections not only because increased managerial opposition has made organizing workers more difficult but also because they have put less effort and imagination into such organizing, or because workers are less interested in unions. In this section we shall consider these issues.

Expenditures by Unions on Organizing New Members

As Bloch has suggested, when unions became established in many industries during the late 1930s and 1940s, the payoff in increased bargaining power from organizing an extra worker in the industry declined, while the union's need to service present workers increased.[38] Thus during the years that union membership increased, we expect a reduction in organizing expenditures, at least as a percentage of the union's total budget. For the period from the early fifties to the late seventies, Voss finds that real expenditures for organizing increased about 20 percent but declined as a percentage of union budgets.[39]

It is likely that since the 1970s total expenditures for organizing have fallen as (1) membership decline has led to less revenue and thus to tighter budgets for most unions, and (2) the prospects for organizing additional workers has declined because of greater opposition from management. Although the AFL-CIO and many of its member unions have been giving a higher priority to organizing activity in recent years, this renewed emphasis has come in a time of declining revenue for most unions.

A reduction in organizing effort, at least relative to the number of non-union workers, may account for some of the difficulty unions have been having in developing more successful NLRB election campaigns. But reduced organizing efforts are probably not the primary explanation. Instead, unions' poor showing in elections may help explain why, at least until recently, they have not been devoting more effort to organizing.

The most obvious reason why unions have had more difficulty in their organizing efforts is the increased opposition of management, which we discussed above. Although there has been some disagreement on the issue, the best evidence suggests that opposition by employers does significantly reduce the success of union-organizing campaigns.[40]

Attitudes toward Unions

Next let us consider changes in how unions are viewed by workers and by the general public. Such changes are likely to affect the ability of unions to organize new workers, both directly and through the effect of public opinion on labor legislation.

The primary source of long-term data on attitudes toward unions is the Gallup poll. These data, presented in Tables 14-3, show that from 1936 to 1965 approximately 70 percent of the public approved of unions and about 20 percent disapproved. Since 1965 approval has fallen to under 60 percent, and disapproval has risen to about 30 percent, with the main decline occurring between 1965 and 1980. This decrease in popular acceptance helps account for the declining political power of unions.

---

[38]Richard N. Block, "Union Organizing and the Allocation of Union Resources," *Industrial and Labor Relations Review* (October 1980), pp. 101–13.

[39]Paula B. Voss, "Trends in Union Organizing Expenditures, 1953–77," *Industrial and Labor Relations Review* (October 1984), pp. 52–63.

[40]William T. Dickens, "The Effect of Company Campaigns on Certification Elections, Law and Reality Once Again," *Industrial and Labor Relations Review* (July 1983), pp. 560–75. A somewhat smaller effect is found in John J. Lawler, "The Influence of Management Consultants on the Outcome of Union Certification of Elections," *Industrial and Labor Relations Review* (October 1984), pp. 38–51.

TABLE 14-3   Ratings of Labor Unions, 1936–85 (percent)

"In general, do you approve or disapprove of labor unions?"

YEAR	APPROVE	DISAPPROVE
1936	72	20
1937	72	20
1939	68	24
1940	64	22
1941	61	30
1947	64	25
1949	62	22
1953	75	18
1957 (Feb.)	76	14
1957 (Sept.)	64	18
1959	68	19
1961 (Feb.)	70	18
1961 (May)	63	22
1962	64	24
1963	67	23
1965 (Feb.)	71	19
1965 (June)	70	19
1967	66	23
1973	59	26
1978 (April)	59	31
1979 (May)	55	33
1981 (Aug.)	55	35
1985	58	27

Source: Gallup polls.

Source: Seymour Martin Lipset, "Labor Unions in the Public Mind," in *Unions in Transition*, p. 300.

Although the general public has negative views of unions and their leaders, as Kochan et al. indicate,

> [A] strong majority of the American public views unions as important and effective vehicles for improving the status and representing the job-related needs of employees at the workplace. That is, more than 80 percent of the respondents agreed that unions are effective in improving their members' wages, protecting job security, and protecting workers against unfair employer practices. . . .
>
> Thus, while most of the American public has a poor image of unions in general, an equally strong majority agrees that the functions unions traditionally have performed for their members and for the larger society continue to be relevant and needed today.
>
> The general endorsement of the need for unions per se does not translate into a search for union representation by a majority of employees in their specific work settings. Indeed, the evidence from numerous studies shows that to induce workers to express a preference for unionizing, takes a combination of (1) deep dissatisfaction with current job and employment conditions, (2) a view that unionization can be helpful or instrumental in improving those job conditions, and (3) a willingness

to overcome the general negative image or stereotype of unions. . . . A majority of workers in a specific bargaining unit must possess these views in order for a union to win a representation election. Yet currently most American workers do not hold these views.[41]

As Farber shows, the percentage of nonunion, nonmanagerial workers who say they would vote for a union has declined from 38.6 percent in 1977 to 32.4 percent in 1984.[42] This decline apparently is the result of an increase in job satisfaction among such workers and a decrease in their perception that unions can improve their wages and working conditions.[43]

Among their members unions have strong support. Three out of four union members tell independent poll takers that they are satisfied or very satisfied with their union.[44]

Among the general public there appears to be considerable concern with corruption among union leaders. Although corruption is important in some unions, especially the Teamsters and some construction unions, and has received considerable publicity at times, most close observers of the labor movement believe that the great majority of unions are run quite honestly.[45]

Attitudes toward union leaders are affected not only by how well they represent their members at the workplace but also by what they do in the political arena. The 1984 presidential election provides evidence that union leaders do not always represent the political views of their membership. In that election the AFL-CIO strongly endorsed Walter Mondale. President Reagan not only won by a landslide but even won about 45 percent of the votes from all union households and probably a majority from households of white union members.[46]

In the late thirties and early forties, when the labor movement was most successful, it was seen by many as the spearhead of a broad, progressive coalition concerned with the welfare of all workers.[47] Since at least the 1960s however, organized labor has come to be seen more as a special-interest group, looking out primarily for the self-interests of its members. Yet as we indicated in Chapter 13, labor's political power is much greater when it seeks to represent the interests of all workers (or all low-income workers) rather than just those of its own members.

---

[41]Thomas A. Kochan, et al., The *Transformation of American Industrial Relations*, pp. 216–17.

[42]Henry S. Farber, "Trends in Worker Demand for Union Representation," *American Economic Review* (May 1989), pp. 166–71, and also his *Science* article, "Recent Decline of Unionization." In the period immediately prior to 1984 there was much publicity about union concessions during the recession, so it is not clear whether this change in perceptions about union effectiveness is primarily a long-run or a short-run development.

[43]Also there is little evidence to support the hypothesis that workers see less need for unions in recent years because of more extensive protective legislation. See Richard B. Freeman, "Unionism and Protective Legislation," *Proceedings of the Thirty-Ninth Annual Meeting, Industrial Relations Research Association,* Madison, Wis.: 1987.

[44]Lipset, "Labor Unions in the Public Mind," p. 305.

[45]Freeman and Medoff, What Do Unions do? Chap. 14.

[46]See A. H. Raskin, "Labor: A Movement in Search of a Mission, in Lipset, "Labor Unions in the Public Mind."

[47]See Michael J. Piore, "Can the American Labor Movement Survive Re-Gomperization?

This change in how the labor movement is viewed politically is related to a broader problem, a decline in labor's missionary zeal. One of the first to note this phenomenon was Richard Lester, who wrote:

> As unions age, they are prone to experience internal adjustments similar to those that take place in other institutions which in their formative years had to struggle for existence and acceptance. In the case of labor unions the gradual alterations that occur through the processes of internal change can be classified under three headings: (1) a decline in the rate of expansion and missionary zeal, (2) a shift of power and control toward the national headquarters, and (3) an alteration in the union's leadership.
>
> As a union's growth curve begins to level off, subtle psychological changes tend to take place. The turbulence and enthusiasm of youth, the missionary zeal of a new movement, slow down to a more moderate pace. Increasingly, decisions are made centrally, as a political machine becomes entrenched, as the channels of union communication are more tightly controlled from the top, and as reliance on staff specialists expands. Along with these changes, the national leadership experiences some modification. As the organization enlarges, the problems of management multiply and the emphasis shifts from organization to administration, negotiation, and contract enforcement. The leaders of the formative years are succeeded by a second and a third generation leadership, who did not experience the early struggles and bitterness. Security for the top hierarchy and the good life on a sizeable salary may be part of a group of corrupting influences. The democratic checks may have weakened with increasing size, centralization, and power in the hands of full-time functionaries. Such developments are natural in the evolution of successful institutions serving as representatives of interest groups.[48]

THE RESPONSE OF THE UNION MOVEMENT

In the 1970s unions were able to maintain good earnings and benefits for most of their members. The union wage differential widened and employment losses were seen as a temporary aberration. In this context unions made few changes in their overall policies or in their organizing strategies. The aging, rather autocratic George Meany was the symbol of organized labor throughout the sixties and seventies. Raskin writes,

> For large sections of the electorate, the stereotypical image of labor remains the caricature cartoonists used to the point of nausea in depicting George Meany in the quarter century of his imperious rule over the federation: a baleful figure with bulging belly and clenched cigar, hurling monkey wrenches at the White House and the Capitol.[49]

Under the leadership of Lane Kirkland, who succeeded Meany as president of the AFL-CIO in 1979, the union movement has been making greater effort to respond to its more hostile environment. Some of Kirkland's first changes have

---

[48]Richard A. Lester, *As Unions Mature*, pp. 106–7.
[49]See A. H. Raskin, "Labor," p. 33.

been in the political arena, reaching out to form new coalitions, organizing mass political demonstrations, and trying to influence the nomination as well as the election of political candidates. Despite these changes, the political influence of labor remains low, especially with regard to any legislative changes that would facilitate the organization of additional union members.

More recently the AFL-CIO has turned its attention to how unions could better represent workers, both those who are already union members and those who might become members through more effective union organizing. A number of quite innovative ideas were presented in a report, *The Changing Situation of Workers and their Unions,* published in 1985. The report emphasized the importance of increasing members' participation in their unions and of improving the labor movement's communication with the general public. Specific suggestions, aimed at both member unions and the AFL-CIO, were made for achieving these objectives, including considerable emphasis on better use of radio, television, and videos by union leaders in communicating with their members and with the general public. The main emphasis of the report was on ways to improve the effectiveness of union organizing. Among its many suggestions were the following:

1. Organizers should be more carefully chosen and trained.
2. Organizers should make greater use of modern technology, including videos, mass media, and polling of workers.
3. Union leaders and rank-and-file members should be more involved in organizing efforts.
4. Organizing targets should be carefully chosen, partly with the aid of polls, to maximize the chance of success.
5. When a unit is organized, unions representing other workers of the same employer should provide more assistance to new units trying to obtain a first contract.
6. Public pressure should be brought to bear to force recalcitrant employers not to interfere with employees' right to organize into a union, a right the AFL-CIO believes is no longer adequately protected by labor legislation.
7. Unions should experiment with new organizing techniques. Specifically, the union "organizer might be more effective in achieving the ultimate end of majority support for collective bargaining if the organizer has first demonstrated the potential of concerted activity by achieving results on a particular issue of concern to the workers in the unit.[50] Such an issue might be a current problem of health or safety at the workplace or a controversial discharge of an employee.
8. New membership categories should be established. For example, union sympathizers and former union members might for a modest fee become asociate members, with the union providing employment-related services (such as job training) and fringe benefits (such as supplemental medical insurance).

Following up on the recommendations of the report, many individual unions as well as the national federation have changed some of their organizing activities.[51]

---

[50]*The Changing Situation of Workers and Their Unions, A Report by the AFL-CIO Committee on the Evolution of Work,* February 1985, p. 28.
[51]Charles J. McDonald, "The AFL-CIO's Blueprint for the Future—A Progress Report," *Proceedings of the Industrial Relations Research Association, 1986,* pp. 276–82.

Unions have been targeting organizational campaigns more carefully; making more effort to chose organizers who are "in tune" with the workers they are seeking to organize; making better use of films, videos, and union volunteers in organizing drives; and making more use of publicity and "demonstrations of solidarity" rather than simply relying on strikes to win first contracts once a certification election has been won. Several unions have also established associate memberships, at lower dues, for those supporting the union but not represented by a union contract. The AFL-CIO has developed a number of service programs for union members, including a Mastercard credit card at a favorable interest rate and with no payments required during strikes.[52] Although there is no sign that these new organizing activities will be dramatically successful, the recognition that change is necessary and that the labor movement should experiment with a variety of new approaches is a useful first step.

Some unions have been making special efforts to organize service workers, women, and others whose share of the labor force is increasing. Pay equity has been a useful issue for public-sector unions in appealing to women, and labor's political agenda now stresses such issues as parental leaves and health insurance that are of at least as much concern to women as to men. Still, in the private sector labor's national leaders do not appear to have been very successful in generating issues or techniques to increase unionization among firms that employ many women.[53]

The situation facing the U.S. labor movement is serious. Historically, unions in this country have focused primarily on collective bargaining in the industries where they were strong, rather than on political activity. But with increasing competition, both foreign and domestic, unions in manufacturing and most other private-sector industries have lost many members and considerable bargaining power. More radical changes may be necessary if the labor movement is to continue to be a strong force outside the public sector. Labor leaders in some other countries regard the new initiatives of unions in the United States to be "ridiculously inadequate" relative to the problems they face.[54] As Freeman indicates, the structure of the U.S. labor movement probably contributes to its inertia.

> A major factor in my view is the otherwise admirable decentralized structure of the American union movement. In the United States, organized labor consists of some

---

[52]The worker's union can have its name prominently displayed on the card and can use the billing system easily to send messages to all its members enrolled in the credit program. Other benefits, such as discounted airline tickets, legal services, life insurance, and investment services, are either in place or planned.

[53]The most innovative approaches have been developed at the local level by groups like Nine to Five that appear to have limited influence among the leadership of the AFL-CIO. For further discussion of techniques used in organizing women clerical workers and their relation to overall organizing efforts by the AFL-CIO, see the discussion of Charles J. McDonald's paper by Maryellen R. Kelley, *Proceedings of the Industrial Relations Research Association, 1986*, pp. 381–89. Also see Karien S. Koziara and Patrice J. Insley, "Organizing Low-Income Women in New Ways: Who, Where, and Why," *Proceedings of the Industrial Relations Research Association, 1981*, and the discussion by Charles McDonald. For an overview of women's issues, see Ruth Needleman and Lucretia Dewey Tanner, "Women in Unions: Current Issues," in *Working Women: Past, Present, Future*, ed. Karen Koziara et al. (Washington, D.C.: Bureau of National Affairs, 1987).

[54]See Freeman, "The Changing Status of Unionism," especially pp. 121–22.

90 or so independent national unions in the AFL-CIO and others outside the federation. Each national has its own problems and agenda. Each contains hundreds of independent locals with their own concerns. Such a structure concentrates union efforts on local or sectoral rather than national issues, guaranteeing slow reaction to problems that affect unionism in its entirety, and making implementation of reforms suggested by the AFL-CIO leadership problematic at best. Without the career option of moving into government, as in countries with labor parties, American union leadership may turn over too slowly and appears to be more risk averse than suits a crisis period.[55]

To conclude, the percentage of the work force that is unionized is not likely to decline over the next few years as it has in the recent past. Because of improvements in the economy, new initiatives from the labor movement, and the normal swings of the political pendulum, the influence of unions on the economy is unlikely to decline significantly as it did in the seventies and early eighties. On the other hand, there is no evidence to suggest that unions will significantly increase their membership and their overall influence. In fact, the increased success of managerial opposition can be expected to lead to still greater opposition, unless there is new legislation or some other drastic change in the industrial relations environment. Together with the shift from blue- to white-collar jobs, this increased opposition suggests that union membership is likely to continue to decline, at least as a percentage of the labor force. As union households represent a declining portion of the electorate, the political power of unions is also likely to continue to decline.

SUMMARY

1. In the private sector the percentage of workers who are union members has declined sharply. In the peak year of 1953, 36 percent of the work force in the private sector were unionized. By 1989 only 12 percent were unionized. The decline has accelerated since 1975.

2. In the public sector the percent unionized has increased from 11 percent in the early sixties to 37 percent in 1988. Large increases occurred in the late sixties and early seventies. Since then there has been a slight decline. Because public employment is a small percentage of total employment, the percent of the total work force that is unionized has declined rapidly since the mid-seventies.

3. One factor partly responsible for the decline in unionization is changes in the composition of the work force. There are fewer workers who are male, living in the Northeast or Midwest, and employed in heavy industry, the areas where unions have been strongest. We need to be careful, however, not to overestimate the importance of the changes in the labor force as *causes* of the decline in unionization. For example, causation can go in the other direction, as is likely

---

[55]Ibid., p. 123.

in the case of geographic shifts in employment. The greater increase in jobs in the South is at least partly the result of employer efforts to avoid unionization.

4. Unionization has been adversely affected by several trends in the economy, including increased foreign competition, deregulation, competition between the North and South, recessions, and an increase in the relative wages of union workers.

5. Many of these economic changes have affected other countries. Since 1970, however, unionization has risen in many countries. Nowhere has it declined as sharply as in the United States. Unionization has increased slightly in Canada, despite its close links to the U.S. economy. In part because of different legislation, firms in Canada cannot oppose unions as effectively as in the United States.

6. Most managers, especially those whose workers are not unionized, are opposed to unionization. Many see unions as arising mainly where managers have not been sufficiently sensitive to the needs and desires of their workers.

7. Nonunion firms often are small companies in competitive industries that cannot afford to pay high wage rates or to provide good benefits. Large profitable firms that wish to remain nonunion generally must pay at least as well as comparable union firms in the same area.

8. Management opposition to unionization increased in the 1970s and 1980s as competition increased, as changes in the economy increased the need for flexibility in the allocation of labor, and as firms learned how to oppose unions more effectively.

9. Because many firms go out of business and plants close each year, unionization will decline unless unions can organize new and expanding firms. In the private sector a union generally must win a certification election run by the National Labor Relations Board (NLRB) before it can represent a new group of workers. If the union wins such an election, it becomes the *exclusive* bargaining representative of the workers in the election unit and must represent all workers in the unit equally, whether or not they are union members.

10. The NLRB must determine who will be in the election unit and must police the tactics of union and management during the election campaign. For example, it is illegal for management to discriminate against union advocates. However, the penalties are modest, and many firms do appear to be firing union organizers. Since the 1970s many firms appear to have resisted union organizing campaigns more vigorously, sometimes within the law and sometimes by illegal activity. Efforts by unions to amend the National Labor Relations Act to avoid damaging delays and to increase the penalties for illegal tactics have been unsuccessful.

11. Even if the union succeeds in winning the certification election, often it fails to negotiate a contract with the employer.

12. Public-opinion polls show a significant decline in the approval rating for unions between 1965 and 1980 but little change since then. Among their members unions continue to enjoy strong support.

13. Union leadership appears to have been slow to recognize the magnitude of the problems facing most unions in the private sector. During the 1980s the AFL-CIO under the leadership of Lane Kirkland took many initatives to try to increase the political power of the union movement and to try to increase the extent and success of organizing efforts. Although these efforts were sensible and sometimes imaginative, they had only a very limited success.

14. There is no evidence to suggest that unions in the private sector are likely to increase their influence very much in the 1990s. On the contrary, the increased success of management opposition in recent years is likely to inspire even greater opposition to union organizing in the future.

KEY CONCEPTS

CERTIFICATION ELECTION   NATIONAL LABOR RELATIONS BOARD

REVIEW QUESTIONS

1. Many different factors have contributed to the decline of unionization in the private sector. In your opinion, which factor is most important? Why?
2. Why are changes in the composition of the work force more plausible as the primary explanation for the decline in private-sector unionization in the 1950s and 1960s than for the decline in the seventies and eighties?
3. Why was management opposition to unions greater in the 1970s and 1980s than in the 1960s?
4. What might unions have done to avoid their decline in the 1970s and 1980s, or at least to have reduced its extent? Comment both on the role of the AFL-CIO and on the role of its member unions. Have some unions been significantly more successful than others in resisting decline? If so, why? Discuss current union efforts to improve their position. How successful do you think these efforts are likely to be? Why?
5. Why do the policies of the National Labor Relations Board (NLRB) play a major role in determining the chances of success of a union-organizing campaign? Discuss the current policies of the NLRB. What changes, if any would you suggest in these policies? Why? Would your suggested changes require any amendments to the National Labor Relations Act?

6. Compare the changes in unionization in the United States with changes in other countries. Go to the library and learn more about what has been happening to the labor movement and to collective bargaining in some other country that interests you.

READINGS

AFL-CIO COMMITTEE ON THE EVOLUTION OF WORK, *The Changing Situation of Workers and Their Unions.* Washington, D.C.: AFL-CIO, 1985.

FREEMAN, RICHARD B., "The Changing Status of Unionism around the World," in *Organized Labor at the Crossroads,* pp. 111–37. Kalamazoo, Mich.: W. E. Upjohn Institute for Employment Research, 1989.

———, "Contraction and Expansion: The Divergence of Private Sector and Public Sector Unionism in the United States," *Journal of Economic Perspectives* (Spring 1988), pp. 63–88.

———, and JAMES L. MEDOFF, *What Do Unions Do?* New York: Basic Books, 1984.

FOULKES, FRED K., *Personnel Policies in Large Nonunion Companies.* Englewood Cliffs, N.J.: Prentice-Hall, 1980.

KOCHAN, THOMAS A., ed., *Challenges and Choices Facing American Labor.* Cambridge, Mass.: MIT Press, 1985.

———, HARRY C. KATZ, and ROBERT B. MCKERSIE, *The Transformation of American Industrial Relations.* New York: Basic Books, 1986.

LESTER, RICHARD A., *As Unions Mature.* Princeton, N.J.: Princeton University Press, 1958.

LIPSET, SEYMOUR MARTIN, ed., *Unions in Transition: Entering the Second Century.* San Francisco: ICS Press, 1986.

LIPSKY, DAVID B., and CLIFFORD B. DONN, eds., *Collective Bargaining in American Industry.* Lexington, Mass.: D. C. Heath, 1987.

PIORE, MICHAEL J., "Can the American Labor Movement Survive Re-Gomperization? *Proceedings of the Thirty-Fifth Annual Meeting, Industrial Relations Research Association,* Madison, Wis. 1983.

———, and CHARLES F. SABEL, *The Second Industrial Divide: Possibilities for Prosperity.* New York: Basic Books, 1984.

REDER, MELVIN W., "The Rise and Fall of Unions: The Public Sector and the Private," *Journal of Economic Perspectives* (Spring 1988), pp. 89–110.

WEILER, PAUL, "Promises to Keep: Securing Workers' Rights to Self-Organization under the NLRA," *Harvard Law Review* (June 1983), pp. 1769–1827.

WILLIAMS, ROBERT E., *NLRB Regulation of Election Conduct,* rev. ed. Philadelphia: Industrial Relations Unit, Wharton School, University of Pennsyvania, 1985.

COLLECTIVE BARGAINING: UNION AND MANAGEMENT GOALS

It is often said that collective bargaining is a relationship between a political organization, the trade union, and a business organization. Before plunging into the details of bargaining procedures, it is desirable to take a broad look at the objectives of the organizations involved. What is the general outlook and thrust of the trade union movement? On the other side of the table, what is the management group trying to accomplish? To what extent are the goals of the parties in conflict, and to what extent do they have common goals that should lead to cooperation?

UNION OBJECTIVES: AN ECONOMIC MODEL

Generation after generation, employers and others have asked, What are the unions really after? In the heyday of union power in the 1940s and 1950s, there were dark suspicions that union leaders aspired to take over the management of industry. In actuality, American union leaders have never had a clear blueprint of the future. When someone asked early AFL leader Samuel Gompers what the aims of the new federation were, he replied, "More, more, more—now!" When another AFL leader was called before a Congressional committee in 1883 and asked about the ultimate objectives of trade unionism, he replied as follows: "We have no ultimate ends. We are going on from day to day. We are fighting only for immediate objects . . . we are opposed to theorists . . . we are all practical men."

This is still quite a good answer a century later; but it is a rather vague

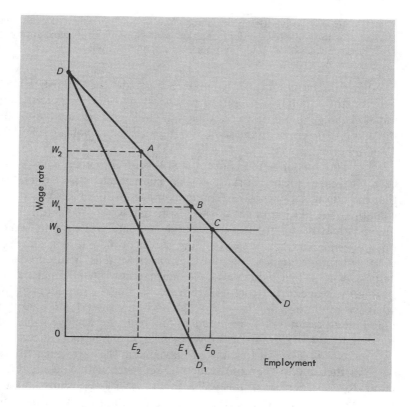

FIGURE 15-1   The Wage-Employment Tradeoff in a Unionized Industry

answer. More of *what?* For what reasons? There are many dimensions of working conditions, of worker satisfaction or dissatisfaction, and of union objectives. In contract negotiations the union is usually bargaining on a dozen fronts at once, trading concessions on some fronts for gains on others. But simplification is necessary in economics, and certainly necessary in the present case. So we narrow the discussion to two policy objectives, which are of prime importance: (1) Wages, by which we mean the total hourly compensation of employees. The division of compensation between direct wage payments and fringe benefits raises additional problems, which we leave until Chapter 20. (2) Employment, by which we mean the number of jobs available to union members.

We start from a simple model, with the following characteristics:

1. The industry is fully unionized, and bargaining is on an industrywide basis.
2. The union bargains only over wages. After the wage has been decided, employers determine employment by moving along the demand curve for labor.
3. The industry's demand curve for labor is D in Figure 15-1. The line D_1 shows the change in the industry's wage bill when the wage rate is reduced just enough to hire an additional worker. It is derived from D in the same way as the marginal revenue

curve is derived from the demand curve for a product. W is the market wage rate for the industry. Under nonunion conditions, then, E workers would be employed at a wage of W, and the industry's wage bill would be OECW.

What will the union do? To analyze this issue, economists have tended to fall back on the familiar concepts of *monopoly* and *maximization.* Employers in the industry can get labor only at a wage that has been bargained out with the union. So the union seems to be in the same situation as a monopolistic seller of a commodity: "Pay my price, or else."

The maximization concept is also central to economics. The business concern maximizes profit; workers and consumers maximize utility. So to the extent that the union is a purposive economic unit, must it not also be trying to maximize something? And what might this be? Note that we are indicating here only what the union would prefer to do. The actual outcome will be influenced by employer objectives and the relative bargaining power of the parties. Some solutions can be ruled out rather quickly. Suppose, for example, that the union chose to maximize *employment,* which would also maximize union membership. This would mean setting the wage at the competitive level W. But the members might then wonder what the union is doing for them and why they should continue to pay dues. The union could disintegrate. In practice, unions try to achieve something better than the competitive wage and, as we will see later, they usually succeed.

Nor is it useful to think of maximizing the *wage rate,* that is, pushing the wage further and further above the market level, with a steady decline in employment. Rational pursuit of this policy might consist of pushing up the wage rate and reducing the level of employment at precisely the rate at which people retire from the industry. Eventually there would be one employee left, working at the very high wage OD. The policy of the United Mine Workers under John L. Lewis, while not this extreme, did tend in this direction. Lewis, a strong leader with unusual ability to dominate union policy, encouraged mechanization of the underground coal mines, which meant a sharp drop in employment of miners. As an offset he demanded large wage increases and large employer contributions to a welfare fund, which among other things provided pensions for displaced miners.

If pushed too aggressively, a rate-maximizing policy would displace prime-age workers as well as those ready to retire, and could cause enough grassroots dissatisfaction to compel a change in policy. Moreover, success of a rate-maximizing policy depends on an assumption that the industry can be kept organized. But as the union rate is pushed higher and higher, there is increased incentive for employers to break away from the union and for new firms to set up on a nonunion basis. A case in point is the construction industry, where escalation of union wage scales has contributed to a relative expansion of nonunion employment.

Two other objectives are somewhat more plausible. The union might try to maximize the *wage bill,* that is, total employee revenue from the industry. The wage bill is maximized where the marginal revenue curve, D_1, crosses the horizontal axis. This would mean choosing point B on the demand curve, with E_1 workers employed at a wage W_1. But why should the union do this? The union does not itself sell labor, nor does it receive the proceeds. The wage bill goes to the workers, not the union. Moreover, this principle could lead to odd results. Over any section of the labor demand curve that is elastic, the wage bill can be increased by *cutting* the wage rate. Union members would probably consider this approach rather unusual and would not be consoled by a lecture on the elasticity of demand.

Finally, the union might try to maximize the *economic rent* of employees in the industry, that is, the surplus of actual earnings over what the same workers would have earned under competitive conditions. This sum is maximized at the employment level E_2, where the marginal revenue curve D_1 cuts the competitive wage line WC. It would mean choosing point A, with a wage W_2 and employment E_2. Again one faces the question, Why should the union choose this particular objective?

The difficulty with such economic models is that they do not explain why the union leaders should prefer one point on the demand curve to any other point. Whatever leaders do, some workers will be satisfied and others will not. If union leaders choose point A, workers over the range OE_2 who continue to be employed will be happy to get the high wage W_2. But workers over the range E_2E_1, who could be employed at a wage of W_1 but are now excluded from employment, will not be so happy. Similarly, for any other point on D above the competitive wage, there will be a fringe of dissatisfied workers who would prefer employment in the industry but are unable to get it.

What we need is a model that brings union members' preferences into the picture. This means using a *political model* of policy formation.

UNION OBJECTIVES: A POLITICAL MODEL

We retain the main features of the economic model in Figure 15-1. The industry is fully unionized and remains so. There is a definite demand schedule for labor. The union bargains over the wage rate, and when this rate is established, employers determine employment by moving along the demand schedule. The only difference is that now we view the union not as a business organization selling labor to employers but as a political organization whose wage-employment objectives are grounded in the preferences of the individual member-voters.

Union leaders are elected by the membership and have an interest in behaving so as to get reelected.[1] A union officer is thus in the position of a member of Congress considering how his or her vote on a tax bill will affect reelection prospects rather than in the position of a company president who can dictate actions aimed at maximizing profit.

But the political analogy goes deeper. The benefits a union wins through

---

[1]In choosing among positions that are equally likely to ensure the union leader's reelection, Atherton argues, the leader may seek to maximize the union's net revenue, which he defines as the difference between its gross receipts, mainly from dues, and the cost of providing services to the membership. See Wallace N. Atherton, *Theory of Union Bargaining Goals*.

negotiation with employers, like the services provided by a governmental unit, are *public goods*. You will remember from elementary economics that a public good has two properties:

1. Nonrivalness in Consumption. If a union reduces dust pollution in a factory by 20 percent, the benefit to one worker does not interfere with all other workers' getting the same benefit.

2. Nonexcludability from Consumption. Just as all citizens can use a public service whether or not they have paid taxes, so all workers in the plant have access to a union-provided benefit whether or not they have helped to finance it by paying union dues. This is the basis for the union argument that all workers in a bargaining unit should either join the union or pay an equivalent amount to the union for its bargaining services. Nonmembers who pay nothing are considered "free riders," enjoying benefits to which they have not contributed.

A private good is sold in a market at a price, and only those who pay the price get the good. A public good, if produced at all, is available to everyone and is apparently free. But since it costs something to produce, it cannot really be free. The "price" citizens pay for government-produced services is their tax bill. And the "price" of union-negotiated benefits is the monthly dues payment.

How much of a particular union-sponsored benefit will be provided? There must be a demand for the benefit among union members; otherwise the union would not bother to negotiate about it. We can imagine a worker's demand curve for the benefit, showing how much he or she would be willing to pay for a specified quantity of it. This curve will slope downward from left to right in the usual way. For a 10 percent reduction in plant heat or noise or a 10 percent improvement in other benefits, the worker might pay a good deal. But for further improvements, demand will decline. By adding all members' demand curves together, we could derive total demand for the benefit. We could also construct the union's cost curve for the benefit, which will slope upward from left to right. To win increasing amounts of the benefit will involve increasing costs—more intensive negotiation, possibly strike costs, possibly a reduction in other demands to win this one. The intersection of the cost and demand curves indicates the optimal level the union should strive to achieve.

But since there is no market, demand cannot be revealed directly. Instead, the union representative must try to estimate it in much the way that legislators in government estimate the wishes of constituents. Here the union leader faces the fact of differences in members' preferences. Some workers would prefer a lot of the benefit in question, while others have lower demand curves. Yet in the end, the same negotiated amount must be provided for all. So there is bound to be dissatisfaction— some will feel that the benefit is being oversupplied, while others will consider it undersupplied.

Remember too that the union is normally negotiating not over a single benefit but over a dozen or more. Again, members will have differing tradeoffs among these objectives. A young, mobile worker may be interested mainly in direct wage payments. A middle-aged worker may be more interested in pensions and protection against layoffs and may be willing to give up some money in exchange.

About all the union officer can do, then, is to judge the preferences of the *average* worker. And the officer had better be right. The penalty for serious misjudgment is likely to be removal from office. This leads to a prediction that turnover of officers will be highest where the membership is unusually *heterogeneous,* so that differences in preference are large and difficult to judge. We can predict also that a certain proportion of the tentative agreements reached between union negotiators and employers will be rejected by the membership when put up for a ratification vote. That seems to be the result in about 10 percent of the cases. These are situations in which either the leadership failed to make an accurate judgment of members' preference or the workers are not realistic about the total gains that can be won.

We see here an important difference unions make in the operation of the labor market. A company tries to offer a package of benefits that will attract the number of qualified workers it needs. It is concerned with the *marginal worker,* who would be attracted by a slight improvement in terms or would leave if the employment package was too thin. The terms that the union tries to negotiate, on the other hand, reflect the preferences of the *average worker.* The average worker is likely to be older, with longer job tenure in the company and a characteristically different preference pattern. The importance of this fact will come out at several points in later chapters.

How does all this bear on union wage-employment objectives? We start from union members' preferences as the basis. The members have an interest in *job security.* Security is greater when employment is expanding than when it is shrinking, with the threat of temporary or permanent layoffs. Members are also interested in *compensation,* and they have information by which they can judge the reasonableness of what they are earning. Especially compelling is information on earnings and prospective increases in earnings for people doing comparable work in other companies. In cases where different groups work closely together—sailors and longshore workers, truck drivers and warehouse workers, lumberjacks and paper-mill workers—unions representing these groups tend to keep pace with each other on wage increases. This tendency was first pointed out by Professor Arthur Ross, who coined the term *orbits of coercive comparison.*

While we can assume that each member has wage and employment preferences, these preferences will differ from one person to another. The two most important sources of difference are probably age and length of service with the company (seniority). As workers grow older, their family responsibilities and need for income rise up to a point, then begin to diminish as children move from being dependents to becoming wage earners. In addition, finding a new job gets harder as you get older, because of a typical employer preference for youth and trainability. Length of service with the same employer benefits the worker as it (1) qualifies the worker for larger benefits, such as longer vacations and larger retirement pensions; and (2) brings greater protection against layoffs, which are usually made on a seniority basis, and (3) provides a greater chance of promotion to a better job.

Thus age and seniority, which are somewhat related, mean that loss of employment is a greater disaster to a senior worker than to a beginner. Employment security will have more weight in the preference system of a fifty-year-old than that of a twenty-five-year-old. Taking into account the age—and seniority—distribution of the work force, the union leader has to shape policies that will satisfy the worker in the middle of the distribution, the median worker. In political analysis this principle is called the *median voter model.* By following this principle the union leader (or the political candidate) can hope to satisfy more than half of his or her constituency, which will contribute to survival in office.[2]

The next consideration is that the median worker's preference system will be influenced by the employer's economic situation—whether product demand and employment are rising or falling, whether profit margins are stable or shrinking, whether best-guess forecasts of the future are optimistic or gloomy. A perceived threat to the jobs of even long-service workers will cause employment security to be weighted more heavily and will cause union policy to tilt in this direction, even at the cost of wage concessions. The threat to employment may come from several sources: (1) a company on the verge of bankruptcy because of mismanagement or other reasons, (2) an entire industry faced with intensified import competition, (3) appearance of new competitors using nonunion labor at lower wage rates, (4) a general economic recession.

Another important factor is the reemployment prospects of displaced workers. A threat of job loss is especially serious if the company is located in a declining area in the "rustbelt," or if a general recession is underway and unemployment is rising. If on the other hand, the company is located in an expanding Sunbelt city, or if a general economic upswing is underway, more workers will reason that jobs lost in one place can be made up for in another place. They will be less willing to trade wage concessions for job guarantees.

Taking these considerations into account, union negotiators select some point on the demand schedule *D* in Figure 15-1 as their preferred target; and this choice may involve only a modest premium over the competitive wage. The employer, of course, will usually prefer a still lower wage, which creates the bargaining problem analyzed in Chapter 16. But our purpose here is simply to define the union objective, which may or may not be achieved.

There is evidence that both wages and employment are important in members' preference functions and consequently in union policy. Two studies of the International Typographical Union (ITU) are relevant in this regard.[3] The ITU is a good union to study for this purpose, since it is unusually democratic; decisions are

---

[2]Unions are more responsive than the market to the preferences of the less mobile, older workers for another reason as well. Workers with more seniority are likely to be more active and influential in union affairs than younger workers. Their greater influence comes partly from greater knowledge and experience. But in addition, they have the most at stake in the union, because quitting and getting another job is a less attractive option for senior workers. Thus they have more incentive to be active in the union.

[3]James S. Dertouzas and John H. Pencavel, "Wage and Employment Determination under Trade Unionism: The International Typographical Union," *Journal of Political Economy* (December 1981), pp. 1162–81; and John H. Pencavel, "The Tradeoff between Wages and Employment in Trade Union Objectives."

made at the local level, thus permitting numerous observations; and the strong position of the union relative to newspaper employers, at least during the period studied (1946–65), makes it reasonable to view the results of bargaining as reflecting (mainly) union preferences. The results indicate that the ITU is concerned with employment as well as wage rates and is not willing to trade off much of one in order to gain more of the other. Both targets appear to be *relative,* that is, set on the basis of comparison with some norm. "It appears to be the excess of wages and employment over some reference levels that is relevant to union behavior." There was also variation of behavior among locals, no doubt reflecting differing economic circumstances. "The relative weight attached to supernumerary wages versus supernumerary employment varies considerably among the locals."

Attention to employment is especially likely if there has recently been a drop in employment. A case in point is the wave of *concession bargaining* during the recession of 1981–82. One study of major contract settlements in these years found forty-six cases of union concessions.[4] The concessions included wage cuts (twenty-one cases), wage freezes (thirteen cases), premature renegotiation of existing contracts (twenty-six cases), and easing of restrictive work rules (11 cases). The industries mainly affected were those in which there had been a sharp drop in demand for union labor, resulting either from import competition (steel, automobiles) or from deregulation and entrance of nonunion competitors (trucking, airlines), as well as from the general recession.

What is apparently required is a drop in employment severe enough to threaten the jobs of relatively senior union members. A drop of 10 percent, which can be met by laying off probationary and short-service workers, may nor arouse much concern. But a drop of 30 percent, with no end in sight, is a different matter. Then the median-service worker, either laid off or threatened with layoff, will place job security ahead of immediate money income, and the bulk of the membership will support union leaders in making some concessions to management demands.

A Qualification: The Partly Unionized Industry

So far we have assumed an industry that is fully unionized. There are such cases, but they are unusual. More commonly the industry is a mixture of union and nonunion firms. The proportion of workers organized may be 80 percent, or it may be only 10 percent. Where entrance to the industry is easy and initial capital requirements are small, as in clothing and other light manufacturing, house building, trucking, and most trades and service industries, it is hard to achieve anything approaching full unionization. This fact places serious constraints on union policy.

In Figure 15-2 *D* and *S* are the demand and supply curves for labor in the industry. *W* is the competitive wage, and *E* is the level of employment at that wage. If all workers in the industry were organized, the labor demand curve *D* would also be the *demand curve for union labor.* But under partial unionization, the two curves

---

[4]Daniel J. B. Mitchell, "Recent Union Contract Concessions," *Brookings Papers on Economic Activity* 1 (1982), pp. 165–201.

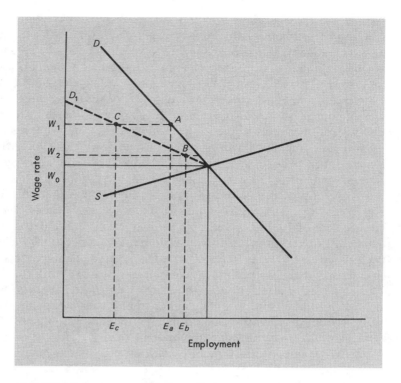

FIGURE 15-2 Demand for Union Labor in a Partly-Unionized
Industry

are different. The demand curve for union labor shows the relation between the union wage rate and the number of union members who will be employed at that wage. This curve is necessarily lower and more elastic than the total labor demand curve D.

Consider what happens as the union raises its wage scale further and further above the competitive level W. If the productivity of labor is equal in union and nonunion plants, a reasonable first assumption, the nonunion plants have lower labor cost per unit of output. They can thus sell at lower prices and take away more and more business from the union plants. In practice the unionized plants may be able to increase productivity somewhat to offset the wage pressure, or they may be willing in the short run to accept lower profit margins. But as the gap between the union and nonunion wage widens, more and more of the unionized companies will have to suspend operations. The demand curve for *union labor,* then, may look like the dashed line D_1 in Figure 15-2.

In considering the wage-employment tradeoff, then, union leaders are operating on D_1 rather than on D. Given the same basic wage-employment preferences on the part of union members, we can predict that the union's wage target will be lower under partial unionization than under full unionization. For example, if the union were fully unionized, the union might prefer point A, with a wage W_1, some 30 percent above the competitive wage, and a moderate decline in employment. But with partial unionization, the wage W_1 would land at point C, with a large cut in employment that would provoke a membership revolt. So the union may prefer to settle at point B, with a wage W_2, 10 percent above the competitive level but with only a small sacrifice of employment.

The research evidence, to be outlined in Chapter 20, confirms this prediction. There is a clear positive relationship between the percentage of an industry that is organized and the size of the union's wage advantage.

Bargaining Over Wages and Employment

We now take another step beyond the models used in earlier sections. In those models, while the union takes into account the employment effect of any wage bargain, it does not bargain directly over the level of employment. It bargains only for a certain wage level. Then the employer, moving along the demand curve, chooses the employment level corresponding to that wage. If the union has estimated the demand schedule correctly, there will be no surprises in this process.

But we know that in practice many unions do bargain over employment as well as over wage rates. They require the company to hire more workers than it would hire voluntarily at that wage, that is, they force the company off its demand curve to the right. Under strict competitive assumptions, such a move would be impossible. The demand curve shows how many workers the company can hire and still earn a competitive rate of return. To require more will put the company out of business.

We can make sense of the observed facts only by supposing that the demand curve D in Figure 15-3 does not indicate the most the employer can do. There is a higher true maximum, shown by the curve D_1, which opens up room for negotiation. But what possible explanations can we find for the existence of D_1, which seems to contradict the normal assumptions of price theory?

1. One possibility is that the company in question is a monopolist or an oligopolist that by controlling product prices and deterring new entrants is able to earn more than a competitive rate of return. Then the union can demand a share of these monopoly gains and can push the company as far as the line D_1. At any point on D_1 the company is earning only a competitive rate of return.
2. Another possibility is that the employer is a government agency. The demand curve D is based on the agency's present budget. But this limit is somewhat flexible—pushing beyond it will not put the agency out of business. The union can bargain for wage-employment terms that require a larger budget, presumably financed by higher taxes. Here the line D_1 could be interpreted as a "taxpayer resistance line," beyond which government officials will not go for fear of political consequences.
3. In many private industries, including automobile, steel, and textiles, unions have worked with industry representatives to lobby for import restrictions to increase the demand for domestic output and thus also for union workers.
4. Let us consider the case where the demand for labor is increasing. At present the labor demand schedule is D, with W_1 the union rate and E_1 the level of employ-

ment. But product demand is rising, either for industry-specific reasons or as part of a general economic upswing. So on the average, over the next contract period, the labor demand schedule is estimated to be D_1. The question facing the union is how this demand increase can best be exploited. Taking up all the slack by an increase in employment would mean moving from point A to point C. On the other hand, taking all the gain in a wage increase, leaving employment unchanged, would mean moving from A to B.

What target will the union select? Presumably, some point on D_1 that is the locus of maximum employer concessions. And probably some point along the segment BC. The reason is that a union is normally more concerned with preventing a worsening of conditions—a reduction in either wages or employment—than with achieving any particular improvement in conditions. This strategy is grounded in members' preferences. Members do not like either taking a wage cut or being forced out of employment. They are more flexible about the form that improvements will take.

The union, then, will be reluctant to move to the right of C or to the left of B. In choosing where to settle along BC, leaders will be guided by median member preferences as explained previously. The union target, of course, will rarely be achieved in full. The employer will resist being forced as far as D_1, and will try to achieve a point some distance to the left. The eventual bargain, then, will be in the

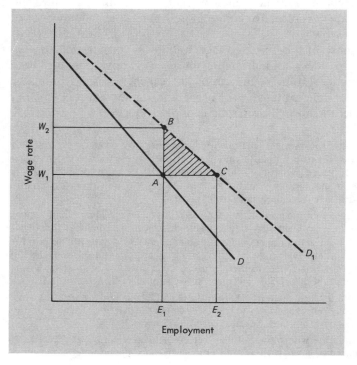

FIGURE 15-3 Bargaining Over Wages and Employment

shaded area *ACB*. But just where depends on the relative bargaining power of the parties, a subject to be examined in Chapter 16.

THE FUNCTION AND OUTLOOK OF MANAGEMENT

Turning to management, we may begin by examining the economic function of the business firm. The picture of the business concern in economic textbooks is considerably simplified, partly because of the emphasis that economists have placed on the theory of pure competition. Under purely competitive conditions the prices that must be paid for all factors of production are strictly determined by the market, and the prices of the company's products are similarly determined. The only decision left to management concerns the method of production to be used. On closer investigation, however, it turns out that management has no real choice even in this respect. By the definition of pure competition, new producers are free to enter the industry at will. Unless a particular company uses the most efficient possible methods, therefore, it will not be able to keep pace with rival producers. It will find itself losing money and will eventually have to go out of business. Under purely competitive conditions, in short, the business concern is a puppet maneuvered by the general forces of supply and demand.

In practice, however, we know that management does do some managing. There is scope for initiative and judgment. The main reason is that most business concerns operate under conditions of imperfect competition. They are sheltered in greater or lesser degree from the full sweep of market forces.

The price of labor, for example, is not completely determined by market forces; it can be altered within limits by management decision or union-management negotiations. Prices of purchased materials and equipment are frequently open to bargaining. The types, specifications, and prices of the products that the company sells can usually be adjusted. Production methods can be altered. The upshot is that competing companies in the same industry may show quite different levels of cost and profit. Every industry has its high-cost and low-cost producers. That is partly due to factors other than management; but managerial skill and ingenuity do make a difference.

The Significance of Profit

Our economy is sometimes described as a *profit system,* or as being guided by the *profit motive.* Economists often assume that each business concern attempts to make as large a profit as possible, the principle of *profit maximization.* How much is there to this, and what is its significance for collective bargaining?

There is a large literature on the motivation of corporate executives and the objectives of the business firm. There is widespread agreement that to maximize profit at each moment of time is an impossible task, mainly because of continual changes in profit and factor markets. Executives aim rather to achieve a "reasonable" or "normal" or "safe" level of profit.

Why is this considered necessary? First, profit provides a margin of security for the company. The higher the company's profit margin, the further it can fall if business turns bad. Second, profit is important as a return to present and prospective investors in the company. Stockholders who find their dividends falling are likely to become discontented with the management and may try to do something about it. A low rate of profit may make it difficult for the company to raise funds for expansion by floating new securities. Third, profits are themselves a source of funds for expansion of plant. Reinvested earnings are the main source of capital for expansion. A low rate of profit may mean that the company will have insufficient funds to finance projects that would help to increase profit. Fourth, profits are an index of management success. The management that is not able to turn in as good a profit rate as other companies in its industry or finds its profit rate declining from year to year is apt to be critical of its own performance. The profit rate is often reflected directly in management salaries and bonuses. Even where it is not, any manager likes to feel that he or she is "up to par" with others.

Some of the difficulties of controlling bargaininig arise from the difference in the way profits are regarded by management and by union officials. In the eyes of management, profit is not merely a legitimate form of income but an essential element in the operation of a private enterprise system. The expectation or hope of profit is a major incentive to managerial efficiency and serves to call forth capital investment in new enterprises. Realized profits are a major source of funds for expansion of existing businesses. A positive rate of profit is thus an essential condition for economic growth and development.

Most union leaders would not quarrel with this idea in principle. Their enthusiasm over profits is more restrained than that of management people, however, and their idea of a "reasonable" rate of profit is apt to be more modest. They sometimes talk as though the net income of a company were a simple surplus performing no function in the economy, a pool into which the union can dip at will without any economic consequence. Management people object strenuously to this view.

There is also a general feeling among management people that profits are none of the union's business anyway. Management believes that the company should pay "fair wages," which usually means fair in comparison with what other employers are paying for similar work. If management can pay fair wages and still make large profits, that is purely management's business. Union officers and members, on the other hand, feel that high profits should be shared with workers in the enterprise through better wages. The workers have helped to produce these profits, it is argued, and hence should be entitled to a share in them. When a company is taking losses, however, the two parties usually switch sides in the argument. The union is apt to argue that the company should still pay fair wages and that its losses are of no concern to the union, while the company will now argue that losses should be taken into account.

A further source of difficulty is that the relevant profit figure in collective bargaining is the estimated profit for the year ahead. Past profits are bygones. The union and management are bargaining over how much the company can afford to pay *next year,* not *last year.* The decision involves forecasts of future sales volume, product prices, material costs, and numerous other things. Sales volume, which depends so largely on general business conditions, is especially hard to forecast in many industries, and a small change in volume may make a large difference in the firm's profit position. Faced with these uncertainties, management typically tries to play it safe, to leave some margin for a possible downturn in business, to make a conservative estimate of probable profits. Union leaders, on the other hand, have a strong interest in taking a rosy view of the future, estimating profits at a high level, and trying to get wages set accordingly. The union, in short, is constantly trying to get management to stick its neck out farther than management likes to do.

This complication is a serious one for collective bargaining. If sales and profits for the next year could be known with certainty, if management could be sure just how much it was giving away and how much it would have left after paying a specified rate of wages, negotiations would be simpler than they actually are.

MANAGEMENT AND UNIONS: CONFLICT AND COOPERATION

We have discussed the views and objectives of both unions and management. Both parties have many common interests. For example, high sales and adequate profits are necessary for a healthy firm, one that can stay in business and provide steady employment for its workers. Despite the common interests that exist between employers and union, the emphasis in negotiation is often on areas of disagreement and conflict. Conflict between the parties, especially when it leads to a strike, is the most dramatic aspect of negotiations and thus receives the most publicity. As we saw in Chapter 14, management became more aggressive in opposing unions in the seventies and eighties, thus increasing conflict between labor and management both at the workplace and politically. Because conflict is important, we turn next to a further discussion of sources of tension between management and unions. Then we return to areas of cooperation and discuss how the bad times in the seventies and eighties led not only to increased conflict but also to many cases of greater labor-management cooperation.

Sources of Tension between Unions and Management

In the modern corporation pursuit of efficiency requires coordination of the efforts of hundreds or thousands of individuals. The business manager is not just an expert in production techniques. He is the leader of an organization, the captain of a team. Successful performance of his function requires that he have wide latitude in making decisions and that he have "cooperation" or "teamwork" from those under him. To most management people teamwork seems to mean mainly fealty—a willing acceptance of managerial decisions and an earnest effort to execute them. It leaves room for tactful and "constructive" criticism of particular decisions but no room for any challenge to management's right to make these decisions. The ideal situation is one in which the manager functions as a benevolent monarch. No one questions her authority, but her exercise of authority is so just and reasonable that her subordinates esteem rather than fear her. The feeling that one has been fair even when one did not have to be is probably one the greatest satisfactions obtainable from a management position.

All this leads to a characteristic management view of satisfactory industrial relations, which has been summarized by Bakke in four major principles:

> Industrial relations are primarily and basically a matter of relations between management and employees, its own employees.
>
> The first objective of industrial relations, like that of every function of management, is the economic welfare of the particular company.
>
> Industrial relations arrangements must leave unimpaired management's prerogatives and freedom essential to the meeting of management's responsibilities.
>
> All parties to industrial relations should be businesslike and responsible.[5]

Trade unionism challenges these cardinal points in management's philosophy. It interposes between employer and employee the trade union, which many managers believe is more interested in its own growth and power than in the economic welfare of either workers or the company. It refuses to accept survival and profitability of the company as the sole aim of business management. It interferes with management's effort to achieve lowest money cost of production and with the freedom of maneuver that most managers consider essential to successful performance of their functions.

Management opposition to unionism is based partly on self-interest. Being human, managers dislike a reduction in their authority just because it is a reduction. Unionism also makes the manager's job harder by increasing the number of people whose agreement must be secured for a given decision and by presenting the risk that agreement may not always be secured. If a lower executive of the company refuses to comply with a decision of top management, that executive can be removed from office; but management cannot fire the union or its officials. Unionism increases the number of conflicting pressures that converge on management. Between the insistent demands of organized workers for more money, customers for lower prices, and the board of directors for larger profits, the manager may be ground to pieces. In all these ways, unionism increases the amount of frustration, personal insecurity, and nervous wear and tear to which management is subjected.

It is too narrow a view, however, to regard management opposition to unionism as entirely self-interested. Most managers believe that unionism, by limiting managerial initiative and discretion, strikes directly at the roots of economic progress and rising national income. Unionism thus tends in the long run to reduce rather than raise the real income of the working class. This conviction is held just as firmly and sincerely as the conviction of union leaders that they are leading a drive for social progress.

---

[5]E. Wight Bakke, *Mutual Survival* (New York: Harper & Row, Publishers, 1946), pp. 2–3.

Another element in the differing outlook of managers and unionists is the difference in their personal background and experience. Most top management officials in American corporations come from business and professional families and have been to college. Only a small percentage have engaged in manual labor at any stage of their careers. The day-to-day problems of the plant worker are something they have read about in business school csaebooks, but have not experienced directly. Contrast this with the background of the union official, almost invariably a former worker, short on formal training but long on plant experience. It is not surprising that the two groups view the world of industry differently and have different conceptions of "proper" personnel management.

The general outlook of management toward unionism, then, is critical and sometimes hostile. Concrete strategies, however, differ greatly from one situation to the next. They range all the way from forcible opposition and a determination to get rid of the union at one extreme, through various shades of reluctant acceptance, to positive cooperation with the union at the other pole.

Labor-Management Cooperation

The emphasis in much bargaining is on conflict, on how to divide a given pie. For example, let us assume that union and management both expect the firm's sales revenue to increase by 10 percent annually for the next three years, with the increase coming equally from the sale of more units and higher prices per unit. Explicit agreement, especially at this level of detail, is most unlikely, but implicit agreement on a qualitative assessment of future trends is fairly common.

Given some agreement concerning future expectations, the parties typically will focus on how much of the explicit increase in sales revenue should be devoted to raising wage rates rather than being left to management for other purposes, including investment in new plant and equipment, reducing present debts, and increasing the compensation of nonunion employees, including top management. Such bargaining is called *distributive bargaining*.

As Walton and McKersie have emphasized, labor negotiations involve much more than distributive bargaining.[6] The major alternative to distributional bargaining is *integrative bargaining*. Such bargaining seeks to increase the total gains available to both parties. Instead of seeking only to divide a given pie, as with distributive bargaining, the negotiators also try to increase the size of the pie.

Unlike most economic transactions, which involve short-term relations between a buyer and a seller, collective bargaining is a long-term relationship. It is more like a marriage than a date. As in a marriage, the two parites can concentrate on what divides them or on how they can live together effectively. The analogy isn't perfect. Obviously, emotional sharing and caring are more important in marriages than in union-management relations. For our purposes, the following differences are most important. First, although the firm can seek a divorce from the union if the relationship turns sour, there is no ready way for it to win such a divorce without the

---

[6]Richard E. Walton and Robert E. McKersie, *A Behavioral Theory of Labor Negotiations.*

workers' consent. The union is even less likely to be able to divorce the firm. The closest it can come to doing so is the occasional case where the union may be able to precipitate a change of management. The union exists to represent the workers in a bargaining unit or a collection of bargaining units. Without the firm, the bargaining unit ceases to exist.

Because neither management nor labor can easily divorce the other, their relationship is usually a long-lasting one. When each party does anticipate a long-term relationship, then it makes sense for each to seek good communication with the other and to look for areas of mutual gain rather than to focus mainly on areas of conflict.

Despite the frequent increase in conflict between labor and management in recent years, there have also been many examples of increased cooperation. The same increase in competitive pressures that has caused many firms to make greater efforts to remain nonunion, if they can do so, has also created greater incentive for management and unions to develop new strategies of cooperation to reduce unit costs and thus to save jobs. Such cooperation is most likely when (1) the firm is in danger of going out of business or at least of having to give permanent-layoff notices to many senior workers, (2) the union has a strong presence at the firm, and (3) when the two parties have proven to be reasonably trustworthy in their past dealings. The secure position of the union is important, since it means the firm cannot expect to eliminate the union by breaking a strike or winning a decertification election. Nor can it expect to significantly reduce the union's influence by expanding production at existing nonunion plants or by building new plants where the union might not be able to organize the work force.

In recent years two types of labor-management cooperation have received the most attention, quality of working life (QWL) programs and concession bargaining.

QWL programs attempt to give workers more control over their jobs. The types of issues covered by such programs range from relatively simple issues involving working conditions, such as lighting and ventilation, to more complex issues of work organization, such as how great a variety of tasks each worker should perform and whether a team or assembly-line approach should be used.

In the early 1980s union-management cooperation became most apparent in the area of concession bargaining, which arose because of the pressures of foreign competition, competition from domestic nonunion firms, and low aggregate demand during the recession of 1982–83. Under concession bargaining a union agrees to help the firm reduce its labor costs by lowering wage rates, allowing more flexible work rules, or making other, similar changes in the contract. The aim is to save jobs, often in return for other benefits, such as profit sharing, so that the workers can share in any of the firm's future gains.

In both QWL and concession bargaining the main gain to the firm is lower labor costs per unit of output. For QWL the main gain for the workers is greater job satisfaction, while the main gain under concession bargaining has been greater employment security. We shall discuss these issues in greater detail in Chapter 17.

SUMMARY

1. Economic models of union behavior treat the union like a business firm, that is, as a monopolist trying to maximize some monetary quality. This is a misunderstanding of how a union operates and does not provide a good basis for predicting union demands.

2. The union is a political organization, whose leaders try to remain in office by correctly estimating the preferences of union members. These preferences differ among members, so the leader must develop policies that satisfy more than half the membership. This approach is usually called a *median voter model.*

3. Assume first that the union bargains only over wages, while the company determines employment by moving along the demand curve. The union's wage target will be some point on the demand curve (above the competitive wage), its location depending on the elasticity of the demand curve and on the wage-employment preferences of the median union member.

4. More realistically, a union often bargains over both wages and employment, that is, it tries to push the company off its labor demand curve. Under strict competitive assumptions, this is impossible, but there are several reasons why it may be possible in actuality.

5. Economists generally assume that the objective of the firm is *profit maximization.* In order to survive, the firm needs to maintain adequate profits. Management and the union typically view profits rather differently, with management seeing the need for a higher profit rate than the union. Management is also likely to be more conservative than the union in its estimates of future profits and thus more skeptical of its ability to pay for the union's wage demands.

6. While union and management have important conflicts in their objectives, they also have many common interests, especially in the survival of the firm and of the jobs it provides. Thus there is an incentive for cooperation as well as for conflict between union and management. Cooperation is most likely if the firm is in danger of going out of business, if the union is securely established at the firm, and if the firm and the union have both proven trustworthy in the past.

7. Two types of labor-management cooperation have received considerable attention in recent years, quality-of-working-life (QWL) programs and concession bargaining.

KEY CONCEPTS

MARGINAL WORKER
MEDIAN VOTER MODEL
PROFIT MAXIMIZATION
DISTRIBUTIVE BARGAINING

INTEGRATIVE BARGAINING
CONCESSION BARGAINING
QUALITY-OF-WORKING-LIFE (QWL) PROGRAM

REVIEW QUESTIONS

1. How does a union's wage-setting problem differ from the price-setting problem of a business monopolist?

2. Describe what factors union leaders typically consider when they formulate their wage demands.

3. Why may workers differ in their preference for money compensation as opposed to employment security? Is it reasonable to suppose that union leaders will be guided by the preferences of the median member?

4. What is meant by "pushing the company off its labor demand curve"? Under what conditions may a union be able to do it?

5. "The profit motive plays a much different role among managers of a large unionized corporation than it does in the typical economics textbook." Discuss.

6. What features of a manager's job produce a natural opposition to unions?

READINGS

ATHERTON, WALLACE N., *Theory of Union Bargaining Goals*. Princeton, N. J.: Princeton University Press, 1973.

DERTOUZAS, JAMES S., and JOHN H. PENCAVEL, "Wage and Employment Determination under Trade Unionism: The International Typographical Union," *Journal of Economy* (December 1981), pp. 1162–81.

DUNLOP, JOHN T., *Wage Determination under Trade Unions*. New York: Macmillan, 1944.

PENCAVEL, JOHN H., "The Tradeoff between Wages and Employment in Trade Union Objectives," *Quarterly Journal of Economics* (May 1984), pp. 215–31.

WALTON, RICHARD E., and ROBERT E. McKERSIE, *A Behavioral Theory of Labor Negotiations*. New York: McGraw-Hill Book Co. 1965.

16

BARGAINING

In this chapter we discuss the collective bargaining process and bargaining theory. First we consider the scope of the bargaining unit; for example, whether it involves one or many firms, whether it is local or national, and what occupations are included. Then we discuss the process of bargaining. Negotiating a new contract is a highly stylized game, with ground rules that are understood and observed by both parties. These include rules about the timing of negotiations, the selection of negotiators, the agenda for discussion, the main stages of negotiation, and the ratification of a new contract.

The outcome of the negotiations depends partly on the relative *bargaining power* of the parties. What meaning can we give to this elusive concept? What are the main determinants of bargaining power? These turn out to be partly economic, but partly structural and tactical, and we'll examine how they operate.

Bargaining usually ends in a new agreement, arrived at peaceably with no interruption of production—usually, but not always. In some cases the discussions end in an impasse or deadlock, and a strike follows. We'll look at the situations that most commonly lead to a deadlock and a strike and discuss the costs of strikes.

THE SCOPE OF BARGAINING UNITS

The size of the bargaining unit affects the complexity of the negotiations and the likelihood that professional negotiators will be involved. In addition, the scope of the bargaining unit is itself a matter for negotiation. Each side generally seeks a bargaining unit whose size and composition will increase its bargaining power.

The scope of agreements is strongly influenced by the area over which employers compete in the sale of their products. The basic distinction here is between local-market industries and industries in which competition is regional or national.

Local Bargaining

Where competition is limited to the immediate locality, citywide agreements are likely to develop. That is the typical situation in housing construction, hotel and restaurant work, printing, local trucking and warehousing, retail trade, laundry and dry cleaning, barber shops, and other local industries.

The individual employer in these industries is typically small and in a weak position to negotiate separately with the union. So after a little experience, employers often decide to pool their strength in a bargaining association. The result is a single agreement reached by bargaining between representatives of the employers' association and representatives of the union.

A master agreement with the union has several advantages from the employers' standpoint. It enables the employers to meet the union on more equal terms. It also places employers on an equal competitive footing as regards wage rates and other items in labor cost; the "chiseler" can no longer undercut the employer who pays a "decent" wage. Moreover, the agreement with the union can often be used to police price fixing and other monopolistic practices within the industry. Union and employers, instead of fighting each other, can unite to levy tribute from consumers.

While there is strong pressure in local-market industries to standardize terms of employment *within* each locality, there is no similar pressure for equalization *among* localities. Bricklaying in Pittsburgh does not compete with bricklaying in Minneapolis, and there is no reason why the union scale should be the same. Union scales in building, printing, and similar industries vary a good deal throughout the country, and national union control over local settlements is loose.

Regional or National Bargaining

Turning to companies that operate on a regional or national basis, we can distinguish three main situations: (1) *association bargaining,* where the union negotiates with an employers' association, usually on a national basis; (2) *company bargaining,* where the union negotiates for establishments operated by a single company; and (3) *pattern bargaining,* where the union negotiates separately with each company, but there is a strong effort to secure similar terms from all of them.

1. Association Bargaining.   This is the standard form of bargaining in most European countries. In the United States, it is the exception, partly because of the continental scope of the economy, partly because of greater individualism and resistance to unionism on the part of employers. Still, association bargaining has developed in a number of industries. Some of these are small-scale, highly competitive industries such as men's and women's clothing, hosiery, pottery, and canning. Here employers have little confidence in their own strength and band together for mutual protection. Both employers and the union find a master agreement convenient in enforcing minimum labor standards and "putting a floor under competition." At the same time these are industries in which union leverage is small. If the union raises wages appreciably above the competitive level, nonunion shops will spring up and flourish. In industries such as clothing, which use little fixed capital, employers often seek to escape the union by migrating to other areas.

Major industries in which association bargaining has developed under union pressure include bituminous coal mining, over-the-road truck transportation, basic steel production, longshoring, merchant shipping, and railroading. In many of these cases, however, association bargaining has declined as a result of the economic pressures of the 1980s.

2. Company Bargaining.   In terms of number of union contracts, this is the commonest bargaining structure. One reason is that union organizing campaigns and National Labor Relations Board (NLRB) elections are on a company-by-company basis. If a union wins the election in a particular company, the NLRB certifies it as bargaining agent *for that company*. The NLRB does not certify multiemployer units, so such units have to be established by voluntary agreement of companies and unions.

In the case of "natural monopolies" the company is the industry, and single-company bargaining follows automatically. Each of the unionized electric power companies negotiates separately. So does each regional telephone company, although the union has pressed unsuccessfully for national telephone negotiations.

Single-company bargaining is also the prevalent form in manufacturing. Large manufacturing corporations, resistant to unionism in general, have been especially resistant to industrywide bargaining, which they feel solidifies the union's position and increases its bargaining power. They also feel strong enough to go it alone. Most unions would probably prefer multiemployer bargaining; but they have not pressed the issue, partly because they can achieve somewhat the same result through the pattern bargaining technique described below.

In the airline industry, unlike other branches of transportation, each company bargains separately. Organization is by crafts, with separate unions for airline pilots, flight engineers, flight attendants, clerical workers, and maintenance mechanics. Also, except for the pilots there are two or more rival unions in each craft. The multiplicity of negotiations and contracts and the constant jockeying for position by rival unions has produced turbulence in labor unions and a considerable number of strikes.

3. Pattern Bargaining.   This is single-company bargaining with a difference. Here the union selects the largest, or one of the largest, companies in the industry and begins its bargaining activitites with that company, calling a strike if necessary. The contract terms eventually agreed on are then held to constitute a "pattern" for the industry as a whole. The union moves on to negotiations with other companies, attempting to secure identical terms from them. As we shall see, however, there is often some divergence from the pattern, especially in smaller companies and in those making somewhat different product lines. Pattern bargaining is thus a matter of degree and shades over into ordinary single-company bargaining.

Craft Units versus Industrial Units

A further issue is whether the bargaining unit should involve all the company's union workers or should be smaller. Should skilled crafts people be grouped with other employees, or should they be entitled to bargain separately?

As we have seen, skilled workers were the first to organize into unions. In industries employing mainly skilled workers each craft union usually bargains separately. This is the traditional pattern in building construction, printing, railroading, and truck transport. In other cases, while all employees bargain as a unit, this unit is dominated by a single craft, such as coal miners or truck drivers.

The choice between craft and industrial units arises most clearly in manufacturing, where most employees are unskilled or semiskilled production workers but where there is also a minority of electricians, carpenters, machinists, and other craft groups. The old AFL, dominated by craft unions, took the view that each craft was entitled to organize and bargain separately; but in fact unions made little progress in manufacturing before the 1930s. This led the leaders of the clothing workers, Mine Workers, and other industrial unions to form a separate Congress of Industrial Organizations (CIO), dedicated to organizing all employees in manufacturing plants into inclusive units. Between 1936 and 1941 the CIO succeeded in organizing the major companies in basic steel, automobiles, tires, electrical equipment, meat packing, oil refining, and a number of other industries.

While industrial units composed of all employees are dominant in manufacturing, the issue is not entirely settled. It arises when the NLRB has to define the scope of the election unit when a union is seeking to organize previously nonunion employees. It arises also in reconsidering the boundaries of old bargaining units. Even though an industrial unit has been recognized in the past, a craft group can petition the NLRB for "clarification," that is, reconsideration of the bargaining structure and possible establishment of a separate craft unit. This arrangment is known as *craft severance*. In considering such petitions the board takes account of the collective bargaining history in the company and industry, the makeup and expressed preference of the craft group, the qualifications of the petitioning union, and other factors. While craft severance is sometimes granted, it is rather unusual.

The economic significance of the issue depends on whether the basis of organization affects the union's wage-raising power. It is usually argued that a craft union has more power to push up the wages of its members, since these wages form only part of the employer's labor costs. But there are counterarguments, to which we will return in Chapter 20.

CONTRACT NEGOTIATIONS: PROCEDURE AND STAGES

Timing of Negotiations

Union contracts in the United States run for a specified period, usually either two or three years; and the approach of the contract expiration date triggers the beginning of new negotiations. There is nothing inevitable about this procedure. In Britain, for example, agreements have no expiration date, and negotiations may be requested by either party at any time. The U.S. procedure is simply a convention, which concentrates bargaining activity into periodic intervals with periods of relative quiet in between.

The contract usually provides that if either party wishes a change in contract terms, it must give notice to this effect so many days before the expiration date. Such notice is almost invariably given, since it is rare for a contract to be renewed without change. There is also a legal provision that the federal mediation service must be notified sixty days before the contract expiration date so that it may have an opportunity to keep in touch with negotiations in important cases.

A further ground rule is that if agreement on terms of a new contract is not reached before the old one expires, a strike results automatically—"no contract, no work." This sets a deadline for the discussions, and negotiations become more intensive and more serious as the deadline approaches. The union may decide, however, to ignore the rule and to keep its members at work while negotiations continue. It might do so, for example, if the expiration date comes at a time of low activity in the industry, when a strike would put little pressure on employers. Or if the parties feel they are very close to agreement when the deadline arrives, the old contract may be extended for a short time by mutual agreement.

Selection and Authority of Negotiators

The next important point is that negotiations are conducted by *delegates* of the parties, who usually do not themselves have power to conclude an agreement. This obviously complicates the bargaining process. Terms that the negotiators themselves would consider acceptable may be vetoed by higher company officials or the union membership. It also enlarges the room for tactical maneuvering. A negotiator on either side may resist certain terms on the ground (genuine or alleged) that he would not be able to "sell" these terms to his superiors.

Who are the negotiators, and how are they selected? On the union side it will be simplest to begin with a local union negotiating with one or more employers in its area. As the expiration date of the old contract approaches, the demands to be served on the employer will probably be discussed at a general membership meeting. A committee will then be appointed to put the demands into better shape and to draft proposed terms for a new contract.

After the drafting committee has done its best, the proposed contract terms are taken back to another membership meeting. There they are discussed at length, perhaps revised, and eventually approved. A negotiating committee is then selected to meet with management. The committee will normally include the chief officers of the local, but it may include other members as well. The national union representative for the area normally sits in on the negotiations and frequently plays a leading role. At some point prior to or during negotiations a strike vote of the membership will usually be taken. This does not necessarily mean that a strike is going to occur. The purpose is to strengthen the union representatives' hand by advance authorization to call a strike if negotiations with the employer break down.

After the union negotiators feel they have won as much as they can from management, they must come back to the membership for approval of the new contract before it becomes valid. In many unions the contract must also be approved by the national office. One reason a national union representative participates is to ensure that the terms will be in conformity with national policy.

Preparation for regional or national negotiations or for bargaining with a major pattern-setting employer is considerably more complicated. National union officers normally take a leading role in such negotiations. Proposed union demands are hammered out by the national executive board and then submitted for discussion to a conference of delegates from the local unions and district organizations. Depending on bargaining practices, this conference may cover the entire industry throughout the country or all local unions dealing with a particular employer, or some other grouping. After revision and ratification of demands by the conference, the union negotiators begin discussions with management representatives. At the end of the process the proposed contract terms must usually be reported back to the conference for further discussion and approval.

On the management side contract negotiations are usually conducted by a small group of top management officials. In a small or medium-sized company the president may serve as chief management negotiator. In large organizations this responsibility is more likely to fall on the executive vice-president or some other line official. The chief counsel and the treasurer frequently participate, and several top production officials normally sit in on the negotiations. The industrial relations director and members of his staff take part as expert advisers. Where the industrial relations director is a forceful individual with high status in the company, he or she may even serve as chief company spokesperson.

The management representatives, like the union negotiating committee, begin to formulate their position well in advance of the start of negotiations. An effort is made to anticipate the main union demands and to determine a position on them. Management may itself want to take the initiative on certain points. Management initiative in presenting demands instead of simply responding to union demands is commoner today than it was ten or twenty years ago. Anything that requires a major change in company policy must normally be ratified in advance by the board of directors or the executive committee. Proposals involving money also require advance ratification. The management representatives go into negotiations with instructions that they may not raise the company's labor costs by more than a certain figure. If they are unable to reach agreement with the union within the specific limits, they must go back to the board for further discussion.[1]

Where there is multiemployer bargaining, representatives of the various companies involved will be called together for a preliminary conference. If there is a formal association, members of the association staff may take a prominent part in working out proposals to the union. Important conflicts of interest may have to be faced and resolved. Some companies, for example, may be in a comfortable profit position and able to afford substantial wage increases. Other companies closer to the margin may feel obliged to fight any increase in costs. These and other differences must be compromised in order to present a united front to the union. After policy has been determined, the actual conduct of negotiations is usually delegated to a small committee of the most experienced and influential company representatives.

The Agenda for Discussion

Negotiations between nations are often two-stage negotiations. The parties first must agree on what they are going to discuss. Each side tries to put on the agenda items on which it hopes to score gains and to keep off the agenda items that might be harmful to its interests or on which it is determined to make no concessions. Only after the agenda is settled do the parties proceed to substantive negotiations.

In collective bargaining, on the other hand, these two stages are merged. There is no advance agenda. At the first negotiating session, the union representatives present their full list of demands, and the management representatives list the changes they would like to see in the new contract. The agenda is obtained simply by combining the "shopping lists" of the parties, and substantive discussion of these items begins at once. Occasionally, one side objects that a certain topic "is not a proper subject for collective bargaining"; but such objections have not been very successful. In general, either side may raise any issue it chooses, and all these issues become part of the bargaining agenda.

The agenda usually includes dozens or scores of items. This leaves room to trade concessions on some items against gains on others. The agenda can be divided broadly into:

1. *Cost items*, including basic wages, fringe benefits, and rules that directly affect labor costs, such as overtime.
2. *Noncost items*, such as union security arrangements or the seniority system, where the cost effect is so indirect that no measurement of it is attempted. Cost items are readily tradable against each other, since each side can measure approximately what it is yielding or getting. Trading between cost and noncost items is also possible.

---

[1] In one case that came to the author's attention the management negotiators were instructed by the board of directors that they could not concede more than five cents an hour. Agreement on this basis appeared impossible, so the vice-president conducting the negotiations came back to the board with an earnest plea that he be allowed to go up to eight cents. After he had made an eloquent statement of his case, the president burst out laughing and said, "Why, that's fine! We were willing to go to ten cents all along!"

A complete draft settlement, including tentative provisions on all major items, is known as a *package,* and both sides usually adhere to what may be termed the *package convention.* The items on the agenda are discussed one at a time—many of them more than once—with each side indicating the concessions and trades it might be willing to make. It is understood, however, that agreement on each item is tentative until agreement has been reached on the total package. If total agreement proves impossible and negotiations break down, each party is free to withdraw these tentative concessions and start bargaining all over again. Realistically, however, the statements that have been made in the course of negotiations cannot really be erased from people's minds.

Stages of Negotiation

Although the course of negotiations is never the same in any two situations, one can distinguish several standard phases. The first of these—presentation of initial demands—typically reveals a wide gap between the positions of the parties. The union wants the moon, while management does not want to concede anything and may want important concessions from the union.

Next comes a period of probing, which in a large negotiation may last for weeks, during which each side questions the other's demands at length. Clause-by-clause questioning of the other party produces various kinds of information; the detailed contents of a particular proposal, the reasons it is considered necessary, the kinds of factual data that have been assembled to support it, sometimes a preliminary indication of the firmness with which the demand is held.

At this stage the negotiating group is usually scaled down to more manageable size—a few key people on each side who have authority to make concessions and decisions. Discussions can move more rapidly in such a group and can also be more frank and informal. Each side continues to probe the other's position while trying to protect its own freedom of maneuver. There may be indications of willingness to make concessions on certain items. Some of the less controversial issues may be resolved and set aside, subject to the general rule that no one subject is regarded as settled until all items in dispute have been settled. For the key issues in dispute, each side may eventually indicate one or more *packages*—combinations of terms—that it would consider acceptable. The contents of these package proposals are significant in indicating which demands the parties are really serious about.

The packages put forward by the two sides, however, are likely still to be some distance apart. What forces further concessions and final compromise is the approach of the deadline date, after which a strike will occur. The imminence of a strike, with the attendant costs and uncertainties for both sides, forces each party to reexamine its position realistically and to ask, "Is it really worth it?" This usually leads to a lowering of union demands and a raising of management offers to the point where they overlap and settlement becomes possible. More than four out of every five contract negotiations carried out in the United States each year result in agreement without a strike. The possibility of a strike, however, is a central feature of the bargaining process and the main force making for ultimate agreement.

A work stoppage, while marking a crisis, does not bring an end to negotiations. The issues in dispute must still be resolved. The only difference is that the costs of a stoppage, which previously were potential, have now become actual. As the strike lengthens and costs mount on both sides, there is growing pressure on the parties to make further concessions to bring the strike to an end. Occasionally a strike ends in a closing down of the enterprise; and occasionally it just dies quietly, with the strikers trickling back to work or being replaced by strike breakers. But the normal outcome is an agreement on new contract terms. A strike is one route to agreement.

Ratification of Agreement

At the end of the road comes ratification of the agreement by company and union. A few unions empower their negotiators to reach a binding agreement. In others, including the United Steelworkers, the agreement is ratified by a policy committee operating at one remove from the membership. By far the commonest procedure, however, is ratification by membership vote.

Ratification by referendum vote involves the possibility of rejection. Although there are no statistics on the frequency with which members reject the terms recommended by their leaders, experienced observers place it at about 10 percent of cases.

Rejection does not always mean what it appears to mean. The union negotiators may pretend to agree to certain terms and may submit them to the membership but openly or secretly urge the members to reject them. The membership vote is a bargaining gambit, used to justify additional demands. In other cases the negotiators may submit a tentative agreement to the members without any recommendation, simply to test membership sentiment. A negative vote in this case is an indication to the negotiators to try for more.

But there are also genuine rejections. The union leaders believe that the terms they have secured are reasonable and acceptable and recommend them to the members; the members proceed to vote them down. When this happens, it is usually because the package lacks certain components highly valued by the membership. Contracts have been voted down because of provisions relating to work assignments, seniority rights, shift preferences, rotation of job assignments, work scheduling, and specific working conditions. The commonest reason for rejection appears to be a failure of communication within the union, so that the leaders' conceptions of what is acceptable fails to accord with reality. In some cases factional strife within the union is a contributing factor. Leaders aspiring to union office urge members to reject terms recommended by those in office, as a step toward displacing the existing leaders.

APPROACHES TO BARGAINING THEORY

Before discussing the theory of bargaining, we should first note two key characteristics of collective bargaining. The first is the pervasive importance of *uncertainty*. Contract negotiations are oriented toward the future, usually toward the next three

·years. Who can say what the economic climate will be over this period? What will happen to general business activity and to the sales and profits of the company engaged in bargaining? What will happen to the consumer price level and hence to the wage increases required to maintain workers' living standards? In addition to these economic uncertainties, there is some uncertainty about the preference systems of union members and about their willingness to strike in support of their demands. Union officials presumably know more about these things than management people, but even they cannot be certain. The opposing positions put forth in bargaining, therefore, rest partly on differing perceptions of the future. And an important feature of negotiations is an effort to change the perceptions of the opposing party, to convince the opponent that your perception of the future is more nearly correct.

A second characteristic is the multidimensional character of bargaining. There are usually several serious issues and a number of minor issues; and bargaining involves trading concessions on one front against gains on another. But to theorize about the process we must make a simplifying assumption: All issues on the table can be reduced to the single dimension of a money equivalent. This presents no difficulty on cost items such as health insurance or other benefits. They can be reduced to a cents-per-hour equivalent, and negotiators commonly talk about a "twenty-cent-an-hour package," including wage and benefit costs. But what about a demand for a union shop? Such demands are often considered matters of principle, which are not capable of compromise. We assume nevertheless that any principle has its price. A union officer once remarked, "Every year I sell the union shop for a nickel."

The Contract Zone

Consider a single buyer of a certain kind of labor confronting a single union, a situation known as *bilateral monopoly*. In Figure 16-1 D is the employer's labor demand curve, while S and MC are his labor supply and marginal cost curves. The diagram is identical with that for the monopsonistic buyer of labor in Chapter 2. We now face two problems: (1) What are the outside limits within which the bargained wage must fall? (2) What determines where it will fall within these limits?

The limits within which the bargain must fall are usually termed the *settlement range* or the *contract zone*. The location depends on the policies of the parties. As regards the employer, we usually assume that a company will try to maximize profit. In the present case, by the reasoning used in Chapter 2, this will mean operating at point B. The most profitable employment is E_M where the marginal cost of additional labor (shown by MC) just equals the marginal revenue product of additional labor (shown by D). We see from the supply curve that E_M workers can be recruited at a wage of W_M.

The analysis so far assumes perfect knowledge about the future. Since the future is uncertain, the management negotiators will probably build in a safety factor, presenting proposals that will safeguard profits if the future turns out worse than expected (e.g., if the demand curve shifts to the left).

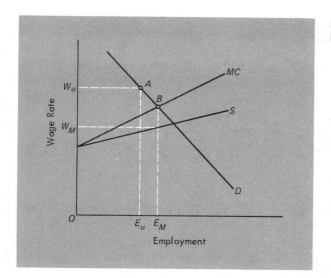

FIGURE 16-1 The Contract Zone under Bilateral Monopoly

Management must also consider the cost of achieving their objectives. As the company's offer becomes smaller, the chance that workers will strike rather than accept it becomes greater; and probable strike costs must be subtracted from possible company gains. The effect of this consideration will be to raise the company's offer somewhat above what management would prefer were the strike threat not in the picture.

Meanwhile a similar process is underway on the other side. Union officers have to estimate not only the median member's preference system but also the willingness of the members to undergo strike costs. The larger the union's demands, the greater the chance of a strike, and the longer it may last. Taking costs into account, therefore, tends to lower union demands.

In this way labor and management negotiators formulate their preferred, or *real*, bargaining positions. Neither party, however, knows the real position of the other, and it is important that the other side not find out too early. An important feature of the negotiations is an effort to conceal and even misrepresent one's true position, that is, the terms on which one would be willing to settle. If you reveal that, then the opponent will insist on at least that much and continue to press for more. Thus the normal first step in negotiations is to demand more than you hope to achieve, to advance *nominal* or "shadow" demands from which you can later retreat.

Assume that management's preferred wage is W_M and that the preferred wage of the union is W_μ. Have we now defined the limits of the contract zone? Not necessarily. The contract zone cannot be *wider* than $W_M W_\mu$ because neither party would want to go outside these limits; but it may be narrower. Suppose the union considers a wage of W_M so unattractive that it would strike indefinitely rather than accept it. Then the bottom of the contract zone, the lowest wage that the union could be forced to accept, will be above W_M. Similarly, the wage W_μ may be so high that the employer would close down permanently rather than pay it, so that the top of the zone is below W_μ. But there will normally be a contract zone, and it will often be wide enough to leave substantial scope for bargaining.

At this point Edgeworth and other early economists were inclined to leave the matter. They said, in effect, "We cannot answer the second question raised above. Within the limits of the contract zone, the actual wage rate is indeterminate." But this means only that *the market variables usually included in economic theory* are insufficient to determine the outcome. A wage rate does get decided, after all, through the negotiating process. In this sense the outcome *is* determinate.

The Hicks Approach

Not all economists have been happy with the Edgeworth pronouncement; and intermittently they have tried to find paths to a determinate solution. One such attempt, by Sir John Hicks of Oxford, is sketched in Figure 16-2. The central idea is that there is a functional relation between the wage that one or the other party will accept and the length of strike that would be necessary to establish that wage. The horizontal axis in Figure 16-2 is a time axis, along which various possible lengths of strike can be measured. *A* is the wage the company would prefer if the union were not in the picture. It will concede more, however, in order to avert a strike; and up to a point its concessions will rise with the length of strike it anticipates. Thus we derive the *employer's concession curve* each point on which shows the maximum amount the employer would pay rather than face a strike of specified length. This curve eventually levels off; that is, there is an upper limit beyond which the employer will not go under any circumstances.

The union's preferred wage would be *B*, provided it could be obtained

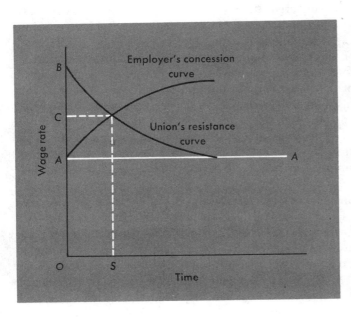

FIGURE 16-2 Hicks's Solution of the Bargaining Problem

without a strike; but the prospective costs of a strike may lead it to accept less. The *union's resistance curve* shows the minimum that the union would accept rather than face a strike of the length indicated, and this minimum declines as the prospective strike becomes longer. The resistance curve also levels off eventually; that is, there is some maximum length of strike beyond which the union would prefer simply to accept the employer's terms.

It seems natural to think that the intersection of the two curves yields a determinate solution to the bargaining problem. *Both* parties would agree to the wage *C* rather than face a strike *S* weeks in length. But what does Figure 16-2 really tell us? The determinate solution rests on an assumption of perfect knowledge. *If* each party knows the other's curve, the path to settlement is obvious. A strike would be settled after *S* weeks at wage *C*. Rather than incur the costs of the strike, the parties could agree to wage *C* without any strike. But the assumption of perfect knowledge is not plausible.[2]

The essence of collective bargaining is uncertainty about the other party's intention. Each side has an incentive to mislead the other. For example, if the union can convince the employer that its resistance curve is higher than it really is, then the union can gain a higher wage. Given this incentive to mislead, each side has reason to be very wary about the truth of the assertions made by its opponent.

Alternatively, the Hicks diagram might be interpreted as charting the course of events over time *after* negotiations have broken down and a strike has begun. With each succeeding week of strike, the union's minimum demand falls, and the employer's maximum offer rises until after *S* weeks, agreement is reached at *C*. This may be a useful way of looking at the history of a strike; but it does not provide a theory of negotiation in advance of strike action.

The Concept of Bargaining Power

Bargaining power is a slippery term, which can be defined in different ways. One interesting definition, developed by Neil Chamberlain, starts from the concept of the *inducement to agree*. Two parties, *A* and *B*, are in a bargaining situation. *A* makes an offer to settle on certain terms, *B*'s inducement to agree is defined as the cost of disagreeing on *A*'s terms divided by the cost of agreeing on *A*'s terms. This will usually be a positive number, greater than zero but not necessarily greater than one. Only if and when it becomes greater than one—that is, when the cost of continued disagreement exceeds the cost of agreement—will *B* be willing to accept *A*'s offer.

The size of the ratio depends partly on the terms offered. By making terms

---

[2]Hicks recognized this difficulty: "If there is a considerable divergence of opinion between the employer and the Union representatives about the length of time the men would hold out rather than accept a given set of terms, then the Union may refuse to go below a certain level, because its leaders believe that they can induce the employer to consent to it by refusing to take anything less; while the employer may refuse to concede it, because he does not believe the Union can hold out long enough for concession to be worth his while. Under such circumstances, a deadlock is inevitable, and a strike will ensue; but it arises from the divergence of estimates, and from no other cause." *The Theory of Wages,* 2d ed. (New York: St. Martin's Press, 1966), pp. 146–47.

more and more attractive, A can raise B's inducement to agree and eventually bring about a settlement. Concession is one route to agreement. But there are other things A can do without altering her offer. A may try to persuade B that the cost of accepting A's terms is less than it seems, thus reducing the denominator of the ratio. Or A may, by bluff or threat, cause B to raise his estimate of the cost of disagreement, and thus raise the numerator.

This leads to a definition: "Bargaining power can be defined as the capacity to effect an agreement on one's own terms: operationally, one's bargaining power *is* another's inducement to agree. If X and Y are in a contest over the terms of their cooperation, X's bargaining power is represented by Y's inducement to agree . . . while Y's bargaining power is X's inducement to agree. . . ."[3] The two are inversely related, Y's bargaining power tending to be less as X's is greater; but the relation is not a simple reciprocal. It is possible that at some point in a union-management negotiation both parties may find themselves with an inducement to agree greater than one. All that is necessary for a settlement, however, is that one party find itself in this situation.

Let us return to Figure 16-1, where the union's preferred wage, W_μ, is higher than W_M, the wage preferred by management, leaving a gap that eventually has to be closed. The union's bargaining power is greater (1) the higher the value of W_M at the outset of negotiations and (2) the greater the union's ability to shift W_M upward over the course of negotiations. Management's bargaining power is defined in the same way—it increases as W_μ is lower and more shiftable.

What Determines Bargaining Power?

Bargaining power may seem to imply personal forcefulness, shrewdness, or tactical skill. So we should emphasize that bargaining power depends mainly on objective circumstances, economic and organizational. Such famous negotiators as John L. Lewis of the Mine Workers and James Hoffa of the Teamsters achieved their results not particularly through superior poker-playing ability but because they actually held good cards.

The relative costs of a shutdown are a key factor in the power relation between the parties. If the strike mainly affects the firm, then the union has considerable bargaining power. If strike costs fall mostly on the workers, then the firm has considerable bargaining power, since it has less reason to be fearful of a strike.

On the union side the costs of a strike to the workers are the wages lost, adjusted for any strike benefits and any extra overtime the workers may earn before or after the strike. These costs depend mainly on the length of the strike and on the extent to which the workers have ways of supporting themselves, such as alternative jobs, earnings of other family members, or savings.

Striking members are usually excused from dues payments and entitled to draw strike benefits, so that a long strike drains the union treasury. Therefore union

---

[3]Neil W. Chamberlain, *A General Theory of Economic Process* (New York: Harper and Row, Publishers, 1955), pp. 80–82.

bargaining power fluctuates over time. A union that has just been through an expensive strike has reduced bargaining power because its treasury is low and the memory of lost paychecks is fresh in the members' minds. As time passes, the union's ability to strike recovers, and its bargaining power rises.

On the employer side the costs of a strike of a given length depend heavily on the product and on the competition. If the company is producing a service or a perishable commodity, sales lost during a strike can never be regained. In an industry that produces a durable good and normally operates below capacity, such as coal mining, what is not produced during the strike will be produced later on. But if potential imports are important, as in steel or automobiles, a shutdown may mean loss of sales to foreign producers; and if U.S. customers find the foreign goods acceptable, this loss can become permanent. In the construction industry builders normally contract to complete a building by a certain date, with a substantial penalty charge for each extra day. A strike called close to the completion date thus becomes very expensive.

The relative bargaining power of unions and management depends heavily on whether aggregate demand is high or low. If it is low, then the bargaining power of the union will be low relative to that of the firm. The firm will probably have low profits and unsold inventories and be under pressure to reduce costs. A generous settlement might force it to go out of business or at least to cut back on its operations. On the other hand, with excess inventory a strike would not be very costly to the firm. In fact, with high unemployment it might be able to break a strike by hiring strikebreakers. But a strike could be very costly to the union. Even if the firm did not hire strikebreakers, it would be difficult for the strikers to obtain temporary jobs with other employers. Moreover, a large wage increase could be costly for the workers if many ended up losing their jobs.

When demand is high, the opposite situation applies, and the bargaining power of the union is greater. A strike would be difficult for the firm to break since there are few unemployed workers. But a strike could be very costly to the firm, since with inventories low, lost output would be translated directly into lost sales and the possible permanent loss of customers.

Apart from the effects of aggregate demand and of intrinsic industry characteristics, each party may maneuver to reduce costs to itself and raise costs to its opponent. For example, a union will not have much power unless it can organize all the workers in both the labor and product markets of the firm. If it has not organized all those in the labor market, then it will be relatively easy for the firm to hire strikebreakers. If all workers in the product market are not organized, then the union can't raise wages significantly at the organized firms without putting them at a severe competitive disadvantage and thus ultimately costing the jobs of union members. As we have seen in Chapter 12, the rise of national markets required the development of national unions. Similarly, the rise of foreign competition in recent years has reduced the power of many unions in the United States.

Bargaining-power considerations also affect the choice of strike targets. For example, will a strike be limited to one firm at a time, or will it close down an entire industry?

The United Automobile Workers (UAW) prefers that a strike, where one eventuates, be confined to one of the auto companies. This plan reduces the cost to the union, since most of its members continue to work and pay dues while only a minority are drawing strike benefits. And it increases the cost to the company, since if Ford alone is shut down many customers will switch to Chrysler, General Motors, or foreign producers.

It is not clear why the automobile companies have been willing to accept this approach. If the firms could negotiate successfully among themselves and thus present a united front in the negotiations with the UAW, then they should be able to achieve better terms. Such interfirm bargaining could be difficult, however, and might lead to either the inadvertent disclosure of confidential information or to antitrust difficulties.

In other industries, the union tactic of bargaining with one firm at a time has sometimes led employers to band together and insist on industrywide bargaining. Occasionally companies have established a system of *strike insurance.* The airline companies, whose strike hazards are increased by the multiplicity of unions with which they bargain, organized a mutual assistance pact in 1958. A company shut down by a strike was entitled to receive payments from other airlines that continued to operate. The plan was approved by the Civil Aeronautics Board (CAB) despite strong union opposition. The unions then asked Congress to forbid the arrangement. This effort finally succeeded as part of the airline deregulation movement. The Airline Deregulation Act of 1978 outlawed the pact in the form originally approved by CAB, permitting only a watered-down version in which the airlines were not interested. Airline enthusiasm for the pact had cooled off in any event, because of the very unequal distribution of benefits. Northwest Airlines proved unusually strike prone, receiving $203 million and paying out only $16 million over the life of the agreement.[4]

The prospective losses from a strike are usually serious enough to serve as a substantial deterrent to both sides. But how can one estimate the probability that insisting on a certain position will actually lead to a strike? It is here that uncertainty becomes critical. If the union knew the management negotiator's true position, it would know that up to some point the probability of a strike was zero and that above some point a strike was a certainty. But the union does not know where these points are. So it will estimate the probability of a strike at something between zero and one, rising toward the upper limit as the wage demand becomes larger.

In an uncertain situation attitudes toward risk influence the outcome. A cautious bargainer may settle for less than could have been gotten. A negotiator who enjoys taking chances may sometimes overstep the mark. Instances of both sorts can be found in the history of collective bargaining. This determinant, unlike those discussed previously, depends partly on the personalities of the negotiators. Increasing experience, however, is likely to moderate extremes of behavior. Nego-

---

[4]For the detailed provisions, see two articles by S. Herbert Unterberger and Edward C. Koziara in *Industrial and Labor Relations Review:* "Airline Strike Insurance: A Study in Escalation," (October 1975), pp. 26–45; and "The Demise of Airline Strike Insurance," (October 1980), pp. 82–89.

tiators who persist in being too cautious or too reckless will find themselves eliminated from the game.

The Tactics of Negotiation

How does the union (or management) negotiator endeavor to improve the opponent's offer? We noted earlier that the first step in negotiations is usually "the big demand"—deliberate overstatement by the union of how much it wants, deliberate understatement by management of how much it will pay.

A long and ambitious list of demands has advantages. It conceals one's true demands and "keeps the other person guessing," which is an important element in bargaining strategy. It provides ample room for negotiation and maneuver, for trading elimination of some items against concessions on others. It serves as protection against a marked change in economic conditions during the course of negotiations. Some negotiations go on for months, during which prosperity may change to recession or vice versa. If your initial demand turns out to be less than would be feasible several months later, you may be criticized for ineptitude.

Although initial demands are expected to be large, they must not be so large as to lose credibility. If the union's minimum demand is a 4-percent raise, it may be good strategy to ask for 6 percent. But to ask for 15 percent would not be taken seriously and would be equivalent to saying nothing. Similarly, in a period of rising prices and profits, a company's insistence on no wage increase would not be credible and could arouse anger rather than amusement.

Starting from the initial positions, each negotiator is trying to accomplish certain things. The union is interested in (1) representing (or in some measure misrepresenting) its own preferences; (2) trying to discover management's preferences; (3) trying to shift management's preferences; and in some cases (4) attempting to alter the preferences of third parties such as the general public or executive and legislative officials. The management negotiator is trying to accomplish the same things vis-à-vis the union.

The available tactics are persuasion and coercion. The union may try to persuade management that a certain wage increase will be more beneficial than management thinks—because labor productivity will rise along with wages, because the economic outlook is brighter than management expects, and so on. Management may argue that the benefit of a large increase is *less* than the union thinks, because it would reduce employment or even force the company out of business.

Such arguments amount to saying to the other party, "You don't really know your own interests." This is not likely to be very palatable. But persuasion should not be dismissed as entirely ineffective. It may convey factual information that the other party did not have at the outset, possibly leading to a shift of preferences. The rationalizations set forth by one side may also provide the other with a ladder by which to climb down gracefully from a position that no longer seems defensible.

The object of coercive tactics is to change the other party's estimate of the costs of disagreement. The union negotiator implies that a strike will result unless certain minimum terms are met. The management negotiator may state that the company will have to shut down or move to another location if the increase exceeds some maximum.

Following Carl Stevens, we can distinguish between bluff and "not-bluff."[5] Not-bluff consists in announcing what you intend to do ("we will strike at anything less than 5 percent"), with the intention of actually doing it if the contingency develops. The difficulty is even though your intention is firm, the other party may not believe it. So one can have the following sequence of events: the union announces a certain demand. The company, if it believed the strike threat, would be willing to concede rather than take a strike. But it does not believe the threat and refuses to concede. The result is a strike that nobody wants.

Bluff consists in announcing a certain course of action even though you do *not* intend to follow it if the contingency arises. Again, there is a problem of credibility. To be effective the bluff must be believed. If the bluff is called and the bluffer backs down, his credibility in future negotiations will be reduced.

One possible method of increasing credibility is *commitment*. Thomas Schelling has argued that a negotiator can strengthen his bargaining position by committing himself in such a way that he cannot later retreat without disastrous consequences.[6] The union negotiator can whip up membership sentiment behind certain minimum demands, take a strike vote, mobilize a strike fund, and make other visible and dramatic strike preparations. The management negotiator may state that the board of directors will not go beyond a certain limit, thus laying their credibility on the line along with his own.

This is a dangerous tactic, because events can get out of hand. What started out as a tentative commitment on one or both sides may harden into a firm commitment, leading to a strike that was not necessarily in the cards at the outset. It is a little like playing a game of "chicken" with the steering wheel locked in position.

Tactical maneuvering on both sides over a period of weeks usually leads to concessions that bring the stated positions of the parties closer to their true positions and also brings the true positions closer together. Making concessions is delicate, since it may be interpreted as weakness, and so concessions are usually signaled indirectly. One side may simply remain silent about a point it has been insisting on; or it may suggest that the point be set aside for the time being, implying that eventual agreement will not be too difficult. One party, having made such an implicit concession, may then wait for the other to take reciprocal action, so that negotiations proceed through a series of moves and countermoves.

Eventually, the approach of the contract expiration deadline forces a final reexamination of positions. As the probability of a shutdown rises, the costs of shutdown are estimated more carefully and taken more seriously. It is no accident that many contracts are renewed at the eleventh hour after hectic all-night bargaining sessions. The fact that it *is* the eleventh hour moves the parties toward a possible agreement.

---

[5] See his *Strategy and Collective Bargaining Negotiation*.
[6] Thomas C. Schelling, "An Essay on Bargaining."

STRIKES: SOURCES, COSTS, PREVENTION

While strikes are sometimes dramatic, they are also relatively rare. In a typical year about 2 percent of the labor force are involved in strikes, and about 0.2 percent of potential working hours are lost on this account. Looking at union members only, about 10 percent are involved in strikes, and the time lost is around 1 percent. In the United States 80 to 90 percent of all collective agreements in the United States are renewed without a strike.

Why Strikes Occur

When a strike occurs the public often asks, Who is to blame? This is not a very useful question, and the answer is never self-evident. The union is often blamed because it makes the first overt move by walking out. But management can always bring on a strike by refusing to make concessions. The mere existence of a work stoppage provides no information about which party is mainly responsible.

A strike occurs when negotiations have not moved W_M and W_μ far enough so that they coincide or overlap. There is still a negative contract zone when the deadline arrives. Occasionally, if agreement seems near, the parties will agree to extend the deadline and continue negotiating. But normally, if the old agreement expires before a new one has been reached, a strike is automatic—"no contract, no work." There are several possible reasons for such an impasse.

1. The assumption that all issues can be reduced to a dollar equivalent may not be warranted. The basic issue may be not the terms of the new contract but the framework of bargaining itself. We noted earlier that the composition of the bargaining unit, and the timing of contract expiration dates can influence the balance of power between the parties. One party may decide that the time has come to force a change in the bargaining framework that will raise its bargaining power in future years.

2. One party may attach positive value to a strike. A company may think that a long strike will break the union and free it of the necessity of collective bargaining. A union leader may consider an occasional strike desirable to maintain the members' morale and to impress the employer with the union's willingness to fight. Unused weapons become rusty.

3. Negotiators may be locked into untenable positions by their respective organizations. An absentee corporation president or board of directors may order a plant manager to take a position that the latter knows will lead to a strike but has no authority to change. A union leader may privately consider some union demands unreasonable; but to retreat might jeopardize his or her own position and may even split the union. Sometimes a rival leader has convinced the membership that the demands are attainable. If the negotiator settles for less, he or she will be accused of a "sellout," the settlement will be voted down by the members, and a strike will result in any event.

4. Finally, one or both parties may misjudge the costs of disagreement. Even when an all-knowing observer could find possibilities of compromise, one side may be unwilling to compromise because it has a low opinion of the other's strength and thinks it can win its point easily and quickly. A negotiating move that is interpreted as a bluff, but turns out not to be a bluff, can bring on an impasse.

To discover which of these situations was responsible for a particular strike requires inside knowledge of the people and issues involved. All one can conclude from the fact of a strike is that there was a failure to reach agreement.

Strike Costs: Private and Social

In assessing the cost of strikes, one must distinguish the costs that the parties inflict on each other from possible cost to the national economy. The striking workers lose wages and other benefits. If the plant is shut down, the company suffers some loss in profits. Even if management tries and succeeds in keeping the plant open, production will usually be lower and operating costs higher than normal.

These are costs the parties choose to bear, at least for a time, rather than accept the opponent's terms. And while these costs are painful, they do contribute to eventual settlement of the dispute. Just as war is sometimes considered "a continuation of diplomacy by other methods," so a strike is "a continuation of negotiations by other methods." As the strike becomes a reality rather than a threat, and as the costs mount up over the course of time, each party is forced to ask itself repeatedly, "Is it worth it?" Their bargaining positions move closer to each other, leading eventually to a settlement. A strike is one route to agreement.

While a strike always involves private costs, it may or may not involve social costs in the sense of a reduced output of goods and services. In many situations a strike involves no loss of national output. In a seasonal industry a strike may simply change the location of the slack season. A strike in men's clothing factories early in the spring season means only that the factories will have to work longer at the end of the season to make up for lost time. In this case there is not even a loss of income to the parties, merely a postponement of income to a later date.

The impact of strikes is mitigated also by the fact that most industries in most years operate below full capacity. If supplies are cut off for several weeks or months by a strike, factories will later work full blast for a time to make up the lost output. The main effect is a shift in the *timing* of production rather than in the *amount* of production.

A slightly different shift occurs when a union strikes selectively against part of an industry. If Ford is shut down, Chrysler and General Motors will sell more cars. Ford and its workers have less income, but other companies and their workers have more income. This assumes, of course, that the other companies have unused capacity and can absorb the additional business. If all plants are operating at full capacity throughout the year, a strike anywhere in the industry will reduce national output.

The main output losses occur in three situations, First, in industries producing services for immediate consumption, production lost today is lost forever. If I do not buy a newspaper or a subway ride today, I am not going to buy two tomorrow to catch up. The seriousness of such losses depends on the kind of service in question. A strike of radio announcers would not affect most people's lives materially. A strike of hospital attendants, public school teachers, garbage collectors, or truckers delivering perishable food to market is a more serious matter. In some cases availability of close substitutes may mitigate the impact on consumption.

Second, there are industries, such as electric power and railroads, whose continuous operation is essential to steady production in other industries. A strike in such an industry may, by crippling production in many other industries, cause a disproportionate drop in national output. Such strikes are often called national emergency disputes, and the Labor-Management Relations Act provides special procedures for dealing with them.

A third possibility, which has become increasingly important with growth of world trade, is that foreign output may be substituted for domestic output. If American automobile production were shut down for any length of time, sales of foreign cars would rise substantially. Moreover, the trade relations established during the strike do not necessarily cease when it ends. The level of imports may remain permanently higher than before, causing a loss of markets to the companies and an employment loss to union members.

Government Intervention: Private Sector

The fact that the social cost of most strikes is low does not mean that it should be ignored.

1. Mediation. Both the federal and state governments try to reduce the number and length of strikes by maintaining staffs of experienced mediators to assist in contract negotiations. Use of these mediators is voluntary. But when the Federal Mediation and Conciliation Service or a state mediation agency offers its services, the offer is rarely refused.

The mediator has no authority. But he or she can be very useful as a communication channel between the parties, especially when direct relations are poor.

One function of mediation is to save face for one or both parties when they have gotten locked into a position from which there seems no graceful retreat. As Stevens points out,

> The mediator may supply a party with arguments which the party may in turn use to rationalize a position (or retreat from a position) vis-à-vis his own constituents . . . the mere fact of a mediator's entrance into a dispute provides the parties with a means of rationalizing retreats from previously held positions, particularly if the mediator can be made to appear to take a part of the "responsibility" for any settlement.[7]

The mediator may help in a situation where a not-bluff by *A*, which is not believed by *B*, creates the possibility of an unwanted strike. Each party is more likely to believe the mediator than to believe the opposing party. The mediator may be able to convince *B* that the not-bluff is genuine, thus averting the strike danger.

The mediator's function in the event of a bluff is less clear. Consider this situation: *A* is bluffing. *B,* if she believed the bluff, would make concessions suffi-

---

[7]Stevens, *Strategy and Collective Bargaining Negotiation, p. 130.*

cient to settle the dispute. If the mediator can convince *B* that *A* is *not* bluffing, this will contribute to a settlement. What is more important for the mediator: to be truthful or effective? Another possibility, of course, would be for the mediator to convince *A* that his bluff is not believed and that he should abandon it.

As the strike deadline approaches, it becomes increasingly important that each side reveal its true position; but this raises the tactical difficulty of "coming clean without prejudice." Each side fears that revealing a willingness to compromise will be interpreted as weakness and will lead the other side to stiffen its position. They may be willing, however, to reveal their true positions to the mediator. When the mediator discovers that the possible compromises coincide or overlap, he or she may call the parties to a joint session and suggest a settlement that each has indicated privately it will accept. The mediator can help to focus the attention of the parties on one solution as most plausible, incidentally providing a rationalization for it and taking a measure of responsibility. Finally, an ingenious mediator can sometimes think of compromise proposals that have not occurred to either of the parties. This is particularly useful in demands that have become matters of principle.

2. Costly Strikes. Some strikes are more serious than others. In the case of rail strikes, the Railway Labor Act provides that the National Mediation Board may intervene in contract disputes at the request of either party or on its own motion. If its efforts are unsuccessful, the president may appoint an emergency board to investigate the dispute, and strike action is forbidden for a sixty-day period. In practice, the procedure provided under this act has been little used in recent years.

The Taft-Hartley Act provides a similar procedure for other strikes, which in the opinion of the President, "imperil the national health or safety." A board of inquiry may be appointed, and strike action is forbidden for an eighty-day period, after which it becomes legal. This procedure has been used in several dozen cases and has usually, but not always, averted a strike. Most of these disputes have involved longshoring, merchant shipping, or coal mining.

A perennial proposal is that unsettled disputes, especially disputes in "essential industries," be submitted to compulsory arbitration by a neutral board. We will see that neutral arbitration is the normal procedure for settling day-to-day grievances arising under an existing contract. But in the private sector most union and management officials are resolutely opposed to using it to write the terms of a new contract. The stakes here are high, and the parties prefer to slug it out on the picket line if necessary rather than entrust their fate to a third party.

Dispute Adjustment in the Public Sector

A strike by public employees is usually illegal, which presents a problem: If contract bargaining reaches an impasse, how can the impasse be broken if the strike option is removed? Most of the state labor relations laws set up procedures for dispute settlement, often several procedures that can be used in successive stages.

1. Mediation. This is the normal first step, and operates in much the same way as in the private sector.

2. Fact Finding. This is normally the next step if mediation fails. The term itself is misleading. The parties already have more than enough facts. What they need and what the fact finder is expected to provide is a set of recommendations on the issues in dispute. Sometimes these recommendations are accepted by the parties, in whole or in part. Even where they are not accepted, the report serves a useful function in clarifying issues and providing a neutral opinion that may be useful at the next stage of arbitration.

3. Arbitration. Most states now provide for arbitration as the final stage in dispute settlement, particularly for essential services such as police work and fire fighting. Arbitration involves formal hearings before either a single arbitrator or a tripartite panel of labor, management, and public representatives, followed by an award that is binding on the parties. This procedure has been criticized on the grounds that it may have a "chilling" effect on genuine collective bargaining. Faced with a possible public hearing, the parties will decline to reveal their real positions or to compromise their nominal positions. Rather than make a concession on a disputed issue, they will pass the buck to the board in the hope of a favorable decision.

To reduce this difficulty, sometimes "final-offer arbitration" is used. In this case the arbitrator is not allowed to split the difference between the parties but must choose one position or the other. This approach provides an incentive for each side to reduce its demands in order to appear to be more reasonable than its opposition, thus increasing the chances that the arbitrator will accept its position.

4. Strikes. These are not supposed to happen but sometimes do. At the federal level strikes are clearly illegal and, in fact, are very rare. In state and local government the legality of strikes varies from state to state, and strikes are almost as frequent as in the private sector. We shall discuss strikes in the public sector in more detail in Chapter 19, where we examine public sector unions.

SUMMARY

1. Bargaining units differ in geographic scope. Local-market industries usually have citywide agreements between the union and an employers' association. In national-market industries, single-company agreements predominate; but one also finds cases of association bargaining and pattern bargaining. Bargaining units differ also in whether they include all company employees (industrial units) or only a particular occupational group (craft units).

2. In negotiations each side must first select its negotiating team and formulate its position. This position should include not only its initial demands but also what it realistically hopes to achieve.

3. The usual stages of negotiation include initial demands; questioning the other side about its demands; concessions; tentative agreement, often just before a strike deadline; and ratification of the agreement.

4. The union seeks a higher wage than management wants to pay. The difference between their positions is the contract zone. Economic theory cannot tell us where within the contract zone the agreement will take place or whether, in fact, an agreement will occur.

5. In the course of bargaining each party tries to shift the opponent's position toward its own position, by a mixture of persuasion, bluff, and threats. Usually at the eleventh hour positions have shifted enough so that agreement becomes possible.

6. If no agreement is reached by the the contract expiration date, a strike follows automatically. A strike inflicts losses on both parties, which exert continuing pressure to shift positions, leading to an eventual settlement.

7. Bargaining power is the ability to reach an agreement on one's own terms. It depends more on such factors as the relative costs of a strike to each party than it does on the personalities of the bargainers.

8. A strike may or may not involve social cost in the form of lost output. Such costs occur mainly when the strike cuts off supply of an essential service, private or public. In such cases government usually intervenes to avert a strike or to ensure quick settlement.

9. In cases where strikes are less costly to the public, the government still tries to reduce the incidence of lengthy strikes by providing mediators, who can work with the parties to facilitate the negotiations and increase the chances that they will reach an agreement quickly. Mediation can improve communication between the parties and can make it easier for either side to make a concession without appearing to be weak.

10. Compulsory arbitration sometimes serves as a substitute for a strike, especially in the public sector where strikes are generally illegal. In contrast to mediation, where the parties need not accept the views of the mediator, an arbitrator can impose a settlement. In the private sector, where strikes are legal, the parties generally have preferred to settle disputes over a new contract by strikes and the threat of strikes rather than to bring in an arbitrator.

KEY CONCEPTS

ASSOCIATION BARGAINING
COMPANY BARGAINING
PATTERN BARGAINING
CRAFT UNIT
INDUSTRIAL UNIT
CRAFT SEVERANCE

CONTRACT ZONE
BARGAINING POWER
STRIKE
MEDIATION
ARBITRATION

REVIEW QUESTIONS

1. Why have multiemployer bargaining units developed in some situations but not in others? Illustrate.

2. Single-firm agreements are the general rule in manufacturing. Why haven't more companies banded together to offset the concentrated power of the union?

3. Where a group of skilled, technical, or professional workers wish to bargain separately rather than as part of an inclusive unit, should they be allowed to do so? Why or why not?

4. What is meant by the statement that under collective bargaining a company's wage level becomes indeterminate?

5. Explain the merits and limitations of J. R. Hicks's approach to wage bargaining.

6. Explain the meaning and outline the main determinants of bargaining power.

7. Construct a situation in which the union negotiator would have maximum bargaining power. Then construct a reverse case that would maximize the management negotiator's power.

8. Why are the parties sometimes unable to reach agreement, leading to a strike?

9. Can the tactical skill of a negotiator appreciably influence the outcome of bargaining? Explain.

10. Why does the cost of a strike to the parties usually differ from the social cost? Under what conditions is there a serious social cost?

11. In what industries, if any, would you consider a stoppage of production to be serious enough to warrant special treatment by the government? Give your reasons.

12. It is often proposed that all unsettled disputes be referred to compulsory arbitration by a neutral party. Do you favor this proposal? Why or why not?

READINGS

CODDINGTON, ALAN, *Theories of the Bargaining Process.* Chicago: Aldine Publishing Co., 1968.

DUNLOP, JOHN, *Dispute Resolution: Negotiation and Consensus Building.* Dover, Mass.: Auburn Publishing Co., 1984).

FEUILLE, PETER, and HOYT WHEELER, "Will the Real Industrial Conflict Please Stand Up," in *U.S. Industrial Relations 1950–80: A Critical Assessment,* ed. Jack Stieber et al., pp. 255–95. Madison, Wis.: Industrial Relations Research Association, 1981.

KENNAN, JOHN, "The Economics of Strikes," in *Handbook of Labor Economics*, vol. 2, ed. Orley Ashenfelter and Richard Layard, pp. 1091–1138. Amsterdam: North-Holland, 1984.

LEWIN, DAVID, and PETER FEUILLE, "Behavioral Research in Industrial Relations." *Industrial and Labor Relations Review* (April 1983), pp.341–60.

SCHELLING, THOMAS C., "An Essay on Bargaining," *American Economic Review* (June 1956), pp. 281–306.

STEVENS, CARL M., *Strategy and Collective Bargaining Negotiation*. New York: McGraw-Hill Book Co., 1963.

WALTON, RICHARD E., and ROBERT B. McKERSIE, *A Behavioral Theory of Negotiations*. New York; McGraw-Hill Book Co., 1965.

YOUNG, ORAM, ed., *Bargaining: Formal Theories of Negotiation*. Urbana, Ill.: University of Illinois Press, 1975.

COLLECTIVE BARGAINING: ISSUES AND OUTCOMES

The outcome of bargaining is a collective agreement, or *union contract*. The matters regulated by the contract vary greatly from one situation to the next, depending on the age of the agreement, the nature of the industry, and the objectives of the parties. Almost every aspect of personnel administration and many aspects of production management eventually become matters of collective bargaining. A list of the subjects covered in the more than one hundred thousand union contracts in the United States would include hundreds of items; and with respect to each of these, many different contract provisions have been worked out to meet differing circumstances.

In the space available here it is necessary to concentrate on a few key issues and, with respect to each issue, describe the commonest contract provisions without trying to display the full range of variation around the norm. The main provisions of a typical contract deal with:

1. The nature of the contract, the rights reserved to management, and provisions for union security
2. Compensation—wages and fringes—a very large area, with many subproblems
3. Job tenure and job security—provisions concerning hiring, training, assignment to work, promotion and transfer, layoff and recall to work, and discharge
4. Working hours, work schedules, and overtime payment
5. Working conditions, including both physical and social dimensions
6. Procedure for adjustment of grievances arising under the contract
7. Issues of labor-management cooperation, including quality-of-working-life (QWL) programs

UNION SECURITY AND MANAGERIAL RIGHTS

Union contracts normally contain a number of procedural provisions designed to set the general framework of relations between the parties. These include provisions concerning recognition and status of the union, rights and prerogatives of management, duration of the agreement and the method of renewing it, and prevention of strikes and lockouts during the life of the agreement.

Status of the Contract

At the outset the contract specifies the date on which it becomes effective and the expiration date. Originally most contracts were for a twelve-month period, but the three-year contract has become the general rule. The advantage is that the trouble and cost of negotiating a new contract, with the ever-present possibility of a strike, occurs only every three years instead of every year. The difficulty is that it is hard to foresee economic conditions for three years ahead, and a union will hardly ever be willing to accept an unchanged wage for such a long period. This problem is commonly met by scheduling a wage increase at the beginning of each of the three years. Additional increases may occur under the cost-of-living provisions to be described later.

Both parties agree to be bound by the terms of the contract. Unilateral changes by the employer are not permitted, even if they would be improvements for employees. The union agrees not to strike during the life of the contract. Strikes in violation of contract, usually called wildcat strikes, were common among newly organized workers in the thirties and forties, but with the maturing of industrial relations in basic industries, they have receded to minor proportions. A wildcat strike is hardly ever sanctioned by the national union, which means that the participants are not eligible for strike benefits; and participants may also be subject to discharge or other discipline by the employer.

Management Rights

Both parties are concerned with status and security. The union tries to ensure its continued existence through the union security provisions to be described in a moment. Management is concerned with protecting its right to manage, which it fears will be eroded as the union demands participation in more and more areas of decision.

Some managements are content with a brief statement that management retains full authority over all matters not covered in the contract. Others prefer a more detailed clause such as the following:

> The Company retains the sole right to manage its business, including the right to decide the number and location of plants, the machine and tool equipment, the products to be manufactured, the method of manufacturing, the schedules of production, the processes of manufacturing or assembling . . . to maintain order and

efficiency in its plants and operations, to hire, lay off, assign, transfer, and promote employees, and to determine the starting and quitting time and the number of hours to be worked; subject only to such regulations and restrictions governing the exercise of these rights as are expressly provided in this agreement.[1]

Although such a clause has symbolic value, its practical effect is less certain. Suppose the union files a grievance on some matter that management regards as within its sole authority. Management may decline to process the grievance, pointing to the management-rights clause as justification. If the issue is of real concern to the union, there will probably be an effort to get it written into the contract at the next negotiation. As a practical matter, the line between actions that management can take on its own and actions it must discuss with the union gets worked out through negotiation.

Union Security: The Union Shop

The position of the union can be buttressed in several ways. A common device in earlier times was the *closed shop,* under which the employer could hire only workers who were already union members. The closed shop was traditional in many of the skilled trades. It enabled the union to ration job opportunities among members of the craft on some equitable basis; and it often furnished employers with a central employment agency. This arrangement is convenient where employers are small, as in clothing manufacture or job printing, or where jobs are of short duration and each employer's needs fluctuate widely, as in building construction. Central hiring is useful also in industries where there is a good deal of seasonal or casual unemployment, such as longshoring and merchant shipping.

In 1946, just before passage of the Taft-Hartley Act, the closed shop appeared in about one-third of all union contracts. Since Taft-Hartley it has been unlawful and has vanished from union contracts. This is not to say that the practice has entirely disappeared. There are no doubt cases in which a bootleg closed shop has continued by tacit agreement between the union and the employer. Where there is a long tradition against union members working alongside nonunion men, it is simpler for the employer to accept this tradition than to assert his rights and lose his labor.

The job referral functions of unions have also continued. Employers in building and other skilled trades often recruit partly or entirely through the union office. Union hiring halls for longshoremen and merchant seamen continue to function. The courts have held, however, that a union employment office is legal only if it serves all comers in a nondiscriminatory way. At most, the union can charge nonmembers "a reasonable fee" for providing employment service. Again, reality may be somewhat different, and the hiring-hall device may serve to protect

---

[1]Cited from Edwin F. Beal, Edward W. Wickersham, and Philip K. Kienart, *The Practice of Collective Bargaining,* 5th ed. (Homewood, Ill.: Richard D. Irwin, 1976), p. 284.

an illegal closed shop. But any such arrangement is open to challenge, and it will normally be struck down by the courts.

More than four-fifths of union contracts contain some provision for union security. Much the commonest provision, found in about 60 percent of all contracts, is a straight *union shop*. This leaves the employer free to hire at will; but after the workers have served a probationary period and become regular members of the plant labor force, they are required to join the union.

Weaker union security provisions, found in some 20 percent of union contracts, include the following: (1) A *modified union-shop* agreement. Under this some groups in the labor force, such as workers on the payroll when the first contract was signed, are exempted from the union membership requirement. (2) A *maintenance-of-membership* agreement. This does not compel workers to join; but if they choose to join, they must remain in for the duration of the agreement as a condition of employment. (3) An *agency-shop* agreement. Under this a worker who declines to join is obliged to pay the union a fee, usually set at the level of the monthly dues, in return for the service rendered by the union as collective bargaining agent. It is sometimes also called a fee-for-service agreement.

In earlier times the union shop gave union leaders a powerful disciplinary weapon over the recalcitrant members. Anyone who fell afoul of the existing leadership could be expelled from the union and would then be out of a job. This system doubtless contributed to the growth of oppressive or corrupt practices in some unions. To correct the situation the Taft-Hartley Act provided that the employer is not obliged to discharge a worker who has been expelled from, or denied admission to, the union on any ground other than failure to tender the regular dues and initiation fees.

The union shop itself is legal under the Taft-Hartley Act. But the act contains a curious provision that where any state has passed a law forbidding the union shop, the state law shall take precedence. It reverses the normal rule that federal law has precedence as regards workers in interstate commerce. Twenty states have laws (usually labeled *right-to-work laws*) that prohibit both the closed and the union shop. These states are almost all in the South and West and include only about 15 percent of industrial employment in the country. Unions have fought these laws vigorously on the grounds that they will destroy trade unionism, while employer and farm groups have hailed them as the Magna Carta of working people. It is doubtful that either claim could be substantiated. Research studies suggest that the practical effect of these laws has been small.[2] Employers who wanted good relations with their unions have usually winked at the law, just as employers in traditional closed-shop industries have winked at the Taft-Hartley Act. Where relations are bad, however, and where the employer wants to mount

---

[2]See Keith Lumsden and Craig Peterson, "The Effect of Right-to-Work Laws on Unionization in the United States," *Journal of Political Economy* (December 1975), pp. 1237–48; Barry T. Hirsh, "The Determinants of Unionization: An Analysis of Interarea Differences," *Industrial and Labor Relations Review* (January 1980), pp. 147–61; William J. Moore, "Membership and Wage Impact of Right-to-Work Laws," *Journal of Labor Research* (Fall 1980) pp. 349–68; and Henry S. Farber, "Right-to-Work Laws and the Extent of Unionization," *Journal of Labor Economics* (July 1984), pp. 319–52.

a drive against the union, an anti–union-shop law may provide an additional weapon.

Some Pros and Cons of the Union Shop

The merits of the union shop have been argued for generations, and the issue arouses strong emotion on both sides. Unionists argue that since everyone in the bargaining unit benefits from the contract terms established by the union, everyone should be required to contribute to the union's support. If there is no such requirement, some workers will receive a "free ride" at the expense of their fellow workers. This situation is as unfair as it would be if residents of a community could decide whether they wished to pay taxes.

A more powerful argument for the union shop is that only if the union's existence is secure can it afford to cooperate with management and play a constructive role in the operation of the enterprise. The union interprets management's denial of the union shop as a lack of complete acceptance of collective bargaining, an indication that management does not consider the union a permanent part of the enterprise and hopes in time to be rid of it. The union must therefore devote much of its energy to keeping its fences mended against employer attack. It must try to hem in the employer by contract restrictions at any point where their employer might try to discriminate against union workers; it must limit management's power to select, promote, transfer, lay off, and discharge. It must manufacture enough grievances to keep the workers convinced that their employer is a tricky fellow and that the union is essential for their protection. It must give good service on grievances to its members and poor service or no service to nonmembers in order to emphasize the practical advantages of union membership; this discrimination makes for unequal treatment and ill feeling within the labor force and may reduce its productivity. On the other hand, many management officials argue that the union shop is coercive and involves an undue encroachment on the liberty of the individual worker. In a free society workers should be able to seek and accept employment with any employers who are willing to hire them, without paying tribute to a third party. The union shop forces them to join an organization of which they may not approve and forces them to pay for the right to work, a right they should enjoy as citizens.

This argument that the union shop coerces workers into unionism against their will appears to have been overdone. Few workers seem to have any conscientious objection to unionism. Most of those who stay out of the union do so simply out of inertia or to avoid dues payments. The coercion involved in requiring them to join the union is mainly financial and is no greater than that involved in levying payroll taxes on them for Social Security or other purposes. There is abundant evidence that where the union shop has been in effect in the past, the great majority of workers favor its continuance. The Taft-Hartley Act originally provided that a union-shop clause could not be included in a union contract unless a majority of the employees in the bargaining unit voted in favor of it in a secret ballot conducted by the National Labor Relations Board. During the first year of the act's operation, some twenty-two thousand elections were held under this section. The union shop was upheld in more than 98 percent of these cases and secured more than 95 percent of all ballots cast. It soon became clear, in fact, that these union-shop referenda were simply an unnecessary expense to the government, and the act was subsequently amended to eliminate the referendum requirement.

Beneath the arguments over the union-shop issue lies the hard fact of a power struggle. A union security clause strengthens the union's position in the shop, renders it less vulnerable to attack by the employer or rival unions, and helps to make it a permanent institution. It also makes the position of union officials more secure and less arduous. Management opposition to the union shop is based mainly on a recognition of these facts. Most managements see no reason to go out of their way in helping the union. That does not necessarily mean they have any hope of breaking the union. Their strategy may be merely to fight an effective delaying action. If the union can be kept busy holding its membership together, it will be in a weaker position to press fresh demands on the employer.

One's attitude toward the union shop is bound to depend on how one answers the following question: Is it desirable to maintain strong, stable, and permanent unions in American industry? If one answers no to this question, the open-shop position follows automatically. If one answers yes, a strong case can be made for a union-shop clause. There seems little doubt that a union is able to function better in a peaceful and constructive way if it embraces most or all of the labor force. It is unreasonable to demand that unions be "responsible" while at the same time denying union officers the control over their membership that would make group responsibility effective.

An issue related to the union shop should be noted in conclusion. Union demands for a union- or closed-shop clause have usually been accompanied by a demand for the *checkoff*. This is an arrangement by which the regular weekly or monthly dues of union members are deducted from their paychecks by the employer and transmitted in a lump sum to the union. Most unions prefer the checkoff, partly because it saves them a good deal of effort and unpleasantness in collecting dues from delinquent members and partly because it still further regularizes and entrenches the position of the union in the plant. Most managements oppose the checkoff, because it involves the company in effort and expense for the primary benefit of the union.

In general, where one finds a closed-shop, union-shop, or maintenance-of-membership provision, one is likely to find the checkoff as well. There are many detailed variations in checkoff clauses. Under some contracts dues are checked off automatically for all union members; under others they are checked off unless the worker asks the company in writing not to deduct dues; in still other cases the dues are deducted only if the worker makes a positive request in writing that this be done. The Taft-Hartley Act provides that a dues checkoff requires the written consent of each employee; but this consent is rarely refused. The whole issue, while presenting many possibilities for technical arguments, is subsidiary to the broader argument over the union shop. The outcome of that argument usually determines the outcome of the checkoff argument as well.

COMPENSATION

Rules governing compensation take up a good part of the union contract. The subproblems that arise in this area include the method of payment and the structure of wage rates; the size of the general wage increase in a particular year and whether the increase should be in the base pay, a lump-sum payment of profit sharing; inclusion or modification of a cost-of-living adjustment (COLA) clause; and changes in the dollar value and kind of benefits.

Job-Control Unionism: Assigning Wages to Jobs, Not Workers

There are a great variety of ways workers can be compensated. As we discussed in Chapter 7, one of the most basic distinctions is between payment for time and payment for output produced. If the firm is unionized, the normal form of compensation is an hourly wage rate that is tied to a particular job. The wage rate for the job may vary some, depending on the seniority of the job holder and possibly on his or her productivity on the job. But a newly hired person will usually start at a fixed wage, regardless of the education, experience, or any other characteristics of the successful job applicant. In contracts negotiated by most industrial unions, each job is defined in some detail and is often rather narrow in scope. In order for the worker to perform different tasks, she must be assigned to a new job, usually with a different wage rate. Such assignments are based on detailed rules that emphasize seniority. Similar rules specify which individual workers will be laid off if management decides a given number of layoffs are necessary.

Most unions are quick to enforce the work rules that define a particular job. If a worker does work that is not in his job specifications, then he is reducing the work available for some other worker. Under the NLRA supervisors are not considered to be in the bargaining unit. Thus unions have a special interest in restricting the kinds of tasks that supervisors can perform. The union seeks to preserve jobs for its members by prohibiting management from gradually shifting work to nonunion supervisors.

The kind of collective bargaining agreement we have been describing is often referred to as job-control unionism. As we saw in Chapter 12, job-control unionism developed in the 1930s and 1940s in the context of mass production, especially assembly lines. Because each worker performed a very limited range of tasks, employers could hire unskilled workers at low wage rates and still provide all the necessary training in a short time. As a result, the individual worker had little bargaining power. With the arrival of unions and collective action, the bargaining power of workers increased considerably. Not only did wage rates increase, but also unions helped to establish rules to protect against instances of managerial arbitrariness and favoritism, especially in promotions and layoffs.

This system of industrial relations, with wage rates based on the job rather than the person, remains dominant in the union sector and among many large nonunion employers. Alternatives do exist, however. In some industries, especially construction, craft unions predominate. Many crafts require a high level of skill, including the ability to perform a wide range of tasks and the judgment to know what needs to be done in a wide variety of situations. Once a worker has acquired the necessary skills, however, he or she is equally valuable to many employers. In contrast to industrial unions with their emphasis on seniority in the allocation of jobs, members of craft unions typically shift readily from one employer to another, sometimes with the assistance of a union hiring hall. Because each worker in the craft has similar skills, there is usually a standard union wage.

Another wage system, called payment for knowledge, has developed in some nonunion firms and has spread to unionized firms in a few cases. In this approach work is performed by small teams, often of six to twenty workers. The team decides which workers should do each task, usually on a rotating basis. Workers who have learned more skills and thus can perform more of the tasks, receive higher pay. Under the team approach workers have more variety in their jobs. The team often has considerable responsibility, much more than similar workers would have under the job-control approach. This increased responsibility comes partly at the expense of the authority of the foremen and of higher-level managers. Because the work force is more flexible and is encouraged to take more initiative, work teams can often help management find better ways to organize the production process. The greater flexibility and broader skills also cause workers to be less threatened by technological change. The team approach thus has much in common with Japanese industrial relations.

The job-control system of industrial relations is best adapted to the assembly line. In contrast, more flexible approaches, such as work teams, that do not emphasize rigid, narrow job specifications are better suited to computer-based technologies. Because machines controlled by computers can easily shift from one operation to another with minor changes in a computer program, such machines typically produce small batches of output and frequent changes in the tasks of the workers. Hence the increasing influence of computers has been one factor leading to pressure on firms to move away from the narrow job descriptions of job-control unionism. Another cause of such pressure is the increasing variability of demand facing many industries as a result of such factors as (1) the greater internationalization of the economy, together with considerable variation in exchange rates; and (2) the high variability in aggregate demand, especially from the mid-seventies through the mid-eighties.

All of these factors have made job-control unionism a handicap for firms in many industries. One result, discussed in Chapter 14, has been the decline in unionization in the private sector. Another important effect has been an increase in the flexibility of work rules in many union contracts. Such flexibility can be increased by having broader job classifications, fewer restrictions on the work that supervisors can perform, and more flexibility for management in transferring workers from one job to another.

With the increase in foreign competition as well as in nonunion competition within the United States, it seems likely that these trends toward greater flexibility will continue. On the other hand, low demand for labor in other time periods, such as the thirties and the late fifties, has led firms to bargain more intensely for flexible work rules. Thus firms' emphasis on achieving greater flexibility during the 1980s may be a result of the severe economic conditions facing many firms during the early years of the decade.[3]

Wage Increases

Wage increases are normally the largest money item involved in a new contract, and they attract most attention among employees and the public. A general increase means that all rates in the wage schedule are increased by so many cents per hour (a *flat rate increase*) or by a certain percentage (a *percentage increase*). Whichever approach is used, the key issue is how large the increase should be. The outcome is shaped largely by external factors: the rate of inflation; whether employment, output and profits in the industry are rising or falling; the size of increases being won by competing or neighboring unions; and the size of the increases being awarded to nonunion workers.

In addition to the general increase, a union will often argue that a particular occupation deserves a further increase because it has been relatively underpaid in the past. There is a "wage inequity," which should now be corrected. The claim is commonly supported by comparisons with rates being paid for the occupation—laborers, machinists, or whatever—by other employers in the area or industry. Depending somewhat on the weight of the evidence, the union claim may or may not succeed. Employers typically resist inequity demands, because of a fear that they can be manipulated to produce a leapfrogging of rates within the plant: a special adjustment for one group this year can create another alleged inequity, which must be corrected next year, and so on.

Lump-sum Payments

During the 1980s a major development was the increased use of lump-sum payments as a partial or complete substitute for general wage increases. In 1988, 43 percent of major contracts provided for a lump-sum payment, up from about 10 percent in 1983.[4] Such payments provide immediate cash for workers, but in the long run they are neither as costly to firms or as beneficial to workers as a corresponding wage increase. For example, many benefits, including pensions, vacation

---

[3]Thomas A. Kochan and Harry C. Katz, "Collective Bargaining, Work Organization, and Worker Participation: The Return to Plant-Level Bargaining," *Papers and Proceedings at the Spring Industrial Relations Research Association* (1983), pp. 524–29. Firms are less willing to take strikes to increase the flexibility of work rules when demand is high, profits are good, and strikes are most costly. With high demand, strikes are more costly, because it is more difficult to meet demand out of inventories. In addition, long-term customers who count on the firm as a reliable supplier may have strong enough demand during a boom period so that they are willing to bear the adjustment costs of switching to one of the firm's competitors. Such switches can have important long-term costs because the customer may not return once the strike is settled.

[4]See William M. Davis and Fehmida Sleemi, "Collective Bargaining in 1989: Negotiators Will Face Diverse Issues," *Monthly Labor Review* (January 1989), pp. 10–24.

pay, and overtime, are tied to the wage rate and generally are not affected by a lump-sum payment. Probably even more important, the lump-sum payment is a one-time bonus, not a permanent wage increase. Thus future wage increases will be added to this year's wage rate, not to the sum of the wage rate and the bonus.

Concession Bargaining

During the early 1980s, job security became an important issue for many unions because of the reduced demand for union labor. All industries suffered from the recession of 1982–83. In addition, many unionized employers faced long-term problems owing to increased foreign and domestic competition. As we have discussed previously, most unions are not too concerned with employment losses if only a few workers are affected or if the losses are expected to be temporary. But permanent layoffs for many workers, including workers with considerable seniority, are a matter of great concern.

To increase the job security of senior workers during the 1982–83 recession, unions were willing to defer scheduled wage increases and in some instances actually accepted declines in nominal wage rates. In return for such wage concessions, some unions were able to negotiate prohibitions against layoffs. Although few employers would go this far, many were willing to negotiate other, less drastic, changes, such as increased severance payments and greater retraining opportunities for those laid off. In addition to assisting workers who did lose their jobs, such policies probably reduced layoffs by increasing their cost to employers. Other policies often negotiated by unions in return for wage concessions include guarantees of minimum employment levels and limitations on subcontracting to nonunion employers.[5]

Two-tiered Wage Structures

When the demand for union labor fell in the early 1980s, another result in some industries, such as airlines, was the development of two-tiered wage structures, where newly hired workers are paid on a much lower wage scale than otherwise comparable workers who were hired during an earlier period. This two-tiered approach has the advantage of providing lower labor costs for employers, especially

---

[5]Concession bargaining has also changed the nature and scope of bargaining. For example, more firms have been willing to share confidential financial data with unions in order to show that they are facing genuine financial problems and are not just "crying wolf" to obtain lower wage rates. In some cases such sharing of information has expanded into other areas, including product development, investment planning, and plans for future employment. A few firms (such as Chrysler) have gone beyond information sharing and allowed unions a role in all the firm's decisions, most conspicuously by allowing a union leader to serve on the firm's board of directors.

Union officials have often been unenthusiastic about sharing directly in the decision making of management, fearing either that they will be coopted or that they will lose support among the rank and file for appearing to be too responsive to the concerns of management. When the jobs of present union members have become more clearly threatened by the investment decisions of firms, however, more union leaders have been willing and even eager to become involved in such decisions.

as hiring increases in the future. At the same time it protects the wage rates of current union members, who elect the union leaders and who must ratify the union contract. Despite these short-run advantages of the two-tiered approach, its popularity has diminished. As the demand for labor has increased, employers need to pay higher wage rates to attract competent workers, and as the demand for output has increased, firms are under less pressure to reduce costs. In addition, union opposition to two-tiered wage rates has increased as the devisiveness of paying different wage rates to workers hired at different times has become more apparent to union members.

Contingency Compensation

When unions have traded off wage increases for employment security at times of unusually low demand, many times they have sought to ensure that wage rates would increase in the future when demand and profits returned to normal levels. Various profit-sharing and employer stock-ownership plans (ESOPs) have been implemented to achieve these objectives. Such forms of contingency compensation make wage reduction more palatable to workers, especially those with high enough seniority to be relatively immune to fears of job loss. At the same time contingency wage increases are not very costly to management, since the firm will not have to pay unless demand for its products improves, in which case paying the higher wage should not present nearly so much of a burden.

Contingency wage increases continue to be important now that the economy is no longer in recession. As firms face greater uncertainty, many appear willing to grant larger increases in compensation if they are not locked into high future wage rates should product demand fall. Lump-sum payments are one way of dealing with this issue. Profit sharing is another.

Cost-of-living Adjustments

Another, more common, form of contingency compensation is cost-of-living adjustments (COLAs) to protect workers from increases in consumer prices over the life of the contract. COLA clauses in union contracts increased sharply in popularity during the inflationary seventies, when they helped provide protection from rapidly rising price levels. The proportion of workers in "major agreements" who were covered by COLA clauses rose from 20 percent in 1966 to 39 percent in 1973 and 60 percent in 1978. With the decline of inflation in the 1980s, however, this coverage fell to 40 percent in 1988.

A COLA clause typically does not recapture the full effect of an increase in the CPI. For example, from the late sixties to the late seventies such clauses offset less than 60 percent of the increase in consumer prices. There are several reasons for this: (1) The formula usually provides an equal cents-per-hour increase for all workers. The commonest provision is a one-cent-per-hour increase for each increase of 0.3 percent in the CPI. This amount may provide full recovery of living-cost increases for low-paid workers, but it will not do so for high-paid workers.

(2) There is frequently a cap of, say, 2 or 3 percent on the total COLA increase permitted in a particular year. In a year of high inflation it will be quite inadequate. (3) There is usually considerable lag in the timing of wage adjustments. While about 40 percent of present COLA clauses call for quarterly adjustment, 15 percent have a semiannual adjustment, and 45 percent adjust only once a year.

Where a COLA clause exists, the contract negotiations will usually involve debate over its provisions. There will be proposals for changes in the basic formula, for addition or removal of a cap, for changes in the frequency of wage adjustment, and other matters. Any changes that are made will usually change the employer's wage costs; and these costs must be counted into the total cost of the settlement package.

Unions without COLA protection will need to negotiate larger general increases, to keep pace with expected inflation. About two million workers in the private sector received wage increases in 1989 under major collective bargaining agreements negotiated in prior years. For those without COLA protection, the average scheduled increase was 4.3 percent, while for those with such protection it was 3.0 percent plus the COLA.

Benefits

The growing importance of benefits in the compensation package was documented in Chapter 7. The main issues that arise in collective bargaining are the following:

1. Health Insurance. In the past few years, health insurance has become one of the most devisive issues in collective bargaining in many industries. Designed originally to cover physicians' services and hospital care, these plans have tended to expand to cover optical care, dental care, and other services. With the escalation of medical care prices, the cost of these contract provisions has soared much above original employer estimates. In recent years many employers have bargained hard to substitute less expensive medical programs and to put some ceiling on costs. Unions naturally resist anything that appears as a reduction of promised benefits.

2. Pension Systems. These are usually quite complex, covering such matters as (a) the relation between length of service and pension rights; (b) the formula for calculating eventual pension payments; (c) the minimum age or length-of-service requirements for retirement; (d) the provision for premature retirement on account of disability; (e) the extent to which money received from other sources, such as Worker's Compensation or Social Security, is deductible from the employee's pension liability; and (f) the extent to which payments to a deceased retiree continue to a surviving spouse or children. These details leave much scope for bargaining and can have a large effect on pension costs.

3. Payment for Time Not Worked, Chiefly for Paid Vacations and Paid Holidays. The length of paid vacation is normally related to length of service, so that workers with two years of service may get a week's vacation, while those with twenty years may get a month. In each negotiation the union usually argues that the list of paid holidays should be lengthened and that length-of-service requirements for vacations should be shortened.

4. Day Care. With the increasing proportion of women with young children in the workforce, the provision or subsidization of day care by employers has become an increasingly important issue. Another related issue is help to family members who must provide care for elderly parents or disabled family members.

We argued in Chapter 7 that direct wage payments and benefits are substitutable in workers' preference systems. So they are also substitutable in union-management negotiations. The dollar cost of proposed benefit changes can be roughly estimated and added to other compensation items to determine the package that the union is demanding or that the employer is willing to concede. A union proposal for a 6 percent general wage increase may, when other cost items are added, amount to a 9 percent package. And different items in the package are tradable in negotiations. On the management side trading is based largely on cost calculations. On the union side it depends also on estimates of members' preference systems—whether, for example, the median member would be willing to trade five cents an hour in wages for a given liberalization of health or pension programs.

WORK SCHEDULES

The Fair Labor Standards Act establishes a normal forty-hour week for most industries and prescribes time-and-a-half payment for overtime work. Union contracts, however, often go beyond this legal requirement. First, the contract regulates daily as well as weekly hours: for example, it may specify an eight-hour day and a five-day week. Thus a worker who put in forty hours during a certain week but who worked ten hours on one day of that week would not be entitled to overtime under the Fair Labor Standards Act, but entitled to two hours overtime under the union contract. Second, the union contract may set a limit of less than forty hours. A number of unions now have standard workweeks in the range of thirty-two to thirty-seven hours, and even fewer hours are encountered occasionally. Third, the contract may impose heavier overtime penalties. Double time is often required for work on weekends and on specified holidays, and even triple time is not unheard of.

The intent of these provisions is to prevent overtime work by making it unduly expensive. The statistics of actual working hours suggest that this intent is usually realized. Weekly hours worked in manufacturing and most other industries have hovered around the forty-hour level since World War II. In contract construction, however, the average week is about thirty-seven hours, while in retail trade it has fallen gradually to below thirty-five hours.

During periods of peak demand many employers face the question of whether to lengthen working hours or hire additional workers. Lengthening the workweek beyond the limit prescribed by the Fair Labor Standards Act or by union contract requires overtime payment. But recruiting, screening, and training new workers also involves costs, usually estimated at several hundred dollars per person. So if the abnormal demand is expected to continue for only a short time, some employers will find it less expensive to offer overtime to the existing work force.[6]

We noted in Chapter 3 that some workers prefer a longer workweek than others. Those with low hourly earnings or high consumption goals or large family responsibilities may be unable to meet their income requirements in forty hours. So when overtime is available, they are eager to apply for it. Indeed, the demand for overtime typically exceeds the amount available, requiring some method of rationing. Union contracts usually specify seniority as the basis for rationing, although some attempt to ensure an equal division of overtime, and some give weight to family responsibilities.

There is a special scheduling problem in continuous-process industries where plants must operate around the clock. Such a plant may work a day shift from 8:00 A.M. to 4:00 P.M., a second shift from 4:00 P.M. to midnight, and a third, or "graveyard," shift from midnight to 8:00 A.M. Even where continuous operation is not essential, two- or three-shift operation produces more output from the same plant, thus lowering overhead costs per unit. The second and third shifts are usually considered less attractive, because they interfere with sleep, recreation, and family life. So the contract usually provides a wage premium for those shifts and also typically provides that as vacancies occur on the more desirable shifts, workers may apply for transfer to them on a seniority basis.

Another group of contract provisions relates to payment for time not worked. In coal mining, for example, it may take considerable time to travel from the pithead to the coal face. The United Mine Workers have negotiated a "portal-to-portal" clause under which workers are paid from the time they enter the mine until they leave it. There is often provision for paid lunch periods and for "wash-up time" at the end of the day's work. Another common provision is for "call-in time," which requires that workers who report for work but are not needed on that day must be paid for a minimum number of hours.

In some industries, such as trucking, workers may lose working time for reasons beyond their control. Over-the-road drivers are usually paid on a mileage basis; but to protect workers assigned to short runs, they are normally guaranteed payment for a minimum number of hours per day, regardless of distance driven. Drivers paid on a trip basis are sometimes guaranteed a certain number of runs per week. The Teamsters' contracts also protect against numerous contingencies inherent in trucking, such as payment for layover time and lodging while waiting for a truck in which to return home; "deadheading," when a driver returns as a passenger; equipment breakdown; and impassable highways.

---

[6]For an analysis of this choice problem, see W. Oi, "Labor as a Quasi-fixed Factor," *Journal of Political Economy* (December 1962), pp. 538–55.

SENIORITY AND JOB SECURITY

An important group of provisions in union contracts concerns the conditions under which individual workers shall have access to vacant jobs, the rules governing their tenure of the job, and the conditions under which they may be separated from employment. So important is this matter that Perlman and others have found in it the key to the growth and persistence of trade unionism. Workers are continually faced with a scarcity of available jobs or, at any rate, a scarcity of "good" jobs; and consciousness of this scarcity molds union philosophy and tactics. The union is a method of controlling the job opportunities in a craft or industry and of distributing these opportunities among union members according to some equitable principle.

The union tries to introduce into industry a "civil service system" of job tenure. The worker ceases to be so many units of productive power, which can be shifted about in the plant or dispensed with altogether at the pleasure of the employer. He or she becomes an individual with a system or rights, which the employer is bound to observe and which can be defended through the grievance procedure. The different matters regulated by this system of rights will be examined briefly in this section.

The Seniority Principle

Over the past forty years there has been increasing acceptance of the principle that a worker's job rights should be related to length of service. Common-sense ideas of equity suggest that a worker who has devoted more years to the company deserves more of the company in return. Seniority is objective, relatively easy to measure and apply, and easy to defend before workers and outside arbitrators.

Seniority appears in the union contract in two main ways. First, it usually governs eligibility for fringe benefits: vacations, paid holidays, pensions, severance pay, sick-leave provisions, insurance and health services, profit sharing, supplementary unemployment benefits, and the rest. In bargaining over these issues, unions and employers have agreed that a worker's entitlement to benefits should vary with length of service. The twenty-year person gets longer paid vacations, larger pension rights, more sick leave, and so on, than the two-year person. Slichter, Healy, and Livernash call this system *benefit seniority*.[7]

The second area they term *competitive status seniority*. Here the problem is one of ranking workers relative to each other. Several workers are in competition to get a promotion or avoid a layoff, and the seniority principle is used to resolve the competition. The most obvious applications are to layoff, transfer, and promotion; but there are also many others. The senior worker may be given first choice in picking vacation periods. He may be given first chance to earn more money through overtime work. She may lay claim to the newest of a group of machines or to the machine in the pleasantest location. Spaces in the company parking lot may be

---

[7]Sumner H. Slichter, James J. Healy, and E. Robert Livernash, *The Impact of Collective Bargaining.*

allocated on a seniority basis. In one company the senior workers are allowed to punch out first on the time clock at the end of the day.

Benefit seniority is almost always calculated from the date of first employment with the company; but competitive status seniority is harder to calculate and apply. Suppose that Bill Jones has been with the company fifteen years, working five years in department *A*, five years in department *B*, and five years in his present job in department *C*. Layoffs now become necessary in department *C*, and it is agreed that they should be in order of seniority. What is Bill Jones's seniority in department *C*? Is it fifteen years or only five years? If he is laid off from department *C*, can he go back to his previous job in department *B* and displace ("bump") some less senior worker? How much seniority does he have in department *B*? The rules have to be spelled out in the contract; and the rules may be different for different problems—one principle for promotion, another for layoff, and so on. These fine details have important effects on employee security and on management's freedom to deploy its work force to greatest effect.

Applications of Seniority

Competitive status seniority comes into play most prominently on two fronts: who shall be laid off if the company's need for labor declines, and who shall have first chance at promotions to better jobs. When labor demand declines, a management that was entirely free to choose might respond in several ways: (1) discharge part of the present work force, with the expectation of hiring new workers when demand recovers; (2) put part of the present work force on temporary layoff, with the expectation of recalling them later on; (3) reduce hours of work; (4) reduce wage rates or at least reduce the rate of increase in wages.

Where a union is present some of these avenues of adjustment are either ruled out or severely restricted. As a result, adjustment through layoffs is substantially greater in unionized firms than in comparable nonunionzed firms, while adjustment by the other methods is substantially less. If the decline in demand is relatively short, most of the laid-off union members will return to their previous employer after a spell of unemployment. During a period of decreased product demand management in effect stores labor outside the firm. This policy is subsidized by the existence of an unemployment compensation system for the laid-off workers. In addition, since it is usually those with least seniority who are laid off, the policy benefits more senior employees. As Medoff points out,

> Adjustments through layoffs are much more favorable to senior workers than are adjustments through across-the-board reductions in [the growth of] real wage rates or hours worked. Thus the choice of layoffs in unionized firms appears to reflect a decision-making process under which the interests of senior infra-marginal workers count a great deal.[8]

---

[8]James L. Medoff, "Layoffs and Alternatives Under Trade Unions in U.S. Manufacturing," *American Economic Review* (June 1979), p. 394.

When layoffs are made, unions typically, and always successfully, insist that they be made on a seniority basis. They argue that workers with greater length of service, in addition to being more experienced and productive, are likely to have heavier family responsibilities. Primarily, however, unions like the simplicity and definiteness of a seniority system, which makes it impossible for the employer or the foreman to use layoffs as an occasion for "taking it out" on certain workers.

It is easier to defend the seniority principle than it is to work out detailed regulations for applying it. A central issue here is the size of the *seniority district.* Should seniority be considered as the worker's length of service in a particular occupation, or in a particular department of the plant, or in plants as a whole, or in all plants of a multiplant company? Under plantwide seniority a worker laid off in one department may be able to shift over and bump a worker in an entirely different department whose seniority is less than his own, who in turn may bump someone in a third department. A single layoff may thus set off a chain of displacements throughout the plant. The more narrowly the seniority unit is defined, the smaller the possibility of bumping, and consequently the smaller the protection afforded to long-service employees. The union will typically argue for broad seniority units in order to achieve maximum employee protection, while management will argue for narrower units in order to minimize the disruption of work teams and the added training time that may result from excessive bumping. Arguments over the drafting of seniority clauses and their application to individual workers consume a good proportion of union and management time in collective bargaining.

Whatever procedure is chosen for layoffs normally applies also to rehiring. Workers are recalled to work in reverse order from that in which they were laid off—"last off, first in." The brunt of unemployment is thus borne by those with the shortest period of service.

Turning to promotion, it is increasingly the practice in modern industry to fill "good" vacancies in the plant by promoting members of the existing work force. New workers usually enter the plant in the least desirable jobs and work their way up as vacancies arise. The concept of "promotion" has more dimensions than might occur to an outside observer. Most obvious is movement to a job involving greater skill and a higher wage. But movement from the night shift to the day shift on the same job would also be considered a promotion by most workers, as would transfer to a lighter but equally well-paid job or even movement to the newest machine or the most pleasant location in a particular work group.

The nonunion employer is free to decide whether to fill a vacancy from the outside or from within and, in the latter case, to decide who should be promoted. Decisions are made unilaterally and without advance notice. A union typically insists, as a minimum, that notice of vacancies shall be posted and that present employees shall have opportunity to apply. This enables workers to know about vacancies as they arise, to decide whether a particular job would be a promotion *for them,* and to make a bid for it if they want to.

Most unions try to make length of service the dominant consideration in promotion as well as in layoffs. Employers naturally resist this demand, which they feel would hamper them in rewarding merit and in selecting the most efficient worker available for each job. Few contracts outside the railroad industry specify seniority as the *sole* criterion for promotion. The usual outcome is a compromise providing that where ability is relatively equal the senior worker shall be promoted, or that the senior worker shall be promoted if competent to do the job, or simply that both ability and length of service shall be considered in making promotion decisions. The meaning of these general statements is then worked out through the grievance procedure in individual cases. Usually the practical outcome is that seniority governs in the absence of marked differences of ability among the candidates. As we discussed in Chapter 14, seniority has also come to play a major role in the promotion decisions of many large, successful nonunion firms. For example, in discussing the policies of such firms, Foulkes writes:

> Although it varies by company and by job, in general much weight is given to seniority in promotion decisions. Some companies have imposed requirements on themselves that seem as strict or stricter than those found in the typical union contract.[9]

Unions have emphasized seniority in promotions, in part because of the difficulty of finding other objective criteria on which managers, union officials, and workers can all agree. The lack of such objective criteria and the effects on worker morale and productivity when employers are suspected of favoritism help account for the diffusion of the seniority principle from union to large nonunion employers.

Discipline and Discharge

One of the most delicate areas of day-to-day administration of the union contract is the application of discipline, including use of the ultimate weapon of discharge. Because seniority now carries so many accumulated rights, discharge is a drastic economic penalty that requires careful consideration. The union is forced to defend its members against discharge except in the most flagrant circumstances. Yet management must retain reasonable latitude to apply discipline and to enforce minimum standards of efficiency.

The union contract normally recognizes management's right to discipline the work force and to take the initiative in applying penalties for "just cause." What constitutes "just cause" may be spelled out in the contract itself or in supplementary rules issued by the company. Standard grounds for discipline include continued failure to meet production standards, disobeying instructions of the foreman, presistent absence from work without excuse, participating in wildcat strikes or slowdowns, fighting, gambling, drinking, smoking in prohibited areas, and other personal misdemeanors. For each kind of offense there is usually a graduated series of penalties, which may begin with an oral reprimand by the foreman for the first offense and then go on to written reprimand, a brief suspension from work without

---

[9]Fred K. Foulkes, *Personnel Policies in Large Nonunion Companies,* (Englewood Cliffs, N.J., Prentice-Hall, 1980), p. 140.

pay, a longer suspension from work, and finally discharge. The worker has thus usually had a number of warnings before incurring the ultimate penalty. Some offenses, however, may be considered so serious that suspension or discharge follows immediately.

If a worker contends that he or she is not guilty of the offense or that the penalty imposed was too severe, the case is taken up through the grievance procedure. Discharges, because of their serious consequences for the worker, are invariably appealed, and a large percentage of them are carried all the way to arbitration. Arbitrators have been reluctant to uphold discharges, especially for long-service workers, unless the offense was serious and the evidence clear. The union's check on management's unfettered right of discipline has doubtless improved plant administration in addition to benefiting employees. In preunion days the right of discharge was often grossly abused. The foreman could take out his temper on those under him without recourse, and favoritism and bribery were common. This climate produced much injustice without necessarily promoting efficiency. Protection against arbitrary discipline and discharge is probably the most important single benefit that the worker derives from trade unionism. More than anything else it makes the worker a free citizen in the plant.

Sharing of Work in Industries with No Steady Jobs

In some industries continuous attachment to a single employer is impossible by the nature of the industry. Seamen are often paid off at the end of each voyage and after a shorter or longer period "on the beach" sign on with another vessel for a new voyage. In longshoring the amount of work coming into a particular pier is irregular, depending on what ships happen to arrive on a particular day. When a cargo comes in and has to be unloaded, it is necessary to hire a gang of longshoremen on the spot; when the vessel is unloaded, their job ends. Clearly, seniority with one firm cannot play a major role in determining a worker's employment security in such industries.

In other industries production is highly seasonal. Building construction tapers off in the late fall and revives in the early spring. Each worker naturally wants to be the last person laid off in the fall and the first one hired in the spring. The men's and women's clothing industries have two production seasons during the year, one for the spring trade, the other for the fall trade. During each of these seasons activity begins slowly, mounts to a peak of production and employment, and then declines. Again, each worker in the industry wants to be the first hired and the last laid off.

In the absence of contract rules concerning hiring, the bulk of the work in such industries would go to workers who were of superior efficiency or who had special "pull" with foremen and hiring officials. Workers who got relatively little work would feel that the union was not serving them effectively and would be tempted to drop out. Partly to preserve the organization, partly out of consideration of equity, the union attempts to ensure that the available work is shared more or less equally among the membership. Where employers are numerous and small, this attempt may require union control over the referral of workers to jobs. It is no accident that the union office has been used as an employment agency in the building, printing, and clothing industries, or that the union *hiring hall* has developed in longshoring and merchant shipping.

The devices used to ensure something like equal division of work vary from one industry to the next. In the shipping industry the man who has been longest "on the beach" gets the first opportunity to sign up for a new voyage; all job vacancies and referrals to work are cleared through the union hiring hall. In longshoring work in Pacific Coast ports, a regular list of *gangs* (work teams) is maintained at union headquarters, and gangs are dispatched to work in the order in which they appear on this list. When a gang comes off the job, it must go to the bottom of the list and wait until its number comes up again before being dispatched to a new job.

In the clothing industries the unions have favored reduction in working hours rather than layoffs as work tapers off toward the end of a season. In this way all workers in a shop get an equal amount of work as long as work is available. In building construction there has been some experimentation with "first off, first on" rules, under which the first person laid off in the fall would be dispatched to the first job opening in the spring. This sort of rule, however, presents certain difficulties. The first workers laid off in the fall may be chronic drunkards or undesirable for other reasons. Experience has shown that where the first employer who starts building work in the spring is forced to hire those undesirables, there is a good deal of jockeying among employers to avoid this unpleasant necessity. Whether for this or other reasons, the building trades have done less than most other unions to enforce formal work-sharing rules.

WORKING CONDITIONS

This range of issues tends to be underemphasized, because its miscellaneous character makes it hard to discuss in general terms. But the environment in which a worker spends half the hours of the waking day can have a large effect on personal satisfaction. The issues include *speed of work,* which can range from leisurely to hectic; *physical conditions* of work, including such things as heating, lighting, ventilation, crowding, safety devices on dangerous machines, and presence of toxic gases, dust, or other substances injurious to health; and *social conditions* of work, relations with fellow workers and supervisors.

Work Speed

We saw in Chapter 7 that the issue of work speed takes a different form depending on whether the company uses time payment or incentive payment. Under incentive payment the issue arises in connection with determining time standards for a particular job. The union will usually insist on participation in the determination of time standards or at least will retain the right to challenge any standard through the grievance procedure. Under time payment it is left to the foreman to keep those under him or her working at a reasonable pace. Where there is disagreement over what is reasonable, it will also be resolved through the grievance procedure.

The economic issue is the same in either case: A faster pace of work means lower satisfaction to workers but lower production costs and prices, and hence greater satisfaction, to consumers. This is a typical economic tradeoff, in which greater satisfaction for one group means reduced satisfaction for the other. In principle, one can define an optimal work speed that would correctly balance worker and consumer interests, that is, would maximize total satisfaction for both groups. But where this optimum lies is bound to be a matter of judgment; and there is no reason to expect it to be closely approached in practice. The interesting question is whether a unionized plant is likely to come closer to the optimum than a nonunion plant.

Physical Conditions

Union officials spend much time negotiating with management over various aspects of physical conditions—heating, lighting, ventilation, and cleanliness of the plant; safety arrangements; reduction of health hazards, dangerous or objectionable features of particular jobs; provision of adequate cafeterias and restrooms; and many other matters. Most of these matters are discussed and resolved informally in the plant from day to day, since they are usually too small to be written into the contract. Taken as a whole, however, these matters are very important to satisfaction on the job.

Some matters formerly left to management direction or union-management negotiation are now regulated by government. The Occupational Safety and Health Administration (OSHA) is charged with detecting safety and health hazards by inspection of establishments and can order employers to correct undesirable conditions. From one standpoint, this reduces the union's role in policing working conditions. But from another standpoint it provides an alternative channel of redress. If the union fails to get satisfaction from management, it can complain to OSHA, press for an inspection, and follow up on results. Improvement of working conditions involves the same economic tradeoff noted earlier with respect to work speeds. The improvement will increase workers' satisfaction on the job; but usually it will also raise prodution costs and prices, with a reduction in consumer satisfaction. So there is the same problem of defining an optimal degree of improvement and trying to achieve it. We return to this point in Chapter 21, as part of our assessment of the economic impact of collective bargaining.

Social Conditions

The most substantial change that unionism brings in this area is the reduction in the authority of the foreman and the protection of the worker against arbitrary discipline or discharge. Here we need say little beyond what was said in an earlier section. The worker's need to cultivate the foreman is somewhat reduced, and the need to cultivate union officials is increased. In particular, it is desirable to stand in well with the shop steward, who is responsible for handling individual grievances. The steward's duty, of course, is to pursue each case on its merit; but judgments about merit are not divorced entirely from personal relations.

ADJUSTMENT OF GRIEVANCES

We return here to the distinction drawn at the outset between *substantive* contract terms governing compensation, working conditions, and personnel practices and *procedural* terms, which set the framework of relations between the parties. The contract clauses that define the grievance procedure are of this second type.

After the contract is signed, union and management officials must live under it for several years, and the agreement must be applied to concrete situations arising in the plant. Contract provisions must at best be rather general. They are often unduly vague, even self-contradictory, because of unwillingness of the parties to face and resolve an underlying difference of opinion. It is easier to compromise on a vaguely worded clause that each party may interpret differently. The necessities of plant administration, however, compel specific decisions in particular cases. For this reason virtually all collective agreements contain a grievance procedure providing for adjustment of disputes arising during the life of the contract.

The grievance procedure serves a variety of functions in a collective bargaining relationship.

1. The most obvious function is to interpret the terms of the agreement and apply them to particular cases. Two or more sections of the agreement may be in conflict. Which is to govern? The contract may be silent on a particular problem, so that grievance adjustment involves closing a gap in the agreement. The language of a particular section may be unclear. What does the section actually mean? Even where the wording is clear, its application to a particular case frequently involves a finding of fact. The agreement may say that smoking on duty is a valid reason for discharge. A foreman discharges a man on this ground. The man says that the foreman's charge is incorrect. Was the man smoking, or was he not? Shall he be discharged, or not?

2. The grievance procedure is also a means of *agreement making* in two senses. To the extent that it reveals problems that are not covered clearly enough or not covered at all in the existing agreement, it helps to build up an agenda of issues for the next contract negotiation. Further, the body of decisions in past grievances itself forms part of the agreement in the broadest sense. There gradually develops, case by case and precedent by precedent, an impressive body of shop law. In long-unionized industries such as railroading and coal mining this body of precedents is much larger than the formal union agreement and is understood by both sides to be, in effect, incorporated in the agreement.

3. The grievance procedure can be a sensitive device for locating sore spots in the plant organization and for pointing up inadequacies of particular foremen or union officials. The fact that an unusual number of grievances is filed in a particular department or on a particular issue may be more significant than the intrinsic merit of the grievances. Several leading students of industrial relations have urged the

wisdom of taking a clinical rather than a legalistic view of the grievance procedure, of seeking to remove sources of conflict rather than to score points or win cases.

4. Where relations between the parties are good, the grievance procedure may be used to adjust virtually all day-to-day difficulties between workers and supervisors, whether covered explicitly by the agreement or not. It can become an orderly and systematic way of examining any disputed personnel action.

5. Conversely, where relations are poor, the procedure may become an instrument of conflict. It may be used

> Not to settle problems between workers and supervisor or union and management but to promote the interests of either or both parties in connection with a future test of strength. . . . In unusually incompatible relationships the grievance process may operate as a sort of guerilla warfare during which the parties keep sniping at each other and endeavor to keep their forces at a martial pitch in preparation for the open conflict which will follow expiration of the contract.[10]

Most grievances relate to rights and duties of individual employees. Discharges, or even less-severe disciplinary penalties, are frequently appealed. The application of complicated seniority rules to a particular worker may be questioned. Any choice by a supervisor that involves giving preference to one worker over another—distribution of overtime work, assignment to day work rather than night work, assignment to a preferred type of work and work location—may become a subject of grievance. Classification of workers or their jobs, for wage purposes—whether a job should be rated as machinist *A* rather than machinist *B*—may be disputed. On occasion, considerable numbers of workers may become involved in a grievance case; it is alleged that the assembly line is being run too fast or that a foreman is speeding up the workers or that work loads throughout a department are two heavy or that piece rates on a certain operation have been set too low. A multitude of such issues, each of them minor from a top-management standpoint but important and emotionally explosive to the workers concerned, get worked out peaceably through the grievance process.

The procedure for handling grievances varies with the nature of the industry. In building construction, for example, the work sites are scattered, jobs are often of short duration, and disputes have to be adjusted quickly or not at all. Each union normally has a *business agent* who makes frequent visits to building sites in his area to check that only union people are employed, to ensure that other contract terms are being complied with, and to hear any complaints by the members. The business agent goes over any grievances with the employer then and there. If no agreement is reached, the workers simply leave the job. This is quite different from the lengthy grievance procedures in manufacturing or railroading.

In most manufacturing industries the basic union official concerned with grievances is the *shop steward,* or *grievance committeeperson.* He is usually elected by the union members in his department, and is normally a plant employee; but he is allowed time off from his job to handle grievances, which in a large department

---

[10]Van Dusen Kennedy, "Grievance Procedure," in *Industrial Conflict,* ed. Arthur Kornhausen, Robert Dubin, and Arthur M. Ross (New York: McGraw-Hill Publishing Co., 1954), p. 240.

can become almost a full-time job. The time spent in handling grievances is often paid for by the company, but in some cases the union bears the cost.

The normal first step in a manufacturing plant is for the worker who is "grieving" to consult her shop steward, who discusses the matter informally with the foreman. Most grievances are, and must be, disposed of at this level. If they are not, higher union and management officials face a hopeless burden of cases, settlements are long delayed, and the procedure becomes a source of annoyance rather than relief. An experienced foreman eventually learns the wisdom of bargaining things out informally with the union, trading concessions that he can afford for offsetting concessions from the union when he really needs them.

A grievance that is not adjusted between the steward and the foreman is generally reduced to writing and then goes to the shop committee on one side and the plant superintendent on the other. The next appeal stage may be discussion between a national field representative and the labor relations director of the company. The final step before arbitration may be discussion between a vice-president of the company and a national union representative. The number of stages in the grievance procedure varies somewhat with the size of the company, and the complexity of its organization. When the procedure is working properly, the case load is gradually whittled down at successive levels, leaving only a small percentage of "hard-core" cases for the final arbitration stage.

The Arbitration of Grievances

Unions generally favor arbitration as the final step in disposing of unsettled grievances. Many newly unionized companies in the thirties and forties opposed it because it allowed outsiders to intervene in personnel decisions. Experience has gradually convinced most managements of the value of the procedure, and its use has increased steadily. Today between 90 and 95 percent of union contracts provide for arbitration as the final step in the grievance procedure.

Both management and the union take a risk under arbitration that they will lose decisions on matters that they consider important. Arbitration has the decisive advantage, however, of making possible a final settlement of grievances without a stoppage of work. Arbitration is also in some cases a convenient face-saving device, particularly for the union. Union officials sometimes have to push a case up through the grievance procedure to satisfy a group in their membership, even though they know the members' demands are unreasonable. If such a case goes to arbitration and is decided against the union, the blame can be put on the arbitrator. Part of the arbitrator's function is to serve as a shock absorber for decisions that are unavoidable but for which one side or the other is reluctant to take responsibility.

It should be noted that we are talking here about voluntary arbitration, agreed to in advance by the parties and limited to interpreting an existing agreement. The arbitrator under a grievance procedure is there solely to say what the existing agreement means and has no authority to change the terms of the agreement or to rule on issues not covered by the agreement.

There are several types of voluntary arbitration clauses. The most common practice is for the parties to appoint an abitrator each time the occasion arises. It is frequently provided that where the parties cannot agree the arbitrator shall be designated by the American Arbitration Association, the head of the Federal Mediation and Conciliation Service, the head of the state department of labor, or some other public official. In some industries it is customary to use three- or five-member arbitration boards; each party appoints one or two members to the board, and these members select a neutral chairman. In large companies or in agreements between a union and employers' association there may be enough arbitration work to justify a permanent arbitrator on a full-time or part-time basis. Such an official is frequently termed an *umpire* or *impartial chairman.*

A properly constructed grievance procedure capped by arbitration should in principle render work stoppages unnecessary during the life of the agreement. In recognition of this fact, most contracts contain clauses denying or limiting the right to strike during the contract year. For example, "Under no circumstances shall there be any strike, sympathy strike, walkout, cessation of work, sit down, slow down, picketing, boycott, refusal to perform any part of duty, or other interference with or interruption of the normal conduct of the company's business during the term of this agreement."[11] What happens if a worker engages in a wildcat or "outlaw" strike during the term of the agreement? Some contracts do not contain any penalty provisions. Many contracts, however, provide that instigators of an outlaw strike may be subject to discharge and that participants may be fined or suspended from work for a time. If there is disagreement over whether a worker did instigate a work stoppage, this is taken up through the grievance procedure in the usual way.

LABOR-MANAGEMENT COOPERATION

Under collective bargaining union and management negotiate a contract, one that is usually long, detailed, and rather legalistic. Often the negotiation process emphasizes the areas of disagreement between the two parties rather than the areas of agreement. Distributive rather than integrative bargaining predominates, as the parties negotiate about how to divide a given pie rather than how to expand the size of the pie.

Once the contract is signed, disputes can generally be settled fairly easily through the grievance procedure. In most cases both union and management cooperate to see that the grievance process moves quickly, efficiently, and equitably. The basic criterion for settling a grievance is the terms of the contract. If either party is sufficiently upset by the outcome, it can try to change the terms of the contract the next time it is up for negotiation.

Thus the collective bargaining process can be viewed as a cycle of conflict and cooperation, with conflict predominating when the contract is being negoti-

---

[11]Agreement between the Turbo Engineering Corporation, Trenton, N.J., and Local No. 731, United Automobile Workers.

ated, especially during any strike; and cooperation predominating between negotiations, as the contract is being administered. In the words of Thomas R. Donahue, secretary treasurer of the AFL-CIO

> I do believe that the adversarial role, appropriate to the conflict of collective bargaining, ought to be limited to the period of negotiation—and during the lifetime of a contract so arrived at, it ought to be replaced by a period of cooperation, aimed at maximizing the potential success of the joint enterprise, i.e., the company's business or production.
>
> The labor relations cycle ought to be one of periods of conflict (limited to the negotiation period) followed by a longer period of cooperation.[12]

Labor-management cooperation can occur for many reasons. One is the technical complexity of many issues, including pensions, health insurance, and occupational health and safety. In recent years efforts to control health insurance costs, while still providing adequate coverage, provide a good example. Because of the complexity of such issues, they often require considerable staff work before the contract is negotiated. Sometimes such staff work can lead to joint union-management administration of the resulting program.

Another reason for labor-management cooperation is a sense of emergency, when the need for integrative bargaining transcends the normal habits of distributive bargaining. Such emergencies range from the concession bargaining of the 1980s to the extraordinary demand for labor during World War II, when many unions gained acceptance from management in return for no-strike pledges for the duration of the war.

Under normal circumstances it has been easy for union and management to develop too close a cooperative arrangement. In most cases there is a long history of conflict between labor and management, primarily at the time of contract negotiations, but also resulting from efforts of many employers to run nonunion as well as union operations and to expand the relative role of their nonunion sector. Such conflict encourages each side to treat the other with suspicion rather than trust, an atmosphere not conducive to cooperation.

While union officials and their industrial relations counterparts in management often do develop cooperative personal relations over time, there are definite limits on how far such cooperation can go on substantive issues. On the union side the rank and file tend to be suspicious of any leader who appears to be becoming too cozy with management. Such a leader will be vulnerable at election time to a charge of "selling out to the bosses." On the employer side many top managers outside of industrial relations are reluctant to see unions playing any significant role in the firm's decision making and are impatient with the length of time involved in consulting effectively with workers, or their unions, on many issues. During the 1970s and 1980s competitive pressures caused many firms to seek to reduce the role of their unions. Such pressures led other firms, usually where unions were more

---

[12]Donahue is quoted by Rudolph Oswald in "Joint Labor-Management Programs: A Labor Viewpoint," in *Teamwork*, ed. Jerome M. Rosow (New York: Pergamon Press, 1986), pp. 26–27.

securely established, to seek greater cooperation from their unions. Rather surprisingly, some firms were able to pursue both strategies simultaneously with some success.

As the pressure on firms from foreign competition and low domestic demand abated a little in the late eighties, both the trend toward greater hostility toward unions and the trend toward greater union-management cooperation appear to have diminished somewhat. There is one area, however, where the trend toward greater cooperation appears to be continuing, namely quality-of-working-life (QWL) programs.

QUALITY-OF-WORKING-LIFE (QWL) PROGRAMS

During the 1970s many firms experimented with programs to involve employees more in decisions affecting how they performed their jobs. These programs, or processes, have many different names, but are referred to most frequently in terms of one of their original aims, to improve the quality of working life (QWL). Most QWL programs are based on two assumptions: (1) that those most directly involved in the production process, the workers, can contribute to making that process more effective and (2) that workers will have greater job satisfaction, better motivation, less absenteeism and lower quit rates if they are treated as mature intelligent individuals and as an important part of the team, rather than as unthinking robots or as shirkers trying to do as little as possible in return for their paychecks. In the words of Irving Bluestone, a leading advocate of QWL when he served as a vice-president of the UAW,

> My feeling was: Damn it, it's about time that workers were given more than just the opportunity to be order-takers. They're not adjuncts to the tool, they're not automatons, they're human beings. They've got to be treated with dignity and they've got to be given the opportunity to use their God-given ingenuity and powers to be creative themselves.[13]

Under the typical union contract management initiates changes, and the union grieves if it believes the changes have violated any provision of the contract. Thus the role of the worker, and the union, in dealing with changes in technology, investment, or other decisions affecting the organization of work is simply a reactive one.

Under QWL, on the other hand, workers have the opportunity to take the initiative and suggest changes in workplace operations, including how best to introduce new technologies. Sometimes the worker involvement may come at a very centralized level, usually through the union. More frequently, however, workers will meet in small groups to discuss how the workplace might be improved, with regard to working conditions (e.g., safety, ventilation, lighting) as well as quality of

---

[13]Quoted by Charlotte Gold, *Labor-Management Committees: Confrontation, Cooptation, or Cooperation?* (Ithaca, N.Y.: ILR Press, 1986), p. 26.

output (e.g., reduction of defects) and productivity (rearranging tasks or equipment, introducing new technology). Such small groups, often called quality circles, do not require the presence of a union and appear to be most prevalent in large nonunion firms. The QWL approach may work more easily in a nonunion environment, where workers cannot effectively challenge management over the share of income going to labor. With this threat largely removed, it may be easier for management to be a good listener, share information, encourage workers to provide new ideas, and try to foster an atmosphere of cooperation and trust. In all cases, however, it takes considerable time and patience to develop the atmosphere of mutual trust that is necessary if QWL is going to be effective.

Although the QWL approach may be more difficult in a unionized setting because of potential conflicts with the union contract and because of a tradition of distributive bargaining, QWL has been successful in some unionized firms.[14] In addition to the productivity and job satisfaction benefits discussed above, in a union setting QWL can also lead to fewer grievances, fewer strikes, and a better atmosphere for integrative bargaining. Bluestone argues that QWL is likely to be most successful when the program is voluntary for each worker, involves no speedup, causes no loss of jobs, includes union representatives, and does not conflict with the union contract.[15] If QWL suggestions do conflict with the union contract, the contract must take precedence. Otherwise QWL is too likely to lose the support of workers and union leaders. Of course, the contract can be modified in future negotiations. Also QWL can successfully address issues that traditionally have been management perogatives or issues that occur on too small a scale to be included in the contract, such as how to rearrange machinery in one small section of the plant.

The problem of increased competition, both foreign and domestic, has contributed to an increase in labor-management cooperation, including QWL. As Gold indicates,

> It remains to be seen whether unions are seeking—and managements providing—such benefits as employee participation in decision making and increased quality of life on the job because (a) they are finding it difficult to give employees major improvements in basic wages and other standard conditions of employment, (b) they are responding to the needs of a new, younger work force that sees these benefits as an essential part of their work life, or (c) they basically believe in the value of joint decision making. There is no doubt, however, that these forces are creating dramatic new changes in the workplace.[16]

After a period of relative stability from the mid-1950s to the late 1970s, labor relations are now in a considerable state of flux. New efforts by firms to seek more

---

[14]For example, see the discussion of QWL at a GM plant in Robert H. Guest, "Quality of Work Life—Learning from Tarrytown," *Harvard Business Review* (July/August 1979), pp. 76–87; and QWL at AT&T, in Raymond Wiliams and Glenn Watts, "The Process of Working Together: CWA's/AT&T's Approach to QWL," in *Teamwork*, 1986, pp. 75–88.

[15]See Irving Bluestone, "How Quality-of-Worklife Projects Work for the United Auto Workers," *Monthly Labor Review,* (July 1980), pp. 39–41.

[16]See Gold, *Labor-Management Committees,* p. 50.

ideas from their workers, to eliminate unions when they can, and to cooperate with unions when they can't avoid them are all being added to the former system of industrial relations.

SUMMARY

1. Several types of provisions appear in a typical union contract. First, the contract specifies the rights and duties of the parties. The most controversial issue is whether all employees should be required to join the union (a union shop) or to pay the equivalent of union dues (an agency shop).

2. Provisions concerning employee compensation are numerous and complex. There are clauses related to the occupational wage structure, overtime, shift differentials, and benefits. Bargaining focuses on the "package cost" of these items, which are tradable against each other to some extent. Wage rates typically are assigned based on the characteristics of the job, not of the worker, although there has been some increase in "payment for knowledge" in recent years.

3. Much of the attention in most contract negotiations focuses on the size of the general wage increase. This increase depends partly on economic conditions and partly on whether the contract includes cost-of-living adjustments (COLAs), lump-sum payments, profit sharing, or increases in benefits.

4. When the demand for labor was low in the early 1980s, some unions were willing to accept wage cuts and more flexible work rules in order to increase job security. Such concession bargaining often also led to more union involvement in the firm's investment decisions and to profit sharing or employee stock-ownership plans (ESOPs).

5. An important group of provisions relates to job tenure and job security. There is usually heavy emphasis on *seniority* in layoffs, recall to work, and promotion to better jobs. Discipline and discharge of employees is also carefully regulated.

6. Other important subjects of bargaining come under the general heading of working conditions. Examples include the speed of work; occupational health and safety; physical conditions, such as heating, lighting, and ventilation; and social conditions, such as protection of workers from arbitrary treatment by foremen or other bosses.

7. Disputes over the meaning of a contract clause or over its application to a particular employee are resolved through the *grievance procedure*. If a dispute cannot be resolved by the foreman and the shop steward, it may go through several higher levels of union-management negotiations. If still unresolved, most disputes call for the final decision to be made by a neutral arbitrator, chosen and paid by the parties.

8. Usually there is a cycle of cooperation and conflict between union and management with conflict dominant during the negotiation of a contract and cooperation dominant while the contract is in place and disputes over interpretation are being grieved.

9. In some industries quality-of-working-life (QWL) programs have become important. Such programs are based on the following two assumptions: (1) because they are directly involved in production, workers are knowledgeable and can contribute to designing more effective production processes, and (2) workers will have greater job satisfaction if they are treated as intelligent, important members of the company team.

KEY CONCEPTS

UNION SHOP	SENIORITY BENEFIT
AGENCY SHOP	SENIORITY, COMPETITIVE STATUS
CLOSED SHOP	SENIORITY DISTRICT
RIGHT-TO-WORK LAW	LAYOFF
OVERTIME	RECALL
SHIFT DIFFERENTIAL	PROMOTION
LUMP-SUM PAYMENT	GRIEVANCE PROCEDURE
COST-OF-LIVING ADJUSTMENT (COLA)	ARBITRATION, GRIEVANCE
SENIORITY PRINCIPLE	SHOP STEWARD

REVIEW QUESTIONS

1. What are the main arguments for and against the union shop?
2. Is it correct to say that the various items in the compensation package are fully interchangeable and that only the package cost matters? Can you think of situations in which this might not be true?
3. In recent years why have lump-sum payments and profit sharing increased in importance while cost-of-living adjustments have become less prevalent?
4. What is the difference between *benefit seniority* and *competitive status seniority?* What are some of the difficulties in defining seniority for the latter purpose?
5. What are the advantages and limitations of the seniority principle in making
   (a) layoffs?
   (b) promotions?
6. What are the main functions of the grievance procedure in collective bargaining?
7. What are quality-of-working-life (QWL) programs? What are the likely benefits and costs of such programs to management? workers? unions?

READINGS

Bureau of National Affairs, *Basic Patterns in Union Contracts,* 11th ed. Washington, D.C.: Bureau of National Affairs, 1986.

Hendricks, Wallace E., and Lawrence M. Kahn, *Wage Indexation in the United States: COLA or UNCOLA?* Cambridge, Mass.: Ballinger, 1985.

Rees, Albert, *The Economics of Trade Unions,* 3d. ed. Chicago: University of Chicago Press, 1989.

Slichter, Sumner H., James J. Healy, and E. Robert Livernash, *The Impact of Collective Bargaining on Management.* Washington, D.C.: Brookings Institution, 1960.

CASE STUDIES IN COLLECTIVE BARGAINING

In this chapter we examine collective bargaining in four important industries—automobiles, farm equipment, steel, and trucking—organized by three of our largest unions—the United Automobile Workers (UAW), the United Steelworkers, and the Teamsters. In each case we shall see that major changes have occurred since 1980, more dramatic changes than over the previous few decades. By looking at these cases in some detail, we can illustrate how collective bargaining works and how it differs from industry to industry and union to union. We will see how it has changed in response to the economic and political changes of the past two decades, especially greater competition from other countries and from nonunion operations in the United States.

AUTOMOBILES

In the peak year of 1979 more than one million workers were employed directly in the automobile industry, either in final assembly or in the production of parts.[1] Most production workers belonged to the UAW, which represented about 8 percent of all union members in the private sector, although not all its members work in the auto industry.

---

[1]The discussion of the automobile industry is based largely on the work of Harry C. Katz. See his book *Shifting Gears: Changing Labor Relations in the U.S. Automobile Industry;* and his chapter "Automobiles," in *Collective Bargaining in American Industry,* pp. 13–53.

The importance of collective bargaining in automobiles is not based solely on the size of the industry. Since 1948 the auto industry has been an important pattern setter, influencing collective bargaining in many other sectors of the economy. Wage increases in automobiles have influenced negotiations most directly in other industries, such as farm equipment, where the UAW represents many workers. In addition, the automobile industry has had some effect on wage rates in most other high-wage manufacturing industries, because auto-worker contracts receive considerable publicity and affect the expectations of many other workers.

The automobile industry has pioneered many important items, including cost-of-living adjustments (COLAs) and supplemental unemployment insurance benefits. More recently the industry and the UAW have played a leading role in negotiating quality-of-working-life (QWL) programs and shifting from assembly-line to production-team approaches. As the demand for labor has fallen, much attention has also been given to job security and to providing training opportunities to laid-off workers. While those in many other sectors of the economy have been concerned with these issues, the auto industry is the only one where union contracts provide significant resources to help train laid-off workers for jobs in other industries.

The Union

The automobile industry is organized by the United Automobile, Aerospace, and Agricultural Implements Workers of America, usually referred to as the UAW. The UAW has achieved national prominence because of its role in the auto industry, which accounts for about three-quarters of its membership. Some other unions also represent auto workers, especially in the supply plants, but the UAW is by far the dominant union in the industry.

Although the UAW is a large union of about one million workers with highly centralized authority, it has a strong democratic tradition. The union first organized the auto industry with the aid of several dramatic sit-down strikes in 1937. After a period of factionalism, strong unified leadership was established by Walter Reuther, who headed the union with energy and imagination from 1947 until his death in 1970.[2]

The Industry

Since 1914, when Henry Ford developed the low-cost model T, produced by a continuously moving assembly line, the automobile industry has been the paradigm case of the large mass-production industry in the United States. Until the 1980s automobiles also symbolized the success of American industry.

The automobile industry in the United States has been dominated by the

---

[2]In addition to his important role in collective bargaining, Reuther was also a leader of the liberal wing of the Democratic party, with considerable influence at the national level as well as in Detroit and Michigan. Since Reuther's death, the UAW has had a succession of leaders who have maintained his tradition of innovative approaches, hard bargaining, and responsiveness to the concerns of union members.

Big Three: General Motors, Ford, and Chrysler. Although these three firms account for almost all the assembly and sales of American cars, they buy many of their parts from independent suppliers. The Big Three are all organized by the UAW, although many parts suppliers are nonunion, and some are located in countries with lower wage rates.

Foreign imports have always been important in sport cars. In the late 1950s the German Volkswagen started providing some competition in the market for passenger cars. Foreign competition increased dramatically in the 1970s with the success of the Toyota, the Datsun, and other Japanese imports. The imports' share of the market increased from 15 percent in 1970 to a peak of 28 percent in 1981. In that year an import quota was negotiated with the Japanese. Under this agreement imports fell to 24 percent of the market by 1985. Partly to avoid the effects of import quotas, the Japanese have established their own plants in the United States, with American workers. Some of these plants have been joint efforts with U.S. firms, while others have been set up entirely by the Japanese. The latter plants, which have been located in geographic areas with little previous unionization, so far have successfully resisted all organizing drives by the UAW. As a result, for the first time since the early 1940s there are now many American production workers in the automobile industry who are not represented by the UAW. Political pressure has led the Japanese to continue their agreement to limit exports to the United States. These limits are no longer of great importance, however, because the Japanese firms can now produce so many cars within the United States.

During the long period when the Big Three dominated a growing American market, the UAW was in a strong bargaining position. Because General Motors, Ford, and Chrysler were all unionized, the UAW could force similar wage increases at each company. With product demand high and growing and no major changes in technology, the union could negotiate generous wage increases without fear of job losses, except for some temporary layoffs during recessions. The industry could pay high wage rates and still earn high profits because it was an oligopoly. Economies of scale in production plus the need for a large distribution system and expensive advertising all limited the potential competition from small firms or from possible new entrants into the market. When new entrants did become a major factor, they came from other countries, first Germany, and then Japan, where firms had already gained the economies of large-scale production. Foreign competition did not become a major threat until the 1970s, however.

Collective Bargaining in Autos Prior to the 1980s

The period from the late forties through the late seventies was one of stability in the automobile industry. Demand for cars was high, except temporarily during recessions. With high product demand, the firms in an oligopolistic industry can afford to pay high wage rates and still earn a good profit. Thus there can be a wide gap between what the firm must pay to attract an adequate work force and what it can afford to pay without being forced out of business. This situation can lead to major conflict in bargaining, as in fact occurred in the auto industry from the late thirties to the late forties except for an interlude during the national crisis of World War II.

Rather than suffer the costs of frequent, lengthy strikes, with great uncertainty about the results of the negotiations, both the UAW and the auto companies had an interest in narrowing the range of disagreement. If this objective could be achieved, it would facilitate long-range planning, because firms could better estimate their future labor costs and workers their future earnings. Such long-range planning was especially important for the auto companies, because it took several years for a firm to plan and then set up the physical capital to produce a new model. In addition to facilitating long-term planning, finding a formula that would reduce the range of disagreement also could reduce the likelihood of lengthy, costly strikes.

1. Formulas For Wage Rates. After World War II leaders of the auto industry recognized that the UAW had become well established and that annual negotiations were very costly. A longer-term contract would reduce the costs of negotiation, including strike costs, and would facilitate long-term planning. In return for a multiyear contract, the auto industry was prepared to offer some significant inducements. To protect the workers against inflation, a cost-of-living adjustment (COLA) was introduced. In addition to the COLA, GM was also willing to pay an annual improvement factor (AIF) so workers' wages would increase with expected increases in productivity.[3]

The COLA was designed to protect workers from part of the cost of inflation. One-hundred percent protection would have increased GM's labor costs too much if the relative demand for automobiles fell, and auto prices did not keep pace with the general rate of inflation, as happened after the oil-price shocks of the 1970s. The AIF was designed so that auto workers could share in the normal productivity gains throughout the economy.

Under neither formula are wage rates intended to vary with changes in the demand for automobiles and auto workers, even though demand in the auto industry is very cyclically sensitive. High unemployment in the auto industry during recessions did not create any effective pressure to reduce wage rates in order to save jobs.[4] Unemployment was temporary for most workers and limited to those with

---

[3]Both the COLA and AIF formulas initially provided for an equal cents-per-hour wage adjustment for all workers. This approach has continued for the COLAs, but the AIFs have been changed to equal percentage increases.

In response to an increase in the consumer price level, the percentage wage increases from the COLA are largest for low-wage workers. Those with relatively low wage rates receive virtually complete protection from inflation, while those with higher wages receive only partial protection. Extra raises have been negotiated for skilled workers from time to time, so that real wage differentials have not declined dramatically with continuing inflation.

[4]If one firm should face unusual financial difficulties and is in danger of going out of business, then the union might be expected to give that firm some breaks in order to maintain the jobs of its workers. The UAW did make some minor adjustments in this regard, as with American Motors in the 1970s. Prior to 1979, however, the union was unwilling to make any major concessions. As we shall see, pattern bargaining did break down under the pressure of severe economic distress in the early 1980s, distress that had a differential impact on the various firms.

little seniority. Supplemental unemployment benefits (SUB) were established a few years later to aid those workers who were laid off.

Trying to adjust wage rates to take account of changes in demand would have involved several problems. First, given the tradition of three-year contracts that developed in the industry and the difficulty of predicting changes in demand, some new formula would have been required. If it had been based on conditions in the automobile industry, then the UAW would have needed to see records that the auto companies strongly desired to keep confidential. Second, varying wage rates with changes in employment would have encouraged the UAW to take greater interest in the firms' policies affecting employment, including decisions on investment, technological change, and pricing. For decades the automobile companies vigorously opposed any union involvement in such issues, successfully resisting Reuther's efforts to extend collective bargaining into these areas. Third, lower wage rates in times of high unemployment would have had an adverse effect on all workers with enough seniority to be in little danger of even a temporary layoff. As long as the short-run labor demand curve is inelastic, then even a sharp decline in demand will cost only a relatively small number of jobs in the short run. In the long run, no jobs would be lost because the declines in demand were only temporary. Under such conditions it is not surprising that the union has favored supplemental unemployment insurance benefits rather than wage cuts during recessions.

The wage formulas established clear expectations about the future and thus helped automobile workers to accept long-term contracts. Before long these basic principles also spread to many other industries. For twenty years, from the late forties through the late sixties, this approach was consistent with a relatively constant wage structure across industries. For example, the average wage rate of auto assemblers stayed about 15 to 20 percent above that of the average private-sector production worker during the period from 1950 to 1965.[5] Even government wage policies, notably the Kennedy-Johnson wage-price guidelines, were based on similar principles.

During the 1970s, however, the relative wage rates of auto workers and of many other unionized workers increased. By 1980 the average GM assembly worker was earning 55 percent more than the average production worker in the private sector. The higher relative wage rates resulted partly from the AIF, which was geared to a productivity growth rate of 3 percent in the economy. As we saw in Chapter 9, for the economy as a whole such a growth in productivity was realistic for the fifties and sixties but much too optimistic for the seventies. Perhaps even more important, productivity in the automobile industry was not increasing nearly as rapidly in the United States as in Japan. Nevertheless, the formulas were sufficiently well established that no appreciable adjustments were made in either the AIF or the COLA clauses of the union contract. In large part, no changes were made because the economic difficulties of the industry and the whole economy were seen as temporary aberrations. As we shall see, it took the even more serious

---

[5]Katz, *Shifting Gears*, p. 22.

problems of the 1980s to force the parties to view the issues as long-term ones that required serious attention.

In addition to wage changes, the negotiations from the forties through the seventies also led to many benefits, including health insurance and pensions as well as supplemental unemployment insurance. Benefits increased from 12.5 percent of the wage rate at General Motors in 1948 to 71.6 percent in 1981.[6] In general, the new benefits came in addition to the normal wage increases. The dramatic rise in the value of benefits over this period increased the compensation of auto workers relative to other production workers. The new and more generous benefits came fairly steadily. Like wage increases, their timing was not significantly affected by changes in sales, profits, or employment in the auto industry.

2. Connective Bargaining. The wage formulas established expectations about how wage rates should change from one year to the next. Another important aspect of collective bargaining in automobiles during the period from the forties through the seventies is how wage rates and labor costs were equalized across companies and across plants within each company. Such standardization is called *connective bargaining.*

Connective bargaining is important, especially for the union. Consider what will happen if contract terms are not standardized. First, any firm or plant that can gain better terms than its competitors will achieve a significant advantage. Thus each firm will push hard to gain terms at least as favorable as those of its rivals. As a result, concessions at any one firm will reduce the bargaining power of the union. In addition to this economic argument, there is also an equity argument. The principle of equal pay for equal work is deeply ingrained in the labor movement. A union is never enthusiastic about having to explain why it cannot win as much for one group of workers as for another. Tensions between groups of union members with differing contracts can be quite divisive and can reduce the power of the union, which depends on the willingness of all members to support each other.

Connective bargaining requires that wage differentials be eliminated both across and within firms. Interfirm differentials were eliminated through pattern bargaining, discussed in Chapter 16. Every three years, when the previous contracts expired, the UAW would pick one of the companies to start the next round of bargaining. Usually it would pick a company that had good sales and high profits. Such a company could afford a generous settlement and would be especially vulnerable to a strike. Once the union reached a settlement with this pattern-setting firm, it would bargain with the remaining companies, forcing each to follow the pattern established with the initial firm. In this way uniform wage rates could be established throughout the unionized sector. For automobile assembly, all United States companies were organized by the UAW so that the only exception to standardization occurred among foreign firms, a small component of the market until the 1970s.[7]

---

[6]Ibid., p. 23.

[7]There is less standardization in the parts-supply segment of the industry, which includes some nonunion firms within the United States as well as foreign firms.

Connective bargaining requires standardization of labor costs across plants within each firm as well as across firms. In the automobile industry wage rates and benefits are negotiated at the national level, with no variation across plants. Still, labor costs can vary from one location to another because production standards, work rules, and health and safety standards affect costs and are negotiated at the local level.

In fact, little variation across plants has been allowed by the UAW in any contract provisions affecting labor costs. With the consent of the companies, the national officers of the UAW established a system where they had to approve all local strikes and also any grievances sent to outside arbitration. The national union was able to use this power to standardize contract provisions across plants, an issue that was important to the union for the same reasons it needed standardization across companies. Long-term differentials in labor costs across plants would provide an incentive for companies to transfer production to the plants with the lowest cost, thus putting pressure on the union to bring labor costs at all plants down to the lowest level established anywhere, in order to protect jobs.[8]

Generally, high and increasing demand in the auto industry helped the UAW to standardize contract provisions during the period from the end of World War II through the 1970s.[9] As a result of high demand, there was little pressure on the union to establish lower labor costs at any plant in order to protect the jobs of its workers.

3. Job Control.   In addition to the wage formulas and the standardization of labor costs across all unionized firms and plants, a third important feature of collective bargaining in the automobile industry has been an emphasis on job-control unionism. As described in Chapter 12, this approach is not limited to the auto industry but is common wherever there are industrial unions. The job-control approach is defined by detailed, lengthy, legalistic contract provisions; a detailed set of job classifications; wage rates assigned to each job, independent of the characteristics of the workers holding the job; rules, based largely on seniority, carefully spelling out transfer and promotion rights from one job to another and the order of layoffs; and grievance procedures to settle disputes over how to interpret the contract in specific situations.

---

[8]The companies were interested in standardization across plants for the opposite reason, concern that the union would use the strike weapon to force all plants up to the most generous standard. Standardization also serves to reduce the range of conflict in negotiations, especially at the local level, and thus makes it easier for negotiators to reach agreement without a strike.

[9]The UAW was quite successful in standardizing contracts across firms and across plants of the same firm. But it could not standardize labor costs and thus eliminate all competitive pressures on such costs. In part, labor costs depend on the amount and quality of capital equipment available to the work force. But investment decisions were the exclusive domain of management and thus were not covered by the union contract. In addition, labor costs depended on the state of labor relations at the plant. Because the quality of such relations could not be legislated, the union could only standardize contract provisions and could not deal with cost differences resulting from interplant differences in the quality of the relation between labor and management.

The history of conflict and lack of trust between union and company officials is one reason for the lengthy legalistic nature of the union contract. Another reason stems from the differing rights of management and labor under the union contract. On any issue management can act without prior approval by the union. Then, if the union thinks that what management has done is in violation of the contract, it can present a grievance. This approach, which is common in most collective bargaining in the United States, encourages the union to negotiate a very detailed contract so that it can establish effective limits on the rights of management. On the other hand, management has tolerated the result as a relatively minor price to pay for keeping unions out of many decisions, such as pricing and investment, in which they might easily have become involved if their role had not been carefully limited to items explicitly covered in the union contract.

Changes in the Automobile Industry Since the 1970s

In the 1970s and 1980s the situation facing the automobile industry changed in many respects. First, foreign competition increased. The Japanese provided especially strong competition, partly because they could provide high-quality, low-cost cars with an extensive network of dealers. In addition, the comparative advantage of foreign producers, including the Japanese, was in small, fuel-efficient cars. The demand for such vehicles became much greater as a result of the large oil-price increases in 1973–74 and 1979. Once car buyers have become used to a foreign car, perhaps because of the oil-price shock, they are much more likely to buy another, even if gas prices have declined and there is less need for fuel efficiency.

When imports from Japan reached 28 percent of the United States market in 1981, import quotas were established. In addition to limiting the amount of imports from Japan, these quotas had several indirect effects. First, they encouraged the Japanese to compete more heavily in the market for relatively expensive cars, where the profits per car were highest. Equally important, the major Japanese firms all built plants in the United States, because cars built in this country would not count under any import quotas. Some of these plants are joint ventures with American auto companies, while others are owned entirely by the Japanese. The latter plants are nonunion, while some of the former have been organized by the UAW. Even among those plants that have been unionized, Japanese principles of labor relations, such as production teams and flexible work rules, play a prominent role.

Increased foreign competition has not been the only factor changing the automobile industry in the 1980s. The recession of the early eighties was very severe and came in addition to the problems caused by increased foreign competition. Primarily because of the recession, employment in the automobile industry fell by almost 40 percent from 1979 to 1981.

Since 1982 employment has increased, as aggregate demand in the economy has expanded. Still there are fewer union members in the auto industry now than in the late seventies. Greater use of robots and computers has led to an increase in output per worker. In addition, more nonunion labor is being used in the production of automobiles made in the United States. As mentioned earlier, Japanese companies, such as Honda and Nissan, that produce cars in this country have work forces that are entirely nonunion. And although all plants operated by the Big Three are union shops, GM, Ford, and Chrysler are buying more of their parts from nonunion suppliers.

The economic environment has changed in another important respect. From the days of the Model T until well into the 1970s, the U.S. automobile industry symbolized the high productivity of long assembly lines. With each worker performing just a few tasks on the line, little skill is required of the work force. Training expenses are low, and it is easy for the auto companies to recruit dependable workers because of high pay.

The assembly line does pose some problems, however. One is the boring, repetitive nature of the work, which would lead to high turnover and absenteeism except for the high wage rates.

Another, more recent problem arises because of the need for large production runs. With a long assembly line, the marginal cost of producing an extra car is relatively small, but the fixed costs of setting up or changing the line are high.

In the fifties and sixties demand was generally stable enough so that the high fixed costs could be recovered with little difficulty over the course of the model year. With relatively stable demand, except for occasional recessions, the companies could do reasonably accurate planning. Starting in the mid-seventies, however, such planning became much more difficult. Gasoline prices shot up in response to oil prices set by the OPEC cartel. As gas prices changed, so did the relative demand for small versus large cars. The demand for American versus Japanese cars also varied sharply over short periods as a result of changes in import quotas and the value of the dollar.

As demand has become more difficult to predict, the automobile companies have become increasingly interested in establishing more flexible production methods. The development of more sophisticated, but less expensive, robots, which can be easily reprogrammed to perform a variety of tasks, has made it easier to shift production from one model to another. With such methods the automobile companies need more flexibility in the allocation of workers.

Collective Bargaining Since 1980

After three decades of stability, collective bargaining in the automobile industry changed dramatically in the 1980s.

1. Chrysler's Near-Bankruptcy. The first break in the old system occurred in the 1979 negotiations at Chrysler, a company on the verge of economic failure. To save the company and avert major costs to the national economy, a $3.5 billion package was negotiated by the federal government, which included almost half a billion dollars in foregone raises by union workers.[10] The primary negotiations occurred in Congress, where the magnitude of the concessions required of each party was determined. If any party refused to accept its required concession, then the federal loan guarantees would not be forthcoming. In return for its concessions, the UAW won a seat on Chrysler's board and an employee stock ownership plan.

2. Wage Concessions at GM and Ford. The problem at Chrysler in the late seventies resulted in large part from bad management by company officials rather than from the changing economy. By the next contract negotiations in 1982, however, increased foreign competition and a severe recession in the economy led to serious problems at all of the auto companies, including the permanent layoff of many workers. The UAW was forced to renegotiate its contracts with GM and Ford before they expired and to make major concessions on both wage formulas and work rules.[11] In contrast to the 1979 negotiations with Chrysler, there was no expectation that these concessions would be taken back at a later time. In return for the concessions, the UAW won several provisions designed to reduce the income and job losses of its members.[12]

3. Breakdowns in Connective Bargaining. The economic difficulties of the automobile industry led to other breakdowns in connective bargaining in addition to the low wage rates at Chrysler. Profit sharing was established at each of the Big Three companies, and extensive work-rules modifications were made at many of the plants that were most in danger of closing.[13]

4. Changes in Work Rules. The work-rule changes have mainly been of two kinds. First, employees can be required to work harder, for example, by speeding up an assembly line. Second, the plant can be allowed to deploy workers

---

[10]The total package included $1.5 billion in new loans guaranteed by the federal government, $650 million in new loans from Chrysler's bankers, $300 million in the sale of Chrysler's assets, $250 million from state and local governments, $180 million from suppliers, $125 million from nonunion employees, and $462.5 million from union workers.

[11]AIF raises were canceled for two years and COLA adjustments for one year. In addition, ten paid holidays were eliminated.

[12]Permanently laid-off senior workers would receive at least 50 percent of their last year's earnings until they reached normal retirement age. More money was put aside to cover the costs of supplemental unemployment benefits. Employment guarantees for 80 percent of the work force were made for some plants, and no plants were to be closed because of "outsourcing," the shifting of production to nonunion suppliers at home or abroad. These job security measures had symbolic as well as practical value, as union and management sought to reassure the workers that they were getting something in return for the concessions from the normal wage formula.

[13]Profit sharing was attractive to the union because it ensured that members would gain higher wage rates as well as more jobs if conditions improved at any of the companies, thus making the wage concessions more palatable. From the company's perspective, profit sharing was attractive because it wouldn't cost anything unless the firm's profits improved considerably, in which case the firm could afford to pay more. On the other hand, profit sharing meant that different rates of pay would develop, between GM and Ford as well as with Chrysler, if one firm developed higher profits than another.

more flexibly. For example, when an assembly line breaks down, the supervisor and nearest workers are permitted to fix the problem rather than wait for a specialized repair worker to arrive.

In some plants more radical changes have been made. Instead of each worker's being assigned a particular job, production is organized by work teams, who decide among themselves how to organize so that all tasks are covered. Under this approach workers are encouraged to learn many skills so they can perform any function for the team. Pay is based on the number of skills the worker has mastered rather than on a particular job classification. The team approach has a number of potential advantages over the more common job-control system, including (1) better worker morale; (2) higher-quality output because of both higher morale and a closer coordination of production and inspection; and (3) greater ease of adapting to new production methods, including both new technologies and shifts from one product to another. There are also some disadvantages for the workers, however. Management may try to play off one team against another. Also older workers lose some of the benefit of their high seniority as pay becomes based more on the number of skills mastered and less on gaining access, through seniority, to a job that is narrowly defined but highly paid.

5. Collective Bargaining in the Late 1980s.   We have seen how the system of collective bargaining that had remained stable for thirty years, starting in the late 1940s, suddenly changed quite dramatically as a result of economic pressures. These pressures included the recession of the early eighties, increased competition from nonunion parts suppliers within the United States, and especially the competition from Japan.

Over the course of the 1980s demand for automobiles increased considerably as the economy pulled out of the recession. Also, quotas, both real and threatened, reduced imports from Japan. On the other hand, nonunion competition remained at higher levels. Perhaps of even greater importance, the Japanese companies succeeded in producing their cars in the United States, with American workers but Japanese management techniques. The Japanese approach emphasizes cooperation and teamwork, both between labor and management and among workers. Except where they have undertaken joint ventures with the American companies, the Japanese plants have succeeded in remaining nonunion, despite the organizing efforts of the UAW. Thus although the economic situation facing the American companies and the UAW has improved, economic problems and uncertainty about the future remain high. Let us look next at how collective bargaining in the automobile industry has changed as a result of this new environment.

As Chrysler recovered its economic health, the UAW was able to win wage increases that reduced and eventually eliminated the differential between wages at Chrysler and at GM and Ford. As economic conditions in the industry have improved, the old wage rules have been partially reestablished. The previous COLA provisions have been restored, but the annual improvement factor has not regained its former level.

Although pattern bargaining across companies within the United States has been restored, the trend within each company has been away from connective bargaining. Nonunion competition is much more of a competitive threat at some plants than at others. For example, many firms supplying parts continue to feel great pressure, while the assembly plants are somewhat less vulnerable. When faced with intense competitive pressures, plants have been allowed to change work rules and make any other adjustments necessary to save jobs.[14]

Prospects for the Future

If demand for new U.S. automobiles continues to improve, then we may see a complete restoration of the AIF formula. But it is unlikely that we shall see any return to the old system of job control with its emphasis on detailed, rigid work rules. A major reason is the success of the Japanese auto companies in producing high-quality, low-cost cars not only in Japan but also in the United States. As long as the Japanese plants in the United States continue to be highly successful, with their more cooperative, team-oriented system of industrial relations, such plants serve as both a model and a competitive threat to GM, Ford, and Chrysler.

The Japanese system of industrial relations has been relatively easy to import into the United States, especially at new plants. Efforts to convert plants from job-control unionism to a more cooperative approach have had mixed success, as workers often have been reluctant to give up the protection of the job-control approach. Still, many successful conversions have occurred.

Major problems remain for the UAW. Its bargaining power is threatened by the increase in nonunion plants among parts suppliers and by the new assembly plants that the Japanese have established in the United States. Moreover, the decline in connective bargaining at GM, Ford, and Chrysler, together with the competitive environment facing these firms, makes it likely that competition will also develop across plants within each company. With radically different approaches to the organization of work at different plants and with major differences across plants in the threat from nonunion suppliers, it appears very difficult for the national union to provide effective coordination. If employment in the union sector continues to expand, however, then pressure may build within the UAW to return to the old system of connective bargaining and job-control unionism.

---

[14]The contracts at GM and Ford also contained other important provisions related to income and employment security. In 1984 a job bank was established whereby a worker laid off owing to technical change, other productivity improvements, or outsourcing would receive full pay until transferred or retrained for a comparable job in the company. Such provisions served to reduce worker fears of efforts to increase productivity and increased the cost of outsourcing to the companies. As conditions improved in the industry, the 1987 contracts went further. There were to be no plant closings for any reason, no layoffs except those resulting from an industrywide decline in sales, and at least half of all job openings due to attrition (e.g., retirements, quits) were to be filled by the companies.

FARM EQUIPMENT

The farm-equipment industry has several important parallels with automobiles.[15] Both are organized by the UAW. Both have dominated the world market, at least for the larger vehicles in their industry. And, historically, output has been concentrated primarily in several large firms.

Foreign competition and competition from nonunion domestic firms have played much less of a role in farm equipment than in automobiles. Japan, for example, does not have a domestic market for the kinds of farm machinery made in the United States because the agriculture of the two countries is so different. Thus it has not been a competitor for U.S. farm equipment. The U.S. firms did shift production of small tractors overseas in the late seventies, but production of large equipment remains mostly in this country. Nonunion firms in the United States do play an increasing role, but sales are still dominated by the big unionized firms. These firms are much more vertically integrated than those in the auto industry. Thus in farm equipment there is no significant part-supply sector, the component of the auto industry where competition from nonunion U.S. firms is important.

In the 1970s high demand for the agricultural products of the United States plus low real interest rates led to great demand for farm equipment. The market collapsed in the early eighties, with sales declining by over 50 percent from 1979 to 1984. The increased value of the dollar reduced exports of agricultural commodities. Farmers did not need new equipment. Moreover, a decline in land prices and increase in real interest rates caused many farms to fail, leading to a surplus of used machinery. In the late eighties a decreased value of the dollar led to a recovery in agriculture, but most farmers remained cautious about buying new machinery for several years.

Collective Bargaining Prior to the 1980s

From the fifties through the seventies collective bargaining in farm equipment largely followed the patterns established in automobiles. Both AIF and COLA formulas were similar in the two industries. Wage levels were lower than in automobiles but still well above the average for all manufacturing.

Pattern bargaining across firms was the norm. Because of greater vertical integration, however, there was less potential competition across plants within a firm and thus less emphasis on connective bargaining across plants than in the auto industry. Perhaps for the same reason, there was greater use of incentive pay in the farm-equipment industry than in automobiles.

Strikes were more frequent in farm equipment than in automobiles or most other industries. One important reason was the timing of negotiations in farm equipment, which in the 1970s occurred in the late fall, after the pattern established

---

[15]The discussion of collective bargaining in farm machinery is based largely on Ronald L. Seeber, "Agricultural Machinery," in *Collective Bargaining in American Industry*, ed. David B. Lipsky and Clifford B. Donn (Lexington, Mass.: D. C. Heath, 1987).

in automobiles. Because the demand for farm machinery was relatively low in the late fall and winter, a strike at this time was not as costly to the companies. Moreover, because the pattern for bargaining was established based on conditions in the auto industry, which frequently differed from those in farm machinery, the companies in the latter industry were inclined to take a strike rather than simply accept the auto pattern without a struggle.

Collective Bargaining in the 1980s

As in automobiles, both the standard wage formulas and pattern bargaining broke down in the farm-equipment industry in the early eighties. The first bargaining round during the period of economic distress took place in 1982. International Harvester was in much greater difficulty than the other major companies and achieved special concessions in both wage rates and work rules. Despite these concessions, International Harvester was not able to recover. Its farm-machinery division was eventually sold to Tenneco, where it remained a relatively small operation with low wage rates.

From 1981 to 1988 there were no wage increases in the farm-equipment industry, except for some COLA increases. As in the auto industry, some profit sharing was established. Since 1988 negotiations have been returning to normal. Pattern bargaining is no longer being challenged by any of the major firms. Wage increases have returned and are above COLA levels but are still largely in the form of lump-sum payments.

In other respects, however, collective bargaining appears to have changed permanently. For example, throughout the 1970s negotiations in farm equipment took place shortly after those in automobiles, and wage changes in the industry generally followed the pattern in automobiles. In the 1980s, on the other hand, the negotiations in farm equipment occurred long after those in automobiles. As wage rates fell sharply relative to those of auto workers, the automobile pattern no longer had much relevance for farm equipment. To increase its bargaining power, the union succeeded in shifting the expiration date for the contract to the early summer, when the demand for labor is higher than in the fall.

Economic distress affected collective bargaining differently in farm equipment than in automobiles. First, strikes decreased in automobiles, but increased in farm machinery. A strike of 205 days occurred at Caterpillar in 1982–83 and one of 159 at John Deere in 1986–87. Second, there has been no comparable shift toward production teams of workers or toward joint labor-management committees in farm equipment.

These differences in collective bargaining between farm equipment and automobiles probably reflect, at least in part, differences in the causes of the economic distress in the two industries. In automobiles the primary problem is nonunion competition, especially from the Japanese companies. This problem will continue now that the Japanese have established their own plants in the United States.

In contrast, the problem in farm equipment has been the depressed condition of American agriculture, which generally was regarded as temporary and has, in fact, improved considerably in the past several years. Thus labor and management have been under less pressure to make long-term adjustments in farm equipment. Instead they appear to have been fighting over how to bear the costs of a temporary decline.

STEEL

Together with the automobile industry, the steel industry has been the major pattern setter in collective bargaining since World War II.[16] Throughout the 1950s and 1960s the United Steelworkers of America was the third largest union in the United States, after the Teamsters and the UAW. As we shall see, economic problems have been even more severe in steel than in automobiles and have considerably reduced the national influence of the Steelworkers.

During the first half of the twentieth century, the steel and automobile industries symbolized the strength of the American economy. High-quality, low-cost steel was an important input for most manufacturing and construction industries, including automobiles. The steel industry in the United States was the most important in the world for many years because of the proximity of coal and iron-ore deposits and the great demand for steel for automobiles, skyscrapers, and many other uses.

Since the 1960s the U.S. steel industry has lost its former position of world dominance. First, steel has declined somewhat in economic importance as other materials, chiefly aluminum and plastics, have been substituted for steel in many products. Second, the steel industry in the United States has suffered severely from foreign competition. Such competition has arisen for many reasons, including (1) the rebuilding of steel industries in other countries after the destruction of World War II; (2) the development of steel production in many less developed countries, partly as a symbol of their arrival in the industrial age; (3) the depletion of the best iron-ore deposits in the United States, especially the Mesabi range in Minnesota, and the distance of our steel-production centers from the best ocean ports; (4) the frequency of steel strikes in the 1950s; and probably of greatest importance, (5) the decision of U.S. steelmakers in the 1950s to invest in large open-hearth furnaces to achieve economies of scale rather than to convert to the new basic-oxygen process, which has proven to be more efficient. As a result of these difficulties, United States ceased to be a leading exporter of steel and by the 1970s was a leading importer, primarily from Japan and from Europe.

Although the U.S. steel industry contains more firms than the auto industry, entry is limited by large fixed costs of production. As in the auto industry, for

---

[16]This discussion of the steel industry is based primarily on the following sources: Jack Stieber, "Steel," in *Collective Bargaining: Contemporary American Experience*, ed. Somers, pp. 151–208; D. Quinn Mills and Janice McCormick, *Industrial Relations in Transition*, pp. 276–97; and John P. Hoerr, *And the Wolf Finally Came*, pp. 317–39, 369–419.

many years steel companies were able to pay relatively high wage rates because of their oligopolistic position. With foreign competition this oligopoly power has decreased considerably.[17] Throughout the period since World War II the steel companies have been slow to respond to changes in the market and in technology. Profits in the steel industry have been relatively low since the late fifties. In the eighties many of the leading companies became highly diversified, as they sought to improve their fortunes outside the declining steel industry. This shift out of steel was symbolized by the name change of the largest company from U.S. Steel to USX. During this period the most successful firms in the industry have been smaller, nonunion producers of specialty steel.

In the automobile industry most jobs have been relatively unskilled assembly-line positions. In steel many jobs have often required more skill and judgment than the jobs on the auto assembly line. In addition, the change from the open-hearth to the basic-oxygen and electric-furnace technologies has increased skill requirements. Most of the skills needed are specific to the steel industry, however, and thus are not very useful if a worker is laid off and must find a different kind of job.

Prior to the 1930s the steelworkers were organized by the Amalgamated Association of Iron, Steel, and Tin Workers. This union represented only a small minority of steelworkers, however, and was unsuccessful in its major strikes. After passage of the Wagner Act in 1935 the industry was organized with the support of the CIO and especially the United Mineworkers of America. U.S. Steel was organized in 1937, but the other leading firms held out until 1941, when high demand for labor increased the bargaining power of the workers.

The United Steelworkers of America has also organized workers in many other industries, including aluminum, other nonferrous metals, and containers. In recent years only a relatively small minority of the union's membership actually are steelworkers.

Collective Bargaining from 1946 to 1980

In the postwar period up through the 1970s collective bargaining in steel was similar to that in automobiles. Both the UAW and the United Steelworkers had considerable bargaining power and were pattern setters for other, smaller industries. Nevertheless there have been important differences between collective bargaining in the two industries.

The initial agreements were negotiated company by company, with U.S. Steel as the most frequent pattern setter. In contrast to the auto industry, however,

---

[17]Both steel and automobiles have been affected by government regulation. Since the 1970s such regulation has focused on antipollution issues. For autos the concern has been mainly with the pollution created as cars are driven. Thus imports as well as domestic cars have been subject to regulation, although antipollution regulations have been one factor increasing the relative demand for smaller cars, a segment of the market dominated by imports. On the other hand, antipollution regulations in steel have applied directly to production, thereby increasing the costs of the U.S. industry relative to at least some of its competitors abroad.

there was a gradual shift to more centralized bargaining. By 1959 the major steel companies were negotiating all issues through a joint committee.

Connective bargaining was important in steel as well as in automobiles. Industry wide bargaining, at least for all the major companies, served to minimize differences in wage rates and other labor costs across companies. Differences across plants within companies were also addressed, for example, by a major job-classification program set up in 1947. The large number of job classifications helped make steel a particularly strong example of job-control unionism. Incentive-pay plans have continued to play a major role in the steel industry, however, in contrast to the successful efforts of the UAW, during the early postwar period, to reduce earnings differentials across similar jobs by eliminating such incentive plans.

Wage formulas were not as clearly worked out in steel as in automobiles, one reason that there were more major strikes in steel. The federal government played a greater role in negotiations than in the auto industry. Steel strikes affected many other industries and during the Korean War also affected our war effort. In addition, increases in steel prices had a significant effect on inflation because steel was an important input in so many other industries.

The most significant steel strike occurred in 1959 and lasted for 116 days. In the late 1950s wage rates in steel had been going up much faster than productivity, leading to higher prices. Partly as a result, the industry was losing sales to imports and to substitute products. Sales and employment had also declined because of the severe recession that began in 1958. The industry sought more moderate wage increases and greater flexibility in work rules, while the union wanted continued good wage increases, better job security protection, and no changes in work rules. The lengthy strike led to somewhat smaller wage increases but no changes in work rules. It also led to a greater increase in imports and substitute products. Consequently, efforts were made to reduce the chances of another serious strike. One of the most important initiatives in this regard was the establishment of a joint Human Relations Committee (HRC) to study and make recommendations on major issues well in advance of the contract deadline.

The development of the HRC helped avoid strikes during the early 1960s. The settlements during this period were relatively modest. One reason was weakness in the demand for steel caused by the long-run effects of imports and substitute products and the short-run effects of low aggregate demand in the economy. The HRC approach also increased the influence of the union staff (e.g., lawyers, economists, and pension experts) at the expense of local and district union leaders. In addition, the rank and file were upset that the settlements were not more generous. Many believed that by reaching a settlement well in advance of the contract deadline, the union had weakened its bargaining power by reducing the threat of a strike. The relatively low wage gains during this period were cited as evidence in support of this hypothesis. Such dissatisfaction contributed to the defeat of David J. McDonald by I. W. Abel in the 1965 election for the union presidency.

Under Abel strikes were averted in the negotiations of 1965, 1968, and 1971, but settlements resulted in reasonably generous gains for the workers and were reached only under the pressure of an immediate strike.

In 1973 the negotiating committee representing both the union and the steel companies announced a major change in collective bargaining. If they could not agree on a settlement when the contract expired the next year, they agreed to submit the dispute to binding arbitration by a panel of arbitrators rather than incur the costs of a strike. This approach was designed to forestall any losses to imports as a result of a strike, losses that might continue if customers established satisfactory relations with foreign suppliers. Binding arbitration had been proposed in 1967, but at that time Abel was not strong enough to gain acceptance for it by the union. By 1973, however, he had consolidated his political position, and binding arbitration was accepted as part of an experimental negotiating agreement (ENA).

Among the other most important provisions of the ENA were the following: Strikes were allowed over local issues; wage increases of at least 3 percent annually were established, in addition to a more generous COLA plan; and a $150 bonus for each worker was established to compensate for giving up the right to strike. If the negotiations did go to binding arbitration, none of the above conditions could be changed, nor could there be any changes in the union shop, dues checkoff, local work rules or working conditions, or management rights.

As a result of the ENA, wage formulas similar to those in the auto industry were established, but they served as a floor for negotiations. Thus the steelworkers were ensured of doing at least as well on wage increases as had become the custom for members of the other most powerful industrial union, the UAW. Prior to the ENA, wage formulas had played a much less important role in steel than in autos.

The ENA was renewed for the contracts in 1977 and 1980 but was terminated prior to the 1983 negotiations. In the 1970s opposition to the ENA occurred primarily among the workers, many of whom did not want to give up the right to strike. In fact, the ENA benefited the workers by putting a relatively generous floor under wage increases. It also allowed them to make additional gains, such as greater income protection for laid-off senior workers (1977) and increased pension benefits (1980).

These gains by the union were achieved through bargaining with the companies rather than through arbitration. Neither side wanted to risk going to arbitration. To avoid arbitration, each was flexible in its negotiations.

By 1980 the union was strongly in favor of continuing the ENA, but the companies were opposed, and the ENA was not included in the contract. Thus a national strike would be allowed after the termination of the 1980 agreement in 1983. The price the companies had to pay under the ENA had become too high. As demand deteriorated and foreign competition increased, the industry could no longer afford 3 percent annual wage increases plus COLA adjustments.

By now it was clear that foreign competition resulted primarily from price differentials and not from the more consistent availability of foreign steel, the problem the ENA had been designed to solve. Steel imports had fallen during the early seventies, perhaps partly in response to greater continuity of domestic supply under the ENA. In the latter half of the seventies, however, imports increased substantially and remained high despite the establishment by the federal government of a "trigger-price" mechanism to keep the price of imported steel from falling below the estimated cost of steel production in Japan, the country that produced steel most efficiently.

The experiment of the steel industry with the ENA was a partial success. Originally established in 1973, it was renewed in the next two contracts. On the other hand, it could not withstand the economic changes that were beginning to overwhelm the steel companies, and it did not spread to any other industries. Compulsory arbitration as an alternative to the strike is important in the public sector. With the demise of the ENA in steel, it is no longer an important factor in collective bargaining in the private sector.

Collective Bargaining Since 1980

In the 1980 agreement the steelworkers continued to gain 3 percent annual wage increases plus COLA benefits. Such increases had been guaranteed to the union as part of the ENA. During 1981 and 1982 the demand for steel fell sharply, as the recession reduced the demand for automobiles, construction, and most other products that used large amounts of steel. Steel production fell from 80 percent of capacity in the spring of 1981 to 30 percent in December 1982. No one had foreseen a decline of this magnitude. Membership in the United Steelworkers fell from 1,200,000 in 1979 to 900,000 in 1982. By 1982 unemployment among steelworkers exceeded 40 percent. In 1981 U.S. Steel bought Marathon Oil for $6.3 billion, a purchase seen by many as a symbol of companies seeking to diversify out of steel despite government efforts to help steel through tax breaks and import protection.

After two unsuccessful attempts, a package of wage concessions was negotiated in early 1983, shortly before the 1980 contract was scheduled to expire. The new contract provided for a pay cut of almost 10 percent. A pay cut of this magnitude was unprecedented in a major industry since the 1930s.[18] In addition to the actual pay cuts, COLA protection was reduced sharply. The union did win increased company financing of supplemental unemployment benefits but had to give up ten paid holidays and also the extended vacation benefits that the union had pioneered twenty years before.

The economic problems of the steel industry also led to the demise of connective bargaining. In order to save as many jobs as possible, the union was willing to settle for greater concessions in the firms that have been in the most serious difficulty. With economic problems much more serious in some firms than others, in 1985 the companies disbanded the Steel Companies Coordinating Committee, which for thirty years had bargained with the United Steelworkers.

Although the economy as a whole had pulled out of the recession of 1982–83, the steel industry was still in great difficulty because of world wide overcapacity during the contract negotiations in 1986.[19] The union bargained separately with

---

[18]In contrast, for example, the concessions in the auto industry were simply lower wage increases than would have been provided under the traditional formulas.

[19]The most dramatic development prior to the 1986 negotiations occurred at Wheeling-Pittsburgh Steel Corporation, a leading steel producer, which was forced to file for bankruptcy in 1985. After a strike that

each company for the first time in over thirty years. The LTV Corporation filed for bankruptcy, the largest company in the United States ever to do so. It settled with United Steelworkers for an hourly pay cut of $3.15. Bethlehem Steel settled for a cut of $1.97 and National Steel for a cut of 42¢. After a six-month strike, USX settled for a wage cut very similar to that at Bethlehem. These contracts also called for the suspension of future COLA increases, limitations on overtime and the use of nonunion subcontractors, and the establishment of profit-sharing and stock-ownership plans for workers.

The next round of contract negotiations began in 1989. By this time there was high aggregate demand in the economy. In addition, voluntary restraint agreements between the United States and producers in other countries continued to restrict steel imports. As a result by 1989 the steel industry in the United States enjoyed much higher demand than it had earlier in the decade. With high demand, past pay cuts were restored and modest additional raises were negotiated, including some protection from future inflation. On the other hand, employment of union members remained low, far below the levels of the 1970s. There was no return to industrywide bargaining. In fact, there was some additional movement away from connective bargaining, since profit sharing became more important at several firms.

Despite the greater demand for steel in the late eighties, the economic difficulties of the steel industry show few signs of significant long-term improvement. Worldwide overcapacity and the relative inefficiency of much of the U.S. steel industry are problems that will remain for years. While the U.S. auto companies remain in the auto industry and are challenged by new Japanese plants in this country, our steel companies diversify into other markets. Foreign competition remains important but does not include any steel produced in the U.S. by foreign firms. The government provides some import protection to the steel industry. Although this protection has increased the price of steel to other industries, including automobiles, it has not been sufficient to encourage any significant new investment in the unionized sectors of the steel industry.

Steel represents a decreasing percentage of sales for many steel companies, and a decreasing percentage of the United Steelworkers of America are steelworkers. Steel, which used to serve as a symbol of the strength of U.S. manufacturing, now serves as a symbol of its weakness. Although the economic difficulties in steel appear more severe than those in automobiles, the steel industry has not been especially innovative in responding to these problems. Industrial relations, which were geared toward a large oligopolistic industry, have been slow to adapt to the new, more competitive environment.[20]

---

lasted almost three months, the company and its creditor banks negotiated a new contract that cut wage rates and benefits by $3.90, from $21.40 to $17.50 per hour.

[20]In response to both the greater uncertainties in the industry and the competitive pressure of the Japanese, the auto industry has been moving away from job control unionism and toward more flexible, cooperative approaches, including production teams. Although there has been some movement in this direction in steel as well, it has been much more limited than in automobiles. The major innovation in steel, the ENA, occurred at the national level and has been discontinued.

TRUCKING

The industries we have discussed have been in manufacturing and have been orga-nized by industrial unions.[21] Although industrial unions have dominated manufac-turing, craft unions are important in many other sectors of the economy, including construction, government, and transportation.

For most of the period since World War II the largest union in the country and one of the most powerful has been the International Brotherhood of Teamsters, whose home base is the trucking industry. The power of the Teamsters has declined considerably, especially in trucking, but the reasons for the decline differ from those affecting the auto workers and the steelworkers. Foreign competition has not affected truck drivers. Instead, the competition has come from nonunion firms. As we shall see, deregulation of the trucking industry has made it easy for nonunion firms to enter most of the industry, and prohibitions on secondary boycotts have made it difficult for the Teamsters to organize such firms.

Increased competition from nonunion firms has also been a factor hurting unions in manufacturing. New plants have been built, primarily in nonunion areas, and have been very difficult for unions to organize, as employers have typically adopted more aggressive antiunion policies. Trucking, however, has probably been more affected than any other industry by domestic nonunion competition. The legal environment has changed more dramatically in trucking than in most industries. Also, trucking is an industry where entry requires little physical or human capital. As a result, it is unusually easy for nonunion firms to enter the industry if there is no regulation by the government.

Unless the Teamsters can develop an effective strategy for organizing such firms, the influence of the union will continue to decline. Although the power of the Teamsters in trucking enabled it to expand to be an important force in many other industries, now the union is stronger in other areas, such as the government sector, where there is less vigorous nonunion competition.

History of the Industry

Trucks began to replace horse-drawn wagons in the early years of the twentieth century. Initially trucking was entirely a local industry, with long-distance shipping limited to boat or railroad. Especially for relatively short intercity routes, trucking offered greater speed and flexibility than its main competitor, the railroads. By 1970 trucking accounted for over 50 percent of all expenditures on freight transportation in the nation. Within the trucking sector over half of total expenditures were for intercity traffic. With the economy growing and with trucking's share of the trans-portation sector expanding, employment steadily increased.

---

[21]This section is based primarily on Harold M. Levinson, "Trucking," in *Collective Bargaining: Contem-porary American Experience,* pp. 99–150; and on Charles R. Perry, *Deregulation and the Decline of the Unionized Trucking Industry.*

Although the trucking industry has had the advantage of generally expanding demand, it did face serious problems during the Great Depression of the 1930s. As already indicated, entry into the industry is relatively easy. Only a few trucks are necessary—one for an owner-operator—so the capital requirements are small. Similarly, the skills necessary to be a driver are easily learned. Consequently, during the depression many who had lost jobs or businesses elsewhere sought to enter trucking. Since the newcomers had not established any reputation in the industry, they often sought to compete by charging low rates. This influx of new, inexperienced people charging low rates put considerable pressure on the established firms. As the demand for their services fell, so did their profits and employment. The railroad industry was also hurt as the cost of moving goods by truck declined.

In response to the problems, the established truckers with assistance from the railroads sought government assistance.[22] Since 1887 the federal government had been regulating railroads through the Interstate Commerce Commission (ICC). Because an enormous investment is necessary to start a new railroad, railroads did have considerable monopoly power, especially in the period before the interstate highway system created considerable competition from trucks. Because of the monopoly power of the railroads, there was a good economic case for their regulation by the government. Trucking was a much more competitive industry and thus much less in need of any price regulation to protect consumers. Instead, regulation of the trucking industry was designed to protect established firms from the rigors of competition from new entrants.

The Motor Carrier Act (MCA), passed in 1935, limited competition by severely restricting entry to the industry and by making price reductions difficult. The Interstate Commerce Commission (ICC), which administered the act, allowed new entrants or price reductions only when there would be no adverse effect on established firms, a criterion designed to reduce most competitive pressures. Such protection enabled profits to be high in the industry for decades, despite high wage rates.

In the late 1970s the Carter administration began to push for deregulation of several industries, including airlines and trucking, as a way of increasing economic efficiency and reducing the rate of inflation. For trucking this effort began with more flexible administration of the MCA and ended with new legislation, the Motor Carrier Act of 1980. This legislation made entry of new firms much easier, allowed existing firms considerably greater freedom in their choice of routes and cargoes, and also increased price flexibility.[23]

As a result of the MCA of 1980, many new firms entered the trucking industry. The combination of increased entry, greater price competition, and the

---

[22]Those in many other industries also sought similar assistance from the government. Partly as a result, the National Industrial Recovery Act (NIRA) of 1933 was passed, encouraging industry groups to combat "destructive competition." The NIRA was declared unconstitutional, however.

[23]Regulation was not eliminated, however. Firms still had to show that they were capable of providing safe, adequate service. But they no longer had to show that their entrance would not hurt any other firm.

recession of the early eighties significantly reduced profits in the industry and drove many established firms out of business.[24]

From the 1940s through the early 1970s employment in the trucking industry expanded continually. With little competition in the industry, layoffs were infrequent. The combination of the OPEC oil-price hike of 1979, the MCA of 1980, and the recession of the early eighties led to significant unemployment in the industry for the first time since the 1930s. Perry estimates that by 1985 the unemployment rate was near 20 percent for union drivers.[25] We shall discuss the implications of these economic developments for collective bargaining shortly. First, however, we show how collective bargaining developed in a more hospitable environment.

Collective Bargaining Prior to the 1980s

The forerunner of the present Teamsters union was founded in 1898 for drivers of horse-drawn wagons. During the early decades of the twentieth century the Teamsters developed considerable strength in a number of large local markets, such as New York, Detroit, Chicago, St. Louis, Seattle, and San Francisco. Initially little effort was made to organize over-the-road drivers. It was more difficult than organizing local drivers, since intercity routes could be driven by men who lived and had their social ties in many different home communities.

Although high unemployment made organizing workers more difficult in the 1930s, changes in the legal environment more than counterbalanced the effects of the economy and made it feasible for the Teamsters to begin organizing long-distance drivers. Three laws were particularly important. As we saw in Chapter 12, the Wagner Act played a major role in the establishment of unions in many industries, including automobiles and steel. It also aided the Teamsters, especially in dealing with many large, financially powerful trucking firms.

The other two laws were of particular importance to the Teamsters. The Norris-LaGuardia Act of 1932 eliminated most judicial restraints on strikes, picketing, and boycotts. This legislation was especially helpful to the Teamsters because union members could refuse to handle cargo that had been handled at any stage by nonunion workers. If the union was strong in one city (e.g., Detroit), such a "secondary boycott" could force truckers in other cities either to unionize or to forego any trucking to or from the Detroit market. Since the Teamsters were already strong in many cities, secondary boycotts could extend their influence to other areas where they were weak. Such boycotts could also exert great pressure on manufacturing firms to unionize if they were dependent on truckers to transport either their inputs or their finished products.

The third legislation of the 1930s that aided the Teamsters was the Motor

---

[24]These pressures were similar to those that led to the MCA of 1935. In the 1980s, however, the political climate was more favorable to economic competition, and unemployment was less severe for the economy as a whole. Thus efforts by the trucking industry and the Teamsters to reestablish significant government regulation were ineffective.

[25]Perry, *Deregulation*, p. 110.

Carrier Act of 1935. This legislation made it easier for the Teamsters to maintain their gains by making it much more difficult for nonunion firms to enter the industry and reap a competitive advantage by undercutting the union wage scale and then charging low prices. Also, the ICC generally was quite willing to increase allowable rates in response to union wage gains, thus reducing employer resistance to union demands.

With the aid of these three laws the Teamsters were able to expand their membership from 75,000 in 1933 to 420,000 in 1939. Together with the growth of the economy and of the relative importance of trucking, Teamster employment continued to increase to 920,000 in 1948 and 1,500,000 in 1964. By the late 1950s the Teamsters had become the nation's largest union.

During the 1950s and 1960s, under the dynamic leadership of Jimmy Hoffa, the Teamsters succeeded in shifting the primary focus of bargaining in the trucking industry from the local to the national level. Most drivers supported regional, and later national, bargaining as a means of strenthening the power of the union and avoiding any efforts by large firms to play off workers in one area against another. For example, when unionization and pay scales were lower in the South, large interstate shippers could try to use nonunion southern drivers on many interstate runs. To consolidate the power of the union, the Teamsters needed to organize all the long-distance truckers. Hoffa saw that "once you have the road men, you can get the local cartage, and once you have the local cartage, you can get anyone you want."[26] With powerful local unions in most large cities and the use of the secondary boycott, it was not too difficult for the Teamsters to organize intercity drivers.[27]

Once the Teamsters had organized a labor market, their bargaining power generally was much greater than that of the employers. Despite the barriers to entry established by the MCA of 1935, all major markets were served by hundreds, if not thousands, of employers, many with very different interests. Thus it was difficult for the employers to unite successfully to challenge the union's influence. In addition, many of the employers had little in the way of cash reserves and thus could not take a lengthy strike. Consequently, it was relatively easy for the union to settle first with some of the weaker employers and then use those settlements to increase the pressure on larger, more financially secure firms. Employers sought to deal with this problem by establishing an employers' association. The longest lasting, the Trucking Employers Incorporated (TEI), was only partially successful.

---

[26]Ralph C. James and Estelle Dinerstein James, *Hoffa and the Teamsters: A Study in Union Power* (Princeton, N.J.: D. Van Nostrand and Co., 1965), p. 100.

[27]While there was little opposition within the union to organizing over-the-road as well as local drivers, there was opposition to centralized bargaining and pay scales. Such bargaining would reduce the power of local leaders and, in the short run, could also lead to lower wage gains among members of those locals that were already receiving the highest pay. In the long run, all drivers might expect to gain from centralized bargaining as the greater unity of labor would increase its bargaining power relative to that of employers. This recognition, together with the personal power of Jimmy Hoffa and the weakness of the employers, led to considerable centralization of bargaining during Hoffa's years as vice-president and president of the Teamsters, 1952–67. His successor, Frank Fitzsimmons, did not complete the national-ization of bargaining, in part because his political position relative was weaker relative to that of local leaders of the union.

For most commodities there was little competition from other modes of transportation or from nonunion truckers.[28] As a result, the Teamsters were able to increase wage rates significantly. Between 1950 and 1973, for example, nominal wage rates increased about 300 percent for Teamsters, compared with slightly over 200 percent for automobile and steel workers. At the start of the period wage rates of Teamsters were 10 to 15 percent below those of the auto and steel workers, while at the end of the period they were about 20 percent higher.[29]

Although the Teamsters have not been pioneers, their pensions and other benefits have kept pace with those of industry leaders, such as the UAW and the United Steelworkers. Until 1977 pension benefits were administered entirely by the union, another indication of its bargaining power relative to employers. There have been many charges of corruption in the use of these funds.

The Teamsters have also negotiated many favorable work rules. These rules have varied from area to area. The one that has had the widest coverage and the greatest effects has been the requirement that over-the-road trucking between cities go from terminal to terminal rather than from the shipper's dock to the receiver's dock. This rule considerably increases the cost of shipping, particularly for intercity trucking that does not involve too many miles. On the other hand, this rule protects the jobs of local drivers and terminal employees from competition by intercity workers. Thus it reflects the concerns and the political power of local Teamsters unions. It has also helped the Teamsters to maintain separate seniority units for local and over-the-road drivers.

In the late 1950s charges of corruption were frequently made against the Teamsters. These charges led to their expulsion from the AFL-CIO from 1957 to 1987. This expulsion caused little harm to the Teamsters and actually helped them in some respects. For example, when they were not in the AFL-CIO, the Teamsters were free to organize workers in other industries without any constraint from AFL-CIO policies on the jurisdiction of each union.

The Declining Influence of the Teamsters

The Taft-Hartley Act had sought to make secondary boycotts illegal. This effort had only limited success. The Landrum-Griffin Act tightened the language in this area and was used with considerably more effect in the courts. The Teamsters now were liable for damages if they participated in boycotts of "hot cargo," goods that had been handled at some other stage by nonunion drivers. Such boycotts of hot cargo had been a major device of the Teamsters to impose unionization on firms regard-

---

[28]In cases like iron and steel, where railroads provided significant competition because large shipments were being made across considerable distances, the Teamsters' bargaining power was weaker. As a result they were often prepared to negotiate "special-commodity" riders, involving lower wage rates. In this way they could keep control of the shipments and provide jobs for dues-paying Teamsters rather than concede the work to the railroads or perhaps even to drivers not organized by the union.

[29]Levinson, "Trucking," p. 120.

less of the preferences of their employees. As it became clear that the Landrum-Griffin prohibition of most secondary boycotts was enforceable in the courts, the Teamsters lost one of their major weapons.

With the prohibition of secondary boycotts, a sizable nonunion sector developed, especially among owner-operators. As a result, membership in the freight division of the Teamsters declined from about 500,000 in the mid-sixties to less than 400,000 by the mid-seventies. Total membership in the union grew from about 1.5 to 2 million over this period, but now no more than 20 percent of the Teamsters were employees in the trucking business.[30]

Collective bargaining in the trucking industry was heavily affected by both the Motor Carrier Act of 1980 and the severe recession of 1981–83. Reduced regulation under this MCA led to the entry of many new, small nonunion firms into the industry as well as to greater price competition among established firms. The extent of new entry can be seen in the increase in firms subject to the reduced regulation of the ICC. In 1981 there were eighteen-thousand and in 1983 thirty-thousand.[31]

Entry of new firms was greatest in the truckload (TL) freight segment of the industry, which involves lower entry costs than the less-than-truckload (LTL) segment, where a new firm must establish its own distribution system. Work rules, such as the requirement that all over-the-road shipping be transported by local drivers to and from centralized terminals, made it easier for nonunion firms to enter the industry. Such nonunion competition led to the failure of many union firms and to fewer jobs for union members. As a result, the Teamsters were under pressure to save jobs by lowering wage rates. On the other hand, union members who remained secure in their jobs did not want the union to "sell out" by making any concessions.

The recession also had a major effect on both the industry and collective bargaining. The recession reduced total employment in the industry by about 7 percent between 1979 and 1981, thus increasing job losses among union drivers. In addition, the recession had other, less obvious effects. For example, it put more pressure on many shippers to cut their costs, thus increasing the percentage who would shift away from established firms with good reputations to take a chance on cheaper nonunion competitors who had not been in business long enough to have developed much reputation for reliability. Also the recession made it easier for firms to recruit nonunion drivers at relatively modest wage rates and with few benefits. As a result of both deregulation and the recession, unemployment among Teamsters drivers increased to about 20 percent in 1981 and 30 percent in 1982.

The failure of many firms and the reduced profits of most others led the trucking association to seek a new union contract, which it obtained shortly before the old one expired in 1982. In addition to providing no regular wage increase over

---

[30]See Levinson, "Trucking," p. 135.
[31]See Perry, *Deregulation*, p. 92.

the next three years, the new contract contained many concessions on work rules, including modification of the requirement that intercity freight be reloaded and shipped by local truckers between the customer and the intercity terminal. Especially for the truckload segment of the industry, additional wage concessions were also made at individual firms that were in danger of going bankrupt.[32]

By the 1985 negotiations the recession had ended, but the competition from nonunion firms remained high, especially in the truckload portion of the industry. The contract reached that year included modest wage increases as well as several clauses making it more difficult for firms to avoid the union by reorganizing, establishing new terminals, or subcontracting to nonunion employers. With nonunion competition remaining strong, the contract negotiated in 1988 included an even smaller pay increase, despite a generally stronger economy with greater total demand for trucking.

Truckload shipping has become predominantly nonunion, largely as a result of the deregulation of the trucking industry. The Teamsters still play a significant role in less-than-truckload shipping, where entry is more difficult for nonunion firms. Even in this sector of the industry, however, nonunion competition has become sufficiently important to reduce considerably the bargaining power of the Teamsters.

As a result of its former great power in trucking, the Teamsters were able to organize extensively outside of trucking. Despite heavy losses among drivers in recent years, the Teamsters remain one of the largest unions in the country with over 1.5 million members. Now less than 10 percent are in trucking, however.

Can the Teamsters remain strong in other areas despite becoming so much weaker in their home base, from which the union has drawn so much of its leadership and its identity? If they do, then the Teamsters will remain a major force in many labor markets. If not, then the Teamsters will be under even greater pressure to reverse their fortunes in trucking. Such a reversal does not appear likely in the present economic and political climate, however.

The laws reducing regulation of trucking and prohibiting the secondary boycott are not likely to be repealed. In addition, there are many drivers who are not enthusiastic about the Teamsters. The most important are owner operators. Having invested in a truck, most owner operators do not want to be subject to a set of rules concerning when, how, or at what rates they can do business. Thus such drivers act more like profit-maximizing small-business owners than employees with a strong sense of worker solidarity. As a result of both the national political environment and the attitude of many drivers, the prospects for any rapid reversal of the Teamsters' fortunes in trucking appear remote.

---

[32]In an effort to reduce the unemployment of union members, the Teamsters negotiated a modification to the national agreement in 1983 to reduce by about 30 percent the wage rates and benefits of laid-off drivers who were rehired. This agreement was overwhelmingly rejected by the union membership, however, and therefore never implemented. In the same year Roy Williams was convicted of bribery in the political battle against the MCA of 1980.

CONCLUSION

In this chapter we have seen how changes in the economic and legal environment have reduced considerably the influence of three major unions. These unions were the largest in the nation in the 1960s and, despite their recent losses, each is still among the top ten.

The steelworkers and the auto workers have been hit primarily by foreign competition. In steel more modern plants in other countries have forced both the industry and the union to focus their attention more heavily on other industries. The competition has been less devastating in automobiles and has been based less on capital equipment and more on labor relations. As the Japanese companies have established successful nonunion plants in the United States, the UAW and its employers have been forced to copy some of the Japanese methods, including greater emphasis on teamwork and on labor-management cooperation.

For the Teamsters the competitive threat has come not from overseas but from domestic nonunion competition, which has greatly increased because of legislative changes, especially the substantial deregulation of trucking with the Motor Carrier Act of 1980. Such competition has significantly reduced the employment and bargaining power of the Teamsters in trucking. Because the Teamsters have become well established in many other industries, the dramatic decline of their influence in trucking has not had any proportional impact on the size or influence of the union as a whole.

As we saw in Chapter 14, most unions in the private sector have been suffering significant declines in recent years. The declines have generally not been as great as those in autos, farm equipment, steel, and trucking. Still membership has been declining in all major private-sector unions during the 1980s.

Unions in the public sector have maintained their strength better in recent years than those in the private sector. Such unions are less subject to the competitive threat of nonunion workers, either foreign or domestic. In the next chapter we examine public-sector unions and discuss how they compare with those in the private sector.

SUMMARY

1. Since 1948 negotiations between the United Auto Workers (UAW) and the Big Three automobile companies have played a major role in our economy, both because of the size of the industry and because the auto industry has been a pattern setter, influencing negotiations in other industries.

2. The UAW and the auto companies pioneered long-term contracts, cost-of-living adjustments (COLAs), and the annual improvement factor (AIF) as well as supplemental unemployment benefits (SUB) and other fringe benefits. To avoid competition based on labor costs, connective bargaining was established in an effort to minimize wage differences across firms and also across plants within the same firm. In addition to wage formulas and connective bargaining, the contracts in the auto industry also emphasized job-control unionism. Wage rates were attached to each job; jobs were defined in detail as part of a job classification system; and rules for promotion, transfer, and layoffs indicated who should gain access to each job.

3. Largely because of increased foreign competition collective bargaining in the auto industry changed considerably during the 1980s. The wage increases due under the formulas were suspended to reduce job losses. Connective bargaining was also temporarily suspended because of the greater difficulties faced by Chrysler in the early eighties. A long-term shift from job control unionism to an approach based on relatively autonomous work teams is occurring at many plants.

4. Because of problems in agriculture during the 1980s the farm-equipment industry, also organized by the UAW, suffered even greater economic difficulties than the auto industry. As negotiations in the two industries became less closely related, wage rates fell in farm-equipment relative to automobiles. With foreign competition playing little role, the problems of the industry were seen as temporary. Thus compared to autos, a bigger short-term but a smaller long-term adjustment was necessary. In this context there were lengthier strikes and less long-term change in collective bargaining in farm equipment than in automobiles.

5. Partly because of foreign competition the steel industry suffered greater, more permanent declines than either automobiles or farm equipment. Wage rates declined in nominal as well as real terms. Connective bargaining disintegrated as the major companies shifted from joint to individual negotiations. The experimental negotiating agreement (ENA), which had required disputes to be settled by arbitration rather than by strike, was terminated prior to the negotiation in 1983 because it led to wage increases that were too costly for the firms and contributed to large job losses among union members.

6. Economic difficulties leading to a decline in union membership and influence have not been limited to industrial unions in manufacturing. Truck drivers, the home base of the large, diverse, and powerful Teamsters union, suffered major losses in the 1980s as a result of changes in government policy, especially the Motor Carrier Act of 1980. Absent legal restraints, trucking is an easy industry for new firms to enter and gain a competitive advantage if they can pay drivers less than the union rate. With workers readily available because of high unemployment in the economy and with legislation no longer creating major barriers to entry, the Teamsters truck drivers suffered substantial job losses. These losses were greatest in the early part of the decade when unemployment was greatest, but continued to be a major problem for the Teamsters throughout the decade.

Because the Teamsters are important in many sectors of the economy, including state and local government, they have suffered less of a decline in total membership than either the UAW or the United Steelworkers. Nevertheless the leadership of the Teamsters has faced difficult problems not only because of the economic situation in trucking but also because of internal dissension within the union and because of charges of corruption being pressed by the federal government.

KEY CONCEPTS

COST-OF-LIVING ADJUSTMENT (COLA)
ANNUAL IMPROVEMENT FACTOR (AIF)
CONNECTIVE BARGAINING

EXPERIMENTAL NEGOTIATING AGREEMENT (ENA)
DEREGULATION
SECONDARY BOYCOTT

REVIEW QUESTIONS

1. Compare the changes that have occurred since the 1970s in collective bargaining in automobiles, farm equipment, steel, and trucking. To what extent have the causes of the decline in union power been similar or different in these four industries? To what extent do prospects for the future look different in each industry? Why?

2. Why have wage rules proved useful in the auto industry? Under these rules why are wage changes not related to changing conditions in the industry? Under what circumstances are the rules most likely to be violated? Why? To what extent have similar rules been developed in the other three industries examined in this chapter? Why or why not?

3. What is connective bargaining? Why did it become increasingly important in the 1950s and 1960s and then decline in significance in the 1980s? What are some of the more important mechanisms for achieving connective bargaining?

4. Human-capital theory emphasizes that the skills of the worker are the primary determinant of wage rates. Yet under job-control unionism wage rates are attached to jobs, not to workers. Is human-capital theory still relevant in industries where job-control unionism is dominant? Discuss.

5. The Teamsters have been hurt more than most unions by changes in legislation. Why has this been true? Do you favor the legislative changes that have been responsible? Why or why not?

6. Investigate collective bargaining in some industry other than those examined in this chapter. What changes have occurred in this industry over the past twenty years? How have these changes affected collective bargaining? How do these changes compare with those in automobiles, farm-equipment, steel, and trucking?

READINGS

HOERR, JOHN P., *And the Wolf Finally Came.* Pittsburgh: University of Pittsburgh Press, 1988.

KATZ, HARRY C., *Shifting Gears: Changing Labor Relations in the U.S. Automobile Industry.* Cambridge, Mass.: MIT Press, 1985.

LIPSKY, DAVID B., and CLIFFORD B. DONN, *Collective Bargaining in American Industry.* Lexington, Mass.: D. C. Heath, 1987.

MILLS, D. QUINN, and JANICE MCCORMACK, *Industrial Relations in Transition.* New York: John Wiley & Sons, 1985.

PERRY, CHARLES R., *Deregulation and the Decline of the Unionized Trucking Industry.* Philadelphia: Industrial Research Unit of the Wharton School at the University of Pennsylvania, 1986.

SOMERS, GERALD G., *Collective Bargaining: Contemporary American Experience.* Madison, Wis.: Industrial Relations Research Association, 1980.

COLLECTIVE BARGAINING
IN THE PUBLIC SECTOR

Earlier chapters have dealt mainly with collective bargaining in private employment, where government is formally a neutral, laying down rules of conduct for unions and employers. We turn next to collective bargaining in the public sector, where government itself is the employer. Although the public work force is much smaller than that of the private sector, one of every six workers is employed by the government at either the local, state, or federal level. We saw in Chapter 14 that the public sector, which was almost entirely nonunion as recently as the 1950s, is now much more strongly unionized than the private sector. Over one-third of all union members are now employed by government. Unionization and collective bargaining in the public sector are important topics in their own right. In addition, by learning more about the public sector, we can develop a broader context for understanding industrial relations in the private sector.

The legal and economic environment of public bargaining differs substantially from that of private bargaining. The decision-making processes of a public employer differ from those of a corporation. The concept of "ability to pay" and the factors affecting ability to pay are different for a public employer. Government is bound legally to represent the interests of all citizens, and this may limit what it can concede to the groups of citizens who are public employees. Use of the strike weapon in public employment is usually considered inappropriate, though strikes do occur. But if the strike possibility is removed, there must be some other method for final determination of disputes in public employment.

In this chapter, we will consider five topics:

1. The differences between public- and private-sector employers
2. The growth of public-sector unions
3. Bargaining at the federal level
4. Bargaining at the state and local level
5. Methods for settling labor-management disputes
6. The effects of collective bargaining in the public sector

DIFFERENCES BETWEEN PUBLIC- AND PRIVATE-SECTOR EMPLOYERS

We have assumed that private-sector employers are profit maximizers. Such an employer sells goods and services, usually in competition with other firms, with the expectation that sales revenue will exceed costs, leaving a profit for the firm's owners.

In the public sector the employer faces quite different pressures. The government does not have to sell its output in a competitive market. Instead, it finances its activities through taxation, which is compulsory. While a firm can go out of business if it misjudges the demand for its product or if its costs become too great, government does not go out of business. Instead, if one set of elected officials are perceived as unsuccessful they will be voted out of office and replaced by another. Thus top government officials are subject to political constraints, in contrast to the market constraints facing executives in the private sector.

Public employers represent the sovereign power of the state, including military and police power. In the United States we have a long history of civilian control of such power, control exercised by elected government officials. Collective bargaining could reduce such civilian control by giving greater influence to police or military personnel, especially if the union includes high-ranking officers. In contrast to the private sector, unions in the public sector do include supervisory personnel. They do not include top officials, however.

From an economic perspective one of the important issues is the elasticity of demand for government services. To the extent that government has a monopoly over any service (e.g., police or fire protection) and the service is considered essential by many people, then the demand for this service will be inelastic. The inelastic product-demand, in turn, will lead to an inelastic labor demand, which increases the bargaining power of the union. Because of the inelastic labor demand the union can seek a high wage rate with little concern for the effect on employment. Equally important, the same factors leading to an inelastic labor demand also imply that a strike will be very costly for the citizenry. As a result of these considerations, legal prohibitions have often been established on the right of public employees to strike, especially for workers in essential areas like police and fire protection.

The elasticity of labor demand in the public sector may not be as great as it first appears, however. First, not all public services are essential. Even those that are, such as police protection, can be provided at different levels depending on cost. Moreover, private-sector alternatives can often be found, ranging from the hiring of private guards to supplement the police to using Federal Express instead of the U.S. mail.[1] Empirical estimates indicate that the wage elasticity of labor demand is somewhat lower in the public than in the private sector but that the elasticity in the public sector is well above zero.[2]

In addition to the sovereignty and monopoly issues, public-sector employers differ from their private-sector counterparts in several other respects. First, because the public sector receives most of its revenue from taxation rather than from sales a strike does not deplete its treasury. In fact, a government will gain financially during a strike because its revenues remain relatively constant while its labor costs diminish.[3] So the pressure on a public-sector official to settle a strike comes primarily through the political process, as a result of services not provided to constituents rather than from financial costs, as in the private sector.

Much of the bargaining power of public-sector unions comes through the political process. In this process union members vote and lobby as well as bargain. Consequently, unions can penalize elected officials for adverse wage decisions. Although the general body of voters has an interest in holding down government costs and tax rates, this interest is more diffuse and therefore usually requires less attention from politicians.

The relative emphasis on lobbying versus bargaining will depend on which approach is perceived to be most effective. Lobbying can be used to shift the labor demand curve as well as to increase wage rates.[4] For example, teachers often bargain about class size as well as wage rates. Such issues can have an important effect on working conditions, job security, and the union's future size and political power. They also may be easier to "sell" politically because they emphasize the community interest in better services rather than just the worker interest in higher earnings.

---

[1]In addition, there are other qualifications. First, public as well as private employers may respond to wage increases by substituting capital for labor or by subcontracting to the private sector. For an interesting study of how such responses have played a major role in sanitation, see David Lewin, "Public Employee Unionism in the 1980's: An Analysis of Transformation," in *Unions in Transition,* ed. Seymour Martin Lipset (San Francisco: ICS Press, 1986), pp. 241–64. Second, high wage rates normally will lead to high tax rates, which can cause citizens to move from one jurisdiction to another, thereby reducing the demand for labor in the high-wage jurisdiction. In addition to these long-run arguments, Freeman emphasizes that in the short run, the elasticity of labor demand may actually be higher in the public than in the private sector. In contrast to private employers, who can pay higher wages at the expense of reduced profits, state and local governments generally face a fixed budget constraint. If the government must pay a wage increase but is already spending all of its revenue and cannot borrow on its current account, then any wage increase must lead to an equal percentage decline in employment. See Richard Freeman, "Unionism Comes to the Public Sector."

[2]For example, see Ronald G. Ehrenberg, "The Demand for State and Local Government Employees," *American Economic Review* (June 1973), pp. 366–79; Orley Ashenfelter and Ehrenberg, "The Demand for Labor in the Public Sector," in *Labor in the Public and Nonprofit Sectors,* ed. Daniel Hamermesh (Princeton, N.J.: Princeton University Press, 1975), pp. 55–78, and Ashenfelter, "Demand and Supply Functions for State and Local Government Employment," in *Essays in Labor Market Analysis,* ed. Ashenfelter and Wallace Oates (New York, Halsted Press, 1979), pp. 1–16.

[3]Revenues will decline somewhat to the extent that a strike by public-sector employees leads to less economic activity, and some taxes, such as those on income and sales, depend on the state of the economy.

[4]See Freeman, "Unionism Comes to the Public Sector," p. 52.

At the start we indicated that private-sector firms attempt to make a profit and usually are assumed to be profit maximizers. Although not a profit maximizer, the public-sector employer is likely to be a cost minimizer. At least for elected officials the political pressure to provide good service at low cost to increase the chance of reelection is likely to be as great as the economic pressure on the private-sector manager to provide a good product at low cost in order to stay in business and reap financial rewards. Of course, lower-level employees may be more accountable to top officials in the private than in the public sectors, thus enabling private-sector executives to be more effective in their attempt to minimize costs. Nevertheless, the most important distinction between public- and private-sector employers is not the distinction between profit and nonprofit orientation but rather the greater emphasis on product markets in the private sector and on taxation and the political process in the public sector.

THE GROWTH OF PUBLIC-SECTOR UNIONS

As shown in Table 19-1, between 1950 and 1980 employment grew at a considerably faster rate in the public than in the private sector.[5] Since 1980 employment has barely grown at any level of government and declined relative to private-sector employment. The absence of any appreciable increase in government employment in the 1980s reflects both an increased opposition to higher taxes and a decline in the number of school-age children and thus in the demand for school teachers. Government employment remains at a fairly high level, however. As pointed out earlier, one of every six nonagricultural employees works in the public sector.

In the public sector union membership has increased even faster than employment. In 1950 less than 5 percent of union members in the United States worked in the public sector. By 1988, 38 percent of all union members were public employees. The increased importance of public employment accounts for some of the increase. Most, however, comes from changes in the percent unionized within the public and private sectors. From 1953 to 1988 union membership increased from 11.6 to 36.7 percent among public employees, while the percent unionized among employees in the private sector declined from 35.7 to 12.9 percent.[6]

As we see in Table 19-2, in 1953, 22 percent of federal workers were union members. Postal workers accounted for over 70 percent of union members among federal employees and over half of all members in the public sector. Outside the postal service unionization among federal workers was only 9 percent. Among state and local employees it was only 5 percent.

In the 1960s unionization among public-sector workers grew dramatically.

---

[5]Employment in state and local government increased sharply, from 9.1 percent of total employment in 1950 to 19.8 percent in 1980. In contrast, federal employment decreased slightly as a percentage of total employment, from 4.3 percent in 1950 to 3.2 percent in 1980.

[6]In addition, the number of workers covered by a collective bargaining agreement is greater than the number of union members, especially in the public sector. In 1988, 43.6 percent of all public employees were union members, while the corresponding figure for the private sector was only 14.2 percent.

TABLE 19-1   Public-Sector Employment

| Year | PERCENTAGE OF TOTAL NONAGRICULTURAL EMPLOYMENT | | |
	All Govt.	Fed.	State & Local
1950	13.3	4.3	9.1
1960	15.4	4.2	11.2
1970	17.7	3.9	13.9
1980	18.0	3.2	14.8
1989	16.3	2.8	13.6

Source: Economic Report of the President.

TABLE 19-2   Unionization among Public Employees

| Year | PERCENT UNIONIZED | | |
	All Govt.	Federal	State & Local
1953	11.6	22.2	4.8
1960	10.8	23.8	5.0
1970	32.0	37.6	30.1
1976	40.2	41.5	39.9
1983	34.1	37.1	32.7
1989	36.7		

Source: Prior to 1989 the data are from Leo Troy and Neil Sheflin, *Union Sourcebook* (West Orange, N.J.: Industrial Relations Data and Information Services, 1985). For 1989 the data are from *Employment and Earnings,* January 1990.

In 1962 President Kennedy issued executive order 10988, which granted federal employees the right to join a union, although it forbade strikes. During the 1960s many states passed legislation making it much easier for state and local employees to join unions. Prior to this period it was more difficult for unions to develop in the public than in the private sector because the provisions of the National Labor Relations Act did not apply to government workers. In the sixties most public-sector employees gained protections similar to those in the private sector. For example, in the federal government and most states agencies were set up to supervise elections to see if workers wished to be represented by a union. If they did vote for the union, then the employer was required to bargain with the union, although strikes were seldom allowed.

During the 1960s union membership grew dramatically among employees of state and local government, especially teachers. In 1960 most teachers were represented by the National Education Association (NEA), which at that time was involved primarily in lobbying and other professional activities unrelated to collective bargaining. In the early sixties the NEA shifted its emphasis to collective bargaining and took on most of the characteristics of a union, although it has never joined the AFL-CIO. Its membership grew to over one million teachers, many of whom were covered by collective agreements. In addition to the NEA, the American Federation of Teachers (AFT), an AFL-CIO union, grew from about 50,000 to almost 200,000 members. Thus while fewer than 100,000 teachers were considered union members in 1960, by 1970 the number had grown to about 1.3 million. Other occupations with strong union representation included police, firefighters, and nurses. Outside of teaching the most important union at the state and local level is the American Federation of State, County, and Municipal Employees (AFCSME), a union that includes workers in a wide variety of occupations.

The 1960s was a period of considerable growth in unionization at the federal level as well. While the two postal unions, the American Postal Workers Union (APWU) and the National Association of Letter Carriers (NALC) continued to expand, the fastest growing union of federal employees was the American Federa-

TABLE 19-3   Public-Sector Union Membership, 1983

Teachers	
Education Association; National (Ind.)	1,444,000
Teachers; American Federation of (AFL-CIO)	457,000
University Professors; American Association of (Ind.)	58,000
State and Local Government	
State, County & Municipal Employees; American Federation of (AFL-CIO)	955,000
Service Employees' International Union (AFL-CIO) (1985)	560,000
Governmental Employees; Assembly of (Ind.)	340,000
Fire Fighters; International Association of (AFL-CIO)	157,000
Police; Fraternal Order of (Ind.)	150,000
Teamsters, Chauffeurs, Warehousemen & Helpers of America; International Brotherhood of (Ind.) (1985)	150,000
Laborers' International Union of North America (AFL-CIO) (1985)	85,000
Communications Workers of America (AFL-CIO) (1987)	85,000
Nurses' Association; American (Ind.) (1987)	25,000
Automobile, Aerospace & Agricultural Implement Workers of America; International Union, United (AFL-CIO) (1987)	25,000
Postal Service	
Postal Workers Union; American (AFL-CIO)	226,000
Letter Carriers; National Association of (AFL-CIO)	203,000
Letter Carriers' Association; National Rural (Ind.)	40,000
Post Office Mail Handlers (Laborers' International Union of North America, AFL-CIO)	40,000
Federal Government	
Government Employees; American Federation of (AFL-CIO)	218,000
Treasury Employees Union; National (Ind.)	47,000
Federal Employees; National Federation of (Ind.)	34,000
Metal Trades Council (AFL-CIO) (1985)	24,000
Government Employees; National Association of (Service Employees' International Union, AFL-CIO) (1985)	23,000
Machinists & Aerospace Workers; International Association of (AFL-CIO) (1985)	12,000

Source: James L. Stern, "Unionism in the Public Sector," in *Public-Sector Bargaining*, 2d ed., Benjamin Aaron et al. (Washington, D.C.: Bureau of National Affairs, 1988), p. 54. Stern, in turn, has derived these figures primarily from Leo Troy and Neil Sheflin, *U.S. Union Sourcebook: Membership, Finances, Structure, Directory* (West Orange, N.J.: Industrial Relations Data and Information Services, 1985).

tion of Government Employees (AFGE). Like AFSCME, the AFGE represents many different occupations, but the AFGE has been less powerful than AFSCME, at least partly because of greater legal restrictions on unions of federal employees.

Unionization among public-sector employees continued to grow during the early seventies. Especially at the state and local level unions took advantage of new legislation, a favorable political climate, and expanding employment to gain new members and in most cases to win significant gains for their members. In the late seventies and early eighties, however, a reaction against both government in general and public-sector unions in particular set in. The result was fewer gains at the bargaining table and a leveling off of membership, as shown in Table 19–2.

The main unions involved in the public sector are listed in Table 19-3.

BARGAINING AT THE FEDERAL LEVEL

Federal authorities long took a negative if not hostile view of employee organization, in part because civil service protection was considered sufficient for government workers. Federal employees, along with state and local employees, were excluded from the coverage of the Wagner Act, while the Taft-Hartley amendments of 1947 specifically outlawed strikes by federal employees: "Any individual employed by the United States or any such agency who strikes shall immediately be discharged from his employment, and shall forfeit his civil service status, if any, and shall not be eligible for reemployment for three years."

The first positive statement of policy came in two executive orders issued by President Kennedy in 1962. The orders guarantee the right of federal employees to join unions, although this right is defined to exclude the right to strike.

Until 1978 labor-management relations in the federal government remained under the jurisdiction of an increasing number of executive orders and was not regulated by any legislation. The Civil Service Commission (CSC) played a large role in administering the executive orders, an arrangement opposed by the federal-employee unions, who saw the CSC as a representative of management.

The Civil Service Reform Act (CSRA) of 1978 provided legislative codification of many provisions of the executive orders and established a new body, the Federal Labor Relations Authority (FLRA), to administer the legislation.[7] Like the previous executive orders, the CSRA sanctions collective bargaining but outlaws all strikes. It covers most federal employees but excludes those involved directly in national security and those who have participated in illegal strikes. In addition, postal workers are covered not by the CSRA but by the National Labor Relations Act (NLRA), which covers workers in the private sector. Like other federal employees, however, postal workers are not allowed to strike.

As with the NLRB in the private sector, one important duty of the FLRA is

---

[7]The three members of the FLRA are appointed by the President for staggered five-year terms, in an effort to keep the FLRA independent rather than serving, or being perceived as serving, as an arm of management.

to determine the appropriate unit for secret ballot elections to determine which union, if any, will represent the workers. If one union receives a majority vote, then it is certified as the exclusive representative of all the workers in the unit and negotiates with the employer on their behalf.

The number of issues to be resolved through collective bargaining is much smaller in the federal government than in the private sector. Specifically, no bargaining is permitted that would modify any federal legislation. Because an agency's mission, budget, and number of employees is determined through legislation, these issues are out of bounds for collective bargaining. In addition, merit procedures have been established by legislation for hiring, transferring, and promoting workers.[8] Although bargaining is prohibited on many topics, it is required on some, especially on procedures for resolving employee grievances. Other topics where bargaining is permitted but not mandatory include the rules, regulations, and technology used by the agency to achieve its mission.

In the private sector a primary issue in collective bargaining is wage rates. In the federal government, however, pay scales are not set through collective bargaining, although unions do play some role. Since 1962 the basic principle underlying wage determination is for the federal government to try to pay the same wage as a "comparable" worker would receive in the private sector. Of course, it is not easy to determine when two workers or two jobs are really comparable. For example, even if the tasks are comparable, one job may involve more responsibility, poorer working conditions, or a greater risk of layoff. In addition, comparable dollar wage rates are set with little attention paid to whether there is comparability in nonwage benefits such as pensions and health insurance. In general, most studies have found that federal employees, especially women, appear to be more highly paid than comparable workers in the private sector.[9] These results are consistent with lower quit rates in the public sector and also with reports of long queues for many public-sector jobs.[10]

To determine how wage rates for white-collar federal employees should be changed each year, the process begins with a national survey of salaries, conducted by the Bureau of Labor Statistics. After receiving these data and the recommendations of top union officials, some of the President's top officials make recommendations. So does a panel of experts from the private sector. On the basis of these recommendations, the President makes his decision, which can be reversed only by a special act of Congress. A similar approach applies for blue-collar employees, except that local rather than national wage data are the standard of comparison.

---

[8]This merit system has been reinforced by the CSRA, which established not only the FLRA but also another independent agency, the Merit System Protection Board (MSPB), to safeguard the merit system.

[9]See Sharon P. Smith, *Equal Pay in the Public Sector: Fact or Fantasy?* (Princeton, N.J.: Industrial Relations Section, Princeton University, 1977); Sharon P. Smith, "Are State and Local Government Workers Overpaid?" in *The Economics of Municipal Labor Markets*, ed. Werner Hirsch and Anthony Rufulo (Los Angeles: UCLA Press, 1983); and Steven F. Venti, "Wages in the Federal and Private Sectors," in *Public Sector Compensation*, ed. David Wise (Chicago: University of Chicago Press, 1987).

[10]James E. Long, "Are Government Workers Overpaid? Alternative Evidence," *Journal of Human Resources* (Winter 1982), pp. 123–31.)

As this process suggests, the primary influence of federal-employee unions is through the political process, not collective bargaining. Unions do play an important role in processing grievances. But because they are not allowed to strike and cannot bargain over many important issues, including wage rates, they are more like lobbying organizations than like unions in the private sector. The main exception is the postal unions, which although they cannot strike, do bargain with the postal service about a wide range of issues, including wage rates.

BARGAINING AT THE STATE AND LOCAL LEVEL

At the state and local level collective bargaining is more important than at the federal level. Yet state and local collective bargaining is difficult to summarize because it is governed by different legislation in each state and because some groups, especially police and firefighters, are often treated differently from other public employees.

Background

Governmental units had systems for managing employee relations long before the appearance of unionism. These older managerial structures have posed serious problems for the development of collective bargaining. We shall comment particularly on practices in local government, where some of the most complex problems arise.

In a private corporation lines of authority are usually clear. The union knows with whom it must bargain; and it knows also that the management bargainer can make good on any commitments he or she makes. Neither of these factors is necessarily clear in bargaining with local government units.

Cities differ, to begin with, in their basic organization. Some have strong-mayor systems, others weak-mayor systems, others a city-manager system. Under any of these systems, the all-important authority over budgets is usually divided between the executive and legislative branches. The mayor or city manager may recommend a budget, but the city council can usually modify or veto it. Who has the dominant influence varies from city to city. The fiscal authority of local officials may be restricted by legislation. Sometimes tax increases beyond a certain size must be approved by the state legislature or submitted to popular referendum. Frequently, important fringe benefits such as pensions, vacation, and sick-leave arrangements are regulated either by state law or by the city charter. Local ability to pay is influenced also by availability of state and federal grants.

This situation presents the union with both difficulties and tactical opportunities. It is often unclear whether the bargainer for the city can actually commit the city to a proposed increase, which implies a corresponding budget appropriation. The bargainer may try to hide behind his limited authority or to pass the buck to other levels of government. Thus one finds the mayor of New York saying to a union group, "I'd be glad to give you the money if the governor would first give it to me" (these two politicians often being rivals). In other cases the bargainer is incapable of making a binding commitment because someone else will have to ratify the budget.

But the division of fiscal authority can also be turned to union advantage. If the city manager or a representative is proving a tough bargainer, the union can sometimes go around the manager to friends on the city council who will ratify a larger settlement. Collective bargaining is thus intertwined with personal and party rivalries in city politics.

A different kind of problem arises from the fragmentation of government units. One often finds semiautonomous agencies with independent authority over wages and benefits. These agencies may have their own taxing power or may be supported by state and federal grants. They are often under no compulsion to coordinate their wage struggles with other city departments or to follow directives of the mayor and council. Los Angeles, for example, has six independent salary-setting authorities, and the mayor and council set salaries for less than 60 percent of city employees. An example from Michigan is the Wayne County Road Commission, which operates in virtual independence of the Wayne County Board of Supervisors. Only about 2 percent of its budget comes from the county, the remainder from state grants and other outside sources. It has complete authority over this budget, including authority to enter into contracts with employees.

Another important governmental body is the civil service commission. Such commissions play a major role in the personnel policies of most states and many large cities. Created as a reaction against the earlier *spoils system*, it attempts to substitute merit for political patronage in public employment. Normally it has authority to establish basic job classifications and descriptions; to compile lists of applicants for entry jobs, and to select from these lists through competitive examination or some other objective basis; to lay down rules for training, retention, and promotion of employees in each classification, making further use of competitive examination as required; and to hear employee appeals from supervisors' decisions. Occasionally, the commission's jurisdiction extends to salary administration and recommendation of salary increases; but more usually its authority is limited to nonsalary matters. The existence and strength of civil service commissions create additional confusion over who can bargain for the public and on what issues.

As we saw in the case of the federal government, unions regard the civil service commission as an arm of the employer rather than as a neutral agency. Commission administration of personnel matters in accordance with its own judgment of merit runs counter to two union principles outlined in earlier chapters: (1) the principle that procedures for recruitment, promotion, layoff, or discharge of employees must be bargained out with the union and administered jointly through the grievance procedure rather than determined and administered unilaterally by the employer; and (2) the principle that seniority should be given dominant weight in personnel decisions. Promotions and demotions based on merit only, with merit decided by the employer, are not acceptable.

Recognition and Bargaining Units

Until the 1960s there was little legislation concerning unionization of state and local employees. State legislatures, particularly in the more agricultural states, were usually critical or hostile to the idea; and some states prohibited unionization of policemen, firemen, or even public employees in general. But usually the decision of whether to bargain was left up to city, county, or state officials. Unions had to make their way by politics and persuasion. Just as in the private sector, this led to numerous strikes over the basic issue of union recognition.

This situation has changed greatly in the past three decades, partly because of changes in the composition of many state legislatures, which now provide less representation to agricultural areas, and partly because of changes in public attitudes, which became more favorable to public-sector unions in the 1960s. Now most states have comprehensive labor-relations statutes covering state and local municipal employees.

A comprehensive statute usually contains an explicit declaration of the right of public employees to organize, to be represented by associations of their own choice, and to negotiate with their employers. Administration is usually in the hands of a public employee relations board, or some equivalent title. This board has the general powers and follows the general procedures of the National Labor Relations Board in defining bargaining units, conducting elections, certifying bargaining representatives, and enforcing the right to bargain. In the larger states the volume of election activity is high; and as a result of the new procedures, recognition strikes have almost disappeared in these states.

Employer Organization for Bargaining

There is often a question of specifying who the employer is for purposes of bargaining. The fragmentation of local-government decision making has frequently led to a corresponding fragmentation of bargaining units, with a union such as AFSCME bargaining separately with many governmental units. Fragmentation also exists because many public-sector unions, including those representing police, firefighters, and teachers, are craft unions, each wanting to bargain separately with the city.

Negotiations between many different unions and many different governmental agencies have considerably complicated collective bargaining at the state and local levels, creating several problems. The bargaining consumes the time of city officials in multiple negotiations. It tends to produce a crazy-quilt pattern of wages and benefits, differing among units and subject to no central oversight or rationale. Multi-union bargaining can pose barriers to ready transfer of city employees among departments using the same kinds of skill. It leads to whipsawing in the bargaining process, as one union wins superior terms on a particular front, and other unions then press for similar treatment. There have been several responses to these problems.

1. A shift of authority for labor relations toward the executive branch, as against the legislature and the civil service commission. This is a move that has clear practical advantages. The executive branch normally prepares and recommends the budget. When it also does the bargaining, any agreements involving money can be coordinated with the timing and content of the budget. Moreover, it is mainly the executive officials who will have to live with the agreement and participate in its administration. They are in the best position to anticipate administrative problems and inefficiencies that may be created by union requests on hours of work, shift arrangements, staffing requirements, transfers of personnel, and other restrictions on managerial authority. City councilors are often part time, usually nonexpert in labor matters, and unavoidably political in outlook, none of which makes them good bargaining representatives.

2. Increased centralization of authority within the executive branch. This is needed to coordinate city policy across the board and reduce whipsawing. It also permits hiring of expert personnel to carry on the bargaining.

3. Transfer of bargaining authority from existing staff officers, such as the budget director or personnel director, to full-time labor relations specialists. The first reaction has often been to assign bargaining responsibility to an existing staff member; but this creates difficulties. Apart from the fact that these officials usually lack expertise in labor relations, the bargaining function involves them in a conflict of roles. The budget director may want to reach agreement with the union; but her main function is to hold down costs to the city. A personnel director, on the other hand, may be willing to make outsize wage concessions if the union will go easy on interfering with personnel management. Increasingly, therefore, the bargaining function is located directly under the mayor or city manager. In smaller communities, the city manager may do the negotiating. In larger cities, there is usually a labor relations office with specialized, full-time personnel.

THE CONTENT OF COLLECTIVE AGREEMENTS

State laws have placed on public employers a duty to meet with unions and negotiate in good faith on "terms and conditions of employment." But what does this mean? In the private sector determination of what are mandatory subjects for bargaining has been left to the NLRB and the courts; and the scope of bargaining has been extended quite far. Any management decision that materially affects job content, job security, or working conditions is likely to become a subject for bargaining.

The situation in public employment is different. The logical problem is to reconcile the sovereign authority of government to make decisions in the interest of all the citizens with the bilateral authority inherent in collective bargaining. This leads to a variety of restrictions on what the public employer may and may not concede: provisions of state constitutions limiting delegation of authority by public officials; municipal ordinances relating to work schedules, pension systems, and other matters; preexisting civil service systems and personnel management rules; restrictions written into the text of state labor relations laws; court decisions interpreting these laws and defining the scope of bargaining.

Discussion of the present rules of the game is more difficult than in the case of the private sector. State laws and practices vary from quite permissive to quite restrictive. Moreover, practices are evolving quite rapidly in this new and experimental area. Space constraints force us to give only a broad-brush picture of where matters now stand.

1. What Is Bargainable? This issue arises most frequently with respect to quasi-professional groups such as teachers, policemen, nurses, social workers. How far can teachers' unions bargain over issues of educational policy? Is class size a legitimate bargaining issue? What about provisions for student discipline? What about curriculum content and assignment of teachers to athletic and other nonclassroom programs?

These subjects affect teachers' "terms and conditions of employment." But they also affect educational standards, administrative efficiency, pupils' welfare, and parents' concerns and interests. The question is whether collective bargaining on such matters provides adequate protection for third parties who have a legitimate interest in the outcome as well as for taxpayers who must pay for program costs.

Similar problems arise with respect to other professional groups. Can a union of social workers bargain over standards and procedures in a city's welfare system? Can a police union bargain for a clause prohibiting establishment of a civilian police review board? This is an issue with strong social and political overtones.

There have been efforts to resolve these issues through appropriate language in state labor relations laws; but the language and the underlying policy vary from state to state. Thus a Maine statute requires local school boards to "confer and negotiate in good faith with respect to wages, hours, working conditions and contract grievance arbitration . . . (and to) meet and consult but not negotiate with respect to educational policies." A Nevada statute defines class size, student discipline, staffing levels, and workloads as management rights. Some other state statutes take the opposite course of enumerating "terms and conditions of employment" in detail; whatever is left out is reserved to management. It has also become increasingly common to write a management rights clause into public employee contracts, confirming the employer's authority to determine agency policy, direct employees, determine the methods and personnel by which operations shall be conducted, and maintain the efficiency of government operations.

But, again, someone—usually the state labor relations board, and ultimately the courts—has to say just what the language means. The courts have tended to develop a "balancing" doctrine, to ask which set of interests predominates. For example, how important is an issue to teachers' well-being relative to its effect on the operation of the school system? There seems also to be a tendency toward gradual expansion of the scope of bargaining under continuing union pressure. Statute language has become less restrictive and has been interpreted in a less restrictive way.

2. Wages and Benefits. As we have seen, unions of federal employees have the peculiarity that they cannot bargain over salary schedules, pension rights, or other money matters, which are determined uniformly for the federal service.

Proposals for change are usually made by the President, and the necessary funds must be appropriated by Congress. On this front, then, union pressure must be exerted through political channels.

At the state and local level, on the other hand, wages and fringe benefits are usually freely negotiable. This involves much jockeying for position among employee groups and between them and the city government. If one union wins a favorable settlement, others will immediately demand the same terms. The city government will often try to delay a settlement with any one group until it can deal with all as a package. In the background, too, is the constraint that increases in wages and fringe costs must be found somewhere in the city or state budget. The people negotiating on the employer side may not have the power to deliver until the state legislature or city council has appropriated the necessary funds.

A government negotiator may even say, "We can't bargain with you at all until we know how much money is available." This position, however, has typically been rejected by state labor relations boards and by the courts. A possible shortage of funds can be used to justify hard bargaining—there is no restriction here; but a shortage cannot be used to justify refusal to bargain.

Pensions are usually included among the bargainable fringe issues; but some commentators have questioned whether they should be. There has been a tendency to write into contracts very generous pension terms—for example, terms that allow firefighters and police officers to retire on full pension after twenty or twenty-five years of service. These provisions build up large money costs for the future. Moreover, some governments, instead of "funding" these obligations—that is, building up a pension fund out of current revenue—have simply pushed them off to be met out of future revenues.

Other expenditure programs that impose large obligations for the future, such as bond issues to finance buildings, roads, sewers, and other public improvements, frequently require taxpayers' approval by referendum vote. It has been suggested that pension costs and the financing arrangements to cover them should be subject to a similar referendum.

3. Job Tenure, Promotion, Demotion. The main problems here arise from preexisting civil service systems at the state and federal levels. The heart of these systems is the merit basis of recruitment, testing, and selection for employment. The merit plan was intended to promote both equity and government efficiency by barring the employment of presumably less qualified people on political grounds. But in the absence of collective bargaining, civil service functions tended to expand into an elaborate body of rules concerning promotion, demotion, discharge, and appeals from employer personnel actions—in short, all the aspects of job rights and job tenure that in the private sector are usually regulated by the union contract. Unions of public employees, however, feel entitled to bargain and to represent their members on these issues as on others. So which should prevail—the old civil service system or the new collective bargaining procedure? The answer to this question varies from state to state. In many cases there is no state legislation, so the answer must be fought out issue by issue and city by city.

Looking to the future, it seems unlikely that public employee unions can be kept completely out of the job-tenure area, an area so central to union activities in the private sector. On the other hand, civil service commissions are not likely to disappear. The most common outcome may be that civil service will be cut back to its central function of advertising jobs, administering tests, compiling eligibility lists, and ensuring initial appointments on a merit basis. But establishing rules about what happens after that and policing allegedly unfair personnel actions by government agencies may become increasingly a collective bargaining function.

4. *Grievance Procedures and Grievance Arbitration*.   Union contracts at the state and local level typically have grievance procedures capped by binding arbitration. Most state statutes permit this system and even encourage it. But the question of whether an issue is arbitrable, as well as the terms of the arbitration award, is subject to court review. In the private sector, as we saw in the last chapter, the courts have been very supportive of arbitration. They limit themselves to determining whether the party seeking arbitration is making a claim that on its face is governed by the contract and do not go into the merits of the dispute. Arbitration may not be denied unless it can be said with positive assurance that the arbitration clause is not susceptible to an interpretation that covers the disputed issue. Arbitration gets the benefit of the doubt. Further, so long as the arbitrator's award can be characterized as drawing its essence from the agreement, the award is final and not subject to judicial review.

In public-sector disputes the courts have been more restrictive, both as to what issues are arbitrable and as to accepting the terms of an arbitrator's award. In a number of cases, the courts have set aside arbitration awards or refused to enforce them on the grounds that some law or public policy precludes the public agency from "bargaining away" or "delegating" its authority or discretion with respect to the issue in dispute. Such cases arise frequently in education, where it has been held, for example, that a school board cannot delegate to the arbitrator authority to make decisions involving tenure. Some courts have also intruded rather deeply into the merits in ruling particular disputes to be nonarbitrable, even to the extent of reversing the presumption of arbitrability that prevails in the private sector. One court held that unless the agreement is specific, direct, and unequivocal about which issues are arbitrable, arbitration may be denied.

The courts have also set aside arbitration awards on occasion, particularly where there was a relevant statute. They have been less tolerant than in the private sector of awards, where past practice is relied on to establish obligations not written into the agreement. Even when there is express contract language, they have shown a greater propensity than in the private sector to overturn an arbitrator's interpretation of this language.

The differences from private-sector practice described above cannot be summarized in any simple way. But it is clear that the scope of collective bargaining is more restricted than in the private sector. For this reason the power of public-sector unions may be less than it appears to be.

The most striking difference from the private sector, of course, is the usual prohibition of strike activity and the special procedures from breaking an impasse in contract disputes. This matter is complicated and important enough to deserve a separate heading.

PROCEDURES FOR SETTLEMENT OF CONTRACT DISPUTES

A strike by public employees is usually illegal and in any event is regarded as undesirable. But this presents a problem: if contract bargaining reaches an impasse, how can the impasse be broken if the strike option is removed? Most of the state labor relations laws set up procedures for dispute settlement, often several procedures that can be used in successive stages.

1. Mediation. This is normally the first step. A government mediator enters the scene and tries to guide the parties toward a settlement but without any coercive power. A certain percentage of disputes, though not a majority, are settled at this stage. The technique of mediation and the factors determining its success or failure are much the same as in the private sector. Success depends partly on the experience and skill of the mediator but also on the objective situation. The chances of success are greatest when there is considerable overlap in the positions of the parties or when the main problem is a breakdown of communications rather than substantive differences. The chances are improved also if there is strong outside pressure to settle, as there often is in public-sector disputes.

2. Fact-finding. A fact-finder is a neutral outsider, like a mediator. But the fact-finder has a broader role. He or she is expected to evaluate the positions of the parties, including the validity of any factual assertions underlying these positions, and then to make public recommendations for a settlement. While undertaking this role, usually the fact-finder will also engage in informal mediation, so a settlement may be reached before the fact-finder issues any formal report. Even if the dispute is not settled, the fact-finding report can help clarify the issues, influence public opinion, and may serve as the basis for a judgment by an arbitrator.

The defect of fact-finding is that it does not ensure a final settlement. Neither party is obliged to accept the recommendations. In order to force a settlement without the economic pressures of a strike sometimes arbitration is necessary.

3. Arbitration. Many states now provide for compulsory arbitration as the final stage in dispute settlement, and there is a trend toward greater use of this technique. The statutes vary considerably in detail. They may apply only to essential services, such as police and fire fighters, or to all public employees.

Arbitration involves formal hearings before either a single arbitrator or a tripartite panel of labor, management, and public representatives. In the latter case, in addition to the formal procedures, there is often continued informal bargaining within the panel and between the panel and the parties; and sometimes a settlement can be reached without issuing a formal award. Most commonly, however, an award is issued, which is binding on the parties.

Arbitration has also been criticized as involving an unacceptable delegation of public authority to an outsider not responsible to elected officials. Thus far most state supreme courts have upheld compulsory arbitration statutes, while some have declared them unconstitutional. In addition, courts have sometimes set aside an arbitration award on the grounds that it conflicted with laws or ordinances governing tenure rights, retirement age, or other matters.

Compulsory arbitration is a formidable procedure, since it takes final settlement of a dispute out of the hands of the parties. A common criticism is that it tends to have a "chilling effect" on collective bargaining—the parties will be unwilling to make concessions in the early stages of negotiation because of fear that this will prejudice them if and when the dispute goes to arbitration. They will remain dug in to fixed positions, and little real bargaining will occur. For example, an arbitrator may split the difference between the positions of the two parties, to avoid offending either and thus to increase the chances of being invited back by the parties to arbitrate future disputes. But if union and management both expect a dispute to go to arbitration and expect the arbitrator to split the difference, then each side will have an incentive to take an extreme position. As a result, little real bargaining will occur.

Although arbitrators do have some incentive to split the difference, it is not clear that they normally act in this fashion. A plausible alternative hypothesis is for the arbitrator to make his or her decision not on the basis of the position of the parties but rather by taking account of the external environment facing the negotiators, especially the wage increases received recently by other comparable workers. If this hypothesis is correct, then union and management have an incentive to reach an agreement by themselves rather than to let the case go to arbitration. This incentive will exist as long as both parties are risk averse and there is uncertainty about the arbitrator's decision.[11] Thus the threat of having to go to arbitration can serve the same function as the strike does in the private sector, since both represent costs the parties would like to avoid but can incur if the other side is being too intransigent in its bargaining demands.

Because of the danger that compulsory arbitration will have a chilling effect, some states have adopted a different approach, called *final-offer arbitration*. Here the arbitrator is limited to choosing either the union's or the employer's final offer, sometimes termed *the last best offer*. It is argued that this tack will make the parties more willing to make concessions, in the hope of making a proposal that will strike the arbitrator as more reasonable than the opponent's proposal. Also, the parties have an incentive to settle rather than risk the chance that the arbitrator will pick the other side's final offer. In some cases the arbitrator must pick the union or management proposal as a package. In other cases he may select the best offer on each individual issue. The New Jersey statute covering police officers and fire-

[11]See Henry S. Farber and Harry C. Katz, "Interest Arbitration, Outcomes, and the Incentive to Bargain," *Industrial and Labor Relations Review* (October 1979), pp. 55–63.

fighters allows the parties to choose from a menu of alternatives, including final offer by package, final offer by issue, final offer on some issues and conventional arbitration on others, or conventional arbitration on all issues.

Detailed studies of final-offer arbitration have been made in New Jersey and in Iowa.[12] Unions are winning about two-thirds of the awards in New Jersey, while the reverse is true in Iowa. In neither state is there any evidence of bias on the part of the arbitrator. Instead, the average union offer is more conservative in New Jersey, and the average employer offer is more conservative in Iowa.

There have been a number of other studies of compulsory arbitration and its consequences. Compulsory arbitration does appear to reduce strikes, although it falls short of preventing them. It is not clear whether compulsory arbitration has any significant chilling effect on collective bargaining. Negotiations are somewhat less likely to go to arbitration, however, when the type of arbitration available is final offer rather than conventional.[13]

4. The Strike.   In the public sector the strike has traditionally been viewed as unlawful. But there has been considerable debate among experts over whether that should be so. There are several shades of opinion. Some believe that the possibility of a strike serves the same functions in public as in private employment and that there should be no legal distinction between them. Others would draw a distinction between essential services, such as police and fire protection, and nonessential services and would make unlawful only strikes in the former category. A third group holds that strikes of public employees should be unlawful under all circumstances.

As to the actual situation, we note first that strikes at the federal level are clearly illegal and are in fact very rare. There was a major postal strike in 1970, when postal workers were still direct federal employees, which was settled only after troops were brought in to sort the mail. The present agreement between the postal unions and the U.S. Postal Service provides for arbitration as the final step in contract disputes.

A dramatic 1981 strike involved the Professional Air Traffic Controllers Organization (PATCO). In 1981 contract negotiations PATCO obtained what might be considered a good government offer. The administration agreed to recommend outsize increases in wages and other benefits to Congress. But the union leadership apparently preferred a strike, counting on support from the other airline unions and on congressional intervention to end the strike. So the executive board of PATCO rejected the proposed contract, and the membership voted it down by a large majority. The rejection proved to be a miscalculation. The administration moved vigorously to maintain service by transferring military air-traffic controllers and

---

[12]See Orley Ashenfelter and David Bloom, "Models of Arbitrator Behavior: Theory and Evidence," *American Economic Review* (March 1984), pp. 111–24; and Ashenfelter, "Evidence on U.S. Experiences with Dispute Resolution Systems," in *Organized Labor at the Crossroads,* ed. Wei-Chiao Huang (Kalamazoo, Mich.: W. E. Upjohn Institute for Employment Research, 1989).

[13]See Freeman, "Unionism," and Craig A. Olson, "Dispute Resolution in the Public Sector," in *Public-Sector Bargaining,* ed. Benjamin Aaron et al.

recruiting new civilian controllers. It discharged all striking controllers and ruled them ineligible for other federal employment, a policy that has been substantially enforced. And it moved to decertify PATCO as bargaining agent under the Federal Labor Relations Act, which was done. The strike received little support from other unions and failed to cripple air transport as had been expected. PATCO went into bankruptcy and eventually dissolved.[14]

In state and local government, however, strikes are common, although data are not available after 1979. In a typical year in the late 1970s there were about five hundred work stoppages, involving over 200,000 workers. Strikes are most frequent by teachers' unions, in part because time lost because of a strike is often made up later in the school year, thus reducing the cost of a strike to both the teachers and the community. For other public employees, such as police and firefighters, where strikes would be much more costly, strikes are forbidden by legislation, and compulsory arbitration is often required if the parties cannot reach an agreement themselves.

Strikes in the public sector are usually shorter than in the private sector. This suggests that a public-employee strike arouses the citizens and generates political pressure for a prompt settlement. Also, some states provide quite severe penalties for strikes by public employees. Imposition of these penalties or fear that they may be imposed gives the union an incentive to settle quickly.

The existence of penalties does not mean that they are always imposed. Whether to involve legal sanctions is a difficult decision, in which a mayor's calculations about political survival may weigh more heavily than the strict letter of the law. Recent studies have found that the combination of antistrike legislation with legislation encouraging compulsory arbitration does reduce strikes but that outlawing strikes without establishing compulsory arbitration has little effect.[15]

THE IMPACT OF PUBLIC-SECTOR BARGAINING

In Chapters 22 and 23, we consider the economic effects of public-sector unions and how these effects compare with the effects of unions in the private sector. In this chapter we consider the political effects of public-sector unions, a more elusive but equally important topic.

The differences between private and public sector bargaining are mainly political rather than economic. Employees do not become different by working in the public sector. The work they do is not distinctively different. The difference lies in the employer. In the case of a private company we do not look into the decision-making process that leads it to take certain positions at the bargaining table. But the decision-making process in government is the central stuff of politics. Government units operate under statutory and constitutional restrictions. Decisions must be

---

[14]For a more detailed account, see Herbert R. Northrup, "The Rise and Demise of PATCO," *Industrial and Labor Relations Review* (January 1984), pp. 167–84.

[15]Freeman, "Unionism," and Olson, "Dispute Resolution."

reached in an orderly way, within fiscal and other limits imposed by legislatures responsible to the public. These restrictions often conflict with the demands advanced by public-employee unions at the bargaining table. In the event of such a conflict, the central question is not how to make collective bargaining work but how to make government work.

Union demands pose a typical conflict of interest among different groups of citizens. This dilemma is clearest in the case of wage and fringe demands, though it exists also with respect to work rules, workloads, staffing requirements, and other things that affect costs and services. Employee compensation typically forms 65 to 70 percent of the city budget. Wage increases usually must lead to some combination of tax increases and reduction of public services, both imposing burdens on the public.

Group pressures exist, of course, even in the absence of collective bargaining. Teachers, police, firefighters, and other employee groups had organizations and engaged in lobbying and election activities long before collective bargaining became general. On the other side are organizations representing those with an interest in controlling government costs and improving public services: taxpayers' leagues, parents' organizations, chambers of commerce. Taxpayers are more numerous than government employees; but the employees have a more concentrated interest in their terms of employment and may exert stronger pressure per person than their opponents do. So it is not easy to judge where the balance of power usually lies.

The next question is, Does the development of unionism and collective bargaining change the balance of power in the employees' favor? Clyde Summers argues that it does, for several reasons. First, the principle of exclusive representation gives public employees a unified and authoritative voice. Second, it gives them special access to the political process. They are no longer limited to speeches and petitions but can argue with government administrators across the bargaining table. Third, because bargaining normally occurs before the budget is adopted, public employees may obtain priority consideration of their interests. Fourth, because bargaining goes on behind closed doors, public officials are confronted by the union's arguments without direct exposure to the counterarguments of other groups. Fifth, the union has resources that can be used politically to defeat officials who resist union demands and to elect others who will be more pliable.[16] As a leading New York labor leader, Victor Gotbaum, once remarked, "We have the ability . . . to elect our own boss."[17]

The mayor and other public officials, who are expected to mediate among conflicting interests in an even-handed way, may not be up to the job. Summers notes the prevalence of "hand-wringing politicians," who claim that they are unable

---

[16]Clyde Summers, "Public Sector Bargaining: Problems of Governmental Decision Making," *University of Cincinnati Law Review* (1976); key portions of this article are reprinted in Getman, *Labor Relations: Law, Practice and Policy* (Mineola, N.Y.: Foundation Press, 1978), pp. 442–52.

[17]Reported in an article on the unusually strong position of municipal-employee unions in New York City: "A Reporter at Large: More for Less," *New Yorker* (August 1, 1977).

to resist union pressure; and also of "buck-passing politicians," who buy off the union by passing the cost on to future budgets and future taxes. The prime example is increased pension rights not funded out of the current budget, so that taxpayers do not realize the size of the eventual bill.

In the late seventies and eighties a counterreaction to public-sector unions developed as voter-taxpayers became increasingly concerned with the high cost of government. This concern led to effective pressure to cut taxes and thus, at least at the state and local level, also to reduce government expenditures. Since there was less money to spend, earnings of government employees could no longer increase rapidly, despite the influence of unions. So the effect of unions on the political process may well be smaller than its proponents initially hoped or than its opponents feared. As we shall see in Chapter 20, it seems clear that unions have not had dramatic effects on wage rates in the public sector.

SUMMARY

1. Public-sector employers are not profit maximizers but are concerned instead with political objectives. Because the public sector receives most of its revenue from taxation, a strike reduces its monetary costs without diminishing its revenue. Thus the pressures for public-sector officials to settle a strike are political rather than economic.

2. The elasticity of demand for union labor typically is lower in the public than the private sector, so public-sector unions need not be quite so concerned with the employment effects of higher wage rates.

3. By 1988, 38 percent of all union members were public employees. Unionization increased dramatically in the public sector in the 1960s and 1970s and was relatively constant in the 1980s, in contrast to the sharp decline of unions in the private sector.

4. Public-sector unions are strongest at the state and local level, especially among teachers, police, firefighters, and nurses. At the federal level the postal unions are the most influential.

5. Unions of federal employees have no right to strike. Their main influence is as lobbyists in the political arena, although they also play a role processing grievances.

6. Collective bargaining is much more important at the state and local level, where the right to strike sometimes exists and where compulsory arbitration is often available when strikes are prohibited. Bargaining takes place over many issues, including wage rates, job security, and promotion policies. Especially in the case of teachers, bargaining also occurs over issues of public policy, such as class size and curriculum, that affect working conditions.

7. Unions achieved considerable power at the state and local level during the late 1960s and early 1970s. Since then a counterreaction has developed, however, as voter-taxpayers have become increasingly concerned with the high cost of government, including expenditures for public employees.

KEY CONCEPTS

FACT-FINDING
ARBITRATION, CONVENTIONAL
ARBITRATION, FINAL OFFER

CIVIL SERVICE COMMISSION
PUBLIC SECTOR

REVIEW QUESTIONS

1. Does your state have a statute governing collective bargaining by state and municipal employees? If so, what are its main provisions?

2. If your college is in or near a city, what unions of public employees exist in the city? With whom in the city government does each union bargain? Appraise the effectiveness of present bargaining arrangements.

3. Is it desirable and feasible to draw a line between bargainable and nonbargainable subjects? If you favor such a distinction, how would you constuct it?

4. What are the main points of conflict between public-employee bargaining and civil service commission procedures? How might this conflict be resolved? (Again, look into what has happened in your own city.)

5. What are the advantages and disadvantages of compulsory arbitration of public-employee disputes? Why shouldn't all unsettled disputes go directly to arbitration, with no prior steps?

6. What should be the legal status of strikes in public employment? Is a policy of banning strikes actually enforceable?

7. Do you think that public-employee collective bargaining, accompanied by strikes or strike threats, unduly distorts the political process in the direction of employee interests? If so, can you suggest any practical correctives?

READINGS

Aaron, Benjamin, Joyce M. Najita, and James L. Stern, eds., *Public-Sector Bargaining,* 2d ed. Washington: Bureau of National Affairs, 1988.

Freeman, Richard, "Unionism Comes to the Public Sector." *Journal of Economic Literature* (March 1986), pp. 41–86.

Lester, Richard A., *Labor Arbitration in State and Local Government.* Princeton, N.J.: Industrial Relations Section, Princeton University, 1984.

Wise, David, *Public Sector Compensation.* Chicago: University of Chicago Press, 1987.

UNION WAGE EFFECTS

We have been studying the process of collective bargaining. Now we shall examine its effects. In this chapter we focus on how unions have affected wage rates and benefits, while Chapter 21 discusses nonwage effects.

We start by looking at the average differential between union and non-union wage rates, the union wage gap. Then we consider the effects of unions on benefits. As a result of these effects on relative compensation, unions also affect the allocation of resources. Then we turn to the effects of unions on the earnings of nonunion workers and on the rate of inflation in the economy.

In the second half of the chapter we see how union effects differ in different sectors, in different industries, and for different workers. We show how the impact of unions differs in the public and private sectors, how the elasticity of demand for union labor affects the ability of unions to gain higher wages, and how unions appear to have reduced the inequality of earnings.

MODELING THE EFFECT OF UNIONS ON WAGE RATES

A union tries—usually with success—to raise the wages of its members above what they would earn under competitive conditions and above the wages of comparable nonunion workers. Let's look first at how unions increase wage rates and then examine the evidence on the magnitude of the effect.

Consider the economy illustrated in Figure 20-1. It consists of two indus-

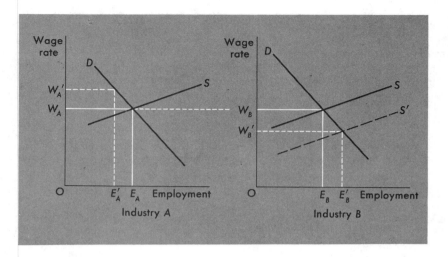

FIGURE 20-1   A Possible Wage-Employment Effect of Collective
Bargaining

tries, A and B, with identical labor supply and demand curves. (This assumption is not necessary but simplifies the exposition.) If we assume a competitive labor market, both industries will pay the same wage, $W_A = W_B$.

Industry A now becomes unionized. The union compels employers to pay a higher wage, W'_A. At this wage employers find it profitable to hire only E'_A workers. So some of those previously employed in the industry, shown by the distance $E'_A E_A$, are out of work.

These workers would presumably rather work in industry B than remain unemployed. So labor supply to industry B increases from S to S'. The wage level of industry B falls to W'_B, while employment rises to E'_B. This increase just equals the decrease of employment in industry A, and everyone is once more employed.

Note that the allocation of labor between the two industries is no longer optimal. The marginal product of labor in industry B ($= W'_B$) is substantially below that in industry A ($= W'_A$). So national output is reduced. This effect is similar to that of monopoly power in product markets.

How is the wage effect of a union to be measured? One obvious approach is to estimate $W'_A - W_A$, the wage in industry A before and after unionization. This difference is often called the *wage gain* for union members. Although it is easy to measure the current union wage, W'_A, it is difficult to measure W_A, the wage in the absence of unionization. Thus empirical studies have focused on $W'_A - W'_B$, the size of the *wage gap* between otherwise comparable union and nonunion workers. To the extent that unionization in industry A may have reduced the wage in industry B by increasing its supply of workers, the wage gap, $W'_A - W'_B$, will be larger than the wage gain for union workers in industry A.

For many issues, including the allocation of resources, the relevant question is, What is the gap between union and nonunion wages? Thus for both theoretical and empirical reasons the literature of labor economics has focused on the wage gap rather than the wage gains from unionization.

In the model presented in Figure 20-1 one industry is completely organized, while the other is completely nonunion. Now consider a situation, common in practice, where an industry is *partially* unionized. How will an increase in the percentage of workers unionized affect the wages of union workers, the wages of nonunion workers, and hence the size of the wage gap?

Unionization of some plants in an industry will raise their relative wages and (probably) unit production costs, reduce employment, and cause some loss of business to nonunion plants. But as the percentage of unionization rises, the amount of business that can be lost to nonunion firms decreases. Thus demand for the product of union firms, and therefore their derived demand for labor, will become *less elastic* than before. This makes wage raising easier, and so the union wage should rise as the percentage organized increases.

The effect on the nonunion wage is less clear, because offsetting tendencies are at work. On the one hand, cost and price increases in unionized plants will shift product demand and hence labor demand toward nonunion plants. The increase in labor demand will tend to raise nonunion wages. Working in the same direction is the "threat effect": nonunion employers may raise wages in an effort to ward off possible unionization. On the other hand, the supply effect of the workers displaced from union plants will tend to lower nonunion wages. We cannot predict *a priori* which effect will predominate. But unless the effect on nonunion wages is strongly positive, we would expect the wage gap to grow as the percentage unionized rises.

Empirical Evidence of Union Effects

So much for possibilities. But what about actualities? Have unions in the United States raised the relative wages of their members, and by how much? It's a hard question to answer. What we want to know is the impact of unionism, *other things being equal*. But other things are never equal. To distinguish the effect of unionization from that of the many other forces bearing on relative wage rates requires complex statistical analysis.

Several different research approaches have been used:

Cross-sectional Studies at a Particular Time. Take an industry like construction, local trucking, or hotels and restaurants, in which the degree of unionization in different areas ranges from zero to 100 percent. Suppose one has data for 1990 on percentage of unionization and average hourly earnings, area by area. One can then examine whether there is a relation between unionization and earnings, after controlling for other variables.

A variant of this method is to use some other group of workers as a reference group. In one study of construction wages, for example, the wage rate for carpenters in each area was divided by the average wage of nonunion common laborers in the area. The study then asked, Is the carpenter's premium over the common laborer, area by area, related to the degree of unionization among carpenters?

Studies of Change over Time.   Suppose we have data on average hourly earnings and percentage of unionization in fifty industries, year by year over the period 1950 to 1990. We then examine whether industries with a greater increase (or less rapid decline) in unionization have had a more rapid rate of wage increase. Again, it is necessary to control for other variables that may have influenced an industry's wage level. At best, this method is not very satisfactory, because the industry categories used are typically broad and include many subindustries and product lines whose behavior may be quite variable. One needs really detailed data to get meaningful results.

Earnings Functions for Union and Nonunion Workers.   A more important line of research tries to explain the earnings of individual workers in terms of their age, sex, race, education, work experience, and other personal characteristics. Here one can include a variable whose value depends on whether the worker is or is not a union member. The question then is whether this variable is associated with significantly higher earnings, independent of other personal characteristics, such as schooling and gender, which also influence earnings. The union variable typically does turn out to be significant and sizable—union workers earn more. This technique can also be used to explore whether unionism raises wages more for some types of labor than for others—for example, for high-skilled workers compared with low-skilled workers or for white workers compared with black workers.

In recent years most studies of the union-nonunion wage gap have used the earnings function approach. After carefully reviewing over one hundred such studies, Gregg Lewis concludes that for the period 1967–79 the best studies indicate a gap of about 15 percent.[1] The evidence from the earnings-function studies is consistent with Lewis's earlier conclusion, based on studies for the 1950s using the first two approaches described above, that the wage gap for that period was 10 to 15 percent.[2]

In another important study Freeman and Medoff, after analyzing a wide variety of data sets, conclude that the wage gap for the 1970s was 20 to 30 percent.[3] Their estimates are a little larger than those of Lewis and also show a more pronounced upward trend. As discussed in Chapter 14, this upward trend is one reason employer opposition to unions increased during the 1970s. The wage gap in the United States for the 1970s also appears to have been slightly larger than in Great Britain or Canada.[4]

For the 1980s there have been fewer estimates of the union-nonunion wage gap. The evidence for the United States does suggest, however, that the gap has not fallen appreciably despite the prevalence of union concessions during the recession

---

[1]See H. Gregg Lewis, *Union Relative Wage Effects, A Survey* (Chicago: University of Chicago Press, 1986), p. 9.

[2]See H. Gregg Lewis, *Unionism and Relative Wages in the United States* (Chicago: University of Chicago Press, 1963).

[3]Richard D. Freeman and James L. Medoff, *What Do Unions Do?* (New York: Basic Books, 1984), Chap. 3.

[4]Barry T. Hirsh and John T. Addison, *The Economic Analysis of Unions* (Boston: Allen and Unwin, 1986), pp. 149–51.

of the early 1980s.[5] In many cases these concessions did not involve actual pay cuts but instead consisted of lower wage increases than had been negotiated earlier, when conditions were more favorable. While the rate of increase of nominal wage rates for union workers was much lower in the 1980s than it was in the 1970s, nonunion wage rates also increased much more slowly in the eighties.

Are the Estimates of Union Wage Effects Real or Illusionary?

We have indicated that the best estimates of the union wage effect are in the 15 to 30 percent range. But despite all efforts of the researchers, these estimates may still be biased. For example, we expect that when unions raise wage rates, employers will be able to hire more productive workers. Some of this effect is captured in the empirical studies, since they control for years of school and experience in the labor force. But other aspects of productivity, such as willingness to work hard rather than quit when the employer demands high effort, cannot be captured in traditional earnings functions. Thus as Lewis has emphasized, the estimates of the union wage gap may be too high. Another possible bias exists if unions are easier to organize where working conditions are difficult and wages high, even in the absence of unions, owing to compensating differentials.[6] High union wage rates may also affect the extent of unionization, either positively by increasing the demand for unionization among workers or negatively by increasing employer opposition to union-organizing efforts.[7]

In conclusion, the estimate of the union wage gap must be treated somewhat cautiously. While economists have done much good work on this topic, all empirical studies are subject to some limitations. On balance, the problems suggest that the estimates may be somewhat too large, but we cannot be certain that the net effect of the various biases is in this direction.

UNION EFFECTS ON BENEFITS

Earlier studies of the wage gap focused on *hourly rates* of pay. But there is now a growing body of microdata from individual establishments that make possible comparisons of *total compensation* per worker-hour, including benefits. Total compensation is a superior measure both of what labor costs the employer and of what the worker receives.

---

[5]See Richard Edwards and Paul Swaim, "Union-Nonunion Earnings Differentials and the Decline of Private-Sector Unionism," *American Economic Review* (May 1986), pp. 97–102; and Richard Freeman, "In Search of Union Wage Concession in Standard Data Sets," *Industrial Relations* (Spring 1986), pp. 131–45.

[6]Greg J. Duncan and Frank P. Stafford, *American Economic Review*, "Do Unions Receive Compensating Differentials?" (June 1980), pp. 355–71.

[7]C. J. Parsley, "Labor Unions and Wages: A Survey," *Journal of Economic Literature* (March 1980), pp. 1–31).

We saw in Chapter 7 that benefits are a large and growing share of total compensation, and that they show some statistical regularities. The size of benefits and their share of total compensation is positively related to size of company. It is also positively related to basic rates of pay. Companies that pay higher wages typically offer larger benefits as well. Because there is intercorrelation among large plant size, unionization, higher wage rates, and a larger benefit share, the *independent* effect of unionism is not easy to estimate.

Using data from the survey of expenditures for employee compensation (EEC), Freeman and Medoff found that benefit costs in union establishments were 68 percent higher than in comparable nonunion establishments.[8] About half this effect comes from the fact that unions raise basic rates of pay, and that benefits vary positively with rates of pay. The other half comes from the fact that unions also raise the *share* of benefits in total compensation. The union's percentage impact on benefits varies with size of firm and with the firm's wage level. It is especially large for small and low-wage firms, that is, for firms that would under nonunion conditions have particularly low benefits. Further, the effect of unionism is particularly large for deferred-compensation plans conferring larger benefits on senior employees, such as pensions, insurance, and health-care plans.

These results imply that studies based on wage rates alone considerably understate the union impact on total compensation. Among establishments in the EEC sample Freeman and Medoff find that the union advantage in straight-time pay was 14.8 percent. In total compensation per hour, however, the union advantage was 17.3 percent.

Why should unionism raise the benefit share of total compensation? An explanation could run in terms of the change that unionism brings in the structure of the labor market. Wage payments and benefits clearly are substitutable, although not perfectly substitutable, in workers' minds. A worker will give up a certain amount in wages to obtain an extra dollar's worth of benefits. Call this the *supply price of benefits*. It is reasonable to think that it will be related to the worker's age and length of service. A young worker, healthy and far from retirement, may not value benefits very highly and will not give up much to obtain them. A more senior worker, getting more benefits currently and also closer to retirement age, will value benefits more highly and will be willing to trade off more in wages.

To the employer the dollar cost of wages and benefits is readily comparable. If paying an extra dollar in benefits will save more than a dollar in wages, that is a good bargain. The nonunion employer, as we observed earlier, is concerned with the preferences of *marginal workers,* the people who can be attracted or retained by a small increase in compensation. If we suppose that these are mainly young, mobile workers whose preference for benefits is relatively low, it will pay to put most of the compensation offer into wage rates and not much into benefits.

It is possible also that the nonunion employer underestimates workers' preferences for benefits. A union is likely to transmit more accurate information on

---

[8]Freeman and Medoff, *What Do Unions Do?* Chap. 4. See also Stephen A. Woodbury, "Substitutability between Wage and Nonwage Benefits," *American Economic Review* (March 1983), pp. 166–82.

members' preferences. Moreover, these will be the preferences of the *average* worker rather than the marginal worker. Policy may even be biased somewhat toward the more senior workers, who as we noted in Chapter 15 are likely to have disproportionate influence in union government. Since preference for benefits increases with age and length of service, we expect benefits to be a larger share of total compensation when employers are unionized.

There are three further considerations. By increasing workers' length of job tenure and reducing quit rates, a union increases the probability that workers will *actually receive* deferred benefits, which will increase their willingness to forgo wages to obtain these benefits. Second, where workers are attached to an *occupation* rather than an *employer* (as in building construction, merchant shipping, longshoring), or where individual firms are rather impermanent (as in the clothing industry), a union may provide the only feasible mechanism for administering benefits. Third, unions increase the relative wage rates of their members. As workers' wages increase, their demand for benefits is likely to increase more than proportionally. At a very low wage workers must spend most of their income for food and shelter. At higher wage rates insurance protection and pensions become relatively more important. In addition, the preferred tax treatment of benefits is worth more to those in higher tax brackets.

THE RESOURCE-ALLOCATION EFFECTS OF THE UNION-NONUNION WAGE GAP

By increasing the wage rate and benefits of their workers, unions may reduce the efficiency of the economy. As we saw in Chapter 5, an employer has a negatively sloped demand for labor. So when a union increases the wage rate, the employer will use less union labor. With fewer jobs available in the union sector, more workers will seek jobs in the nonunion sector.

If in the absence of unions we assume that the economy is reasonably competitive, then this shift of labor from the union to the nonunion sector will reduce national output and thus reduce economic efficiency. Let us see why. If the economy is competitive, then each worker is paid the value of his or her marginal product. As we saw in Figure 20-1, workers who would otherwise have worked in the union sector at wage rate W_A must now settle for jobs in the nonunion sector at the lower wage of W'_B. Since the wage rate in each sector is equal to the value of the output produced by a marginal worker, the shift of workers to jobs at lower wage rates also means a shift to jobs that produce less valued output. Thus the total national output is reduced. This argument that unions cause labor to be allocated inefficiently has been emphasized by critics of unions.[9]

The magnitude of this misallocation of resources depends on the number of

---

[9]For example, see Milton and Rose Friedman, *Free to Choose* (New York: Harcourt Brace Jovanovich, 1980), Chap. 8; or Henry C. Simon, *Economic Policy for a Free Society* (Chicago: University of Chicago Press, 1948).

workers affected and on the difference in the value of their output in the union and nonunion sectors. Estimates of the cost of this misallocation are rather modest, about 0.2 percent of GNP.[10] This cost represents about $10 billion, or about $40 per capita. If higher union wage rates lead to increased unemployment rather than lower nonunion wage rates, the resource allocation costs of unions are considerably higher. To evaluate the overall contribution of unions to the economy and to society, we need to consider a wider variety of issues.

THE EFFECT OF UNIONS
ON NONUNION WAGE RATES

We have concentrated on the effect of unions on the gap between union and nonunion wage rates for two reasons. First, this wage gap is what is most relevant for considering the issue of resource allocation. Second, many empirical studies have been made estimating the wage gap. Although the wage gap is of interest, it is also important to know the extent to which unions have actually raised the wage rates of their members, relative to the wage rate that would have existed in the absence of unionization—the wage gain due to unionization. Going back to Figure 20-1, we seek to estimate the wage gain, $W'_A - W_A$, rather than just the wage gap, $W'_A - W'_B$. The wage gain cannot be measured directly, because we do not know what union members would have earned in the absence of any unionization. Instead we must estimate $W'_A - W_A$ by noting that it depends on both $W'_A - W'_B$ and $W'_B - W_B$, where $W'_A - W'_B$ is the union-nonunion wage gap, and $W'_B - W_B$ is the effect of unions on nonunion wage rates. Only in the special case where unions have no effect on the wage of nonunion workers will the union-nonunion wage gap be identical with the increase in wage rates that unions have won for their members.

Recall that there are two primary reasons why unions may affect the wage rates of workers who are not union members. First, by increasing wage rates and thus reducing the number of workers in the union sector, unions increase the supply of labor to the nonunion sector. This increase in supply is expected to reduce nonunion wage rates. The resulting decline in nonunion wages is called the *spillover effect*. On the other hand, nonunion employers may pay workers at or near the union scale in an effort to keep their workers from becoming unionized. This *threat effect* will increase nonunion wage rates, at least for some workers. The threat effect is likely to be greatest for firms that operate large plants or that have monopoly profits, since such firms make especially good targets for union organizers.

We have seen that the high nonunion wage rates in large firms and in firms with monopoly power provides some empirical support for the threat effect. For

---

[10]See Robert H. DeFina, "Unions, Relative Wages, and Economic Efficiency," *Journal of Labor Economics*" (October 1983), pp. 408–29; Freeman and Medoff, *What do Unions Do?*, Chap. 3; and Albert Rees, "The Effect of Unions on Resource Allocation," *Journal of Law and Economics* (October 1963), pp. 69–78.

evidence on the relative importance of the threat and spillover effects, we can examine whether nonunion wage rates tend to be higher or lower in labor markets with high unionization. This approach has been taken in studies by Kahn, by Holzer, and by Freeman and Medoff.[11] They find that the typical nonunion worker gains higher wages in standard metropolitan statistical areas (SMSAs) where unionization is high.

The empirical studies do find some support for the spillover effect, however. Employment is lower and unemployment is higher when unionization is high. In addition, unionization has a negative effect on nonunion wages for blacks and women, workers who on average are most likely to be employed in secondary labor markets. Because of low turnover and high job commitment in the primary labor market, the threat of unionization is high unless the employer pays good wage rates. Not only will the threat effect be important but there will be little spillover effect in primary labor markets, because the wage normally exceeds the level needed to clear the market. In secondary markets, however, turnover is high, the threat of unionization is relatively low, and wage rates are more flexible so long as they are above the legal minimum. So it is not surprising that evidence for the spillover effect should occur among workers who are employed disproportionately in secondary labor markets.

THE EFFECT OF UNIONS ON INFLATION

If unions have no effect on productivity, then the effect of unions on inflation depends on (1) changes in the union wage premium, (2) the effect of changes in union wage rates on nonunion wage rates, and (3) the effect of changes in wages on costs and thus also on prices.[12]

Note first that unions will have an inflationary effect only when the union wage effect is *increasing.* Even then the direct effect of unions on inflation will be small because labor's share of total costs is small. Thus unions will have a significant effect on inflation only if there is a rapid increase in the union wage premium or if changes in union wage rates have an important effect on nonunion wage rates.

In the 1970s the union wage premium did rise, but this increase appears to have been responsible for only a small part of the high inflation during this period.[13]

---

[11]Lawrence M. Kahn, "The Effect of Unions on the Earnings of Nonunion Workers," *Industrial and Labor Relations Review* (January 1978), pp. 205–16; "Union Spillover Effects on Unorganized Labor Markets," *Journal of Human Resources* (Winter 1980), pp. 87–98; Harry J. Holzer, "Unions and the Labor Market Status of White and Minority Youth," *Industrial and Labor Relations Review* (April 1982), pp. 392–405; Freeman and Medoff, *What Do Unions Do?* pp. 158–59; and Edward Montgomery, "Employment and Unemployment Effects of Unions," *Journal of Labor Economics* (April 1989), pp. 170–90.

[12]The effects of union on productivity are discussed in Chap. 21.

[13]Freeman and Medoff estimate that even though the union wage premium increased by nine percentage points between 1975 and 1981, unions increased inflation by only a little over two percentage points (3 percent of a total increase in inflation of sixty-eight percentage points from 1975 to 1981.) See *What Do Unions Do?*, pp. 58–59.

In fact, the high inflation may have led to the increased union premium rather than vice versa.

As we saw in the last section, there has been relatively little study of the effect of unions on the level of nonunion wage rates. There has also been little study of the effect of *changes* in union wage rates on *changes* in nonunion wages. The few studies that have been done generally conclude that union wage increases do lead to greater wage increases in the nonunion sector but that the effects are quite modest.[14] Given these results, it appears unlikely that unions have had any large effects on inflation in recent years.

UNION WAGE EFFECTS IN THE PUBLIC SECTOR

We have been discussing the effects of unions on the average worker. But union effects are not the same for all workers. Let us look at the effects of one important group of unions, those whose members work in the public sector. In order to investigate this issue, we look first at how wage rates are set by the government in the absence of unionization. The federal government and most lower government units have legislation requiring them to follow the *prevailing wage principle*—that is, to adjust their rates of pay to those prevailing for comparable work in the private sector. Experienced observers have argued, however, that there are biases in government wage-setting procedures that tend to produce a higher wage level for public employees.[15]

First, there is usually a range of private wage rates for any occupation. The wage surveys used in ascertaining the "prevailing wage" tend to exclude the smaller, relatively low-wage employers and thus contain an upward bias. Second, for occupations with active unions (such as the building trades) the prevailing wage is almost invariably interpreted as the union scale, regardless of the actual prevalence of that scale in the private sector. Third, focusing attention on equality of wage *rates* ignores other important characteristics of public employment, such as year-round work and greater security of job tenure, which might under competition lead to a compensating wage differential in favor of the private sector.

Do Government Workers Earn More?

The hypothesis that government tends to pay more for comparable work is supported by the statistical evidence.[16]

---

[14]See Robert J. Flanagan, "Wage Interdependence in Unionized Labor Markets," *Brookings Papers on Economic Activity* (1976), pp. 635–73; and Daniel J. B. Mitchell, "Recent Union Contract Concessions, *Brookings Papers on Economic Activity* (1982), pp. 165–201.

[15]See, in particular, Walter Fogel and David Lewin, "Wage Determination in the Public Sector," *Industrial and Labor Relations Review* (April 1974), pp. 410–31.

[16]For an overview, see two studies by Sharon P. Smith, *Equal Pay in the Public Sector: Fact or Fantasy?* (Princeton, N.J.: Industrial Relations Section, Princeton University, 1977); and "Are State and Local Workers Overpaid?" in *The Economics of Municipal Labor Markets* ed. Werner Hirsch and Anthony Rufulo (Los Angeles: UCLA Press, 1983), pp. 59–89. For a review of studies for individual occupations, see Richard B. Freeman, "Unionism Comes to the Public Sector," *Journal of Economic Literature* (March 1986), pp. 41–86.

After adjusting for schooling, experience, and other worker characteristics, the following results have been found.

1. Federal employees earn more than private-sector workers, with the difference greatest for women. At the state and local level the situation varies a good deal from area to area. On the average, female state-local employees earn considerably more than comparable private-sector employees; but there is no appreciable difference for male workers. The situation also differs by occupational levels. Governments show a tendency to overpay at the bottom of the wage structure and to underpay at the top, that is, to maintain a more compressed wage structure than exists in the private sector. This underpayment for managerial and professional occupations makes it hard for government to compete with private employers for the best talent.

2. The *earnings* differential in favor of government workers is considerably larger than the wage differential, because of the greater regularity of government employment. Benefits also are higher in the public sector. Retirement pensions are the largest benefit for federal workers, but they are important also at the state level, and for police and firefighters at the local level. Paid time off—paid holidays, vacations, sick leave, and so on—is also distinctly more generous than in the private sector.

In short, most government employees have some advantage over private-sector workers in wage rates, a larger advantage in annual earnings, and a still larger advantage when benefits are included.

Do Unionized Government Workers Earn More than Nonunion Workers?

Granted that government employees already enjoy some advantage over private sector employees, does unionism serve to increase this advantage? Do government workers who are organized earn more than nonunion government workers?

Public-sector unions face less competition from nonunion employers, but they do face considerable taxpayer opposition to high wage rates. Also they are less free to strike. Thus there is no clear theoretical expectation as to whether unions will have a greater effect on wage rates in the public or the private sector.

The empirical evidence suggests the following:[17]

1. The effect of public-sector unions on the wage gap is somewhat smaller than in the private sector, perhaps less than 10 percent. Before concluding that unions in the public sector have less effect on wages, we need to consider several important qualifications. First, public-sector unions probably have a more positive effect on nonunion wage rates than their counterparts in the private sector because nonunion wage rates are so heavily influenced by "prevailing wages." Thus the union wage gain may be as high or higher in the public sector, even though the wage gap is lower. Second, many of the estimates of the effect of public-sector unions are for the 1970s, when such unions were just becoming established. As the unions became better established, the wage effects may have risen. Third, public-sector unions represent a much higher percentage of white-collar workers than do unions in the private sector. For blue-collar workers the effect of unions on the wage gap appear

---

[17]The empirical evidence discussed in this section is summarized in Freeman, "Unionism."

to be roughly comparable in both the public and the private sector. The smaller effects in the public sector are primarily for white-collar workers, such as teachers.

2. Unionism has an especially strong effect on earnings of those who would otherwise be lowest paid. The less educated benefit more than the more educated. Black workers benefit more than white workers. Women benefit more than men. Thus inequality of individual earnings is somewhat reduced. For all state and local government employees in 1981, the standard deviation of wages was 0.54 among non-union members but only 0.41 among union members.

3. As for the makeup of the compensation package, public-sector unions raise benefits by considerably more than they raise wage rates, as is also the case in the private sector. Retirement systems, in particular, are often quite generous, perhaps partly because the burden of financing them is shifted to the future. Elected officials have a short time horizon, often not extending beyond the next election. So they may hold back on wage increases that affect their current budget, while being more generous on pensions and other benefits that their successors will have to pay for.

4. Public-sector unions strive to maintain or increase employment as well as to raise wages. They do this partly by staffing requirements written into union contracts: two police officers in every patrol car, a minimum number of firefighters in each fire station, a maximum pupil-teacher ratio in the school system, workloads or work schedules that require hiring of additional employees, and so on. They also lobby actively for increases in departmental budgets, which make it possible to finance wage increases without reducing employment. Studies indicate that public-sector unions probably increase, or at least do not decrease, employment. At the state and local level government deficits on current account are usually impossible. Thus if unionization increases wages with a zero or positive effect on employment, then either the government must spend less on other items, such as equipment, supplies, or transfer payments, or else revenue must increase, usually through higher taxes. There is some empirical evidence showing an increase in government budgets as a result of unionization, suggesting a corresponding increase in tax rates. Because there is little evidence that public-sector unions reduce productivity, it appears likely that they increase output. Whether this shift from private to public sector improves resource allocation obviously depends on whether one views the public sector as too big or small relative to the private sector.

VARIATION IN UNION WAGE EFFECTS

In both the public and private sectors the ability of unions to influence wage rates varies considerably for different kinds of workers. In the private sector differences among industries are especially impressive. For example, one study of sixty-two industries found a small wage effect of less than 5 percent in thirteen of these industries, a moderate effect of 5 to 15 percent in seventeen industries, a large effect of 15 to 35 percent in twenty-four industries, and very large effects of 35 percent or more in the remaining eight industries.[18]

In discussing the model of how unions raise wages, we showed that unions are likely to have a greater effect on the wages of their members and on the union-nonunion wage gap the greater the extent of unionization in the industry. Freeman

---

[18]See Freeman and Medoff, *What Do Unions Do?* p. 50.

and Medoff tested this hypothesis for manufacturing and construction.[19] For rather narrowly defined industries (the three-digit level) they ran separate regressions for union members and nonmembers, with the percent of industry employees who are organized as an independent variable. For union members the percent organized had a sizable positive effect on wage rates. In manufacturing an increase in the organized percentage from 20 percent to 80 percent raised member wages, on the average, by 10 percent. In construction, a similar increase in organizational strength raised wages by 16 percent. For nonunion workers, on the other hand, there was no significant relation with percentage organized. Thus greater unionization does increase both the union wage gain and the union-nonunion wage gap.

The Elasticity of Demand for Union Labor

Let us look more carefully at some of the reasons why there are such large differences in the effect of unions on wage rates.

A prime consideration is the *elasticity of demand for union labor.* We noted earlier that unions show some concern for employment as well as for wage levels. If labor demand is elastic, so that a wage increase will cause a substantial drop in employment, the union will tend to moderate its wage demands. But if demand is quite inelastic, so that wage increases will cause little loss of employment, the union will demand and obtain a larger wage premium.

The demand for labor is a derived demand, whose elasticity depends on the factors outlined in Chapter 5. The main factors are, first, the elasticity of demand for the final product. The more elastic product demand is, the more elastic—other things equal—will be the demand for the labor employed in making it. Second, the ratio of labor cost to total cost of production is important. If the ratio is only 20 percent, a 10 percent wage increase will raise unit production cost by only 2 percent. But if labor costs are 80 percent of the total, the same 10 percent increase will raise unit costs by 8 percent. Prices will have to adjust more in the latter case, and the impact on employment will be larger. Thus a union in oil refining, which has a low labor cost ratio, is in a stronger position than one in clothing manufacture, where labor costs are relatively larger. A third consideration is the ease or difficulty of substituting capital for labor in the production process. The larger the possibilities of substitution, the more elastic will be the demand for labor (i.e., the larger will be the drop in employment resulting from a given wage increase).

Actually there seems to be a two-way relation between union strength and elasticity of demand for labor. There is evidence that unions are most likely to be established and to survive in situations where elasticity of demand for labor is low (i.e., where the potential gains are largest). Oswald concluded that the likelihood of unionization in a competitive industry is inversely related to the price elasticity of product demand, the relative cost of labor in the final product, and the ease of

---

[19]Richard B. Freeman and James L. Medoff, "The Impact of the Percent Organized on Union and Nonunion Wages," *Review of Economics and Statistics* (November 1981), pp. 561–72.

capital-labor substitution.[20] Another study by Freeman and Medoff tested the hypothesis that unionism is more prevalent in industries where substitutability of other inputs for labor is low, and hence labor demand curves are more inelastic.[21] They found that ease of substitution (measured by the elasticity of substitution technique) is about one-third less in union than in nonunion establishments. Thus unions are more likely to be established where demand for labor is inelastic; and once established, inelasticity of demand increases their ability to raise wages.

We must next consider that elasticity of demand for *union labor* may differ from elasticity of demand for labor in general. First, the union may aim only at a segment of the labor force, whose wages are a small part of total cost. The salaries of airline pilots are a small part of airline operating costs, so the bargaining power of the Airline Pilots Association is strong, and it has been able to win salaries as much as double those of comparable nonunion pilots. This kind of clout is the traditional argument for organization by individual crafts in building construction, printing, and other areas of skilled employment.

As against these cases, in which demand for union labor is *less elastic* than demand for labor in general, there are cases in which demand for union labor is *more elastic*. The commonest reason is inability to organize all competing firms in an industry, or to keep them organized. Consider a situation in which the union has been able to organize only 40 percent of the workers in an industry while the remainder continue nonunion. If the union raises wage rates in union firms much above the nonunion level, the nonunion firms, with lower production costs, will be able to sell at lower prices and expand their share of the market. The output and employment of union firms will shrink. Thus the demand curve relating the *union* wage rate to *union* employment will be quite elastic, and the union wage premium will be small. Nonunion competition is a constant threat in partially unionized industries, which includes most of consumer-goods manufacturing plus coal mining, housing construction, and (currently) trucking and air transport. This threat explains the positive relation between the percentage of an industry that is organized and the size of the union wage premium in that industry.

Competition versus Monopoly in Product Markets

Do unions make larger wage gains in monopolistic than in competitive industries? Two separate issues are involved here. First, is industrial concentration favorable to a high degree of unionization? Second, given the same degree of unionization, is a competitive or monopolistic market structure more conducive to union wage gains?

---

[20]A. J. Oswald, "The Microeconomic Theory of the Trade Union," *Economic Journal* (September 1982), pp. 576–95. See also Edward P. Lazear, "A Competitive Theory of Monopoly Unionism," *American Economic Review* (September 1983), pp. 631–43.

[21]Richard B. Freeman and James L. Medoff, "Substitution between Production Labor and Other Inputs in Unionized and Nonunionized Manufacturing," *Review of Economics and Statistics* (May 1982), pp. 220–33.

The answer to the first question appears to be positive. Highly concentrated industries (basic steel, automobile assembly, aluminum, heavy electrical equipment, aircraft manufacture, and so on) tend also to be large-scale industries. In an earlier chapter we noted reasons why large plants are more susceptible to union organization than small ones: economies of scale in running an organizing campaign, greater worker alienation, inability of a large plant to escape the union by moving, higher barriers to the entrance of new nonunion competitors.

On the second question research suggests that where degree of unionization, plant size, labor-force characteristics, and other relevant variables are held constant, the "pure" relation between concentration and wage level is not significant. The threat of possible unionization has probably led to high wage rates in concentrated industries that have not been organized.

An important aspect of market structure is the height of entry barriers to the industry. If entry is easy and if new firms come in as nonunion in the first instance, this will tend to undermine the union's position. But entry may be difficult, because of large plant size and heavy startup costs (as in basic steel or automobile assembly) or because of government regulation (as in commercial trucking and airline transport before 1980). Companies sheltered from new competition can maintain a profitable price level, either through oligopolistic cooperation (steel and autos) or through government-sanctioned price fixing (airlines and trucking). There will then be some tendency toward soft bargains with the unions, because of a belief that wage increases can readily be passed on in price increases. Thus it is not surprising that steelworkers, auto workers, teamsters, and airline personnel were able to maintain large wage premiums through the 1970s.

In the eighties, however, these cozy arrangements were severely shaken. In the case of steel and automobiles, the cause was rising imports of lower-cost products. With transportation costs decreasing and tariff rates relatively low, the market for most manufactures is increasingly a world market. Even if U.S. companies are able to control domestic competition, they can readily price themselves out of international competition. In trucking and airlines, barriers to new entrants were lowered by the deregulation of air transport in 1978 and of trucking in 1980. This brought a flood of new nonunion companies, intensified price competition, and led to the failure of many trucking companies and even some airlines. Competitive pressures led to smaller union wage premiums in these industries. We are thus reminded that the union wage premium in a particular industry is not graven in stone but changes in response to economic circumstances. Changes in union leadership are also relevant, as demonstrated by the United Mine Workers.

WAGE DIFFERENCES
WITHIN A UNIONIZED INDUSTRY

In this chapter we have focused on how unions affect the wage rates of their members, relative to the wages of other, comparable workers. As we have seen, much of this effect comes from a few industries where the percent unionized is high.

Next let us look at the effects of unions on relative wages within a unionized industry. As we shall see, unions generally reduce intraindustry earnings inequality.

There are several reasons why wage differences within a unionized industry tend to be smaller than in a comparable nonunion industry. They include (1) the union policy of establishing a *standard rate* for each job; (2) a related principle which states that employers competing in the same product market should pay the *same* job rates. Where the product market is national in scope, this usually means narrowing or even eliminating geographic wage differences; and (3) a tendency to raise wages of the lowest groups faster, on a percentage basis, than wages of the highest-paid groups, with a consequent compression of occupational differentials.

The Standard Rate

Even in nonunion establishments there is usually a normal starting rate for each job. But how fast and how far a worker moves above this rate may depend on personal characteristics, on when the worker was hired, on supervisors' judgments of ability, even on the possibility that a superior worker may quit to take a better job. This system of personal, or *merit,* rates typically leads to considerable variation in wages among people in the same job classification. Employers feel that it provides incentive for good work and enables them to reward superior performance. Unions usually argue that it opens the door to favoritism and discrimination.

A cardinal union principle is "rate the job, not the person." If a job is judged to deserve so many dollars per hour, then everyone on the job is entitled to that amount. This principle of the standard rate has a long history in union thinking and practice. It rests on considerations of fairness and also on a desire to restrict supervisors' power over wages, which could be used to discourage union membership or simply to reward personal favorites.

Rather than a single rate for a job, union contracts often provide a range of rates and also specify the conditions under which a worker may move up in the range. A common provision is for an automatic annual increase, conditional on satisfactory job performance. Thus if turnover is low, most members of a work group will eventually be concentrated at the top of the range, which becomes the effective job rate.

As we discussed in Chapter 17, a two-tier wage system was established in a number of union contracts following the recession of 1982–83, especially in airlines and trucking. It occurs most frequently where firms are under great long-term competitive pressure to reduce costs but where workers are more willing to abolish the standard rate than to accept substantial wage cuts. Under a two-tier system, workers hired after a certain date, usually the beginning of the new contract, receive lower wage rates than present employees. This lower wage can be either permanent, as in the airlines, or limited to the first few years on the job, as in trucking. Although the two-tier wage system does represent a significant move away from the principle of the standard rate and the concepts of equity and worker solidarity that underlie it, this system does have one point in common with the standard rate. Both avoid the potential favoritism by bosses and discrimination against union leaders that cause unions to be very wary of merit pay.

Intercompany Wage Differences

In a nonunion industry one often finds considerable variation in company wage levels. Different regions of the country have characteristically different wage levels. There are further differences among communities of varying size within each region. There are also differences related to a company's wage-paying ability. Low-wage companies tend to be so, not because their managers are especially greedy but because for one reason or another their productivity is relatively low.

Unions generally view these intercompany differences with distrust. They fear that a low-wage company will be able to achieve lower unit costs of production, which will enable it to cut prices, which will in turn put downward pressure on price and wage levels in competing companies and limit the possible union gains in those companies. The only safe course, they feel, is to "put a floor under competition" by brining all companies up to a common wage level. This policy, to be sure, is not inflexible. If a company can prove that it really is suffering from low efficiency and low profits and that paying the standard wage will put it out of business, the union will usually consider concessions. But the burden of proof is on the company.

The area within which the union seeks to eliminate intercompany differences depends mainly on the area over which companies compete in the product market. Where competition is limited to a locality, as in house building and repair, retailing, and many service industries, and where bargaining is conducted locally with little supervision by the national union, the union will try to bring all employers in the local area to a common wage level. But there is no reason to expect wage equalization among localities.

In manufacturing industries selling in a national market, on the other hand, geographic differentials have usually been reduced and in some cases virtually eliminated. In addition to the economic pressures for wage equilization, there is usually political pressure from union members. Bargaining is typically on a national basis, and delegates from all parts of the country serve on the wage-policy committee. Delegates from lower-wage areas are bound to feel that their members should receive as much as workers in the highest-wage plants of the industry; and national union leaders are under pressure to effect a gradual leveling up of area differences.

Employers, on the other hand, tend to feel that wages in a particular plant should be in line with the *community* wage level.[22] If a company has been lucky or astute enough to locate in a low-wage area, it should be entitled to reap the benefit. So where geographic leveling has occurred under collective bargaining, it must be attributed to union pressure overriding employer resistance.

---

[22]That is true, at any rate, of employers in heavily capitalized and hard-to-enter oligopolistic industries, where wage differences do not threaten the price level. It is not necessarily true of more footloose and competitive industries such as textiles and clothing. Northern employers in such industries often urge the union to make a maximum effort toward raising southern wage levels.

Most unions in the majority of industries have probably had little effect on geographic differentials, either because of the local-market character of the industry or because of union weakness in one or more regions, or because the union has not found it expedient to aim at geographic equality. On the other hand, in truck driving, coal mining, basic steel, automobiles, and some other branches of heavy manufacturing, geographic differentials have been reduced and in some cases eliminated.

This result, of course, would also be achieved in a purely competitive labor market. Companies buying the same kind of labor end up paying the same wage rate. But under competition it tends to occur as a result of *factor movements*. Labor flows from low-wage areas to high-wage areas, while capital flows in the opposite direction; and the movement continues until returns to both labor and capital are equalized. To the extent that a union levels up wage differences prematurely, as it were, the incentive to such movements is decreased, with a loss in economic efficiency. Rees comments:

> The economist puts primary emphasis on efficiency, and views "equal pay for equal work" as a pleasant by-product of achieving efficient allocation. The unionist, for a combination of idealistic and selfish reasons, puts primary emphasis on geographical equality. He is either unaware of the loss of efficiency from achieving equality too soon . . . or considers this a reasonable price to pay for achieving his primary goal.[23]

Occupational Wage Differences

Market forces have been tending to reduce the percentage premium for high-skilled jobs over low-skilled ones. So if we find that differentials have narrowed in an industry where rates are set by collective bargaining, we cannot conclude that union pressure was responsible. It is difficult to distinguish the impact of unionism from that of other factors in the situation.

Where skilled, semiskilled, and unskilled workers are employed in the same enterprise, one can assume that demand for the skilled workers will be more inelastic. Their wages form a small proportion of total cost; it is less easy to replace skilled workers with semiskilled workers than vice versa; and skilled workers are also less easily replaced by machinery.

One might expect this economic fact to be reflected in bargained wage structures; but the outcome will depend also on the form of organization. A common situation is that in which the skilled workers have one or more craft unions that bargain separately from another union of the lower-skilled workers. Thus in building construction the carpenters, bricklayers, and so on are organized separately from the laborers and hod carriers. In the railroad industry the train-operating crafts are organized separately from the shop crafts and the maintenance-of-way workers. In such cases one might reason that the skilled groups will exploit their demand curves and raise differentials to some equilibrium level beyond which,

---

[23]Albert Rees, *The Economics of Trade Unions*, rev. ed. (Chicago: University of Chicago Press, 1977), p. 60.

barring major changes in technology or labor supply, differentials will remain stable. But maximizing models may not yield correct predictions. One can find cases, such as the printing industry, where the premium of compositors over bindery workers and other low-skilled groups has been well maintained. But there seem to be more cases, including building construction, railroading, and paper, where differentials have fallen substantially over the past several decades despite the prevalence of craft organization. In construction, for example, the wage advantage of the top skilled trades over the laborers has fallen from about 70 percent in 1950 to 40 percent today.

Perhaps the most interesting case, and the one most frequently studied, is that of the industrial union including all levels of worker from laborer to craftsperson. If the union behaved as a monopolist—trying, for example, to maximize the wage bill—it might exploit the demand situation by establishing a relatively higher wage for the skilled workers than would exist under nonunion conditions. It is a familiar principle that a monopolist selling in two or more distinct markets will maximize profit by charging the highest price in the market whose demand is least elastic.

On the other hand, the union is a political body, whose leaders must be responsive to membership sentiment. Since the bulk of the members are low skilled, they might be expected to press for policies that would bring them closer (percentagewise) to the skilled wage level. On the basis of this "democratic" reasoning, it has often been assumed that industrial unionism makes inevitably for a narrowing of occupational differentials.

But this view is also rather simplistic. The skilled workers will certainly feel that their "traditional" differential over the less skilled is right and proper and should be perpetuated; and since custom has considerable weight in workers' thinking about wages, many of the less skilled will accept this reasoning. The skilled workers also, because of their standing in the plant hierarchy and their personal qualities, will usually carry more than proportionate weight in union discussions and furnish more than their share of the union leadership. Finally, the skilled workers can exert leverage by threatening to form their own union and bargain separately if their views are not given sufficient weight.

The results of speculative reasoning, then, are inconclusive. In actuality, industrial unionism seems to have made for a reduction of the skilled-unskilled differential. In basic steel the COLA formula, which has provided uniform cents-per-hour increases to everyone, has reduced occupational differentials, especially during periods of rapid inflation. This has been partly offset by periodic increases in the cents-per-hour increments between job classes. Still, differentials have fallen considerably over the past forty years.

The United Automobile Workers also attached great importance in the early years to raising the bottom of the wage structure and insisted on equal cents-per-hour increases for all workers. The effect was to reduce the *percentage* differential between various grades of labor. By the mid-1950s that had produced considerable restiveness among the skilled tool-room and maintenance workers, who constitute about one-quarter of automobile employment. Some craft groups threatened to withdraw from the UAW and bargain separately. The union responded to this pressure by negotiating larger cents-per-hour increases for the skilled workers from 1955 onward and by giving craft representatives a greater voice in negotiations and contract ratification. Since that time the skilled-unskilled differential has not changed appreciably.

A broader study of manufacturing industries by Sherwin Rosen also found that unionism had raised laborers' wages considerably more than craftsworkers' wages, leading to a reduction of the skill differential.[24] More recently Freeman and Medoff have confirmed this result. They used multivariate regression analysis to compare wages of union and nonunion workers, controlling for age, sex, race, education, and other relevants. Unionized laborers earned 28 percent more than nonunion laborers. For crafts workers, however, the union premium was only 19 percent, and for operatives only 12 percent.[25] The implication is that under unionism, crafts workers have gained somewhat, relative to semiskilled operatives, while laborers have gained relative to both groups.

Overall Effect

When we add together the effect of standard rate policies, of reduced intercompany spreads, and of reduced occupational spreads, what is the total impact on wage inequality of union as against nonunion workers? Freeman and Medoff analyzed this question for a sample of some thirty thousand blue-collar workers in the Census Bureau's current population survey and reported that

> In terms of the standard deviation measure of inequality . . . inequality is 25 percent lower in union manufacturing than in nonunion manufacturing and 20 percent lower in union nonmanufacturing than in nonunion nonmanufacturing. . . . about 20 to 30 percent of the difference in inequality is due not to union wage policies *per se*, but rather to the fact that union workers are more alike in terms of age, education, and so forth than are nonunion workers. . . . Even so, the effect of unionism on the inequality of blue-collar organized workers remains substantial: We estimate that union wage policies reduce inequality by 15 to 20 percent among otherwise comparable workers.[26]

Another interesting finding, derived from data on some sixty-five hundred establishments, is that unionism brings blue-collar workers' wages considerably closer to white-collar workers *within the same establishment.*

> In the average nonunion establishment, the white-collar worker earns about one and half times as much as the blue-collar worker. In the comparable union establishment, the white-collar worker earns about one-third more than the blue-collar worker.[27]

---

[24]Sherwin Rosen, "Unionism and the Occupational Wage Structure," *International Economic Review* (June 1970), pp. 269–86.

[25]Richard B. Freeman and James L. Medoff, *What Do Unions Do?* (New York: Basic Books, 1984), p. 49.

[26]Ibid., p. 86.

[27]Ibid., p. 90.

Obviously unions have had some success in their goal of achieving a more egalitarian society. Other evidence that unions decrease the inequality of earnings is provided by looking at differences in inequality across labor markets. As Hyclak has shown, there is less inequality in labor markets where unions represent a high percentage of the workforce.[28] In addition, as we saw in Chapter 9, earnings inequality has increased in recent years, a trend that may well be related to the declining influence of unions.

SUMMARY

1. The wage effects of unions can be measured either as the *wage gain,* the difference between what union members are earning and what they would have earned if they were not unionized, or the *wage gap,* the difference between the wage rates of union members and comparable workers who are not unionized. The wage gap differs from the wage gain in that the latter includes the effect of unions on the wage rates of those who are not union members.

2. The union wage gap is éasier to measure than the wage gain. Empirical estimates of the wage gap generally range from 10 to 30 percent.

3. Unions raise benefits even more than they raise wage rates and thus raise the benefit share of total compensation. One reason is that union demands reflect the preferences of the *average* union member who, older and having more seniority, is more interested in benefits than the short-service or *marginal* employee whose preferences weigh heavily in the nonunion labor market.

4. The effects of unions on relative wage rates and benefits create costs to the economy from the misallocation of resources, but such costs appear to be relatively small.

5. Unions may either increase or decrease the wage rates of nonunion members, as a result of threat or spillover effects. Empirical estimates suggest that the threat effect may be greater than the spillover effect.

6. The effects of unions on inflation have probably been quite modest.

7. Comparisons of unionized with nonunion government workers suggest that for blue-collar workers the wage-raising effect of unionism is about the same in the public sector as in the private sector, but it is somewhat weaker for teachers and other white-collar groups.

8. In the private sector the union wage gap varies widely among industries, from near zero in some cases to 50 percent or more in others. The key determinant of

---

[28]Thomas Hyclak, "The Effects of Unions on Earnings Inequality in Local Labor Markets," *Industrial and Labor Relations Review* (October 1979), pp. 77–84.

wage-raising ability is the *elasticity of demand for union labor.* It depends on elasticity of demand for the product, the extent of union organization in the industry, whether it is easy or difficult for new nonunion firms to enter the industry, and the ratio of labor costs to total production costs.

9. Within a unionized industry unionism reduces the inequality of wages by applying the principle of the *standard rate,* by reducing occupational wage differentials, and by reducing wage differentials across firms.

KEY CONCEPTS

UNION WAGE GAIN	STANDARD RATE
UNION WAGE GAP	THREAT EFFECT
DEMAND FOR UNION LABOR, ELASTICITY OF	SPILLOVER EFFECT

REVIEW QUESTIONS

1. You are asked to design a research study to determine whether wages in the automobile industry are higher than they would have been in the presence of unionism. Outline at least two ways you might approach this problem.

2. Why might one expect a significant relation between the elasticity of demand for union labor and the wage gain of a particular union?

3. Why may elasticity of demand for union labor differ from elasticity of demand for labor in general?

4. How would you appraise the effect of union wage gains on the distribution of personal income in the United States?

5. You are national president of an industrial union, whose membership consists of 25 percent skilled workers, 60 percent semiskilled workers, and 15 percent unskilled workers. What policy would you pursue on occupational wage differentials?

6. "The policy of paying everyone on a job the same standard rate discriminates against the more capable workers and removes any incentive for top performance." Discuss.

READINGS

FREEMAN, RICHARD B., "Unionism Comes to the Public Sector." *Journal of Economic Literature* (March 1986), pp. 41–86.

———, and JAMES L. MEDOFF, *What Do Unions Do:* New York: Basic Books, 1984.

HIRSH, BARRY T., and JOHN T. ADDISON, *The Economic Analysis of Unions.* Boston: Allen & Unwin, 1986.

LEWIS, H. GREGG, *Union Relative Wage Effects, A Survey.* Chicago: University of Chicago Press, 1986.

PARSLEY, C. J., "Labor Unions and Wages: A Survey." *Journal of Economic Literature* (March 1980), pp. 1–31.

NONWAGE EFFECTS
AND THE BALANCE SHEET

The effects of unionism and collective bargaiing penetrate into most areas of personnel and production management. These nonwage effects are often discussed in impressionistic terms, with heavy reliance on particular cases. But the growth of microdata on companies and workers and the ease of manipulating this material have made substantial progress in quantitative analysis possible. On many questions that used to be discussed in qualitative terms, we now have a growing body of statistical evidence.

Not everything, to be sure, can be related to the measuring rod of money. The quantitative evidence relates mainly to the characteristics of union and nonunion workers; the characteristics of union and nonunion plants; rates of labor turnover and especially voluntary quit rates; average length of service on the job; labor productivity, usually measured by output per worker-hour, in union and nonunion establishments; and the effect of collective bargaining on company profits. From this relatively solid base we move into a variety of less tangible effects: on working conditions, including both physical conditions and human relations; on workers' satisfaction with their jobs; on management structure and policies; on the balance of political power in the community. The difficulty of judging these intangible effects is frustrating but at the same time intriguing, since it permits differing judgments on the social value of unionism.

As background, we note first some organizational effects of unionism—on management practices and on the operation of the internal labor market. We proceed then to the more measurable effects of collective bargaining—on worker quit rates, length of job tenure, productivity, and profitability. At the end of the chapter we shall speculate on some of the less tangible consequences of union activity.

UNION IMPACT ON MANAGEMENT ORGANIZATION

In preunion days most managements did not attach major importance to the industrial relations function. The director of industrial relations, in those days commonly called the personnel director, was usually not an outstanding person and did not rank high in the management hierarchy. In large measure the line officials made personnel policy through their day-to-day decisions, which the personnel department had little power to influence. Many managements, either deliberately or through inadvertence, left wide latitude in decision making to lower levels of supervision. Thus actions on a particular subject might vary widely from one department to another; and top management might know little about what was actually happening at the grassroots.

The coming of a union changes the situation drastically. Personnel actions are no longer solely a matter of management discretion. They are governed by provisions of the union contract, and the union is there to police observance of the contract. It has its own information network throughout the plant, can detect discrepancies in management's actions, and is then likely to demand that the most favorable practice in any department be extended to all other departments—a tactic commonly known as *whipsawing*. Moreover, unsettled grievances between the union and management are normally referred to an outside aribtrator. So management must try to ensure that its decisions are consistent and will stand up under outside review.

Unionism, in short, compels *management by policy* rather than by off-the-cuff decisions. A newly unionized company usually reacts in three ways. First, it has to strengthen its industrial relations department, both because there is more work to be done and because top-flight people are needed to deal with the professional union leaders. Second, it may decide that personnel decisions should be made at higher levels of management, in order to ensure uniform interpretation of company policies and union contract provisions. Third, this normally means that industrial relations officials will have greater voice in decisions and line officials will have less. Some managements, indeed, have panicked to the point of virtually abolishing line authority over personnel actions and work standards and turning these matters over to the industrial relations department for handling.

Although greater centralization of decision making and greater staff authority are natural first reactions, they have their own disadvantages. Foremen know what is happening on the plant floor and are in closest touch with the facts on which correct personnel decisions should be based. They are also the people in charge of production. To hold them responsible for production results while depriving them of disciplinary authority over the work force is scarcely feasible in the long run. So many companies have been moving back toward decentralization, toward pushing

decisions down to the plant floor, and toward reconstituting the authority of line supervisors.[1]

Another typical result is a raising of production standards and a tightening of shop discipline. When a union comes in and (usually) raises wage rates substantially, this serves as a cold shower to management. If workers are to be paid more, they can reasonably be expected to produce more. So more attention is paid to worker recruitment, selection, and training. Work methods are reviewed, standards of acceptable performance are raised, and these standards are policed more carefully. These productivity-raising efforts of management are aided by the fact that the relatively high wage level attracts superior job applicants and that workers who are hired realize they have a good job that they don't want to lose.

As we discussed in Chapter 14, there are many different kinds of nonunion firms. Some, especially those that are relatively small, pay low wage rates and manage their workers quite informally. Others, however, pay high wage rates and devote considerable attention to personnel policies. Such firms have adopted many of the policies pioneered in the union sector, including a strong emphasis on seniority.[2] It is not clear whether the primary motivation for these policies is to increase worker productivity (e.g., by increasing morale and reducing turnover) or to keep the firm from becoming unionized. If union avoidance does play an important role, then unions are having an important indirect effect on the behavior of these nonunion firms.

THE INTERNAL LABOR MARKET

We noted in earlier chapters that large organizations are characterized by internal labor markets—an expectation of a continuing employment relationship, vacancies filled mainly from within, benefits that accrue with length of service, and so on. In a nonunion company, however, personnel actions are still a matter of management discretion rather than established rights. A worker may be unpleasantly surprised by a personnel decision and, if aggrieved, has no appeal.

A union formalizes and restructures the internal market in several ways: (1) outside recruitment is more severely restricted; (2) workers' job tenure is protected by limiting the right of discharge; (3) seniority becomes the dominant factor in job assignments as well as benefit entitlements; (4) the worker now has a channel for bringing pressure to improve his or her job without the necessity of quitting the job. While these points are familiar from earlier chapters, it will be useful to review them and to consider their consequences for turnover and productivity.

1. Restrictions on Outside Recruitment. A nonunion company may choose to fill most vacancies by internal promotion; but it always has the option of outside recruitment. Under unionism this option is largely excluded. The contract usually

---

[1]See on this point Sumner H. Slichter, James J. Healy, and E. Robert Livernash, *The Impact of Collective Bargaining on Management* (Washington, D.C.: Brookings Institution, 1960), Chap. 29.

[2]For example, see Fred K. Foulkes, *Personnel Policies in Large Nonunion Firms,* (Englewood Cliffs: Prentice-Hall, 1980).

provides that when a vacancy arises, "insiders" shall be given an opportunity to apply for the job before "outsiders" are considered. There are often detailed rules on posting notices of a vacancy, who is entitled to apply, and the criteria to be used in selecting among applicants. Only in the event that no present employee is interested may the company look outside. This limits outside recruitment almost entirely to entry-level jobs.

2. Protection for Workers from Arbitrary Discharge. A worker who performs poorly on the job or violates plant rules is subject to varying degrees of discipline, including the ultimate sanction of discharge. Because seniority now carries so many accumulated rights, discharge is a drastic economic penalty, especially for older workers who may have trouble finding new employment. In a nonunion plant, discipline is exercised in the first instance by the foreman, subject to possible review at higher levels. This puts the foreman in a position to exercise varying degrees of favoritism, oppression, and unjustice.

The union reduces the foreman to a constitutional monarch, materially increasing the worker's security of tenure. Indeed, a knowledgeable union officer once remarked, "The greatest benefit a union brings to the worker is the ability to tell the boss to go to _____ ."

3. The Role of Seniority. Even in a nonunion plant length of service is an important consideration in personnel decisions. But under unionism its role is formalized and enhanced. The discussion of seniority rules in Chapter 17 need not be repeated here. Briefly, seniority operates in two ways. First, it increases the worker's entitlement to certain benefits, such as length of vacation, accumulated pension rights, disability benefits, possible provision for early retirement. If the demand for labor declines, those with the least seniority are laid off first. Thus a job becomes more valuable with increasing years of service, which must strengthen the worker's reluctance to leave it.

Second, seniority becomes the dominant consideration in movement up the promotion ladder. Management would usually prefer freedom to promote according to its own judgment of individual ability. The usual outcome of bargaining negotiations is a compromise clause that mentions both ability and length of service as relevant criteria. In applying the clause to particular cases, however, the union will usually argue for the more senior person, carrying the case to the grievance procedure if necessary. The practical result is usually that seniority governs in the absence of marked differences of ability among the candidates, and where management believes there is a marked difference of ability, it must be prepared to prove its case.

4. Increased Voice for Workers. A final major charge in labor-market operation can be viewed in terms of Hirschman's schema of *exit* versus *voice* as ways of redressing unfavorable conditions.[3] A nonunion worker dissatisfied with some con-

---

[3] Albert O. Hirschman, *Exit, Voice, and Loyalty* (Cambridge, Mass.: Harvard University Press, 1971).

dition of employment has two alternatives. The worker can complain to the foreman or the personnel office; but this may endanger his or her job, and so direct complaint is discouraged. Alternatively, the worker can quit. The model of a competitive, nonunion labor market relies heavily on *exit* to balance workers' preferences against employers' offers.

From the worker's standpoint, however, exit is usually not the preferred option. A job is an asset, whose value typically increases with length of service. Quitting imposes a heavy penalty on a long-service worker, whose age may be a serious barrier to new employment. Quitting is also less viable when demand for labor is low than when it is high. What the worker wants is some way of bringing pressure on management *without* quitting.

Unionism meets this need by giving the worker a direct *voice* in the determination of working conditions. Workers' preferences are clarified through discussion, channeled through the union organization, and brought to bear on management through both contract negotiations and informal day-to-day contacts. Thus conditions can be improved without recourse to the unpleasant exit alternative.

Even from a management standpoint, union voice has advantages over exit as a signaling device. When an experienced worker leaves, the company loses its investment in recruitment and training. Further, the information transmitted by quits is limited and ambiguous. An abnormal rise in the quit rate signals that something is wrong in the multidimensional employment relation; but it does not indicate just where the trouble is. Exit interviews, in which a departing worker is asked why he or she left, are quite unreliable, since there is no incentive for the worker to give an accurate response. The union provides a different and possibly superior information source for management. Union representatives can pinpoint sources of discontent and even suggest possible remedies, thus helping to head off quits before they occur.

Although the union can provide valuable information to management, the employer normally would prefer to operate without the constraints imposed by a union. Therefore many large nonunion companies have attempted to institute communication and feedback mechanisms that do not depend on an independent worker organization that can exert pressure through collective bargaining. Such communication mechanisms include attitude surveys, company newspapers, and regular meetings between workers and top executives. There are several reasons why good two-way communication with workers is likely to be valuable to the employer. First, a worker who understands why decisions are being made is more likely to support the decision and thus be a more motivated productive worker. Second, workers can often provide valuable information to management about how both personnel policies and production processes can be improved. Third, by becoming aware of workers' problems before they become too serious, the firm has a better chance of avoiding a successful union-organizing drive. Fourth, a worker who has a personal problem (e.g., alcoholism, family difficulties) may be able to get assistance from the company and thus become a better worker.

Although there are many advantages to having good communication, workers will be willing to present their views only if they believe they are being heard and that they will be better off as a result of having spoken up. If worker comments are ignored or, worse yet, if management retaliates against a worker who makes negative comments, then the firm can expect to receive little useful feedback from its workers—except perhaps through union-organizing drives or high quit rates.

TURNOVER AND LENGTH OF TENURE

Turning to quantitative evidence, there is now considerable information about quit rates and length of job tenure among union and nonunion workers. This information comes mainly from worker samples but also from establishment samples. To estimate the net effect of union attachment, it is of course necessary to compare workers at the same wage level and to control also for occupation, age, sex, and other personal characteristics.

Freeman and Medoff, from an examination of seven worker samples, concludes that quit rates are invariably lower among union workers, typically by about one-third.[4] This is in line with earlier studies, which consistently show quit rates about 40 percent lower among union workers—other things equal. This lower quit rate can be attributed partly to the labor market changes outlined in the previous section: the availability of union voice on working conditions as an alternative to quitting; the existence of a grievance procedure to adjust individual complaints; and the emphasis on seniority, which increases the incentive to stay with the job as length of service increases. On the other hand, the causation may run from a low quit rate to a high unionization rather than from high unionization to a low quit rate. For example, if quit rates are high because other jobs are readily available or because the work force moves in and out of the labor force frequently, then workers have less of an incentive to join unions. Also union organizing campaigns are more difficult if the organizer has to continually convince new workers of the benefits of unionization, as will be the case when there is both high turnover among workers and considerable delay from the initial organizing to the time of a certification election.

Unionism also raises wage rates by a typical 20 percent or so, and a higher wage by itself is associated with lower quits. The reduction in quit rates arising from a 20 percent higher wage, however, is somewhat less than 10 percent, which suggests that the *exit-voice* effect of unionism in reducing quits may be considerably stronger than the *monopoly wage* effect.

If quit rates are lower under unionism, it follows that average length of service in a job must be longer, and this is also confirmed by the worker samples. The average tenure of union workers is typically 25 to 35 percent longer than that of nonunion workers at the same wage level.

It is interesting to ask *whose* tenure is increased most by union member-

---

[4]Richard B. Freeman and James L. Medoff, *What Do Unions Do?*, Chap. 6. This is a basic source, referred to hereafter in this chapter as Freeman and Medoff.

ship. There is not much difference by race or sex, but the age variable is important. Average tenure is increased by 38 percent for workers aged fifty or older, compared with only 8 percent for those under age thirty. The reason must mainly be the seniority rules in union contracts, under which older workers are entitled to larger current benefits and are also closer to the point of receiving pensions and other deferred compensation. Unionism also raises the tenure of less-educated and less-skilled workers more than that of the more educated and more skilled: 28 percent for laborers, 8 percent for craft workers; 39 percent for those with less than high school graduation, 17 percent for those with education beyond high school. Freeman and Medoff comment:

> This finding reflects the fact that under unionism formal work rules cover all employees, so that supervisors cannot treat those with better outside market opportunities more favorably than those with worse outside opportunities. By applying the same standards to all workers, unionism improves work place conditions more for those at the bottom than for those at the top of the firm hierarchy and has a greater effect on their exit rates.[5]

A lower frequency of job changes has cash benefits to the worker, which Freeman and Medoff estimate at about a 2 percent increase in wages. Since recruitment and training cost money, and since worker productivity tends to increase with experience, reduced turnover also benefits the employer, by an amount estimated at 1 to 2 percent of production costs.

We should note at this point an apparent paradox in union members' behavior: They quit less but complain more. Several studies have asked samples of workers whether they were very satisfied with their jobs, moderately satisfied, moderately dissatisfied, or very dissatisfied. The proportion expressing dissatisfaction with the job is usually *higher* among union than among nonunion workers. Follow-up questions indicate that this is not mainly dissatisfaction with wages. Since union wages are relatively high, one would expect union members to be at least as satisfied with wages as nonunion members; and that is confirmed by the studies. The complaints of union members tend to focus more on working conditions, health and safety hazards, and relations with supervisors. Satisfaction with the job and satisfaction with the performance of the union are quite highly correlated. Older workers in general express higher levels of job satisfaction than younger workers do.

When there is a conflict between what workers say and what they do, it seems best to rely mainly on what they do. The lower quit rates of union workers suggest that they are *not* more dissatisfied in the operational sense of looking around for other jobs. A plausible interpretation is that they feel freer to complain than nonunion workers do, since they are not subject to the penalty of arbitrary discharge. Further, one function of a union is to mobilize and focus worker complaints with a view toward improving conditions. Union leaders must be able to say

---

[5]Ibid., p. 98.

convincingly to management, "Look, our people are unhappy—with this, that, or the other." It is reasonable that members should strengthen their leaders' hand by voicing an appropriate degree of dissatisfaction.

PRODUCTIVITY

The traditional view is that unions tend to reduce productivity by restricting management's choice of the most efficient production methods. Unions of skilled workers have often imposed burdensome work rules in order to create additional employment for their members. Industrial unions have also on occasion resisted technical change, though this is usually no more than a delaying action. On the other hand, some recent studies find higher productivity in union than in nonunion plants in the same industry. We will look first at restrictive union practices, then consider recent statistical findings.

Make-Work Rules and Policies

The effort to create employment or to prevent a shrinkage of employment takes many forms. The practices described in this section, however, all have the intent of increasing the number of worker-hours of labor that employers must hire. For this reason they are often termed *make-work policies*.

1. Limiting Daily or Weekly Output per Worker. This is a widespread practice in both nonunion and union shops, particularly where the workers are paid on a piecework or incentive basis. The motive for limitation of output is partly to make work, partly to avoid rate cutting and speeding up by the employer.

2. Limiting Output Indirectly by Controlling the Quality of Work or Requiring Time-Consuming Methods. These techniques are best illustrated in the building trades. Although the unions have done a useful service in combating shoddy construction by the less reputable contractors, they have frequently insisted on needlessly high quality in order to justify spending more time on the job. The gradual decline in the number of bricks laid per hour by bricklayers, for example, is usually justified by the union in terms of the care that must be taken to ensure perfect accuracy and soundness in the product. It would seem, however, that this argument has been overworked. Plastering, lathing, and other processes are often done more thoroughly than necessary in order to create additional work.

Another frequent device of the building trades is to require that work be done on the construction site rather than in the factory. Painters often require that all window frames and screens be primed, painted, and glazed on the job. Plumbers in many cities prohibit the cutting and threading of pipe in the factory and refuse to install toilets and other fixtures that have been assembled at the factory. There has been some movement toward prefabrication of plumbing fixtures, kitchen cabinets, and even whole kitchen units as a means of reducing production costs. This movement has been resisted by the construction unions. The prefabrication of the whole house structure has been resisted even more vigorously and with greater success.

3. *Requiring that Unnecessary Work Be Done or that Work Be Done More than Once*. Switchboards and other types of electrical apparatus, for example, were in earlier days always wired on the job. The recent tendency has been to have this equipment wired in the factory, where the work can be done at considerably lower cost. The New York City local and certain other locals of the International Brotherhood of Electrical Workers have refused to install switchboards and other apparatus unless the wiring done in the factory was torn out and the apparatus rewired by union members.

4. *Requiring Standby Crews or Other Unnecessary Workers*. This practice is often termed *featherbedding*. The Musicians' Union, for example, attempted to enforce a rule that radio stations that broadcast recorded music or that rebroadcast programs originating elsewhere must employ a standby orchestra to be paid for doing nothing. This led eventually to passage of the Lea Act of 1946, which made it unlawful to compel a licensee under the Federal Communications Act to employ unnecessary people, or to refrain from using unpaid performers for noncommercial programs, or to limit production or use of records.

The theater is especially vulnerable to featherbedding because picketing can so easily interfere with attendance. The Stagehands' Union requires a minimum crew to be hired for any theatrical performance, regardless of whether their services are actually needed, and so does the Musicians' Union, the Electricians' Union, and other groups. The resulting inflation of production costs and ticket prices has contributed to the disappearance of commercial theaters in many cities.

The Motion Picture Projectors' Union has tried for years to require two operators for each projection machine and has succeeded in some cities. The Operating Engineers assert jurisdiction over all machines and engines used in building construction, regardless of their source of power. Even if the power is purchased from an electric company, a union member must be there to push the button or turn the switch, which may constitute his or her whole day's work.

5. *Requiring Crews of Excessive Size*. This is a common practice among the printing pressmen, longshoremen, musicians, and a number of other unions.

A major controversy in this area concerned the use of firemen on diesel locomotives. On high-speed passenger trains, safety considerations might dictate having a second person in the cab as a backstop for the engineer. But the union insisted also on use of firemen in freight trains and even in yard switching. This controversy continued for decades, causing several railroad strikes. The union agreed to eventual elimination of fireman positions on diesel freight locomotives through attrition. The existing force of about 18,000 firemen on freight trains were guaranteed jobs until they were promoted to engineer, retired, resigned, or died.

6. Requiring That Work Be Done by Members of a Particular Occupational Group. The object is to enlarge job territory of the group so that there will be the maximum amount of work available to be divided among its members. Pursuit of this objective takes various forms. A common rule prohibits employers or foremen from working at the trade. This rule prevents supervisors from reducing the amount of work available to employees by doing it themselves and from acting as pacesetters by working alongside the workers. Another common rule requires that skilled workers be used for semiskilled or unskilled work. The Typographical Union frequently requires that proof be read and revised by union members before going to anyone outside the composing room. The building trades often require that material handling be done by craft workers rather than laborers.

Some Teamsters locals, on the other hand, prohibit drivers from assisting helpers in unloading their trucks. This rule creates more jobs for helpers, so that total employment is increased. Longshoremen in some ports refuse to shift from ship to dock work or even from one ship to another of the same company, thus compelling use of multiple crews.

The Industrial Unions and Technical Change

The quickened pace of mechanization and automation since World War II has reduced employment opportunities in basic steel, automobiles, and numerous other industries and has caused unions in these industries to be concerned for the job security of their members. In general, their reaction has not taken the form of trying to block technical change, a policy that would have little chance of success. The new equipment in these industries is so labor saving and cost reducing that employers have a powerful incentive to install it, and the unions could at most fight a delaying action for a limited period. So they have concentrated instead on ways of cushioning the impact on their members.

In automobile production the United Automobile Workers has not opposed technical change as such. The industry has a tradition of annual model changes, rapid technical innovation, and wide management flexibility in production methods. The union has tried, however, to cushion the decline of auto employment by speeding the exit of older workers from the industry and by spreading the available work among those remaining. Exit is speeded through liberalization of retirement benefits and reduction of the retirement age.

In meat packing the Armour Company maintains a joint program with the union under a neutral chairman, who has usually been a labor economist. The program includes research on the company's future labor requirements, advance notice of plant closings or cutbacks in employment, preferential hiring rights for displaced workers in other plants of the company, assistance with moving and relocation costs, and assistance in finding other work for those who prefer to remain in their home community.

In the mass-production industries, then, things have moved in the direction of a trade, in which management gets reasonable flexibility in changing production methods, while the union gets provisions to cushion the impact on its members' jobs. The cushioning devices include liberalized pension provisions, a reduction of the retirement age, and other efforts to encourage early retirement; severance pay for workers released permanently; work sharing through reduction in the number of days and hours worked per year; outright guarantees of lifetime employment in some cases; and arrangements under which workers in a plant that is closed down permanently can "follow the work" to other plants of the same company, with preferential hiring rights. The assumption is that the number of production jobs in these industries will continue to decline; and the object is to ensure that the shrinkage of employment will be orderly and will do minimum damage to the present labor force.

This tradeoff of greater freedom for the employer against employment guarantees for the worker is not limited to manufacturing but has occurred also in other industries. The diesel fireman agreement has already been noted. In the printing industry the New York newspaper publishers had long sought to introduce modern composing-room technology, which would reduce both the number of employees and the level of skill required. After many years of opposition, the International Typographical Union agreed to a settlement. Management got a free hand with regard to automation, staffing requirements, job assignments, and elimination of bogus type. In return, all regular and substitute employees received a guarantee of employment until retirement. Retirement provisions were liberalized, and a bonus was provided to anyone retiring within six months of the contract date.

Quantitative Research

There have been a number of recent attempts to compare output per worker-hour in union and nonunion establishments in the same industry. This is a harder task than may appear at first glance. Some studies measure output in value terms, but the results may be distorted by differences in product mix and competitiveness of pricing. More reliable are physical-output measures, but they can be obtained only for industries producing a standardized product, such as cement or pig iron.

There are likely also to be significant differences between union and nonunion establishments. Because the rate of unionization has been declining, we might expect the average unionized plant to be older than the average nonunion establishment. There are also some significant differences in size and capital intensity.[6]

Statistical comparisons of productivity try to adjust for differences in the capital-labor ratio; but the adjustment may not capture the full effect. The same thing is true of possible differences in quality of the labor force. The higher wage level of the union plant gives it a longer queue of job applicants, presumably including a larger number of superior workers; and there is an incentive to select superior workers as a partial offset to the higher wage level. Thus even though one standardizes for such measurable characteristics as age, sex, education, and work experience, some quality differences may still slip through the statistical net.

---

[6]Freeman and Medoff, "Substitution between Production Labor and Other Inputs in Unionized and Nonunionized Manufacturing," *Review of Economics and Statistics* (May 1982), pp. 220–33.

The results thus far can only be described as mixed.[7] A study of underground bituminous coal mining found a large positive effect of unionism on productivity (tons of coal per worker-day) as of 1965. This effect is no doubt related to former UMW president John L. Lewis's policy of favoring mine mechanization and trying to capture the benefit in higher wages, even though it meant a gradual decline in employment. In recent years, however, the positive union effect had turned into a decided negative effect, with productivity in union mines 14 to 18 percent below the nonunion level. This change may in part have reflected serious disorganization of the union and a partial collapse of the national bargaining system.

An important study of large manufacturing firms by Kim B. Clark found a slightly negative effect, with union productivity estimated on average at 2 percent below the nonunion level.[8] This effect is not inconsistent, of course, with higher union productivity in particular industries. Another study by Clark of cement plants[9] where good physical-output measures are available found output per worker 6 to 8 percent higher in union plants. Further, former nonunion plants that had been unionized had experienced on average a 6 percent increase in productivity.

The idea of a union *raising* productivity is counterintuitive. Where it has happened, what might account for the result?

1. There is the possibility noted earlier that the higher capital-labor ratio and the probable higher quality of the work force in union plants is not fully allowed for in the statistical analysis.
2. The longer average job tenure of workers in union plants, noted in an earlier section, could account for some increase in productivity, which normally rises with increasing experience. Also, by putting more emphasis on seniority unions provide experienced workers with a greater incentive to train new workers.
3. Perhaps more important, however, is the tightening up of management practice in response to union pressure for higher wages. Management is forced to demand more of workers, and it gets more.[10]

Some indication of how management gets more out of workers can be found in Clark's study of cement plants before and after unionization.[11] There was a clear impact on management performance. There was a new plant manager in all six cases, many new supervisors, usually an increased supervisor-worker ratio, and often a new industrial relations specialist, accompanied by introduction of production targets and better monitoring of performance. As one manager remarked,

[7]For reviews of such studies, see Freeman and Medoff, *What Do Unions Do?* Chap. 11; and Barry T. Hirsch and John Addison, *The Economic Analysis of Unions*, Chap. 7; and their article, "Union Effects of Productivity, Profits, and Growth: Has the Long Run Arrived?" *Journal of Labor Economics* (January 1989), pp. 72–105.

[8]Clark, "Unionization and Firm Performance: The Impact on Profits, Growth, and Productivity," *American Economic Review* (December 1984), pp. 893–919.

[9]Clark, "The Impact of Unionization on Productivity: A Case Study" *Industrial and Labor Relations Review* (July 1980).

[10]See the discussion in Chap. 7 of the effect of high wage rates on morale, work effort, and productivity.

[11]Ibid. pp. 451–69.

"Before the union this place was run like a family; now we run it like a business." Clark notes:

> [There was] A more professional, businesslike approach to labor relations by front line supervisors. . . . In four of the six plants we found attempts to increase work effort and work group efficiency, primarily through introduction of formal methods of organization control. . . . They amounted to a system of production goals or targets accompanied by procedures for the review and monitoring of performance . . . often . . . in newly introduced staff meetings."[12]

There are indications that productivity under unionism depends partly on the quality of the day-to-day relations between union and management officials, whether relations are cooperative and constructive or, on the contrary, hostile and confrontational. Quality of the industrial relations climate is not easy to evaluate, but there are proxy measures such as the number of grievances per hundred workers and the proportion of grievances that go to arbitration instead of being resolved at lower levels. A high grievance rate and a high proportion of unsettled grievances suggest poor union-management relations. Several studies of different unionized plants in the same industry have found an inverse relation between grievance rates and output per worker.

PROFITABILITY

We have seen that unionism raises wage rates substantially and raises total compensation even more through the effect on benefits. Unionism also appears to be associated in some cases with higher output per worker. Does the second effect offset the first, so that union firms have as low unit labor costs and as high profit rates as nonunion firms?

The answer apparently is no. There is typically a negative effect of unionism on profitability. The estimated size of the effect varies among studies. Profitability can be measured in several ways, including the rate of return on capital and the size of the margin between price and unit variable costs. And there are several techniques of estimation, including direct comparison of union and nonunion establishments, and cross-section analyses of industries or states with differing degrees of unionization.

Regardless of method, however, the union effect is almost invariably negative.[13] The reduction in profitability attributable to unionization is typically of the order of 15 to 20 percent, though both lower and higher estimates appear in various studies. This suggests that the general opposition of American businesses to union-

---

[12]Ibid., p. 467.

[13]For example, see Clark, "Unionization and Firm Performance"; Richard S. Ruback and Martin B. Zimmerman, "Unionization and Profitability: Evidence from the Capital Market," *Journal of Political Economy* (December 1984), pp. 1134–57: Freeman and Medoff, *What Do Unions Do?* Chap. 12; and Paula Voos and Lawrence Mishel, "The Union Impact on Profits: Evidence from Industry Price-Cost Margin Data," *Journal of Labor Economics* (January 1986), pp. 105–33.

ism is not just a matter of ideology; it has an economic rationale. Executives anticipate correctly that unionism will injure the bottom line.

Freeman investigated the question of whose profits are hit hardest, with particular attention to differing degrees of industrial concentration.[14] The results are suggestive. In the less concentrated industries, where pricing is presumably competitive, the union effect on profitability was small or negligible on average. In the more concentrated industries, on the other hand, the negative effect was substantial, on the order of 20 percent. A reasonable interpretation is that highly concentrated industries, which usually have substantial barriers to entrance and "cooperative" pricing among the established firms, are able to set prices well above cost and earn monopoly profit. Unions, as we noted earlier, find it easier to penetrate and organize such industries than is the case in more competitive industries. And once inside the protected framework, the union manages to appropriate part of the companies' monopoly gains. Profits are not necessarily reduced to the competitive level but are brought somewhat closer to it.[15]

WORKING CONDITIONS

In the familiar trilogy of "wages, hours, and conditions of employment" there is a tendency to focus on wages and to overlook working conditions, partly because the latter are numerous and often unmeasurable. Yet the conditions surrounding the worker from day to day can make a large difference in job satisfaction.

Some of these conditions involve human relations, particularly relations with one's immediate supervisor. We have already noted that unionism increases the worker's ability to talk back, to question the foreman's decisions, to pursue complaints through the grievance procedure, without fear of reprisal. This no doubt makes the foreman's life more difficult. But the worker feels this increase in personal freedom as a substantial benefit.

Other conditions are physical: temperature in the work place, lighting, cleanliness, degree of crowding, risk of accidents from dangerous machinery, presence of dust, fumes, and other health hazards. Speed of work is often an issue, taking such varied forms as assembly-line speed (automobiles), number of looms to be tended by each weaver (textiles), number of pieces to be produced per hour under piece-rate payment. In a nonunion plant decisions on these points are made with a view to minimum cost. If an improvement in conditions will yield an increase in productivity

---

[14]Richard B. Freeman, "Unionism, Price-Cost Margins, and the Return to Capital," working paper no. 1164 (Cambridge, Mass.: National Bureau of Economic Research, 1983). Also see the summary of these results in Freeman and Medoff, Chap. 12. Among the large firms in Clark's data set, market share is negatively related to the magnitude of unionization's negative effect on profits, perhaps because firms with a very large market-share price below the point of short-term profit maximization and thus can most readily respond to higher union wages by increasing prices. See Clark, "Firm Performance."

[15]For an alternative view, see Barry T. Hirsh and Robert A. Connolly, "Do Unions Capture Monopoly Profits?" *Industrial and Labor Relations Review* (October 1987), pp. 118–36; and John T. Addison and Barry T. Hirsch, "Union Effects on Productivity, Profits, and Growth: Has the Long Run Arrived?"

sufficient to cover the cost, it will be made; otherwise it will not. But conditions determined on the basis of money cost may be unpleasant from the worker's standpoint. In a perfectly competitive labor market management would presumably have to pay a higher wage to compensate for the unpleasant working conditions. There is something to this—we noted in Chapter 7 that unusually dangerous jobs do tend to carry a higher rate of pay. But the labor market is rather a blunt instrument and can scarcely be counted on to achieve perfect compensation on all points. Moreover, it implies that workers must always be ready to use the exit sanction—complaining by quitting—which is usually unpleasant and sometimes unfeasible.

Unionism supplements the exit alternative by providing a worker voice on working conditions as well as wages and other matters. Major issues, such as work speeds and safety precautions, may be regulated by the union contract. Smaller problems are worked out through informal day-by-day negotiation in the plant. Thus in a variety of ways the union makes the plant a pleasanter place in which to live and work.

Do unions go too far in this regard? What do we mean by "too far"? Consider the following case: A plant uses hot processes that produce a normal plant temperature of ninety degrees. Workers complain and ask that temperature be reduced to seventy degrees. The union negotiates a compromise under which management reduces the temperature to seventy-five degrees by additional expenditure on cooling equipment. Assume for simplicity that there is no effect on productivity, so that production costs rise by the full amount of the added expenditure. Assume also that the cost increase is passed on to consumers in higher prices. The union, in effect, has taxed consumers a certain amount in order to improve the daily lives of its members in the plant. Is this action economically harmful or beneficial?

Any answer involves balancing the satisfaction of consumers from more output at a lower price against the satisfaction of workers from pleasanter conditions. As temperature is reduced below ninety degrees, it seems likely that for a while the benefit to workers will outweigh the cost imposed on consumers. But at some point—call it temperature X—that will cease to be true, and costs will begin to exceed benefits. We can thus call X the optimum temperature for the plant, and if we know enough about the utility schedules involved, we can determine its location. If it turns out to be seventy-five degrees, then the negotiated settlement is in accord with economic criteria. Only if it is higher has the union "gone too far."

Is temperature X—and equivalent measures of other working conditions—more likely to be approximated under union or nonunion conditions? This question can be answered only on a case-by-case basis; and the answer will depend not only on the kind of policy involved but on the degree to which it has been carried out. Down to a certain point, for example, a reduction in work speeds brings more benefit than cost; beyond that point the reverse becomes true. The problem in each case is to strike a correct balance between the interests of a particular producer group and of society at large.

There is some reason to think that in the absence of union organization the balance is tilted too far in the direction of minimizing money costs of production, that is, of sacrificing the interests of workers to those of employers and consumers.

Most workers lack detailed information on working conditions when they are first hired and find mobility costly after being with a firm for several years. There is equally little doubt that unions, in attempting to redress the balance, sometimes overshoot the optimum and saddle industry with unduly high costs. On the whole, however, it seems likely that we come closer to a proper balancing of producer and consumer interests with collective bargaining than without it.

THE BALANCE OF POLITICAL POWER

While collective bargaining is the main task of American unions, there is also an important side current of political activity, as we discussed in Chapter 13. Individual unions, city and state federations, and the AFL-CIO participate in the political process in several ways:

    1. By Endorsing Candidates for Public Office. In national elections labor normally endorses candidates for the House and Senate and also a presidential candidate. The AFL-CIO nod has invariably gone to the Democratic presidential candidate, though the Teamsters and a few other unions have supported the Republican candidate on occasion. The endorsement has usually come after the two nominating conventions. In 1983, however, the AFL-CIO endorsed Democrat Walter Mondale well in advance of the primaries and the convention, in the hope of solidifying labor behind his candidacy; and labor support did contribute to his success in several important primaries. But his later defeat in the general election illustrates the limits of union influence.

    2. By Contributing Funds and Other Forms of Support to Endorsed Candidates. A union, like a corporation, is forbidden to contribute to political candidates. So it is necessary to channel funds through separate organizations, of which the most important is the AFL-CIO's Committee on Political Education (COPE). Labor contributions are large, though not as large as those of business groups. In addition to cash contributions, unions contribute the time of staff members and volunteers for distributing election material, organizing campaign meetings, registering voters, and getting out the vote on election day. The value of these free services probably outweighs the cash contributions.

    3. By Lobbying Government Officials. Staff members of the major unions and AFL-CIO devote much time to lobbying activity. This includes not only lobbying Congress and the state legislatures but also maintaining pressure on administrative agencies. The effect of a law depends a good deal on how it is interpreted and how vigorously it is enforced by the agency in charge. So if the U.S. Department of Labor or the NLRB or EEOC or OSHA makes a decision that is adverse to labor interests, union representatives will be quick to protest and seek a reversal, either from the agency itself or conceivably in the courts.

Political effectiveness, however, is judged by results rather than by effort. Here labor's influence appears to have declined considerably in the 1970s and 1980s, as the country has become more conservative and as the percentage of union members in the electorate has fallen.

What kinds of measures do the unions support? Many of the bills in question can be classified as general social legislation—expenditures for welfare, food stamps, Medicare and Medicaid, public housing, job training, public-employment programs, unemployment compensation, and other types of transfer payment. These programs may bring some benefit to union members; but the main benefits go to the bottom 20 percent of the income distribution, to people living near or below the poverty line. In supporting such legislation, labor is part of a broader coalition including black and Hispanic organizations, community action groups, liberal Democrats, and others.

Quite different are laws that protect or subsidize a particular industry. Here the unions typically line up with employers in defense of industry interests. Thus the Teamsters have supported the trucking associations in opposing deregulation of the trucking industry and, after this battle was lost, in advancing proposals for reregulation. The steel and automobile unions have lined up with employers in demanding import quotas and other restrictions on foreign competition. The maritime unions have supported subsidy programs for U.S. shipbuilding and ship operation. Unions employed in defense industries are among the most active lobbyists for larger defense appropriations. Where those who stand to lose (taxpayers, consumers) are numerous and poorly organized, the bill is likely to pass. The business groups involved would frequently be able to achieve this result on their own; but the support of unions with members scattered across many congressional districts, certainly strengthens their efforts.

Unions have also been quite successful in supporting wage-fixing legislation. They are the mainstay of support for the federal minimum wage, which affects only a limited number of union members in low-wage industries but is regarded as an article of faith. The building trades unions have also been successful in maintaining the Davis-Bacon Act, which requires payment of "the prevailing wage" (for which, read "the union scale") on federal construction projects.

Where unions have been least successful is on measures designed to advance or to curb union power. Here they stand largely alone and are opposed by powerful business lobbies which usually prevail. The unions failed to block the Taft-Hartley Act of 1947, which was generally proemployer. They similarly failed to block the controls on internal union government imposed by the Landrum-Griffin Act in 1959. They failed to pass the mildly prounion Labor Reform Bill in 1978. Their main success has been in blocking bills that would have imposed more severe restrictions on union political activity.

As usual, then, we come up with a mixed verdict. Unions do constitute an influential interest group. They have often joined successfully with employers in advancing industry interests. They have helped to tilt social legislation in the direction of the "welfare state." But they succeed mainly as part of a broader coalition.

When they stand alone, supporting measures designed simply to increase union power, they are normally outvoted.

THE BALANCE SHEET OF TRADE UNIONISM

It is a curious fact that both critics and defenders of unionism have based their case mainly on wage-employment effects. These subjects bulk large in textbook discussion because we have theories about wages and employment, while we lack equally precise tools for analyzing working conditions and social relations in the plant. But the fact that we have conceptual difficulty in grappling with these problems does not mean that they are less important. The review of nonwage issues in this chapter should help to put matters in better perspective.

There are two difficulties in constructing an overall balance sheet. The first is that alongside any list of union effects that are economically harmful, one can set another list of effects that appear beneficial. The wage effects described in Chapter 20 might well be considered adverse to economic efficiency. The sizable gap between union and nonunion wages distorts resource allocation—too little labor and too much capital in the union sector, too much labor and too little capital in the nonunion sector. It also introduces an arbitrary element into the distribution of personal income and brings little benefit to the poor, who are largely nonunion. Union legislative activities, too, like those of other pressure groups, often seem to operate against the public interest. Unions generally favor restriction of competition in product markets, whether from domestic or foreign sources, and cooperate with employers in taxing the consumer.

On the other hand, the establishment of worker voice as an alternative to exit in regulating terms of employment appears as a gain; and so do the things that flow from it—lower turnover, longer job tenure, possibly productivity improvements associated with greater experience. Protection against arbitrary discharge is a very substantial benefit. We have suggested also that physical conditions of work are likely to be closer to optimum with a union than without it. Whether the items on this second list outweigh those on the first list is necessarily a matter of judgment.

The second difficulty is that some effects cannot be assigned clearly to either the pro or con list. In some cases the jury is still out. For example, unions appear to have reduced productivity in some cases and to have raised it in others. Which effect preponderates is not clear. The same might be said of reliance on seniority in job promotions, which has costs as well as benefits. In still other cases a judgment about the desirability of union effects can scarcely be divorced from one's political orientation. Union support of "welfare state" legislation will not be viewed in the same light by liberal Democrats and conservative Republicans.

Unionism and collective bargaining are here to stay. But over the long run, judgments on the merit of trade unionism will help to shape the economic and political future. We have deliberately refrained from suggesting any conclusion. We have tried rather to provide facts and ideas that you will find helpful in making your own evaluation.

SUMMARY

1. The presence of a union produces substantial changes in management organization: upgrading of the personnel function, greater effort at consistency in personnel policies, raising of production standards, and other productivity-raising changes.

2. A union also formalizes and restructures the internal labor market: outside recruitment is more severely restricted, job tenure of present employees is better protected, seniority is given greater emphasis in job assignments as well as benefit entitlements.

3. Unionism typically reduces quit rates and increases workers' average length of service with the company.

4. The traditional view is that unions reduce productivity by imposing burdensome work rules; and one can point to many such rules imposed by skilled craft groups. Recent studies, however, have turned up cases of higher productivity under unionism, partly associated with greater management effort. The net effect on productivity for the economy as a whole is uncertain and probably small.

5. Unionism typically reduces company profits. This effect shows up especially in concentrated industries, where unions are apparently able to force some sharing of monopoly gains.

6. The cost of improvements in working conditions won by unions is normally passed on to buyers of the product. The result may be a better balancing of worker and consumer interests, but this is not certain.

7. Unions devote considerable effort to electing political candidates who are sympathetic to labor, but labor's record of legislative success is not impressive, especially for measures designed to defend or increase union power.

KEY CONCEPTS

MANAGEMENT BY POLICY   FEATHERBEDDING
MAKE-WORK POLICIES

REVIEW QUESTIONS

1. Compare *exit* and *voice* as ways of regulating terms of employment.
2. Why might one expect quit rates to be lower in union than in nonunion establishments?

3. Collective bargaining seems in some cases to raise output per worker rather than to lower it. How might one account for this result?

4. "In industries where product prices are controlled, either by private market power or by government regulation, unions often succeed in appropriating part of the monopoly profit. Good for them." Discuss.

5. Why is it difficult for unions to resist technical change in manufacturing industries? What provisions have unions negotiated with employers to cushion the labor-displacing effect of such changes?

6. A union requests that a company install insulation to reduce unpleasantly high noise levels in the plant. By spending more money, the company can reduce noise to any desired level.
   (a) What principles could you apply to define an optimal noise level?
   (b) Would you have enough information to apply your definition in practice?

7. "Union political power is considerably overrated. It is still well below the power of organized business groups." Do you agree?

8. Considering everything you have learned in this book, do you think the benefits of unionism outweigh its disadvantages? Why or why not?

READINGS

BOK, DEREK C. and JOHN T. DUNLOP, *Labor and the American Community,* New York: Simon and Schuster, 1970.

BROWN, E. H. PHELPS, *The Economics of Labor.* New Haven, Conn.: Yale University Press, 1962.

FREEMAN, RICHARD B. and JAMES L. MEDOFF, *What Do Unions Do?* New York: Basic Books, 1984.

FREEMAN, RICHARD B., "Unionism Comes to the Public Sector." *Journal of Economic Literature* (March, 1986), pp. 41–86.

HIRSH, BARRY T. and JOHN T. ADDISON, *The Economic Analysis Of Unions,* Boston: Allen & Unwin, 1986.

REES, ALBERT, *The Economics of Trade Unions,* rev. ed. Chicago: University of Chicago Press, 1989.

SLICHTER, SUMNER H., JAMES J. HEALY, and E. ROBERT LIVERNASH, *The Impact of Collective Bargaining on Management.* Washington, D.C.: Brookings Institution, 1960.

GLOSSARY OF CONCEPTS

ability curve: a curve showing how, for a person of given ability, the return for investment in human capital declines as the amount invested increases; a person with more ability has higher ability curve.

accession rate: new hires per month, as a percentage of total employment.

added worker effect: unemployment of one family member leads another family member to seek employment.

adjustment assistance: retraining and mobility programs designed to fit displaced workers into available jobs.

affirmative action: positive steps to meet targets for employment of women and minority workers.

agency shop: contract clause providing that nonmembers of the union must pay a prescribed fee for union services as collective bargaining representative.

amnesty: policies proposed to allow illegal immigrants to become legal residents if they have been in the United States for some years.

annual improvement factor (AIF): a concept developed in the automobile industry where wage rates increase during each year of a multiyear union contract; such increases are designed so that workers can share in expected productivity gains.

arbitration: a procedure for settling labor-management disputes by having the decision made by a neutral third party, the arbitrator.

arbitration, conventional: arbitration where the arbitrator has the freedom to make any award that he or she considers appropriate.

arbitration, final offer: arbitration where the arbitrator must choose the position of one of the parties, either in its entirety or separately for each issue in the dispute.

arbitration, grievance: neutral arbitration as normal last step in the grievance procedure.

association bargaining: collective bargaining between a union and an employers' association.

average hourly earnings: actual earnings divided by hours worked.

bargaining power: capacity to effect an agreement on one's own terms; A's bargaining power is B's inducement to agree.

base rate: minimum hourly rate for a job, exclusive of overtime or incentive earnings.

benefit reduction rate: the rate at which the benefits of an income maintenance program decline as the recipients' earnings increase.

benefits: include payment in goods, such as leisure time and health care, and deferred compensation, such as disability and retirement pensions.

bracero: a worker under the bracero program, where many seasonal agricultural workers were admitted to the United States from Mexico between 1942 and 1964.

brain drain: the cost to a sending country when many of its most-educated workers emigrate to other nations.

break-even level: the lowest earnings at which welfare benefits are zero; given by G/r, where G is the guarantee and r is the benefit reduction rate.

budget constraint: alternative combinations of income and leisure available to a worker at the market wage.

bumping: a more senior worker is entitled to displace a less senior worker in the event of a reduction in staff.

certification election: an election, supervised by the National Labor Relations Board, to determine which union, if any, should be certified as representing a group of workers; also called a representation election.

Civil Service Commission: a commission that makes and enforces rules regarding selection, promotion, pay, and other issues of employment in many governmental units; with the development of public-sector unions, conflicts have developed between collective bargaining and Civil Service regulations.

closed shop: provides that only union members will be considered for employment.

cobweb model: where training time is substantial, market wage and numbers in training may fluctuate above and below equilibrium levels.

codetermination: inclusion of worker representatives on boards of directors, or other steps to increase worker voice in company policies.

collective benefit: a benefit received by each member of a group, regardless of who pays for it; unions provide many collective benefits.

collective voice: responding to job-related problems by voicing one's concerns as a group; voice is likely to be more effective and less subject to possible retaliation when it is done by a large group of workers rather than by an individual.

company bargaining: collective bargaining between a company and a union.

company offer curve: terms on which a company is willing to trade fringe benefits for cash compensation.

comparable worth: rates of pay should depend on job characteristics rather than on whether the job is held predominantly by women or men.

comparative advantage: the principle that all countries can gain through trade if each produces those goods where it has the greatest relative advantage.

compensating differences: differences in wage rates to compensate workers for differences in the nonpecuniary attractiveness of jobs; if the labor market is competitive, these compensating differences should make all jobs equally attractive to a marginal worker.

concession bargaining: bargaining where the workers agree to take a wage cut, or make other concessions, in return for greater job security during periods of declining demand for labor.

connective bargaining: bargaining that results in the standardization of wage rates and labor costs across companies and across plants within each company.

conspiracy doctrine: held that concerted action by workers constituted an illegal conspiracy under common law.

contingent workers: a worker in a job with little security, especially a temporary worker or one employed by a subcontractor to a large firm.

contract zone: extends from the union's preferred wage level to the employer's preferred wage level.

core worker: a worker with a relatively secure job in an internal labor market; a worker employed in the primary sector of the dual labor market.

Cost-of-Living Adjustment (COLA):   a provision in a union contract under which wage rates are adjusted automatically in response to increases in the Consumer Price Index; the adjustments can be made in various ways, but usually represent less than 100 percent protection from the effects of inflation.

craft severance: provision that a group of skilled workers may organize and bargain separately from a larger employee group.

craft unit: collective bargaining unit limited to a particular category of skilled employees.

decision criterion, for job search: decision whether to accept a job offer depends on estimated probability of obtaining a better offer by continued search, and also on search costs.

deferred compensation: fringe benefits to be received in the future; for example, pension benefits.

demand for labor, change in: upward or downward shift of a labor demand schedule.

demand for labor, elasticity of: percentage change in employment resulting from one-percent change in the wage.

demand for labor, firm: schedule relating wage rate to quantity of labor demanded by one employer.

demand for labor, long-run: more elastic than the short-run schedule because the factor-substitution effect operates as well as the scale effect.

demand for labor, market: schedule relating wage rate to quantity of labor demanded by all employers in the market.

demand for labor, short-run: for a firm, demand schedule is identical with the marginal revenue product schedule.

demand for union labor, elasticity of: percentage change in employment of union members resulting from a one-percent change in the union wage; may differ from elasticity of demand for all workers.

deregulation: reduced governmental regulation of trucking, airlines, and communications has allowed new firms to enter these industries more easily, thereby increasing competitive pressure on prices and on wage rates.

discouraged worker effect: belief that jobs are unavailable may lead some unemployed workers to leave the labor force.

discrimination, labor market: lower earnings of one group of workers than another, where the earnings differential cannot be attributed to any difference in productivity.

discrimination, monopoly: exercise of market power, usually by white males, to exclude women or minority groups.

discrimination, preference: workers', employers', or customers' dislike of associating with workers of a particular race or sex.

discrimination, statistical: employers judge job candidates by average characteristics of the group rather than by individual characteristics.

disparate impact: a policy's adverse effects on the employment opportunities of women or minorities; until 1989 a policy with a disparate impact was illegal unless it resulted from standards that were clearly job related.

distributive bargaining: bargaining over how to divide a pie of a given size, assuming that there is a fixed total gain available to the bargaining parties.

earnings inequality: differences in the amount people earn; such inequality has increased since the 1960s.

education voucher: a cash grant, usable only for school tuition, which enables a student to pay for education at the school of his or her choosing.

efficiency unit of labor: an hour of labor of average or standard efficiency.

employer sanctions: policies proposed to penalize firms that employ illegal immigrants.

employment and training program: any government program to reduce unemployment by providing subsidized jobs or job training opportunities.

employment tax credit: a tax credit or other payment for each additional worker hired.

equilibrium, labor market: exists when quantity of labor demanded at the prevailing wage equals the quantity offered.

equilibrium analysis, general: analysis of the mutual determination of equilibrium in interrelated markets.

equilibrium analysis, partial: analysis of equilibrium in one market, conditions in other markets assumed constant.

equilibrium wage: wage that equates the quantities of labor demanded and offered in a particular market.

exclusive jurisdiction: principle that only one union is authorized to organize a particular category of workers.

exit: responding to job-related problems by quitting one's job.

experience rating: a company's tax rate under unemployment insurance as related to the amount of unemployment attributable to the company.

Experimental Negotiating Agreement (ENA): an agreement in the steel industry during most of the 1970s to use compulsory arbitration as a substitute for a strike, if the negotiators could not agree on the terms of a new contract.

extensive margin of search: a worker searches at the extensive margin by seeking additional job offers.

external effect: a benefit (or cost) to others that is not reflected in the price system; government subsidies, out of tax revenue, often appropriate for goods and services with positive external effects.

fact finding: normal intermediate stage in public-sector disputes; involves hearings, reports, and recommendations by a neutral party.

factor-substitution effect: a rise in the cost of labor relative to the cost of capital will lead capital to be substituted for labor in production.

featherbedding: requirements in union contracts that firms employ more workers than needed.

firm investment in workers: sum of recruitment, screening, and training costs.

firm-specific training: training that increases a worker's productivity at only one firm.

fiscal substitution effect: the reduced hiring of regular employees by state and local governments when cheaper workers are available through a federally subsidized public employment program.

flextime: within some limits, hours of work are scheduled by the employee.

free rider: a person who receives a collective benefit but does not pay any of the costs necessary to attain that benefit.

full income: value of time used in household production plus time sold in the market.

gain sharing: a compensation plan where earnings depend partly on the performance of the employer (for example, its total revenue or its profits) rather than just on the employee's hours of work, as under a wage system.

general training: training that increases a worker's productivity at more than one firm.

grievance procedure: a multiple-step procedure for resolving disputes over rights of a worker (or occasionally an employer) under the union contract, normally culminates in arbitration.

guarantee: the benefit available from a welfare program to a family with no other source of income.

guest workers: temporary workers from Southern Europe invited by several Northern European countries with a high demand for labor; such programs ended with recession of 1973–74.

hours of work, optimal: for an individual, defined by tangency of the budget constraint to the highest attainable indifference curve.

household production: combination of time with market purchases to produce consumer goods.

human capital: increased productive capacity achieved through investment in education, job training, and work experience.

immigrant: a person moving permanently into a new country.

immigration quota: a limit on the number of people who can immigrate into a country.

implicit contract: worker expectation of future employer behavior, involving continuity of employment and no reduction in wages.

implicit control mechanism: a firm may seek to influence its workers through peer pressure and the development of self-motivation rather than relying solely on monetary rewards and punishments.

import quota: a limit placed on the number of cars or other products that can be imported from a country or group of countries.

incentive work: compensation based on individual or group output.

income, labor share: the percentage of total income going to labor.

income effect, on labor supply: an increase in real income leads an individual to offer fewer hours of labor (buy more leisure).

income-maintenance program: a program that provides income support to those in need.

incomes policy: an effort to slow the growth of money incomes by persuasion or pressure.

incomes policy, tax-based: tax measures designed to encourage compliance with incomes-policy targets.

indifference curve: alternative combinations of two goods which yield equal satisfaction.

industrial policy: a set of government policies to channel resources to some industries and thus away from others.

industrial unit: collective bargaining unit including company employees in many job categories.

inflation: a rise in an index of all prices.

inflation, anticipated: inflation that people do expect; it has less effect on real economic outcomes than does unanticipated inflation.

inflation, unanticipated: inflation that people do not expect; it leads to a redistribution of income and wealth.

inflation, underlying rate of: rate of increase in money wages minus rate of increase in labor productivity; equals increase in labor cost per unit of output.

injunction, labor: court order prohibiting certain conduct by a union or its members, violations punishable as contempt of court.

in-kind benefits: assistance to low-income families in the form of specific consumption items such as food, housing, and medical care rather than cash assistance that can be spent on any goods or services.

integrative bargaining: bargaining that seeks to increase the total gains available to the parties, rather than focusing primarily on how to divide up a fixed pie.

intensive margin of search: a worker searches at the intensive margin by seeking additional information on a job offer already received.

internal rate of return: interest rate at which discounted value of additions to future earnings equals the cost of education or other human capital.

intertemporal substitution effect: substitution of work hours across time periods to maximize lifetime satisfaction.

investment in education: amount spent on education by an individual, including implicit cost of student's time.

investment in education, return on: present value of increase in future earnings attributable to education, as a percentage of investment in education.

job competition model: employers compete for labor by tightening or loosening their hiring standards rather than (or in addition to) changing wage rates.

job evaluation: determining relative worth of different jobs by developing rating criteria and assigning point scores.

job segregation: heavy concentration of female workers (or black workers) in a limited range of occupations.

Job Service: public employment offices operated by the states.

labor: human effort exerted in production.

labor cost per unit of output: total compensation of employees, including benefits, divided by units of output.

labor economics: analysis of the supply, demand, allocation, and remuneration of labor.

labor force: includes persons working or actively seeking work.

labor force participation rate: percentage of people in a particular age-sex group who are in the labor force.

labor grade: classification of jobs into categories for wage-setting purposes.

labor market: interaction of demand for and supply of labor services.

labor market, competitive: free entrance and exit by buyers and sellers, no collusion or government regulation.

labor market, guild: permanent attachment to a craft rather than to an employer, as in building construction.

labor market, internal: procedures for filling job vacancies by promoting present employees.

labor market, primary: marked by substantial firm investment in workers, relatively high wage and skill levels, and long job tenure.

labor market, secondary: marked by relatively low wage and skill levels and short job tenure.

labor shortage: quantity of labor demanded exceeds quantity offered; implies wage rate below equilibrium.

labor surplus: quantity of labor offered exceeds quantity demanded; implies wage rate above equilibrium.

layoff: reduction in labor requirements met by laying off some employees, usually on a seniority basis.

layoff rate: workers laid off per month as a percentage of total employment.

lifetime employment: an employment relation between employer and employee that is expected to last until the employee's retirement; lifetime employment is common in Japan, but not in the United States.

lockout: employer closure of a plant in pursuance of a contract dispute.

lump-sum payment: a payment to workers that does not affect the base wage; a one-time bonus that does not affect pension, vacation pay, overtime, or future wage rates.

make-work rules: rules negotiated by a union in order to increase the amount of labor that a firm must employ.

management by policy: management by rules and formal policies rather than in a casual "off-the-cuff" manner.

marginal cost of labor: addition to labor cost resulting from employment of an additional unit of labor.

marginal physical product: additional product resulting from employment of an additional unit of labor.

marginal productivity schedule, national: relates the marginal physical productivity of labor to the number of workers employed.

marginal productivity theory: holds that a firm's demand schedule for labor depends on estimated marginal productivity.

marginal rate of substitution: the rate at which one is willing to substitute one commodity for another, for example, income versus leisure; the slope of an indifference curve.

marginal revenue product: addition to revenue resulting from employment of an additional unit of labor.

market demand schedule: a schedule showing, for each wage rate, the total demand in the labor market for a particular kind of labor.

market offer curve: terms on which all employers in a market are willing to trade fringe benefits for cash compensation.

median voter model: union negotiators' demands reflect the preferences of the average union member.

mediation: participation of a neutral mediator in union-management negotiations.

minimum wage: a law prohibiting employment of labor at less than a specified hourly rate.

monopsony: one buyer of labor in a particular market.

national federation: includes national unions of various trades and industries, as in the AFL-CIO.

National Labor Relations Board: a board, established by the National Labor Relations Act, to supervise union certification elections and to prosecute unfair labor practices.

nondiscrimination requirement: legal prohibition of discrimination in recruitment, hiring, promotion, or wage rates.

normative economics: analysis of the welfare consequences of alternative government policies.

occupational licensing: licensing by the government restricting entry into many occupations, for consumer protection and/or monopoly privilege to occupational incumbents.

opportunity cost: the cost of an opportunity foregone; opportunity cost of leisure time is earnings that could have been gained had leisure time been spent working for pay.

opportunity curve: a curve showing how the cost to an individual of borrowing money for human capital investment increases with the amount that must be borrowed.

organizational rule: imposed by management or collective agreement, governing employment or remuneration of labor.

overtime: employment of a worker for more than the standard workweek.

pattern bargaining: a practice of bargaining first with selected companies in an industry, and then extending the result to other companies.

pay equity: pay that depends on characteristics of the job, rather than on whether the job is held predominately by women or by men; also called comparable worth.

payment in goods: current compensation received not in cash but in free or subsidized goods, such as leisure or health care.

permanent-income hypothesis: consumption and work decisions depend on expected long-term income rather than current income.

ports of entry, to a company: jobs normally filled by outside recruitment rather than internal promotion.

positive economics: analysis of how the economy operates.

poverty line: annual income required to buy a minimum budget of consumer goods; varies with family size and urban or rural location.

poverty rate: individuals or households below the poverty line in a particular year, as a percentage of all individuals or households.

present value: present value of future income is obtained by discounting the income by the rate of compound interest; if income to be received n years in the future and interest rate is i, then discount factor is $\frac{1}{(1 + i)^n}$.

productivity slowdown: the decline in the rate of growth of productivity that has occurred, especially since 1973.

profit maximization: the goal assumed in most models of the firm.

promotion: transfer, to a job perceived by the worker as superior, based on ability and/or seniority.

public interest labor law: legislation, such as the Occupational Safety and Health Act (OSHA), designed to provide direct government protection of workers, rather than to rely on unionization as a means of protection.

public sector: the sector of the economy where the government is the employer; it includes federal, state, and local governments.

Quality-of-Working-Life (QWL) Programs: programs to give workers more influence over their jobs, generally to increase both job satisfaction and productivity.

quit rate: workers leaving jobs voluntarily, per month, as a percentage of total employment.

rate curve: relates labor grades to hourly rates of pay.

rate of return, private: considers only educational investment by, and future returns to, the individual.

rate of return, social: considers total costs of education, government and private, as well as possible external benefits of education to the community.

recall: return to work by laid-off workers, usually in order of seniority.

replacement rate: worker benefits under unemployment insurance, as a percentage of previous earnings.

representation election: an election, supervised by the National Labor Relations Board, to determine which union, if any, should represent a group of workers; also called a certification election.

reservation wage: wage below which a worker will not accept a job offer; tends to decline with length of unemployment.

right to work laws: state laws (in twenty states) prohibiting the union shop.

scab: a worker who is willing to replace someone who is on strike; a strikebreaker.

scale effect: a rise in the cost of labor, other things equal, will raise the relative price of the product, hence will reduce sales, output, and employment.

secondary boycott: a strike or boycott against one employer in order to put pressure on another employer with whom the union is having a dispute.

seniority, benefit: length of service as a criterion of eligibility for vacations, pensions, or other fringe benefits.

seniority, competitive status: length of service as a criterion in decisions concerning promotion, transfer, layoff, and recall to work.

seniority district: range of jobs within which seniority rules apply to layoff, recall, and promotion.

seniority principle: use of length of service as a major criterion in promotion, layoff, and recall, and in defining benefit rights.

separation rate: workers separated from employment, per month, as a percentage of total employment.

shift differential: extra pay for workers who are assigned to work the evening or nighttime shifts.

shop steward: lowest level of union representation in the shop; usually handles first step in the grievance procedure.

signaling model of schooling: schooling valued in the labor market as a signal of ability and motivation rather than because of any skills learned in school.

social insurance: an income-maintenance program, financed with payroll taxes, where benefits are provided to reduce the income lost when a worker's earnings are reduced because of such factors as old age, disability, or unemployment.

spillover effect: union wage increases leading to lower wage rates in the nonunion sector as fewer jobs are available in the high-wage union sector and workers shift to nonunion jobs.

standard rate: principle that workers employed on the same job should receive the same wage rate or wage range.

state federation: includes locals of various trades and industries in a particular state.

statutory rules: legal controls over union and management behavior, enacted by Congress or state legislatures.

strike: results from a failure to agree on new contract terms.

substitution effect, on labor supply: an individual tends to buy less of any good, including leisure, that has risen in price relative to other goods.

supply of labor, change in: upward or downward shift of a labor supply schedule.

supply of labor, firm: schedule relating wage rate to quantity of labor offered to one employer.

supply of labor, market: schedule relating wage rate to quantity of labor offered to all employers in the market.

take-home pay: cash receipts after deduction of withholding taxes, employee share of payroll taxes, and other employee payments.

tariff: a tax on imported goods.

tax, progressive: a tax which takes an increasing proportion of income as income rises.

tax, proportional: a tax which takes the same proportion of income at all income levels.

tax, regressive: a tax which takes a decreasing proportion of income as income rises.

tax rate, average: percentage of all income taken by a particular tax, or by all taxes.

tax rate, marginal: percentage of a specified *increase* in income taken by a particular tax, or by all taxes.

technical change: increases the output obtainable from the same quantities of inputs.

tenure-earnings profile: relation between employee earnings and years of service with same employer.

threat effect: the effect of unions on nonunion wage rates as some nonunion employers pay high wage rates in an effort to remain nonunion.

time study: used under incentive payment to determine a reasonable time allowance per unit of output.

time work: compensation based on amount of time worked.

total hourly compensation: average hourly earnings plus the average hourly cost of fringe benefits.

trade adjustment compensation: a proposal where workers who have been displaced by foreign competition would be given a subsidy equal to hours worked times some percentage of the difference between their hourly pay on the new job and on the job that was lost.

trade union: continuing association of workers aimed at improving their terms of employment.

unemployment: persons are unemployed if they are not employed but are actively seeking work or are not working because of a temporary layoff or because their jobs haven't yet started.

unemployment, deficient-demand: arises because job vacancies fall short of the number of available workers.

unemployment, frictional: arises because workers quitting, laid off, or discharged require time to locate new jobs.

unemployment, full-time: unemployed people desiring full-time work.

unemployment, nonaccelerating inflationary rate of (NAIRU): unemployment rate below which the inflation rate begins to rise.

unemployment, part-time: unemployed workers desiring part-time work plus part-time workers desiring additional hours per week.

unemployment, rate of: the number of workers who are unemployed as a percentage of the total labor force.

unemployment, structural: arises because of a mismatch between the qualifications of unemployed workers and those required on vacant jobs.

unemployment insurance: operated by the states under federal supervision; provides cash benefits to unemployed workers for a limited period.

unfair labor practice: a union or management practice prohibited by the Labor-Management Relations Act.

union, craft: includes workers with a particular craft skill, as in the building and printing trades.

union, industrial: includes most or all employees of a particular company, regardless of skill level.

union, local: includes workers in a particular company or a particular local area.

union, national: includes local unions of a particular industry or trade throughout the country.

union shop: provides that all employees must become union members after a probationary period.

union wage gap: difference between the wages of a union worker and a nonunion worker with the same personal characteristics.

union wage gain: the amount by which a union raises a worker's wage rate, relative to what it would be if there were no unions in the economy.

value of the dollar: the rate at which the dollar can be exchanged for the currencies of other countries.

variable proportions, law of: as increasing quantities of a variable factor are applied to one or more fixed factors, the resulting additions to output will eventually decrease; also termed *law of diminishing returns*.

voice: responding to job-related problems by voicing one's concerns and trying to work with others to solve the problem.

wage rate, money: payment per unit of time for a particular job.

wage rate, real: money wage rate adjusted for changes in consumer prices.

welfare: income-maintenance programs that limit eligibility to those with low family income and provide benefits that are unrelated to previous employment.

work test: a requirement that welfare recipients be actively searching for work (and accept any suitable offer) in order to continue receiving benefits.

worksharing::   reduction in labor requirements met by reducing weekly hours for all employees.

INDEX